The Latter day luminary. Volume 1 of 6

American Baptist Foreign Mission Society. General Convention of the Baptist Denomination in the United States.

Asahel Davis's Book. Sept 27 1823

THE LATTER DAY LUMINARY;

BY A COMMITTEE

OF THE

BAPTIST

BOARD OF FOREIGN MISSIONS

FOR THE

UNITED STATES.

"I AM COME A LIGHT INTO THE WORLD" JOHN xii 46.
"IN THY LIGHT SHALL WE SEE LIGHT." PSALM xxxvi. 9.
"All kingdoms, and all princes of the earth
"Flock to that light. COWPER
"Attempt great things, expect great things" CAREY

VOLUME I.

PHILADELPHIA:

PRINTED FOR THE BOARD BY ANDERSON AND MEEHAN,
NO. 59, LOCUST-STREET

1818.

INTRODUCTION.

MAN, since the apostacy, is characterized by spiritual ignorance, depraved affections, and a train of consequent calamities. If, according to Mr. Locke, he has no innate ideas, he has innate propensities, which lead him to contemplate and embrace evil as his chief good, and folly as his highest wisdom. To remedy this state of wretchedness, the great JEHOVAH, in ages past, sent his prophets and apostles, to record his holy will, and to develop the best interests of our race, through a series of generations; until his volume of revelation was closed and sealed with a curse on the man that should dare to "add unto these things," or "take away from the words of the book of this prophecy."

It is certainly among the most favourable of the signs of the present time, that the friends of revealed truth have associated themselves in bands, unnumbered, united, and mighty, to spread the Bible through the earth without note or comment. Millions of copies are put into the most promising circulation, and growing funds and labouring presses, will soon send out their millions more. In the age in which we have the honour to live, the art of stereotype has been invented, and employed in the service of religion.

The Scriptures have themselves been translated into more than fifty languages, in which before they had never appeared. Mission societies rejoice in all the vigour of youth, and new missionaries, with each succeeding year, are seen elevating the ensign of the Cross in regions degraded with superstition and defiled with crime.

The diffusion of Bibles and the publishing of the everlasting Gospel, are, without doubt, the grand means which the Spirit of the Lord will employ for subduing the nations to the dominion of the Son of God; but there are other means which have been succeeded with his blessing, and have conduced to the moral welfare of thousands. Incidental publications, such as are issued by religious tract societies, and periodical ones, such as magazines, have contributed greatly to the circulation of evangelic truth. They have now become popular. The benevolent mind is left to regret that they were brought into operation no earlier.

Miscellaneous pamphlets, appearing at stated periods, were first enlisted in the service of politics and philosophy. The earliest work of this description was the "Journal des Sçavans," printed at Paris, for the use of such as were "too busy or too indolent" to read larger productions. This was succeeded by the "Gentleman's Magazine," which has been issued monthly, from January 1, 1731, to the present time. It was not until nearly half a century had expired, that the friends of Christianity adopted a medium calculated so extensively to promote habits of reading, and to inform the public mind.

Magazines, by what name soever distinguished, have given rise to a new epoch in the history of intellectual improvement. They come to the purchaser on terms so reasonable, and at periods so regularly distant, as to render the procuring of them a circumstance unattended with inconvenience. Like the painters of Montezuma, they portray and transmit characters and events as they daily occur. A respectable writer observes, that "many young authors, who have risen to considerable eminence, have here made their first attempt in composition." They convey information through regions which larger publications cannot reach. Properly conducted, and devoted to evangelic purposes, they stand as heralds of God for the defence of the Gospel. Though destitute of holy inspiration, they bear some resemblance to "the Acts of the Apostles," while they exhibit the power of the Divine word, and the success of his servants in converting the heart and sanctifying the life. They are calculated to inspire the supplications, elevate the joys, command the benevolence, and invigorate the toils of all who are waiting till the "enemies" of Messiah and his kingdom "shall lick the dust," and "they that dwell in the wilderness shall bow before him."

At a time when numerous magazines are spreading through society, an attempt to add to their number might seem to demand an apology. But, a reflecting and observant mind will readily perceive, that that number, great as it may appear, is far too small. Large sections of our country, and especially in western and southern regions, are almost destitute of such channels of intelligence, and are yet anxiously desirous to possess them. The prophecy that, in the latter days, "Many shall run to and fro, and knowledge be increased," will probably be illustrated as really in magazines as in preachers. The lamps of heaven need not be multiplied; they amply display the Creator's glory; but luminaries on earth must, in proportion as the kingdom of the Mediator widens.

The Baptist Board of Foreign Missions, among other periodical works issued by their brethren, have contemplated with pleasure the American Baptist Magazine, conducted by the superiour talents of their much esteemed friends Dr. Baldwin, Mr. Sharp, and Mr. Winchell. They have been instructed by the information, and refreshed by the devotional spirit that excellent work has exhibited. They wish it an extensive circulation, and regret that the terms on which it is issued forbid its reaching the distant parts of our country, lying remote from the sea-board, without incurring to the publishers a positive expense. They are anxious that the Latter Day Luminary be considered as an associate of that valuable work. If, in particular districts, like some rivers in Asia, they run hundreds of miles side by side, in others their evangelical current will move alone.

The work which now is presented to the friends of the truth as it is in Jesus, will be enriched by occasional essays. It will delight to become useful as a biographic, obituary, and ecclesiastical intelligencer. But its leading design is to show the state and promising advance of Christian missions, whether foreign or domestic, and more particularly of such as are connected with the Board.

The very extensive correspondence of the Secretary and Agent of the Board, throw into their possession a large body of interesting letters from societies and brethren throughout the Union. These not only record measures that relate to their own economy, but often present the most animating information concerning local revivals of religion, and still more frequently contain bright ideas relative to the growing empire of Jesus, and the fervours of holy desire for his universal reign. It must be obvious that communications of this nature ought not to be consigned to the silence of the bureau. They are among the most precious materials for magazine publication.

It is said that, under the Jewish economy, men were employed on the tops of the surrounding mountains to watch the first appearing of the new moon. No sooner was it discovered, than a fire was kindled on the summit of mount Olivet. This was seen by the men on other hills, who had their combustible wood prepared, and by these means the inhabitants all over the land in a short time were admonished to praise the name of Jehovah for the blessings of the past moon, and to rely on his gracious providence during the progress of the present. Magazines are the fires of the present times. They convey to each other, and to observing thousands, the joyous news that the feast of the Lord is come, and invite his servants to the exercise of devotion and thanksgiving.

The Publishing Committee enter on this work, they hope, with humility of heart, and an humble dependance on the gracious assistance of the God of Missions. They will be sincerely grateful for communications from their christian brethren; and anticipate the pleasure not only of deriving aid from the publications of their fellow-labourers in the north, but that the efforts of their southern and western friends will contribute to the important object. America has abundant talent, and ought to "occupy till" the Master "come." In modern magazines it has become, in a great degree, unnecessary to defend what have been called the outworks of Christianity.

> The Infidel has shot his bolts away,
> Till his exhausted quiver, yielding none,
> He gleans the blunted shafts that have recoiled,
> And aims them at the shield of Truth again.

It is now the happiness of the saint to mark the triumphant progress of the chariot of his Redeemer, to see voluntary captives of all nations in his train, while righteousness goes forth as brightness, and salvation as a lamp that burneth.

PHILADELPHIA, February, 1818.

THE LATTER DAY LUMINARY;

BY A COMMITTEE

OF

THE BAPTIST BOARD OF FOREIGN MISSIONS FOR THE UNITED STATES.

COMMUNICATIONS.

ON THE HISTORY AND CHARACTER OF RUTH.

THE histories in the divine word are all instructive. They are generally concise, embracing frequently, in a few pages, numerous events of the most interesting character. The story of Ruth is remarkable for its simplicity. The charming poet, Mr. Thomson, was aware of its beauties, and from it collected materials for his elegant Summer tale of Palæmon and Lavinia.

A famine occurred in the land of Judea. As no such calamity is on record during the history of the Judges, but that which was felt in the days of Gideon, it is probable that about the time of his call to office, the transactions mentioned in the book of Ruth took place. In Bethlehem Judah lived Elimelech; he had a wife, whose name was Naomi, and two sons, Mahlon and Chilion; their names, signifying sickness and consumption, were probably given either on account of the feebleness of their constitution, or the calamity at the period of their birth. This man and his family left Judea, and went into the country of Moab. The Moabites, descendants of one of the sons of Lot, were called by Moses, on account of their superstitious adherence to their false divinity, "the sons of Chemosh." The conduct of Elimelech in leaving the land of promise for an idolatrous country, appears to have been deserving of censure. He could not have been pressed sorely with the famine, for Naomi on her return says, "I went out full." Other Israelites were willing to endure the chastisements of the Lord, and in due time enjoyed deliverance. The distresses that befel the good man and his family, were probably the consequence of his unnecessary flight.

Elimelech soon died. So uncertain are earthly prospects. The two sons took to themselves wives. Their names were Orpah and Ruth. It is probable these females were, at their marriage, idolaters. If so, the step on the part of the young Hebrews was unwarrantable. The divine law forbade it. Deut. xxiii. 3—5. & vii. 3, 4. The mischievous effects of such intermarriages were experienced in the days of Israel's sovereigns. 1 Kings xi. 1. 7. 33.; and one of the most laborious and painful services of the reformation by Nehemiah, was the purifying of the people by the rejection of such prohibited alliances. The instability of worldly relations, and the rectitude of God, who will, in one way or other, chastise the persons who depart from his commands, are seen in this portion of the history. No posterity sprung from these connexions, and both the husbands died.

When Socrates was requested to escape from his prison, he asked, "Can you take me to a country where men do not die?" Elimelech fled from the land of Israel to avoid death; but he that by unhallowed means seeks to save his life, loses it. Poor Naomi! who would not feel for a situation such as hers! Her husband and her sons dead, and buried in a land of strangers. Yet some sources of consolation were still left opened. She seems to have been pious, and had the Lord for her refuge, and her daughters-in-law appear to have been amiably duteous. Her distresses create a desire after home. And the more so, because she heard that "the Lord had visited his people in giving them bread." Often does the God of mercy allure his children to his sanctuary and himself, by removing their secular comforts.

Herself and daughters set out together. She dissuades them from the journey, for they had mothers in Moab, who had *homes*. She gives them a mother's blessing. "The Lord deal kindly with you, as ye have dealt with the dead." She wishes them a future settlement in life, and states that the hand of the Lord had gone out against her; an affliction which, for their sakes, she deeply deplored. To a mother-in-law and a daughter-in-law what beautiful lessons of wisdom and love are here suggested! Orpah was persuaded, not without difficulty, to return. They wept together. Orpah kissed Naomi, and departed; but Ruth, the faithful, tender Ruth, clave unto her. "Entreat me not to leave thee," she cries. My heart is resolved; I will journey with thee; I will lodge with thee; I will own the same people with thee; I will worship the same God; with thee I will die, and a common tomb shall enclose us both. Nay, she expresses her resolution by an oath. "The Lord do so unto me, and more also, if aught but death part thee and me;" as if she had said, May God desert me, if I, my poor dear mother, ever desert thee! Among the resolves the virtuous Ruth adopted, a pious mind is forcibly struck with the determination, that the God of Naomi should be hers. She had been trained up a worshipper of Chemosh, an idol, the same with Baalpeor, represented by some as a gnat, by others as the sun, by almost all writers as the god of uncleanness.

Men have their numerous gods—my god—thy god. Human ingenuity and activity in making to themselves divinities is astonishing. They have selected them from angels and from demons, from heavenly bodies and from air, earth, and ocean. The Persians adored the wind, the Finlanders worshipped stones, and the Scythians, iron. The ancient Druids paid religious veneration to the oak-tree, and the Egyptians to the leek and the onion. The God of the Hebrews, the great Jehovah, the refuge of Naomi, the choice of Ruth, is to be preferred above them all. His existence is real, and not like that of an idol, imaginary. He possesses infinite perfections, and has performed the most marvellous works. His favour can make us happy, or his frown miserable, for ever. This Naomi knew—this Ruth was learning.

It is possible the truth may be ascertained by an individual whether this great God be really his or not. He is certainly our creator and preserver; but is he our father and friend? He is *ours*, if he be the God of our choice. Men, by nature, choose not the Lord; but ask, with the haughty tyrant of the Nile, "who is Jehovah, that I should obey his voice?" But if the heart be inclined to love and delight in God, it is because his sacred Spirit has regenerated its powers. He is *ours*, if he be the God of our hope and confidence. He has revealed himself as the God of salvation. He has sent his Son to be a Prince and Saviour, who, having assumed the nature of man, honoured the law of heaven, offered the sacrifice for transgression, and vanquished the powers of darkness, has ascended to heaven, and ordained the publication of life through His name. These truths were seen by Ruth and Naomi only in shadows and types, yet " under his wings" they put their trust. This God is *ours*, if he be the object of our reverence and worship. To acknowledge Jehovah, and not to adore him, is an absurdity. Moses, at the Red sea, is heard saying, " He is my God, and I will prepare him a habitation, my father's God, and I will exalt Him." David says, " I will extol thee my God, O! King." " Our God," exclaimed the intrepid three, " Our God, whom we serve, is able to deliver us." The people that find pleasure in his law, his sabbaths, his ordinances, his sanctuary, his servants, are at liberty to rejoice and say,

"This awful God is ours,
Our Father and our Love."

The favourite theme of heathen conversation, all over the world, is, the gods they adore. On these their poets exhaust the powers of imagination and verse. Naomi, though in Moab, never lost sight of her God; and it is highly probable her pious instructions and example were sanctified to the conversion of her daughter-in-law. Was she afflicted? It was "the hand of the *Lord*" that had "gone out against" her. Was the kindness of Boaz recognized? she said unto her daughter-in-law, "blessed be he of *the Lord* who hath not left off his kindness to the living and to the dead."

The choice of Jehovah for our God, is greatly to be desired and peculiarly amiable in early life. To the youthful reader, the example of this interesting Moabitess is offered for imitation. The difficulties she had to surmount were numerous. A mother's house must be abandoned. A sister-in-law's example was quite unpropitious. Orpah went back to her country and her gods, but Ruth "*clave.*" Her only companion was a widow mother, "empty," all impoverished. The country into which she was going, was a country unknown, and she had to enter it, in a manner, alone; without so much as a solitary countrywoman with her. But these impediments were nothing. The young stranger was determined in her choice " to suffer affliction with the people of God." The pain of singularity was of no consideration when contrasted with the pains of perdition. She knew the unknown country was the land of vision, Immanuel's land.

The advantages which arise from an early choice of the Lord to be our God, are innumerable. Ruth was honoured with a happy settlement in life. Boaz, the pious, " the generous, and the rich," became her husband, amid the blessings of the elders of the people. She had the honour to be the mother of Obed, the father of Jesse and grandfather of the man after God's own heart. She was one of the highly-favoured mothers from whom our Lord Jesus descended—while the character of her sister Orpah is lost in forgetfulness from the moment she retired from her distressed mother-in-law's side.

The departure of Ruth from Moab has been viewed as an emblem of the calling of the Gentile nations to the knowledge and adoration of the living and true God. It is worthy of observation that Rahab, one Gentile, was the mother of Boaz, and Ruth, another Gentile, his wife

The truth is unquestionable, that Gentiles with their forces shall come to the light of the Redeemer, and his church. The everlasting gospel is spreading, and the frequent convert is embracing the joyous missionary and exclaiming, "Thy people shall be my people, and thy God my God!"

ON THE INFLUENCES OF THE HOLY SPIRIT.

THE testimony of scripture, the history of our species, the observation we are making daily on men around us, and the knowledge we possess of our own hearts, confirm the melancholy truth, that man is every where polluted and guilty. The miseries consequent on sin in the present life are felt on every side, while those which are reserved in eternity for the finally impenitent, properly realized, must create the most serious alarm. Under the Old Testament the promise which encouraged the hope of a better state of society was the advent of Jesus Christ. Under the New Testament, the promise of the Spirit encourages our expectation, for it is He who shall convince the "world of sin, of righteousness, and of judgment." It is His to take of the things of Christ, and reveal them to the sons of men. He is the Spirit of holiness and truth; of power and wisdom, the agent by whom the heart is regenerated and enriched with heavenly graces. He is the Spirit of adoption and of prayer; the guide of his saints, who leads them through the wilderness, "for his mercy endureth for ever."

In many parts of our earth, in the age in which we live, we have heard of the effusions of the influence of the good Spirit of the Lord, and have witnessed the blessedness with which they have been accompanied. Let "the spirit be poured from on high" on the ministers of the gospel; secular aims vanish, the mind rises superior to mortal frowns or smiles; zeal for the salvation of men glows like the perpetual fire on the altar of the Lord, and a missionary passion is inspired. Let the holy influence descend on a church of Jesus Christ; its members will abound in love; they will fear the Lord, and speak often to each other. Prayer meetings will become crowded; an anxiety will generally be felt for the conversion of sinners, associated with desires to become useful in the world. The hand will be opened to communicate to the relief of the poor, and for the spread of the Saviour's kingdom; and circumspection and holiness mark the life and conduct. Let it descend on a family; parents become affectionate, children respectful, servants obedient, while the domestic altar flames with a sacrifice morning and evening to Him in whom "the families of the earth" are " blessed." Does it descend on the ungodly ? hypocrisy hurls away her mask, sabbath breaking is ended, swearing is no more; falsehood and deceit, envy and malice, are supplanted, and their seats in the heart occupied with integrity and good will; infidelity hides its head, confounded; youth relinquishes its vain expectations and follies, and age its obduracy and avarice. This blessed influence is the rod of Moses on the rock, which produces penitential streams: it is the shadow of Peter, that, "passing by," heals all manner of disease: it is the sling of David, before whose energy the enemy of Zion falls. Sacred Spirit! forgive these low allusions! it is thyself brooding on the face of the waters.

It is pleasing to observe how variously the influences we are now contemplating, approach the recipient. Sometimes they descend imperceptibly, like the dews of evening; at others unexpectedly, like the unlooked for visit of a friend. Here they come suddenly, as a summer shower; and there periodically, as torrents in mountainous countries. They are always effectual, like the opening of spring, and demonstrate, like the rains of heaven, that God is their father.

President Edwards remarks, that it has been God's manner in every new establishment of his visible church, to give a remarkable outpouring of his Spirit. Such displays of divine influence were enjoyed in the days of Enos, on the establishment of the Hebrews in Canaan, at the time of the restoration of the Jews from the bondage of Babylon, and especially at the introduction of the Gospel dispensation. The grand period, however, of holy effusion, yet remains. " This is the word of the Lord unto Zerubbabel, saying, not by might, nor by power, but by my Spirit, saith the Lord of Hosts." Where this grand and bounteous influence shall be first felt, we cannot say. The rise of bible and mission societies are probably among the providences that, after the example of John the Baptist, shall prepare the way for the coming of the Lord. When this sacred power shall descend, the earth, that has for ages been a wilderness, shall be converted into an Eden—righteousness shall prevail—peace shall flow like a river, and the church of God enjoy her long expected repose. With Ezekiel we behold an " open valley full of bones very dry," but the preaching of the word, and the inspirations of the Spirit, shall produce from the desolation " an exceeding great army." A new heaven and a new earth shall appear. The final jubilee shall be sounded, and its liberties, its honours, and its joys, endure for ever.

INTRODUCTION OF THE GOSPEL INTO ENGLAND.

TO be made acquainted with the means by which we have come into the possession of that invaluable treasure, the BIBLE, cannot be uninteresting or unacceptable. Nor can intelligence of this kind be lost in the momentary gratification of curiosity. A disclosure of the fact, that our own ancestors, having received the Gospel as the result of evangelic missionary effort, were thus rescued from the debasements and miseries of an idolatrous state, and have handed down to us this source of innumerable benefits, will strongly impress the conviction of reciprocal duty. This, too, will inspire the determined, vigorous, active, benevolent resolution, to employ all the means the kindness of Providence may throw into our hands, in a similar manner, to impart these unspeakable blessings to our brethren of the whole human family.

Joseph of Arimathea, the same who laid the body of 'our Lord in his own new tomb, hewn out in the rock,' is represented by ancient tradition, as the first who announced in the British isles the Gospel of salvation. Having been furnished by Philip the evangelist with eleven associates, or missionaries, about sixty-three years after the incarnation of our Saviour, and thirty after his ascension, he proceeded to Britain, to destroy the barbarous rites of the Druids, and introduce the religion of the Prince of Peace. Aviragus, the British king, permitted them to settle at Glastonbury, and allowed them *twelve hides* of land for their support. *Thus, by missionaries, was the knowledge of the Gospel communicated to our forefathers!*

In the year 43 the emperor Claudius visited in person this country; and an ancient inscription has created the belief that Pomponia, the wife of Plautius, one of his generals, made known the Gospel, not only to her domestics, but to a large circle of acquaintance, whilst resident in the country. Some, therefore, and not, certainly, without very plausible reasons, would attribute to this excellent lady the honour of having first introduced to our ancestors the knowledge of salvation by the atonement of Christ.

The apostle Paul, a distinguished and successful missionary to the Gentiles, or heathen, is by many supposed to have visited England. This opinion is conceived to be rendered highly probable, by a quotation from Clement, a cotemporary of this apostle. " Κηρυξ γινομενος εν τη ανατολη και εν τη δυσει—δικαιοσυνην διδαξας ολον τον κοσμον και επι το τερμα της δυσεως." " *He became a herald to the East and to the West;*

he taught the whole world righteousness, coming even to the boundaries of the West." Bishop Stillingfleet is confident that by "BOUNDARIES OF THE WEST," Britain is intended.

Without descanting on the supposition that St. Peter, or that Aristobulus, mentioned Romans xvi. 10. was the first who conveyed the knowledge of the gospel to England, it appears indubitable, not only by the concurrent testimony of history, but by *regal ordinances*, that the British were early converted to the Christian faith. The very *charter* granted by Henry II. in 1185, for rebuilding Glastonbury church, which had been burnt, denominates it *Mater sanctorum et tumulus sanctorum, quam ab ipsis discipulis domini edificatum,* "*the mother and burying place of the saints, founded by the very disciples of* Lord."

An additional testimony from Tertullian, who flourished near the middle of the second century, might be introduced here, and is omitted only for want of room, proving, unequivocally, the fact of the establishment of the gospel in England, in that early period. A quotation from Origen, about the year 220, might also be introduced in support of the same fact. Athanasius and Chrysostom might both be brought forward to the same effect, while the accounts of different councils held there to regulate the affairs of their churches, may be regarded as placing the matter beyond the legitimate bounds of controversy.

It would be both pleasant and interesting to pursue the track of this particular portion of history, and survey as we passed along the beneficial results of the Bible in England, from that early period of the Christian era, down to the present day; but this must be deferred to a future opportunity. Mean-time, let ours be the sacred gratification, while with devout thankfulness to our Creator we review those missionary labours which, by imparting the knowledge of salvation through a Redeemer, rescued our ancestors and ourselves from superstition, delusion, turpitude, and wo, to bring into action every sympathy that feels for our fellow-beings, every sentiment that loves what is truly desirable, and every faculty allotted us by the benevolence of the Deity, in carrying forward the cause of the exalted Son of God!

ALEXANDER, EMPEROR OF ALL THE RUSSIAS. AND PRINCE ALEXANDER GALITZIN.

FEW characters, if any, of the present day, are gazed at with a more sincere or more delighted admiration, than the Emperor of Russia, and his excellent friend and minister prince Alexander Galitzin. Few, if any, appear now on the theatre of the world, to whom a more interesting part appears to be assigned in those scenes which are so obviously prelusive of the millennial glory on earth! The following *short account of the commencement of the serious and religious impressions and their effects, on the minds of these distinguished personages*, will not, therefore, be unacceptable to the readers of the Luminary; nor can the Publishing Committee deny themselves the pleasure of acknowledging their obligation to the politeness of a respectable member of the society of Friends, a citizen of Philadelphia, for this interesting narrative.

"For many years a great friendship had existed between the Emperor of Russia, and prince Galitzin. It is said they were unbelievers. Beyond a doubt they were both opposed to the influence of vital religion, as appears by the following relation.

"The office of "Minister of Religion" having become vacant, the Emperor was inclined to dispose of it to a person whom he esteemed; but, understanding he was attached to the Bible, altered his intention, and with some difficulty prevailed upon prince Galitzin to accept the place. The prince early felt himself in a very awkward predicament, not knowing how to execute with any propriety the trust imposed on him. He was therefore under the necessity of sending for the bishop of the diocese, to ask his advice how to proceed in this arduous, and to him novel undertaking. The bishop referred him to a certain book, in which, he assured him, might be found every necessary instruction, and which he entreated him to study; repeating the assurance, that if he did so, faithfully, he would experience no difficulty in rightly proceeding in his new situation. This book was the Bible. To this his mind was opposed, and he objected against it to the bishop; but in a short time secretly obtained a Bible, and read it with much attention. The more he read, the more he was impressed with the importance of the subject—his understanding became enlightened, and a conviction fastened on his judgment of the truth and excellence of the sacred scriptures.

"This was but a short period previous to the entrance of the French army into Russia. When information of that event reached St. Petersburg, the Russian court were in great alarm; every one seemed to carry terror in his countenance. The prince alone appeared calm and serene. This circumstance caused universal surprise, known, as it was, that the sincerest attachment existed between the Emperor and himself. The former had observed it, and could hardly suppose it possible any one should be thus tranquil under circumstances which seemed to threaten ruin to the Russian empire. Yet he could not believe his friend a traitor, or that he was insensible to the pressing difficulties of the occasion.

"The Emperor one day called on the prince, and asked him, how it was that "he should be so composed, while every one else was in dismay?" to which he replied, that he had of late read the scriptures, and they had fortified his mind against every danger—giving him a firm trust in Divine help and protection. The Bible lying on the table, he urged his majesty's perusal of it, believing it would have the same calming influence on his mind, as he had been favoured to experience; at which the Emperor was displeased, and with violence pushed the Bible from him on the floor. It lay open on the ground; the prince took it up, and entreated his majesty to let him read the part which was then open, to which he agreed. It was the ninety-first Psalm. The Emperor was much struck with its appropriate and consoling language.

"When the Russian army was about departing from St. Petersburg to meet Napoleon, the sovereign and his officers went to church, as is the usual custom previous to an army's going on an expedition. The Emperor was greatly astonished when that part of the service of the Greek Church was read, which was a portion of the scriptures, that it should prove to be the ninety-first Psalm. He apprehended that prince Galitzin, who was with him, had desired this; but, on questioning him upon the subject, he declared he had not seen the person who had read the service, nor had he directly, or indirectly, had any communication with him since the conversation they had had about the scriptures.

"This circumstance made a strong impression on the mind of his majesty, and a reverence for the Bible began to impress itself on his feelings. While in the camp afterwards with his army, he sent for a chaplain of one of the regiments to read to him. His surprise was now very great; for the portion of scripture selected was the ninety-first Psalm. He inquired of the chaplain who told him to read that particular Psalm? to which he replied, "God;" for on being told on what account the Emperor had sent for him, he had most earnestly prayed that the Almighty would instruct him in what part of the scriptures he should read in order for the religious improvement of his august sovereign; and that it was from a Divine impulse he had read what he had. The Emperor now became more and more delighted with the Bible, and his subsequent conduct has amply attested the happy influence of these religious impressions on his mind."

It is quite remarkable that Beza, an eminent character of the Reformation, and author of a Latin translation of the New Testament, was, while young, and providentially in the church of Charenton, much impressed by an exposition of the *ninety-first Psalm*. He was enabled to believe that the Lord would fulfil to him all the promises of it; at death he declared that he had found it so indeed.

It is stated on authority not to be questioned, that the Sister of Alexander has become the happy subject of experimental piety and the gracious operations of the holy Spirit. In addition to the foregoing detail of Providential circumstances, which, by the blessing of God, have induced one of the most powerful of earthly monarchs to become one of the most active, as he is one of the most illustrious, and able patrons of the Bible, it would be particularly gratifying to insert at large, could the limits of this work allow of it, the distinguishing exercises of the mind of his Sister connected with her becoming acquainted with "the truth as it is in Jesus," and possessed of that "faith" which "is the substance of things hoped for, and the evidence of things not seen." May her life be as splendid by religious attainment, as elevated by rank, and, like lady Huntington, lady Erskine, and other excellent females, may she be the angel of mercy, of peace, and salvation to many.

UKASE,

ADDRESSED TO THE LEGISLATIVE SYNOD AT MOSCOW, BY ALEXANDER, EMPEROR OF RUSSIA,

Dated from Moscow, October 27, 1817.

"During my late travels through the Provinces, I was obliged, to my no small regret, to listen to speeches pronounced by certain of the clergy in different parts, which contained unbecoming praises of me; praises which can be ascribed only unto God. And as I am convinced in the depth of my heart of the Christian truth, that every blessing floweth unto us through our Lord and Saviour Jesus Christ alone, and that every man, be he whom he may, without Christ, is full only of evil; therefore, to ascribe unto me the glory of deeds, in which the hand of God hath been so evidently manifested before the whole world, is to give unto man that glory which belongeth to Almighty God alone.

"I account it my duty, therefore, to forbid all such unbecoming expressions of praise, and recommend to the Holy Synod to give instructions to all the diocesan Bishops, that they themselves, and the clergy under them, may, on similar occasions, in future, refrain from all such expressions of praise, so disagreeable to my ears; and that they may render unto the Lord of Hosts alone, thanksgivings for the blessings bestowed upon us, and pray for the out-pouring of His grace upon all of us; conforming themselves in this matter to the words of Sacred Writ, which requires us to render to the King Eternal, Immortal, Invisible, the only wise God, honour and glory for ever and ever.

"ALEXANDER."

SCRIPTURE CRITICISM.

In this thing the Lord pardon thy servant, that when my master goeth into the house of Rimmon to worship there, and he leaneth on my hand, and I bow myself in the house of Rimmon; when I bow down myself in the house of Rimmon, the Lord pardon thy servant in this thing. 2 KINGS, v. 18.

RIMMON was an idol: whether the sun, or some other elevated object, is to us unimportant. The Christian, in controversy with the Infidel, has often in substance said, point to the passage in the sacred writings that connives at sin, and we will admit the Bible is not holy and divine. Naaman was healed of leprosy by obeying the instructions of Elisha. He discovers a heart converted to the belief that an idol is nothing—that Jehovah is the true God. "He said, behold, now I know that there is no God in all the earth, but in Israel." Yet in the words above, as taken from our translation, he asks leave to join his master in idolatrous service. He hopes God will pardon him for the sin he intends to commit; and the prophet bids him " go, in peace."

Surely there is a difficulty here that requires solution. It is far from satisfying honest inquiry, because far from honouring the holy word, to assert, that the bowing in question was not religious, but merely civil and political, as Abraham's bowing, Gen. xxiii. 7. Still less acceptable is the pretence that to worship idols was forbidden only to the Israelites. The ingenious remark of Mr. Scott, that " we should always fear losing our advantages by prematurely grasping too much," is about as satisfactory as Mr. Henry's, who says that, " perhaps, all things considered, this might be excusable in Naaman, though not justifiable;" or as Beza's, who, on the words ' *Go, in peace,*' observes, " the prophet did not approve Naaman's act, but, after the common manner of address, bids him farewell." We would rather say with Mr. Brown, " Holy gratitude disposeth to a careful performance of duty, both *towards* God and man. It disposeth to *remember past transgressions with grief, and to resolve for the future to abstain from all appearance of evil."*

What shall be done with this difficulty? The observations of the Assembly of Divines in their " Annotations, &c." deserve attention.

" In this thing pardon thy servant, that when my master went into the house of Rimmon to worship there, and leaned on my hand, and I bowed myself in the house of Rimmon; that I bowed myself in the house of Rimmon, the Lord pardon thy servant in this thing."

They add, " the very words of this place are, in other places, translated by the time past, as כבוא, *when he went*, Psalm li. 1. & lii. 1. & liv. 1." So, as to the words " leaned, 2 Samuel i. 6. and bowed down, Exod. xxxiii. 10."

Admit this translation, and all is easy, all is beautiful. The convert and the prophet each acts a consistent, natural, and most interesting part. Calmet evidently adopted this rendering. He says, " Naaman the Syrian confesses to Elisha, that he had often been in the temple of Rimmon with the king of Damascus, his master, who leaned on his arm while he paid his adorations." We are happy to find the venerable Dr. Gill of our opinion. Naaman's " request to the prophet or to the Lord, is not for pardon for a sin to be committed; nor to be indulged in his continuance of it; nor to worship the idol along with his master; nor to dissemble the worship of it when he really worshipped it not; nor to be excused any evil in the discharge of his post or office: but for the pardon of the sin of idolatry, which he *had been guilty of*, of which he was truly sensible, now sincerely acknowledges, and desires forgiveness. And so Dr. Lightfoot and some others interpret it. To this sense the words may be rendered; *When my master went into the house of Rimmon to worship there*—which was his usual custom—*and he leaned on my hand*—which was the common form in which he was introduced into it—*and I worshipped in the house of Rimmon*—as his master did, for the same word is used here as before—*inasmuch*, or, *seeing, I have worshipped in the house of Rimmon*—have been guilty of such gross idolatry—*the Lord, I pray, forgive thy servant in this thing:* the language of a true penitent."

The original text conveys a very lively idea of the feelings of the converted Naaman. לדבר הזה.—יסלח נא יהוה. For this thing, (hac re, condonabitne. Vid. Pol.) For this thing, will Jehovah indeed forgive me?—will he dissolve my chains? *Naaman, he will!* is the implied language of Elisha—" Go, in peace." Such are the tidings the missionary of Christ has to convey to the embarrassed heart of every heathen convert.

MISSIONARY INTELLIGENCE.

FOREIGN MISSIONARY DEPARTMENT, CONNECTED WITH THE BOARD.

MISSION TO BURMAH.

THIS mission, from the time of Mr. Judson's arrival at Rangoon, has presented an object of increasing interest and promise to all who " pray for the peace of Jerusalem," and are longing for the period to arrive when " all flesh shall see the salvation of God." To know the origin of this undertaking, as it regards the occupancy of the station at Rangoon by American missionaries, will be gratifying to all, and tend to secure a patronage in its support, which liberal minds ever incline to bestow on objects of whose propriety they entertain a distinct and enlightened persuasion.

As far back as the year 1807, a few young men, having the Gospel ministry in view, then students in William's College, Massachusetts, began to converse together on the subject of missionary labours. Messrs. Samuel J. Mills, Gordon Hall, James Richards, Luther Rice, and others, were of this number; several of whom came to the deliberate resolution of devoting their lives to the service of the Gospel among heathen portions of the human race. This was previous to the existence of any thing like a public impression on the subject; before either " The Star in the East," or the "Christian Researches in Asia," of Dr. Buchanan were printed in this country; while the operations of the baptist mission at Serampore were little known in the United States, and every thing in the case was as remote as possible from notoriety, the very meetings of the young men for prayer and conversation on the subject being without the observation or even knowledge of their fellow students.

As the result of these impressions, views, and purposes, and similar ones, not far from the same period, although the persons were in different places, on the minds of Messrs. Samuel Newell, Samuel Nott, Adoniram Judson, and others, a memorial, in the spring of 1810, was addressed to the General Association of ministers of Massachusetts, held that year not far from Andover, the seat of a Theological Institution, at which most of the persons, whose names are mentioned above, were at that time pursuing studies connected with the ministry. In consequence of this memorial, was formed the same year, " The American Board of Commissioners for Foreign Missions."

Under the patronage of this excellent and highly respectable society, early in 1812, the Rev. Messrs. Gordon Hall, Samuel Newell, Samuel Nott, Adoniram Judson, and Luther Rice, having been, for that service, solemnly ordained and set apart, sailed from their native country for the East Indies.

While on their voyage to the East, Mr. and Mrs. Judson were induced to commence a re-examination of the points in controversy between the baptists and their brethren of other denominations. Mr. Rice, although in another vessel, was also drawn, in some measure, to a fresh consideration of the same points. Sometime after arriving in Bengal, Mr and Mrs Judson, and not many weeks later, Mr. Rice, were baptised—all of them in Calcutta, by the Rev. Mr. Ward, one of the baptist missionaries associated in the establishment at Calcutta and Serampore.

The measures adopted on the part of the British East India Company's government, were such as rendered it necessary for the brethren Judson and Rice to go from Bengal to Mauritius, or the Isle of France. Mr. Newell, owing to similar measures, had gone to the same place before them. Thence, it was judged expedient, and his duty, for Mr. Rice to return again to the United States, the consequences of which are well known.

After the departure of his colleague, Mr. Judson, with his excellent lady, left Mauritius for Madras, in the expectation of proceeding thence to Penang, and of commencing there his missionary labours with reference to the Malays, a people whose language is easy, and who have spread themselves extensively along the coast of the eastern peninsula of India, and the adjacent Islands. Such, however, were the arrangements of the overruling providence of God, as rendered it necessary for them to proceed from Madras directly to Rangoon—*the very point had in view by the whole mission on leaving the United States for the East!*

The incidents affecting that mission in any considerable degree since the providential manner of Mr. Judson's being conveyed to that station, have been so fully communicated in the Annual Reports of the Board, as to render it unnecessary to introduce them here. The state of it by the latest information may be seen in the following documents. *Seventeen millions of idolators, five millions of whom can read, call aloud on the Christian public to put them in possession of the Scriptures of Truth!*

FROM MR. JUDSON TO THE CORRESPONDING SECRETARY.

RANGOON, *March* 7, 1817.

REV. AND DEAR SIR,

Since the beginning of this year we have printed two tracts; the one, a view of the Christian religion—7 pages 1000 copies—the other a catechism of 6 pages, 12mo.—3000 copies. After which, finding that we had paper sufficient for an edition of 800 of Matthew, we concluded to undertake this one Gospel, by way of trial, and as introductory to a larger edition of the whole New Testament. I am now translating the 11th chapter, and in the printing-room, the 3d half sheet is setting up. Having premised thus much concerning the present posture of our affairs, I proceed to mention the circumstance which induced me to take up my pen at this time. I have this day been visited by the first inquirer after religion, that I have ever seen in Burmah. For, although in the course of the last two years, I have preached the Gospel to many, and though some have visited me several times, and conversed on the subject of religion, yet I have never had much reason to believe that their visits originated in a spirit of sincere inquiry. Conversations on religion have always been of my proposing; and though I have sometimes been encouraged to hope, that truth had made some impression, never, till to-day, have I met with one who was fairly entitled to the epithet of *Inquirer*.

"As I was sitting with my teacher, as usual, a Burman of respectable appearance, and followed by a servant, came up the steps and sat down by me. I asked him the usual question, Where he came from? to which he gave no explicit reply, and I began to suspect, that he had come from the government-house, to enforce a trifling request which in the morning we had declined. He soon, however, undeceived and astonished me, by asking, "How long time will it take me to learn the religion of Jesus?" I replied, that such a question could not be answered. If God gave light and wisdom, the religion of Jesus was soon learnt, but without God, a man might study all his life long, and make no proficiency. But how, continued I, came you to know any thing of Jesus? Have you been here before? "No." Have you seen any writing concerning Jesus? "I have seen two little books." Who is Jesus? "He is the Son of God, who, pitying creatures, came into this world, and suffered death in their stead." Who is God? "He is a being, without beginning or end, who is not subject to old age and death, but always is." I cannot tell how I felt at this moment. This was the first acknowledgment of an eternal God, that I had ever heard from the lips of a Burman. I handed him a tract and catechism, both which he instantly recognized, and read here and there, making occasional remarks to his follower, such as, "This is the true God—this is the right way," &c. I now tried to tell him some things about God and Christ, and himself, but he did not listen with much attention, and seemed anxious only to get another book. I had already told him two or three times, that I had finished no other book, but that, in two or three months, I would give him a larger one, which I was now daily employed in translating. "But," replied he, "have you not a little of that book done, which you will graciously give me now?" And I, beginning to think that God's time is better than man's, folded and gave him the two first half sheets, which contain the five first chapters of Matthew, on which he instantly rose, as if his business was all done, and having received an invitation to come again, took leave.

Throughout his short stay, he appeared different from any Burmans I have yet met with. He asked no questions about customs and manners, with which the Burmans teaze us exceedingly. He had no curiosity, and no desire for any thing, but "MORE OF THIS SORT OF WRITING." In fine, his conduct proved that he had something on his mind, and I cannot but hope, that I shall have to write about him again.

March 24th. We have not yet seen our inquirer, but to-day we met with one of his acquaintance, who says, that he reads our books all the day, and shows them to all that call upon him. We told him to ask his friend to come and see us again.

March 26th. An opportunity occurs of sending to Bengal. I am sorry that I cannot send home more interesting letters. But I am not yet in the way of collecting interesting matter. I have found, that I could not preach publicly to any advantage, without being able, at the same time, to put something into the hands of the hearers. And in order to qualify myself to do this, I have found it absolutely necessary to keep at home, and confine myself to close study for three or four years. I hope, however, after Matthew is finished, to make a more public entrance on my work, than has yet been done. But many difficulties lie in the way. Our present house is situated in the woods, away from any neighbours, and at a distance from any road! In this situation, we have no visiters, and no passing travellers, whom we could invite to stop and hear of Christ. My attempts to go out and find auditors, have always occasioned such a waste of time, and interruption of study, as would not often be indulged in or justified. We are very desirous of building a small house near town, on some public road, but do not venture to incur the expense. We wish further instructions, and further explanations of the views and intentions of the Board. The approaching triennial Convention, also, we contemplate with the deepest interest. May God give abundant wisdom, and zeal, and holy spirit!

Permit me to close with a word in behalf of Eastern missions. Great Britain and the United States appear to be the only countries which can, at present, take a very active part in missionary concerns. The British are fully occupied with India, Africa, and the South sea Islands. East of the British possessions in India, are Burmah, Siam, several other Indo-Chinese nations, the great empire of China, Japan, thence north indefinitely, and southward, the numerous Malayan isles. With all these countries the British are no more connected than the Americans. The British are under no greater obligations to evangelize them, than the Americans. They are no nearer the English, in point of transportation, than the Americans. And furthermore, throughout all these countries, the British are suspected and feared; but not the Americans.

The idea that the Western continent belongs to the Americans, and the Eastern continent to the British, however plausible at first sight, cannot bear a moment's examination. I apprehend, that all the north western Indians, and the inhabitants of those parts of South America which are accessible, will scarcely outnumber the inhabitants of this single empire of Burmah. And on what principle can the Americans, who are perhaps half as numerous as the British, be let off with one twentieth or one thirtieth part of the work? But when we apply the case to the baptists, it is still more decisive. There are about 500 baptist churches in Great Britain, which average one hundred members each. There are 2000 in America, which average about the same. Behold Ireland also, almost as destitute as South America. And suppose the British should say—This is the proper province of our missionary exertions. Let us leave Asia and Africa to the Americans, and "not send our young men to the antipodes!"

Yours, respectfully,

A. JUDSON.

Rev. Dr. STAUGHTON, Cor. Sec. &c. &c.

FROM MR. JUDSON TO THE CORRESPONDING SECRETARY.

RANGOON, *June* 18, 1817.

REV. AND DEAR SIR,

The translation of Matthew was finished the 20th of last month, and the printing soon after. The books are now ready for distribution. The tracts, which are already in circulation, have begun to excite considerable inquiry. I generally go out every morning, and distribute a few, as opportunities offer, and sometimes say a few words to those I meet. In several instances, those who have received tracts have come to inquire further, and there are a few who have visited us several times, professing a desire to become acquainted with the religion of *Yeeshoo Creet.* The man whom I mentioned in my last as having given much encouragement during a single interview, lives, I find, at a considerable distance from Rangoon, and was here on a visit merely. On Sunday a few come together, mostly people who live in the yard, with whom I converse on religion. Mrs. J. does the same with a little company of women. Our lonely situation in the woods, at a distance from the town and any public road, together with the rainy season, which has just commenced with violence, prevents much intercourse with the natives. If our pecuniary supplies permitted, we should procure a more advantageous situation. In present circumstances, having neither money for this purpose, nor money to purchase paper and types, and other means of carrying on the printing of the New Testament, I have concluded, at the request of brother Hough, to devote the ensuing six months to revising and putting in order the materials of a Burman dictionary, which I have been long collecting. To this I am urged by the consideration of the present illegible and confused state of the manuscripts, which would render them useless to any other person: whereas, if revised and carried forward to that state of improvement, which the labour of six months will accomplish, they will, I calculate, occasion a saving of at least one year to every missionary who shall hereafter undertake the language. At the expiration of this time we hope to receive such supplies of men and money, as will enable us to go forward in our work.

The brethren at Serampore stand ready to comply with all our wishes, and to forward us all that we require, but we hesitate at sending them orders to a large amount, when the remittances from America in our favour, are not sufficient to meet the bills which we are obliged to draw on them for bare subsistence. They have given us advice of having received one thousand dollars in our favour, granted June 1816. You will be able, however, to obtain a more correct idea of the probable expense of this mission, from our joint communication, made soon after brother Hough's arrival, a copy of which we transmitted to Serampore, and received in reply a letter, from which I extract the following, viz.

"Very dear brethren,—We have been highly pleased on reading your late communications. The specimens of your printing, your family rules, your prospect of putting the New Testament to press, &c. all gave us great joy; and we were quite pleased to see a translation [rather a Burman catechism] from the pen of our beloved sister Judson. The Lord spare you long; bless you greatly; and make you a holy and most blessed family. In all these matters, very dear brethren, we are wholly with you; and, to the utmost of our power, will strengthen your hands. May we all be strong in faith: then we need not fear man, nor distrust God.

"We are indeed yours,

"W. CAREY, J. MARSHMAN, W. WARD."

[After communicating in detail, with too much length and particularity to be copied at large, an account of difficulties which it had been their lot to encounter at Rangoon, and their severe disappointment at finding, upon a more careful and accurate attention, that the attempts at translation and at the preparation of a dictionary and grammar, by those before them in that station, were too imperfect to be useful, Mr Judson adds:]

On perusing this letter the members of the Board will perhaps be able to enter a little into the distresses and trials which myself and my wife solitarily and silently sustained for two or three years. I do not wish to revive the recollection of scenes which for days together deprived us of appetite and sleep. I hope that we were enabled to pass through them in a meek and Christian manner, and to bear what our heavenly Father was pleased to lay upon us, trusting in His wisdom and goodness, whose prerogative it is to bring good out of evil, and light out of darkness.

With our earnest prayer that the Holy Spirit may be granted, both to guide th counsels of the Board, and to make their missionaries faithful and persevering
I remain,
Your missionary, A. JUDSON

Rev. Dr Staughton, Cor. Sec. &c. &c.

EXTRACT OF A LETTER FROM MRS. JUDSON TO MRS. S———.

Rangoon, *June* 18, 1817.

My Dear Mrs. S———,

Amid all our trials and privations it has been a source of thanksgiving and praise that Providence had brought us to Burmah, and it is our constant and ardent prayer that we may live and die among this people.

It is unnecessary for me to write any thing relative to the mission, as Mr. Judson is writing to Dr. S———. I have a little meeting of females, to whom I read tracts, and some part of Matthew, and try to teach them how to pray to the living God. They sometimes ask pertinent questions, and one of them, I hope, is seriously feeling the need of a Saviour. I visited her yesterday, as she was confined to her house by sickness, and inquired particularly respecting the state of her mind. She told me she prayed every day to the true God, to give her a new heart, and enable her to believe on his Son. We have so frequently had our hopes and expectations raised by similar cases, that we hardly dare promise ourselves much from this. We doubt not God will, in his own time, convert the Burmans, and that he is now preparing the way for the promulgation of the gospel here. We see no ground for discouragement, but feel rather that the circumstance that no Burman has yet been converted, should be a fresh stimulus to double our diligence; and a new excitement to our friends, at home, to be more in prayer for this great blessing.

I frequently visit the viceroy's wife. She has given orders that I shall be admitted into her private apartments whenever I wish. I gave her a tract a few days ago, and she asked me to read some of it. I began to read to her a description of the character of God. She heard me through a few lines, took the book and laid it down, and said it was very good, and she would hear me some other time. I presume she has never looked at it since. It is extremely difficult to hold a long conversation with her, as she is always engaged in business. O, that God would touch her heart, and make her a monument of his mercy! Very few of the females here know how to read; consequently they think it a great acquisition in me to be able to read their language.

I doubt not, my dear Mrs. S———, you constantly pray for us, and long to hear of the conversion of the heathen around us.

Our temporal wants are comfortably supplied, health is preserved to us, we are happy in our employment, and would not change situation with any person in the world.

When I reflect on the perishing state of the Burmans; when I see how much there is to be done, and how few to do it, conscience tells me that all inferior gratifications must yield to the great work of the mission. How happy should I be to receive a long letter from you! Do gratify and comfort us a little in this way. We still love America, and feel a deep interest in every communication from our native land. Excuse my freedom, and permit me to subscribe myself,

Your unworthy sister in Christ,

NANCY JUDSON.

FROM MR. HOUGH TO THE BOARD.

RANGOON, *June* 19. 1817.

DEAR BRETHREN,

My mind being now relieved of an anxiety of several months' continuance, and my hands of a laborious duty in the printing office, I feel myself constrained to communicate to you the manner of my entering upon the work for which I was sent to this place, and the reasons which induced me to proceed as I have.

Soon after my arrival in Bengal, a letter was received by Dr. Carey from brother Judson, mentioning his having written a tract, and inquiring whether or not it could be printed at Serampore. The receipt of this letter so soon after my arrival, was such a coincidence as could not be viewed in any other light, than indicative of what I ought, in duty, to do. This, in the opinion of the brethren at Serampore, in which I could not but cheerfully concur, was, that I should take a printing press and types with me to Rangoon, and accomplish in the field of our mission, what otherwise must be done out of it, viz. printing the scriptures, religious tracts, &c. Their benevolent and pious aid was exhibited in the valuable donation of an apparatus for commencing the printing business. At that time I understood that the press taken to Ava by Mr. F. Carey had not been put in motion, and on my arrival at Rangoon the fact was amply corroborated that it had not been in use either for missionary or other purposes.

When arrived here, after adjusting the temporal affairs of my family, I commenced the study of the language, with this limitation, to pursue a knowledge of it no further, at this time, than would be requisite for conducting merely the manual labour of printing. This could be done when the language could be read with a little degree of accuracy.

In this the views of brother Judson and myself were one. It was thought that the time had fully come, when the Burmans generally should be made acquainted, not only that this mission really had an existence here, but also of its important design. Hitherto it had not been possible for brother Judson, a solitary missionary among surrounding thousands, to do more than strive after communication with the Burmans, by obtaining, through means at most scanty, and at brightest, obscure, such a knowledge of the language as would qualify him to speak and write it intelligibly. We both felt it immoveably impressed upon our minds, that, at least, as an intimation of the way of life, through a Saviour, could be made, at that time, to a people sitting in darkness and in the shadow of death, such an intimation could not consistently be withheld. Add to this, brother Judson's ardent desire to appear more publicly in the work, and be more generally known. In order for this he felt the need of something more than his voice, a tract or two, and a portion or two of the word of God, he thought would strengthen him. With this he was not supplied Whatever had before been written and translated in the Burman language, we had the inconvenience of finding was unintelligible, which their authors had left the field without experiencing. Besides, it was thought that a dictionary, materials for which had been collected from various sources by Mr. Judson, and which he purposed to arrange, when the translation of Matthew should be completed, would be of such utility to me and others in acquiring the language, as to place me, at a year's end, in as high a state of forwardness, as that which could be obtained, without that facility, by applying myself without any interruption. Calculating on this, together with the good which might result to the Burmans, from the contemplated operations of the press for a few months, we had no alternative but a decision upon those measures which we have, each of us, since pursued.

After studying the language a few weeks, and making the necessary preparations, I began work in the office, where I have continued until a few days past. On the 25th of January I finished striking off the first tract, 1000 copies. February 5th, finished a small catechism, 300 copies June 3d, completed Matthew, containing 104 pages large 8vo 500 copies, which is now ready for distribution. Pray with us, dear brethren, that this precious little portion of the scriptures may make many Burmans " wise unto salvation." This labour has been done by my own hands, excepting that in striking off a part of the sheets of the translation, we employed a Burman to use the *balls*.

"By the good hand of our God upon us," having been enabled to accomplish our wishes thus far, I have again set down to the study of the language.

When the printing of the New Testament will again be resumed, we are unable to determine, casting a waiting and wishful eye, at present, on your appropriations for means of conducting it, not having received the least intimation how far you intend to uphold us in the blessed work of giving the scriptures to this poor, perishing people. Should you find appropriations for other purposes, to be more practicable, and should duty seem to call your attention another way, still, while feeling ourselves your servants for the Lord's sake, and bound to you by the most endearing ties, we shall put our trust in the treasures of Him, whose is the earth, and the fulness thereof.

We have some hopes of three or four Burmans, that there is upon their minds a slight influence of Divine radiance; but whether our hopes will be like an early cloud which vanisheth away, a higher ascent of the orb of light must determine. O! that our hopes may abide!

Dear brethren, be mindful of us as we are of you, and pray for us that our labours be not in vain

Your servant for Christ's sake,

GEORGE H. HOUGH.

SAILING OF MORE MISSIONARIES FOR BURMAH.

COMMUNICATIONS from our beloved brethren in Boston, have announced the sailing of Mr. Wheelock, and Mr. Colman, with their wives, for Calcutta, on their way to Rangoon. The morning on which the anchor was weighed, about 200 of the brethren and sisters assembled at the ship. Suitable lines were sung and a prayer presented by Dr. Baldwin, in which every bosom joined, for their safety and usefulness. The breezes of heaven blew fresh and fair. It is supposed that during the first twenty-four hours, they had made, at least, 180 miles of their passage. The parting was unusually tender. All seemed agitated and in tears, excepting the dear missionaries themselves, in whom all other ideas appeared lost, excepting such as were connected with the honour of becoming missionaries of the cross, and the prospect of doing good to millions of degraded and perishing Burmans.

Mrs. Colman observed to a sister present, that she would not exchange her situation with any. One circumstance, mentioned by brother Sharp, was of a nature peculiarly affecting. The father of Mr. Wheelock, just before the vessel moved, cried out "my dear Willard, let me see thy face once more!" Wheelock came to the side. His father saw him, and unable to sustain the sight, ran through the crowd, and hastened to his habitation to commend his dear son, now offered on the sacrifice of faith, to the arms of a Father, who is present in every region. Mr Colman uttered some expressions as the ship was moving, but they were not distinctly heard. About the same time Mr. Wheelock was understood to say, " If I forget thee, O Jerusalem, let my right hand forget her cunning If I do not remember thee, let my tongue cleave to the roof of my mouth; if I prefer not Jerusalem above my chief joy———"

Public prayer meetings the sabbath before the vessel sailed, were held in Boston, New York, and Philadelphia. At an early season, another prayer meeting was held by our Boston friends, at which the brethren officiating enjoyed unusual enlargement, and the congregation, though the services were protracted until 10 in the evening, were unwilling to break up. Sacred consolations! how do they attend and recompense missionary endeavours! What a feast of sympathy and joy do they spread for every enlightened and benevolent mind! Scenes, such as these we describe, must interest the transports of cherubim, and command the gracious smiles of that Redeemer, whose name they are designed to honour!

> "Soft airs and gentle heavings of the wave,
> Impel the "ship," whose errand is to save,
> Let nothing adverse, nothing unforeseen,
> Impede the bark that ploughs the deep serene,
> Charg'd with a freight transcending in its worth,
> The gems of India, nature's rarest birth,
> That flies, like Gabriel on his Lord's commands,
> A herald of God's love to heathen lands."

Missionary Instructions.

FROM MR. WHEELOCK, A SHORT TIME BEFORE SAILING.

BOSTON, *October* 18, 1817.

REV AND VERY DEAR SIR,

You have probably heard, that brother Colman and myself have been ordained as missionaries to the heathens. O, sir! how interesting was the scene! The solemnities of that day can never be forgotten, while memory retains her seat in my bosom! Our beloved tutor, Mr. Chaplin, preached the sermon from Gal. ii 9. Our venerable Dr. Baldwin gave the charge, and our dear Mr. Sharp, the right hand of fellowship. Yes, my dear sir! on the very self-same day in which, six years before, in the same house, the first time I ever entered it, my mind was arrested by Divine truth, I was there again to be *set apart* to the sacred and glorious work of a missionary of the cross! O, how shall I express my gratitude to our heavenly Father for his great goodness and mercy towards me! " Bless the Lord, O my soul, and forget not all his benefits!"

We expect to sail in about six weeks.

Accept, dear sir, my unfeigned thanks for your fatherly advice to make the blessed bible, as much as possible, *my own* I feel this to be of the first importance. The Greek, and Hebrew, and geography, will, I expect, occupy the principal part of my time before sailing.

"I remain, dear sir, your unworthy, but affectionate,

EDWARD W. WHEELOCK."

INSTRUCTIONS

Of the " Baptist Board of Foreign Missions" to their young friends, Mr. Wheelock, and Mr. Colman, about to commence their voyage to Calcutta, on their way to Rangoon.

BELOVED BRETHREN,

The Board contemplate with pleasure, the work on which, in the name of the Lord Jesus, you are now entering. They fervently pray, that the "arm of the Lord," may prove your firm support under all your trials, and that the same sacred arm may be made bare, to give success to your anticipated labours in the empire of Burmah. They are convinced, that you have already received the judicious counsel of the brethren who undertook the charge of your outfit, and that in Burmah you will enjoy such valuable advice, as the experience of the brethren there has qualified them for imparting. They nevertheless, conceive it a duty to address to you a few lines. And the delicacy, lest it should seem to interfere with the province of the worthy committee, above referred to, who superintend your departure, is removed by the following passage in a letter to the Secretary from Dr Baldwin. "It has been usual, I believe, in every instance, when our missionaries have been sent out, for them to receive particular instructions from the Corresponding Secretary, as the organ of the Board. If you should think proper to address them, it would be very pleasing to us, and, I presume, highly gratifying to our young friends."

It is the wish of the Board that the general sentiments and recommendations, contained in their second annual Report, be considered as directed, in substance, to yourselves, as well as to the brethren already at the mission station.

In a land of darkness and enemies you will perceive the importance of combining your interest and affections to the utmost possible extent. Unity of temporalities in missionary projects has been the vital pulse of the wonderful establishment at Serampore. In reference to Burmah, we would urge that such a union "is not a vain thing for you, because it is your life." While the members of the mission feel themselves "One in Christ Jesus," and while the Board is fully convinced, that no disposition exists in the brethren in India to assume an improper influence, they affectionately urge you, to pay that respect to their sentiments, which superior age, and an actual residence at Rangoon, obviously claim.

The Board has received most pleasing testimonials, relative to the amiableness of your dispositions, and has confidence in your prudence and piety; but youth is a season of inexperience, and the suggestions of years will not be despised. Be circumspect and conciliating in your conduct on board the Independence. Missionaries of the cross sometimes derive encouragement to future service from the blessings which follow their intercourse with those who sail with them. A respectable and useful minister of Christ, now connected with the Philadelphia Association, was brought to the knowledge of the truth, under the pious instructions of Rev. Mr. Biss, while passing in the ship from America to Calcutta. May the honour be yours, as instruments in the hand of the Lord, to rescue some thoughtless mariner from the error of his ways, and thereby "save a soul from death."

Appreciate the counsels of the millennial band at Serampore, observe their habits, and cultivate their friendship. They are the medium of intercommunication between the Board and Burmah, and are entitled to respect and gratitude.

Above all, dear brethren, may you and your companions in Christ abound in personal religion. The prosperity of your own souls will be the surest presage of success in your missions. Familiarity with the throne of grace will confirm your faith, sustain your hopes, beguile your tribulations, and animate your zeal.

The Board will be happy often to hear from you. Write at large, either by way of letter or journal.

Be assured that your necessities and comforts, together with the demands for publishing tracts, the scriptures, &c. will engage the constant and solicitous attention of the Board. Ample funds, no doubt, by the liberality of the public, will be offered; and He, who is the Proprietor of the silver and the gold, has promised his blessing.

On the behalf of the Board, much beloved brethren,

Yours affectionately,

WM. STAUGHTON, *Cor. Sec.*

PHILADELPHIA, *November*, 1817.

MISSIONARY INTELLIGENCE.

DOMESTIC MISSIONARY DEPARTMENT, CONNECTED WITH THE BOARD

MISSION TO THE WESTWARD OF THE MISSISSIPPI RIVER

UPON the service of this mission the brethren John M. Peck, and James E. Welch, having been solemnly *set apart* for it last May, have zealously entered. Communications from them while journeying to the field of their labours, and since their arrival at St. Louis, have been received. A particular account of the monies contributed and put into their hands for missionary purposes by the liberality of the churches and people, as they passed along, and the societies they assisted in forming to promote the same object, will be presented in the next annual Report of the Board.

FROM MR. WELCH TO THE CORRESPONDING SECRETARY.

LEXINGTON, Ky. *October* 9, 1817.

REVEREND AND DEAR SIR,

Allow me to present to you, and through you to the Board, a short detail of the course pursued by me since my appointment as their missionary to the west.

Pursuant to the instructions of the Board, I proceeded immediately to prepare for my journey; left Philadelphia the 19th of June, and arrived the 27th, in Orange county, Virginia. Being detained a few weeks in that quarter, an opportunity was offered of making frequent collections, and the 15th day of July allowed me the happiness of aiding in the formation of the "Union Society, auxiliary to the Board," whose annual subscription on the day of its constitution amounted to 235 dollars, besides donations.

Renewing our journey on the 16th of July, taking, as I passed along, a missionary collection in a presbyterian meeting house, in Rockbridge county, it was with considerable difficulty, owing to sickness and inclement weather, that myself and companion reached Kentucky, in time for me to meet the Elkhorn Association the second Saturday and Sabbath in August. The liberality of this respectable body in favour of the general object, together with the kind reception of friends, more than rewarded for every privation and suffering.

The next Saturday and Sabbath I was at the South District Association in Mercer county, preached a missionary sermon, and received a collection; and the following Saturday and Sabbath was at the Tate's Creek Association, where I also preached on the subject, and received a collection for the mission cause. Meantime, arrangements were made with several brethren of Madison county, Kentucky, for the formation of a mission society in that quarter.

The first Saturday and Sabbath in September, at the Bracken Association,

Mason county, was witnessed a very happy display of liberal feeling in behalf of the perishing heathen. On Thursday evening following, in Lancaster, Ohio, a missionary sermon was delivered and a collection taken, and on the second Sabbath in September, a like service was performed in the morning in the baptist church at Mayslick, and in the afternoon in Washington, at both of which places collections were taken in aid of the mission funds.

The 25th of September was formed the "Madison Society of Kentucky Auxiliary," &c. And on the Saturday and Sabbath following, a kind Providence conferred on me the favour of attending the Salem Association, Nelson county, Kentucky. With feelings not easily expressed I witnessed the zeal and liberality of this large and respectable Association. On Monday evening of the same week, a sermon was delivered in Bardstown, and a public collection received, as also on Wednesday at Springfield.

On Sabbath, the 15th of October, we joyfully welcomed the arrival of brother Peck and family. We spent the Sabbath with the baptist church at David's Fork, and received a collection.

I should do violence to my feelings were I not to acknowledge in this short detail, the kindness of many individuals, while pursuing the great object of my appointment. And particularly the liberality of col. James Johnson, of Scott county, in franking the passage of Mrs Welsh and myself in his stage from Kentucky to Lancaster, Ohio, and back to Kentucky again, a journey of about 250 miles.

With sentiments of sincere regard to yourself, sir, and the Board of missions,

I subscribe myself yours, in missionary labour,

JAMES E. WELCH.

FROM MR. PECK TO THE CORRESPONDING SECRETARY.

LEXINGTON, Ky. *October* 10, 1817.

DEAR SIR,

The period has elapsed which renders it proper that some account of my labours and pursuits, since my appointment as a missionary, should be laid before the Board. This is the more necessary, as the labours of my worthy associate, brother Welch, have been pursued in a course separate from mine.

Immediately after my appointment I left Philadelphia for Litchfield, Connecticut, to make the necessary arrangements for removing with my family to the field designed for our future labours.

Some weeks being requisite for preparation, it was deemed desirable to spend as much of the time as possible in visiting Associations, and by other means to forward the general object of the mission. Accordingly, the 4th and 5th of June afforded me the satisfaction of meeting the Shaftsbury Association, and it is hoped not without some advantage to the cause. The following Sabbath gave me the opportunity of preaching a missionary sermon in Albany, at which time a collection was received. Besides visiting Catskill by request, to preach the annual sermon of the Catskill Female Mite Society, and preaching in several other places, the 25th of June brought me to Galway, Saratoga county, to meet the

Saratoga Association. A sermon on missions was delivered, and a collection taken, to which were added a valuable pair of gold ear rings and a finger ring.

In the vicinity of this Association the mission spirit is fast advancing. Female societies are springing up in almost every church.

The following week was spent in the southern part of the Shaftsbury Association. On Lord's day I visited West Stockbridge, baptised five persons, received a small collection for the mission, and assisted in arranging a Female Mission Society. The four following days gave the privilege of preaching in Egremont, East Hillsdale, West Hillsdale, and Canaan, in each of which places mission societies were formed. Friday, July 4th, preached on the subject of missions, and assisted in arranging the Columbia and Berkshire Society Auxiliary to the Board. The next Sabbath, in Amenia, Dutchess county, New York, after reading some of the annual Report, a collection was taken for the mission. Going to New Haven the following week, and spending the Sabbath with the church recently constituted in that city, another opportunity offered to plead the cause of missions, and receive the liberality of the public.

On the 25th I gave the parting hand to my aged parents, and, with my family, set out for St. Louis. Upon reaching Peter's Creek, Washington county, Pennsylvania, rest being necessary after crossing the mountains, I embraced the opportunity of visiting Pittsburgh, where I spent a Sabbath, and received a collection. The week following, opportunity offered to plead the cause of missions before the Redstone Association; on which occasion that body displayed their wonted liberality in a contribution which was put into my hands. The next Sabbath a collection was taken in Washington. The Tuesday following, I had the pleasure of seeing the Weldsburgh Mite Society, at Weldsburgh, Brooke county, Virginia. Several Mite Societies have been since formed, I learn, in the neighbourhood of the Redstone Association.

Passing through the state of Ohio, two or three opportunities presented to plead the cause of missions, particularly in Zanesville, and Chillicothe. October 5th brought us to David's Fork, near Lexington, Kentucky, where we had the high satisfaction of meeting brother and sister Welch.

Thus a gracious Providence has safely conducted myself and family about 1000 miles on our journey,—supported us through many difficulties, granted us (except my youngest child during a part of the way) an unusual share of health—preserved us through many dangers, and brought us into company with our dear brother and sister Welch, with whom we expect to be associated the rest of our journey.

While procuring our outfit, and while journeying, it has been my desire, as much as possible, to avoid expense, though more has been necessary than what I was aware of at the time of my first engagement with the Board, and much more would have been incurred, had not the repeated kindness and hospitality of friends been enjoyed, to whom I shall feel myself under lasting obligations of gratitude.

With very affectionate christian regard to the Board, permit me to subscribe myself,

Your unworthy missionary,

JOHN M. PECK.

FROM THE MISSIONARIES AT ST. LOUIS

BY a communication from brother Welch, under date of December 29, 1817, we have the pleasure of learning that our beloved missionaries have arrived at their station.

From Shawnee town brother Peck and family went by water. Brother Welch, travelling by land, arrived ten days before him. Two weeks previous to his arrival brother Peck was taken ill. His situation, and the circumstances of his lady, have given to our brother and sister Welch an unusual pressure of care, as the charge of the family of brother Peck devolved upon them. It is hoped the valuable life of our afflicted, excellent brother, may be prolonged. When it is said in the writings of David, that for the Messiah "prayer shall be made continually," it must surely involve the duty of praying constantly and with fervour, for the life and health of the men of God who have gone forth to proclaim the riches of his grace.

Brother Welch has commenced his endeavours as a herald of truth. He expected at the beginning of 1818, to open a school, which, before the expiration of the first quarter, he anticipated will be as large as he can, with convenience, manage. Rent, living, and wood, at St Louis, are high. Our brother says, with that decision and glow of heart in which we cannot but rejoice, "*Under a full conviction that I am in the path of duty, I am determined to live and die in the cause of God and missions.*"

NEW ORLEANS AND VICINITY

FROM MR. RANALDSON TO THE CORRESPONDING SECRETARY.

NATCHEZ, *September 2, 1817.*

REV AND DEAR BROTHER,

IN my letter to the Agent of the Board, the 28th of May, I stated some of the difficulties and perils which lay before me, as well as the prospects opening around for more extensive usefulness. A Sunday school has since been established in the city of New Orleans, under the most encouraging circumstances. There are now nearly a hundred children in the school, catholic and others, who are conducting with remarkable order. This school has had the happiest effect on the minds of the children, and some of the parents. After being well organized, I left it under the fostering care of our amiable young brother Estes, my Lancasterian teacher, and proceeded to Natchez. On the 28th of June, we formed the "Mississippi Society for Baptist Missions Foreign and Domestic." The society unanimously appointed me their agent, in which capacity I consented to act till I should receive communications from the Board.

Before my return to New Orleans, I had the opportunity of preaching four missionary sermons for the benefit of the society. The spirit of missions seemed to be kindled in every bosom! Every heart was disposed to contribute something towards the *great work!* and the subscriptions were swelled to more than 1300 dollars!!

I returned to New Orleans the last of July, to remove my suffering family. I there received your interesting letter of the 11th of June, informing me of my appointment from the Board to labour in New Orleans and its vicinity. This appointment I accept with great pleasure and satisfaction, being unwilling to relinquish this important field of exertion.

Finding it expedient and even necessary to take my family out of the city, I thought proper to retire to the next most important missionary ground, which is considered to be the parish of Feliciana. This station is rendered highly important from its local advantages, its proximity to New Orleans, and its immense population of Americans, *wholly destitute* of the gospel! Schools and bibles are wanting in every part of Florida. Ignorance and vice prevail, and "darkness visible on all sides round." Yet present indications in Divine providence encourage the hope, that "the Spirit of the Lord" will ere long "lift up a standard" in Louisiana, where "the enemy" has "come in like a flood."

As long as I remained in New Orleans, the prospects were brightening. The congregations were serious and solemn, but little servile labour done in the streets on the Sabbath, a gradual increase in the schools, and much affection manifested from the parents and pupils. It grieved me much to leave this people; yet there was no alternative. As a token of their love and esteem, they sent me 419 dollars, besides other donations. I hope, and think there is reason to believe, that my removal out of the city, will contribute to the furtherance of the gospel, both in New Orleans and its vicinity.

As ever, yours, &c.

JAMES A. RANALDSON.

FROM THE SAME TO THE AGENT OF THE BOARD.

St. Francisville, La. *Dec* 30, 1817.

MY DEAR BROTHER,

Your favour of the 6th ultimo, was received a few days since. The 'Latter Day Luminary" will, I trust, shed light upon this region, too long accustomed to the ignorance and darkness of heathenism. I have to lament, however, that among the people so few are in the habit of reading.

Your letter of the 24th June I received at Natchez, and wrote to you from that place to Nashville the 1st of September. Since that time Natchez has received an awful visitation. About three hundred of its citizens were in a short time numbered with the dead, being cut off by the malignant fever!! A great number died with the yellow fever in New Orleans, and other places, but it is supposed to have been more fatal in Natchez than in any other place. The goodness of God has been very manifest to myself and family. We have enjoyed good health through the sickly season, with the exception of our dear little son. I might speak of the tender mercies of our Redeemer, who has promised to be with his servants "always, even unto the end of the world," for He not only led us safely through a waste howling wilderness, and delivered us from sore afflictions; but has opened a door for us to enter in and serve him among the heathen of our own dear country. Ah! my dear brother, I knew but little of the real condition of thousands of our countrymen! I now see more clearly the necessity and the importance of missionary exertions, both at home and abroad. Whilst the natives of the land are astonished at the doctrines of the Cross, I cannot but be astonished at their ignorance in these things.

My engagements at present will not permit me to write a long letter. I wish this to go to the office immediately, that it may reach you in time. I expect to write to Dr. Staughton, in a few days, and give him some information of importance.

Yours in the bonds of love,

J. A. RANALDSON.

FROM THE REV. DAVID COOPER.

WOODVILLE, Mi. Oct 24, 1817.

MY VERY DEAR BROTHER,

LAST spring I spent a few weeks in the city of New Orleans, where I had the pleasure of an acquaintance with brother Ranaldson. It was my opinion that it was the duty of brother Ranaldson to remove his family from Orleans. I advised him to turn his attention to the parish of Feliciana; he has done so, and will, I have no doubt, be well received. It is a large and populous settlement, almost entirely destitute of the gospel, except the little attention they have received from your unworthy servant, and is, of course, good missionary ground.

Your sincere friend and humble servant,

D. COOPER.

AMERICAN INDIANS

THE views of the Board in relation to the native tribes of the west, as well as in relation to other calls for exertion, in which it has been deemed their duty to engage, may be collected from the following

GENERAL CIRCULAR

To the Baptist Associations throughout the Union, the numerous Missionary Societies who with them are uniting their exertions to promote the interests of evangelical piety and virtue, and to all who commiserate the calamities of man, and long and labour for the arrival of the day when the knowledge of the Lord shall cover the earth as the waters cover the sea,—

THE BAPTIST BOARD OF FOREIGN MISSIONS FOR THE UNITED STATES,
Present affectionate gratulations:

EVER since their origination, the Board has kept in view the best aims of the CONVENTION whom they represent, particularly the important duty of endeavouring to diffuse religious knowledge, not merely on the wretched and benighted plains of Burmah, &c. but also along the western frontiers of our country, and through the depths of the wilderness, from the Mississippi to the Pacific ocean. They have ever considered the service of sending the everlasting gospel to the aborigines of the west, as devolving with peculiar reasonableness and force on American christians. These occupy a large portion of lands once the possession of the natives, and can point them to no surer and brighter a recompense then the "inheritance incorruptible and undefiled" beyond the grave.

In an age like the present, when, for the circulation of the gospel, christians of every name are coming forth with all the beauties of the morning, and all the promise of the spring, it can create no surprise that several societies have taken the condition of the Indians into serious and active consideration. The field is wide and encouraging. The number of those who sow in hope, and who shall reap with joy, can scarcely be excessive. The efforts of the Baptist Mission Society in Kentucky, communicated to them through the medium of the Rev. Mr. Trott and the Rev. Mr. Noel, deserve affectionate commendation. The Board wishes them ample success. The magnitude, however, of the object embraced, calls for *general* rather than *local* resources. Such resources are thrown into the possession of the Board, who will find its happiness in their faithful appropriation to the purposes for which the generous contributors have designed them. In every effort for the spread of civilization and piety, and particularly through western regions, the Board earnestly solicits, and will gratefully welcome, the counsel and co-operation of their western brethren.

The Board are alive, with all the ardours of the most sincere thankfulness, to the christian zeal, in favour of the untaught Indians, discovered by Col. R M. Johnson, and beg his acceptance of their fraternal acknowledgments. They have perused the eloquent and informing letters addressed to him by Thomas L M'Kenney, esq. with no common interest. They pray that the God of missions may abundantly remunerate these excellent men, and grant them, in the diffusion of the principles of truth and holiness, all that an enlightened and benevolent heart can desire. They are persuaded that ten thousand more, and particularly the India agents through our country, are waiting only for an opportunity of accelerating the common design.

The circumstances which gave birth to the general Convention of the Baptist denomination of the United States, and of consequence to their officiating Board, will not be forgotten. Two excellent men, brother Judson and brother Rice, were, in the providence of God, thrown on their patronage and support. They were welcomed as brethren beloved. Brother Rice has, by the decided approbation of the Board, been continued to advance the interests of missions in the United States. Brother Judson and family are in Eastern India. The wretched, dismal, desolate condition of the Burmans, has been pressed on the zeal and piety of the disciples of the Redeemer in the United States. The voice of heaven has not been heard in vain. Funds for the support of the amiable missionary have been liberally contributed and transmitted. He has asked for associates. Brother Hough and family have been sent to Rangoon.—Brethren Wheelock and Colman are waiting in Boston for a vessel, [*they have since sailed*] having been approved as missionaries, that they may unite in their labours. This field is highly important. The God of mercies is, in fact, saying to America, "I have set before you an open door, and no man can shut it." It is a voice distinct and forcible as that of the man of Macedonia to the apostle of the Gentiles. Communications from Rangoon are of the most encouraging nature. Mr. Judson is in possession of the language, has his whole heart in the work, and has already issued a tract in Burman, exhibiting, with lucidity and faithfulness, the way to the paradise of God. The Board feel themselves bound by all the ties of duty, honour, and affection, to give to this sphere of missionary exertion, and to the brethren who occupy or may enter it, their cheerful and firm support.—God grant that in those miserable regions " the heavens" may " drop down righteousness, and the earth bring forth salvation."

But it was never contemplated by the Convention and Board that their endeavours should be circumscribed by *eastern* lines. The WEST has lain with weight on their minds. Nor have they been backward at expressing their feelings. They need appeal only to the several " Reports" of the Board, and to the " Proceedings of the Convention," for confirmation. Five missionaries are already under their patronage in the western and south-western sections of the country; all of whom have ultimate reference to the savage tribes. Ranges of destitute frontier are kept in view, but they are regarded as inlets to Indian wigwams and Indian *talks*. The missionaries are instructed, not merely to make inquiries respecting the aborigines, but to plunge into the depths of their superstitions, and to direct their views to the " GREAT FATHER," who receives with expanded arms the penitent prodigal.

The Board are solemnly impressed with the high advantage that must result from imparting education, particularly in the English (or French) language, to the children of the natives. They purpose making application to Congress, should it be found adviseable, for a site or sites where seminaries may be established with the hope of success, and where the arts of civilized life—agriculture, domestic economy, &c. in conjunction with the doctrines and duties of the gospel, may be inculcated. The states of Louisiana, Mississippi, Indiana, and Ohio, together with the territories of Missouri, Illinois, Alabama, and Michigan, exhibit plains for spiritual culture, that the eye of pious sympathy can never survey without the tear of pity, and a heart prepared for exertion. Efforts for the salvation of the Indians have hitherto been of a character too solitary. Elliot, Brainerd, Edwards, and others, laboured too much alone. It is no more the design of Heaven in christian missions, than in the toils of the rustic, that forests should be prostrated by the strokes of an individual.

The Board would beg leave respectfully to solicit the opinion of their excellencies the governors of the several states and territories above mentioned, and of the respective Indian agents, as to the most eligible means of attaining the great object. They wish information in reference to the number, location, and temper of the tribes; whether any of their youths could probably be obtained for the purpose of receiving christian education; whether, if found practicable, it would be more eligible that they should be educated at a mission establishment in the neighbourhood of the Indians, or in the midst of white population, industry, economy, and refinement. Should situations among or near themselves be thought preferable, the Board would feel a sense of extreme obligation in having such spots designated as might appear most promising.

A publication denominated THE AMERICAN BAPTIST MAGAZINE, has for a considerable time been published in Boston. It has circulated widely through the New England States, and extensively along the seaboard of the country. It is conducted by men of superior talent, possessing ardent zeal for the cause of God and missions. The names of Baldwin, Sharp, and Winchell, are a praise in the churches. The consideration alone that the terms of that valuable work forbid its effusion through the west, and southwest, without incurring a positive expense to the Board, has induced the latter to propose another work, which they wish to be considered a *sister*, but by no means a rival, of the former, to be denominated "THE LATTER DAY LUMINARY." It will be published quarterly. The terms may be collected from the circulars. Its profits will be sacred to the interests of the mission.

Perhaps in relation to eastern and western missionary attempts, the prophecy of Zechariah is actually accomplishing. "It shall be in that day, that living waters shall go out from Jerusalem, half of them toward the former sea, and half of them toward the hinder sea, in summer and in winter shall it be: and the Lord shall be king over all the earth. In that day there shall be one Lord, and his name One."

The Board is grateful for the liberal assistance that from every part of the union is pouring into its treasury. A faithful statement of every item of expenditure will be annually exhibited. The work is great, but unity, beneficence, ardour, and a steadfast perseverance, with the blessing of the Lord, will accomplish wonders. Let the ministers of heaven "speak to the people that they go forward," and let all unite in the prayer of the prophetic David, "Arise, O God, judge the earth, for thou shalt inherit all nations."

By order of the Board,

WM. STAUGHTON, Cor. Sec.

October, 1817.

It would be particularly acceptable, did our limits admit of it, to publish at large the interesting correspondence between Col Johnson and Esq M'Kenney, referred to in the foregoing circular. The latter has thus written to the Corresponding Secretary since.

OFFICE OF INDIAN TRADE,
Georgetown, D. C. November 14, 1817.

REVEREND SIR,

I HAD the pleasure of an interview with Rev Mr. Rice, and received from him a package of your general circular. One of them was addressed to myself by Mr. Rice, in which he expressed a wish that I would forward a copy to each of the Governors of the States and Territories mentioned in the circular, and to the Indian agents, accompanied by such remarks as the subject might give rise to.

I have forwarded a copy to each of the Governors, except to his excellency Governor Claiborne of Louisiana, and to him also one should have been transmitted had the number held out. To each of the Indian agents it would be proper to send a copy, inasmuch as they are centered in the Indian settlements, have much of the confidence of the respective tribes, and could aid greatly in furthering the design of reformation. If you will furnish me with, say twenty copies, I will forward them immediately.

I sincerely wish the Baptist association, and all other associations of benevolent men, whose efforts tend to relieve the calamities of man, all that success which the importance of such undertakings merits

I enclose you a copy of the remarks which accompanied the printed circulars to each of the Governors,

And am, sir, with sentiments of very great respect,
Your obedient servant,
THOMAS L. M'KENNEY.

OFFICE OF INDIAN TRADE,
Georgetown, November 4th, 1817

SIR,

I HAVE had transmitted to me copies of a general circular issued by the Baptist Board of Foreign Missions for the United States, with a request to forward one of them to you.

In complying with the request of this benevolent body, whose purpose is to meliorate the condition of our brethren of the forests, and to convey amongst them, in addition to the lessons which shall improve them in the arts, and in domestic life, those nobler views which relate to futurity, I do nothing more than what I conceive to be my duty. Not a duty which devolves upon me by reason of my official tenure; but a duty which arises out of my conviction that we all, as Americans, owe the aborigines a debt, which cannot be more acceptably or justly cancelled, than by the promotion of those means which tend to civilize and christianize them. And what means are more likely than those which are used by men who go amongst them as *messengers of peace and good will?* They go without mercenary considerations, or desire of gain, but only to impress upon them the superior excellence of the civilized over the savage state, and the happy consequences which follow a life of virtue, in the future world.

In asking you to correspond with the Board, on those parts of the circular which relate to the information they request, I do no more, I am sure, than put it in your power to do a service no less acceptable to your own feelings, than it will prove beneficial to the views of the Board.

Accept the assurances of high regard, &c.
THOMAS L. M'KENNEY.

THE Chickasaw Indians, when the circular from the Kentucky Mission Society was presented to them, suggested the idea of a school of the kind with that contemplated by the Board, and expressed their wish for such a school in their neighbourhood, at which their children might receive education. Accordingly, the Board has resolved on commencing an establishment there, as soon as, in Divine providence, it shall be found practicable. Other tribes, as appears by the following communications, possess similar views.

FROM MR. M'KOY TO THE CORRESPONDING SECRETARY.

Maria, Ia. *January* 14, 1818.

DEAR BROTHER,

Permit me to inform you that on the 1st instant I had the happiness to assist in the formation of the Bruceville Missionary Society Auxiliary to the Board; also of assisting, at the same time, in the formation of the Bruceville Female Missionary Society, whose objects are the same with the former. I am happy to say the zeal manifested on this occasion exceeded my most sanguine expectations. How much strength will be derived to the missionary cause from these societies, I dare not venture to predict.

It will, I am persuaded, afford pleasure to the Board to know, that since my last, the situation of the Wea and Kickapoo Indians has attracted my attention materially. They have heard the proposals of the Kentucky Missionary Society, "to take some of the children of each tribe to Kentucky to be educated at a school instituted for that purpose." These proposals were made to the Weas through the agent. After several weeks' deliberation on the subject, they returned for answer that "they were unwilling to send their children to Kentucky to be educated, because that, in obtaining an English education, they would lose their mother tongue, and if they had learned any thing profitable, they would be unable to communicate it to their friends at home; but if schools could be established in their neighbourhood, where their children could get an English education, it would be agreeable to their wishes." This answer might have been anticipated. They will always be alarmed by so great an innovation as seemed to be threatened by the proposals above mentioned.

I have made known to his excellency Thomas Posey, who has the agency of the Weas and Kickapoos, the wish of the Board to introduce the gospel to the Indians, and my plan for effecting it amongst these two nations.

Governor Posey is not only philanthropic, but religious. He is of opinion that a school establishment may be made; and has promised all the assistance in his power, in the accomplishment of this undertaking. The plan contemplated is, to propose to these tribes at their next meeting, which will probably be in March, to open a school convenient to them, say a little above Fort Harrison, where they will not be subjected to the inconvenience of losing their mother tongue. They will at the same time be assured that their present scattered situation will be no objection to the establishment, as their children will be supported at the expense of the Board; and, provided a few children can be obtained, the institution to go immediately into operation.

Should it be thought necessary at the time, they may be assured that their children will be instructed by an Indian. There is a Brothertown Indian, now in the neighbourhood of Fort Harrison, who is a baptist, and has an English education, who may be hired at a reasonable rate; yet I would choose to take the oversight of the institution myself, until the Board could make other arrangements. As it is probable the Indian school would not at first be numerous, it is presumed that a number of white children might be educated at the expense of their parents. I hope the Board will not delay to give me more particular instructions on this subject than I have yet received.

Should we make an agreement with the Indians, the least failure on our part would be attended with injurious consequences. *What shall I do?* The subject is now agitated amongst them. There is at least some prospect of success. Dare I let the opportunity pass unimproved?

I wish you to be apprized, however, that there are serious difficulties attending our scheme, which, to the eye of human reason, may seem to threaten its very existence. Amongst these the capricious disposition of the Indians, and the interest of traders, are not the least. But, although we are not sure of success, there appears sufficient reason to hope for it to justify the making of an effort; even should matters assume quite another aspect by the time I write again, let us not too soon be discouraged.

I am happy to find that a missionary spirit is spreading beyond my expectation. Requesting the prayers of the Board that I may be directed in the right way,

I subscribe myself, sir,

Your obedient servant,

ISAAC M'KOY.

FROM THE SAME TO THE AGENT OF THE BOARD.

MARIA, Ia. *January* 19, 1818.

DEAR BROTHER,

There are now about seventy members in the Bruceville Missionary Society, which was constituted the 1st instant, and nearly as many in the Bruceville Female society formed at the same time. I hope also that a little missionary fire has been kindled in two other neighbourhoods, which, with the blessing of God, may be fanned into a flame.

I suppose the Board did not expect me to do much among the Indians; but, upon making inquiry, I found the prospect so flattering, that I concluded it would be criminal in me to let the opportunity pass unimproved.

The Weas (Miamis) and Kickapoos will probably meet in March to receive their annuities, when I expect to make proposals for opening a school amongst them, on a plan that they have already said would be agreeable to their wishes. Governor Posey, the agent, thinks the Indians will accede to my proposals, and he has promised me all the assistance in his power. Yet the influence of certain individuals, whose interest it is to keep them in ignorance, is so great, that I sometimes "tremble for the cause." I have written to the Board on the subject, and have confidence that they will be directed by wisdom from above.

Your brother in gospel bonds,

ISAAC M'KOY.

FROM MR. POSEY TO THE CORRESPONDING SECRETARY.

HAYWOOD Co. N. C. *August* 26, 1817.

REV. AND DEAR BROTHER,

With particular sensations of gratitude to God for his great goodness towards me, and a strong impression of your christian regard, permit me now to answer your kind letter of the 23d of June. I am sorry that it is not in my power to give information of a more satisfactory nature relative to my neighbours the Cherokees.

In 1802, I joined the baptist church in Greenville district, S. C. About that time my mind was very much exercised in relation to the Indians; and I thought, if any way opened, I should feel it my duty to labour among them. A few years since, I made an attempt; but after visiting the Indians twice, left them for want of encouragement. I have still, however, an earnest desire to see something done for them; and, at the request of the Board, am willing to make another effort, believing the case by no means a hopeless one. The following is the course which I purpose to pursue; viz. as soon as practicable I will go among them, and see if they will permit schools to be set up; and will preach to those who can understand English; by the assistance of an interpreter will endeavour to impart some knowledge of divine things to those who are not acquainted with the English; and, on my return, will give you an account of the success.

I am persuaded that no method would be more likely to succeed than this. They must first be prepared by learning the English language; but great care should be taken in the choice of teachers. If one so unworthy as myself can do any good, I know that the Lord must have all the glory.

What support may be necessary, you will learn, after the business is commenced. Should it be found expedient to engage schoolmasters, it would be my endeavour to obtain young men of good morals, and of the baptist denomination. However, in your instructions to me, you will have the goodness to communicate to me the wishes of the Board on every subject.

I am happy to inform you, that on last Lord's day the missionary spirit was kindled in our Association, and a collection taken. Although the people were not apprized of it, and our country is very poor, there was nearly thirty dollars contributed to aid the general missionary fund.

Your very affectionate brother in Christ,

HUMPHREY POSEY.

FROM THE SAME TO THE CORRESPONDING SECRETARY.

Haywood, N C. *Nov* 6, 1817.

DEAR BROTHER,

According to the request made, I have taken two journies among the Cherokee Indians, much to my satisfaction. I find them anxious that I should continue to visit them. I have preached, and had one sermon interpreted by a certain Edward Tucker, who is a native by birth, but a mulatto. He told me they said it was good. This man accompanied me through several towns, and took a great deal of pains to inform the Indians about my business. They almost universally appeared pleased, and I conversed with them about schools. I had a spelling book, and called over the letters, which a number of Indians, large and small, who could not speak a word of English, named after me. The children fondled on me, and seemed to look up to me as one who knew more than their people. One little girl, probably 4 years of age, who had known me on my first visit, as soon as she saw me coming again, ran out and rejoiced as though I had been a particular friend, telling her people who I was, and that she was not afraid of "Yunaka," that is, whiteman.

A white man accompanied me both times, who, from the reports he had received, was opposed to missionary exertions. He lives on the edge of the nation, and has been a smith amongst them many years. Near him is a large settlement of whites. When I started to visit the Indians the first time, I appointed a meeting near his house, and, not knowing the thoughts of any, told them I would try to preach a short missionary sermon. I did so, and his prejudices were removed, so that he offered to conduct me as far as I would go into the nation. We went on through various towns, until we arrived at Mr. Tucker's, as mentioned before. Though I was told he was a swearing man, and at times drank to excess, yet I was not discouraged, for he had been upon my mind, as one that was to become useful in some way, for probably three years before I saw him. I told him my business, and that he must quit swearing, and drinking to excess. He was entirely ignorant of the way of salvation, but acknowledged there was a God, and said that all the Cherokees do this; but who He is, or how to be worshipped, he and they were ignorant. I told him, he had a soul that must be eternally happy or miserable in another world. He said, he did not know. I told him he should pray to the Almighty to give him instruction, and save his soul. He said, he did not know how. I said, if you were condemned to be hanged for murder, and was told that the governor, or some great man, had power to release you, and you had only to plead with him, what would you say? He answered, I do not know; but the nature of the case would give me words. I said, that is true; and this is your case. You and all of us are condemned by the righteous law of God; you should, therefore, improve your time. I heard him say, "Lord have mercy on me." I told him, that was a very scriptural prayer, and if uttered from a real sense of need, would be heard.

When I came the second time, I found him determined to forsake bad company. He told me he had thought a great deal about our former conversation, and that he knew he should feel much happier if he only had the christian's hope. I want you, my dear brother, and the brethren around you, to pray for the salvation of Ned Tucker, and the benighted Cherokees. I desire you will let me know as soon as possible, whether I may venture to establish schools among them. I have agreed to have one at Tucker's, and one or two more for three months, even should I pay for them myself, in order to see how they will answer. If the Board should undertake on a large scale, a great deal, I am persuaded, may be done in these regions.

I am at present at the command of the Board, as respects these people, and should rejoice to learn what measures are adopted.

Yours, in the bonds of the gospel,

HUMPHREY POSEY.

FROM THE SAME TO THE CORRESPONDING SECRETARY.

ASHEVILLE, N. C *Nov* 14, 1817.

REV. AND DEAR BROTHER,

I WROTE you by the last mail, but on receiving yours of the 16th October, I felt it my duty to send you an immediate answer.

I wish to communicate to the Board, that with gratitude I accept the appointment of missionary to the Cherokees, humbly requesting that they will bear me up in their prayers, and beseech the blessed Jesus to ask for the poor blinded Cherokees as a part of his immediate " inheritance."

As it respects my compensation, suffice it to say, I am fully satisfied with the decision of the Board on that subject.—I shall endeavour to begin about the first of December—shall keep a regular journal of my proceedings, and communicate the same quarterly or oftener.

The confidence placed in me by the Board, while it makes me feel small, still binds me to them in a manner not easily to be expressed, and I hope never to be forgotten.—May heaven smile on you, my dear brother, and may the happy period speedily roll round, when the earth shall be full of the knowledge of the Lord, and his high praises be sounded in every place

Yours, in the bonds of the gospel,

HUMPHREY POSEY.

ADDITIONAL RESPECTING THE INDIANS.

BESIDES what the "Baptist Board" have undertaken in relation to the aborigines of our country, other denominations are directing their attention zealously the same way. An establishment, with great promise, has been commenced among the Cherokee Indians by the Rev. Cyrus Kingbury, under the patronage of the " American Board of Commissioners for Foreign Missions." The Rev Mr Gambold, under the patronage of the " United Brethren," or Moravians, is also, if our information be correct, among the Cherokees.

Esqr. M'Kenney, in his valuable letter to Col Johnson, mentions the Rev Moses Crume, who " was appointed, by the last annual Conference of the Methodist Episcopal Church, to preside in the Miami district; and it became a part of his duty, by the direction of that body, to make arrangements with the friendly Indians within the agency of John Johnson, Esq. for opening schools among them. In conformity with his instructions, Mr Crume proceeded to open his mission to the principal men of Mr. Johnson's agency, and was received in a manner highly flattering to his hopes"

" I cannot," continues Esq. M'Kenney, " withhold my commendation of the efforts of this minister, or deny myself the pleasure of pronouncing upon his merits."

" *The United Foreign Missionary Society*—composed of the Presbyterian, Reformed Dutch, and Associate Reformed Churches," which was constituted in New York last July, has specially for its " object to spread the gospel among the Indians of North America," together with " the inhabitants of Mexico and South America."

Nor are efforts of this kind in vain, as appears by the following quotation from " *The late proceedings of the Synod of Pittsburg and Western missionary Society,*" and from many other extracts that might, if our limits permitted, be offered.

" Mr Oldham has been employed for another year. The number that attend in school has been lately increased, and their progress has been equal to our expectations. The most of them can spell words of five and six syllables, and read easy lessons. Some of them write a very good copy hand, and we are not without animating expectations, that if their education can be effected, the advantages resulting from it may, through the divine blessing, descend to generations yet unborn."

" We must also remark, that the Indians are beginning to pay a more marked attention to the arts of civilization than formerly They cultivate the ground with more industry, and they raise much larger crops of corn, oats and potatoes, and are beginning to raise wheat and rye The women are beginning to pay more regard to cleanliness and decency in their houses, and, in their domestic economy, imitate Mrs. Oldham, who is now employed by this Board to pay a more pointed attention to the women than formerly."

GENERAL MISSIONARY INTELLIGENCE.

FROM THE REV. DR. CAREY.

CALCUTTA, *June* 30, 1817.

MY DEAR BROTHER,

I WROTE to you about three weeks ago, but having just received a note from the supercargo of the Wm. Savery that the ship is on the point of sailing, I cannot persuade myself to let the opportunity slip, though I can command only a few minutes. This is the day for our public disputations at the college, in the oriental languages, and upon these occasions I have always a post of importance to maintain, being moderator of the disputations in two languages, and having a public speech to deliver in both. This year we have no Sungskrit disputation, which has eased me of one half of my burden; but to me the day is always a day of care and anxiety.

The cause of our glorious Redeemer, I believe, is gaining ground in this country in a variety of ways, and in none, perhaps, more than in the entire revolution which has taken place in the sentiments of Europeans respecting the utility of missions. Schools for the instruction of youth upon the plans of Lancaster and Bell, are now originating in almost every direction, and proper persons to superintend them are much more difficult to procure than funds for their support. A society for the purpose of translating, or composing, and publishing books on education in the different languages of the east, has lately been formed, which promises to be of great utility. Several additional attempts to spread abroad the light of truth have been lately made, and are making.

Two missionaries from the London Missionary Society have recently arrived. They are, I believe, men of God, and will be useful. Two from the Church Society are here also. Their sphere of activity will be greatly circumscribed, but I think they will ultimately be of great advantage to the cause. We are all well, and are carrying on our plans as usual. I rejoice at all the good that is going forward in America. May the Lord prosper all our and your undertakings, that they may end in his glory and the advancement of the honor of his name.

I am, very affectionately, yours,

WM. CAREY.

FROM MRS. ROWE TO MRS. S———.

DIGAH, Hindosthan, *April* 13, 1817.

MY EVER DEAR FRIEND AND SISTER,

I FEEL as if I wanted to answer every item of your letter, but what would be the use of it? let me feast on it, and give you something in return. The Lord's work goes on gradually in India. Mr. Rowe lately baptised six persons belonging to the 24th regiment of his majesty's army in India; and sixteen candidates are expected to join at the next baptismal season. There are four native inquirers who attend morning daily worship at our house in Hindee, together with about six native brethren and a few others. There are only two native sisters here, one of whom now lies very ill. I went to see her this evening, and sent her some comforts when I returned. All the native christians, and inquiring natives, that appertain to this station, live on our premises.

I have one native scholar, a little girl, whose parents brought her to me, requesting that I would teach her to work and read Hindee. The father is an inquirer, and therefore associates with the christian brethren, and lives at our expense. I keep the child close to me, and do every thing for her myself, lest the parents of the fair children should become dissatisfied with her being in the school. If I had more of this kind of scholars, I would teach them at a separate house. I cannot, however, expect any but the children of christian natives.

This mission is very prosperous, through God's mercy. I want nothing but more grace to enable me to fill my station better. Pray for me.

Mr and Mrs Hough are comfortably situated at Rangoon. The government is relaxing in its rigour, and already the condition of our friends there is meliorated. See God's grace! Our sister Judson shines like a star of primal magnitude in the east. She has translated into Burman, and brother Hough has printed, a tract; while brother Judson has something else in readiness for the press.

There has lately been a tract on the subject of public schools published by the brethren at Serampore, which has so taken with all denominations, that many persons, unsolicited, have sent large donations.

This morning another little native girl came to learn with the former. As there are now two, I must keep them separate from the English school, so that I have three separate schools to conduct, in three different apartments, the boys' English school being in a separate bungalow. This anecdote may please you;—two natives were talking about religion, one, who was a christian, asked the other, who was a heathen, how he thought the spirit of goodness, or religion, manifested itself? He answered, "In clothing the naked, feeding the hungry, and doing good to the needy."

How then does it become missionaries to magnify the religion of Christ, and win souls to it, by such works!

Your ever affectionate friend and sister,
CHARLOTTE H. ROWE.

FROM THE SAME TO THE CORRESPONDING SECRETARY.

Digah, *April* 21, 1817

EVER DEAR SIR,

Your letter, dated Oct. 1st, 1816, together with a parcel, came safe to hand last week. The duplicates I have put up to send brother Hough, with a letter.

They have afforded us much refreshment. Such receipts from afar, give a spring to missionary ardour. We behold the dawning of the day when "Hosanna to the Son of David!" will be the universal acclamation. O, may it shortly silence the festal shouts to the praise of the *son of Mahomet*, prevalent in the East!

The glorious things you relate concerning the churches in America, remind us of what remains to be done for God and the good of souls, in heathen lands.

I cannot but approve the conduct of the Board of Missions at their late meeting. I would not wish brother Rice to abandon a work, which he is well calculated to execute; and there is no reason why the remoter parts of America should remain unattended to. Beholding things on the enlarged scale it does, he could with difficulty confine his mind to unravelling the dark page of an unlearned language. I think he is doing more for Rangoon by remaining where he is. Nor, since brother Hough's arrival, is the situation of brother and sister Judson lonely, as heretofore, to call specially for his return to them. They will now do very well, at least till you are able to send others to their assistance. Brother Hough has printed a tract of sister Judson's translating into Burman.

I know not in what relation to themselves, the Board now consider me; or whether my union with the English mission by marriage will, in their estimation, dissolve the bond between them and me. I can only say, I wish still to be regarded as a daughter of the American mission, and to hold some filial affinity and intercourse with it, though I need not its pecuniary supplies.

It is now my sole desire to be enabled to devote my every talent to the gracious Giver, and to serve his cause all my days and hours. I wish to die working for the welfare of Zion. I have been blessed with health since my arrival, and feel all alive in my work.

Desiring a respectful remembrance to each of the members of the Board, and requesting the prayers of all who love the prosperity of the Redeemer's kingdom, permit me to subscribe myself,

Your sincere friend and sister in Christ,
CHARLOTTE H. ROWE.

FROM THE REV. MR. WARD.

SERAMPORE, *July* 3, 1817.

MY DEAR BROTHER,

I now send some more of the circular letters, as they will supply you with the principal articles of news respecting us and our work.

Brother Carey is now firmly recovered from a long sickness, in which his life appeared to be threatened, sometimes by the violence of the disorder, and at other times by its obstinate continuance and lingering nature. Blessed be God, he is now, I think, as well as he has been for several years.—Blessed, blessed be God! he survives, and the most precious life on earth is still spared!

I rejoice, and so do we all, in the great things God is doing for Zion in your happy country. Our affairs here are making that progress which might be expected after ages of universal impenetrable darkness, and an institution like the *cast* to overcome. You have two blessed men at Rangoon. We gave them a press and types, and it was at work in the porch of their house, in a few hours after its arrival. A wonderful work is going on among the Mugs on the borders of the Burman empire, and these people talk the Burman. This may encourage you.

I am, my dear sir, ever thine,
W. WARD.

FROM THE SAME TO THE CORRESPONDING SECRETARY.

SERAMPORE, *July* 4, 1817.

VERY DEAR BROTHER,

You will kindly convey to the Baptist Board of Foreign Missions our acknowledgement of the receipt of 1000 dollars for the translation of the scriptures under our direction, and 1000 for the brethren and sisters at Rangoon, by Mr J. Smith, and our thanks for this donation to the translations.

Wishing our dear brethren composing the Board every spiritual aid, and the hearts of all the American churches, I am, dear brother,

Yours for the brethren, in everlasting bonds,

W. WARD.

FROM THE REV. MR. MORRISON.

CANTON, China, *February* 25, 1817.

MY DEAR SIR,

Your kind letter of December 1814, I did not receive till January last, after my return from Peking. I am happy to have the pleasure of hearing again from you and your family.

The liberty which you enjoy, and which is enjoyed in my native country, to preach and to teach the doctrines of Jesus, is a blessing, for which none can be sufficiently thankful. The rulers of this land are hostile to the name of Jesus. My original object was the acquisition of the language, for the purpose of rendering into it the sacred scriptures. To that object, I have constantly adhered, and still adhere. My labours are in my study.

My brother Milne at Malacca, is better situated. He teaches school, or rather superintends a large free school, for Chinese children, and publishes in Chinese a small magazine containing religious papers, monthly. He has baptised the person who prints his magazine.

I rejoice in the success of your zealous endeavours to diffuse the knowledge and love of our Saviour. May every scriptural means be abundantly blessed.

With christian regard to Mrs. Staughton, and the other members of your family,

I remain affectionately yours in the faith of our Lord,

ROBERT MORRISON.

FROM THE REV. DR. HINTON.

OXFORD, England, *Nov* 7, 1817

DEAR BROTHER,

Our annual missionary meeting was held here October 1st crowded beyond measure. Preachers, Birt, senior, Hughes, and R Hall, all excellent. I resigned my secretaryship—health, pastoral duties, &c left me no alternative. Mr. Dyer, a faithful and able brother, is chosen unanimously assistant to Dr Ryland.

I rejoice in what the Lord is doing in America. *Ten thousand* added to your churches! Glory to God! The Lord make them ten times as many still, for millions know not yet the glories of our Emmanuel.

Your affectionate

JAMES HINTON.

PROPAGATION OF THE GOSPEL IN IRELAND.

FROM the "*Third Report of the Baptist Society* (in England) for promoting the gospel in Ireland, by establishing schools for teaching the native Irish, for itinerant preaching," &c &c we regret that our limits in the present publication forbid our making more copious extracts. In a future number we hope to be able to offer to our readers still more abundant gratification.

One of the worthy men who itinerate as readers of the Irish testament, though far advanced in age, says, "that during the last two years he has travelled 2,000 miles on foot, and 200 miles on horseback." In a letter, dated April, 1817, he observes, "that, excepting in two places, he met with no opposition, and that there is no place he has left, where he has not had the most pressing calls to go again." Another reader says, "Within the last year I have known seven men and two women, who were made acquainted with the gospel, and died in sure and certain hope of salvation, who, three years ago, had neither seen nor heard of it." Another says, "The people not only desire me to send the sabbath readers to them, but even go themselves at night to the house of O H., causing him to rise from his bed to read the Irish testament to them."

Under the head of *Irish day schools*, the Committee mention the following interesting fact. "It will scarcely be credited, that a beggar woman, pretending to witchcraft, has lately much disturbed their schools, by declaring that she had received a revelation from the Virgin Mary, informing that the Baptist Irish Society had a wicked design to entrap all their children, and send them off by a ship into a foreign land! When the people were asked if they believed this woman, they replied, that for the most part, they were inclined to believe her, as it was unreasonable that any people would go to such cost, without some such intention. 'This gave me,' says the inspector, 'the greatest advantage to read and speak to them, showing them from the scriptures, that we are arrived at that time when the gospel must be published to all nations in their own language.' Such is the alarm that prevails, that the inspector has not been able, since this report has gotten into circulation, to visit the schools on the shores of the Atlantic ocean, as the children would all run away on his approach, supposing him the captain of the ship. Notwithstanding this opposition in the province of Connaught, there are in daily attendance in the Irish schools nearly 2000 children." One of the inspectors in a letter to the Committee remarks, that "it is impossible to calculate the good which is likely to result from teaching the children of the poor in this country to read the word of life. Ireland has been a land of *beads* for many centuries, but I am convinced the beads must soon give way to the *Bible*."

"The Committee have reason to think, that the opposition made by some of the Roman catholic priests will be encouraged and stimulated by their highest ecclesiastical authorities. So far, however, from feeling dismayed by these portentous circumstances, they recommend the Society to persevere fearlessly, and as far as possible, inoffensively to the catholic priesthood of Ireland, in enabling the people to read and to understand the scriptures."

GLASGOW MISSION SOCIETY

"The Glasgow Auxiliary Society in aid of the Baptist Mission and Translations in India," issued, during the past year, their *first annual Report*—Every page of it is replete with interesting matter. We cannot withhold the following extracts

"Your Committee consider it impossible to give too much publicity to the fact, that one half of the whole funds (employed for translating the scriptures &c at Serampore) say *seven thousand pounds annually*, arises from the personal labour of the missionaries and other brethren in India, who have all adopted and steadily adhered to the noble and disinterested principle of restricting themselves to a very limited expenditure, and devoting the rest of their income to the cause of God."

Several eloquent addresses were delivered at the annual meeting, from which we should delight to make selections, or, if practicable, insert the whole. The Rev Dr. Burns, the Rev Dr. Mitchell, the Rev. George Barclay, the Rev Greville Ewing, Mr. Cunningham, and the Rev Mr. Anderson, were the principal speakers. This last gentleman, after remarking that there were other parties in the hall, who deserved the thanks of the present meeting, he alluded to the Ladies' Association for promoting the Oriental Translations, who had contributed to the funds of this Auxiliary Society 126*l*. 4*s* 7*d* sterling, added, "It is not unworthy of remark, that the idea of supporting the native ministers of the gospel in India, while preaching the good news of salvation, originated with a lady. *Miss R. (now Mrs. Dr. Carey,) first proposed, out of her own private fortune, to support a native preacher:* and her suggestion, conveyed home to this country with admiration, by one of the missionaries, first gave rise to the delightful idea of individuals in Britain acting in like manner."

PARTICULAR DETAILS of the operations and their success of numerous other missionary bodies, Foreign and Domestic, among different denominations—of Tract Societies—of Education Societies—of Sunday Schools,—various communications from Female Mite Societies;—an account of the baptism of the Jailor's household in Goochland county, Va.—of the revival of religion in Mecklenburg and Muhlenburg counties, and other places in the same state—of the revivals in Kentucky—those in the state of New York and in New England,—an Essay on Prayer,—some of the Ordinations, and Obituary notices,—Reviews,—several pieces of Poetry;—an introductory number to a compressed and succinct History of Missions,—and many other interesting particulars, which we anxiously wish our readers to possess, are unavoidably postponed to a future opportunity.

To the Publishers of the Latter Day Luminary.

HAVING observed in the third annual Report of the Board, a passage in a letter from the Rev. Dr. Carey, in which he intimates, that the "AFFGHANS" are "*undoubtedly the remains of the ten tribes*" of Israel by adducing any evidence of this idea that you possess, you will confer an obligation on

AN ISRAELITE

BIBLE SOCIETIES.

THE THIRTEENTH REPORT OF THE BRITISH AND FOREIGN BIBLE SOCIETY, MAY, 1817.

THIS "Report," with its "Appendix," occupies 340 pages, besides the "List of Contributors," which takes up 20 pages more; and an "Abstract of the Cash Account," displayed on about a dozen pages. It presents us with information drawn from more than a hundred distinct and different sources, and of the most interesting and animating kind, in addition to statements and details, in the "Report" itself, which astonish and delight the reader. With heartfelt pleasure the following extracts are offered.

"It might reasonably have been expected, that, during a season of uncommon embarrassments and privations, the British and Foreign Bible Society would have felt its influence, in a temporary abridgment of its means, as arising from the public benevolence. But your Committee have no regret to express on this account, on the contrary, it will appear, from the specification of the sums contributed by the auxiliary societies since the last annual meeting, that the pure flame of charity has continued to glow with undiminished ardour. And it cannot fail to be highly gratifying to the members of the Institution to learn, that during the last year, to the period when the Society's accounts are annually made up, the contributions from auxiliary societies amounted to no less a sum than 52,0$\mathit{}$. *l.* 9*s* 8*d*. [*more than two hundred thousand dollars,*] notwithstanding the accession of new societies has been inconsiderable, compared with former years, owing to the ground having been previously occupied."

"To what has been said in former Reports on the subject of Bible associations, which have so essentially contributed to enlarge the funds of the Society, your Committee will only add the following observation: that the very principle of those associations is calculated to operate as a monitory and restraining influence on the members of them. They see and feel the inconsistency of a life devoted to licentious indulgences and immoral habits, with the open and reiterated veneration for that Book which so explicitly condemns them, while their regulated orderly meetings, and their weekly and monthly contributions for promoting the circulation of it, tend to invigorate those feelings, and render them habitual. And when this influence is considered as extending (as from the active participation of females, and the young, it will naturally) to the families of the members of these associations, the consideration opens a new source of exhilarating hope, with respect to the rising and future generations."

"The general statement of the copies of the scriptures issued from March 31, 1816, to March 31, 1817, is 92,239 bibles, 100,782 testaments; making the total issued from the commencement of the Institution to the last mentioned period, 746,666 bibles, 929,328 testaments, in all 1,675,994 copies, exclusive of nearly 100,000 circulated abroad at the charge of this Society, making more than a *million and three quarters* of copies circulated by the British and Foreign Bible Society in twelve years."

"The infancy of this Society gave the promise of a vigorous maturity, which the progressive growth of thirteen years has amply confirmed. For complete and satisfactory evidence, that it has hitherto answered its designation and end, it is only necessary to advert to the extent to which the holy scriptures have been circulated, and to the numerous institutions in different and distant parts of the world, now actively co-operating in the distribution of them. And while, on the one hand, the associations which have thus been formed on its example, may be deemed a gratifying homage to the pure and benevolent principle of the Society, they come nearer to the feelings and expectations of its members, when considered as a provision for extending and perpetuating the benefit derived from it."

"Devoutly ascribing these auspicious results, so astonishing by their magnitude, and so incalculably beneficial in their uses, to the Divine favour alone, your Committee may be permitted to indulge the satisfaction of contemplating them as the pleasing fruits of christian union, founded on a lively sense of an identity of interest in the promises of the gospel, and animated by the charitable desire to make all mankind partakers of its blessings."

"It is from the active influence and energy of this union, that the British and Foreign Bible Society derives its means, and information to direct their employment; labourers of every soil, coadjutors in every quarter of the globe, in a word, its support, encouragement and success. No association, formed on a narrower basis than that of universal benevolence, which is the characteristic of the religion of Jesus, could have effected what it has accomplished."

"Having but one object in view, and that not only simple and intelligible, but also involving a duty which christians of all denominations must admit to be of paramount obligation, this catholic union requires no compromise of its members, and exacts no sacrifice of principles, and hence is less liable to be disturbed by the collision of human passions and prejudices."

"Consolidated and enlivened by a constant reciprocation of christian hopes and feelings, it exhibits and encourages those endearing sympathies which mark the source whence they spring, and which, if universally cultivated and improved, would render the nations of the earth, what the gospel was designed to make them—a holy brotherhood, a community of love and peace."

"That the moral and religious influence of the scriptures has had a considerable and extensive operation, both in this and foreign countries, is too obvious to be questioned or denied. The salutary and efficacious counteraction which it has opposed to the increase of scepticism and infidelity, and to the progress of immorality and vice, together with all the evils which follow in their train, may be fairly enumerated among those of its general and ascertained effects, which have contributed in no small degree to the preservation of social peace and order. Nor is evidence wanting, in addition to what has been adduced in the body of the Report, of its influence with respect to a more important consummation. "Many who never acknowledged the real value of this blessed volume," observes the noble President of the Swedish Bible Society, "have been enlightened by the

Spirit of God, and look upon the holy scriptures with a more pious regard. The spirit of levity and mockery that prevailed as to the doctrines of revelation, has considerably given way to a more serious and devout attention to their more important concerns." This testimony is strengthened by that of a correspondent in Swabia, who asserts, that "a growth of divine knowledge, and an increasing faith and love to Jesus Christ, are already visible in many thousand souls."

"If the preceding facts and reflections suggest the most encouraging motives for perseverance in the great undertaking to which the Society has pledged itself, they will receive additional weight from the consideration, that, if the British and Foreign Bible Society had never existed, a large portion of the millions who, it may be presumed, have been benefited by its exertions, might have lived and died without possessing a copy of the sacred volume, to whom therefore the charter of salvation would have been as if it had never been revealed. That it has pleased the Almighty, in his gracious dispensations, to awaken mankind, in so remarkable a degree, to a sense of the superior importance of his holy Word, and in times when his afflictive judgments were calculated to give it a peculiar impression, and that He has so particularly favoured this country, by selecting from it his instruments for exciting this feeling, and giving operation to it, are motives of grateful adoration and praise. That the labourers in this vineyard are increasing all over the world, is no less a subject of joy and devout thanksgiving. Their zeal, their exertions, their rivalship, their success, will ever be hailed by the Society which inspired them, with fraternal congratulations, and a cordial disposition to encourage and assist them."

"Such, indeed, is the interest which the British and Foreign Bible Society has excited, that the prayers and benedictions of thousands attend its progress, and are offered up for its success, and a suspension of its functions would be felt and lamented as a calamity in every quarter of the globe. In the mutability of human affairs it is possible, however, that the existing favourable opportunities for circulating the holy scriptures may suffer some diminution; and it is certain, that, in a few years, both those who have devoted themselves to this benevolent duty, and those for whose more immediate benefit it has been undertaken, will be overshadowed by that night in which no man can work. This, in addition to the awful considerations already stated, appeals most powerfully to the feelings and principles, the benevolence and pity, of every believer in the scriptures, to lose no opportunity in communicating to all who want it, the blessing of that divine revelation which an all merciful God designed for the whole human race. The call for the scriptures is more than ever extensive, loud, and importunate: by the blessing of God the call shall be answered, and the desire shall receive its accomplishment. It has appeared to not a few, when contemplating the wonderful success of the bible institution, and the facilities opening to its progress, "That the angel having the everlasting gospel to preach to them that dwell on the earth, and to every nation, and kindred, and tongue, and people, has commenced his flight in the midst of heaven."

"Whether this sublime vision is now offered to the eyes of mankind, or is to diffuse its lustre over the days to come, we may be allowed to enjoy the hope which it inspires, and to anticipate the blessedness which will flow from its realization."

'With these feelings it remains only to offer devout supplications to Almighty God, that he will perfect the work which he has so abundantly prospered; that the zeal which he has inspired may never relax, until the spiritual wants of every believer in revelation shall have been supplied, until the tidings of salvation shall have been communicated to every inhabitant of the earth."

† "APPENDIX.—*The British and Foreign Bible Society has printed, or aided the printing or circulation of the scriptures, in part or in the whole, in* SIXTY SIX *different languages or dialects.*"

To this astonishing Institution, "*There are 570 Auxiliary and Branch Societies (or upwards) within the* British *dominions.*"

The expenditures of the Society last year, that is, from March 31, 1816, to March 31, 1817, were 89,230 pounds sterling, and a fraction over, but little short of 400,000 dollars. "Total, from the commencement of the Institution, 541,504*l*. 1s. 10*d*.," but little less than TWO MILLIONS AND A HALF of dollars.

The "*Bible Societies established in foreign parts, encouraged by pecuniary aid from the British and Foreign Bible Society, or by its example*," amount among the various nations of Europe, to at least *forty six*, with many auxiliaries and branches to these, besides *six* in Asia, and *four* in Africa.

On the American continent are more than 150 Bible Societies. These, with the numerous principal, auxiliary, and branch societies in other quarters, swell the whole number, it is confidently believed, to *more than one thousand* at present in the world. The prodigious sums employed by all these annually in the diffusion of the sacred scriptures, WITHOUT NOTE OR COMMENT, may possibly, at first thought, impress the idea on the minds of some, that exertion is already sufficiently ample, and that it is unnecessary to attempt increasing the amount of effort in this particular direction. *Let no one think thus till every human being in the world possesses a bible!* Notwithstanding all that has yet been done, see what remains to be accomplished! It is estimated that there are *one thousand millions* of mankind now upon the earth, only *one hundred and seventy five millions* of these, *not two out of every ten*, belong even to what are called christian nations, and not *one sixth* of this small proportion are supplied with the bible! *Not* FULL *out of every* ONE HUNDRED *of the human family, have in their possession that invaluable book!!!* Who then will say that exertion to multiply and circulate the sacred scriptures need not be augmented, and that to the utmost extent possible?

ZEAL OF CATHOLICS IN GERMANY FOR THE SCRIPTURES.

For the following communications, taken from the "*Monthly extracts from the Correspondence of the British and Foreign Bible Society*," the Publishing Committee feel much pleasure in acknowledging their obligations to the politeness of their excellent friend Robert Ralston, Esq. of this city.]

From a Catholic Professor of Divinity at ———, July 20, 1817.

"FOR this fortnight past, a disorder in my eye has prevented me from writing and reading; and the first use I make, with thanks to God, of my recovered sight, shall be to discharge the sacred duty of conveying to the revered Bible Society the sentiments of superlative joy in the Lord, and heartfelt gratitude, which abound, not in me only, but in many thousands, languishing after scriptural food. Writing, however, can give but a faint idea of these overflowings, beheld and interpreted by God alone."

"And how shall I sufficiently praise the Lord, for his wise and unsearchable ways, in disposing of all events, who changes night into day, and darkness into light, and is able to make friends out of foes; in whose omnipotent hand, opposition and obstruction become instruments of bringing forth that which is good, and accomplishing his eternal decrees! For never did I disseminate, in so short a period, such a vast number of copies of the New Testament, as since the time of the late bible publications, and no where have I perceived a more lively and ardent desire after the word of God, than in those very places where infatuated men strive to dry up that fountain of living water, or to prevent the people from having free access to it!"

"The physicians advise me to use the bath for the benefit of my health; but I can hardly spare so long a time from bible distribution. However, after much earnest prayer for Divine direction, I have resolved, instead of going to a bathing place, to make a biblical tour. My aim will be to strengthen and confirm many friends of the Bible, to reconcile enemies, and to scatter the blessed seed of the word, on the right hand, and on the left."

From the Catholic chaplain at ———, March 25, 1817.

"I HAVE completely gained my three neighbouring ministers over to the good cause of the Lord. They are afraid of no man who lays obstacles in the way of their distribution of the New Testament, and are ready, should it so happen, to endure the humiliation, and bear the cross of Jesus Christ. But here, in Prussia, particularly as the king protects and values Bible Societies, endeavours to obstruct their progress will avail nothing."

"From a Catholic bishop.———May 7, 1817.

"I CONTINUE to take the warmest interest in all that is doing for the advancement of religion and morality among men; and have often in my closet blessed the disinterested and unwearied exertions of those noble minded men, who, together with you, reverend and worthy sir, labour in the great work of promoting the happiness of mankind, and, by disseminating the holy scriptures of the New Testament, spread far and wide that most important declaration of St Peter, that "there is no other name by which men can be saved, than the name of Jesus of Nazareth."

"Fully convinced that mankind in general would be greatly improved in their moral condition, by being refreshed with the pure fountain of everlasting life, I have not without regret observed endeavours to throw obstacles in the way of the great work, which I attribute to the blind religious zeal of uncalled for critics, who torture words to a different meaning from that which they actually bear. On the other hand I have observed with sincere delight, and ascribe it to a true regard and zeal for religion and morality, that the noble Britons, with unexampled disinterestedness, rouse all the talents of ingenious and learned men in Germany, to assist in the increasing dissemination of the BOOK OF BOOKS."

"I also have endeavoured to do this in my diocess, and feel not the smallest reluctance, warmly and impressively, to recommend the holy scriptures to my clergy."

TOBOLSK BIBLE SOCIETY IN THE CAPITAL OF SIBERIA.

FROM THE REV. R. PINKERTON.

"ON the the 25th of June, a day memorable in the annals of Siberia, the foundation was laid of the Tobolsk Bible Society. The archbishop and clergy, together with the chief governor, and a vast number of the citizens of all classes, being assembled in the palace of the archbishop, the cathedral priest Zemlenitzen, addressed the meeting in a speech of which the following is an extract:—"

"At length Siberia also, though distant in her situation from the imperial throne, yet ever near the heart of the august monarch who sits upon it, puts her hands, with gladness, to labour in the blessed harvest of the word of God. Already the inhabitants of this city, at the call of the Deliverer of kings and of nations, with sentiments of sacred joy, hearken to the friendly invitation to enter on this course, and stand here prepared to join the multitude of those who, with one heart, and one mind, are pushing towards the mark—and is not this mark the glory of God, and our salvation? For out of what source are we to derive right knowledge of that glory which is due unto Him, and of the means of salvation for ourselves, but from the words of God himself? Let us put upon these words the sure seal of faith, that its light may illumine our hearts. 'O Lord!' to whom shall we go? Thou hast the words of eternal life!'—Thus spake one of the genuine disciples of the faith, whose spirit ardently longed to imbibe the doctrine of grace from the mouth of God."

"The Saviour himself has pronounced those blessed who hear the word of God, and obey it. And the light of God's word, which is now shedding abroad its animating rays upon all, is destined soon to shed them upon the most distant parts of Siberia also, in order to enlighten, sanctify, and glorify, all those who hunger and thirst after righteousness. Then these strange tribes, who know not the true God, but fall down and worship corruptible gods, graven images, the work of mortal hands, shall be illumined by hearing and reading the word of God; those who were once foolish, shall become wise, and those who formerly were darkness, shall become light in the Lord. The numerous tribes on every hand, shall all join in extinguishing the torch of superstition, and overthrowing their abominable idols, and shall become co-partakers of that faith which comes from God and brings salvation to man. Doubtless, you all, distinguished personages and respectable citizens, will join in showing examples worthy of your enlightened minds and honourable feelings, by promoting the present most auspicious undertaking, in every possible way; and demonstrate that Siberia also has its zealous lovers of the word of the true God; that Siberia also knows how to appreciate the wise laws of the wise legislator of Russia, Alexander the First, by adopting the surest means for disseminating the light of the gospel of divine grace in every part of Russia: a work, in which they who sow, and they who reap, shall one day rejoice together."

"The regulations of the proposed Institution having been read, the venerable gray headed archbishop Ambrosius rose; and in the midst of the crowded audience pronounced the following concise speech."

"Most respectable meeting! Once, the Lord, the Upholder of all things, in his wrath threatened the children of Israel for not obeying his commandments, with a famine, not of bread, and of water but of hearing the word of the Lord.

The weight of this just indignation which overtook that people, and draws after it spiritual destruction, has lain even until now, on the necks of our own fellow countrymen. But in our day, this most gracious and merciful God, moved with compassion at the weakness of man, in the midst of wrath hath remembered mercy, and as he sent manna to the hungry in the wilderness, so has he sent his life giving word unto us, to strengthen weak and famished souls. Now the grace of God abounds towards all men. The Most High has made choice of his anointed servant, our most pious Emperor, to satisfy with heavenly food, those in our native land that hunger after salvation. And, behold, to our unutterable joy, his imperial majesty's will has extended unto us also! He accounts us worthy of being promoters of his paternal designs towards those tribes which inhabit this country, sitting in darkness and in the shadow of death. How high is our vocation! What unspeakable honour is appointed unto the conscientious promoters of this cause! Let us commence our labours, therefore, in obedience to the will of our gracious God, and of our Emperor and Father. Let us spare neither exertion nor property, in order to bring these our unfortunate brethren who know not the true God, to the knowledge of him, by means of his word, and thereby prove ourselves worthy of the name which we bear,—Sons of our beloved country, and sons of the Most High."

"To this proposal a unanimous consent was heard throughout the whole assembly, the sincerity of which was demonstrated by the liberal subscription on the occasion amounting to about 6000 rubles." (Equal to $4333.33.)

MISCELLANEA.

ORDINATIONS.

ON the 4th of October, 1817, brother Joshua P. Slack, from the church in Sansom street, was ordained in the baptist church at Pennepeck, Lower Dublin, Pa.

The Rev. Thomas B. Montanye preached the ordination sermon from 1 Cor. iv. 1. and offered prayer during the imposition of hands. The usual questions were proposed and the charge delivered by Rev. Dr. Staughton.

At the same time brethren Thomas Holmes and John Foster were ordained deacons of the church.

From the Rev. Mr Richards, Mecklenburg county, Virginia.

ON the fifth Lord's day in November, I had the pleasure of assisting in the ordination of brother Silas Shelburn, to the important work of the ministry.

I have likewise had the happiness of assisting in examining and licensing four other candidates for the ministry, viz. William Hatchett and Pleasant Barnes in Ready Creek church, Lunenburg county; John Leigh and James Jeffries, in Tussakiah church, in the same county.

CHURCHES AND MEETING HOUSES.

From the Rev. Mr Sharp, Boston, Massachusetts.

ON Christmas day, a neat and elegant meeting house was opened at Cambridge Port, and a church was constituted. Dr. Baldwin preached, and Mr. Grafton delivered an address and gave the right hand of fellowship. In the evening I preached from Psalm cxviii. 25.—The services were interesting and pleasing.

NEW MARKET STREET BAPTIST CHURCH, PHILADELPHIA.

THE circumstances which led to the formation of this church show decisively the overruling agency of that Almighty Being, who is "wonderful in counsel, and excellent in working." The Budd street church, having been deprived of their pastor, and finding it difficult to obtain a successor in whom all could happily unite, concluded it best that a new church should be formed, their number being sufficiently large to justify, if not imperiously to require this measure. In August last, the Rev. James M'Laughlin was elected pastor. On the 10th of September, in the meeting house in Budd street, 76 persons, who, for that purpose had been dismissed from the mother church, were constituted the *New Market Street Baptist Church* in the Northern Liberties of Philadelphia. The Rev. John P. Peckworth preached on the occasion from 1 Pet. ii. 5. the Rev. Dr. Staughton propounded the necessary interrogatories, and the Rev. Dr. Allison delivered to the newly organized body a solemn and affectionate address.

At their first church meeting they elected as their pastor the Rev. Jacob Grigg. On the 11th of October, *one month and one day only* after their constitution the CORNER STONE, with the name of the church and that of their pastor engraved upon it, was laid; by the 11th of November the roof was raised; by the 29th of December the building was in readiness for public worship; and, on the first day of January, this church, constituted *not four months* before with 76 members, having increased to more than a hundred, and having erected a building 60 feet by 54, had the gratifying opportunity at once to hail the arrival of the *New Year*, open their HOUSE OF PRAYER, and solemnly dedicate it to the service of GOD! The pastor introduced the exercises of the occasion with select portions of the sacred scripture, Mr M'Laughlin led in prayer, the Rev. Mr. Montanye preached from Psalm v. 7., Mr Peckworth from Mal. iii 1, and Dr Staughton closed the services of the day with a sermon from Is. xxxii 15. The assembly was large, the season highly interesting, and it is sincerely hoped that a blessing will follow.— "O, that men would praise the Lord for his goodness, and for his wonderful works to the children of men!"

ANECDOTE OF QUEEN ELIZABETH.

WHEN queen Elizabeth passed through London from the tower to her coronation, a pageant was erected in Cheapside, representing TIME coming out of a cave, and leading a person clothed in white silk, who represented TRUTH his daughter. TRUTH had the English Bible in her hand, on which was written "*verbum veritatis,*"—*the word of truth.* She addressed the queen, and presented her the book. Elizabeth kissed it, held it in her hands, laid it on her breast, greatly thanked the city for their present, and added, that she would often and diligently read it.

More than this is seen in the age in which we have the happiness to live. Time has *actually* brought Truth from her cell. She has scattered millions of bibles, and millions have to their bosoms pressed the heavenly treasure.

God has a large family, but, as is observed by bishop Hall, "none of his children can go alone."

OBITUARY.

DIED, at Walnut Hill, on Wednesday, the 14th ultimo, Mrs MARY CURWEN, consort of JOHN CURWEN Esq. of Lower Merion township, Montgomery county, Pennsylvania. Her remains were interred on the succeeding Friday, in the burying ground belonging to the baptist church of Merion, and on Lord's day, the 18th, her funeral sermon was delivered by the Rev. Horatio G. Jones, from James iv. 14 "What is your life? It is even a vapour, that appeareth for a little time, and then vanisheth away."

Mrs. Curwen was a daughter of John and Sarah Fisher, of Thornthwaite, in the parish of Crosthwaite, and county of Cumberland, England. During a residence of more than thirty years in America, her character became well known, and was held in high estimation. As a friend, her virtues shone with distinguished lustre. Though moving in the first circles of life, she regarded with peculiar kindness and urbanity, the *virtuous* and the *good*, whatever might be their situation. But that which more particularly demands our attention, is, the honour which her *exemplary* life, and *triumphant* death, reflect on the cause of the Redeemer. She was educated under the auspices of the establishment in England. Her mind, however, soared above those limited views which, too often, attach the disciples of the Saviour, exclusively almost to the denomination they prefer. With her, it was a cardinal point to worship God in the "solemn assembly," and very rarely, when her health permitted, was she absent from the meeting in Merion. Her piety, though not *ostentatious*, was *substantial*, and such as will stand the test "*when consternation turns the good man pale.*" When seized with the disease which terminated her mortal career, she was fully sensible of the "destroyer's" approach; but viewed him with calm intrepidity. —A friend having suggested to her his hope of her recovery, she replied, "*What will it avail? Death is certain! The respite can be only of short duration! It becomes us all to stand prepared!*" The favourite topic on which she conversed with her friends, was the Saviour's atoning blood. Exulting in the prevalence of his intercession, she occasionally appeared to forget the pains with which she was afflicted, and desired ardently to glorify God in her death.

A short time previous to her decease, speaking of the vanity of life, and her hope of immortality, she named the passage from which she desired her funeral discourse to be delivered. In the address, the pastor of the church remarked that "he had seen many encountering the "*last enemy*," but never had he seen *that* enemy so effectually baffled and disarmed of his terrors."

If such is the victory piety can achieve, who does not wish to be religious? who can refuse to say,

"The chamber where the good man meets his fate,
"Is privileged beyond the common walk
"Of virtuous life,—quite in the verge of heaven!"

POETRY.

ON THE DEATH OF MY MOTHER.

Yes, thou art gone! the morning dream,
   The fleeting vapour's passed away!
The spark of life has lost its gleam!
   And night has closed upon the day!

The bliss of love, and friendship's glow,
   So richly felt, are felt no more!
And every throb thy heart could know,
   When sorrow pressed, alike is o'er!

Yes, thou art gone! but, as the sun,
   When gold and azure deck the west,
And all his radiant course is run,
   In peaceful glory sinks to rest:

So gently sunk, in skies as bright,
   Where angels watched, thy honoured head;
And all the heavenly way was light,
   That Judah's Star benignly shed.

January 31, 1818.   C.

LATTER DAY GLORY.

Hail, holy light! the bard divinely sung
As rays celestial o'er his vision hung.
Hail holy light!—let men and angels say,
The light that flushes on the latter day.
   Of gloomy darkness long has been the reign,
And deep the galling of her heavy chain,
Since that tremendous, sad, and awful hour,
When first in Eden's heavenly planted bower,
The chief of hell assailed with blackest art,
And won the empire of the human heart.
How have we wandered in a world of woe;
The Lord who made us for His praise our foe!
What thousands have, on hateful altars, bled,
To demons raised, where monsters vile have fed!
How has the earth been filled with dire alarm!
And man 'gainst brother, bared the murdrer's arm,
Till fell destruction, and her compeer death,
Were *almost satisfied*, and paused for breath!
   Hail, then, the light! all hail! the sacred ray!
Prelusive to that bright and blessed day,
Which favoured seers, by heaven inspired, of old
In strains of hallowed rapture have foretold;
When He, the man of sorrows and of grief,
Who came to give the sons of men relief,

The Lamb of God, who bowed his lowly head,
And guiltless for the guilty freely bled,
The Lord of life, who once in weakness died,
Then rose in power to God the Father's side,
And lives, no more to weep, to bleed no more,
But sway the sceptre prostrate thrones adore,
Shall come again, salvation from afar
Beaming resplendent on his winged car,
And riding forth illustrious in his might,
Shall put the legions of his foes to flight,
With shouts of joy his rightful empire gain,
And bind the opposer with a lasting chain!

Thy kingdom come, O Lord! thy servants cry;
Thy kingdom come, the angel hosts reply.
Desire of nations, come! the sceptre's thine,
And wide unfurled thy radiant banners shine
We range beneath them, ours the glorious aim
To spread the honours of thy mighty name.
Crown, crown our weak endeavour with success,
And every kindred band of brothers bless,
And let our eyes with raptured gladness see,
All men on earth, adoring bow to thee,
And light, and glory, and the beams of love,
Reflect the image of thy realms above!

C

HYMN.

"*He brought streams out of the rock.*" Ps. lxxviii, 16

Israel the desert trod,
  Sustained by power divine;
While wondrous mercy marked the road
  With many a mystic sign.

When Moses gave the stroke,
  From Horeb's flinty side
Issued a river, and the rock
  The Hebrew's thirst supplied

But, O! what nobler themes
  Does gospel grace afford,
From Calvary gush superiour streams—
  There hung the smitten LORD.

Of every hope bereft,
  Sinner, to Jesus go,
Behold the rock of ages cleft,
  And living currents flow.

Here may my spirit bathe,
  Here may her joy abound,
Till, passed the wilderness and death,
  She tread celestial ground!

THE LATTER DAY LUMINARY;

BY A COMMITTEE

OF

THE BAPTIST BOARD OF FOREIGN MISSIONS FOR THE UNITED STATES.

Vol. I.   MAY, 1818.   N. II.

COMMUNICATIONS.

OBSERVATIONS ON THE TERM MISSIONARY.

IT is reasonable to expect that, as new events and services present themselves, in the advance of the kingdom of Christ to its promised perfection, new terms will be employed by which they shall be designated. Of these, in the days in which we live, none is more popular, none more deserving investigation, than the term Missionary.

Among the Romans the word mission was used in a restricted sense. It intimated the compassion of an emperor, discovered by his sending orders to rescue a wounded gladiator from his triumphant antagonist Ainsworth gives us as the first sense of the word missionary, the latin word *emissarius*, or emissary The interpretation appears highly exceptionable. Both the latin and english expressions are, we believe, commonly used in a bad sense, indicating a spy or a traitor; a sense totally repugnant to the character and aims of an ambassador of the cross of Jesus Christ. The term might be applied to a minister plenipotentiary who is sent by his nation to negotiate with foreign powers; to an individual commissioned, as was Parke, to trace the origin of rivers, and the political state of unknown tribes; or to the lover of botany, mineralogy or zoology, who, patronized by public institutions, travels with a view of enlarging the empire of science. But in these senses the term is not used. It is employed to indicate a man who, zealous for the conversion of others, and especially of the heathen, relinquishes the endearments of friendship, and the consolations of *home*, to diffuse the knowledge of evangelic truth. The societies under which such persons go forth, contemplate not, for a moment, any dominion over the faith of their brethren in the Lord. They are content to be helpers of their joy. They are happy to encourage a spirit of liberality that shall assist in the accomplishment of their glorious design, and cheerfully responsible to their constituents for the prudence and integrity with which funds entrusted to their management are ever employed.

It may be worth observing, that a mission is sometimes ascribed to things as well as persons. Thus, Mark iv. 29. " when the fruit is ripe, he putteth forth (αποςελλει, he commissions) the sickle." So Acts x 36 " The word which he sent (απεςειλε, which he commissioned,) unto the children of Israel, preaching peace by Jesus Christ." In such a view the passages may be contemplated found in Acts xiii 26 "whoever among you that feareth God, to you is the word of this salvation *sent;* and in Rev. i 1. " the revelation of Jesus Christ—*sent* and signified by his servant John." But the words are here used in a figurative sense, and not applicable to our subject.

The true character of a christian missionary may be understood, by contrasting it with the office of a prophet, an apostle, and an ordinary minister of the everlasting gospel.

Prophets were frequently qualified to write scripture, missionaries are not. Prophets could foretel future events, missionaries are unable. The predictions of the seers of God related chiefly to circumstances that are to occur during the lapse of time; the missionary has to point to the solemnities of eternity. Several of the prophets performed miracles; missionaries have no such power. Prophets usually obtained their instructions by dreams and symbols, by visions and voices; missionaries derive theirs from the completed volume of revelation. The sphere of prophetic toil was usually restricted. The labours of Isaiah, for example, were chiefly confined to the tribe of Judah, and those of Amos to Israel. Jonah and Nahum had principally in their view the city of Nineveh, and Joel the city Jerusalem. No prophet had a general commission, but missionaries obey his instructions who said, " Go ye into all the world, and preach the gospel to every creature;" " Go teach all nations." Prophets foretold a Saviour to come, missionaries declare that " the Life is manifested." The ministration of prophecy was mingled with obscurity; that of the missionary is clear and effulgent.

No character approaches so near to the missionary as the apostolic. It may indeed be surely asserted, and supported by a variety of considerations, that apostles were ancient missionaries, and missionaries are modern apostles. And yet a difference may be traced. Apostles were subjects of the infallible inspirations of the Holy Spirit; missionaries are exposed to errour, and have need to offer perpetual prayer, and to employ incessant circumspection, that they may "sow wholly a right seed." It seems to have been a requisite qualification in an apostle, that he should have seen Christ, in person, after his resurrection, 1 Cor. xv. 8.; missionaries are not warranted to expect any such preparation for office. Though the commission of the apostles was general, yet it had certain limitations. Peter was the apostle of the circumcision, Gal. ii. 8., Paul of the gentiles, Rom. xi. 13., yet not exclusively; Peter had the honour of instructing the family of Cornelius; and Paul, as is evident from a variety of proofs, wrote an epistle to the Hebrews; but to the missionary there is "neither Jew nor Greek, circumcision nor uncircumcision, bond nor free." The apostles were endowed with extraordinary gifts, and particularly with the gift of tongues; missionaries must proceed to the acquisition of languages as other men, by patient labour, by gradual advance, by the compilation and use of the grammar and dictionary. With the exception of Paul, the apostles were generally unlettered men; modern missionaries, for the most part, enjoy before they enter the fields of service, the advantage of an education which enables them to read the holy scriptures in their original languages; an acquisition happily qualifying them to become enlightened expositors and faithful translators. Yet are apostles and missionaries alike the servants of the Lord Jesus; they alike appear in the end of the world; they alike have the assurance of divine assistance, and of ultimate success.

The services of the minister of the gospel and those of the missionary are, in many respects, the same. Their common aim is the exhibition of the guilt, depravity, and helplessness of fallen man, and the suitableness, sufficiency, and glory of the Redeemer. They equally teach the consolations of grace, and the obligations of its subjects to be holy as God is holy. But the minister labours usually among the professed friends of christianity, the missionary among its adversaries, who are attached to far different systems. Ministers commonly, like Apollos, water, missionaries, like the apostle of the gentiles, plant. The ambassador of Christ in the sanctuary, delivers his views in the form of sermons; the ambassador among the heathen, must employ familiar intercourse, colloquial argument, and assuasive expostulation. A talent for social converse is as desirable in the latter, as in the former are lucid arrangement and flowing elocution. The minister continues usually in the country, perhaps in the city of his nativity;

the missionary traverses the ocean, plunges into the depths of the forest, climbs the frosted rock, to reach the dwellings of the wretched, or wanders over inhospitable sands. He is not left, like the minister, to enjoy the facility of addressing his fellow mortals in his maternal tongue; but must use a foreign one: a tongue which he has attained notwithstanding the inconveniences of a memory which manhood obdurates, and in the midst of enemies, privations, and sorrows. The ardour of mind and the degree of solicitude sufficient to produce the ordinary minister of the gospel, are not equal to those which form the missionary. If they were, thousands of preachers would be seen crowding our harbours, and negotiating for passages to distant regions. The missionary feels a sacred necessity laid upon him, to live, and labour, and die among the heathen, and them that know not God. It is a holy fire, hurled from the altar of heaven, which some happy spirits have caught; a passion peculiar to these latter days, which thousands are destined to feel, and which the rising generation are gradual" and forcefully imbibing. It is realized not only by the subjects, but by affectionate and godly parents, who, not without tears, but without hesitation, offer their sons and daughters as first fruits unto the Lord. It is an eminence of character, an apostolic inspiration, reserved for the commencement of the universal reign of Jesus, and a fulfilment of the prophecy, "Many shall run to and fro, and knowledge be increased."

JESUS CHRIST THE FIRST OF MISSIONARIES, AND THE ENCOURAGER, EXAMPLE, AND SUPPORTER OF ALL SUCCEEDING ONES

DEPLORABLE in the extreme was the condition of the world, when the son of God appeared in the nature of man. The gentile nations were involved in the gloom of ignorance, idolatry, and perplexity, and the Jews in a condition very little above them. They were enslaved by the Roman power, over them the cloud of divine displeasure hung dark and portentous, and they were characterized by the spirit of covetousness and hypocrisy, infidelity and devotion. The moral condition of the world did not materially differ from what is seen, at the present day, in the general situation of Jews and heathen

At length, in the fulness of time, agreeably to the voice of ancient prophecy, the GREAT MISSIONARY came. Servants of the eternal Father had been before commissioned, but last of all he sent his Son, invested with the office of the apostle and high priest of our profession, and entrusted to reveal to man the glories of the Father. Others, as Dr. Owen observes, were merely *anteambulones*, forerunners, intended not to represent his person, but to prepare the way of the Lord. The gracious Saviour delighted to exhibit himself as a messenger from God. In his memorable prayer for his disciples, he says, "I have given unto them the words which thou gavest me, and they have received them, and have known surely that I came out from thee, and they have believed that thou didst send me," and afterwards, "as thou hast sent me into the world, even so have I also sent them into the world." The same idea runs through the apostolic writings "In this was manifested the love of God towards us, because that God sent his only begotten Son into the world, that we might live through him."

It is asserted by the evangelist John, that he came unto his own; meaning his own nation, who were *his*, as Craddock observes, by *choice*, Deut. vii. 6.; by *redemption*, Exod. xx. 2.; by *covenant*, Deut. xxvi. 17; and by *kindred*, Rom ix. 5, and among *his own* his labours were chiefly, but not exclusively, confined. He " was a minister of the circumcision for the truth of God, to confirm the promises made unto the fathers," yet so as ' that the gentiles might glorify God for *his* mercy." Romans xv. 8, 9.

In various ways the condescending Redeemer revealed the will of heaven. Sometimes he had recourse to private conversation. He taught Nicodemus, a pharisee, who came to him by night, the necessity, the nature, and the manner of regeneration, and declares himself the only revealer of evangelic mysteries, the only Saviour of miserable sinners. He discovered to a woman of Samaria her need of "living water," and that he alone could supply it. He developed the immorality of her life, exhibited the spirituality of the divine nature, and prepared the way for an exposition of the advance of his kingdom, and the blessedness of those who were sowing and reaping in the harvest field. He instructed a few inquiring Greeks who came to a solemn feast at Jerusalem, and who desired an interview with him, in the doctrine of his passion and his empire, and illustrated both by the familiar figure of the casting of a seed corn into the earth. He pressed on their minds that all who would be his disciples must after his example, prepare for suffering, and that after the same example they might look for a glorious immortality. Sometimes the addresses of Christ were public. Frequently he taught in synagogues, and occasionally in the temple; twice he preached to the multitude from a mountain, and twice from a ship. He often entered the principal cities of Syria. Nazareth and Capernaum, Jerusalem and Bethany, Sidon and Tyre, Sychar and Jericho heard his informing, alarming, and consoling voice. At other times we find him engaged in extensive and laborious tours, partly through Samaria, but more especially through "the regions of Galilee." "He went through every city and village, preaching and showing the glad tidings of the kingdom of God," Luke viii. 1. Often he explained his doctrine by parables, and often by the most striking miracles confirmed its truth.

How much a missionary spirit was the spirit of Jesus, may be inferred from the commissions he gave to his disciples. First he sent forth the twelve, and besides giving them power to heal all manner of diseases, to cast out devils, and to raise the dead," directs them to preach "that the kingdom of heaven is at hand," that "the Messiah has come." Afterward he commissioned seventy, to go to all the places which he meant himself to visit, " to heal the sick," and say to the people, "the kingdom of God is come nigh unto you," and instructs these very seventy, as if to inspire them the more with missionary ardour, from the consideration that " the harvest truly is great and the labourers few," to " pray the Lord of the harvest that he would send forth labourers."

On leaving the world he authorized his apostles to " go and teach all nations, and " commanded them that they should not depart from Jerusalem, but wait for the promise of the Father." The promise was fulfilled. The spirit descended, and "they went forth, and preached every where, the Lord working with them, and confirming the word with signs following."

To attempt a contrast between our Lord Jesus and the missionaries of his cross, were absurd, if not blasphemous. It were much like comparing " Socrates and Jesus." What is a missionary brought by the side of him that is " the brightness of the Father's glory, and the express image of his person," but dust and ashes, meanness and vanity? Yet from the example of Jesus missionaries may deduce many instructive lessons. He is a pattern of willingness and labour, of fidelity and self denial, of prudence and fortitude, of pointedness in argument, and patience in suffering. He instructs us, not only by his own missionary efforts, but by his influencing others to become cities on hills, lights of the world, and the salt of the earth. To him his faithful servants may direct their prayers for graces and gifts, for the exertions of his regal power in affording protection to them, and in controlling their adversaries. They may chase their despondencies, and fire their expectations, by the thought, that he who has called his missionaries into the field, will make mountains and hills break forth before them into singing, and when their testimony is finished, receive them to himself to behold his glory.

Christ's Travels as a Missionary.

HOW FAR, AS A MISSIONARY, DID JESUS TRAVEL?

	Miles.
1 FROM Nazareth to Galilee, to John, to be baptised by him at Bethabara, near the part of the river which was miraculously dried up. See Joshua iii. 16. and Judges xii. 6. – Luke iii. 23. "Jesus himself began to be about 30 years of age."	35
2 From Jordan to the wilderness, perhaps in the part near the sea of Galilee, he was "returning" to Nazareth, Luke iv. 1. say,	15
3. From the wilderness to Jordan, John i. 29. Here he had some temporary residence, John i. 39.	15
4 He leaves Jordan for Galilee, John i. 43 and was present at a marriage at Cana.	38
5. "After this he went down to Capernaum," John ii. 12. where he tarried "not many days"	25
6. The passover being at hand he went to Jerusalem, John ii. 13.	72
7 Jesus and his disciples went into the land of Judea, at some distance from the capitol, uncertain how far, say	25
8 He left Judea after a residence of seven or eight months, and by the way of Samaria went into Galilee, John iv. 3, 4, 5. to Cana, John iv. 46.	70
9. He went from Cana to Nazareth, Luke iv. 16	12
10. He left Nazareth and came to Capernaum, Matt vi. 13.	23
11. Leaving Capernaum he made a circuitous tour, Matt iv. 23 "Jesus went about all Galilee," probably through its extreme parts, for "his fame went through all Syria," Matt. iv. 24. He visited the neighbouring towns, Mark i. 38.	300
12. His fame increasing, he was obliged to be without in desert places,	30
13. He returned to Capernaum, Mark ii. 1.	15
14 He went to the sea shore, Mark ii. 13	6
15 "There was a feast of the Jews, and Jesus went up to Jerusalem," John v. 1.	70
16. He returned to Galilee Compare Mark iii. 7 and Luke vi. 12, 13. with Luke vii. 1.	60
17. He visits Capernaum again, Luke vii. 1.	30
18 He went into the city called Nain, Luke vii. 11	25
Carried over	896

		Miles.
	Brought forward,	896
19	He travelled " through every city and village, preaching and showing the glad tidings of the kingdom of God," Lu. viii. 1.	300
20.	He returned to the side of the sea of Galilee, Matt. xiii. 1. and taught in a ship,	10
21.	He passes over the sea, Mark iv. 35.	8
22.	He returned back again, Matt. ix. 1.	8
23.	He visits Nazareth, Mark vi. 1.	15
24.	He made a circuitous tour, " about all the cities and villages," Matt. ix. 35.	300
25.	Again he crosses the sea of Tiberias, Luke ix. 10.	8
26	He returns to Capernaum, walking on the sea, Matt. xiv. 26. "This was thought so impracticable, that the picture of two feet walking on the sea, was an Egyptian hieroglyphic for an impossible thing."	18
27.	He withdraws to the coasts of Tyre and Sidon, Mark vii. 24.	45
28	These regions he leaves, and comes to the sea of Galilee, Matt. xv. 29.	45
29.	Entering a ship with his disciples, he crossed the sea, and came into the parts of Dalmanutha,	10
30.	Here crosses the Tiberian sea, Matt. xvi. 13.	8
31.	He visits the towns of Cæsarea Philippi, towns that had lately been rebuilt by Philip the Tetrarch, Mark viii. 27.	40
32.	After these things he walked in Galilee, John vii. 1.	100
33	He visits Jerusalem about the middle of the feast of Tabernacles, John vii. 14	90
34.	He takes a last circuit through Galilee. It was by far the most successful and glorious, Lu. xiii. 31-33. John x. 40-42.	300
35.	He returns to Jerusalem, John ix. 1.	90
36.	The Sanhedrim agreeing that for raising Lazarus he should be put to death, he retires to Ephraim, John xi. 47. in the N. E part of the lot of Benjamin,	18
37.	Sets out on his last journey to Jerusalem, taking Jericho in his way, Mark x. 32. Matt. xxii. 29. (the last two miles he rode on an ass,)	18
38.	Retires to Bethany, John xii. 20—30.	2
39.	Returns to Jerusalem, John xii. 44	2
		2331

His occasional visits added, probably, one half in distance to the above aggregate.—It will be remembered that these journeys were almost entirely performed on foot. Absolute accuracy is not pretended to; but such as will with the greatest care examine the above account, it is believed, will be best satisfied of its general correctness.

A VISION.

SITTING a few days ago in my easy chair, and meditating with sorrow of heart on the miserable condition of the race of man, I insensibly fell asleep. Whether the sleep were induced by a despairing conclusion that human miseries would not soon be abolished, or whether, as physicians frequently assert, grief lulls the body to slumber, and had such an effect on me, I cannot determine. The world was scarcely shut out from my senses before I heard a voice louder than thunder, in which majesty and sweetness, decision and energy were combined, utter the sounds, "Behold I create all things new." A chorus instantly succeeded, loud and harmonious, the theme of which was "good will toward men." I felt as though I were in a new world. Involuntarily I looked up to the heavens. The moon was setting, a few stars were still visible, and the increasing crimson of the east gave assurance that the morning sun was about to throw over the earth its reviving lustre. But what, thought I, of novelty is there here? These glorious luminaries may hereafter become useless in the system of things, and the power that framed may destroy them; yet as they are not subjects of moral turpitude, whence the necessity of creating them anew? Occupied in reflection, I heard again the music of heaven in sounds more combined and vigorous than before. I saw a form descend, mild and trailing as a shooting star; he came nearer, sustaining a roll in his hand, and suppressed my alarm, by saying, "Child of dust, dismiss thy apprehensions he who sits on the rainbow has seen thy sorrow. Believe me, I am the genius of prophecy, and am sent to show thee scenes which in a few years shall be amply realized: ascend with me" He took me by the hand: my body became light as air, the instant he touched me. I ascended. "Seest thou yon hill?" said my instructor. "Mark it well." Its summit was rugged and barren; but down its sides, in every direction, I saw—for we flew round the hill—falling the most beautiful currents. The celestial messenger seemed as though he could have continued gazing on the spot for ever; and indeed, when we left it, I remarked, that, with a countenance beaming with joy, and bespeaking a heart occupied with contemplation, he would often look back. I could not help observing that, wherever the streams directed their course, the soil, otherwise sterile, was covered with flowers and fruits. I was sorry to observe that after a while the waters appeared to run under ground, excepting here and there a narrow stream threw back the rays of the sun. At length, after miles of desolation, they again broke up, and continued with some interruptions gradually to swell "Extend thy vision," said the genius; when, I know not by what enchanting virtue, or by what unperceived elevation, I saw the earth, far as the eye could reach, yielding her increase. The cattle fed in large pastures. The vine gave her fruit; and the heavens their dew. I was particularly delighted to observe the interest which a number of cherubim took in the beautiful scene. Now they were flying through the air, and now apparently alighting on the ground, as if such a soil they could wish to inhabit. I could hear them saying, partly in the voice of proclamation, and partly in song: "The glorious Lord will be unto us a place of broad rivers and streams." I could not forbear asking the name of the hill whence these blessings issued. I was answered, "It is Calvary, where the Lord was crucified: but come," said the genius, "let us draw nearer to these happy regions." But how shall I describe what I had the felicity to observe! I could not help exclaiming,

> O! scenes surpassing fable, and yet true,
> Scenes of accomplished bliss!

In one place I heard the sound of ponderous hammers; thousands were busily employed. They were beating swords into ploughshares, and spears into pruning hooks. They sang as they laboured; and at the end of every stanza, the air rang with the chorus, "there shall be war no more." I saw in the same pasture the kid and the lion sporting, and children fearlessly playing with adders and asps. The countenances of the inhabitants every where exhibited the appearance of vigorous health. There was not one weak or sickly among them. Many were far advanced in age; a century or more had passed over them. They bent like the grain of harvest; showing themselves richer, because older, than those around them. It was gratifying to see bands of youth crowding around the aged; some offering their arms to sustain them; others presenting them milk and fruits, and all listening to their pious instructions. Nearly every one had under his arm a book, which my guide told me was the volume of inspiration. Some of them had the book open, and were offering observations more sublime, evangelic and lucid, than any thing I had ever heard before. Even the youth seemed to possess the mental vigour and clear discernment of manhood. I asked the genius whence this wonderous illumination had proceeded? He told me the temple of God was opened in heaven, and that this happy people had seen in his temple the ark of his testament.

My instructor perceived my attention directed to a particular class of men, that were almost every where to be traced. They seemed greatly to excel in the spirit of wisdom and love. They always walked arm in arm. The attachment of the people to these men was surprising. Some of the men were on their knees, and with eyes bright with tears of rapture, cried, "Lord, it is enough!" A few were engaged in public addresses, but most of them were saying to the people, "In every place your faith to God-ward is spread abroad, so that we need not to speak any thing." I was informed they were ministers of the gospel, who had lived to see the answer of their prayers, and the fruit of their ministrations.

I was struck with observing at some distance, immense volumes of smoke ascending in the air. My director invited me to approach the spot. In one place were large furnaces, with prodigious crucibles, into which were cast gods of gold and silver. The workmen were so zealous in their employ, that one melting pot could scarcely be poured, before they wanted to throw in other gods. The matrices gave to each ingot characters which every one might read, "the silver and the gold is the Lord's." In another place blazed a prodigious fire, which at first appeared composed of logs of wood; but, on nearer inspection, I found them gods from the forest. I recognized in them the forms of Brumha, and Kishnoo, and Shivu: and mentioned them to the genius. "Yes," added he," and here are the representations of Indru, and Sooryu, and Guneshu. and Kariketu, and Ugnu, and Puvunu, and Vuroonu, and Yamu, and Gaudana, and all the three hundred and thirty millions of Indian gods at once on fire." Many similar piles were seen in every direction. It was really delightful to observe with what eagerness men were carrying their idols to the pyre. The women and children, and old men were no less active than the rest. "This," said the guide, "is the way in which God will purge the earth, by *the spirit of burning.*" One stream of fire ascended more vivid than the rest. I supposed the reason to be, because the materials were more combustible. I arrived just in time to spell out some few characters, for I found them to be papers, rolls and books. I distinctly discovered the words Koran, Veda, Shastra. "Come with me," said the genius, "to the other side of the pile." I went, and saw amid the fire the names of Chubb, Collins, Herbert, Shaftsbury, Hume, Gibbon, Paine, and several others that I do not distinctly recollect. On a neighbouring spot were burning beads and crucifixes, dispensations and mitres. As I was contemplating the fiery mass, I heard a voice from the sky, "These the Lord shall consume with the spirit of his mouth and shall destroy with the brightness of his coming." Seeing at a distance some vessels very deeply laden, I asked my instructor what these meant? He said, "Come and see." We hastened to the rivers, and passed in our way many heathen temples, over each of which were written the words, *empty, void and waste.* We discovered that the vessels were filled with gods of stone and clay, which, with shouts of joy, the seamen threw into the depths of the ocean, to be seen no more.

Walking among the inhabitants I could not but remark that they had some familiar terms in conversation, that I never found used so much before. I often heard the words, *showers, wind, waters of the sanctuary, jubilee, year of release, mountain of the Lord's house, latter days,* and the like. I ventured to speak with one of the happy people, with which I saw my conductor was not displeased. I asked, do you keep the sabbath? The answer was, " Sir, ours is perpetual sabbath, the seven thousandth year of the creation of God is come." Are there any hospitals, or alms houses in your regions? " No, disease is not." Have you any courts of judicature, or prison houses? I was told, the former still remain, the latter are demolished, for " the people are all righteous." I had proceeded, but the genius said, " Come, let us survey at large the glorious landscape." We ascended, and pursued our way. The seas were covered with ships, but on every pendant were such mottoes as *joy, love, peace, zeal, holiness, the end is come,* &c &c. In one situation I saw multitudes of Chinese occupied in evangelic devotions. There Tartars in immense congregations were celebrating the name of Jesus. Hindoos and Bengalees, Gentoos and Burmans, were hailing the light of the glorious gospel. Ethiopians were lifting up their hands to the heavens. Indians of the west were rejoicing that to their deserts the excellency of Carmel was given. The face of the Jew was without a veil; and the names of Mecca and Medina were in a manner forgotten.

" These," said my director, " are some of the glories of future times, which I have been instructed to unfold to thee, but the half has not been told. Return to thy station in life; believe in the Lord, and bid adieu to thy griefs." The thought of losing the delightsome vision seemed intolerable. I said, How long, my inestimable instructor, shall it be before these glories shall be universally realized? He replied, " Come with me, I will show you the hill of prophecy." Turning to the east I beheld the most magnificent eminence I had ever seen. Its base was granite, coral and gold, on which were engraved, as with a pen of iron on the rock, in letters which time had not in the least degree defaced, " HATH HE SAID, AND SHALL HE NOT DO IT?" The mountain rose sublime and awful, in some parts it showed a steady resplendence, in others it was involved in clouds which seemed gradually vanishing. A bright effulgence descending from above rested on its summit, on which stood forty or fifty venerable forms. Several of them bore standards waving long and beautiful. On two that flamed with red, I saw the figures 666 and 1000. But several, which my guide pointed to me, were of the purest white. On one was written " his times," on another, " time, times, and the dividing of a time ;" on a third, " forty and two months," on a fourth, " twelve hundred and sixty days." I regretted that a part of the ensigns seemed wound round the staffs that supported them, so that I could not ascertain the dates, whence to calculate the period intended. On expressing my sorrow on this account, my instructor said, with the greatest tenderness of manner, " You remember, child of dust, the words of your Lord and mine, ' it is not given to you to know the times and seasons.'" But, said I, may we not hope that in one hundred and a few years all these things shall come to pass? He smiled. I understood the smile to say *Yes*, thou hast rightly divined. He however only said, opening the scroll he held in his hand, " Read this." I saw in golden letters, Moravian Missions, Baptist Mission Society, London Mission Society, Bible Societies, Sunday Schools, &c ; and the names Elliott, Brainerd, Vanderkemp, Kircherer, Carey, Marshman, Ward, &c. I was continuing to read the opening roll, when the prophets on the hill struck with their lyres and uttered with their voices such rapturous strains, that, overpowered with their sweetness, their fulness, and their harmony, I awoke.

TO THE EDITORS OF THE LATTER DAY LUMINARY

GENTLEMEN,

OBSERVING in your last number a request, that any evidence possessed may be communicated, relative to the sentiment of Dr. Carey, that *the Affghans are undoubtedly the remains of the ten tribes*, I beg leave to submit a few ideas, which you may make use of as you please.

ARE THE AFFGHAN TARTARS THE DESCENDANTS OF THE ANCIENT ISRAELITES?

WRITERS on the subject of the Israelites may be divided into three classes. The first are those who believe that after they were made captives by Shalmaneser and carried away into Assyria, (see 2 Kings, chap. 17.) their identity as a people was lost; the second conceive that their descendants still exist, and use their penetration and industry to discover them; while a third regard the whole as a thing of entire uncertainty, and are ready to say with Mr. Brown, "What has become of them since their captivity—whether they removed eastward with the Tartars, and partly passed over into America, or how far they mixed with the Jews, when carried into Babylon, we know not."

The opinion of Prideaux, was in favour of the first of these classes. He says, "the ten tribes of Israel, which had separated from the house of David, were brought to a full and entire destruction, and never recovered themselves. For those who were thus carried away, as well in this as in the former captivities, (excepting only some few, who, joining themselves to the Jews in the land of their captivity, returned with them,) soon going into the usages and idolatry of the nations among whom they were planted, after a while they became wholly absorbed and swallowed up in them, and thence utterly losing their name, their language, and their memorial, were never more spoken of." It has been thought that they wasted away, until at length, mingled with the nations, as rivers with the sea, they totally disappeared, according to the celebrated passage, "Israel shall be broken that it be not a people." Is vii 8 (Vid. Pol in loc.) It was also the opinion of Mr. Henry, that we have no reason to credit the conjecture of some that they remain a distinct body in some part of the world.

Such as believe the ten tribes are still somewhere in being, urge the prophecies that relate to their restoration, as Isaiah xi. 11, 12 "The Lord shall assemble the outcasts of Israel, and gather together the dispersed of Judah:" and Jeremiah, iii. 18. "Judah shall walk with Israel, and they shall come together out of the north, to the land which I have given for an inheritance to their fathers." Ezekiel was ordered to join together two pieces of wood, as a symbol of the reunion of Israel and Judah, see chap. xxxvii. 16. In Amos ix. 14 God says, "I will bring again my people Israel from their captivity." In Hosea xi. 11. are the words, "They shall tremble as a bird out of Egypt, and as a dove out of the land of Assyria: and I will place them in their houses, saith the Lord." &c Some stress may be laid on the circumstance, that when Ezra celebrated the passover, a sacrifice was offered of "twelve he-goats for the whole house of Israel, according to the number of the tribes,"—see chap. vi. 16, 17. and viii. 58. Paul speaks of the twelve tribes which serve God day and night, Acts xxvi. 7. James writes to the twelve tribes scattered abroad, i. 1.; and the sealing of the tribes is mentioned in the Revelation of John.

But if the Israelites really exist, where are they? It has long been regarded as not improbable, that they are found in the aborigines of our country. The reasons assigned for this opinion are sufficiently known. Such as their division into tribes—their reckoning time by lunar months—their using parables—their discovering traces of the more important Jewish festivals, such as the passover, the day of atonement, and the feast of tabernacles—the supposed resemblance of the Indian and Hebrew languages, &c. &c.

The opinion, however, seems gaining ground, that they are to be sought, not in western forests, but among the *mountains* of the east. Whether the Affghan Tartars are they or not, is the subject of our present inquiry.

It may be proper to mention, that Affghanistan is a mountainous country between Persia and the Indus. The inhabitants are martial and untractable. Cabul is their capital city; it is walled, nearly two miles in circumference, and situated at the foot of the Hindookoo mountain, near the river Kameh, in lat. 34° 30′ north, and in long 68° 35′ east.

Sir William Jones probably first suggested the idea that the Affghans are descendants of Israel. "We learn," says he, "from Esdras, that the ten tribes, after a wandering journey, came to a country called Arsaxeth, where we may suppose they settled. Now Affghans are said by the best Persian historians to be descended from the Jews; they have among themselves traditions of such a descent; and i. is even asserted that the families are distinguished by the names of Jewish tribes, although since their conversion to the Islam, they studiously conceal their origin. The Pushtoo language, of which I have seen a dictionary, has a manifest resemblance to the Chaldaic, and a considerable district under their dominion is called Hazareh or Hazaret, which might easily have been changed into the word used by Esdras." He adds, "I strongly recommend an inquiry into the literature and history of the Affghans."

There is a work translated from the Persian by Mr. Vansittart, which is itself an abridgment of a more early production, written in the Pushtoo language, called *the Secrets of the Affghans*, in which they state, that they are the descendants of Melic Talut, or king Saul, and Affghan, who had a military command under Solomon. In the second volume of Asiatic Researches, some curious particulars may be found. The Affghans not only call themselves the posterity of Talut, or Saul, but state that, in a war which raged between the children of Israel and the Amalekites, the latter being victorious, plundered the Jews, and obtained possession of the ark of the covenant. Considering this as the God of the Jews, they threw it into the fire, which did not injure it. Unable to destroy it, they placed it in their temple, and all the idols bowed to it. At length they fastened it to a cow, which they turned loose in the wilderness. They are said to have applied to Samuel after their defeat by the Amalekites. The angel Gabriel gave Samuel a wand, teaching that the person whose height equalled the wand should be their king. Melic Talut, or Saul, a herdman, had lost a cow; he applied to Samuel for assistance. Samuel, observing his lofty stature, asked his name; he answered Talut: upon which, having measured him with the wand, he said to the children of Israel, " God has raised Talut to be your king." After Talut obtained the kingdom, he seized part of the territories of Jalut or Goliath, who assembled a large army, but was killed by David. Melic Talut they say had two sons, one called Berkia, the other Irmia, who served David, and were beloved by him. The son of Irmia was *Usbec*, the son of Berkia, AFFGHAN. The latter made frequent excursions to the mountains, where his progeny, after his death, established themselves, built forts, and exterminated the infidels.— See Rees's Cyclopædia, article AFFGHANS.

Mr. Hanway, in his history of the Revolution of Persia, vol. 3. observes, that " the Affghans have an utter aversion against marrying their daughters to strangers." Bernier, a learned Frenchman, who visited the Affghan country, observes, that the inhabitants which he saw in the first village, appeared to him to be Jews in their air and deportment, and in that " indefinable peculiarity which enables us to distinguish one nation from another." The name of Moses was much in use among them, and a small ancient edifice on the summit of a lofty hill, they called the throne of Solomon. Several Jewish writers are of the opinion that there are tribes of Israelites in Tartary, particularly Benjamin of Judea, a celebrated traveller of the twelfth century, who relates that several Jewish tribes migrated beyond the rivers of Chaldea, and lived after the manner of Tartars, accompanied by their flocks and dwelling in tents. We will remark only that the studiousness of the Affghans, who are now professors of the Mahometan religion, to conceal their origin, and their remoteness from European research, may account for their character as Israelites having been developed no earlier.

To present the preceding arguments in a concentrated point of view, let it be observed,

1. They call themselves descendants of Talut or Saul.

2. Their traditions on this point are obviously founded on scripture history.

3. Their families are distinguished by the names of Jewish tribes

4. They are careful not to suffer their daughters to intermarry with strangers

5. They have a fondness for Old Testament names

6. The Pushtoo, or Affghan language, resembles the Chaldaic

7. The testimony of the best Persian historians supposes the Affghans to be the Israelites.

8. Several learned Jews are of the same opinion.

9. Nothing absurd or mysterious is found in the circumstance that they have not been discovered earlier.

As the recesses of Asia are every year penetrated in an increasing degree, it is not to be doubted that new light will soon be thrown on this interesting subject, of which both the Hebrew and Christian world will be happy to avail themselves. I consider the testimony of Dr. Carey, who has long resided in Asia, next to demonstration on the point in question.

AN ISRAELITE'S FRIEND.

ON PRAYER.

MAN, from the dawn of reason, feels that he is a dependent being. Conscious that he is not the architect of himself, and entered into life without any agency of his own, it is impossible for him to extinguish the conviction that he is amenable to a superior power. The structure of his body, and the operations of his mind, alike proclaim him the workmanship of a God, to whom gratitude and reverence are due:

From the belief of an all-powerful, and benevolent Deity, arises the feeling of obligation to bow the knee in homage, and to pour forth the heart in prayer. When blessings flow in rich profusion from the hand of Providence, and bliss mantles round our brow, emotions of thankfulness should fill the heart. When danger lowers in our sky, and the elements convulsed menace destruction to those whom they were destined to subserve, conscience beckons us for assistance to him who "rides in the whirlwind and directs the storm!" Then, indeed, prayer is resorted to both as a duty and a refuge. It is such at all times, and enlists in its performance attendant pleasure and consequent blessings.

The injunctions of the christian code on the subject of prayer, though sometimes perverted, have seldom been denied. Even those who, by a general sweep, have removed every ceremony which could distinguish one system of religion from another, have not altogether rejected the obligation of prayer. While to the humble and enlightened believer in revelation, guarded by the awful sanctions of divine authority, the important nature of this duty becomes too apparent, and the precepts for its observance too imperative, for the one to be controverted, or the other neglected.

> "Prayer ardent opens heaven, lets down a stream
> Of glory on the consecrated hour
> Of man in audience with the Deity."

Responsible beings, endued with freedom of volition, though subject to the sceptre of the Almighty, are encouraged to make known their holy desires, in order to cherish in themselves a becoming sense of *his* goodness and *their own* dependence. This is the natural tendency of prayer. It keeps alive in their breast those sentiments of devotion which are acceptable to God, and profitable to man. It elevates the mind above the humiliating scenes of earth, and teaches it to share the converse and anticipate the bliss of heaven. It conducts the aspiring soul into the presence of the Most High, and encourages it to gaze upon the glories that encircle his throne.

Nor is this all. To obtain blessings at the hand of the Creator, is one important object in the prayers of the saint. Jehovah, in the language of the poet, has

> "Still wrought by *means* since first he made the world."

He has been pleased to make prayer a medium for the conveyance of those favours which He bestows on men. The fervent aspirations of the devout heart ascend to the throne of grace, and bring down the choicest mercies. The blessed God himself assures us, that, for the numerous bounties of his providence, and the riches of his grace, he will be *inquired of* by the creatures of his hand. *The effectual fervent prayer of a righteous man availeth much.*

With a deep and solemn impression of the importance of this duty, as connected with the progress of the Redeemer's kingdom on earth, and the best interests of the human family, it is gratifying to mark the prevalence of a spirit of prayer throughout the brotherhood of christianity. The flame is sacred, and should be scattered wherever there are souls to be recovered from death. It has been kindled by an irradiation from the brightest glories of the Godhead, and shall increase in splendour till the world shall be filled with the light of divine truth.

Monthly prayer meetings for the dispersion of the christian faith over the wide surface of the globe, form a most interesting feature of these gospel times. Such assemblies, where saints of different professions bow together before one common shrine, to supplicate for one common good, furnish a peculiarly animating indication of the approach of that happy day, when all distinctions shall be merged in the excellence of christian principle, when man shall be arrayed in the livery of grace, and the whole earth be responsive with the anthems of love.

Christians! it is your privilege, as it is your duty, to invite the approach of this predicted bliss. Your prayers are demanded. Constantly importune the Father of Mercies to hasten the chariot of that sun who is to ride in such majesty through the heavens. For the achievement of this sublime end, be zealous—be unwearied. Let your nightly pillows be witnesses of your petitions, and usher in the day-spring with the same supplications.

The good which we have reason to believe has already eventuated from the prayers of the pious, is a powerful inducement for more active exertions. Infidelity may scoff, but we are not ashamed to avow our belief that the unprecedented victories which are daily bringing fresh laurels to the temple of Zion, and the brilliant prospects which now gladden the souls of the faithful, are given in answer to the confederated petitions of the christian community. How strong the encouragement!—how imperative the duty!

A

INTRODUCTION OF THE GOSPEL INTO ENGLAND.

OF this matter some account has been given in the preceding number of the LUMINARY. Proof was there adduced that the gospel had been planted in Britain at a very early period of the christian era. But whether Joseph of Arimathea, or Pomponia, the wife of one of the generals of Claudius, or the apostle Paul, was the angel of mercy in an event so important to the welfare of our ancestors and ourselves, cannot, perhaps, with certainty, be decided. It is, indeed, not improbable, that each of these imparted the knowledge of the christian faith to a portion of the inhabitants of that country, without any acquaintance at the time with what was done by the others—almost simultaneously. Not very remote from the same period, possibly earlier, christianity appears to have found its way into Wales. In support of this fact, the following quotation from the *Appendix to the third volume of Howell's History of the Bible*, is offered.

"The most calamitous events are often, through the wise direction of a superintending Providence, productive of the most important and happy consequences. Caractacus, king of the Britons, was, through the treachery of Cartismandua, queen of the Brigantes, betrayed into the hands of his enemies, and carried captive to Rome. His father, Bran (or Branus), his wife, children, and brothers, shared in this calamity, and remained prisoners there for seven years, while the great apostle of the gentiles was successfully planting the standard of the gospel in the capital of the world. An opportunity thus afforded to those illustrious Britons, of attending the first preachers of christianity, Branus, and others of his family, were converted to the faith, and on their return, introduced the gospel into Wales. On this account, Bran or Branus, is called, in the venerable and uncorrupted chronicles of Wales, one of the three blessed sovereigns of Britain. Cyllin, or St. Cyllin, son of Caractacus, and Eigen his daughter, were also among the first to establish christianity among their unenlightened countrymen. The latter is accounted the first female saint in Britain. On their return from Rome, they brought with them, A. D. 70, Ilid, a Jewish christian, and Cynday, another convert, to assist in preaching the gospel.

"Towards the close of the second century, Lleirwg, the son of Coel ab Cyllin, called Lleuver Mawr, and Lles, or Saint Lucius, prince of the Silures, formed the laudable design of diffusing the knowledge of the Christian faith generally over his dominions. In order to further the grand design, he sent over to Rome for the assistance of some able teachers; whereupon Eleutherius sent Dyvan, Fagan, Medwy, and Elvan for that purpose. The first Christian church was built by Lleirwg, at Llanday, "under national protection, right, and privilege." On this account, Lleirwg was ranked with Bran and Cadwaledr, under the appellation of the three blessed princes of the isle of Britain.

"This account is found in authentic documents still extant in the ancient British language, called, "Trioedd Ynys Prydain," the Welsh Triads; and "Bonedd y Sant," The Genealogy of the British Saints. See the above names in the Cambrian Biography, by Mr. W. Owen, F.A.S. Evan. Mag November 1806, p. 506, 507. See also Tertullian contra Judaeos, Venerable Bede, Gildas the Briton, and Fox in his Martyrology, who all agree, that the gospel was planted in Britain at a very early period, and, most probably, during the first century."

REVIEW.

DR. CHALMERS' DISCOURSES.

THE design of presenting the readers of the LUMINARY with a review of the astonishing discourses of Dr Chalmers of Glasgow, had been contemplated. Upon further reflection, however, it was apprehended, that our limits could scarcely admit a review sufficiently extended, for an adequate consideration of the unusual manner and unusual track pursued by the author. Let the discourses themselves be read: though not beyond the reach of legitimate criticism, they carry with them their own eulogy. At the same time, the following extract from BLACKWOOD's Magazine, it is believed, will not be unacceptable.

"In every step of his progress he seems to dissolve, by the touch of his magic wand, that stony sleep of lethargy in which some noble feeling of our nature had for a season been entranced. He gives us no new arguments, no new images, but he scatters the vivid rays of poetic splendour over those which, by the very frequency of repetition, had ceased to have any power either upon our reason or our fancy. We are lost in a vague maze of wonder, how it should happen that all these things seemed so trivial to us before—how arguments so convincing should have appeared weak, or images so appalling should have passed tamely and dimly before our eyes

"It arises not from the weakness, but the will of Chalmers, that he very seldom keeps us long at the summit of this elevation He seems to be insensible that the splendours which he has revealed to us are either new or dazzling. His genius regards the universe as its birthright, and he has no undue partiality for the richer and more magnificent regions of his domain With the same overpowering sweep of mastery, he brings us at once from the heaven to the earth, and from the earth to the heaven; and however majestic may have been his elevation, he has not the air of feeling any degradation from his descent. He compels us indeed to follow his footsteps into the basest tracks of mortality, and lays open the infirmities, the frailties, the errours, the vilenesses of our nature, with the keen indignation of a Juvenal, no less willingly than he has already inflamed and purified our spirits with the angelic enthusiasm of a Milton. But there is diffused over the humblest of his representations a redeeming breath of Christian sublimity, a thousand times more ennobling than all the stern and unbending dignities of the Porch. He does not, like the philosophers of old, confine all grandeur to contemplation; he clothes with majesty the most common offices of life, and teaches that the meanest of his christian hearers may exert, in the bosom of his family, and in the manly perseverance of painful labour, virtues more lofty and divine than were ever called up by the pure spirit of the Stagyrite, or ever floated among the mystical and foreboding dreams of Plato. These are things which fill the walls of his church with crowds the most mingled, yet the most harmonious, that were ever collected together for social enjoyment or social good. It is this that makes the wise and the great come to have their souls fed like infants by the liberal hand of his genius, and makes the poor man and the ignorant steal from the precious moments of his week-day toil, that his spirit may be sustained and kindled by the inspiring voice of Chalmers. He is not the preacher of any one class; he is the common orator of man.

"Were our hearts, indeed, as dead and as cold as monumental marble, they could not fail to sympathize with such a preacher. He has given up his soul to the full sway of his emotions, and he summons from the depths of a convulsed spirit things more awful, as well as more lovely, than could ever be dreamed by the ordinary mind of man. We need only to look upon him, to see that his heart is bursting with the deluge of his zeal. His countenance glares with the feeling of unutterable things; his voice quivers, and his limbs tremble: and we perceive that he is in the agony of inspiration.

"It has, we know, been said by some, that Chalmers has in his noble Astronomical Discourses, all along combated a phantom, and that those objections to the truth of christianity have never been raised, which it is their object to overthrow. On this very account are his discourses invaluable. The objections which he combats are not so much the clear, distinct, and decided averments of infidelity, as they are the confused, glimmering, and disturbing fears and apprehensions of noble souls, bewildered among the boundless magnificence of the universe."

THE HISTORY OF BAPTISM,

BY ROBERT ROBINSON,

First published in England in 1790, has again been ushered into public notice. It has appeared in the course of the past year, edited by David Benedict, A. M., a brother whose labours in collecting a history of our denomination, have been justly appreciated by all our churches. A review of this volume may be found in the American Baptist Magazine. We have been edified and delighted with the discriminating acumen, the impartial statements, and the enlightened orthodoxy the review discovers. Such a production we consider to be as necessary and seasonable, as it is ingenious and correct. Its length, extending at least through fifteen or sixteen pages, renders the insertion of the whole impracticable.

When treating on parables, divines have taught us to distinguish between their *scope* and their *drapery*. The scope of Mr. Robinson's work we have always admired, but the drapery has been ever exceptionable. He has hung round the fair form of christianity and the beautiful institute of baptism, the garments of purple, and has crowned them with thorns. He has presented us with a medley cargo of gold and silver, apes and peacocks. He has endeavoured to dash the sacred chalice of the sanctuary with the poison of error, or, to use words of the late Mr. Fuller, quoted in the review before us, it is probable " that the subversion of what is called orthodoxy, and the vindication or palliation of every thing which in every age has been called by the name of heresy, were the objects of Mr. Robinson in writing his History of Baptism, and what has since been published under the title of Ecclesiastical Researches."

We are gratified to observe, that Mr. Benedict has excluded from his edition a number of the author's geographical whimsies, and still more so to find he has enriched it with a few valuable observations; and by translating several of the notes of the author, has placed their sense within the reach of the unlettered reader. Still the work bears resemblance to the sweep-net mentioned in Matt. xiii. 47. It has " gathered of every kind." To collect the " good into vessels," and " cast the bad away," is the duty of all who peruse it. The writer of the review, we have good reason to believe, was the reverend Ira Chase, a young brother of sound learning, of evangelic principles, and of correct discernment, whose health and life we trust will long be preserved, as a blessing to the church of God.

While the talents of Mr. Robinson, his literary acquirements, and his opportunities for obtaining information are fully admitted, the author of the review justly observes, that the work " has much *redundant* matter. It sometimes presents minute, critical remarks, that are but little to the purpose, and seem to be of no possible use but to exhibit the author's acquaintance with languages. He wanders often from the subject, and bewilders the reader by leading him aside to view a multitude of objects which have no special connexion with a history of baptism." The reviewer refutes a notion entertained by the author, that the original Greek word for baptism cannot be translated, and that John did not know Christ until after he had baptised him. Several mistakes relative to Tertullian, Cyprian, the Donatists and Augustine are properly corrected. The erroneous views of Mr Robinson relative to the divinity of Christ, and the depravity of man, are ably and ingeniously exposed. The sentiment that private christians may administer the ordinance of baptism, and that churches require no "fundamental articles," are, in own judgment, fairly and fully refuted.

Had an abridgment of "the History of Baptism" been published similar to that which we know—having seen the copy—the late Dr Jones, of Lower Dublin, Pennsylvania, actually prepared for the press, in which all exceptionable passages were expunged, and only mere matters of fact supported by incontestible authorities retained, we are convinced that its usefulness would have been superiour. The work, however, as now issued, deserves not indiscriminating censure. It contains many most interesting passages, and merits the perusal of all the disciples of Jesus who are desirous of knowing the will of their master, and who wish to collect a body of unquestionable facts relative to the history of one of the sacred institutions which his wisdom and goodness have ordained to be observed in his church to the end of time. The baptist denomination most decidedly agree with their evangelic brethren, in asserting and defending the doctrines of the apostacy of man, and the proper divinity and infinite sufficiency of the son of God. Mr Robinson was once professedly of their number. He was the author of several popular gospel hymns, and, if our memory serve, of a Plea for the Divinity of Christ. His sun was for a long time brilliant, but, alas! it suffered a melancholy eclipse, and went down in a cloud of darkness.

MISSIONARY INTELLIGENCE.

MISSION TO THE WESTWARD OF THE MISSISSIPPI RIVER.

THIS mission appears likely to obtain footing at St. Louis, and the prospect of usefulness is great and animating. From the missionaries at that place, communications have been received, from which the following extracts are furnished.

From Messrs. Peck and Welch to the Cor. Sec. dated St. Louis, Feb. 21, 1818.

Accompanying this, we transmit a subscription, &c. the object of which you will at once understand. [The object of this subscription paper is, to procure funds for the erection of a suitable building for public worship. It is sincerely hoped the effort will not be in vain.]

We have constituted a baptist church of eleven members. But we have no house in which to worship God, except a school room, and that we rent. Our hearers continue to increase, so that "the place has become too strait for us," and we are ready to say, "give place, that we may dwell."

Although we have a subscription in circulation, so few appear on the Lord's side, in St. Louis, that, unless our friends from a distance lend their aid, an object so desirable in the commencement of our mission cannot, we fear, be attained.

Notwithstanding the frequent calls of this kind in your city, we still cherish the hope that some will be disposed to contribute their bounty, to be sent over to this western Macedonia for our relief. Let them remember, that "the liberal soul shall be made fat," and that "he that watereth, shall be watered himself," while our prayer shall continually ascend for their prosperity.

It is no small pleasure to inform you, that the health of brother Peck is once more established. He is quite hearty, but not quite as strong yet as before his sickness.

Our affairs as it respects the mission are more prosperous than we anticipated. We must acknowledge the hand of the Lord is with us. Yesterday we found that one of our students was under serious impressions. He is a sober, intelligent young man, and apprenticed to one of our church members.

The second sabbath in March, we commenced a sabbath school for the Africans. Brother Welch has preached several times in the country, from ten to fifteen miles distance, and we have recently heard that a man there is convicted of sin. Still we wish not to be elated. We have our trials and difficulties. It is no small trial to us that our expenses are so great, but we make it a rule to purchase nothing but absolute necessaries. It is hoped our school, next quarter, will begin to afford us some profit.

From Mr. Welch, dated St. Louis, Feb. 10, 1818.

Those who live in this place, and those who fill up the vast extent of country between this and Boon's Lick, as properly *need* the gospel, as do the Indians or the Burmans.

Let us take the field before us, and if the "Lord of the harvest" should send forth a sufficient number of labourers, and crown them with success, I would gladly continue on to the west, and willingly lay my bones in some lonely Pacific isle.

Brother Peck, even before being able to walk much, having entered the school, I obtained an interpreter, and went a little way up to visit the encampment of the chief of the Sacks tribe, from Rock river. All I could learn was, that he could not think of admitting English teachers into his nation, without first consulting his fellow chiefs. The interpreter, however, told me he heard the chief say he had two sons whom he wished to send to school. I am to have another interview with him to-morrow.

When I commenced meeting in the school-room about a month ago, while brother Peck was sick, only six or eight persons made up the congregation. Now, the room will not hold them.

My brother, ask our patrons—ask our fellow students, and all our missionary friends and brethren, to pray for us, for I feel as though we were in the very place where the Lord would have us be. We are encouraged, too, by the increase of the congregation, and the solemn attention manifested, and are led to believe that God has much people in this place. The appearance in the country is equally flattering.

From Mr Peck, dated St. Louis, January 23, 1818

St. Louis contains more than three thousand souls, many of whom are quite ignorant of the gospel of Christ. Here is a wide field, besides several places in the country, only a few miles distant, where much good may be done. We have a meeting and school established, which promise to increase.

In case we should obtain any Indian youth, which we have hopes of, to attend our school, an establishment back in the country would be indispensable, as they could not be supported in St Louis. With respect to schools, I think there is a wide field opening, but the charity of the public must be received to effect any important good. Also, a system must be adopted and pursued. But to carry this system forward, money is necessary, which it is desirable to obtain, as far as practicable, without resorting to the mission funds. Will not the liberality of the public supply us? We need a school-house, a dwelling-house, and some land at the mission station. Books for the school must be had. If we have Indian scholars, considerable expense will be necessary for their support. By what I have been able to learn, the Delawares and Shawnees, two tribes of Indians about twenty or thirty miles to the northwest and southwest of Cape Girardeau, and one hundred and forty from St Louis, are willing to have schools established among them, and are even desirous that their children should receive instruction. If a few Indian youth could be qualified for teachers, who knows what good might be done?

From Mr. M'Coy, near Vincennes, March 2, 1818.

Mr M'Coy appears actively engaged in arranging and entering on a plan of extensive and energetic operation among the Wabash Indians. The prospect appears inviting, especially to one whose vigour of mind, and zealous determinations, become more prompt and decisive in view of difficulties and obstructions. In a recent letter, he observes, that he is sensible of his duty to communicate to the Board his plans, hopes and prospects, without reserve, and is determined to be governed by their instruction. He is aware that if his scheme fails entirely, he will, like many better men, upon attempting great things, be obliged to bear the sport of his enemies, and pity of his friends. But when foreboding and apparently insurmountable difficulties "threaten to plunge all in ruin," he proposes going with Zerubbabel to see the great mountain levelled to a plain. When Sanballat and Tobiah, by insidious attempts and false rumours, would make him afraid, he proposes going in company with Nehemiah. When he realizes pain and hardship, he will visit Gethsemane! And, should he have the happiness to see the fruit of his labours, it will be his joy to say, *not unto us, not unto us, but unto thy name, O! Lord, be all the glory.*

From Mr. Ranaldson to the Cor. Sec. dated St. Francisville, Jan. 19, 1818.

I SHOULD have written several weeks sooner, but was induced to defer it, in order to communicate at this time, certain information of importance. In September last, after writing to you from the city of Natchez, I finished my tour through the Mississippi state, for the purpose of preaching to the destitute, and of making collections for the mission, and returned to this neighbourhood, where I have been chiefly engaged in preaching at the graves of the deceased, or from house to house, where the open doors of hospitable families invited my reception. Solemn attention has been paid generally to the public worship of God. A few souls among us, who have been long waiting for the consolation of Israel, have been refreshed with the presence of the Lord; whilst some others, who were considered strangers from the covenants of promise, appear now to be inquiring the way to Zion with their faces thitherward. My field of labour is constantly enlarging. I would cry for help in the language of the man of Macedonia, if my feeble voice could be heard by my brethren, for truly the harvest is great, but the labourers are few!

In October I attended the Mississippi Association, which convened on Bogue Chitto, about eighty miles from this place. It was my wish and intention to go on, from that meeting, to the Creek nation, pursuant to the instructions I had received from the Board, to visit, if practicable, such Indian settlements as might not be found too remote. But the sickness of my family at the time prevented me from going. The matter, however, being submitted to the association, excited deep and general interest in that body. The propriety of doing something without delay, was urged by the manifest dictates of divine Providence, which moved the association to appoint two brethren, the Rev. Thomas Mercer, and Benjamin Davis, to visit the Creeks.

These brethren accordingly set out on their mission, the 26th of October, with instructions from the association and, on the 11th of November, they arrived at Tucabatcha, the chief town of the nation, and seat of the Big-warrior. After explaining to him the benevolent object of their visit, they baptised one of his slaves named William, (a negro of good character and much esteemed by his big-master) and then proceeded to Curnels's settlements, 15 miles from the chief town. They were accompanied by a brother, Laprade, a merchant who resides in Fort Jackson, is well known among the Creeks as a trader, and appears to have their entire confidence. The company of this brother as interpreter, contributed in no small degree to the unsuspecting reception of our missionaries. They were permitted, on the 12th, to preach in Curnels's house, to a mixed crowd of Indians, half-breeds, negroes, and a few whites. The next day, they heard the gracious experience of seven blacks, (four men, and three women) and baptised them. These were immediately constituted into a church. Charles was ordained their pastor, and Tyler their deacon. Both are preachers; but neither of them can read. Charles is said to be quite intelligent, and has a happy faculty for communicating his ideas, both in the Creek and English languages. These poor disciples rejoiced with exceeding great joy, that white men were sent to them to instruct them more fully in the ways of the Lord. From the best information, it appears, that these negroes were raised among the Creeks, and received their knowledge of christianity from a religious slave who belonged to Col Hawkins, the former agent. William, the slave of the Big-warrior, is a preacher likewise.

General David B. Mitchel, the present agent of the Creeks, is about to establish a school at the agency, having already consulted the chiefs on the subject. The Big-warrior has consented for our missionaries to establish a school also, when recommended by the agent. The Rev Isaac Suttler, who lives on the west side of the Talepoosa, and about twenty five miles from the *Creek African Church*, has agreed to visit them every third Sabbath, for the current year. He is both a farmer and a gunsmith, works for the Indians, is familiar to their customs, and seems to possess their confidence and affection.

Except the present hostility of the Seminoles, all other circumstances appear to me favourable to the undertaking of a Creek mission. At a time when christian denominations are much engaged to civilize, and to evangelize the poor aborigines of our flourishing country, when the general government yields a favourable countenance to Indian reform, by offering pecuniary assistance to missionary exertions; surely something *must* be done for that long *neglected*, severely *persecuted* race of human beings!

The Lord has, I trust, begun a good work in this region, and I esteem it a happiness that my lot has been cast among the *destitute* by a wise and benign Providence.

On the second of November, we constituted a church with the assistance of Rev D Cooper, which is the first in this section of the country. The number was small, but equal to that saved in Noah's ark, and not to be despised; for *a little one shall become a thousand, and a small one a strong nation.* Yesterday I preached in my own hired house (one mile from town) from Acts the xxii. 16th, and administered the ordinance of baptism to *two ladies*, the first baptised converts in the vicinity. The place selected for baptising was not the Mississippi river, because there is too much water there; but it was a beautiful pool in my yard. Much curiosity was excited on this occasion. Though a rainy day, a solemn congregation encircled the water, to see the ordinance performed. Baptism was thought by many to be a certain *kind of dipping* which would provoke ridicule and laughter. But I saw no laughing, no kind of levity in the crowd. On the contrary, the solemnity of death was depicted in every countenance! I observed more weeping around the watery grave, than what I had seen at the late funeral solemnities of deceased relatives! The heavens seemed to be opened, and tokens of love and affection poured out, whilst the female disciples rejoiced in their baptism, and *went on their way rejoicing.* Eleven [slaves] more are wait ng for baptism, waiting with impatience, and bowing with suppliant knee to masters for permission to follow the imitable examples of the blessed Jesus.

An old negro slave called Billy, has been an instrument of blessing to many of his fellow servants in this neighbourhood. Before the Americans had possession of West Florida, he was not allowed to teach or pray vocally, even in his own hut. But of late he has been permitted to teach the poor negroes the way of salvation through the Mediator.

We enjoyed a happy season of refreshing at the association in October. The business was conducted with great harmony and brotherly affection. The association entered into a resolution to publish a "Summary of Church Discipline." They also with unanimous consent agreed to raise by subscription, an "education fund for the benefit of gospel ministers." About eight hundred dollars were subscribed, including a donation of five hundred dollars from Rev. David Cooper, who is a zealous promoter of this benevolent object.

GENERAL MISSIONARY INTELLIGENCE

From Rev. Dr. Carey to the Cor Sec dated Calcutta, 25th November, 1817.

I HAVE omitted writing to you till I am ashamed, yet it has not arisen from indifference to you, but from absolute inability for want of time, principally occasioned by my many avocations, and by a number of family circumstances which have demanded a more than ordinary degree of attention. You are dear to me, and have been ever since we first met together, a little before my first sailing to this country.

Little did either you or I suppose at that time, that the ensuing quarter of a century would have been productive of the great things which we have witnessed; for when I compare the present time with the state of religion then, I must call what we now see *great things*. A mission was then *ventured on*, as a kind of experiment, with fear and trembling, and was in its infancy preserved, though in extreme weakness, by the kind providence of God, from sinking into ruin; for scarcely any thing of even the most necessary nature, for the support of this mission, was provided. We were actually cast at first upon Providence, not that our brethren were unconcerned about us, they cared very affectionately for us, but merely from their inexperience. God, however, provided, and he did much more, he inclined the hearts of our brethren of different denominations to engage in similar undertakings, and we have seen in England the rise of the London Mission Society, the Edinburgh Society, the Church of England Society, and that of the Methodists. The impulse hence given to the religious feelings of the christian public, in time produced the British and Foreign Bible Society, which ramifying in every direction, has filled the world with its different branches, or with similar institutions. Thus we now see England and America abounding with Missionary Societies, and the whole world with Bible Societies, and there is a prospect that in a reasonable time, all the nations of the earth will read in their own tongues the wonderful works of God. Russia may be said to have undergone a religious revolution. The efforts of the Russian Bible Society will meet with those now making in India on the tops of the Himaluya mountains, the Imaus of the Greeks; and it is probable, will embrace all the nations on the continent of Asia. I am also happy to be able to say that I am acquainted with more than one who is engaged in translating the word of God into the different dialects of the Malay language, which we now confidently expect will soon be followed by translations into the other languages of the islands.

When the work was first engaged in, it was uncertain whether it was practicable to preach the gospel to heathen nations. It was not certain that there was an open door for this work upon the earth: but so graciously has God superintended this work, that every door has opened, almost at the first attempt, and there are now but few places on the earth where natural or political obstacles operate to any great extent. So anxious are the inhabitants of India to obtain bibles and other books, that no efforts at present within the power of all the presses in India united, can do any thing like supplying the demand.

An uncommon concern for the education of the rising generation, now prevails in India. We have at least a hundred schools belonging to our mission, all supported by funds raised in India, and there are many belonging to those of other denominations. Some time ago a society was formed, called the Calcutta School Book Society, the object of which is to translate or otherwise furnish in the vernacular languages of India, school books, from those containing the first rudiments of science to those which lead to the very highest branches of it. Already the abridgments of Goldsmith's History of England, and of Rome, are in a course of translation by this society. I have undertaken the superintendence of them, and by ourselves several valuable works on education have been printed independently of the School Book Society.

We have to lament that the work of conversion does not keep pace with the increase of ministers. There is, however, still a great want of men to publish the gospel. I mean men who know the language, and feel deeply for the conversion of the heathen. I rejoice that all power is in the hand of God, and that the Saviour who laid down his life for the church, is the head over all things, for the church, which is his body. As things are, it would do your soul good to be present sometimes when inquirers come to my house. This evening I had seven, four of whom, a Brahman, a Soodra, a Mussulman, and one called a Portuguese, but in reality of no cast, came for the first time; they have heard the word for months, and appear truly hopeful.

From Mr Lawson, dated Calcutta, June 23d, 1817.

We have many things to mourn over; but, thanks to our Redeemer, we have also some things to rejoice in. Our labours are not in vain amongst the soldiers. If spared to next month I hope to baptise 13 or 14 persons; Europeans, natives, Portuguese, and what is here called country born. I am now able to read the scriptures in public, and to talk a little about Jesus in private.

Brethren Judson and Hough are doing very well for the Burmans. I know not of two more industrious and persevering missioners. They possess great faith, and I think God will reward that faith with souls; for I never have seen a strong exercise of faith labouring long without some success. Mrs White (Rowe) seems to be very happy, and I suppose very useful at Digah. That station was much in want of such a person.

Could you not contrive to blow across the mighty ocean, some of the blessed spirit which seems to enliven you in America? I read the account of revivals in your baptist magazine to the soldiers in Fort William, and longed to "hear the sound of his going in the tops of the mulberry trees." And truly we were much refreshed. It would have done you good to see a number of stout men, who never trembled at the cannon's mouth, shed the honest tear of thankfulness to God for doing such wonders among your western christians.

Extract of a letter from Mrs. Rowe, dated Digah, Oct. 17, 1817.

WITH regard to the spread of the gospel among the Hindoos, we have hope that its influence is greater than appears ostensibly, as their prejudices are giving way, and a strange face often appears among those who come up hither to worship the true God; and the attempt to afford instruction to them, in its effects, bears a strong analogy to the "leaven hid in three measures of meal." In addition to my labours in our boarding school at Digah, I am endeavouring to do what I can toward informing a few native females who come at regular school hours to sew, and to read their mother language. From the small beginning of one little girl, (Simatria) two other little girls and two women have come, one of whom is a mother, and brings her infant at her breast. They all belong to the native christians and inquirers on our premises. For this purpose there is not as yet any specific fund, but to enable and encourage me to persevere in the undertaking, a few of the ladies at Dinapore have offered a yearly subscription. The known friends of the cause who possess means, are too few to form a society for its support to any great extent. Should any society in America be disposed to contribute toward the support and enlargement of this infant native female school, a little pecuniary aid from time to time, will be acceptable in its behalf, and what money may not be wanted immediately, shall be conscientiously funded and put to interest for this object.

From Mr. Chamberlain, to the Cor. Sec'y. dated Monghyr, April 30th, 1817.

I CANNOT express how interested I feel in all that respects your happy, highly favoured country, but especially in all that relates to the progress of Immanuel's kingdom therein, for on this depends the harmony, unity, stability and prosperity of the states. The moral misery of the people in the western country, must be very great, destitute of the bible as it appears they have always been, but, it is rejoicing to the heart, to see their day dawning, and to expect the rising of the Sun of Righteousness upon them.

Our Divine master has wondrously succeeded your efforts, and, I think, far exceeded your former most sanguine hopes. You will meet with opposition, especially from those who may be termed the irreligious religious. They like to live on the king's bounty in cantonments, but have no heart to take the field in his majesty's service; they prefer sitting in the shade, to *pelting* in the sun. We must leave them and "go forward." The good Lord in his mercy bring them up in the rear, that they may have some portion in this glorious work, and though late, better late than never—better among the last, than not at all.

Much of my time has been taken up in the work in which I am engaged, i. e. in preparing two translations. Many things occur to obstruct my progress, but the work is progressing, though so slowly that it is a daily trial to my sanguine disposition. One of the translations, (the Brij Bhasha) I write, and to the other I employ an amanuensis. This I have not long began. But Matthew and Mark are ready, and Luke is in hand, in which I have been at work all this day, and have got over from the 25th of the 10th chap to the close of the 11th chap. In the evening I rode out and preached to a few poor people, boat builders, who heard with great attention. In the beginning of the year I accompanied a friend up the river as far as Mirzapore, and was out about two months. During which time I had a grand campaign, both among Europeans and natives. To the former I preached at three stations, 12 or 13 sermons, and was otherwise engaged amongst others, to promote the cause of truth and righteousness with much encouragement. Amongst the natives I was regularly engaged in preaching and distributing the gospel and tracts, almost daily, now on this side of the river, and now on that. A large chest of ammunition was expended. Three cities were attacked, and with considerable success Ghazeepore, Benares, and Mirzapore. Every where I found the people willing to hear, and frequently very eager to receive tracts and gospels. Probably two thousand tracts, and two or three hundred gospels were sent abroad in this journey amongst an immense population. Benares itself contains 7 or 800,000 souls. The journey and the work, with the kind attentions of my friend, were very beneficial to my body, as well as refreshing to my soul.— Preaching to the poor heathen has always been to me both gladness and health.

At Monghyr, I am much engaged at home, especially during the present season of the year, as the heat is great and the wind in general very unfavourable to the work in the streets or highways.

Mingham Misser, a person who was at first employed as a school master, but owing to his attachment to the sacred Scriptures did not succeed, is employed as a reader of the holy book; in which work he is very diligent, and affords me abundant satisfaction. At present he is not baptised; why he delays I know not exactly, but in all other things he appears to be a truly converted man. He is a man of respectable connexions, though in reduced circumstances, with a considerable family. Some of his relations oppose him much; others think well of him still, and esteem him, but are afraid to associate with him. He is a Brahman, well known all over the country around, and his decided conduct thus far, has had an astonishing effect upon the people, in exciting their fears and suspicions. How it would delight your heart to see him, coming a good mile every morning to worship, with his New Testament, tracts, and hymns under his arm, and here sitting with all the gravity, and modesty, and humility, and cheerfulness of a christian, uniting in the solemn exercises! He is daily engaged in reading and conversation with persons who call on him from all the places around. He has read the New Testament through twice, with uncommon attention, and the Pentateuch, Job, Psalms, and Proverbs, and the historical books through once, and repeats some of the principal facts or topics with great precision. Blessed Saviour, be merciful to him, and speedily bring him into thy church, and place him with thy saints! Two or three others are engaged in reading the words of Jesus, which are spirit and life. I rejoice in hope

BIBLE INTELLIGENCE.

FROM THE CORRESPONDENCE OF THE BRITISH AND FOREIGN BIBLE SOCIETY.

Extract from the Sixth Report of the Calcutta Auxiliary Bible Society.

"TO the members of this and every other Bible Association, as well as to all persons entrusted in the diffusion of that knowledge which alone can be instrumental to the eternal happiness of man, it must afford the highest gratification, that many of the nations of India, Mahommedans as well as Hindoos, evince not only a willing, but a solicitous disposition to receive and peruse such versions of the Holy Scriptures as are intelligible to them. And the friends of the British and Foreign Bible Society will rejoice to hear, that of 500 copies of the late Rev. Henry Martin's Hindoostanee translation of the New Testament, which were printed in the Persian character at the expense of that Society in the year 1814, so few now remain undistributed, that the Corresponding Committee, at this Presidency, have already found it necessary to order another edition, to the same extent.

"The noble example given to Europe and Asia by the Russian Bible Society, its patronage in church and state, its numerous auxiliaries, the activity of its members and agents, the wide field of its labours, and above all, the spirit and zeal which prompt and direct its operations, render it an object of peculiar interest. That interest is most lively to those who have contemplated the spread of the gospel in the oriental parts of the globe; and the members of this local association, in particular, cannot but feel the purest satisfaction in finding themselves addressed by a sister community from Russia, in the following terms:—
"However far separated, we consider ourselves as fellow labourers with you, in the great and glorious work of extending the knowledge of our Lord and Saviour, by disseminating the oracles of divine truth; and great as is the distance between St Petersburgh and Calcutta, we hope, ere long, to meet you, in sowing the word of eternal life, in Armenia, Persia, and Tartary."

From Frankfort, November 6, 1817.

I CANNOT let this opportunity pass, without giving you some account of what took place at the commemoration of the third centenary of the Reformation. To add to its solemnity I had some time before submitted a proposal to our committee, whether it would not be advisable, on the day of that festival, to make, at the principal Lutheran church, a public distribution of bibles to young people, and particularly to those whose parents, on account of the heavy pressure of the times, had it not in their power to procure a bible for them. This proposal was, to my great joy, very readily agreed to; and I was commissioned to provide the requisite number of copies. Although it was thought that two hundred, at most, might be sufficient, I took care to have five hundred bound; and though the notification of our intention could be issued only a few days before it was to be carried into effect, such a number of children presented themselves in order to partake of the proffered boon, that they amounted to upwards of four hundred; in addition to which, the parents of some, in decent circumstances, offered to pay with pleasure, for the copies, that the bible on that day might be given to their children, as a lasting memorial of the festival of the Reformation.

The Rev. Mr Bencknard, a member of our committee, opened the solemnity, at four o'clock, with an address; after which the distribution of four hundred and seventy-five bound copies took place. Pious emotions pervaded the whole assembly. The children received the bibles with tears of joy and gratitude.— A pious lady of rank made her way through the crowd to the altar, carrying her little boy in her arms, in order to have the gratification of receiving a bible. A thousand bibles would not have been sufficient to satisfy the desire of all Parents and children appear every day, and anxiously inquire after a bible In short, there is a general longing after the bible; and on this occasion it has been shown, that the sacred volume is more scarce in many families than could have been supposed.

A person of rank brought me a donation of 60 florins, (about $26 60 cts.) and many parents paid double the price for a copy. This circumstance will, no doubt, increase the number of members, as many will now be made more acquainted with the real object of the Bible Society.

From a Calmuc Prince to the President of the Russian Bible Society.

On the 10th of the first Tiger month, I received with pleasure the letter you wrote me on the first day of the Mouse month, in the last Wooden Swine year, together with two copies of the history of the merciful God, Jesus Christ, translated into our Mongolian language; one bound in yellow, the other in red. You desire me, for my own benefit, to read in this book, which contains the word of God, and to afford my subjects an opportunity to hear it, and learn from it also.

In obedience to this command, I have not only myself read the word and doctrines of the all merciful God, Jesus Christ, but have given one of the copies to our lama, who reads it with the priests.* Respecting my subjects, I wished to assemble them together, this winter, in order to have this book read to them; but on account of the severity of the season, that is not practicable.

In the course of four months, the chief part of my people will go upon a pilgrimage, to be present at the celebration of a religious festival, and assemble for the purpose of praying. At that time, I shall have the book read to the people congregated for such a pious purpose, and in this manner obey your injunctions.

I shall not neglect, through the grace of God, giving you an account of the effect produced, and pray to Him, that he may have mercy on me.

(Signed,) TUMEN DSHIR-GALANG

Written in mine own solid habitation, in the island of Shambay, the first of last Tiger month, of the Fire Mouse year [JANUARY 4, 1817.]

Inquiry excited among the natives of Ceylon

In the district of Jaffna, several Hindoos have shown a desire to possess and read the New Testament, Buddhists, and even Buddhist priests, apply frequently for Cingalese scriptures; and Mahometans have begun to manifest an inclination to receive instruction themselves, and to permit their children to partake the benefit of an improved education. Daniel Theophilus, the Mahometan whose conviction was noticed in the appendix to the second Report of this Society, has been zealously employed among his late brethren, who begin to look upon him with more complacency than they did. He has just completed an elaborate work, in which he has collected a great many passages from the Koran, which he gives both in Arabic and Tamul, with the passages out of the Bible from which they were evidently copied.

DOMESTIC INTELLIGENCE.

To the Corresponding Secretary of the Board, from the Corresponding Secretary of the Washington Mission Society, transmitting the Report of the Directors of that Society.

I AM specially instructed to communicate to you, and through you to the general Board, the warm approbation of this society in the measure lately adopted by them of uniting *domestic* with *foreign* missions, so far as a surplus fund may remain, unnecessary for the due support and enlargement of the foreign mission, which is of course the primary object, and to state the pleasure they would experience, should it be in your power to strengthen the stations already established, and to establish others, on our destitute frontiers.

Report, &c.—The board of directors of the Washington Baptist Society for Foreign Missions, according to their annual custom, beg leave to report to the society, that since their last annual meeting, the general Convention of the baptist denomination for the support of foreign missions, have held their first triennial meeting in Philadelphia, which appears to have been numerously attended by delegates from almost all parts of the United States. It appears from the printed report of their proceedings, that their meeting was harmonious, and strongly evidenced a becoming zeal for the enlargement of the Redeemer's kingdom and the salvation of the heathen. It also appears that the missionary spirit has been widely diffused throughout our country, and is still spreading; from which circumstance we are more and more convinced that "the good hand of our God is upon us," and that our "labours of love shall not be in vain." The funds of the general Convention are prosperous beyond all anticipation; they had at their last meeting more than twenty-three thousand dollars on hand after meeting the large expenditures necessary for the support and enlargement of the mission to Burmah. This prosperity, so evidently owing to the blessing of the Lord upon the exertions of his people, has induced the Convention to enlarge the contemplated field for missionary labours, by instituting new stations among the destitute inhabitants of Louisiana and Missouri, and sending missionaries to preach to them and to the Indians bordering on the waters of the Mississippi. Will the Lord thus furnish the means and the missionaries, without having determined to bless their labours? We trust not: on the contrary, we feel assured that the "time has come, the time that the Lord's house should be built," and that he is greatly honoured who is permitted to bring but a handful of goats' hair to this fabric, whose duration shall be eternal. Among the numerous indications that the Lord's time is come to favour Zion, we would mention the establishment of many societies similar to our own in all parts of the Union, and throughout the Christian world, many others, whose object is the translation, printing, and diffusing of the holy scriptures into every language and into every clime. Many mite societies, composed exclusively of pious and benevolent females, one of which we notice with pleasure has been recently established in this city, and which promises considerable aid to the missionary cause.

While we reflect on these encouraging appearances, and consider how many prayers are daily ascending to the throne of grace, to own and prosper these exertions, and how many hands are held out for their support, we have the greatest encouragement, brethren, to persevere in the good cause, and trust that our exertions will not cease so long as we have a mite to cast into the gospel treasury.

(Signed,)   O B. BROWN, *Pres't.*
                               E. REYNOLDS, *Cor Sec*

In proportion as the pages of the LUMINARY can possibly admit of it, with unfeigned satisfaction will the letters from any of those useful associations of ladies, in the form of Mission Societies, Mite Societies, Cent Societies, or by what title soever designated, whose object is to encourage the missionary cause, be introduced.—Nor is it too much to expect, that the amiable and zealous language of these communications, will happily conduce to the increase of a missionary spirit.

From the Directress of the Catskill Mite Society to the Board.

IMPRESSED in some degree with the worth of immortal souls, and with the obligation we are under to serve God, and to do good to our fellow men, we have adopted a constitution presented to us by our beloved brother J. M Peck, and formed a society called the Catskill Female Mite Society for Missionary purposes. Our object is to assist in sending the gospel to the heathen, by aiding the funds of the Baptist Board of Foreign Missions; and also to advance, in any way that may appear expedient, the cause of the Redeemer.

We are convinced that God is able to carry his purposes into effect without our assistance, yet we believe your missionaries cannot live without bread · and we believe if our motives are right, that our actions will be right also, and that God will reward our labours of love. Nor can we fail to derive encouragement to the exercise of charity, from the approving declaration of our blessed Saviour to his disciples concerning the poor widow who cast only two mites into the treasury of the Lord We rejoice in having fellowship with the saints of God, and that we have it in our power to do something for the cause of Christ in this world. As Phebe, servant of the church at Cenchrea, was bearer of the epistle of Paul to the Romans, and Priscilla and Chloe were helpers, so also would we reach forth a helping hand and assist in carrying into effect your laudable design. Our aim at present is to aid the mission in Burmah, not forgetting, however, our dear brethren Peck and Welch, and their dear families; but praying that God may protect them, and make their labours abundantly successful. We trust you have our prayers that your exertions may be blessed to the upbuilding of the Redeemer's cause, and that every missionary effort may have its desired effect, and may you all be blessed with the peaceable fruits of the spirit of God. Amen!

In behalf of the society,
KETURAH HILL, Directress.

Catskill, N. Y Nov. 12, 1817

From ANSTIS TITUS, *Sec of the Baptist Female Miss Soc in Troy, to the Board*

WE can but express our gratitude to God for his evident smiles on your laudable and interesting Institution, having for its object the glory of God, the dissemination of the word of life, and the salvation of immortal souls. O! that holy, fervent love to God, to truth, and the souls of our fellow *men*, might more abundantly pervade and influence our hearts! It afforded us no small degree of joy, to hear that our dear brother Hough, with his family had, through a kind Providence, safely arrived at Rangoon. No doubt but their arrival produced joy to brother and sister Judson, and will very much serve to encourage their hearts, and strengthen their hands, in the great and glorious work of the Lord. We hope we can add, that our prayers continually ascend to God on their behalf. We hope our two brethren lately chosen and destined to the same place may be safely wafted to them, and prove a great acquisition to the missionary cause. It was peculiarly gratifying to us to hear also, that the Indian tribes in our own land have not been forgotten by the Convention, and hope that the great Head of the church may be pleased to bless and prosper our brethren destined to a western mission. It is an important consideration to such as are engaged in missionary efforts, that it is a cause which must prosper, for it appertains to a kingdom which can never be abolished; having the power, grace, truth and faithfulness of Jehovah Jesus for its support, and in which his own glory is concerned.

We shall transmit to your treasurer by the earliest opportunity, the amount collected during the last year, being $71 50 cts. which you will please to consider as a token of our well wishes to the cause of missions, and should be happy were the amount much larger. We presume that you, like our Divine master, will not despise the day of small things.

From ANNA BUSHNELL, *Sec. of the Fem. Mite Soc Lex N Y to the Board.*

IMPRESSED in some measure, as we humbly trust, with a sense of God's goodness to us, in that we enjoy the invaluable blessing of a preached gospel every Lord's day, and at other seasons; and realizing, as we hope, in some degree, the dark and dismal state of those who do not enjoy this blessing, we feel it as a duty we owe the poor heathen, to cast in our mites, which, though small, may do something towards sending the gospel to those who are perishing for lack of vision; and considering ourselves stewards, we cannot, without penalty, dispense with making the best use of what God has committed to us, and as no man can call what he possesses, his own, we think it highly becomes us to try to honour God with our substance. He has assured us that he will give to his Son the heathen for his inheritance, and the uttermost parts of the earth for his possession, and that the gospel must be preached to all nations and as he will bring this about by means, we feel animated, while witnessing the great exertions many are making for the spread of the gospel, and the upbuilding of the Redeemer's kingdom. Thankful to our heavenly Father for having put it into our hearts, we cheerfully contribute our mite, $16 63 cts and a gold pin, which we beg you will accept, and appropriate to missionary purposes. We hope the Lord will raise up and send forth many faithful labourers into his vineyard, and grant them many souls as seals of their ministry. We wish you grace, mercy and peace, and may God crown your labours with abundant success.

EDUCATION.

Report of the Massachusetts Baptist Education Society, September, 1817.

PERMIT us to address you on this third anniversary of the Education Society. The prosperity of this new Institution has exceeded the hopes of its patrons, and claims the grateful acknowledgments of its friends, but as it is yet in its infancy, it needs the cheering patronage and united exertions of the churches.

The expenses of the last year amount to upwards of $600. We have $110 85 remaining in the hands of the treasurer. The present number of scholars is ten. Hence the expenses of the ensuing year will probably increase, which circumstance ought to quicken our zeal. When we consider the improved state of society, in literature, we should consult the most proper means to render its progress useful. It is a laudable charity which aids men in the pursuit of those studies which may improve their minds, and promote their piety and usefulness. By reviewing the history of our species, we shall see how various capacities have been unfolded by education, and their characters formed for eminent usefulness. In early ages, many plans were devised to accomplish this end. In process of time they combined the wisdom of their sages, and established schools, that they might conveniently instruct the ignorant, and transmit their acquirements to posterity.

The Israelites set up seminaries of sacred learning, in which they instructed the youth, and thus furnished the nation with able and faithful teachers. In the days of Samuel, Najoth in Ramah was the seat of literature, in which the prophet bore a very distinguished rank. In the time of Elijah, Bethel was celebrated as a place of learning, and Jericho was resorted to for literary advantages. Jewish learning was highly cultivated about eight hundred years before the birth of our Saviour. The prophet Isaiah received a literary polish which rendered him one of the most sublime and elegant writers the world ever knew. The Chaldeans, the Egyptians, the Persians, the Greeks, the Romans, and various other nations, owed their elevation, in a great measure, to their literary improvements. We may generally trace the rise of their greatest characters, to these founts of learning.

In the early stage of the Christian church, schools were deemed necessary for the diffusion of knowledge. A theological school was founded at Alexandria in Egypt, where the celebrated Clemens formed an imperishable character, and greatly promoted the increase of knowledge. In this school the learned and eloquent Origen lectured, and to this institution the African churches in early times owed their literary eminence. In the glorious reformation from popery, Luther, Malancthon, Calvin, Zuinglius, Beza, and many others, held learning in high estimation. Luther and Melancthon, though pressed with numerous duties, yet devoted much of their time in the college of Wurtemburg. Calvin, though fervently engaged in the progress of the reformation, and officiating as pastor of a numerous church, yet discharged the duties of Theological Professor in the seminary at Geneva, and was one of the most able writers of the age. An improper use of human acquirements has led some to denounce literature, as useless or pernicious; but such persons do not consider that the abuse of the best things is no argument against their worth. We cannot be insensible that the present state of the times calls for the exertions of all who are friendly to the spread of religious knowledge, and urgently presses the duty of liberally aiding in the good cause. New efforts are operating, and will probably effect a religious change among the nations. Persons of dissimilar views seem to forget their animosities, and combine to spread religious knowledge. The charities of many are concentrated in Bible Societies, which have mysteriously risen with the aid of princely power and liberality, and present the most formidable arrangement of the holy warfare that the world ever beheld. What will be the ultimate issue of these unparalleled efforts we cannot precisely define.—But shall we be indifferent at such a crisis? or what is worse, shall we withhold our liberality? Can we refuse to assist our young brethren who give evidence that they are called to preach the gospel, but are struggling under poverty and frowns, to surmount the obstacles to their necessary education? Let us consider our responsibility in this age of inquiry, to diffuse correct knowledge, to extirpate errour, and benefit the world. Think for a moment on the miseries of those countries where the faint traces of religion are debased by all the terrors of superstition, or the licentiousness of idolatry. View the moral feelings of our fellow creatures, sinking under the dominion of imposture, and sacrificed to the purposes of priestcraft and delusion. Surely there is much to be done, and a review of the vast mixture of errour, and the dreary face of the heathen world, should be no discouragement to our exertions. There are many encouraging circumstances to excite our generous efforts. It appears that the light of salvation is preparing to rise over a darkened world. Doubtless the time is hastening when millions who are divided by seas, and separated by languages, will unite in one common sentiment of praise.

We live, dear brethren, in an age of great events. Different scenes have passed before us in rapid succession. Since the indefatigable Carey arose with this maxim, "Attempt great things, expect great things," the saying has been verified beyond human calculations. The religious world is re-invigorated, thousands have emerged from indifference, and we may expect to see great things hereafter.

By the intelligence recently received from various quarters, it seems that the predicted period is come, when many shall run to and fro, and knowledge be increased. According to the last Report of the Baptist Convention, ten thousand have been added to the Baptist churches in the United States the past year. Should one out of a hundred be called to preach the gospel, it would take $15,000 a year to defray the expenses of their education; which sum, if proportioned among the churches, would give a tax of about eight cents a year upon each member. A small retrenchment of needless expenses would amply suffice.

But while we advocate the advantages of learning, let us not be insensible to the importance of guarding the rising genius against extravagances which disgrace the christian name. Learning and humility adorn human nature. Piety, extensive knowledge, and zeal to do good, are laudable; while pride, self-importance, and illiberal disdain are debasing, and are doubly mischievous, when pointed by education. In a seminary where none are patronized but pious and promising youth, who profess to be called to preach the gospel, there is less danger of misapplying our endeavours to promote literature, than in a promiscuous school. While we therefore solicit the aid, we wish to excite the vigilance of the churches to guard against the errours which corrupt the minds of youth, empoison and debase society. May the great Head of the church raise up suitable candidates, and direct in all our measures to promote the interest of Zion, which is the sincere desire of your brethren in gospel affection.

Signed, W. BATCHELDER, Secretary.

EARTHEN VESSELS.

Mr. Henry, in his sermon on the death of the Rev Mr. Daniel Burgess, from 2 Cor iv. 7, has the following excellent closing observations. As the sermon is not generally known, the ideas may afford to our readers much entertainment.

1. This doctrine may be instructive to us, who are ministers

Are we *earthen vessels?* Then we have reason to be low in our own eyes, and to take care that we never think of ourselves above what is meet, but always—soberly.

Are we *earthen vessels?* Then let us not be indulgent of our bodies, not of their ease, or appetites. What needs so much-a-do about an earthen vessel, when, after all our care and pains about it, we cannot alter the property of it? Brittle it is still, and must be inevitably broken after a while

Are we *earthen vessels?* Then let us not be empty vessels. A vessel of gold or silver is of considerable value though it be empty, but an earthen vessel, if empty, is good for little, but is thrown among the lumber.

Are we *earthen vessels?* Then let us be clean vessels. It is enough that, as earthen, we are mean by nature—but let us not make ourselves vile by sin. Eli's sons not only made themselves vile, but made even the sacrifices of the Lord to be abhorred, as good food is in a dirty vessel.

Are we *earthen vessels?* Then let us take heed of dashing one against another.

Are we *earthen vessels?* Then let us bear contempt and reproach with patience, and not think it strange, and fret at it Those who over-value themselves, cannot easily bear to be under-valued by others. What can earthen vessels expect, but to be despised and thrown under foot?

Are we *earthen vessels?* Then let us often think of being broken and laid aside, and prepare accordingly. We are in use for a while, and it is our honour and delight to be employed in the service of Christ and souls. But what is our strength, that we should hope to be long thus employed? Is *our strength the strength of stones? or is our flesh of brass?* No! we are earthen vessels, and are hastening to the dust.

2 This doctrine may be of use to all —are ministers *earthen vessels?*

Thank God for the gospel treasure, though it be but in an earthen vessel nay, thank God that it is in such vessels, that it may be the nearer you, and the more within your reach

Esteem the *earthen vessels* for the treasure's sake that is put in them. Throw not those vessels to the ground hastily, because in something or other they do not please you; for, remember, they are earthen vessels, and they are your own.

Bless God that the breaking of the *earthen vessel* is not the loss of the heavenly treasure. Ministers die, but the word of the Lord endureth for ever.

Let the glory of all the benefits you have by the ministry of the gospel, or may have, be given to God; to him only, to him entirely; for from him the excellency of the power is

Let the consideration of the frailty and mortality of your ministers, quicken you to make a diligent improvement of their labours while they are continued to you You have the treasure in *earthen vessels,* therefore delay not to make it yours, lest the vessels that are most likely to convey it to you should break, and others such should not be raised up.

It is rather singular, that Dr. Mayo, the continuator of Mr Henry on the second book of Corinthians, has not introduced these ideas into his able exposition

STATE OF RELIGION.

Revival of religion in Mecklenburg and Muhlenburg Counties, Virginia.—From Rev. WM. RICHARDS, *Mecklenburg county, Dec.* 16, 1817.

In compliance with your request, permit me to give some account of the work of God in this vicinity. A year ago last March, I was on a visit at Lunenburg, in the bounds of elder Shelburn's labours, at Coolspring meeting-house, where a most gracious gale of heavenly influence was afforded. A considerable number appeared to be sensible of their lost state, and came up near the stage, and falling on their knees, requested the prayers of the pious. Among them was elder Shelburn's youngest son, for the first time. From this period the work appeared to increase and spread in different directions; nurtured by the faithful labours of father Shelburn, and brother James Robertson, his assistant in the ministry, until July, when twelve came forward, were baptised, and united with the church. The precious work has continued, until the number added to that church amounts to between eighty and ninety; among whom we hope there are three chosen vessels to bear the glad tidings of the gospel to a world of perishing sinners. It is still progressing in one arm of the church more rapid of late than heretofore. There has likewise been a considerable revival in Tussakiah church, in the same county, under the care of elder Johns. About thirty or forty have been added to that church; among whom may be found a number of amiable young men, and two who are now candidates for the ministry. Brother Johns will probably write more fully respecting that part of the revival.

I now come to my beloved people in this county. In the spring of 1816, there were some small appearances, but nothing very singular until August, when elder Shelburn's labour was evidently owned and blessed of God, among the people. Several young men in the bloom of youth came forward in the presence of the congregation, and begged the prayers of the people of God. From this time the work increased, though at first among the young men principally, but in a few months it progressed with such rapidity, that it was not uncommon to see one fourth of the congregation on the floor, of different ages and sexes, crying for mercy. They seemed to be sensible of their utter helplessness, and resolved through grace to live and die at the feet of Jesus. Their dejected countenances bespoke the anguish and sorrow of their hearts.

About Christmas four young men came forward and made declaration of their faith in Christ, which had a very solemn effect among their young companions, many of whom were at that time groaning under the spirit of bondage. I baptised them on the twenty-seventh of December. Not long after, I baptised six more young men, with others. From that time, I have been frequently called to this precious service. The number added to this church [Bluestone] is a little upwards of one hundred. The precious work still appears to be going on. I baptised nine yesterday, and there are many more anxiously inquiring the way to Zion. The other two churches which I supply in the counties of Charlotte and Lunenburg, viz. Sandy Creek and Meherrin, have likewise had considerable additions, but not equal to the church named above. Truly the Lord has done great things for us in this quarter, for which we ought to be unfeignedly thankful.

JAILOR'S HOUSEHOLD.

Extract from a letter dated Richmond, Va. Nov. 20, 1817

Within the present year, (the exact date not recollected), the Rev. Mr. Bryce of this city, baptised, on the profession of faith in Christ, the household of the jailor of Goochland county, himself excepted, consisting of nine children, and a son-in-law, the youngest of whom was about eleven years old.

Since that period, the jailor himself has professed to have a hope in the Lord Jesus, and offered himself a subject for the sacred ordinance and no doubt, like the Philippian jailor, rejoices " believing in God with all his house"

The Lord has been gracious to this place Numbers in the course of the year past have been brought, as we trust, to a knowledge of the truth Various parts of this state have also been visited with the refreshing influences of Divine mercy. O! that all might know the love of our precious Redeemer!

MISCELLANEA.

ORDINATIONS.

ON Friday evening, the 2nd of December last, at the baptist meeting house in Sansom street, Philadelphia, the Rev SAMUEL CORNELIUS, member of said church, was solemnly ordained to the full office of the christian ministry. The service was opened by the Rev. Mr. Grigg, who delivered a very impressive sermon, founded on Eph. vi. 19 The usual questions were proposed by the Rev Dr Staughton. The rite of imposing hands was then performed by Dr. Staughton, and the Rev. Messrs Proudfoot, Billings, and Walker; during which solemnity the Rev Mr. Strawbridge offered the ordination prayer. The Rev Mr. Proudfoot then presented him the bible, and gave him the right hand of fellowship, welcoming him into the toils and consolations of the ministry. The same pledge of christian regard being tendered to the candidate by the rest of the officiating ministers, Dr. Staughton followed, with a solemn and affectionate charge. The whole of the services were peculiarly impressive and interesting.

On the 25th of January, 1818, the Rev. JOHN C MURPHY, a student under the patronage of the Baptist Education Society, was ordained to the pastoral care of the baptist church in Frankford.

The ordination sermon was preached by the Rev. John P. Peckworth, from Rom. x. 14, 15 "How then shall they call on him in whom they have not believed and how shall they believe in him of whom they have not heard? and how shall they hear without a preacher? and how shall they preach except they be sent?"

Hands were imposed, and the Rev Mr Peckworth offered the ordination prayer A charge was then addressed to the candidate, by the Rev. William Staughton, D D

GREGORY, in his book *de pastorali cura*—on pastoral care, observes, that Paul, writing to TIMOTHY, bids him *not strive*, but be *gentle* to all men, and to reprove with *all long suffering*. But writing to TITUS, he bids him rebuke *sharply*, and reprove with all *authority*, for which he gives this reason: "Titus was a man of a mild disposition, and needed a spur. Timothy, more sanguine, needed a bridle."

BOYLE, the great philosopher, speaking of the scriptures, said, "I prefer a single sprig of the tree of life, to a whole wood of bays."

AFTER the art of printing was introduced into England, Latin, Hebrew, and Greek bibles, and particularly copies of the New Testament, became much more common. Accordingly, a vicar of Croydon, in Surry, is said to have expressed himself to this purpose, in a sermon preached at St. Paul's Cross about this time, "We must root out printing, or printing will root out us."

GALILEO states, as the result of his calculations, that some spots in the sun are larger than Asia and Africa put together. Had he known the sun's parallax and distance as precisely as it has been determined by later philosophers, he would have found them larger by far than the whole surface of our earth. The young believer in Jesus Christ, conceives the spots that defile his person and services very large, but only the christian made wise by observation, experience, reflection, and the teachings of the Spirit of the Lord, discovers their real and enormous magnitude.

HISTORIANS mention a poor family in Germany, who were in danger of perishing during the prevalence of an alarming famine. In the anguish of his heart the father proposed to his wife, that one of their dear children should be sold for a little bread. The wife, after long hesitation, reluctantly consented. But here a difficulty offered they knew not how to surmount; which shall they part with?—not the eldest, *he* was their first born—not the second, *he* was the exact image of his father—not the third, *her* every feature was her mother's—and, oh! by no means the fourth—*he* was their youngest, and the darling of their declining age. They resolved they would perish together rather than be separated. And did affection thus hesitate?—thus resolve? How boundless the love of our heavenly Father, who gave His dearly beloved, His only begotten Son, freely for us all—that with Him also he might freely give us all things!

DR HERSCHELL conceives that the sun is an opaque body, surrounded with an atmosphere of clouds. Of these clouds he supposes there are two strata, the lower stratum protecting the sun from the heat and lustre of the upper, which last throws light and warmth through all the system. One cannot help remarking the correspondence between the conjecture of the philosopher, and the creed of the Unitarian. With the latter, the sun of righteousness is a mere man, an opaque body like ourselves, encircled indeed with a nebulous radiance, but it is a radiance not properly his own. The orthodox believer finds his contemplations enlarged, and his hopes sustained, by the firm persuasion that Jesus Christ is, in himself, independently of extraneous effulgence, the brightness of the glory, and the express image of the person of his Father. Heaven has no need of the sun, neither of the moon, to enlighten it—for "*the Lamb is the light thereof.*"

Wonders of the Microscope.

Upon examining the edge of a very keen razor by the microscope, it appears as broad as the back part of a pretty thick knife, rough, uneven, full of notches and furrows, and so far from any thing like sharpness, that an instrument so blunt as this seemed to be would not serve even to cleave wood.

An exceeding small needle being also examined, the point thereof appeared above a quarter of an inch in breadth, not round or flat, but irregular and unequal, and the surface, though extremely smooth and bright to the naked eye, seemed full of ruggedness, holes, and scratches. In short, it resembled an iron bar out of a smith's forge.

But the sting of a bee, viewed through the same instrument, showed every where a polish amazingly beautiful, without the least flaw, blemish, or inequality; and ended in a point too fine to be discerned.

A small piece of exceeding fine lawn appeared, from the large distances or holes between its threads, somewhat like a hurdle or lattice; and the threads themselves seemed somewhat coarser than yarn wherewith ropes are made for anchors.

Some Brussel's lace, worth five pounds a yard, looked as if it were made of a thick, rough, uneven hair line, intwisted, fastened or clotted together in a very inartful manner.

But a silkworm's web being examined, appeared perfectly smooth and shining, every where equal, and as much finer than any thread the finest spinster in the world could make, as the smallest twine is finer than the thickest cable.—A pod of this silk being wound off, was found to contain nine hundred and thirty yards; but it is proper to take notice, that as two threads are glued together by the worm through its whole length, it makes really double the above number, or one thousand eight hundred and sixty yards; which being weighed with the utmost exactness, were found no heavier than two grains and a half. What an exquisite fineness was here! and yet this is nothing when compared to the web of a small spider, or even with the silk that issued from the mouth of this very worm when but newly hatched from the egg.

Let us examine things with a good microscope, and we shall be immediately convinced, that the utmost power of art is only a concealment of deformity, an imposition upon our want of sight; and that our admiration of it arises from our ignorance of what it really is.

This valuable discoverer of truth will prove the most boasted performances of art to be ill shaped, rugged and uneven, as if they were hewn with an axe, or struck out with a mallet and chisel; it will show bungling, inequality, and imperfection in every part, and that the whole is disproportionate and monstrous.— Our finest miniature paintings appeared before this instrument as mere daubings plastered on with a trowel, and entirely void of beauty, either in the drawing or the colouring. Our most shining varnishes, our smoothest polishings, will be found to be mere roughness, full of gaps and flaws. [*Baker on the Microscope*

Who, after such a survey, but must assume the language of David, Psalm cxi 2. "The works of the Lord are great, sought out (or as Dr. Derham would render the word דרש, heedfully and deeply pried into, solicitously observed and inquired out) of all them that take pleasure therein." They are found

"As full, as perfect in a hair, as heart"

AN ANECDOTE,

As received from a gentleman in the County of King and Queen, Va.

"That after himself and his gay associates had been engaged in mirth and music until it became dull, he calls on an old solitary slave, that belonged to him, which was the only baptist in his large family,—to change the scene and refresh their minds. He demands a song from the slave, at which she most solemnly repeated and then sung this verse.

"Death, 'tis a melancholy day
"To them that have no God,
"When the poor soul is forc'd away,
"To seek her last abode"

After which he never rested until he was hopefully converted, and become a happy associate with the old slave."

A Bible bought by a Drunkard.

A person whose intemperance had reduced his family to poverty, was in the habit of attending all the public vendues in his neighbourhood, where liquor is obtained *gratis*. He uniformly came home drunk. At one of these places, a bible was put up for sale, for which he gave *a bid*. The buyer, *out of fun*, said, —it is yours, and gave it to him. He put it under his arm and travelled off home. He began to read it carefully. The Lord was pleased to impress it with power on his heart. He has now become a sober man. His habits are highly serious, and his family are maintained in excellent credit. The alteration is of considerable standing, and it is believed will continue as long as he lives.

"Thy word I've plac'd within my heart,
To keep my conscience clean,
And be an everlasting guard,
From every rising sin."

As the Rev. Matthew Henry was returning home after one of his Lord's day evening lectures, he was stopped by four men, within half a mile of Hackney, who took from him ten or eleven shillings, upon which he makes the following pious reflections. "What reason have I to be thankful to God, that, having travelled so "much, I was never robbed before!—What abundance of evil this love of money is "the root of, that four men should venture their lives and souls, for about half "a crown a-piece! See the vanity of worldly wealth, how soon we may be "stripped of it!"

On *Revelation* ii 9. "I know thy works and tribulation."—Mark, (saith one,) the conjunction *works and tribulation*. Active, stirring christians, are likely to suffer much. Of Sardis and Laodicea only, we read not of any troubles they had!—*Vid Trappe in loc.*

OBITUARY.

THE Rev. Mr Wm Batchelder of Haverhill, Mass has lately finished his testimony, and entered, as we have reason to believe, into the joy of his Lord. In a letter dated April 18, 1818, the Rev. Mr. Bolles of Salem says, "There is a great call for labourers in the Lord's vineyard in this part and in all parts of our country, and though some are entering upon their services, others are ceasing from them for ever. The last week our brother Batchelder, of Haverhill, was conveyed to the grave The breach occasioned by his death is wide He has left a large family, and an extensive field of usefulness. As a preacher, he was very active His labours in destitute places, many miles north and east of him, were abundant" His death seems to have been accelerated by the toils he underwent in soliciting subscriptions for a new Baptist theological school at Waterville, in the district of Maine May He, in whom the widow and fatherless find mercy, support his bereaved family, and the Head of the church pity and relieve the sorrows of his afflicted congregation.

" 'Tis God that lifts our comforts high,
Or sinks them in the grave:
He gives, and blessed be his name,
He takes but what he gave."

" Blessed are the dead who die in the Lord."

The subject of this notice, Mrs Elizabeth Booth, was born in London, 1772 Her parents were respectable and religious After coming to the United States, she resided principally in Philadelphia till her decease, which took place on Saturday, the 9th of October last. She had been for many years a professor of the religion of Jesus Christ, and had adorned her profession by a corresponding life of piety. We trust she sleeps in the Redeemer.

The following particulars are presented by a female acquaintance.

"Mrs. Booth's conversation during the whole of her last illness was very evangelical. All her dependence was on Jesus ; from him she sought and found that peace of mind which none but the real followers of Christ know any thing of. She was never known to murmur or repine, but her constant prayer was, "thy will be done." One day, when she was in extreme agony, she was heard to say, blessed are the dead that die in the Lord, for they rest from their labours! Oh that I may die the death of the righteous, and that my last end may be like his! She often repeated the hymn, "Dear refuge of my weary soul," &c. On Thursday preceding the evening that she was struck with death, she called her son and daughter to her bed-side, and after beseeching them to walk in the way of the Lord, she bid them an affectionate farewell. She repeated the hymns, "Jesus, lover of my soul," "Jesus can make a dying bed, Feel soft as downy pillows are," &c. From Thursday evening she lay unable to speak, until Saturday morning, nine o'clock, when she expired."

POETRY.

I will be as the dew unto Israel.—Hos xiv. 5.

FROM realms of eternity, blessed and bright,
   Where thrones and dominions enraptured adore,
Salvation his garment, and man his delight,
   The Angel of Mercy descends to restore.

The Angel of Mercy! how joyful the sound!
   Messiah, thy name is a balm to the soul!
Its sweetness shall fall on the Gentiles around,
   And Jews shall submit to its peaceful control.

Ah! long have they wandered forlorn and afar,
   In darkness have wandered a wilderness way;
Unknowing the bright and imperial star,
   And hating the beams of Immanuel's day.

But mercy, the rainbow that arches the skies,
   Through clouds, and through darkness effulgent shall shine;
Oh! Israel, the nations no more shall despise,
   For rich is the promise that follows thy line.

"Compassion and goodness, still swelling above
   Thine offences, thy constant rebellion shall heal,
For freely, most freely, I give thee my love,
   And vengeance no longer her arm shall reveal!

"As dews upon Zion their freshness distil,
   My heavenly grace shall descend upon thee,
And fair as the olives which mantle the hill
   That looks upon Salem, thy beauties shall be.

"Thou shalt grow as the lily the pride of the vale,
   Where life giving waters are flowing along,
And, like the tall cedar, resisting the gale
   On the mountain of Libanus, thou shalt be strong.

"Thy branches shall spread and thy fruit shall be fair,
   And sweet as the odours of exquisite wine:
Thine outcasts shall then to thy shadow repair,
   And I will regale them with banquets divine."

C.

Out of Zion, the perfection of beauty, God hath shined.

THE Lord of lords, and King of kings,
   In realms of bliss exalted reigns:
Ah! who can touch the trembling strings,
   And hymn his praise with equal strains?

The grandeur of his works may show,
   In beams of lasting, heavenly light,
To all who love their radiant glow,
   His wisdom and his boundless might:

But, Zion! on thy portals fair,
　　His wondrous name resplendent shines,
And every child of wisdom there
　　Shall read it in the clearest lines.

Yes! there we learn that God is love!
　　The lucid truth let angel choirs,
Circling the shining throne above,
　　Resound upon their golden lyres.

With deep astonishment they saw,
　　Immanuel, the virgin's son!
And heard with fixed and sacred awe,
　　The Lord of glory cry—'tis done!'

But quit the endless theme, my soul,
　　And wait resigned, a brighter day,
Above mortality's control,
　　To wake a more enraptured lay.

The 'crown of life,' the 'harp' of gold,
　　And 'palm of vict'ry,' all proclaim,
That nobler songs shall yet unfold
　　The glories of Jehovah's name.

　　　　　　　　　　　　　　　C.

ON THE SPRING.

*"Thou sendest forth thy Spirit, they are created;
and thou renewest the face of the earth."*

Thou Power Supreme! thy works I see
　　In almost pristine glory shine!
O! let them lift my soul to thee,
　　And with their praise accept of mine.

Thy spirit moves upon the earth,
　　And life assumes her joyful sway,
As when creation first had birth,
　　And starry hosts attuned the lay.

The universal song, that swells
　　With raptured gladness, breathes of thee,
Thy kindness every flow'ret tells,
　　Thy goodness every blooming tree.

Most happy they who dwell around
　　The throne of radiant light above,
And raise in strains of nobler sound,
　　Their anthems to the God of love.

The God of love! oh, blissful name!
　　Bright angels, hymn your glorious king;
But man may urge a further claim
　　To praise;—and God the *Saviour* sing!

Yes! Lord of suffering mercy! yes!
　　The blood bought gift of life divine,
Thy saints with glowing powers shall bless,
　　Whilst heaven's eternal ages shine.

　　　　　　　　　　　　　　　G.

THE LATTER DAY LUMINARY;

BY A COMMITTEE

OF

THE BAPTIST BOARD OF FOREIGN MISSIONS
FOR THE UNITED STATES.

THIS NUMBER CONTAINS

THE FOURTH ANNUAL REPORT OF THE BOARD

| Vol. I. | MAY, 1818. | No. III. |

ADDRESS.

THY kingdom come! has been the devout and benevolent aspiration of every true disciple of the Lord and Saviour Jesus Christ, from those who caught the prayer from his gracious lips, to those who now utter the fervent ejaculation, with hearts animated by the delightful prospect of its extensive accomplishment, and souls illuminated and fired by the blaze of the Divine glory, as the millennial sabbath dawns. In the execution of the vast and important, yet truly grateful task of directing the liberality of thousands of their brethren to the objects by them designed, and in their endeavours faithfully, in every point, to attend to the duties delegated to them by the general Convention, the efficacy of the supplication has been made evident to the Board; and they now acknowledge it, with sentiments of heartfelt gratulation to their brethren in Christ, and of devout thankfulness and praise to the Lord God Omnipotent, who, riding forth in the chariot of salvation, deigns to make them fellow-workers with himself in the magnificent design of redeeming from the dominion of darkness, and the bondage of sin, out of every kindred and tongue, and people and nation, the sanctified, the sacramental host, who shall ultimately join the universal choir in ascribing "blessing, and honour, and glory, and power, unto Him that sitteth upon the throne, and unto the Lamb, for ever and ever."

Conceiving that nothing could contribute more to the generous ardour of enlightened benevolence, and to the excitement of extended christian sympathy, than the diffusion of missionary intelligence, the Board have commenced a periodical publication, entitled the Latter Day Luminary: from this, and the documents annexed to the present address, may be collected every information respecting the number of missionaries under the patronage of the Board, their destination, their operations, and their prospects of usefulness. It may not, however, be improper here to present a concise statement of the transactions of the preceding year.

Our agent, Mr. Rice, has continued persevering in those active exertions for the advancement of the missionary cause, which so essentially contributed to its rise: and, whilst prosecuting this course, "in labours more abundant," "in journeyings often," "in weariness and painfulness," "in watchings often," he has our warmest sympathies, and we recommend him to the patronage of every friend of Zion.

Brethren Peck and Welch, whose designation to the western mission was announced in the last Report, have arrived at St Louis, constituted a church of believers, whom the providence of God had conducted thither before them; opened a school; and made excursions among the Indians in the surrounding country; and found them generally willing, even solicitous, that their children should be instructed.

Brother Ranaldson has been actively employed in the states of Louisiana and Mississippi, in preaching the gospel to bond and free, with a success that has rejoiced our hearts; and has established a church in the former state. Though unable, from the sickness of his family, to visit the Creek Indians, pursuant to the instructions of the Board, his representation to the Mississippi Association produced a mission from that body, which eventuated in the formation of a *Creek African Church.*

Among the Cherokees inhabiting the wild mountainous country which lies on the borders of North Carolina and Tennessee, the Rev Humphrey Posey has communicated evangelic instruction with acceptance, and has established several schools for the education of their children. Having similar objects in view with respect to the Indians inhabiting the state of Indiana, and territory of Illinois, the Board appointed the Rev. Isaac McCoy, near Vincennes, to missionary service in that quarter.

Two young missionaries, Messrs. Wheelock and Colman, whose hearts are devoted to the cause in which they are engaged, whose desires are to live for the conversion of the Burmans to God, and to die among them, have sailed to join their brethren Judson and Hough in Rangoon.

In this limited view of the proceedings of the Board, it may be observed, that the destitute places of the earth have been sought out, and cultivated by the faithful servants of Christ: the wretched, ignorant, wandering race, whose inveterate habits of savage life have often palsied the efforts of those who were warmest in their cause, are now induced to submit to the fostering hand of civilization, and listen to that gospel which has brought life and immortality to light. The poor African, once as "dark in things divine" as the complexion which Providence has stamped upon him, now beholds the "light of the knowledge of the glory of God in the face of Jesus Christ." In personal bondage, he is Christ's freeman; and, without a country in all the world he can call his own, his expectations are raised to one that is heavenly. And the devoted missionaries in Rangoon who have planted the standard of Christ in the empire of darkness, and invaded "the habitations of cruelty," will soon, it is hoped, receive an accession to their number.

Such extended operations, it may well be conceived, could not be carried on without great expense; and the Board, ever regarding economy in the use of the funds by the liberality of the public entrusted to them, have, nevertheless, been compelled by a sense of duty, to make large appropriations for these several objects. The calls of Providence were too plain to be misunderstood. They would not resist, they could not but promote the ardent wishes of those into whose hearts God had infused the holy desire of sacrificing almost every earthly consideration to his sacred cause. They confided in His faithfulness who has promised to accomplish what they are labouring by his blessing to achieve. They trusted, too, that there existed in those who have hitherto favoured them with their patronage, a spirit that would not suffer them to grow weary in well doing; but which, regarding the success that has crowned their efforts, would only find in each renewed demand upon their benevolence, a fresh inducement for contributing to such heavenly purposes.

Much has been done, but more, much more remains to be accomplished. We have only planted our standard on the field; the battle is yet to be fought. The various stations which have been chosen, are only strong positions from which must be carried on a more extended warfare. If we faint here, our strength is small indeed! If we sit down satisfied with such partial achievements, the laurels already gathered will wither on our brows If steady, ardent, persevering efforts do not succeed these measures, we have but laboured in vain. What are *four* missionaries in Rangoon against a host of *seventeen millions?* and these too under the strong influence of the god of this world, and shielded by the grossest darkness! Take up the map of North America. Trace the range of the 'everlasting hills' which divide the waters that roll to the Atlantic from those that discharge themselves into the gulf of Mexico. One missionary is stationed there; more solitary than the eagle that builds upon their rocks. From thence look southward upon the vast extent of country inhabited by the Cherokees, Creeks, Chickasaws, and Choctaws, and one or two may be discovered shining like stars amid the general gloom. Then extend your view across the Mississippi to the town of St. Louis, two missionaries have fixed themselves there. But follow this river in its course for thousands of miles; trace its mighty tributary streams, and you will find their banks lined with tribes of Indians, almost as ignorant of the God who made them, as the animals on which they subsist. When shall these " floods clap their hands?" when shall these valleys sing, and the mountains repeat the joyful sound of salvation? Can such mighty effects be produced by the efforts of *two* men, however pure their aims, however unwearied their exertions?

We repeat it, the work is but in its commencement. Those self denying men, who, confiding in the promises of God and the fidelity of his friends, have gone forth to their glorious task, must be ably supported. For *success* in their endeavours they look to *Him* whose privilege alone has power to make darkness light, and raise the dead to eternal life; but for the *means* which shall enable them unceasingly to persevere in their labours, they look to *us*. And who will refuse " a cup of cold water" to the disciple of his Lord, when fainting with the extremity of toil? Let us rather say, who will not count it a happiness, for which he is bound to give thanks to the Father of mercies, that an opportunity is afforded of participating in that noble design which invites the contemplation, and engages the attention of the happy spirits who " are sent forth to minister to those who shall be heirs of salvation?"

There is one circumstance which the Board are particularly desirous of impressing upon the mind of every friend to humanity. Our British brethren in India have found, by the experience of more than twenty years, that " civilization and salvation go hand in hand;" and if this be true respecting a people in some degree enlightened, it obtains with a ten-fold consideration when applied to the aborigines of our country, destitute of a written language and every art of cultivated life. It follows that schools for their instruction must be established if we would do them any real and permanent service; and an additional expense proportionate to these objects must ensue. But let not any one be discouraged on this account. By teaching them to read, and placing in their hands the word of God, which by the power of his Spirit is able to make them wise unto salvation, we shall greatly prepare the way of the Lord, and facilitate the progress of his missionary servants. It is but following the bright path that marks the progress of redeeming love on the fields of Europe and the extensive plains of Asia. By this method such as were ready to perish, even in lands where the gospel had long been known, have been nourished with the bread of life. By this method the heavenly manna distils upon the wilds of Tartary. And it is by disseminating religious tracts, and such portions of the Scriptures as they have, in the short period of their residence in Rangoon, been able to translate into the Burman language, and publish, that our beloved brethren there are diffusing the knowledge of God with success; and their hearts are gladdened with inquiries for "*more of this sort of writing.*"

Brethren of our own denomination! brethren in Christ and friends of humanity of every name! whilst thus we press upon you the mighty objects yet to be attained, we are not unmindful of what you have already done. We thank you, from our hearts we thank you, for the liberal support you have afforded in the common cause of our master; and we feel a pleasure in reflecting that our thanks are the least recompense that shall be given to every one who thus serves him. If we have "used boldness" in urging upon you the necessities of ever increased exertions, it is because we are sensible, that such only can be crowned with success. We ask not your gold or silver for our own purposes, but for His who is Lord of both. Our missionaries, content with what may subserve the ordinary support and decencies of life, prefer to all the charms of wealth, the privations which their duties impose, and find their comforts in the consolations of Christ—their luxuries in doing good. There is, indeed, one subject upon which they are importunate, and we cannot but request your attention to it. Their constant cry is, "*Pray for us.*" This duty a Lazarus may fulfil, and even the most wealthy will find themselves enriched by the exercise. They who cast their bread upon the waters shall find it after many days; but the devout supplication of the pure in heart of itself diffuses the joys of heaven through the bosom of man. We close our address with the wish, that in this, as in every good word and work you may continue to abound; and that all engaged in the glorious enterprise of extending the empire of the Redeemer, may realize the prayer of Moses, the man of God—" Let thy work appear unto thy servants, and thy glory unto their children. And let the beauty of the Lord our God be upon us; and establish thou the work of our hands: yea, the work of our hands establish thou it."

TO THE CORRESPONDING SECRETARY OF THE BAPTIST BOARD OF FOREIGN MISSIONS FOR THE UNITED STATES.

DEAR SIR,

A MERCIFUL God has preserved me in health and safety through the various journeyings and exertions of another year. While recognizing his great goodness with devout gratitude, permit me to present to you, and, if you think proper, to the Board, the following statements, connected with the services allotted me by that venerable body.

These statements will have reference—1st, to the publishing of the proceedings of the Convention and third annual Report of the Board, and a tour through the western country last summer—2nd, to the circumstances connected with issuing proposals for the publication of the Latter Day Luminary, including a journey to Boston—3rd, to a tour through the middle and western states last fall and winter—4th, to the issuing of the first number of the Luminary, and a late excursion to Virginia and North Carolina.

1st. From the first of my employment in the service of the Board, it has been my endeavour to keep steadily in view, and to prosecute with undeviating perseverance, the great object of *effectuating arrangements for keeping up a regular intercourse between the Board and all the Associations and Mission Societies in the United States*, as designated in your second annual Report, 1816; combined with efforts *to excite the public mind more generally to engage in missionary exertions, and to assist in originating Societies, or Institutions, for carrying the missionary design into execution*, as expressed in my original appointment, in 1814. Of the importance of attaining this object, in addition to my confidence in the wisdom of the Board, I have ever felt a deep conviction, and have only lamented, while wearing away the best part of my earthly existence in the business, that it has not been in my power to carry forward these systematic arrangements with greater rapidity, to a larger extent, and with much more vigour and success.

After the publication of the proceedings of the second meeting of the general Convention, and the third annual Report of the Board, and the accomplishing of a general distribution of the same, I proceeded, conformably to instructions, on a tour to the westward. Although so late as the 8th of July before it was practicable for me to set out, and notwithstanding the badness of roads and the extreme heat of the season, I arrived at the Green River Association, in Barren county, Ky. the 27th of the same month. The following Saturday and Sabbath, I was with the Concord Association, Smith county, Tennessee; the next, with the White Water Association, Franklin county, Indiana, but in the evening of the same Sabbath preached in Cincinnati, Ohio, and received a contribution for missionary purposes; and the Saturday and Sabbath after, was again in the south part of Kentucky, at the Stockton's Valley Association, in Barren county, and on Monday, the day following, was at the close of the South District Association, in Mercer county, a hundred miles from the place of the meeting of the Stockton's Valley Association. Here, although brother Welch had received a liberal collection the preceding day, another was willingly offered.

On Thursday of the same week, I set out from Lexington, Ky. for this city, to be present at the quarterly meeting of the Board, the first Monday in September, conceiving it my duty to lay before my honoured patrons various considerations and facts relative to some important modifications of the plan now moving into operation Nor could I avoid thankfully to mark the event as specially providential, that it should be practicable for me, without losing any opportunity of visiting associations, to meet the Board at a juncture which actually formed a crisis of no ordinary moment to the system of intercourse between that body and the baptist denomination throughout our country. I visited just on the bank of the Ohio river, on the Ohio side, the Teass Valley Association, on my way; and, in ten days and a half, having passed the distance of 760 miles, arrived in Philadelphia.

At the White Water Association, a meeting was agreed on for the purpose of forming, in that part of Indiana, a mission society, which was to take place in February; of the result, advices have not yet been received. A meeting was also appointed, before my leaving that quarter, for the purpose of originating a mission society, in the county of Madison, Ky. Brethren Peck and Welch, on their way to St Louis, were present at that meeting, and a society was organized

At each of the associations mentioned in the foregoing, as well as at each of those yet to be mentioned as visited by me in the course of the past season, a contribution was made to assist the missionary funds, and each of them consented to a correspondence with the Board.

2nd. Permit me now to introduce statements having reference *to the circumstances connected with the issuing of proposals for publishing* The Latter Day Luminary, *including a journey to Boston.*

This part of the business has been regarded on all hands as possessing singular importance. Your condescension, therefore, will indulge me a few moments in adverting to the circumstances, the contemplation of which inspired the resolution and imparted the strength that brought me in so short a time from so great a distance, to your quarterly meeting in September.

A short period previous to the assembling of the late Convention at their first triennial meeting, the proprietors of the American Baptist Magazine and Missionary Intelligencer, as you are well acquainted, conceived the noble and herculean design of giving to that valuable work, a complete circulation throughout our country. The state of things and pressure of other weighty concerns, prevented this matter from undergoing a discussion in the Convention, and a deliberate, extended investigation of the practicability of attaining the object contemplated by the proprietors of the Magazine, on the plan adopted by that publication; or whether, even if practicable, it would not be more eligible for a publication on this enlarged scale, to emanate directly from the general missionary body, that might conduce to display and strengthen its relations with all parts of the community; or, whether, if not practicable, some other plan could not be discovered, suited to the accomplishment of an object of so much interest, and so much to be desired.

The case, however, as it will be recollected, although not regularly gone into in any formal discussion, could not, from its very nature and bearings on the cause of missions, be suffered to pass wholly without notice. Solicitous that the useful information spread uniformly over its pages, should be diffused as widely as possible through the community, the Convention strongly recommended the Magazine to general acceptance and patronage. Founded on the same solicitude an arrangement was proposed, and acceded to, which should render the Board, in part, proprietor of the publication, in the hope and belief that this would give such invigoration to the means of circulating the work, as should secure the object, at least to a very gratifying extent

Soon, however, on applying to this arrangement, from which so much had been anticipated, the test of experiment, it was discovered that the plan could not succeed. The smallness of the Magazine and its price, together with the frequency of its publication, left the concern unable to diffuse it through all the wide spreading regions westwardly and south-westwardly from this place, unless on the principle of employing other resources for this purpose, besides such as the work itself should supply. At the same time, as this deficiency of means for the ample circulation of the Magazine through the extensive sections of country referred to, without incurring expense, was discovered, another plan, of a larger work, of course higher in its price, and less frequently issued, revealed itself in all the light of obvious practicability, and certain ultimate profit to the missionary interest. The solemn alternative distinctly offered, whether a plan, the feasibility of which was shaded not by a solitary obscuring doubt, should be adopted, or leave the numerous population alluded to, still unsupplied with the information which it is so affectingly important they should possess!

These views constantly present, and pressing with daily accumulating weight upon my mind, impelled a hasty return from Kentucky, that the facts, so far as they had fallen within the scope of my observation, might be stated, fully, to the Board. Nor was it in any small degree consoling, to find that I had not been contemplating the matter in an erroneous light, as their unanimous decision still supports me in believing.

It was deemed expedient, however, to postpone the prospectus till the Editors of the Magazine should be consulted. But so urgent was the case, that it was judged advisable for me to omit several associations it had been my design to visit, and proceed to the eastward on this errand. In prosecuting this measure, some additional expense was incurred, while the opportunity of receiving collections in a number of instances, was lost, but it was an object greatly desirable to bring this matter to a happy conclusion.

Early the next morning after the meeting of the Board, I set out on an excursion to Virginia; visited the Shiloh Association in Madison county on Friday and Saturday of the same week, was with the Goshen Association in Orange county on Sabbath and Monday; and, wheeling to my right, met the Baltimore Association the Friday following, at Sideling Hill, Bedford county, in this state; the Wednesday after, was with the New Jersey Association at Trenton, N. J.— and arrived in Boston on Saturday, the 20th of the month. After accomplishing the object of my journey thither, I had the pleasure to be with the Hartford Association at Weathersfield, Connecticut, on Wednesday, the first of October, on my return; and was present at the meeting of the Board, on Monday the 6th. Of my reception by the worthy brethren in New England, and the results of my journey to that quarter, it is unnecessary here to say any thing. Your expectations were not disappointed.

3rd *Statements relative to my tour through the middle and western states, last fall and winter*

Proposals for the Latter Day Luminary being issued by the publishing committee appointed by the Board, the day after their meeting, I went to the Philadelphia Association at Southampton; and on Saturday evening of the same week, was at the Dover Association, King and Queen county, Virginia. The contribution by the assembly present at the missionary sermon on the Sabbath was 272 dollars In a fortnight, having taken a circuitous route through a part of that state higher up, and a part of Maryland and Pennsylvania, for the purpose of scattering subscription papers for the Luminary, I attended the Salisbury Association in Sussex county, Delaware. The next Saturday and Sabbath, was with a mission society in Fredericksburg, Va. and the Saturday and Sabbath following, with the Raleigh Association in Wake county, North Carolina.

Leaving this place the 10th of November, having been at fifteen associations in the course of the season, I crossed the country by Lynchburg, Romney, and Uniontown; reached Pittsburgh the 23d, and received in a Presbyterian meeting house a contribution for missionary purposes The young ladies had formed a Mite Society not long before The next day I proceeded to Washington, Pennsylvania, and the day after to Wheeling, Virginia; thence through Zanesville, Chilicothe and West Union, Ohio; Maysville, Washington, Lexington, Georgetown, Harrodsburg, Bardstown, Louisville, Shelbyville, Frankfort, Versailles, Richmond, Campbellville and Glasgow, Kentucky, Nashville, Franklin, Murfreesboro, Lebanon, Liberty, Sparta, Knoxville, Jonesboro and Blountville, Tennessee; Fincastle, Lynchburg, Lexington, Staunton, Harrisonburg, New Market, Luray, Milford, Front Royal, Zion, Winchester, Charleston to Harper's Ferry, Virginia. In each of these places I had opportunity, in connexion with preaching, to introduce the subject of missions, and receive assistance. The collections, although not large, commonly manifested the liberality of the people, as the meetings were often such as could be obtained after my arrival at the place at the close of a day's ride, without any previous notice. In Lynchburg I spent less than forty hours, and assisted to originate two mission societies, and received by contributions in the Presbyterian and Methodist meeting-houses, more than $200.—At Winchester was commenced a Female Mite Society in the school of the Rev. Mr. Sedwick.

From Harper's Ferry coming on through Fredericktown and Lancaster, I arrived in this city the 2nd of February. A principal object of this tour was the disposing of subscription papers for the Luminary, and arranging for its conveyance. The returns furnish the best comment on the probable success of the undertaking.

4th. In relation *to the circumstances connected with the issuing of the first number of the Luminary, and a late excursion to Virginia and North Carolina*, it is unnecessary here to say much

In the proposals for the publication first printed, it was thought proper to allow separate columns for the Luminary and the annual Report; and the plan of semi-annual payments was adopted, in order to obtain a sufficient amount in advance to enable the publishing committee to commence the work, inasmuch as this concern was, in the outset, to keep entirely clear of the funds belonging to the Board, and the responsibility and risk to rest on the committee, personally, not on the body by whom they were appointed and authorized The prospect, however, soon became so fair and promising, that the Board assumed the responsibility; and it was judged advisable to drop from the paper the column for the annual Report, and regard that as one in the series consisting of five numbers a year, accommodated, as most convenient, to the basis of annual payments, rather than semi-annual. So many had subscribed for the Report, that what would be found in it could not with propriety be introduced into the Luminary, as in that case such would pay for the same matter twice, while, if any omitted taking the Report, there would be a chasm in their information. New subscription papers were, therefore, issued. These are in operation, and it is probable the number of subscribers will be considerably augmented. Much, if any profit, cannot be expected this year; but ultimately, no doubt, something handsome will be derived from this source to the mission funds.

The discretion to me confided by the Board, to employ persons in different parts of the country to assist in systematizing the circulation of the work, I shall feel it my duty to exercise with great caution. None have as yet been employed; but arrangements are in train on which is founded the expectation that some will be in the course of the season ensuing. In all these cases it may justly be calculated that direct advantage to the funds of the Board will be secured, besides assistance to the regular circulation of the Luminary.

On obtaining from the press the first number, I proceeded southwardly, in the hope of being able to go as far as Milledgeville in Georgia. A quantity of the publication had been shipped for Richmond, Va. to be taken along to the south, and distributed all the way, but the vessel did not arrive time enough for me to accomplish the journey intended. Indeed the detention was so great, owing to this failure, as to prevent my going farther in that direction than Raleigh, N C Turning to the left, I visited Edenton and Norfolk, on my way back to this place.

While in Richmond, Va. I had opportunity of attending the annual meeting of the Female Mission Society—the African Mission Society—the Richmond Mission Society—of preaching a sermon for a collection to aid the funds of the Juvenile Female Cent Society—of witnessing the beginning of a Youth's Mite Society—and of witnessing the zeal of the ladies to form an Education Society. It afforded me much pleasure, indeed, to observe the zeal, and intelligence, and capacity, and success, discovered in the African Mission Society. The fact too, that the little girls from 6 or 7, to 12 or 14 years old, had formed a society, to save from the purchase of little delicacies their mites to assist the glorious object of giving the knowledge of the gospel to all the world, and that their lovely example was producing something similar among the little boys, could not fail to awaken emotions peculiarly delightful, anticipations the most lively and interesting In Raleigh it is probable a similar little ladies' Cent or Mite Society, may ere this have been instituted. In Norfolk I am confident a Female Society will soon go into operation, probably has already In Edenton the ladies have an Education Society:—these, besides the Mission Societies before existing in and about Norfolk and Edenton

In Alexandria has recently been originated a Female Missionary Society, and one in Washington city; one at Chapawamsick, one at Wellsburg on the Ohio river, and one at Bruceville, in the state of Indiana, besides the Bruceville Mission Society While in Virginia, on his way to the westward, brother Welch assisted in the formation of a mission society in Madison and Culpeper counties. How many more have been formed during the past year, I cannot with certainty at this moment say, but will endeavour to make out a list of them on a separate paper; also, an account of monies received, and of the expenditures incurred in the business assigned me by the Board.

My expenses have been greater than formerly, owing to the journey to Boston, the necessity of travelling so much in expensive parts of the country, and of frequently resorting to stage and steam boat conveyance as the only mode sufficiently rapid to answer the purpose

Mean-time the collections taken have not swelled to the amount they might have done, had not my course of visiting Associations been interrupted by the circumstances already mentioned, or had I been able to prosecute my late southern excursion to the extent originally designed. Very little attention have I been able to bestow on the important object of securing a permanent fund for the secretary department. This matter, however, may now be offered to the public, in a light, I trust, to be pursued with vigour and success.

Since the date of my letter to you, the 6th of May, 1817, I have travelled 9359 miles, and received 5443 dollars 57 cents. The expenditures connected with this course, including my allowance of $8 per week, distribution of the last annual Report; paper, printing, and distribution of the Luminary; paper for the Report this year; postages, &c &c. have amounted only to 1963 dollars 67 cents.

In closing this communication, it causes me to feel peculiar satisfaction to declare my unshaded conviction that the missionary spirit is still gaining ground, and extending its benign influence. May the period soon arrive when "*all flesh shall see the salvation of God.*"

As ever, with most affectionate and christian salutations,

Permit me to subscribe myself, your Agent,

LUTHER RICE

Rev. Dr. Staughton, Cor. Sec &c
Philadelphia, April 30, 1818

INSTITUTION FOR IMPROVING THE EDUCATION OF PIOUS YOUNG MEN, CALLED TO THE CHRISTIAN MINISTRY.

AMID the range of interesting efforts recommended by the baptist Convention to the Board of missions, the education of youth destined for the work of the ministry, is one of the highest importance. It is demanded by the improved state of society; it supplies to the young minister himself numerous and solid advantages, and is, with the blessing of God, in every case useful; but as relates to the business of translation, it is of indispensable value to the foreign missionary. The manner in which this duty was pressed upon the Convention by the venerated President, at its last session, will not soon be forgotten. All that zeal for the honour of God and the prosperity of the churches, all that correct conception, impressive eloquence and decision of feeling could suggest, were employed to arouse the minds of the brethren to this necessary measure.

The Board has felt the weight of the charge that has been to them committed. So far from fearing that in this business they have come forward too early, they apprehend most from their apparent delay. They owe it to truth to avow, that their difficulty has arisen from the want of funds to carry the object, to any considerable extent, into execution. What of late they have observed with reference to the public impression on this point, creates an assurance that to obtain funds competent and ample, nothing is necessary but a direct appeal to the liberality of their fellow christians throughout the Union. To this they were the more inclined, as the Baptist Education Society in Philadelphia, so early as July last, addressed to them a letter, offering their immediate co-operation in accomplishing the objects contemplated by the Convention.

At the late annual meeting of the Board, the subject was fully and in all its various bearings discussed, and a committee appointed to consult with a committee of the Education Society. The Rev. Dr. Staughton has been elected Principal, and the Rev. Ira Chase, A. M. Professor of Languages and Biblical Literature. The Board calculate much on the talents, piety, and devotedness of brother Chase, and it affords great pleasure to announce that he has accepted the appointment.

A suggestion of the honourable judge Tallmadge, one of the vice-presidents, on his return from the south, has been welcomed and recommended—that a meeting of the Board, as numerous as possible, be called, to put into immediate effect the wishes of the Convention, and to elicit all the aid that can be procured for the accomplishment of the important design. The second Wednesday in July has been fixed upon for this purpose. In the mean-time, brother Rice, the agent of the Board, is instructed to obtain all the subscriptions he can, that may contribute to the supplying of means for the accomplishment of an object so conducive to the prosperity of our churches, the interests of missions, and the glory of our common Lord and Saviour.

It may be thought unnecessary in the present state of society to assign any reasons to prove the utility and importance of education in assisting the minister of the sanctuary in the discharge of the public and solemn duties of his office. When, however, it is recollected that the most valuable principles fail in their effect unless frequently reviewed, " line upon line" may be found advantageous.

The bible in its popular translation ought unquestionably to engage the laborious attention of the candidate for pulpit labours. The saints of God are accustomed to its phraseology, and find in its words a savoness which accords with the most gracious exercises of their hearts. It has become venerable for its antiquity, and is received among christians as their guide to heaven.

It is our happiness that as a translation the scriptures are most excellent; but still they are a translation. They supply the best remedy for the evils which the confusion of tongues has created, but the words are not those which the Holy Ghost first employed in conveying revealed truth to man. An acquaintance with the original scriptures qualifies the minister of Christ for contemplating the sentiments delivered in the sacred volume in a variety of lights. It enables him to correct errours which mistaken friends or avowed enemies of divine truth may have introduced. The baptists in determining and defending the real import of the term by which they are denominated, and the nature and government of a church of God, are deeply interested in giving to their public teachers an acquaintance with the scriptures in their original tongues.

Besides the oracles of God in their translated and original forms, the public speaker ought to become familiar with the grammar of his own language. Logic will assist him to reason with accuracy, and rhetoric to convey the result of his investigations and the fervours of his heart with acceptance. Without an acquaintance with profane history he can never explain the prophecies which are on record, and ignorant of ecclesiastical, he can never trace to their sources the mischievous errours that prevail. Geography, ancient and modern, is of importance, the former will aid him in his public expositions, and the latter serve to animate and direct the enlarged zeal of his heart, for the extension of the Mediator's kingdom

The able minister is made such by the Holy Ghost, and only those who in the judgment of the churches are subjects of grace will be admitted to the benefits of the institution. When science would assume the seat of vital religion, let her be treated as was Hagar when she would become the mistress of Sarah; let her be turned out of doors. But it is certain the Holy Spirit works by means. Who will argue that preaching is unnecessary because God alone changes the human heart? Timothy had received a special gift at the laying on of the hands of the presbytery, and yet he is exhorted by an apostle, who, in zeal for the doctrines of grace and the honour of the Holy Ghost, was by none exceeded, to "give attendance unto reading"

The same blessed Spirit who assisted the apostles to speak with tongues, employs and blesses human acquisitions to the honour of the divine name. Was not Paul under the inspiration of the Holy Ghost when he quoted from heathen writers the following passages, certain of your own poets have said, for "we also are his offspring"—"The Cretans are always liars"—"Evil communications corrupt good manners." The divine Spirit in employing our English bible for the conversion and sanctifying of the people of God, condescends to make use of the instrumentality of human learning. Had our translators been ignorant of gender and case, of mood and tense, of syntax and government, the bible in the vernacular tongue had never been ours. The venerable Carey and his associates are consecrating their learning to the important work of translating the word of life. They translate not from translations, but draw the waters of life from the sacred fountains of original scripture. Some of our young men feel a necessity laid upon them to become missionaries too. Who would not regret dismissing them from their native shores without possessing talents for extended usefulness, such as the bounty of zealous christians could supply, such as the good Spirit of our God has singularly blessed?

That there are in the church eminent ministers of Christ whose opportunities of mental improvement have been small, furnishes occasion for holy joy. Never let human acquirements be regarded as indispensably necessary for pulpit duties. Should it however be inferred that mental improvement is of no moment, the inference is no more correct than that because sometimes God converts men by a thunder storm the ministry of the gospel may be laid aside. Ask those excellent men who, without literary aid, have become great in the church of Christ, their ideas of the value of education, and without an exception you will hear them deplore the want of it. If their eminence and usefulness have been great without learning, what would they have been had they possessed it? Who are the divines whose works stand in the world for the defence of the gospel, above all others? It need not be answered they were men signalized for the variety and extent of their erudition, as well as for their soundness in faith, the riches of their experience, and the purity of their conversation.

But learning makes men proud! Alas, such is the frailty of the human heart, that pride will spring as a noxious plant, whether the soil in which it grows be cultivated or not. Pride is not the associate of wisdom only. The most unlettered professors may sometimes be classed among the proudest. The preacher may be as proud, while from the pulpit he is inveighing against that learning which he does not possess, as he who before his congregation opens a thousand of its stores. Superficial literature may produce vanity; but sound learning, sanctified attainments, originate and maintain unaffected humility.

It is hoped that the churches of our denomination are becoming more and more convinced of the duty of assisting pious youths in their education, and do we need arguments to strengthen this conviction? Had ancient prophets their schools for the edification of their youth, and shall we not endeavour to have Naioths and Bethels now? Enemies of christianity are employing learning for its overthrow, and shall not the champions of the Cross be assisted to meet them on equal ground? Did not much of the superstition and folly of the dark ages of the church arise from an unlettered ministry? Has not the reformation, under God, sprung from the intrepidity of men who have been as eminent for learning as for zeal and piety? Is it not the interest of the churches that their spiritual guides possess every possible qualification for advancing their knowledge of divine subjects? Have not the churches, already, realized many important advantages from the literary institutions which exist in our connexion? And ought not such considerations to animate to new and continued exertions?

Youth is undoubtedly the best period for mental improvement, not only because it is a season of inexperience, and freedom from care, but because the memory is then the most tenacious. The habits of study and reflection which are commenced in early life, usually become permanent. Early improvement promises extensive usefulness. Many young men in our churches are anxiously desirous to avail themselves of those advantages which a literary and theological institution supplies. They are not able to support the inevitable expenses of their subsistence, clothing, washing, books, &c. without the aid of their christian brethren. Let then the churches of Christ zealously exert themselves. How soon their worthy pastors that go in and out before them may be removed they cannot tell. Their liberality may be rewarded, richly rewarded, by obtaining from the candidates they have assisted equal successors in pastoral office. Let generous and pious individuals offer of their substance to the sanctuary of the Lord. Let the rich encourage education societies by their contributions and by their bequests. Such as have duplicates of useful works in their libraries are respectfully and importunately requested to favour this institution with their supernumerary volumes, towards the formation of a library for the use of its students.

The cause is the Lord's. Its aim is the prosperity of the churches, and its supporters will find ample consolation in committing the whole to the protection of the Supreme Head of the church, and in a holy and resolute perseverance to expend their talents and substance to the praise of his glory.

TRANSLATION OF THE SCRIPTURES INTO THE LANGUAGE OF BURMAH

The Baptist Board of Foreign Missions for the United States, with respectful and anxious importunity, address the friends of the holy scriptures. They rejoice that the day has arrived when thousands have their hearts engaged to give universal circulation to the sacred volume. The importance and efficiency of combined exertion are abundantly evinced, and afford encouragement for new endeavours.

Among other indications of human ignorance and misery, it is a fact deserving pity, and which should command beneficence, that the Burmans, a people upwards of 17,000,000 in number, are destitute of the Bible. Missionaries are at Rangoon, among whom is Rev. Mr. Judson, who has made himself master of the language, and is proceeding to translate the holy word; but what will a translation avail without the means of circulating it? Paper must be obtained, and expenses attendant on the printing encountered—and at this moment assistance is loudly called for. And will the christian world permit this important service to be impeded in its career? It is believed they will not! Bible societies it is hoped will afford their aid. Possibly translation societies may be formed, or at least private contributions and public collections obtained, which would immediately facilitate the design, and ultimately accomplish it. The Board affectionately request that their christian brethren will direct their immediate attention to this point, and communicate the sums they may obtain, as early as practicable, to John Cauldwell Esq. the treasurer of the Board, to Rev Luther Rice, its agent, or to

Wm STAUGHTON, Cor Sec

May 7, 1818.

SUBSTANCE OF THE MINUTES OF THE BOARD,
From the time of the meeting of the General Convention to the present time.

AT the quarterly meeting of the Board, on the first Monday in June 1817, pursuant to the recommendation of the Convention on the subject of education, a committee was appointed, consisting of the Rev. Drs. Staughton and Allison, and the Rev Mr Jones, seriously to consider the plan which had been offered to that body by their President, the Rev. Dr. Furman, and to report upon the subject

The following is the result of the deliberations of said committee.

The committee appointed to consider the plan of education submitted to the Convention by the venerable President, the Rev. Dr Furman, beg leave to report:

That, owing to the importance of the subject, and the necessity of waiting the openings of Providence, and the indications of the liberality of their brethren in various parts of the union, they have not been able to return their ideas so fully, or so soon, as they could have wished

They approve, in the main, highly, of the plan the President proposed, and are of opinion that it will ultimately, in substance, probably in a few years, be found in successful operation. They, however, beg leave to state, that until it can be accomplished, and for its accomplishment very ample funds must be obtained, something may be done that will prepare the way for more comprehensive measures. As far as their information extends, and they believe their information correct, many worthy and wealthy friends of Zion are waiting for an opportunity to contribute of their substance for the tuition of pious young men. Were a system commenced, they think several thousands of dollars might easily be collected. At least they feel it a duty respectfully to recommend a trial. If at first the resources were small, they would hope that, like a rill from the foot of a mountain, they would gradually and greatly increase.

The committee believe that no adequate reason can be assigned for farther delay. The public are entitled to expect some vigorous attempt on the part of the Board. For this they are anxiously looking. The Convention has left this business to their sacred charge. Numerous youth are waiting to avail themselves of the privileges of a literary and theological Institution, and the widening sphere of missionary effort already undertaken, renders an accession of godly and educated youth highly desirable. The liberal spirit of the times the committee regards as very favourable to immediate exertion, and they cannot but hope that the blessing of the Lord will accompany an attempt designed, so immediately, for the glory of his holy name.

WM STAUGHTON,
BURGISS ALLISON,
HORATIO G. JONES.

At the quarterly meeting of the Board the first Monday in September last, as it appeared that the American Baptist Magazine and Missionary Intelligencer, recommended to general patronage by the Convention, and designed by the Board, as in part proprietor, to be extensively circulated through the west and south-west, could not be thus circulated without expense instead of profit to the funds, therefore,

Resolved, That the Corresponding Secretary be instructed to write to the Editors of the Magazine on the subject, and that brother Rice also be instructed to proceed to the eastward as soon as practicable to see the members of the Board, particularly in New-York and Boston, about this matter, to acquaint them in detail with our views, and learn theirs, relative to the issuing of a periodical publication under the auspices of the Board, designed to circulate missionary intelligence.

Resolved, That a Circular by the Corresponding Secretary be sent to the Mission Societies, Associations, &c exhibiting the general views and operations of the Board, and particularly what they have done in relation to the western Indians, and the measures they have yet in contemplation.

A letter was received from the Rev Isaac M'Coy in reply to a communication to him, stating his willingness to accept a missionary appointment on the Wabash, whereupon,

Resolved, That he be appointed to that service, and allowed $500 a year, to enable him to carry forward his operations, if possible, among the aborigines in that quarter, and that the Corresponding Secretary be requested to write to him accordingly

A communication was received from the Baptist Education Society in this place, expressing their willingness to co-operate with the Board in the business of education, which was referred to the committee on this subject appointed at a former meeting.

At a meeting of the Board the 6th of October, a communication from the Editors of the American Baptist Magazine, on the subject of a periodical publication by this body being read, and the subject having been fully discussed,

Resolved, unanimously, That this Board enter as soon as convenient upon the prosecution of such a work.

Resolved, That a committee be appointed to carry the above resolution into effect, and that brethren Staughton, Allison, Jones, and Rice be that committee.

At a meeting of the Board October 13th, a letter was received from the Editors of the Magazine, explicitly announcing their acquiescence in the publication of a periodical work by the Board.

A letter from the Rev. Humphrey Posey relative to missionary labours among the Cherokee Indians was read, whereupon,

Resolved, That he be employed in that service, and allowed $500 a year to enable him to carry forward his operations with vigour and effect.

At a meeting of the Board Dec. 18th, letters from our missionaries at Rangoon, brethren JUDSON and HOUGH, dated in March and June 1817, communicating most important and interesting intelligence respecting the state of the mission in Burmah, were read.

Also was read, a letter from the Rev. Dr. Carey at Serampore, with which the Board was highly pleased.

A letter from the Rev. Wm. Ward, Serampore, acknowledging the receipt of $1000 for the translation of the scriptures, and $1000 for the use of the missionaries at Rangoon, was read.

[These have been published in the first number of the Luminary.]

Resolved, unanimously, That in future our transmissions of money to our missionary brethren in the east, shall be one year in anticipation of their demands.

A letter from brother Judson being read, conveying very important information relative to the translation of the bible into the Burman language, and the operations of the press in that empire,

Resolved, unanimously, That the Corresponding Secretary communicate to him with how lively an interest the Board enter into his feelings, and appreciate his labours, and that brethren Staughton and Jones be a committee to devise and bring into effect measures for promoting the translation of the scriptures into the language of Burmah, and to facilitate and enlarge the operations of the press in that country.

Brother Judson having stated the inconvenience resulting from the remote and secluded situation of the mission-house, which prevents that instruction of the natives which might be given in familiar intercourse, and having expressed his wish that they might be enabled to build a house in or near Rangoon:

Resolved, unanimously, That $1500 be appropriated for that purpose.

A letter was received from Thomas L. M'Kenney Esq. Superintendent of Indian

Trade, declaring his readiness to co-operate in the measures adopted by the Board relative to the instruction of the Indians, whereupon,

Resolved, unanimously, That the thanks of the Board be presented to Thomas L. M'Kenney Esq. for his kind and zealous attention to the concerns referred to him by the Board.

At a meeting of the Board the 4th of February, 1818, a communication was received from the Agent relative to the subscription papers, and the means of extensively circulating the Latter Day Luminary - referred to a committee for consideration, viz. brethren Staughton, Peckworth, and Curwen.

The committee, after mature deliberation, reported, that they recommend the subscription paper submitted by our Agent, and that he be authorized to employ assistant agents in certain cases to arrange the business for obtaining subscribers and circulating the Luminary in particular sections of the country.

Resolved, unanimously, That this report be accepted.

Resolved, That the attention of the Board be directed to the obtaining of a suitable person, to commence a school among the Chickasaw tribe of Indians.

ANNUAL MEETING OF THE BOARD, APRIL 29, 1818.

At this meeting were present.—THOMAS SHIELDS Esq. 1st Vice President, WILLIAM STAUGHTON D D Corresponding Secretary, Rev HORATIO G. JONES, Recording Secretary, Rev. JAMES M'LAUGHLIN, Rev JOHN P PECKWORTH, and Mr JOHN BRADLEY of Philadelphia, Rev THOMAS ROBERTS, and Mr GEORGE F CURWEN near Philadelphia, Rev JOHN HEALEY of Baltimore, Rev SPENCER H CONE of Alexandria; and Rev ELISHA CUSHMAN of Hartford, Connecticut.

The meeting was opened with prayer by the Rev Mr Healey.

The Rev Mr JUDSON of Plymouth, Mass father of the Rev ADONIRAM JUDSON, missionary at Rangoon; the Rev Mr CHASE from Vermont, the Rev Mr BRIGGS, from Hudson, N Y and the Agent of the Board, Mr. RICE, being present, were invited to sit with the Board.

The proceedings of the Board from the time of the late triennial Convention were read.

A general letter from the Agent of the Board was communicated by the Corresponding Secretary.

Burman Mission.

An account of the expenditures attending the outfit and passages of brethren Wheelock and Colman for Burmah, transmitted by the Rev Dr Baldwin, chairman of the eastern Committee to whom this business had been referred, was laid before the Board, and gave great satisfaction.

An appropriation of $1500 voted at a former meeting for the purpose of enabling the missionaries to procure or build a house, greatly needed for their accommodation and usefulness, in Rangoon, or quite near it, was considered; and the Board, under a persuasion of the importance of the object, expressed a willingness to enlarge the sum should that appropriation be found insufficient.

Resolved, That all the monies now in the hands of the Treasurer specially designated *for the translation* of the scriptures, and the additional sum of $1000 be transmitted to India for the use of our missionaries in the translation and printing department of the mission.

Resolved, That the Publishing Committee be instructed to prepare and publish an address on the subject of the translation of the scriptures into the language of Burmah, and the operations of the press in that empire.

A letter from the Rev Jonathan Price, soliciting the patronage of the Board as a missionary to Burmah, with the view of going to that country in the character of a physician, was communicated by the Corresponding Secretary.

Resolved, That he be requested to present himself for examination at the next meeting of the Board, and that, if approved, he be accepted, and instructed to enter, as our missionary, upon the study of medicine.

Western Missions

A LETTER from the Rev Mr Ranaldson, communicating very important information from Louisiana, and soliciting additional missionary aid, transmitting at the same time five hundred dollars from the Mississippi Mission Society, was read, whereupon,

Resolved, That the Corresponding Secretary convey through Mr Ranaldson, to the aforesaid Mission Society, our grateful acknowledgment for their liberal aid, and that the Board will find pleasure in sending more missionaries into that quarter as soon as practicable, and that the Secretary also make known to Mr Ranaldson the high opinion we entertain of his useful and active services in Louisiana.

A letter from the Rev. Mr Posey, missionary among the Cherokees, was read, giving an interesting description of the country and the natives where he labours. He has set up four schools for the instruction of the Indian children, at an expense of forty dollars per quarter for each assistant teacher.

Resolved, That it is expedient to support these schools.

The mission to St Louis was taken into consideration. Letters from brethren Peck and Welch at that station, of a very interesting nature, and very satisfactory, together with a transcript from their journal, were laid before the Board. In reply to these communications,

Resolved, That the Board regard with the warmest approbation their solemn articles of agreement in a missionary family or society, that we possess a lively satisfaction that they have, by the mercy of the Lord, succeeded in forming a church in that place, and are taking measures for the erection of a place for public worship; and that, in relation to Indian schools, the Board earnestly press upon them to prosecute the measure to the utmost. They conceive, however, that such schools will be best supported in the vicinity of the tribes, as this will be most likely to excite a desire after education generally, and to satisfy such desire. In special cases some might with advantage be instructed in the higher branches of learning, to qualify them to teach others.

Resolved, That, conformably with the importunate pleadings of the missionaries at St Louis, for more labourers in that field, the Board will send others into that quarter as soon as practicable.

A communication from the Rev. Mr. M'Coy was referred to the next meeting of the Board, in the expectation that further information from him will then have come to hand.

Brethren Cone and Cushman were appointed a committee to audit the accounts of the Agent.

This committee reported that, upon careful examination, they found that the

Agent had received 5443 dollars and 57 cents; that the expenditures connected with the business allotted him, amounted to 1963 dollars and 67 cents. All appeared correct, and displayed great minuteness and accuracy.

Resolved, That, conformably to a request of the Treasurer, John Cauldwell Esq of New York, whose indisposition did not permit him to meet with the Board, a committee be appointed to audit his accounts in that city, and that the Rev Messrs Cone, Williams, and Maclay be that committee.

Institution to Promote Education

Pursuant to the recommendation on the part of the Convention, of the plan submitted to that body by the President, and the report of the committee to whom that important subject had been referred,

Resolved, unanimously, That it is expedient to enter actively into the prosecution of vigorous measures to improve the education of pious young men, possessed of gifts and graces suited, in the judgment of the churches, to the christian ministry.

Resolved, unanimously, That, in addition to the co-operation proffered by the Baptist Education Society in Philadelphia, a union with which, it is believed, may prove a germ whence many important advantages may grow, the education societies existing in different parts of our country be affectionately invited also to co-operate in the present effort to accomplish the important object in view.

Resolved, unanimously, That the Agent be instructed to encourage the formation of other education societies, auxiliary if they think proper to the Institution connected with the Board, and that he make such collections, and obtain such donations, as he may be able, for the advancement of this interesting concern.

Resolved, unanimously, That a committee of five be appointed to make arrangements with the Education Society relative to the Institution contemplated, and to carry the intentions of the Board into full effect, and that brethren Staughton, M'Laughlin, Jones, Peckworth and Curwen be that committee.

Resolved, unanimously, That the Rev Dr Staughton be appointed Principal in the Institution, and the Rev Ira Chase, a young brother of piety, talents and learning, Professor of Languages and Biblical Literature.

Resolved, unanimously, That, inasmuch as the enlarging of the missionary operations, the editing of the Luminary, and the concerns of the Institution for improving the education of pious young men called to the ministry, make great and increasing demands on the time of the Corresponding Secretary, the Agent be authorized and instructed to press his solicitations for augmenting the special fund provided for in the constitution for this department, and at discretion request public contributions for this object, and that wealthy and liberal individuals, and the public at large, be invited to aid this important design.

Resolved, That the Rev H G Jones prepare an address, and that the Publishing Committee issue without delay the annual Report. Adjourned.

TABLE OF ASSOCIATIONS.

Associations	Sts	C.	M	Bap	Tot.	Correspondents	Times of meetings	Places of meeting
Bowdoinham	Me.	36	31	301	2090	Thomas Francis, Leeds, Kennebec co	4 Wed. 23 Septemb.	1h. 2nd ch in Bowd.
Lincoln	Me.	52	35		29 7	Phinehas Pilsbury, Nobleboro Lincoln co	3 Wed. 16 Sept	Last n. m. not recd
Cumberland	Me.	26	24	470	1902	John Tripp, Hebron, Cumberland co	Wed af 4 Wd 30 Sep	Portland, Cumbr d
New Hamp.	N H	24	26	60	2051	Timothy Hodson, Hollis, York co. Me	3d Wednes. 10 June	Wells 1 pa Yorke
Meredith	N H	9	11	26	1004	Stephen Pilsbury, Hebron, Grafton co	2 Wed. ies. 9 Sept	Lyme, Grafton co
Dublin	N H	16	11	48	775	John Parkhurst, New Ipswich, Hills co	3 Wednes. 20 Oct	Westmoreld. Che
Shaftsbury	Vt	32	23	510	3363	Ely. F. Willey, Lansingbg. Rens co. N.Y	1 Wednes 3 June	Shaftsb'ry, Bennin
Woodstock	Vt	25	2	178	2141	Gen. Abner Forbes, Windsor, Windsor co	Last Wed 30 Sep	New Lon. New Har
Vermont	Vt	7	5	366	1540	John Conant Esq. Brandon, Rutland co	1 Wednes. 7 Oct	Pultney, Rut. coun
Fairfield	Vt	15	6	209	848	Roswell Meers, Georgia, Franklin co	1st Wed. 26 Aug	Enosbrg. Franklin
Barre	Vt	13	6	65	453	Elijah Huntington, Brainard, Orange co	3 Wednes. 16 Sept	Bethel meeting hou
Danville	Vt.	7	5	124	297	Daniel Mason, Craftsbury. Orleans co	3 Wednes. 17 June	St. Johnsbury ch Lam
Leyden	Ms.	26	23		1746	Elijah Montague, Leverett, Franklin co	2 Wed. 14 Oct	Last m m. not recd
Sturbridge	Ms.	25	2	150	2433	Zenas L. Leonard, Sturbridge, Wor. co	1st Wed. 26 Aug	Sturbridge, Worces
Boston	Ms.	35	28	399	3609	Lucius Bolles, Salem, Essex county	3 Wed. 16 Septemb	Woburn, Middlesex
Westfield	Ms	10	8	76	643	Elijah Arnold, Westfield Hampshire co	1st Wed 2 Septemb	Russell
Warren	R I	30	37	251	47-2	Nathan Waterman Esq. Providence	Tu ast 1 Wen. 8 Sep	Bridge tr Plymou
Stonington Meet	R I	17	14		1395	Philo Slade, Swansey, Bristol co Mas	1nd b.2 Sab 1 Sep	Last m m not reed
New London	Ct.	16	23	226	2 11	Jonathan Goddard, Mansfield, Wind co	3 Tuesday 20 Oct	2 ch. Saybrook, Mid
Stonington Un.	Ct.	10	11	15	1452	Roswell Burrows, Groton, New Lon co	Wed 1.3 Sab 24 Ju	Ft. Hill, 2d Gro N la
Hartford	Ct.	26	22	114	2120	Elisha Cushman, Hartford, Hartford co	1st Wednes. 7 Oct	Bristol, Hartford
New York	N. Y.	25	2	125	1775	William Parkinson, New York city	Last Wed 27 May	Scotch Plns 1 sca N
Warwick	N. Y	10	10		1403	Aaron Perkins, near Poughkeepsie	1 W d. 3 June	Last m m. not reed
Otsego	N. Y	30	13	409	2000	Caleb Douglass, Whitestown Oneida co	1st Wednes 2 Sep	2d ch Burlgtn Ones
Chemung	N. Y	14	13		710	Thms. Snyden, near Milton, Northumb. co	1 Wed. 7 Oct	Last m m. not rea
Rensselr.	N. Y	18	16	69	1341	Dea. Hiland Hill, Catskill, Green county	2nd Wednes 14 Oct	Lexington, Greene
Cayuga	N. Y	22	19		3010	Hiaugh Comstock Owasco, Cayuga co	3 Wed. 16 Sep.	Last n m. not recd
Essex	N Y	7	2		426	I L. Stone, Jay, Essex county. New York	3 Wed. 21 Oct.	Last n m. not rec.
Saratoga	N Y	23	17	77	3479	Edward Barber, Greenwich, Wash co	Last Wed. 24 June	Balls. Sprngs Sarat
Black River	N Y	17	12	23	11	Jacob Osgood Rupert Herder Jeff co	2nd Wed. 10 June	Watertown, Jeffer
Madison	N Y	44	33	870	4560	John Peck, Cazenovia, Madison county	2d Wednes. 9 Sep	Delphi in Pmp Ones
Lake George	N. Y.	5	4	64	240	Jehiel Fox, Chester, Warren county	3 Wed 16 Sep.	Athol
Union	N Y	13	9	30	534	Job Fuss, Dover, Dutches county	1 Wed 2 Sep.	N. m. h. Stamford
Franklin	N Y	20	18		170	John Lawrence, Hartwick, Otsego co	3 Wed 17 June	Last m m. not reed
Holland Pur	N Y	14	4		495	Joy Handy Fredonia, Chatauque county	Last Wed 27 Aug.	Last m m. not reed
St Lawrence	N. Y.	5	4		59	Jonathan Payne, Gouverneur, St Law co	3 Wed 20 Jan	Last m m. not recd
Ontario	N Y	48	23	437	2711	Solomon Goodale, Bristol Ontario co	4th Wednes 23 Sep	Mendon, Ontario
Hudson Riv.	N Y	6	0	273	1267	Lewis Leonard, Poughkeepsie, Dutches co	1st Wednes. 5 Aug	Milly n, St. m. N
New Jersey	N. J	24	15	160	2000	Joseph Sheppard, Salem, Salem county	3rd Tues. 15 Septem	New Mills, Bridge
Philadelphia	Pa.	25	32	134	3184	George F. Curwen, Walnut Hill, Pa	1st Tuesday 6 Oct	Bud st. m h Phil
Redstone	Pa.	30	24	54	1015	James Estep, Mt. Pleasant, Westmore. co	1 Tues 1 Sep.	Connelsvill Fayett
Abington	Pa.	4	3	12	280	John Miller, Abington, Luzerne county	1st Wednes. 2 Sep	Bethany, Wilk
Delaware	De.	8	5		570	Israel Dodge, Wilmington, Delaware	Sat. b. 1 Sab 5 June	Last m m. not recd
Salisbury	Md.	14	7		450	Stevens Woolford, jr. Laingers Dor. co	Sat. b. 1 Sab 24 Oct.	Last m m. not recd
Baltimore	Md.	20	20	168	1206	Sumner B Cone Alexandria, Dist. Col	Thus. b. 2 Sb 10 Sep.	Patapsco m h. 1 ak
Ketockton	Va	38	14	154	2382	Thornton Stringfellow, Fauquier co	1st b 3 Sab 13 Aug	Grove m. h. Fauq
Strawberry	Va.	21	10			John S. Lee, Lynchburgh Campbell co	As year before	Not known
Dover	Va.	43	20			John Biver, Richmond, Virginia	2nd Saturday 10 Oct	Mattews m h
Middle Dist.	Va	9	9			Benjamin Watkins, Powhatan county	2nd Sat. 10 October.	Liberty m h Am
Roanoke	Va	30	19		2840	Jul n Jenkins, n. Grasty's store, Pittsyl co	As year before	Last m m. not recd
Portsmouth	Va.	21	15	263	2321	James Mitchell, Norfolk, Virgin	Sat b. 2's b. 3 June	Norfolk, Norfolk co
Albemarle	Va.	11	11			Martin Dawson, in Warren, Albem. co	As year before.	Last m m. not recd
Goshen	Va.	26	15			Absalom Waller, Spotsylvania county	1st Tuesday, 5 Sep	Loster's Cr. Louisa
Shiloh	Va	20	13	54	1625	Richard I. Tutt Esq. Culpepper county	Fri b. 1st 5 b 4 Sep	Smith's cr. m h. Sh
New River	Va	8	5		325	Jesse Jones, W. fork, Lit. Riv. Mont. co	2d S. t. 11 June	L k's cr Montgt
Mayho	Va.	15	14			Ezy Jewell, Rockingham county N C	A year b june.	Last m m not recd
Appomattox	Va.	15	15			Richard Dabbs, Keysvile, C lott co	4th h 1st Sab.2 May	Bucking rh Pur
Meherrin	Va.	18	8	130	571	Dan. J Saunders, n. Perce d's, Brunsc co	at b 4 sb 25 April	Laurel Hill, Bruns
Union	Va	18	9		517	Joshua Hickman Morgantown	1 b last Sab 2 Aug	Buckhannon Law
Green Brier	Va	5	5		119	Joseph Osborn, Lewisburgh, Green B co	Fri b. 25 sb. 11 Sep	Big Levels Chur
Accomack	Va.					Thomas Costin Lower Do thing to	Sat 3 Sab. 15 Aug	Me tompkin m h.
Washington	Va.	15	6	27		Eby Gillingwater, Esq. Washington co	2nd Friday 11 Sep	N York m h. Wash
Tears Valley	Va	12	9			John Young, n. Greenupsburgh, Ky	Fri b 4 Sab. 21 Au	Last m m. not recd
Sandy Creek	N C	11			701	Robt. P Daniel n. Pittsboro, Chatham co	Sat. 24 Oct.	Last m m not rec
Kehukee	N. C				175	Isaac Reed n. Halifax, Halifax county	Sat. b. 1st Sab 3 Oct	Iskewark y mdav
Yadkin	N. C				510	Josh Wright E q. Hampton ville S co	1st Sat. 3 October	Bethell m h. Ire
Flat River	N C	10	9	17	11	Elijah Bards, Oxford, Granvill count	1 b 3 Sab 17 Oct	Cedar Creek mh
Neuse	N C					Thomas P Biddie, n. Newbern, Craven co.	Sat b. 3 Sab 17 Oct	Sandy Bottom, L

Associations	Sts	C	M	Ba	Tot.	Correspondents	Times of Meetings	Places of Meetings
Mountain	N. C.	14	12		646	Reuben Coffey, n. Ft. Defiance, Wilkes co	4th Satur. 22 August	Mulberry m h Wkes. c.
Cape Fear	N. C.	29	8	48	1476	Charles M'Alister, Esq. n Fayetteville	Sat. b. 1st. Sab. 3 Oct	Limestone m h Dup c.
Chowan	N. C.	22	13	138	2013	George Outlaw, Esq. Bertie co.	Sat. b. 4 Sab. 23 May	Sawyers cr.m h Cam. c.
Country Line	N. C.	12	11		1031	Geo. Roberts, n. Brown's store, Caswell co	3d Satur. 15 August	last m. not come to hand
Raleigh	N. C.	18	10	20	731	John Purify, near Raleigh, Wake county	Sat. b. 2 Sab. 7 Nov.	Union m.h. Johnson co.
French Broad	N. C.	15	12		598	James Whitaker, Esq. n. Buncombe county	Day b. 4 Sab. 22 Aug.	last m. not come to hand
Pee Dee	N. C.	10	7		637	John Culpeper, n. Allentown, Montg. co.	Sat. b. 3 Sab. 17 Oct.	last m. not come to hand
Charleston	S. C.	37	27	262	3695	Wood Furman, Esq. Charleston, S. C	Sat b.1 Sab. No.31 Oc.	H Hills of Sant. Cl. Dis.
Bethel	S. C.	36	29		2159	Sam M'Creary, Beckamville, Ches. Dist	Day b. 1 Sab. 3 Oct	last m. not come to hand
Broad River	S. C.	26	18		1519	Wm. Lancaster, Esq. Mt. Astrea Spart. D.	Fri. b. 3 Sab. 16 Oct.	last minutes not rec'd
Saluda	S. C.	27	10	11	1143	James Crowther, Abbeville District	Sat. b. 2 Sab. 8 Aug	Hopewell m.h. Pen. Dis.
Edgefield	S. C.	42	13	21	2445	Joseph King, Edgefield District	Sat. b 3 Sab 19 Sep.	Div cr m.h. Edge. Dis
Moriah	S. C.					Mr Pegg, Chester District	The minutes of this	have never been obt'd
Georgia	Geo.	36	24	36	2951	Jesse Mercer, Powelton, Hancock county	Sat. b. 2 Sab. 10 Oct.	Powelton, Hancock co.
Hephzibah	Geo.	31	19		1827	Charles I. Jenkins, Esq. near Louisville	Sat. b. 4 Sab. 25 Sep	last min. not obtained
Sarepta	Geo.	47	21	35	2830	Isham Goss, Oglethorpe county	Sat. b. 4 Sab. 24 Oct.	M tts Hill, Clarke co.
Savannah R	Geo.	33	9	195	5771	Thomas S. Winn, Riceboro, Liberty co.	Sat. b. 4 Sab 24 Oct	H Spring Barn D.S.C.
Emulgee	Geo.	39	21	26	2411	Frances Flournoy, Madison, Morgan co	Sat. b. 1 Sab. 5 Sept.	Crooked cr Putnam co.
Ebenezer	Geo.	19	11		681	Ezek. Taylor, Esq n. Hartford, Pulaski c.	Sat. b. 2 Sab. 12 Sept	last min. not obtained
Piedmont	Geo.	5	2	3	109	Wilson Conner, Sarepta ch.	Sat. b. 2 Sab. 10 Oct.	Wesley ct m.h. M'In c.
Sunbury	Geo.					Charles O'Scriven, Sunbury, Liberty co.	Sat. b. 4 Sab. 7 Nov	Sunbury, Liberty co
Flint River	Ala.	22	16	9	1213	Willis Hopwood, n. Shelbyville, Bed. c. T.	Sat. b. 1 Sab 3 Oct.	Fount. cr m h Mau. c. T.
Rigby	Ala.	5	3		118	Jacob Parker, Wayne county, Ala. Ter	Sat. b. 1 Sab 3 Oct	last min. not obtained
Mississippi	Mis.	31	21		1144	Wm. Snodgrass, Esq. Natchez, Adams co	Sat b. 3 Sab 17 Oct.	last min. not obtained
Holston	Ten.	18	19	148	1985	Jona Mulkey, Buffaloe Ridge, Wash. co.	2d Friday, 14 August	County Line m h Gre
Tennessee	Ten.	29	41	50	1675	W Walker, on Clynch 20m.f.Knoxv.Knoxc.	1st Satur. 3 October	Dumplin cr. m.h. Jef c.
Cumberland	Ten.	29	30	26	1555	Garner M'Connico, n. Franklin, Winson c.	Sat. b. 3 Sab. 19 Sep.	W Harpeth m h Wm. c.
Red River	Ten.	24	23	36	1995	Sugg Fort, Port Royal, Montgomery co	Sat. b. 2 Sab. 8 Aug	Barren Sp Chris. co. K.
Elk River	Ten.	27	13	21	1412	Hardy Holeman, Lincoln county	2 Sat. 12 September	New Hope m h Bedf c.
Concord	Ten.	35	26	90	2372	R.C. Foster, Esq. Farmer's Joy, Dav'dson c.	Fr. b. 1 Sab 4u 31 Jul	Wilson's cr. m.h. Wn c.
Stoney Fork	Ten.	11	12	17	472	George Dawson, Esq. Sparta, White co.	4 Sat. 26 September	Parker's m.h Bledsoe.
Re formed	Ten.					Garner M'Connico, near Franklin	Sat b 1 Sab. 5 Sept	Barton's creek m h. Je.
Elkhorn	Ky.	30	12	503	3205	Silas M Noel, Oakley, Franklin county	2nd Satur. 8 August	S. Elkhorn m h Fay. c.
Salem	Ky.	31	12	153	1809	Gen. Joseph Lewis, Bardstown, Nelson c.	4th Frid 25 Septem.	Simpson's cr m.h Ne Lc.
Tate's Creek	Ky.	18	16	32	1153	Wm.Goodloe, Esq. n.Richmond Madison c.	4th Satur. 22 August	Mt. Nebo, Madison co.
Bracken	Ky.	15	12		958	Walter Warder, May's Lick, Mason co.	1st Sat. 5 September	last min. not obtained
Green River	Ky.	17	9		1143	Michael W. Hall, Esq n. Glasgow, B. co.	Fri b. 4 Sab 24 July	last min. not obtained
North Bend	Ky.	17	15		868	Absalom Graves, Bulletsburg, Boone co.	4 Frid. 25 September	last min. not obtained
North District	Ky.	31	11		1311	James Mason, Esq n. Mt.Sterling, Mont. c.	4 Saturday, 25 July	last min. not obtained
South Dist.	Ky.	17	8	122	1164	William Sturman, Perryville, Mercer co.	3d Satur. 15 August	Union m.h. Mercer co.
Long Run	Ky.	33	26	621	3117	George Waller, Buck creek, Shelby co	1st Frid. 4 September	Drinn's cr m New.H.c.
Russell's Cr.	Ky.	18	15	45	1019	J Chandler, Stuart's cr.n.Campbellsv.G.c.	3d Satur. 19 Septem.	Brush cr m.h. Gree. c.
Stockton's V.	Ky.	15	8	17	762	Wm.Wood, Esq. Stockton's Val. Cumb. c.	3d Satur 15 August	Spring cr. m.h. Ow c T
Emancipat.	Ky.	7	9		213	David Barrow, n. Mt. Sterling, Montg. c.	Sat. b. 2 Sab. 12 Sep.	Gilgal, Shelby county
Licking	Ky.	21	7	24	874	Ambrose Dudley, n. Bryan's Stat. Fay. co.	2d Satur. 12 Septem.	Mill cr. m.h. Harrison c.
Cumb. River	Ky.	18	13	5	720	Thos. Paschal, Esq. Somerset, Pulaski co.	1st Satur. 5 Septem.	Fishing cr. m h. Pulas. c.
Gasper River	Ky.	25	18	12	1099	Dea. Ed. Collins, n. Russellville, Logan c.	Sat. b. 4 Sab. 22 Aug.	Walton's cr. ch. Ohio c.
Little River	Ky.	31	29		1013	Thomas Ross, near Dover, Stuart co. Te	Sat. b. 3 Sab 15 Aug.	last min. not obtained
Burning Spr.	Ky.	12	10	3	359	Samuel Hanna, Buffaloe Shoal, Floyd co.	1st Satur. 3 October	Red river m.h. Floyd c.
Union	Ky.	6	4		340	Arche. Vanhook, Esq Cynthiana, Har. c.	3d Satur. 19 Septem.	last min not obtained
Franklin	Ky.	12	9	351	1083	John Scott, n. Port William, Gallatin co.	1st Friday, 7 August	S. Benson m.h. Frank. c.
Union-South	Ky.	8	5		242	Peter Engle, Esq. Barbourville, Knox co.	Frid b. 4 Sat. 25 Sep.	Barbourville, Knox co.
No one.	Ky.					James H. L. Moorman, Breckenridge co.	Time of meeting not	known, min. not rec d.
Miami	Ohio	28	14		1083	John Mason, Sugar cr. Warren county.	Sat. b. 2 Sab. 12 Sept.	last min. not obtained
Scioto	Ohio	13	10	27	457	Samuel Comer, n. Lancaster, Fairfield co.	Sat b 4 Sab. 26 Sept.	Deer cr m.h. Ross co
Beaver	Ohio	18	9	66	701	William West, Youngstown, Trumbull co.	Thur b.4 Sab.20 Aug.	Wooster ch. Wayne co.
Straight Cr	Ohio	6	4		103	Thomas Ellrod, n. West Union, Adams co.	Fri. b. 4 Sab. 21 Aug	last min. not obtained
Muskingum	Ohio	16	12	70	684	Jacob Drake, Delaware, Delaware county	Th. b. 4 Sab. 20 Aug.	Hopewell ch. Furfd. c.
Mad River	Ohio	14	14		366	John Thomas, Urbanna, Champaign co.	Fri. b. 4 Sab. 18 Sept.	last min. not obtained
Little Miami	Ohio	8	4	47	381	James Jones, Indian Hill, Hamilton co.	Sat. b. 1 Sab. 5 Sept.	Clough—co. not known
Grand River	Ohio	5	4		160	Azariah Hanks, Chardon, Geauga county	2nd Wed 9 Septem.	Kinsville—co unknown
Wabash	Ind.	12	7	20	380	Isaac M'Coy, n. Vincennes, Knox county	Sat. b. 1 Sab 3 Oct.	Patoka m h Gibson co.
White Water	Ind	18	12		998	Ezra Ferris, Lawrenceburg, Dearborn co.	Frid b. 2 Sat. 7 Aug.	last min. not obtained
Silver Creek	Ind.	14	9	118	401	Rice G. M'Coy, Charleston, Clark county	4th Satur. 22 August	Silver creek m house
Blue River	Ind.	17	12	70	581	James M'Coy, Esq. Salem, Washington c	2d Satur. 12 Septem.	Sinking Sp m h. Wa. c.
Illinois	M.T.	9			216	John M. Peck, St. Louis, Missouri Ter	Not known	min. not yet obtained
Missouri	M.T.	6			114	James E. Welsh, St. Louis, Missouri Ter	Frid b. 4 Sat 21 Oct.	Femme Osage, St. Ch. c.
Ab. Gen. Con.	USA	10	11		1934	William Stillman, Hopkinton, R Island	Thur.b.2 Sab. 10 Sep	last min. not obtained

* Bethel, 7 churches, Missouri Ter. Todd's Fork, 6 churches, Ohio Total, 138 associations—2682 churches—
? ministers—12,270 baptized—172,085 members in 125 associations; probably, in all the associations, 190,000

BAPTIST BOARD OF FOREIGN MISSIONS IN ACCOUNT WITH J CAULDWELL, ESQ. THEIR TREASURER

Dr.

1817.		D. C.
May 10	To draft for Stationary &c. to Dr. Staughton, (for 3 years)	54 00
10	do for Sexton for attending Convention	11 06
10	do Mess Peck and Welch, Missionaries 1000—to two bad notes 10	1010 00
June 5	Curcier & Co as per order	360 00
28	Rev L. Rice as per order 62 50—to a counterfeit Baltimore note 10	72 50
July 9	freight, &c. of Reports 2 75—to order for printing Reports 498 56	501 31
9	porterage of Reports	25
Aug 18	cash draft for outfit of Mess Colman and Wheelock	400 00
Sept 16	Mr Rice as per order	15 00
Oct 2	W W Woodward on account of Rev J. A Ranaldson	250 00
23	Exchange of Foreign notes	10 49
26	do on a remittance from the Redstone Association	8 43
28	cash as per order of the Board, May 15	1560 00
28	do for passage of Mess C & W 800—to counterfeit note Maryland 5	805 00
Nov. 10	cash Mess Judson & Hough, as per order of the Board, May 15	3000 00
22	cash for 5000 New York State Stock Com &c.	5087 69
24	loss on tickets from Catskill	2 81
Dec 1	draft by the President	513 00
1818		
Jan 29	dolls. per ship Edward 3240—premium on do. 113 40—commission 8 32	3361 72
29	shipping expense, &c	3 00
Mar 16	cash J A Ranaldson	250 00
19	cash Mess Peck and Welch	600 00
Apr 16	Rev Isaac M'Coy, Missionary 109 50—postages 7 46½	116 96½
24	postage	54
May 4	dft Rev L Rice 1967 67—to do Rev Cushman 34	2001 67
4	do Mr G Curwin 20—to do. Rev Mr Healy 18—to do S. H Cone 24 56	62 56
4	ballance due	3292 60½
		23860 60

CONTRA,

Cr

1817		D C.
May 10	By balance due the Board	10051 63
13	Rev Dr Furman from Mrs H Townsend, Charleston, S Carolina	100 00
13	Mr Thomas Swain, New Mills, New Jersey, F M S	114 66
14	Rev L Rice, Washington Baptist Society, F M S	300 00
21	Rev S Goodale, Ontario, N. Y. do	62 00
21	Rev A Bechec, Skaneateles, Onondaga county, N Y F. M S	100 25
27	Rev Jesse Mercer, Powelton, Hancock county, Geo.	550 00
27	do. do. do. Ocmulgee Baptist Society, Geo. do	310 19
27	do. do. do. Sarepta do Geo. do.	100 00
27	do. do Georgia Association	57 00
29	A. Runyan, esq East Jersey, F M S	100 00
31	B Hastings, esq. Westfield Association	7 00
June 2	L S Law, esq Sunbury, Geo. F M. S.	113 25
2	do do Female Mite do. do	101 00
2	do do Coloured Brethren do.	21 00
2	Rev B Bates, Bristol and Newport Evangelical Society	13 00
30	J Conant, esq Vermont, Foreign Mission Society	150 00
30	do. do. Addison, Vt do. do do.	10 00
July 5	July quarter Interest on U. S Stock	167 08
8	J Wilson, esq Worcester co. Mass.	100 00
14	Interest on Bank Shares	7 50
14	Rev Dr Furman, Charlestown, from Rev. J. King, Edgefield Associ.	80 00
May 11	Rev B. Watkins, Mid Dist Association, Powhattan county, Va.	121 00
11	Rev J Bryce, Richmond Female Mission Society	250 00
Sept. 22	Hon Mark Harris, Portland, Cumberland Female Mission Society	140 00
23	Hon S. Eddy, Warren Asso 48 77—do. African Mite Soci Providence	12 27
	Amount carried up	13159 73

			D. C.
1817.		Amount brought up	
Sept. 23	By Hon. S. Eddy, Individuals		3 00
26	Rev. J. Segar, Red Stone Association, Penn.		167 00
Oct. 4	Oct. quarter Interest on United States' Stock		167 98
13	J. Skelding, esq. Female Foreign Mission Society		71 50
13	Rev. William Gammel, Mass Female Mission Society		60 00
16	General A. Forbes, Windsor Union Society		200 00
20	Rev. Caleb Douglas, Utica, N. Y. do.		767 38
Nov. 14	Deacon H. Hill, Catskill Northern District Society		149 93
14	Mrs. K. Hill, Catskill Female do.		43 37
15	Rev. S. Goodale, Holland Purchase Association		65 70
15	do. do. Ontario do.		31 00
15	do. do. Female Society, Farmington		10 00
15	do. do. Ontario Female Mission Society		29 30
28	El. Parson, a donation from Mr. Abn. Mitchell, Turin, Lewis co. N.Y.		75 00
Dec. 2	Rev. L. Austin, Leyden F. Mission Society		100 00
24	James Loring, esq. Boston do. do.		500 00
1818.			
Jan. 2	Interest on United States' Stock		167 98
2	do. do. New York do.		75 00
2	Bank dividend		7 50
29	sale of 2000 6 per cent. 5¼ deducting commission		2099 74
Feb. 17	Rev. J. Mercer, Powelton, Hancock county, Georgia		143 00
Apr. 1	Interest on Public Stock		212 98
3	D. Adams, esq. Charleston F. Mission Society		639 00
3	do. do. Mrs. M'Nair, towards a Theological Seminary		100 00
3	do. do. Mr. Lawson, translation		10 00
3	Rev. E. Barber, from an unknown person		2 00
10	Female Cent Society, Sunbury, Georgia		200 00
15	Rev. J. W. Griffith, Middleton, Rockland co. N. York		20 00
22	John Torry, Western Con. donation		10 00
22	Joseph B. Gilbert, esq. Cont. Auxiliary Society		300 00
22	Mrs. H. Wildman, Stratfield Mite Society		40 00
24	Rev. William Brantly, Beaufort, South Carolina		50 00
24	Female Board of Foreign Missions, Fredericksburgh		100 00
24	Auxiliary Society at Chapawamsick		40 26
27	J. Wilson, esq. Mid. District Society, Poughkeepsie		100 00
28	Mr. E. Arnold, Westfield 12—do. sale of Reports 2		14 00
28	do. do. translation		1 00
May 4	Rev. L. Rice		3387 67
			23350 60¾
May 4	balance due the Board		3292 61¼

We the subscribers being appointed a committee to audit the Treasurer's accounts, do certify that we have carefully examined the receipts and expenditures as stated in the above accounts, and do find the balance in the hands of the Treasurer to be three thousand two hundred and ninety-two dollars sixty-one and a quarter cents, and also certificates of Stock in the hands of the Treasurer, amounting to fourteen thousand four hundred and ninety-nine dollars and fifty-four cents.

ARCHIBALD MACLAY,
JOHN WILLIAMS,
SPENCER H. CONE.

New York, May 4, 1818.

AUXILIARY SOCIETIES, &c. &c.

New Hampshire,	The Foreign Mission Society in Hebron	5 —
	The Female Cent Society in Hebron	15 —
	The Foreign Mission Society in Lyme	7 50
	The Foreign Mission Society in Canaan	5 —
	The Female Cent Society in Canaan	8 —
	The Female Cent Society in Rumney	4 64

These sums, with the addition of 9 86, have been sent by Mr. Pillsbury to the treasurer. *In Maine,* besides the societies mentioned last year, we notice, The Female Mite Society in Fayette, do. in Topsham, do. in Readfield; do. in Brunswick, and the Female Charitable Society in Wayne. These with others in that quarter send their contributions to Dr. Baldwin Boston, through whose hands they go into the missions funds.

MONIES RECEIVED BY THE AGENT OF THE BOARD SUBSEQUENT TO THE
OF MAY, 1817, AND ONWARD TO THE 30th OF APRIL, 1818, VIZ

1817.

			D C
May	10	By the hand of Gen. John S. Gano, of Cincin. Ohio, from the Mad River asso. (omit. bef. by mistake)	40 00
	10	By letter, from the Washington Bap. Soc. for Foreign Missions, District of Columbia,	300 00
June	9	By Deacon Geo. Allen, from the church in Burlington, New Jersey, for preaching,	2 00
	16	By collection, Salem, N. J. credited to the Baptist Missionary Society of New Jersey,	21 00
	16	By a worthy person of the denom. of *Friends* 2—a man of colour 15 cts.—a woman of col. 6 cts	
	16	By Elder Sheppard, from the congregation, for preaching, 12—two other persons 50 cts. each,	13 00
	16	By sale of the third Annual Report of the Board, at different times and places,	1 00
July	28	By collection at the Green River Association, Sinking Creek church, Warren county, Ken.	34 00
Aug.	1	By col. in the court house, Carthage, Smith co. Ten. 18 85—by Mr. Nunley from a man of col. 25 cts.	19 10
	2	By Mr. Harris Bradford, Smith co. Ten. 10—by a methodist preacher, to encourage mis 25 cts.	10 00
	3	By collection, at the Concord Association, Hickmans cr. Smith co. Ten 25 52—by Mr. Brown 25 cts.	25 77
	10	By collection, at the White Water Association Cedar Grove, Franklin county, Indiana,	45 00
	10	By Elder Ferris, from the church in Lawrenceburg 2—from Mr. Wm. Martin 1 do	3 00
	10	By col. in the Baptist meeting house, Cincinnati, Hamilton county, Ohio,	50 00
	11	By Gen. John S. Gano, Cincinnati for the *Education Institution*,	
	12	By Mr. Hewitt, Georgetown, Ky. on being presented with a copy of the Report 1—others 1 50	2 50
	13	By Mr. Ben. Stout Lexington, Ky. per sale of Report 5 58—from others 75 cts	6 33
	17	By col. at the Stocktons Valley Association, Mill Creek church Barren county, Ky.	24 00
	18	By col. at the South District Association Salt River, Mercer co. Ky. (besides one the day before)	10 00
	18	By sale of Report, at South District Association 5 87—by M Smith 2, Kentucky,	7 87
	20	By the hand of James Mason, esq. Montgomery co. Ky. from Mr Nolin for third Report of the Board,	9 00
	21	By capt. Harrison, Mount Sterling, Montgomery co Ky *5 personal*, 5 for the mission, &c.	10 00
	23	By col. at the 'Teass' Valley Association, Storms cr. ch Ohio 28 80—J. Morris 2, *personal*	30 80
	27	By El. Thos. Buck, Rockingham co. Va. on being presented with the Report 1—others elsewhere 1	2 00
Sept.	6	By collection, at the Shiloh Association, Robertson River, Madison co. Va. 41 46—Report 3	44 00
	8	By collection, at the Goshen Association, Zion, Orange co. Va. 122 50—by Mrs. Taylor 1	123 50
	8	By hand of Elder Hiter, from a lady 6 25—another lady 5—another lady 5—Report 6 75	23 00
	12	By col. at the Baltimore Association, Sideling Hill, Bedford co Pa. 4 89 sale of Report 1 25	6 14
	17	By col. at the New Jersey Associat on, Trenton, N. J. credit the Bap. Mission. Society of N. J.	
		By the hand of Elder Boswell, Trenton, N J afterwards, to be added to the same collection,	1 40
	24	By collection in the Baptist m. h. Woburn, Ms. 7 18—by a lady 5—another 50 cts Report 25 cts	12 93
Oct.	2	By collection at the Hartford Association, Wethersfield, Hartford county, Connecticut,	22 00
	8	By collection, at the Philadelphia Association, Southampton, Bucks county, Pennsylvania	35 00
	13	By collection, and added afterwards, at the Dover Association, King and Queen co. Va.	277 00
	17	By Wm Wilson esq. treasurer of the Baltimore Mission Society, Baltimore, Md	29 00
	19	By collection in the Baptist meeting house, Wilmington, Newcastle co. Delaware,	8 00
	26	By collection, Laurel, Sussex county, Delaware, in the methodist meeting house	4 00
	27	By collection, at the Salisbury Association, and part of the collection for visiting ministers,	20 00
Nov.	4	By persons at a meeting at Mr. Red's, 5 87 Caroline co Va—Mr Th Nelson 5, Hanover co. Va	10 87
	4	By Mrs Price 1—Miss Robinson 2—another person 50 cts. Hanover co. Va.	3 50
	4	By Mrs. Frances Greenhow, 4 50—and Miss Mary Daniel 3, for *education*—two Reports 50 cts.	8 00
	6	By collection, at the Raleigh Association, at the Cross Roads meeting house, Wake co. N C.	37 00
	11	By Rev. Elisha Battle, Battle Hall, Granville county, North Carolina,	1 00
	12	By Rev. Wm. Richards 2—Mrs. Richards 1—near Spanish Grove, Mecklenberg co. Va.	3 00
	17	By col. in a methodist m. h. 6 13 Harrisonburg, Rockingham co. Va.—Rev. D. Baker, presb. 2	8 13
	19	By Anthony Miller 50 cts.—Wm Warder 50 cts. *Luminary*, near Finville Mills, Hardy co. Va	1 00
	23	By col. in a Presbyterian m. h. Pittsburg, Pa. 46 60—hand of Mr. Belden 50 cts.—Mr. Prentice 3	50 10
	24	By collection, in the court house, Washington, Washington county, Pennsylvania,	12 00
	25	By collection, at an evening meeting in Wheeling, Ohio county, Virginia,	9 00
	27	By collection, at an evening meeting in the Presbyterian m. h. Zanesville, Ohio,	11 00
	30	By collection, Chilicothe, Ohio, 23 50—a little boy *for the missionaries* 25 cts.—another 50 cts.	24 25
Dec.	1	By persons at an evening meeting 4—Mr Armstrong 5—Mr Luckey 3—West Union, Ohio	12 00
	2	By Mr. Wheatley 50 cts—persons at a meeting, Maysville, Ky. 5 50—Washington do. 10	16 00
	2	By Rev. Robert Wilson, Washington, Mason county, Kentucky for the *Luminary*,	1 00
	5	By persons at an evening meeting, Georgetown, Ky. 6—Col. J. Johnson, Great Crossings 10,	16 00
	7	By persons at Shawney Run meeting 4 56—Harrodsburg 3 57—Capt Moore 5, Ky	13 13
	8	By persons at an evening meeting, Bardstown, Nelson county Kentucky,	6 00
	9	By collection, in the methodist meeting house, Louisville, Jefferson county, Kentucky,	23 00
	10	By collection, in the methodist meeting house, Shelbyville, Shelby county, Kentucky,	14 00
	12	By collection, Versailles 13—collection in the Presbyterian m. h. Frankfort 47 43	60 00
	15	By collection in the Lancasterian school room, Lexington, Fayette county, Kentucky,	25 00
	15	By persons at an evening meeting, Richmond, Madison co. Ky. 13 62—Mr Joseph Lees 4,	17 00
	16	By Mrs. Barnett, Madison county, Kentucky, 1—Wm. Wood, esq. for Reports 1	2 00
	17	By persons at an evening meeting, Campbellsville, Green county, Kentucky,	4 50
	18	By persons at an evening meeting, Glasgow, Barren county, Kentucky,	13 00
	21	By collection, of which 2 are for the African mission, Nashville, Davidson co. Ten.	25 00
		Amount carried up	1736 00

Fourth Annual Report of the Board.

		D.	C.
	Amount brought up	1736	47
1817.			
21	By Elder James Whitsett, from the West Tennessee Baptist Auxiliary Mission Society	50	00
22	By collection at an evening meeting in Franklin, Williamson county, Tennessee	30	50
23	By Elder M'Connico, for Report 20—collection in Murfreesborough, 10 50, Tenessee	10	50
24	By Solomon Beasley, esq. near Murfreesborough, Rutherford county, Tennessee	1	00
27	By Mrs Lewis, near Nashville, Ten. 3 75—sale of Reports of the Board 50 cts.	4	25
28	By persons at Cedar Lick meeting, Wilson co. 3 20—Mr Betts, near Lebanon, 1—others 1	5	20
28	By Thomas Edwards, Lebanon, Wilson co. 4—Henry H. Howell 1—Mrs Bartlett 50 cts	5	50
29	By persons at an evening meeting at Capt Dale's, Liberty, Smith county, Ten.	2	50
30	By persons at an evening meeting 3 77—Mr. Dawson 2—Report 50 cts. Sparta, Ten.	6	27
1818.			
January 2	By Elder West Walker, Knox co. Te. on a subscription for the Luminary	9	50
3	By collection in the Methodist m. h. Knoxville, Te. 7—Rev. Mr. Sherman, 5	12	00
4	By persons at a meeting at Col. Roddye's Jefferson co. Tennessee	2	00
4	By Dr Deaderick, secretary of Holston Association Mission Society, auxil. to the board	193	00
4	By Elder Isaac Barton, near Panther springs, Jefferson co. Te. for Luminary	1	35
5	By sale of Reports 75 cts.—collection 13 06, Jonesboro, Washington co. Te	13	81
6	By Mr King, near Blountville, Te. 5—collection in Blountville, 10 14	15	14
8	By E. Gillingwaters, esq. from Elders Thomas Colley and Wm. Laswell, Va. for Report	1	00
8	By Mr Hubbell, after preaching, 1—Mrs. Hubbell, 1—another 50 cts—another 13 Washington co Va	2	63
12	By Mr. William Holmes, near Newbern, Montgomery co. Va.		62
14	By persons after preaching, at the house of Mr Absalom Dempsey Fincastle, Bottetourt co. Va.	1	38
15	By persons at a meeting at Mr Jac. Eckhols, Liberty, Bedford co. Va. 8 65—another 1 afterwards	9	65
16	By Mr. Eckhols 2—and from Rev. Mr. Leftwich 5—on a subscription for the Luminary	7	00
16	By persons, after preaching, at the house of Mr. John Teass, New London, Campbell co. Va.	3	25
17	By the hand of Rev. John S Lee, Lynchburg, Campbell co Va. from a lady	5	00
18	By collection in the Presbyterian m. h. Lynchburg, ea. to the Mission and Mite Societies there	127	00
18	By collection in the Methodist m. h. Lynchburg, cr. as above to the two Societies there	77	00
19	By collection in the Presbyterian m. h. Lexington, Rockbridge co. Va.	21	76
19	By Mr. Valentine Mason, Lexington, Rockbridge co. Va. on a subscription for the Luminary	8	50
20	By Mrs. Steele, near Lexington, Rockbridge co Va.	5	00
21	By collection in the Presbyterian place of worship, Staunton, Augusta co Va.	14	66
21	By Mr. J. C Sowers, after, from a poor lady 12 cts.—others 10 dolls.—subsc. for the Luminary 2	13	12
21	By collection in Harrisonburg, Rockingham co. Va. in the Methodist meeting house	13	60
21	By Mr. John Lincoln 2—on sub. for the Luminary 2—Rev. Thos. Buck on sub. for Luminary 1 50	5	50
22	By collection in the Baptist m h. New Market, Shenandoah co Va	13	82
22	By Elder Jacob Hirshberger, near New Market, Shenandoah co. Va sub. for Luminary	6	10
22	By collection, Luray, Shenandoah co. 17 50—four persons afterwards 1	18	50
22	By Wm. R. Almond, Luray Shenandoah co. Va on subscription for the Luminary	5	00
23	By persons after preaching at the Baptist m h. near Center Mill and Milford, Shenandoah co Va.	9	25
23	By collection in the Methodist m. h. Front Royal, Frederick co. Va.	16	26
23	By Rev S.O.Hendron, near Millwood, Fred co Va 7 50—Rev. Wm C Buck, near Strasburg 3 for Lum.	10	50
24	By Thomas Buck, esq. Front Royal, Frederick co. Va from the Ketocton Association	150	31
24	By the same from the Rev. Thornton Stringfellow, Fauquier co. for a parcel of the annual Report	14	50
24	By the same for a parcel of the annual Report 2 63—for the Luminary 5	7	63
24	By collection at Zion m. h. Frederick co. Va. 30—by four persons in Winchester 1	31	00
26	By collection in the Lutheran m. h. Winchester, Frederick co Va.	22	65
26	By collection in the Presbyterian m. h Charleston, Jefferson co Va	21	68
26	By the Rev Mr. Walton, Charleston 1—Mr. Robert Lemon 40 cts. for the Luminary	1	40
26	By collection at Harper's ferry 12 35—afterwards by the hand of J Reser and others 7 50	19	85
27	By Francis Moore 1—and J. Resor 11 25 for the Luminary—Jos. Stubblefield, esq. 5	17	25
31	By the hand of El. Roberts, Great Valley, Pa from an aged lady anxious to assist the translation of the Bible	10	00
Feb. 2	By Messrs (for the Luminary) Kenard 3 75—Clopton 5—Ranaldson 10—Garnett 8—Shelburn 5	31	75
2	Lilly 3—Cosley 1 50—Barrow 10—Battle 4—Purify 4—Norris 10—Calgan 4	39	50
2	Richards 4—Wood 4—Winn 5—Dossey 3—Elton 5—Campbell 2—Fife 35—Crocker 5 50	63	50
2	Woolford 5—Costin 7—Goss 16 50—Galusha 4—Posey 12—Newton 4—Madison 2 50—Gammell 1—Fox 2	54	00
3	By Chas. K. Mallory, esq. 31 25, of which 11 25 is for the Luminary—subscribers in Philad. 1 25	32	50
4	By Messrs Waples 4—Darter 2—for the Latter Day Luminary	6	00
5	By Mr John Samuel, Ky. 10—Asa Runyon, esq. N. J 8—for the Latter Day Luminary	18	00
7	By Deacon Hiland Hill, Catskill, New York, for the Latter Day Luminary	1	00
9	By Elder Bostwick, N. Y. 1—Elder Grinsted, Ky. 5—Mr. Barksdale, Va 6 25—Luminary	12	25
10	By Dr. Wm. H Deaderick, Cheek's x roads, Hawkins co. Te. for the Luminary	2	00
12	By Dr Christian B. Fleet of Virginia for the Latter Day Luminary	3	00
14	By Mr. Jeremiah Dale, Zanesville, Muskingum co Ohio, for the Luminary	10	00
15	By a friend, after preaching, at Lower Dublin meeting house, Pennsylvania	2	00
16	By M. C. Rogers, Te. 4—hand of Dr Staughton from a person at Marcus Hook 4—for Luminary	8	00
18	By Elder Berry Mon Hicks, N. C 1 50—Elder Thomas Hill, Md 4—for Luminary	5	50
19	By the hand of Dr. Staughton from Elder Jesse Mercer, Ga. for 3d annual Report	17	50
22	By Deacon Allen 1 50—collection in the Episcopal m. h. Bristol, Penn. 8 50	10	00
25	By a subscriber in Philadelphia for the Luminary	1	25
28	By Mr. Curwen 20—subscriber in Philad 1 for the Luminary—El J Morris, Va. an Report 10	31	00
	Amount carried up	3162	16

1818.		Amount brought up,	D. C
Feb.	28	By letter from Wm. R Almond, esq. Luray, Va. to be added to the collection taken there in Jan.	1 8
March	2	By Mr Curwen, for *Luminary* 10—Elder Thos. Roberts, per collection, Great Valley, Pa. 22 50	32 5
	4	By the Rev. John Bryce, Richmond, Va for the *Luminary*	40
	6	By Elder Jehiel Fox, N. Y. annual Report and collection 12—Mr. Logan, Salem, Va. for *Lumin* 3	15
	7	By Mr Curwen 1 25—Mr. Ashton 4—subscribers in Philad. 3 25 for the *Luminary*	8
	11	By subscribers in Baltimore, Maryland, for the *Luminary*	4
	13	By Elder Sedwick Dumfries, Va. from Miss Catharine Smoot, Chopawamsic church, Md	7
	13	By the Rev Spencer H Cone, Alexandria, D C for a number of the 3d annual Report	5
	16	By Miss Jane Daniel, Treasurer of the Juvenile Cent Society of Richmond, Virginia	5
	19	By Mr George Greenhow 20— Mr Wm Crane 2, Richmond, Va for the *Secretary fund*	22
	23	By a friend 1--Rev. John H. Rice, Richmond, Va. 1 25 for the *Luminary*	2
April	2	By Mrs Maria O Marshall, Richmond, Va. for *Secretary fund* 20—for *Luminary* 7 50	27
	3	By Mr Crane, Richmond, Va for Report 1 50 Mr Roper 5 Dabney 2 Mr. Jones 1 25 for *Sec fund* 9	
	4	By the hand of Mrs Frances Greenhow 20 Mr Pope 3, for *Sec fund* Mrs Moreton 1 25 for *Lumi* 2	
	13	By collection in Raleigh, N. C. and 1 afterwards by a lady, and 50 cts by Mr. Shaw	
	13	By sixteen subscribers for the *Luminary*, Raleigh, N. C.	
	14	By the Rev Josiah Crudup and Mr Davis, for the *Luminary*	2
	17	By Thos. Brownrigg, esq. 10 Rev Mr. Farnsworth 10, for the *Luminary* ch. 1, Edenton, N. C	
	20	By collections in the two Baptist places of public worship in Norfolk, Virginia,	
	22	By letters for *Luminary*, El Stevens, Woolford 3 Mr. Corns. Payne 35 Wickes & Harsberger 5	
	22	By do El W Castin 1. El J Landers 6 25 G. Luckey, esq 11. El G.Evens 2 D Robertson,esq.49 6	
	22	By do from El Isaac M'Coy, by Isaac Montgomery 3 W Latham 3 Lemuel Baldwin 3 Indians 9	
	22	By do do by James Tweedle 2 Samuel Adams 3 50 Thomas Martin 50 cts *for translation*	
	22	By do. do. by Thomas Martin 50 cents, also, *for civilizing the Indians*	
	23	By letters from Elder James Bailey, for *Luminary*	
	24	By Mrs. Allen, from the Burlington Female Mite Society, for missionary purposes	100
	24	By the same 3. by Dr. Staughton from Elder Hastings and Elder Boss, for *Luminary* 1	4
	25	By letters for *Luminary*, Elder Th. L Henley 18 Mr George Hugill 1 Elder David Philips 5	
	25	By do. do Mr Mic. Finifield 12 J I Sherwood, esq 4 El J. Estep 2 El G Waller for Rep. 20	
	26	By collection in Frankford, near Philadelphia	
	28	By John M'Alister, esq 10 25, Jonesboro', Tennessee, for *Luminary*	
	29	By the hand of Dr Staughton, from D. Barrow from the Kehukee Association, N. C.	11
	29	By do. from the same from the North Carolina Baptist Society for Foreign Missions	20
	29	By do. from Thomas Brownrigg, esq from the Chowan Baptist Mission Society, N. Carolina,	100
	29	By do. from the same from the Baptist Female Mission Society, Edenton, N C	20
	29	By do. from Isaac Howell, from the Franklin Association, New York	50
	29	By do. from the same from the Milford Baptist Female Society, New York	
	29	By do. from Mr. Roger Watkins 6, of which 3 *for translation*	
	29	By do from Mr. Lowry from the Cincinnatti Female Baptist Mission Society, Ohio	15
	29	By do. from Mr Wm Goodloe from the Tate's Creek Association, Kentucky	6
	29	By do. from Wm Lancaster esq. from the Broad River Association, South Carolina	14
	29	By do. from Elder William P. Biddle from the Neuse Association, North Carolina	14
	29	By do. from Rev Mr. Maclay from Mrs. Holt, Bermuda	
	29	By do by the hand of B. W Lester from Captain Thomas Peters	
	22	By do from Rev J A Ranaldson from the Mississippi Mission Society, La	500
	29	By do from Elder John Miller, Abington, Pennsylvania, for Report	
	30	By Elder John Bryce from the Richmond Foreign and Domestic Baptist Mission Society	
	30	By the same from the Richmond Female Society to aid Foreign and Domestic Missions	25
	30	By the Rev. Spencer H. Cone from the Alexandria Female Missionary Cent Society	100

Total to the time of the accounts being audited by a committee and approved by the Board   54

In the foregoing   designated for *civilizing the Indians*   50
                    designated for an *African Mission*   2 —
                    designated as *personal*   7 —
                    designated for the *translation*   16 —
                    designated for the purpose of *education*   17 50
                    designated for the *Secretary fund*   73 25
                    by sale of the last Annual Report   123 08
                    by subscriptions for the Luminary already paid   653 10
                    by remittances from societies, collections, donations, &c.   4551 14

Overpaid last year 95 see 3d annual Report, p 149, *personal* 7   102 —
Paid after Treasurer's account was audited last year, *ibid*   300 —
Transmitted 4th of May   3387 67
To be transmitted in a few days   1653 90

30 Expenditures up to this date, connected with the range of business assigned the Agent, including weeks' service at 8 dolls. per week., travelling expenses; distribution of the 3d Annual Report, printing, stitching, and circulating the first number of the Luminary, subscription papers, paper the second and third numbers of the Luminary, and the 4th Annual Report, postages, &c &c 19

Fourth Annual Report of the Board. 143

Received since the Committee audited the accounts.

	D.	C.
1 By the Rev. Mr. Peckworth, from the Phila. Southern District Bap. Soc. for For. & Dom. Mis.	100	00
1 By letters from W. Kimsey 4—G. Darter 2—T. S. Winn 5—and by R. Anderson 35 for *Luminary*,	46	00
2 By Mr. Cushman 10—Mr. Healey 10—Mr Briggs 10—Mr Curwen 2 50 for *Luminary*,	32	50
2 By Mr Briggs 5—Mr. M'Call 25 cts. for *Secretary fund*—By Mr. Curwen from Miss Thomson 1 50	6	75
2 By Mrs Staughton, from the Sansom st. Bap. Female Society for promoting For. Evangel Mis.	202	00
2 By the same from Mrs. Elizabeth C. Walker from a Female Society at Marcus Hook	61	00
2 By Rev. Jos. Mathias, from the For. & Dom. Miss. Soc. of Montgomery, N Britain, & Hilltown	100	00
3 By Mrs. Mary Watts, from the Bap. Female Mite Society of Lower Dublin for For. Missions	50	00
4 By Rev Jos Mathias 13—by Mr. Deadrick from Valentine Sevier, esq. 11 25 for *Luminary*	24	25
4 By letter from Mr. Mercer, from Mr. Perryman for third Annual Report	5	00
5 By Mr. Schucker 1 25 Mr M'Call 50 cts. for *Luminary*	1	75
6 By Mr. Curwen 1 25 hand of Miss Staughton from Mrs Conroe 50 cts for *Luminary*	1	75
7 By letter from James Whitaker, esq. from French Broad Association, North Carolina	29	25
7 By individuals next day 1 Elder S. Morgan, *personal* 2 Mrs. Brayer, do 50 cts. for Report 7 25	10	75
9 By letter from Mr. Price 10 by Mr Hansell, from Mr. Jeffries 8 for *Luminary*	18	00
11 By letter from Eld. D. Barrow from the church at Bracken 10 at Lawrence ct. 3	13	00
11 By do do. per collection at Emancipat. Asso 8 25 Mrs. Suddoth 1 Report 2 75	12	00
11 By do. from Mr John Reson 20 by Mr Samuel Weasey 1 50 for *Luminary*	21	50
16 By Dr. Staughton, from Joseph Forman, treasurer of Washington Ky Mission Society	160	00

Received by Mr. Peck before going, and on his way to the Westward.

	D.	C.
5 By Rev Dr. Staughton, corresponding secretary of the Board	600	00
5 By a few persons, after sermon, at Sand Lake, Rensselaer county, New York		67
8 By collection in the Baptist meeting house, Albany, New York	23	12
10 By brother Fish of Ohio 1 by Mrs. Hildreth, a poor but pious widow 6 cts. Hudson, New York	1	06
29 By collection West Stockbridge, Massachusetts	2	00
2 By a few individuals after sermon in East Hillsdale, New York	1	36
6 By collection in the Baptist meeting house, Amenia, N Y 6 by Miss Morgan, Sharon Ct. 1	7	00
6 By collection in the Baptist meeting house, New Haven, Ct. 6 43 by sale of Report 75 cts	7	18
3 By a friend in Burlington, New Jersey, *personal*	3	00
4 By collection at the Redstone Association 56 45 for copies of constitution 63 cts	57	08
4 By collection in the Baptist meeting house in Pittsburg, Pennsylvania,	13	00
7 By collection in the Baptist meeting, Washington, Pennsylvania	17	00
8 By Hugh Wilson, a little boy, 25 cts Rhoda Wilson 50 cts Mr Read 1 a stranger 2	3	75
9 By collection in Charleston, Brooke county, Virginia	3	50
11 By a few persons after sermon, Cadiz Harrison county Ohio, 3 36 Report 50 cts	3	86
22 By collection after missionary sermon in the court house, Zanesville, Ohio	13	10
28 By collection after missionary sermon, Chilicothe Ohio	14	50
Total	831	16

1817. *Expenditures of Mr Peck connected with his outfit and journey to the Westward*

	D.	C.
24 To expenses from the 17th of May up to this date, including horse hire, travelling expenses, &c	48	08
24 To expenses of family and several articles of outfit for journeying to the Westward	70	48
24 To clothing 75 83 Horse 95 Waggon 96 60 Harness 23 83	291	26
9 To travelling expenses from Litchfield, Con to Lexington, Kentucky, with a family,	102	43
0 To the transportation of a box with books linens, &c to Pittsburg	27	50
0 To printing 500 copies of constitutions for Mite Societies	7	50
0 To portable Map of the United States 10 price - 1 50 deducted by Mr. Mellish	8	50
0 To loss on counterfeit and bad bills	1	06
Total of expenditure	566	64
Balance in favour of the Board	204	52

1817. *Received by Mr Welch before going, and on his way to the Westward*

	D.	C.
19 By the hand of the Rev. Dr Staughton, corresponding secretary of the Board	400	00
10 By collection at Orange court house, Virginia	44	87
11 By collection at Zion meeting house, Orange county, Virginia	19	25
13 By collection Zoar in h Orange co. 13 25 do a presbyterian m h Rockbridge co 12 22	25	47
10 By a stranger, who refused to give his name, but said your *Master knows me*	5	00
16 By collection at South District Association, Kentucky	48	75
17 By cash by the hand of B. Bell, esq Danville, Kentucky	2	00
24 By collection at the Tates' Creek Association, Kentucky 16 18 Report 1 25	18	13
26 By collection in the Presbyterian meeting house, Lexington Kentucky	28	00
7 By collection at the Bracken Association, Kentucky	84	25
11 By collection in Lancaster, Ohio	11	75
14 By collection Mays Lick 15 Washington 11 87, Kentucky	26	87
15 By cash by the hands of Walker Reed, esq	3	00
18 By several persons in the republican m h Woodford county Kentucky	4	50
9 By collection in the court house, Versailles, Woodford county, Kentucky	7	00
20 By the Rev John Scott, corresponding secretary of the Franklin Association	3	50
25 By collection in Richmond, Madison co. 13 50 Mrs. Barnett 1 Report 75 cts.	15	25
Amount carried up,	747	59

		Amount brought up,	747 5
Sept.	27	By Gen Jos Lewis, corresponding secretary of the Salem Association, Kentucky	5 0
	28	By collection at the Salem Association 93 25 hand of brother Benjamin Edwards 5	98 25
	29	By collection Bardstown 12 19 : J. W. Ogan esq. 1 Report 1 Kentucky	14 19
Oct.	1	By several persons after preaching at Springfield, Kentucky	8
	5	By collection at David's Fork meeting house Fayette county, Kentucky	1 0
		By the hand of brother Benjamin Stout, collected at the Elkhorn Association	94 2
		Total	978 34

Expenditures of Mr. Welch connected with his outfit and journey to the Westward.

1817.			
May	18	To clothes trunks, boxes, horse hire, necessaries for the journey &c &c	100 0
June	28	To gig and harness 180 a horse 120 travelling expenses to Orange county, Va 35 75	335 0
	28	To travelling expenses from Virginia to Kentucky, with additional clothing	75 0
	28	To carriage and storage of 2 boxes, containing books, &c. from Philadelphia to Kentucky	55 0
	28	To repairing gig, harness &c for postage, medicine, &c	44 0
	28	To counterfeit bills taken in collections	9 0
		Total expenditures	621 15
		Receipts 978 34 expenditures 621 15 balance in favour of the Board	357 3

Expenditures of brethren Peck & Welch, from Kentucky to St Louis, and after arriving there

1817.			
Oct	11	To various articles of necessity for family use 67 41 bad bills 5 77	73 7
Nov	7	To travelling expenses from Lexington, Ky. to Shawnee, Il. 1 47 37 while there 12 50	59 8
	21	To travelling exp of br. Welch and lady from Shawnee to St. Louis 22 38 after arriving 13 75	36 1
Dec.	1	To passage of br Peck from Shawnee to St. Louis 25 other expenses 12 21	37 2
	3	To transportation of a box and trunk from Pittsburg to St Louis	5 8
	20	To freightage on two boxes from Kentucky to St. Louis	20 5
1818			
Jan	9	To horse keeping 15 70 To room for school and meeting 32 13	47 9
	9	To rent of a room for br. and sister Welch, 16 80 expense for clothing 18 32	35 1
	20	To all other necessary expenses of the two families up to this date	19 9
		Total	404 5

CONTRA,   Cr.

1817			
Oct	11	By balance in the hands of br Welch, 357 19 do. br Peck, 204 53	551 0
	12	By collection in the baptist meeting-house Providence Jessamine county, Kentucky	25 0
	19	By collection in Friendship meeting-house, Clarke county, 8 55 do Winchester, 17 45	26 0
	21	By collection after sermon, Frankfort, Kentucky	6 0
	26	By collection in Elizabethtown, Harden county, Kentucky	4 0
1818			
Jan	10	By Dr J. Young, 3 report, 75 cts subscription for the Luminary, 6 25	10 0
		Total,	651

The Baptist Board of Foreign Missions in account with Thomas Baldwin, Lucius Bolles, and Daniel Sharp Committee, to whom was referred the outfit, &c of brethren Wheelock and Colman for Burmah

THE BOARD,   Dr

1817			D C
Nov.	1	To cash paid Bridge and Renough for dolls 1560 in specie	1591 0
	1	To White for packing the same	1 0
	4	To cash paid Captain Drew for passage for two missionaries and their wives	700 0
	13	To cash paid Mr Bolles for articles purchased by him for the missionaries	137 0
	13	To two mattresses, 18 29 cheese for Rangoon, 5 41 do for passage, 2 81	26 0
	13	To cash paid for 3000 specie bought at Branch Bank	3000 0
	13	To Osburn for packing the same	3 0
	3	To the truck-man for the trunks, and porterage of specie going on board	4 0
	13	To Lincoln and Edmonds' bill for books, *as per bill*	195 0
	13	To cash paid for Brown's History of Missions	6 0
	13	To cash paid Dr. Torrington for medicine, &c. *as per bill*	84 0
	13	To Miss Ditson's bill for making clothes for the missionaries, *as per bill*	20 0
	13	To Mr Sharp's bill for boarding Mr Colman, and for one medical book, *as per bill*	85 0
	13	To Mr Kuhn for plaid cloak for Mr. Wheelock, *as per bill*	16 0
	13	To expense of horse and chaise in settling business for Mr Colman	6 0
	13	To amount of articles purchased by Mrs Baldwin and Mrs Sharp for the missionaries	381 0
	13	To cash paid Mr. Sharp for a trunk	2 0
		Total	6266

CONTRA,   Cr.

1817			D C
Aug.	9	By draft from the treasurer, John Cauldwell, Esq	400
Nov.		By do do.	2360 —
		By do do.	3000 —
Dec.	5	By do do.	513 —
	5	By cash of 2 friends, 5 Mrs Bradford, 1 by Rev. Mr. Batchelder, 9 25	15 25
		Errors excepted	6288

Boston, Dec. 1817.   THOMAS BALDWIN

FOREIGN MISSIONS

MISSION TO BURMAH.

From the missionaries at Rangoon, no communication later than what has been published in the Luminary has come to hand. Intelligence, however, has arrived which announces that they were well and going on prosperously, as late as October last. By the present time, it is hoped, brethren Wheelock and Colman have joined them. We here introduce the *tract* composed by Mr. Judson.

The following Tract in Burman and English, needs no other remark than, that the Burman is the original, and the English a translation. This may apologize for the inelegance or uncommonness of some of the phrases and sentences in English, the version being made as literal as possible.   A JUDSON.

There is one Being who exists eternally, who is exempt from sickness, old age and death; who was, and is, and will be, without beginning, and without end. Beside this, the true God, there is no other God. The true God is diverse from all other beings. Uniting three in one, God the Father, God the Son, and God the Holy Ghost, these three are one God. God is a spirit, without bodily form. Although omnipresent, it is above the heavens that He clearly discovers His glory. His power and wisdom are infinite. He is pure and good, and possessed of everlasting felicity. Before this world was made God remained happy, surrounded by the pure and incorporeal sons of heaven. In order to display His perfections, and make creatures happy, God created the heavens, the sun, moon and all the stars, the earth, the various kinds of brute creatures, and man. The first man and woman, at their original creation, were not liable to sickness or death; they were exempt from every kind of evil, and their mind was upright and pure. Afterwards, because, by violating the command of God, they transgressed against their Benefactor, the sum of all perfections, beyond compare, the light of the divine countenance disappeared; and those two, together with all their posterity, became darkened, and unclean, and wicked; they became subject, in the present state, to sickness, death and all other evils; and they became deserving of suffering, in the future state, the dreadful punishment of hell. Above four thousand years after mankind was thus destroyed, God, being moved with compassion for man involved in misery, sent to the earth, the abode of man, God the Son, the second yadana among the three *yadanas* [any thing superlatively excellent—In the present application, it conveys no additional idea; but is requisite in Burman to the intelligibility of the sentence.] The circumstances of his being sent were thus:—God the Son, uniting the divine and the human natures, without destroying or confounding them in the land of Israel and country of Judea, in the womb of a virgin, was conceived by the divine power, and was born. This God-man, who is named Jesus Christ, being man, endured in our stead, severe sufferings and death, the punishment due to our sins; and being God, is able by virtue of having endured those sufferings, to deliver all his disciples from the punishment of hell, redeeming them with his own life, and to instate them in heaven. On the third day after Jesus Christ suffered death, his soul re-entered his body, and he lived again. For the space of forty days he remained giving instruction to his disciples, after which he commissioned them thus—' Go ye into all countries on earth, and proclaim the glad news to all men. He that believeth in me and is baptised, shall be saved; he that believeth not, shall be damned, or shall suffer endless punishment in hell.' Then in the presence of many of his disciples, he ascended to heaven, and took up his abode in the place where God displays his glory. According to the final command of Jesus Christ, his disciples, beginning with Judea, travelled about through various countries and kingdoms, and proclaimed the glad news; and many believed, and became disciples of Jesus Christ. The true religion afterwards spread into the countries of the west; and now to this country of Burmah, among the countries of the east, a teacher of religion, from the country of America, has arrived, and is beginning to proclaim the glad news. About one or two hundred years hence, the religion of Boodh, of Brahma, of Mahomet, and of Rome, together with all other false religions, will disappear and be lost, and the religion of Christ will pervade the whole world; all quarrels and wars will cease, and all the tribes of man will be like a band of mutually loving brothers. [*End of Part* 1.

A disciple of Jesus Christ is one that is born again; the meaning of which is, that the old nature, which is successively inherited from the first man and woman, begins to be destroyed, and the new nature, which is implanted by the Holy Spirit, is obtained. The unrenewed man loves himself supremely, and seeks his own private interest. The renewed man loves the true God supremely, and desires that the divine glory may be promoted. He loves all others also as himself, and seeks their interest as his own. The desire of the unrenewed man is to enjoy sensual pleasure, worldly wealth, fame and power. The renewed man contemns sensual pleasure, &c. His desire is to be pure in mind, to be replete with grace, to be useful to others, to promote the glory of God, and to enjoy the pure and perpetual happiness of heaven. The unrenewed man, influenced by pride, hates the humbling religion of Jesus Christ. When seized with alarm, he endeavours to perform meritorious deeds, in order to make atonement for his sins, and obtain salvation. The renewed man, knowing surely, that man having sinned against God, and contracted great guilt, cannot perform meritorious deeds, firmly fixes in his mind, that it is on account of the God-man, Jesus Christ alone, that sin can be expiated, and the happiness of heaven obtained; and therefore, through supreme love to Jesus Christ, and a desire to do his will, endeavours to avoid evil deeds, and to perform good deeds only, according to the divine commands. Sometimes, when through the assaults of the remaining old nature, he slides and transgresses the divine commands, he repents that he has sinned against his superlatively excellent and lovely Lord, and trusting only in the death of Christ, he humbly confesses the sin he has committed, and begs pardon of God. He who is unrenewed, and therefore is not a disciple of Christ, in the present life, obtains no true wisdom; his sins are numerous and heavy. And because he has no regard to the Lord, who can deliver from sin, he will, in the present life, obtain no refuge or resting place; but soul and body will fall into hell, as his sins deserve; and having transgressed against an eternal God, he must accordingly for ever suffer eternal misery. He who is renewed, and becomes a disciple of Jesus Christ, in the present life, is acquainted with true wisdom, and attains the state of a *Thoutahpan* [one that has acquired a new and excellent nature, which will issue in final salvation.] And when he changes worlds, his soul having obtained the pardon of sin through the death of Christ, will, through the grace of God, enter into the divine presence. The body also, though it be burnt with fire, or consumed in the earth, and thus destroyed for a time, will, at the end of the world, by the power of God, with whom nothing is impossible, live again, and thus soul and body united, will for ever enjoy eternal happiness in the presence of God. [*End of Part 2.*

The commands of Jesus Christ are as follows:—Repent, or be changed in mind; that is, extirpate the old nature and cultivate the new. Have faith in the Saviour, the Lord Jesus Christ. Love God supremely. Love others as yourself. Set not your heart on worldly goods and riches; but look forward to, and long for those riches which are free from defilement, and eternal in the heavens. Suppress haughtiness, pride and insolence, and cherish an humble, meek and lowly mind. Return not evil for evil, but have a disposition to forgive the faults of others, and to bear injury with patience. Love your enemies, and pray for them. Be compassionate to the poor and needy, and give alms. Covet not the property of others, therefore take not by violence, steal not, defraud not in trade, trespass in no manner on the property of others. Speak no falsehood. Bear not false witness. Without being invested with governmental authority, take not the life of man. Drink not intoxicating liquor to excess. Despise not marriage, whether of a teacher of religion, a ruler, or a private person. Beside your own husband or wife, have no desire for any other man or woman. Honour parents, and willingly assist and support them, according to your ability. Listen reverently to the instructions of religious teachers, and make offerings for their support. In regard to rulers, whether disciples of Christ or not, honour them, pay them tribute, pray for them, and obey their lawful commands. Pray to God always. On the first day in seven, assemble to worship God, and hear his word. On becoming a disciple of Jesus Christ, receive baptism in water. Afterwards in memory of his flesh and blood which he gave for the sake of his disciples, reverently, from time to time, eat bread and drink wine. Use all diligence, that your relations and neighbours, and countrymen, who are not disciples of Christ may be converted. With a compassionate mind, use all diligence that the inhabitants of towns, and countries and kingdoms, that are in darkness, not having obtained the light of the knowledge of the true God, may become disciples of Christ. The above are commands of Jesus Christ. [*End of Part 3.*

The teacher who composed this writing, seeing the great evil which is coming on the Burmans, left his own country from compassion, and from an immense distance, has arrived by ship, to this, the country of Burmah. He desires neither fame nor riches. Offerings and gifts he seeks not. The disciples of Christ, in his own country, moved with compassion for the Burmans, make offerings sufficient for his use. He has no other motive but this. Being a disciple of Christ, and therefore seeking the good of others, as his own, he has come, and is labouring that the Burmans may be saved from the dreadful punishment of hell, and enjoy the happiness of heaven.

In the year of Christ 1816, in the Burman year 1178, in the 967th day of the lord of the Saddan elephant, and master of the Sakyah weapon; and in the 33d year of his reign, in the division Pashoo, on Tuesday, the 12th day of the wane of the moon Wahgoung, after the double be , this writing, entitled *The Way to Heaven*, was finished. *May the reader obtain light. Amen.*

DOMESTIC MISSIONS.

MISSION TO THE WESTWARD OF THE MISSISSIPPI RIVER.

The missionaries brethren Peck and Welch with their families, arrived at St. Louis, it appears, about the first of December last. In a few days they addressed a communication to the Corresponding Secretary of the Board, giving a detailed account of the numerous difficulties that had opposed and retarded their progress to that place, and the many kindnesses they had received. In the conclusion they observe—"It is easily perceived by us, though we have been here but a short time, that the state of things is truly important. *Lord help us! All our help must come from thee!*"

Under date of December 28, Mr Welch thus writes—"The time has already passed, at which a second communication ought to have been made; but such were the difficulties, the unusual and unexpected length of our journey from Kentucky, and such the embarrassments attendant on our first residence in this place, that I have not had it in my power to make my report, as the Board had a right to expect.

"On the first of January, as per agreement already made, I expect to commence teaching a small school, which I calculate by the close of the first quarter will become sufficiently large." [At this time Mr Peck was very sick, and Mr. Welch remarks] "Be not surprised if in my next I shall have to perform the painful task of announcing the death of my partner in missionary labour."

In a joint communication, on Mr. Peck's becoming convalescent, they observe, "that the mission has been deprived of the labours of brother Peck since his arrival at this place, but we feel thankful to our gracious heavenly Father that he is now, though slow, regaining his health and strength. In the town of St Louis are a number of persons who have professed religion. Amongst these are several baptists, with whom we hope soon to unite in church fellowship.

"There is a small presbyterian church in this place, constituted some months ago. They have a meeting established in a commodious school house in one part of the town, and the Rev Mr. Giddings, a missionary from the eastern states, preaches to them. He also teaches a school in the same house. There is another minister of the denomination called "*Cumberland Presbyterians*," who resides in town, and occasionally preaches to the people. On our first arrival here brother Welch occasionally preached in the house occupied by Mr. Giddings, as he was then absent on a missionary tour in the country. But after we had obtained a room for the school in quite a different part of the town, it was judged expedient to establish another meeting. In this our highest expectations have been exceeded. The meetings are tolerably well attended, both on the Sabbath and on Wednesday evenings. The people give a solemn attention, and the number of hearers continues to increase. On the whole, we are encouraged with the prospect, and pray that the Lord may accomplish a gracious work here. One person we hope has experienced religion of late, and we trust one or two others are thoughtful."

Fourth Annual Report of the Board. 149

To the Corresponding Secretary, St. Louis, M. T. March 12, 1818

DEAR SIR,—

THAT the Board may have entire knowledge of our prospects, our trials, and every occurrence relative to the mission in this region, we think it would not be improper to forward the following extracts from the mission records or journal

JANUARY 29th, 1818.—The missionaries having formed an acquaintance with several brethren and sisters, met according to previous agreement, to consult on the propriety of uniting in a church relation. Eleven persons presented letters and other testimonials of their good standing in churches whence they had removed, and we proceeded to adopt a covenant as the basis of union.

FEBRUARY 5.—The missionaries and brethren again met for consultation We unanimously adopted articles of faith, and resolved to be constituted as a church of Christ the following Sabbath.

It is highly gratifying to contemplate the union and cordial sentiments of those brethren and sisters who have agreed to become thus united This may be regarded as the first effort of the missionaries to establish and spread the visible kingdom of Christ in this western land In the result, thus far, they acknowledge the special mercy of God. The meeting established increases in the number of hearers, and the solemn attention given One or two instances of awakening appear. The school continues to prosper, and the pupils make considerable progress in learning. The prospects are encouraging

FEBRUARY 8th,—*Church constituted* Brother Peck preached on the occasion from 1 Cor. iii. 9 'Ye are God's building'

Brother Welch produced and read the covenant and articles of faith, and after imploring the protection and blessing of the Great Head of the church, in the name of the Father and of the Son and of the Holy Ghost, and in the presence of many witnesses, solemnly pronounced them a visible church of Christ.

Brother Peck made the dedication prayer and gave the right hand of fellowship, and brother Welch gave the charge.

Then after 'showing forth our Lord's death,' we closed this interesting service with praise to God

FEB. 12. The church appointed a committee, consisting of brethren Peck, Welch and Jacoby, to prepare a memorial, accompanied with a subscription, to be presented to the public, soliciting aid to build a house for public worship

MARCH 1st.—It was concluded that it would be most conducive to our own individual comfort, and to the prosperity of the western mission, that we form ourselves into a society.

Impressed with the importance of employing every means in our power to accomplish the great object for which we have come into this western country, WE the undersigned being under the patronage of *the Baptist Board of Foreign Missions for the United States*, agree to adopt the name of '*the Western Baptist Mission Society*,' and to be regulated by the following PRINCIPLES

1st Having devoted ourselves to the Lord Jesus, we give ourselves to one another by the will of God, and *agree* to be kindly affectionate one towards another with brotherly love, realizing that we have our master even Christ, and that all we are brethren.

2d. We agree that our sole object on earth is to promote the religion of Christ in the western parts of America, both among the whites, Africans, and Indians, and that the means to be employed are, the preaching of the gospel, distributing the holy scriptures, religious tracts, &c. and establishing and promoting schools for the instruction of the youth, and the education of such persons as may be selected to aid us either as preachers, catechists, or school teachers.

3d. We agree to engage in no business for the purpose of individual interest, to resign all private right to remittances from the Board, avails of labour, compensation for services, donations whether public or private, and in a word all monies arising from any quarter shall go into the common funds of this society.

Provided, that nothing in this article be understood as affecting our private right to inheritances, or personal favours not made in compensation for services.

4th. This society shall have a secretary to record its proceedings, publish documents, &c. who shall be treasurer *ex officio*.

5th. The funds of the society shall consist of the following branches, viz.

All monies or property, specially designated for the benefit of schools, shall form the *Education fund*, to be appropriated only for that particular purpose.

All monies and property specially designated for the maintenance and instruction of Indian youth, shall form the *Indian fund*, to be appropriated for that object.

All monies or property specially designated for the erection of buildings for the mission or for schools, shall form the *Building fund*, to be used only for that purpose.

All monies or property coming into our hands without such special designation, shall be appropriated to the common expenses of the mission as circumstances dictate.

6th. All appropriations from the mission funds shall be made by a majority of the brethren united in this compact, subject however to the inspection of our patrons, the Board.

7th. We agree that all members of the mission family have equal claims upon the mission funds for equal support in similar circumstances—the claims of widows and orphans not to be in the least affected by the death of the head of the family. But it is to be understood that no one shall have a right to adopt a child into the mission family so as to entitle it to the claims secured in this article, but by consent of the brethren.

J. M. PECK,
J. E. WELCH

St. Louis, M. T. March 2d, 1818

MINUTES OF THE WESTERN MISSIONARY SOCIETY.

Voted, That brother J. E. Welch be secretary to this society.

March 4.—The missionaries opened a Sunday school for the instruction of Africans in this village, and it is with peculiar satisfaction that they record the attendance of no less than fourteen the first day.

To the Cor. Sec. dated St. Louis, March 14, 1818.

In addition to the foregoing communications permit us to forward also the following remarks respecting the southern and interior parts of this territory. This information has been obtained from several persons, but more particularly from a baptist minister by the name of *Edwards*, who has resided on this side of the Mississippi most of the time since 1811. Last year he spent some time in itinerating in the lower part of the territory to examine into the state of religion. In this tour he rode more than 1000 miles, visited all the principal settlements on the Arkansas, the St. Francis, and the White rivers. In some places the people are not only destitute of ministers of any denomination, but deplorably ignorant of the gospel. In other settlements some attention is paid to religion. Baptist professors are scattered through the different parts of the country. They have removed from Kentucky and other western states, but now are deprived of the gospel. In some settlements churches might be formed, could there be ministers obtained to oversee them. This part of the territory is rapidly settling, but unless missionaries go amongst them they must be destitute of the gospel for some years to come. Between St. Louis and the above mentioned region are seven small churches, situate mostly in cape Giradeau county. These united in an association in 1815, calling themselves the " Bethel Baptist Association."

Pursuant to our instructions from the Board, we have neglected no opportunity in which we might obtain information relative to the Indian tribes in this western land. The Delawares and Shawnese, the remnants of once powerful tribes, live from 20 to 40 miles from cape Giradeau. They are not numerous, perhaps two or three hundred of each tribe.

The Delawares have expressed a desire to have their children instructed in English, and that if a teacher is sent amongst them they will build a schoolhouse. A band of the Cherokees have lately removed from their tribe east of the Mississippi, and are settled on the Arkansas. This was in consequence of an exchange of lands by the United States' government. The Cherokees, Shawnese, and Delawares are leagued together, and agree mutually to support each other. Within a few months past they have made war upon the Osage nation, and 'tis said have destroyed a considerable village. A gentleman who saw and conversed with their warriors as they returned from the fight, told brother Peck, that they had about one hundred scalps, which they showed as trophies of victory. The cause of this war is said to be the murders and other depredations which for years have been committed by the Osages upon the Delawares and Shawnese.

There is a settlement of about 150 Indians on the Merrimac river, about 50 miles west of St. Louis. Their chief is a white man by the name of Fish. Some of this band converse in English. They have comfortable dwellings, and are said to have made considerable progress in civilization.

Another small settlement of natives are in the neighbourhood of St. Louis, not more than 10 miles distant. One of us expect to visit this band in a few days.

The Osages live more than 300 miles west of St. Louis, on and beyond the Osage river. They are a numerous nation, but scattered over an extensive country. They are more generally represented as a peaceable and well disposed nation, and inclined to become civilized, though some persons give them a different character. The Sacks (pronounced Soks,) and Foxes, (a band of the Sacks or Saukies) are settled betwixt 150 and 300 miles up the Mississippi. Some are scattered through the upper part of the Illinois territory. They are not very friendly, though not on terms of hostility with our government. A short time since *Quoshquomme*, a chief of a band of the Sacks from Rock river, with a number of Indians, were in this village. Brother Welch obtained an interview with the chief on the subject of education, the introduction of schools, &c. among the tribe. It was understood from the interpreter who was employed, that the chief had two sons whom he wished to have educated in English. The interview closed without any thing decisive, as we had no funds to support the youth, and the chief prudently declined giving an answer relative to the establishment of schools amongst their nation, without consulting the other chiefs.

Other tribes, as the Winnebagoes to the north, and the Sioux, Ottoes, Mandans, &c. to the west, live more remote, and are less likely to receive immediate attention.

By this statement the Board will understand, that the Indian tribes who are populous and extensive, live at a distance from us; that a large population of whites, quite ignorant of the gospel, are scattered through the country for 3 or 400 miles betwixt us and the Indians, and that if we attempt to carry the gospel immediately to these tribes, we must pass over multitudes more likely to receive the gospel than are the savage and uncultivated Indians. It is hoped, however, that some good may be done amongst local tribes, without lessening our usefulness amongst the whites.

Hitherto we have said nothing on the importance of increasing the number of labourers in this western harvest. But we now venture to raise the Macedonian cry, 'come over and help us.' Could the Board, but more especially the public at large, be made fully sensible of the vast work that lies before us, and the importance of strengthening our hands by one or two additional labourers, our cry would not be unavailing. If one or more young men of ardent piety, and a good education, could receive an appointment from the Board the present season, by the time of their arrival we might be prepared to enlarge our sphere of effort.

Another added to this mission, in a little time would not much increase its expense, as the school department might then be rendered more profitable.

Praying the Great Head of the church to guide in all the deliberations of your respectable body, we subscribe ourselves your unworthy servants in the mission cause,

J. M. PECK,
J. E. WELCH.

UNDER date of March 28, 1818, the missionaries thus write: "We have not much additional news to communicate. We have enlarged the plan of our school. At our public examination yesterday, our students performed remarkably well. Several gentlemen of respectability of the village, since they have been made acquainted with our object in this country, appear to interest themselves in our cause.

"Our African Sunday school has more than 50 on the roll, most of whom are very attentive and strive to learn.

"The first Sabbath in April we expect to baptise a candidate. This, we believe, will be the first time the ordinance was ever attended in St. Louis. We have ascertained that five persons at least have manifested a hope of religion within less than three months past. Thus grace begins to triumph here."

The fifth of April Mr. Welch says: "Last evening was our church meeting. Additions were received by letter, and experience. To-day at nine o'clock a sermon was delivered on the banks of the Mississippi, and two candidates baptised —*late work of grace!* You can scarcely imagine the happiness we this day enjoyed around the table of the Lord, while bidding welcome to all the privileges of the house of God four new members. Prospects are flattering. I hope the Lord is about to commence a great work in this quarter."

LOUISIANA

From Rev. M. Ranaldson to the Cor. Sec. dated St. Francisville, March 20, 1818.

IT is my duty as your missionary to make frequent communications. In this I have been deficient. But I can assure you it has not been for want of disposition. The whole of my time has been occupied. My field of labour is still enlarging, and the work is increasing on my hands daily.

I wrote to you on the 19th of January, which I hope you have received. Having just returned from the first annual meeting of the Mississippi Society for Baptist Missions Foreign and Domestic, it is necessary for me to forward communications by the next mail, that you may receive them in time for the annual meeting of the Board.

Our society has been formed on missionary ground. There are pressing demands for active and general exertions. Four missionaries are already employed by the society for the term of three months; and one for a year. Rev. Isaac Suttle, whom I mentioned in my last, is appointed to preach in the African church recently formed in the Creek nation, for the current year. It is hoped that the present hostilities of the Seminoles will not defeat the object of his appointment. L. Scarborough is appointed for a circuit on the west of the Mississippi river; N. Morris for the eastern section of West Florida, J. Flower for the frontier settlements in the Mississippi state, and Benjamin Davis for the coloured people in New Orleans. This last appointment was made in consideration of the poor in this city who manifest a disposition to receive the word with gladness; for a number of them are truly pious. Whilst missionary exertions are making for the Asiatics and aboriginal Americans, the poor Africans in our country who bear the heat and burden of the day, should not be neglected. It truly requires the wisdom of the serpent blended with the harmlessness of the dove, to teach this wretched race of human beings! But we feel a confidence in the prudence and zeal of our brother appointed to the work. He has a faculty for teaching the blacks; and should the city corporation yield a favourable countenance to the undertaking, I hope it may soon be said, that *the poor of New Orleans have the gospel preached to them.*

The society having attributed a great share of their success to the agency of your missionary, agreed to remit the sum which was appropriated for his use by the Baptist Board of Foreign Missions. I therefore inclose to you a check on a bank in Philadelphia, for *five hundred dollars.*

I hope the employment of domestic missionaries will never diminish your treasury, but rather replenish it. Permit me to tender my very grateful acknowledgments to the Board, for the seasonable supplies they have given, which enabled me to make a decided stand in the midst of the strong hold of Satan, and to preach among the gentiles of Louisiana the unsearchable riches of Christ. Although I could not maintain my first position in the city of New Orleans, on account of its expensiveness, yet I am persuaded I could not occupy a more important missionary ground in the state, and one which promises more immediate and general usefulness as respects the mission, than the present station. I am happy to say that the prospects, as relates to my future support, are such as to supersede the necessity of the continued patronage of the Board. I have reason to expect that the generosity of the people whom I serve in the gospel, will enable me still to give myself wholly to the work of the ministry. Your patronage therefore may, and will I hope, be extended to another in my place. Not that I wish to withdraw from the delightful services of the Board, or shake off the pleasing responsibility of the mission. No, I wish still to be the missionary, and still to act under the advice and auspices of the Board, at least so far as to maintain an intimate connexion with that honourable body.

This letter must soon close for the mail. In my next I will endeavour to give farther information concerning this country, &c. &c. There are thousands around us starving for the word of life. Several important stations are ready for the reception of missionaries. With affectionate importunity I would solicit the attention of the Board to be directed this way. O send us help, that we may lift up a standard for the people in the name of the Lord of hosts! We want at least six missionaries whose lips are touched with a *live coal*, whose hearts are sanctified with the love of God, whose bowels yearn for the salvation of men, whose fortitude and piety can resist the temptations of filthy lucre, and, in a word, whose abilities may be competent for the defence of the gospel, among ingenious and learned infidels, and before powerful adversaries of the doctrines of the cross. Aid such in their commencement, send them out under your patronage, and in a short time they may remunerate the Board by returning the loan with good interest.

It is expensive to live in this country. The enormous price of cotton raises every thing else to its par. House rent and the hire of servants are remarkably high. And in these two articles there is but little difference between this place and New Orleans.

Such is the state of society, that it appears unquestionably a duty incumbent to pay some attention to the education of the young. And although the whole of my time, strength and abilities, are required for the ministry of the word, yet I shall be obliged by the united petitions of the people to give a small portion of it to the instruction of their children. They wish me, however, merely to superintend an academy, and employ other teachers, able to sustain the laborious functions of the school. This plan should, in my humble opinion, be recommended to all our missionaries to the west, as the religious education of children is of the highest importance, and will probably contribute in a very great degree, to the acceptation of the gospel among a heterogeneous mass which has been collected from the four quarters of the globe.

May the God of missions prosper and succeed your pious labours to send the gospel among all the nations of the earth.

CHEROKEE INDIANS.

From the Rev. Mr. Posey to the Corresponding Secretary, dated Haywood County, North Carolina, March 13, 1818.

HAVING commenced legally in the work of the mission on the first of December last, I now take the liberty of addressing the Board, through you, in order that you may know something of the manner in which I have spent my time. I shall first give a brief view of the country. The paths through this wilderness are generally difficult to pass, like the bye ways of Deborah—and the traveller will experience as great a variety in one day, probably, as curiosity itself could desire. Over this wide extended tract of country, I have been mostly traversing, through the course of the winter, preaching to the whites, and by an interpreter to as many Indians as I could convene from time to time; though the winter has been so excessively cold as to prevent my progress at times, yet I have got four schools started. In this business I found it difficult to obtain such teachers as I would wish; I have however employed such as are capable of teaching them the first principles of the language, and they understand some of the Cherokee language, which appears of use in the beginning of the business. I draw my articles with them in such a manner as to prevent them from trading, and confine them to use every exertion to instruct the Indians in every thing necessary, and they are liable to be turned off, if they are guilty of any immorality. The progress of the Indians surpasses my most sanguine hopes—I visited one school on the day after its commencement, and found a number able to show any letter in the alphabet and name it. One man and his wife, in another school, who did not talk English at all, had learned in about nine days to spell the words of three letters. Their anxiety appears great to obtain information; they know there is something in the bible to which they are strangers, and they want to understand it. When I am amongst them, it is impossible to describe my feelings; there I view a number of fellow creatures, looking up to me for instruction, and anxious to hear as much as possible. Some of them go a considerable distance to meeting, and appear very attentive. I have kept a kind of a journal, and if the Board requests it, I will send a copy of it in my next letter.—I have only engaged the teachers for three months at forty dollars each, and I hope to obtain considerable aid in defraying the expenses in these parts, and if they continue anxious for learning, of which I have no doubt, I wish the school to continue. However, I still wish communications from the Board on the subject. It appears as if it will be attended with great expense, to do any thing to the purpose among them.

Pray for me my dear brother, that my feeble labours may be blest, and that I may be faithful in the cause of my precious Saviour—may heaven smile on you and the Board in general.

Our brethren in Georgia, particularly of the Sarepta Mission Society, are directing their attention also towards the Cherokees, and we are happy to hear favourable accounts from their labours.

From the Rev. Isaac M'Coy nothing has come to hand later than what has appeared in the second number of the Luminary. It is hoped that the vigorous prosecution of his plans relative to the Wabash Indians, will be accompanied with a blessing.

GENERAL STATE OF RELIGION.

It is lamented that our limits do not permit us to present that comprehensive and detailed view of this subject which the importance of it, and the interest it has in every christian bosom, would render at once so proper and so gratifying—not in relation to one denomination only, but to all. A very brief, though general survey, only, can be here attempted. In this it will be necessary to mark regions of barrenness as well as those favoured by the refreshing visits of divine mercy. The Rev. Thomas Smiley justly observes, that "it would be a useful part of information to publish where there are declensions in religion as well as revivals, and where churches after great revivals have become extinct, let it be known, and what seemed to be the leading cause of it as this may have been mostly owing to our own imprudence, a faithful account of such things might serve as a warning both to ourselves and others. Also where ministers have apostatized, I have often noticed that in their best days there appeared to be a lack in them; and it would be but justice that, when they show themselves as they are, it should be known how they came into the ministry, their conduct while in it, together with their fall, which would serve as a future caution."

This subject is so intimately connected with that of missions, or with exertions to spread the everlasting gospel, that, in the review here submitted, no care will be taken to keep up between them a distinct line of demarkation.

MAINE.—In this quarter much mercy has been experienced the past year. Among the churches of the *Bowdoinham association* about 300 have been baptised on profession of faith and repentance; among those of the *Cumberland* nearly 500. At the last session of the former 95 dollars and 29 cents were furnished from various sources for missionary objects; on the minutes of the latter, the funds of the *mission society* exhibit an amount of 387 dollars and 77 cents. Had the minutes of the *Lincoln* come to hand, with accounts from other mite and mission societies, additional information of this nature might have been offered. In

NEW HAMPSHIRE and VERMONT—much that is grateful to christian feeling is observable. To all the associations accessions have been gained of such as profess an experience of grace in the heart; to some of them the accessions have been very numerous, in one instance 510, in another 666. Female mite societies and other indications of the prosperity of Zion are multiplying. Extracts from letters and minutes, exhibiting notices of *societies, contributions,* &c. with many animating passages relative to revivals, and some complaints of coldness and negligence in religion, are unavoidably here omitted. The *associations* in

MASSACHUSETTS, RHODE ISLAND and CONNECTICUT—have received additions, but some of them small, while others have been very considerable. Although, in reference to particular places, there is great reason for lamentation and distress on account of the low state of religion, and disregard of the ordinances of the house of God, others have experienced precious reformations. The mission spirit also is in active operation, as the contributions from mite societies, churches, congregations, and individuals mentioned in their minutes amply testify.

NEW YORK State.—Upon this region we advance with unfeigned delight. Here the Spirit of the Lord has been largely shed abroad. Numbers have been brought out of the darkness of sin into marvellous light. Many have been baptised into the name of HIM who was crucified, and who rose from the dead. Of course, zeal for missions abundantly prevails. It is regretted that the minutes of several of the *associations* the past year have not been obtained. Those that have come to hand, as well as letters from that quarter, exhibit the most animating indications of the progress of the cause of Zion. In the churches of one Association have been baptised 409—another, 437—another, 733—and another, 870. Extracts from letters will be introduced into a future number of the Luminary, as soon as practicable. Some of the churches in the

NEW JERSEY—*Association* have been favoured with refreshing influences from on high. Others mourn a state of coldness in divine things, praying with the prophet, *O Lord, revive thy work!* The ladies of the Burlington *Mite Society*, as well as others, continue to display a laudable zeal for missions—while one, lately of their number, now shares in the toils of the missionary field westward of the Mississippi river. Large additions the past year were not made to any of the churches connected with the *associations* in

PENNSYLVANIA.—A number of them, however, both in the city of Philadelphia and the country round about, as well as those at a greater distance, have worn a pleasant aspect, and realized a gradual increase. Several missionary societies have been formed. Within the limits of the *Abington Association*, a revival, it is understood, has commenced. But in various sections of the commonwealth missionary aid is pressingly needed. Relative to the *associations* in

DELAWARE and MARYLAND.—but little can be here introduced. Notwithstanding a degree of coldness in religious matters much to be deplored, and that many are to be met with who seldom hear preaching, some things are observable to sustain and animate our hopes. In one of the churches in Baltimore, 46 have been baptised, and in that in Alexandria 58, besides the zeal for missions, *foreign and domestic*, in these places, in Washington city, and in other portions of country now under review. A survey of

VIRGINIA—awakens emotions at once joyous and painful. Several of the churches in different parts of the state have been richly visited with the showers of divine goodness. Happy and extensive revivals have been witnessed. Much zeal for missions continues to be displayed; and societies for missionary purposes have multiplied. Some sections, however, are but partially supplied with the preaching of the gospel. Similar observations will apply to

THE CAROLINAS and GEORGIA.—Although various places exhibit a degree of barrenness which it is mournful to view, considerable ingatherings have gladdened some of the churches; favourable prospects have for a time warmed the hearts of the brethren in others; and a zealous activity and liberality in favour of the missionary cause has been manifested. In the

ALABAMA TERRITORY and STATE OF TENNESSEE—the gospel appears to be gaining ground. To the associations in this quarter large additions have not been made. In a few instances the Lord has shed forth a spirit of revival; at Mobile a Sunday school has been originated by the ladies; missionary efforts are increasing; still here is a wide field for faithful labours in the Saviour's service.

KENTUCKY—has been greatly favoured the past year. Powerful and extensive awakenings have been experienced; the number of mission societies has been augmented; and much concern for imparting the blessings of civilization and christianity to the native tribes of the forest, is here discovered. An abundant reward for these evangelical solicitudes, and their attendant liberalities, it is hoped, will be enjoyed in the continued and increasing displays of the divine favour.

OHIO and INDIANA—appear not to have been signalized by any remarkable outpourings of the Holy Spirit, the year past. Some of the servants of the Lord have seen happy times; others have had their hopes raised and expectations excited for a season; but have reason to lament the want of preachers, and *the ways of Zion mourn* that so few attend the solemnities of divine worship.

ILLINOIS and MISSOURI TERRITORIES—present extensive fields for missionary labours. Churches however have been formed; and there are some, besides the missionaries under the patronage of the Board, proclaiming the *unsearchable riches of Christ.*

MISSISSIPPI and LOUISIANA.—The state of things in this quarter is best exhibited in the communications from the Rev Mr. Ranaldson, published in this and former numbers of the Luminary. Missionaries are there greatly needed

By the returns on the minutes as exhibited in the *Table of Associations,* the number baptised the preceding year must have exceeded 12270, that number is actually returned from 80 associations, while from 50 associations no returns of those baptised have been furnished The churches are 2682, preachers, 1859, the whole number of members about 190,000

From this estimate it is obvious that there is far from being a sufficient supply of ministers even for the churches, besides loud and pressing calls from destitute sections of the country. While, therefore, we have much cause for devout thankfulness to the Father of goodness for his manifold mercies, we have also great reason for deep humility, and fervent supplication that the *Lord of the harvest would send forth labourers.*

The preceding remarks have reference to the state of religion in our own denomination. Others, blessed be God! have, in multiplied instances, been highly favoured with the reviving influences of divine grace We regret that our limits do not allow us to introduce a more particular and extended survey We wish to know, and wish our readers to know, as accurately as possible, the state of every religious denomination in our own country, and throughout the world.

THE EDUCATION of pious young men, who in the judgment of the churches, as well as in their own judgment are called of God to the work of the ministry, deserves to be taken into the account in a general view of the *state of religion.*

The necessity that the preacher of the everlasting gospel should "*give attendance to reading,*" as well as "*to exhortation*" and to "*doctrine,*" should "*meditate upon these things,*" should "*give himself wholly to them,*"—that he should "*study*" in order "*to show himself approved unto God, a workman that needeth not to be ashamed, rightly dividing the word of truth,*" agreeably to the solemn and repeated injunctions of Paul to Timothy, is becoming more and more apparent Enlightened by the scriptures on this subject, the churches feel its importance In all directions a kindling zeal is producing vigorous exertion

Our brethren in the eastern states have already made considerable advancement. As appears by the minutes of the *Boston Association* at their last session, they received 765 dollars to assist the funds of the Baptist Education Society Among the contributors we are happy to notice two *Female Education Societies* A dozen or fourteen young men are studying with the Rev Mr Chaplin, of Danvers, Mas In the course of the past season another institution has been originated in that quarter, and located in Maine, the design of which is understood to be both classical and theological, and the prospect of its utility flattering

Besides the Education Society in the city of New York, one has been formed in the interior of that state, where very considerable zeal appears to exist, with competent means, for the prosecution of this interesting object.

In Virginia and North Carolina something, on an enlarged scale, it should seem, is about to be attempted Education societies, particularly among the ladies, have already been there established.

Our brethren in South Carolina connected with the Charleston association, have for a long time employed a zealous activity, and given to this business successful operation. The minutes of their last session exhibit receipts from societies, churches, and individuals, to the amount of $635 93½ for the *Education Fund*, besides $928 99½ for missions. We notice, too, with particular satisfaction, the donation of $100 by Mrs. Elizabeth M'Nair, towards the Theological Seminary proposed by the Convention, and about to be carried into effect by the Board.

Another education concern, it is understood, has been originated in the same state among the churches belonging to the Savannah River Association. Our friends in Georgia, we are persuaded, will not, with their ample means, refuse themselves the happiness of assisting a cause so obviously important to the interests of religion.

In Mississippi an education society has already been formed, and one in Ohio; nor will we for a moment admit the idea that our worthy brethren in the wealthy and flourishing country between, will suffer others to carry forward these benevolent and useful plans without their assistance. Meantime let all unite in supplicating the blessing of God on every pursuit undertaken for his glory.

POETRY.

For the following communication the publishers are indebted to Miss SALLY GANO *of Poughkeepsie, N. Y. who received it from the author, Mrs* HOUGH, *when on her voyage from America, twenty days from Calcutta.*

"The other evening I sat reflecting on the past, and my absent friends shared much in my meditations; sadness pervaded my mind, and I almost involuntarily poured forth my soul in song. Possibly the simple effusions of your friend may amuse you, and perhaps a sympathetic feeling will pervade your bosom as you read the following lines.

ON MELANCHOLY.

When absent friends invite
  The silent tear, the tender sigh,
When Memory throws her light
  On scenes of joy passed swiftly by:
Then Melancholy flings
  A sombre sadness o'er the mind,
She strikes the tender strings
  Of sensibility refined.

She bids the tears to speak,
  To tell the latent grief she feels,
Their language is too weak,
  'Tis what the deep-fetch'd sigh reveals
But, Melancholy, why
  Hang all thy tender charms o'er me?
I would not always sigh
  For worldly joys, which transient be.

Though time and distance join
  To part me from the friends I love;
If Jesus is but mine,
  'Tis joy which changes cannot move
Then, Melancholy, go—
  Thy power can never bind my soul,
Thou tender nurse of wo,
  I yield thee not supreme control."

PSALM LXXII

To Christ the Lord, fair Zion's king,
Judgment and righteousness we bring;
The poor shall bless the faithful throne
Of our anointed Solomon.

Hence shall the bow and chariot cease,
And hills to mountains echo peace;
He shall the needy children save,
And bind oppression in the grave.

Long as the sun shall rule the day,
Or moon effuse her silver ray,
His fear shall sway the ransom'd heart,
And every meaner fear depart.

He shall descend like spreading rains
That fertilize a thousand plains,
His saints shall hail the rich increase,
And bind their ample sheaves in peace.

From seas to earth's remotest ends
The glory of his throne extends;
In him the wilderness shall trust,
And foes, as adders, lick the dust.

Sov'reigns of Tarshish and the Isles
To him surrender all their spoils,
Before him Sheba's monarchs bend,
And universal hymns ascend.

Though death against his empire strive,
For ever shall that empire live:
For him perpetual prayer be made,
To him immortal honours paid.

No more the thistled earth shall mourn,
The hills shall smile with bowing corn,
While from their sides the seed shall spread,
And peopled cities fill with bread.

Blessings in him shall mortals find
To heal and elevate the mind;
Earth be a Paradise again,
And loud as thunder, shout—*Amen!*

Such were the strains of Jesse's son—
'Twas inspiration gave their tone.
"Be this:"—he said,—"my whole desire!"
And threw away his useless lyre.

THE LATTER DAY LUMINARY;

BY A COMMITTEE

OF

THE BAPTIST BOARD OF FOREIGN MISSIONS FOR THE UNITED STATES.

VOL. I.   AUGUST, 1818.   No. IV.

BIOGRAPHY.

THE REV. ANDREW FULLER.

IN selecting characters for our biographical department, the publishers of the Luminary are desirous of portraying such, especially, as have distinguished themselves in the mission cause. Of these, the late Mr. FULLER is among the most prominent. For more than twenty years he was the faithful and laborious secretary of the Baptist Mission in England. He classed with the most active of the venerable men who planned the measures that have been so extensively executed in India, and by his death has occasioned a chasm, which only the God of missions can remove.

This extraordinary and excellent man was a native of Wicken, a small village in Cambridgeshire, where his ancestors on his father's side had long resided. He was born on the 6th of February, 1754. Impressions of a religious nature were received at an early age. He had serious thoughts relative to a future state, when only fourteen years old. They were deep, various, and pungent, and at the age of sixteen terminated, as he trusted, in real conversion. "From this time," he says, "my former wicked courses were forsaken.—My soul, said I, with joy and triumph, is as a weaned child! I now know experimentally what it is to be dead to the world by the cross of Christ, and to feel an habitual determination to devote my future life to God my Saviour." In April, 1770, he was baptised, and joined the church at Soham, then under the pastoral charge of the Rev. Mr. Eve. A Mr. Joseph Diver, a man, pious, thoughtful, and much devoted to reading, was baptised with him. An intimacy with Mr. Diver was valued by Mr. Fuller, as one of the greatest blessings of his existence. The succeeding autumn an unhappy breach occurred in the church, which issued in Mr. Eve's removal. His brethren soon discovered talents in young Fuller, promising usefulness in the Christian ministry. An elderly lady of the church dying, in the year 1774, expressed her wish, if it could be done with propriety, that Mr. Fuller should preach her funeral sermon. Previous to the funeral, the church, who were of one mind on the subject, after a day of prayer and fasting, called him to the ministry, in which he continued until he finished his testimony.

In 1775, he accepted the pastorship of the Baptist church at Soham, where he laboured between seven and eight years. A circumstance occurred about this time, which, as it may prove useful to persons in similar embarrassment, deserves to be mentioned. "A friend, of slender abilities, being asked to pray, knelt down, and Mr. Fuller and the company with him, when he found himself so embarrassed, that, whispering to Mr. Fuller, he said, "I do not know how to go on." Mr. F. replied in a whisper, "Tell the Lord so!" The rest of the company did not hear what passed between them; but the man, taking Mr. Fuller's advice, began to confess his not knowing how to pray as he ought to pray, begging to be taught to pray, and so proceeded in prayer to the satisfaction of the company.

> Have you no words—ah! think again,—
> Words flow apace when you complain.

The removal of Mr. F. from Soham was attended with numerous and painful exercises of mind. Dr. Ryland, his biographer, judiciously remarks, that "Men who fear not God, would risk the welfare of a nation, with fewer searchings of heart, than it cost him to leave a little dissenting church, scarcely containing forty members, beside himself and wife." His difficulties at Soham, arose in part from the unkindness of some of the members, and in part from his receiving an income which neither the opening of a small store, nor the keeping of a school, could render equal to the frugal demands of an increasing family. By the Rev. Robert Hall, of Arnsby, author of the "Help to Zion's Travellers," the church at Kettering were first incited to try if he could not be obtained as their pastor. After a series of painful emotions, solemn meditations, frequent prayers, and the concurrent advice of his brethren in the ministry, among whom were men whose praise is in all the churches, he consented to a removal. This took place on the 7th of October, 1783. A passage in his confession of faith, delivered on taking the pastorship of the Kettering church, has so direct a bearing on his future, unanticipated relation to missions, that, without supposing it prophetic, it must be acknowledged remarkable. "I firmly and joyfully believe that the kingdom of Christ will yet be gloriously extended, by the pouring out of God's spirit upon the preaching of the word: and I consider it as an event, for the arrival of which, *it becomes all God's servants and churches most ardently to pray!* It is one of the *chief springs of my joy* in this day of small things, that it will not be so always."

At some periods of his life, Mr. F. kept a private diary. Such extracts as have come to light, demonstrate no common degree of holy watchfulness, spiritual conflict, and anxiety for the success of his ministry, and the spirituality of those committed to his pastoral care.

Monthly prayer meetings for the spread of the everlasting gospel through the earth, were introduced to the attention of christians by the Baptist association in Nottingham, June 3, 1784. At the end of a sermon on " *walking by faith,*" the first publication Mr. F. ever issued, various " persuasives to a general union in extraordinary prayer" were introduced. Their effect is visible in the supplications of thousands. They have contributed to introduce a periodical service, that may be considered as the *new moon* of the latter days.

The character of Mr. Fuller, as a controversialist in theology, is sufficiently known. Whatever difference of opinion may be entertained as to some of his productions, his Calvinistic and Socinian systems compared as to their moral tendency," his "Gospel its own Witness," his "Letters on the doctrine of Universal Salvation," and his " Strictures on Sandemanianism," are, we believe, among our churches, every where welcomed and admired His " Memoirs of the Rev Samuel Pearce" affectingly address the heart of the real christian, while his "Expository Discourses" are calculated to illumine and enlarge the understanding. Single sermons, on different occasions, that have appeared through the press, are numerous.

In his missionary exertions we behold an example which commands our admiration, and invites our efforts. The immediate origin of a Baptist mission is to be traced to the solicitude of Mr. (now Dr.) Carey, for the salvation of the heathen; but it is certain that Mr. F. caught the flame when only in an incipient state. At a ministers' meeting in Clipstone, 1791, an uncommon degree of attention was excited by two sermons; the first preached by Mr. Sutcliffe, on being "jealous for the Lord of Hosts," the other by Mr. Fuller on "the pernicious influence of delay." These sermons were printed, together with a third sermon delivered at an association in Nottingham by Dr. Carey, from Is. liv. 2, 3. enforcing the obligations of Christians to *expect great things*, and to *attempt great things*. The society was formed on the 2d of October, 1792. The labours of Mr. Fuller for the promotion of this great object, became indefatigable. He had reason to believe that they induced a paralytic affection, by which, in the year following, he was deprived for a short time of the use of one side of his face. His brethren were alarmed at the prospect of losing such a man. In about two weeks the symptoms subsided, leaving a headach, which he never wholly lost. As the mission soon went into operation, it became necessary to provide funds for its support. Mr. F. began to journey and preach, with a view of obtaining collections. In this service he occupied, for several years, nearly a fourth part of his time. Besides frequently visiting London and the different parts of England, once he went to Ireland. He was on this business five times in Scotland. He almost ever returned with monies more ample than himself or his friends had expected. As the mission in the East Indies enlarged the place of its tent, and stretched forth the curtains of its habitation, it became by degrees an object which the English government began to recognize. Its officers, and those of the East India company, he had occasion repeatedly to visit. Though a stranger to the manners and arts of a courtier, the solemnity of his address, the perspicuity and sagacity of his observations, and the resolute devotion of his whole heart to the work, commonly enabled him, with the blessing of his God, to ward off impending danger, or secure existing privilege. His defence of the baptist and other missionary societies against the pernicious and illiberal publications of Mr. Twining, major Scott Waring, and a Bengal officer, was keen, intrepid, and effective.

Mr. Fuller was twice married. His first wife was a miss Gardiner. He had by her eleven children, "three of whom were buried at Soham, five at Kettering, one in the sea, and two survive." Such as are dead, with the exception of two, expired in infancy. One of these was a lovely daughter, who died May 30, 1816, aged six years and about six months; giving pleasing evidence of a change of heart. The removal of this child was a sore affliction to Mr. F. but he learned to be resigned in tribulation. In some artless but sentimental lines, which he wrote on the providence, he says:

"But—must we part, and can I bid farewell?
We must—I can—I have—I kiss'd her dust;
I kiss'd her clay-cold corpse, and bade farewell,
Until the resurrection of the just."

The other was his eldest son, who, at a proper age, was placed under the care of a merchant in London. The hopes which accompanied the earlier years of his life, were in a short time blasted. The temper of the youth was unstable and restless. He preferred the tumult and dissipation of the life of a soldier or a marine, to the quietude of mercantile occupations. His conduct pierced the heart of his father with many sorrows. He died on the seas in March, 1809. One of the severest of the trials which befel Mr. Fuller, was the death of his companion. This occurred shortly after the birth of a daughter. Hysterical affections deprived her for some time of her senses, so that she could not be prevailed upon to believe that her husband, her children, or her home was *hers*. Her mourning husband wrote the following epitaph, designed for her grave-stone.

"The tender parent wails no more her loss,
 Nor labours more beneath life's heavy load,
The anxious soul, released from fears and woes,
 Has found her home, her children, and her God"

Mr. Fuller's second wife, who survives him, was miss Ann Coles, the only daughter of the Rev. William Coles, late pastor of the Baptist church at Maulden, in Bedfordshire. By this marriage he had six children, three of whom died in infancy, and three are living. In both these connexions it was his happiness to have found intelligent, amiable, and godly partners

The messenger which was commissioned to put an end to the labours of this excellent man was a disease in the liver, brought on by one of the bilious attacks to which he was subject. He appears to have entertained very little hope of recovery. "The complaint I have upon me," said he in a letter to a friend in America, "will, I expect, before long lodge me in the grave." In the later stages of his disease, it was thought adviseable that he should visit Cheltenham, but the progress of the disorder rendered the attempt impracticable. Dr. Kerr, an eminent physician of Northampton, who was sent for to see him, informed a friend he was satisfied his liver was as black as his hat, and as hard as a table. On the 28th of April, 1815, he dictated a letter to his affectionate friend, the Rev. Dr. Ryland of Bristol, in which he says, "I have no other hope than from salvation by mere grace, through the atonement of my Lord and Saviour. *With this hope I can go into eternity with composure.* Come, Lord Jesus, come when thou wilt. Here I am—Let him do with me as seemeth him good."

On the afternoon of the day on which the letter was dictated, he observed to one of the deacons of his church, that his bodily depression was almost intolerable. The brother replied, "I do not know any person, sir, who is in a more enviable situation than yourself—a good man on the verge of a blessed immortality." He modestly acquiesced. He then lifted up his hands and exclaimed, "if I am saved, it will be by GREAT AND SOVEREIGN GRACE;" which last words he repeated very emphatically—BY GREAT AND SOVEREIGN GRACE! To record all the expressions which have been preserved from his dying lips, would swell our article beyond its bounds; but we must subjoin a few. He would often say during his affliction, My mind is calm—no raptures, no despondency. About nine days before his death, while attempting to get up, as he sat by the bed-side, he observed, "all my feelings are sinking, dying feelings!" Seeing his wife affected, he said, "we shall meet again" and added, "it will be well." On another occasion he used an expression highly characteristic: "My hope is such that I am not afraid to PLUNGE into eternity." On the Lord's day morning on which he died, May 7, 1815, he said to his daughter Sarah, "I wish I had strength enough!"—she asked him "to do what?" he replied "to worship, child!"—Soon after, his daughter Mary entering the room, as soon as he understood who it was, he said, "Come, Mary, come and help me."—He was then raised up in bed—and for the last half hour appeared to be engaged in prayer. His children surrounded his bed, listening attentively, to catch, if possible, the last words of their dying parent, but nothing could be distinctly heard but "HELP ME!" Then, with his hands clasped and his eyes fixed upwards, he sunk back and expired.

COMMUNICATIONS.

THE RESTORATION AND CONVERSION OF THE JEWS.

IN the present age the salvation of the Gentiles has not alone engaged the zeal of the disciples of Christ; they have cherished a serious concern, and entered on vigorous endeavours, with the blessing of the Lord, for the everlasting welfare of the Jewish nation. At least seven millions of this people are spread over the earth, particularly throughout Europe, Asia and Africa. Every where they adhere to the law of Moses, not only among Christians who admit the divine appointment of Hebrew rites as fully as the Jews themselves, but also amid the errors and follies of idolaters. No lustrations in the Ganges, no popular veneration for Birmah and Vishnoo, prevails on the Jews in India to abandon the religion of their fathers.

Doris amara suam non intermiscuit undam.

In relation to this wonderful people, two things present themselves on the page of prophecy.

1. Their restoration to the country of Judea. This may be inferred from the words of Moses—Deut. xxx. 1. "And it shall come to pass, when all these things are come upon thee, the blessing and the curse, which I have set before thee, and thou shalt call them to mind among all the nations, whither the Lord thy God hath driven thee, and shalt return unto the Lord thy God, and shalt obey his voice, according to all I command thee this day, thou and thy children, with all thine heart, and with all thy soul, that then the Lord thy God will turn thy captivity, and have compassion upon thee, and will return and gather thee from all the nations, whither the Lord thy God hath scattered thee. If any of thine be driven out unto the outmost parts of heaven, from thence will the Lord thy God gather thee, and from thence will he fetch thee: and the Lord thy God will bring thee into the land which thy fathers possessed, and thou shalt possess it; and he will do thee good, and multiply thee above thy fathers. And the Lord thy God will circumcise thine heart, and the heart of thy seed, to love the Lord thy God, with all thy heart, and with all thy soul, that thou mayest live." Later prophets foretel the same event; particularly Isaiah and Ezekiel. See Isaiah xi. 12. "He shall set up an ensign to the nations, and shall assemble the outcasts of Israel, and GATHER TOGETHER the dispersed of Judah from the four corners of the earth." See also Isaiah xxvii. 12. "And it shall come to pass in that day, that the Lord shall beat off from the channel of the river unto the stream of Egypt, and ye shall be gathered one by one, O ye children of Israel." Ezekiel dwells much on this occurrence, Ezekiel xxxvi. 24. "I will take you from among the heathen, and gather you out of all countries, and bring you into your own land." Chap. xxxvii. 21. "Thus saith the Lord God, behold, I will take the children of Israel from among the heathen, whither they be gone, and will gather them on every side, and bring them into their own land; and I will make them one nation in the land upon the mountains of Israel, and one king shall be king to them all, and they shall be no more two nations, neither shall they be divided into two kingdoms any more at all."

Many circumstances render the event probable in itself. They are a people almost every where oppressed; and consequently their attachment to the countries in which they live must be feeble. They every where entertain an assured and cheerful expectation of entering their land. With each other they correspond all over the earth. They generally speak and write Rabbinical Hebrew, and have therefore a language through which they can enjoy immediate intercourse;

and it is remarkable that they value personal above real property. Their wealth consists in money and jewels, which are capable of easy transportation. They have been called " *the brokers of the world.*"

But the prophecies which more deeply interest the feelings of Christians, embrace

2 Their conversion to the faith of the gospel. From numerous passages of this description, we select three Jer. xxxii. 37, &c. " I will gather them out of all countries whither I have driven them in mine anger, and in my fury, and in great wrath, and I will bring them again unto this place, and will cause them to dwell safely, and they shall be my people, and I will be their God: and I will give them one heart and one way, that they may fear me for ever." Hos. iii. 4. " For the children of Israel shall abide many days without a king, and without a prince, and without a sacrifice, and without an image, and without an ephod, and without teraphim. Afterward shall the children of Israel return, and seek the Lord their God, and David their king, and shall fear the Lord, and his goodness in the latter days" Romans xi. 25—31. " For I would not, brethren, that ye should be ignorant of this mystery, lest ye should be wise in your own conceits; that blindness in part is happened to Israel, until the fulness of the Gentiles be come in. And so all Israel shall be saved. as it is written, There shall come out of Sion the Deliverer, and shall turn away ungodliness from Jacob: for this is my covenant unto them, when I shall take away their sins. As concerning the gospel, they are enemies for your sakes: but as touching the election, they are beloved for the fathers' sakes. For the gifts and calling of God are without repentance. For as ye in times past have not believed God, yet have now obtained mercy through their unbelief; even so have these also now not believed, that through your mercy they also may obtain mercy."

A society in London has for several years been engaged in seeking the salvation of the Israelites. It is composed of men high in respectability and wealth. Their plans appear founded in wisdom and piety. They have issued a copy of the New Testament in the Hebrew language, which has been distributed through various parts of Europe and Asia. It was completed only in December last, and yet a new edition is demanded A very respectable member of the society of Friends, thus   ct, in an address to the editors of the Jewish Expo   , 1818. " It is, I assure thee, with great pleasure   ong faith, that I look forward to the effect of the general reading   the New Testament among the Jews. The Hebrew character, which they consider a sacred one, will ensure an attention to it, that no other character in which it may be presented can induce them to pay; and although a great multitude of the Jews are but half acquainted with the Hebrew tongue, a great proportion remain who thoroughly understand it, and whose minds, I trust, will be enlightened while they survey its doctrines—doctrines which, whilst they abolish the law of Moses, magnify and make it honourable."

In the United States some pious ladies have taken the lead in this service of love. A "Female Society" exists in Boston and its vicinity, "for the promotion of Christianity among the Jews." From their second annual report it appears, that by subscriptions, donations, &c. $533 62 were obtained the past year. One hundred dollars have been sent to Bombay, for the education of Jewish children there, and one hundred pounds sterling have been transmitted to the London Society, to aid in the translation of the New Testament into Hebrew. "With great satisfaction they announce that another auxiliary has been added, composed of a large proportion of the ladies in Portland, (Maine,) and called the Portland Female Association for the promotion of Christianity among the Jews." Such interesting examples ought to be imitated.

Dr. Gill indulged the opinion that "the conversion of these people will be sudden, and of them altogether a *nation shall be born at once.*" He adds, "It looks as if their conversion would be like that of the apostle Paul; and he seems to hint that it will, when he says, that he, in obtaining mercy, was *a pattern to them which should hereafter believe;* meaning perhaps his own countrymen that should believe in Christ in the latter day, whose conversion should be similar to his: that as his conversion was sudden, in the midst of all his ignorance, unbelief and rebellion, and without the word, by the immediate power and grace of God, so will theirs be in like manner; nor is it likely that their conversion should be by means of the word, since there is such an aversion in that people to the hearing of it; and a rare thing is it to see a Jew in a Christian assembly." It must, however, be recollected, that with the exception of the time of the Pentecost, and a few days succeeding, Jews in the primitive age of Christianity were converted to God as other men. Late reports as to the spread of divine truth among them encourage the expectation, that, as Gentiles are turned to God, so shall they be; and certainly no conjectural interpretation of scripture should wither the energies of Christians, or depress their hopes.

CHARGE DELIVERED TO MESSRS. WHEELOCK AND COLMAN,

BY REV. MR. SHARP,

WHEN THEY WERE SET APART TO THE OFFICE OF MISSIONARIES OF THE CROSS OF CHRIST, FOR THE KINGDOM OF BURMAH.

My dear young brethren,

THIS day you have been set apart to a very solemn and arduous work. It is an important event in the life of a minister to be ordained as the pastor of a regularly organized church in his own land, but it is an event of peculiar importance when individuals receive the imposition of hands in the full expectation of soon bidding adieu to their kindred and friends, and of going far off to the heathen, never to return. We know that you are not insensible to the ties of country, of kindred, and of friendship, which the scenes of youth and the associations of early life produce. To you, therefore, the services of this day must assume an importance and an interest, which language cannot express.

We trust, however, you have seriously reflected on the sacrifices you will have to make, and that the great principle which has prompted you to offer yourselves as missionaries, is love to the souls of the poor Burmans, who are bound in the chains of idolatry; "sitting in darkness and the shadow of death."

Many esteem the service in which you hope to be engaged, as a novel employment. This is not the case, for although ages have passed away in which Christians appeared to forget their obligations to the heathen, it was not always so. The apostles and disciples of our Lord were missionaries. The ancient cities of Greece and Rome, and there is reason to believe the ancient Britons, were indebted for the gospel of the grace of God, to the travels and labours of these servants of the Most High. Many contemplate missionary exertions with scorn. They say that all our prospects of success are visionary; that an Ethiopian can as soon change his skin, or a leopard his spots, as that the heathen should ever embrace the gospel of Christ. It is said that their habits are too deeply rooted, their natures too debased, and their attachment to idolatry too strong, ever to be overthrown.

We grant, if it depended on human exertions alone, we should despair of success. But God has promised his Son that he will give him the heathen for his inheritance, and the uttermost parts of the earth for his possession. You may therefore rely with confidence on the faithfulness and power of a promise-giving God.

He who has presented the strongest assurances of the universal extension of Messiah's empire, has not excited our hopes, induced our prayers, and called forth our exertions, in vain.

He can, with the most perfect ease, bring order out of confusion; light out of darkness; and create purity where licentiousness reigned. He that giveth man knowledge, can pour a flood of spiritual light into the most benighted mind. He who made the heart, can, with a word, transform that heart into his own moral image.

Let every doubt as to the conversion of the heathen vanish, from a recollection that nothing is impossible with God.

Encouragement to missionary exertions may be derived from facts. Brahmins have relinquished the honours and emoluments of their priestly office, and have become humble followers of Christ. Hindoos have broken their cast, and burnt their idols in the fire. We therefore believe that the work to which you are attached is the work of the Lord, and most sincerely bid you God speed.

When James, Cephas, and John perceived the grace that was given to Paul and Barnabas, they gave to them the right hand of fellowship that they should go unto the heathen.

Your fathers and brethren in the ministry, persuaded of your personal piety, your intense desire to labour in India, and the uprightness of your motives, have requested me to give you, in their behalf, the right hand of fellowship. Take it as an expression that we most cordially approve of the cause, in which you expect to spend all your strength and all your days. Take this hand as an expression of the confidence we have in you as men of God, and of the deep interest which we feel in your future prosperity and happiness. If, in the course of Providence, you were this day placed over some of our neighbouring churches, we should endeavour to redeem the pledge we have given you, by habits of personal intercourse, and by an interchange of ministerial services. We would give you our best advice. We would mingle our tears with yours when you were called to weep, and would rejoice with you in your prosperity. But these pleasures will be denied us. Do not think, however, that as soon as you are absent you will be forgotten! No, my dear brethren, the cause you serve, as well as a personal friendship strengthened by an intimate acquaintance, will secure to you a place in our memories and our hearts. When it is well with us, we will remember you. Mighty oceans will cut off the possibility of social interviews, but they will not cut off the brotherly affection we feel for you. Though placed at the distance of thousands of miles, we shall not be indifferent spectators of your proceedings. The intelligence we receive from you, will lighten up our countenances with joy, or swell our hearts with grief. Whatever instruction, comfort, or encouragement we can impart by our correspondence, rest assured it will be imparted.

A short time before those venerable men of God, Thomas and Carey, went to India, at an interview with their friends Pearce, Fuller, Sutcliffe and Ryland, they said, "We are like men going down into a well, you are on the top, and have got hold of the rope, do not let us fall!" They unitedly exclaimed, We never will! Do you view your situation similar to theirs, and are you saying, Do not let us fall! Take this hand as a pledge, that whether others withdraw their aid or not, "we will not let go the rope!"

When life was fast ebbing away, and Lawrence was in the arms of death, his last words were, "Dont give up the ship!" Are you ready to say, Dear fathers and brethren, dont give up the mission! We solemnly assure you we will not give up the mission.

I cannot deny myself this opportunity, my brethren, of giving you my hand as a public expression of my unceasing regard and affection for you. An intimacy which has subsisted for years, in which I have had an opportunity of witnessing your conduct, has endeared you to me by ties which will not readily be broken. Wherever you go, my prayers will go with you. Let your demeanour towards that worthy man who has already published a tract in the Burman language, be such as I have uniformly witnessed, and you will secure his confidence and his love. We need not remind you, that if, you would be happy and useful, you must live near to God. Never forget, that whatever exertions you make, you can do nothing without the blessing of God. While we assure you of our fellowship, let it be a fixed persuasion in your own minds, that you can do no good in India, unless you walk with your brethren in harmony and love. Never allow a spirit of competition, envy, or jealousy, to have a place in your breasts. An unyielding spirit, on one side at least, rendered it necessary for Paul and Barnabas to separate. Let the motto of the father of your country be inscribed, in large characters, on some part of your mission house, "UNITED WE STAND, DIVIDED WE FALL!" I trust at some distant period it will be said of you, my brethren, as it was of Saul and Jonathan, "they were lovely and pleasant in their lives."

May the Lord Almighty bless you, dear brethren. Go forth in his strength, and the power of his might. Enter the highways and hedges of a dark world, and compel sinners to come in, that they may partake of the feast which heaven has prepared; and whatever good may result from your efforts, ascribe the whole to that divine Spirit, who descended on the primitive missionaries, qualified them for their work, and rendered efficacious the messages they proclaimed.

MISSIONARY INTELLIGENCE.

MISSION TO BURMAH.

Extract of a letter from Rev. Mr. Judson, dated July 30, 1817.

"I AM entirely engaged in the dictionary, and shall be for several months to come. Brother Hough is getting on in the language. He is, however, rather out of his element since the printing has been suspended.

"My attention has lately been turned toward Siam. This is a great kingdom; the next accessible beyond Burmah, on your way to China. The people are superior to the Burmans in every respect. Is there no young man in the American churches who will feel that he is a debtor to the Siamese? He can come to Rangoon, and acquire the language under very considerable advantages. There are hundreds of Siamese in Rangoon, and churches and priests. Afterwards he must go to Bengal, and form a connexion with some commercial house who would open a trade with Siam. Such a thing has been mentioned to me. It is desired by some. O, that I had another self! This is the enterprise to which I would devote him: but my present self is devoted to Burmah."

[Siam, the country to which Mr. Judson alludes, before the recent extension of the Burman empire, was regarded as the principal state of the Thither India. Its precise boundaries are not ascertained. It embraces a tract of country from five to six hundred miles long, and from two to three hundred broad. The capital of the kingdom, as well as the kingdom itself, is called Siam: the natives, however, call it Yuthia, or Juthea. It stands on an island formed by the Meinan river. The system of legislation among the Siamese, is said to resemble that of the Burmans. Mutilation or death is the punishment of minor offences. Their religion, if it may be so called, is the doctrine of Boodh. They burn their dead. White elephants among them are held in adoration. God, in his providence, will introduce his gospel among this people. How soon, we are unable to ascertain; but we have often had reason for observing, that *impressions* on the minds of the servants of God, are frequently the forerunners of missionary adventure.]

From Mr Hough to the Cor Secretary, dated Rangoon, September 1, 1817

RECENT letters sent to you from Rangoon, preclude my affording you much additional information relative to the mission. Our printing office is now unoccupied. What we have been employed about, you will have heard before this reaches you. I shall send you a copy of each of the publications.* They will prove

---

* The Board acknowledges the reception of the Gospel by Matthew, translated into Burman by Mr Judson, together with a copy of the first religious Tract circulated in that country, and a Catechism, each in the Burman tongue.

to you that two missionaries can do a little, and, by the rule of proportion, you can calculate, that as two, already here, is to the little done, so would four be, were they here, to as much again. Slow and tedious are the first advances of a mission in a heathen country; particularly in this, where every step must be taken with the nicest circumspection, and where idolatry and pagan madness, speaking in human weakness, are desperate. I cannot, I dare not, however, admit a discouraging thought, and I trust and pray that you will not, for our assurance of success rests upon this basis—"the Lord reigneth."

There is yet no proof of any permanent impression of truth being made on the mind of any Burman. On reading this fact, I am sure your heart will not sink lower than mine does in writing it, but let us not faint. The Lord converts sinners, and the manner how, and the person who, are his own choice. He tries us by what we call a delay, in the work of conversion, and perhaps our Saviour had something of this in view, when he commanded "not to faint in praying always." If our prayers were immediately answered, the injunction would be needless; and if success immediately followed exertion, why be required to "wait on the Lord?" "Wilt thou now restore the kingdom unto Israel?" if considered as a prayer, rather than a question arising out of an expectation which the existing circumstances might suggest, was indicative of a zeal, which, though godly in itself, was so hasty as to require a check, and that not by positive denial, neither in a way to prohibit a future repetition of it, but by a reference to humble reliance on God, who hath put the times and seasons in his own power.

We have lately had a few European transients here, who have attended worship with us on Lord's days, and also two or three Americans. They have heard the gospel among us. May God give it success.

You wish me "success in studying the round O language." I thank you, for I know your wishes are sincere. Could you realize the labours a mind must suffer in ascertaining new signs for its ideas, and then giving those signs birth in sounds so strange as almost to appal your ears, you would appear to yourself as undergoing a transformation. It was the remark of a learned man, that a person in obtaining a new language, acquired another soul. If this be not literally true, it certainly appears, that a new language gives an impress of new features on the soul already possessed. To enter into the genius and idiom of the Burman, is my greatest difficulty. I hope I am gradually mounting up the rugged steep, and your wishes encourage me. I will give you a little specimen of the language, in the Lord's prayer, with its pronunciation in the English character, together with its idiom, as near as I can represent it to you. In pronouncing it, sound the *g* hard, and the initial *ng* as perfectly nasal, as when final in the English. The figures over the vowels correspond to those in Walker's Dictionary. All the words in which there is not a hyphen are monosyllables.

Koung geng wá ná dau mó thau kyn-ók dó è á-hpá; kóy-dau è ná-má dau
Heaven   in   dwellest   who   our   Father;   thy   name
gó yó thá lá myat thé hpyèt tsá thau, kóy dau è ncing ngan dau dé thé
reverenced   be   may it;   thy   kingdom
hpyèt tsá thau, kóy dau è á-ló dau thé; koung geng hneit pyè tsòn thá kai
be may it;   thy   will   heaven   in,   fulfilled   as
thó. myá gyè á-pyéng hneit pyè tsòn thé hpyèt tsá thau. á-thèt shèng
earth   surface   on   fulfilled   be may it.   Life   [for]

láuk	thǎ hmyǎ	ǎ-tsǎ	gǒ lě	kyr-ǒk dǒ	aǎ	yǎ nǎ	pǎ	thǎ-nǎ	dau mǒ	bǎ.
is sufficient	*as much as*		*food*			*us*		*to to-day*	*give*	

kyn-ǒk dǒ ǎ pyet hnia thau mo tǎ ba dǒ ¢ a-pyět dǒ go kyn-ǒk dǒ thĕ
us against err who others of sins we

khan thǎ kai thǒ kyn-ǒk au ¢ a-pyět dǒ gǒ kǎ-nya shlǒt dau mǒ bǎ.
bear as our sins be pitiful deliver from

ǎ-pyět dǒ gǒ teik twǒn shlě tsa hkeyngmǎ shě, ma koung ma thěng thau
sins to instigating deceptive be not, is not good is unfit which

ǎ-hmǒ ǎ-ya hning k—ng lwǒt aung tsaung mǎ thǎ-nǎ dau mǒ bǎ pǒ-rǎ.
work deliver from free from in order to protect have mercy O God!

Reversed thus.—Our Father, who dwellest in heaven; thy name, may it be reverenced, thy kingdom, may it be, thy will, as fulfilled in heaven, may it be fulfilled on [the] surface [of the] earth, food, as much as is sufficient [for] life, give us to day, be pitiful, deliver from our sins, as we bear sins of others who err against us, [that there] be not deceptive instigating to sin, and in order to free, deliver from [a] work which is unfit, not good, protect, have mercy, O God!

It will be gratifying to you, and our other friends, to know, that we lack not much of worldly comfort. It is not difficult, at present, to obtain good and healthy food, and sickness does not frequently visit our habitation, neither are our trials many or severe. I beg you to use your influence in obtaining for the use of the mission, Rees' Cyclopedia. We need it much. Also do write to me very often, as letters from our friends form the only society we have, of which we are exceedingly fond.

STATION AT ST LOUIS.

Letter from Mr. Peck to the Corresponding Secretary, dated April 25, 1818.

SINCE my recovery from my long and tedious illness, my health has been remarkably good, as well as that of my family. I now begin to feel myself at home in the delightful work assigned me, and I view it as one of the most favourable events of Providence I have ever enjoyed, to advance my individual happiness in this life. Surrounded with young minds whose desire for knowledge stimulates me forward to fulfil the important task of a teacher; and, favoured with the confidence, the prayers, and the friendship of many, what desire can I have but to live for the good of my fellow creatures!

By intelligence from brother Welch you have probably heard of our baptising, which took place on the first Sabbath of the present month. Since that period things have gone on well. When I look back on the short time of our residence here, and view the hand of God in accomplishing many events, and opening several channels of usefulness, I am filled with wonder and gratitude. Our prospects of immediate usefulness are opening on every hand, and calls from different quarters are more numerous than we can possibly supply. Our African Sunday school consists of more than 90 scholars, of all ages, from 5 to 40 years. The greatest number are adults. The good that is likely to issue from this department is incalculably great. Sunday is the only day that the poor degraded

Africans can call their own. On this day they used formerly to assemble for amusement or mischief. It is now evident to the most superficial observer, that a great change has already taken place in regard to their morals. In most instances they are attentive to school on every Sabbath, and the avidity with which they seize every moment's leisure through the week, evinces the desire they have to learn. The school has been continued seven Sabbaths, and most of them have entered since its commencement, and yet more than half who began the alphabet, can now spell words of four and five letters, and some of two syllables Several, who had learned a little previous to attending school, can now read in the bible. I have been most happily disappointed in respect to the Africans. As soon as my recovery admitted, I began to turn my attention to devise some way to instruct these miserable beings in the knowledge of Christ and his salvation A Sunday school appeared the most favourable, and, indeed, the only method Brother Welch hesitated as to the practicability of the measure, but agreed I should make the trial. The school was proposed to the public, and opened I expected to engage in a task by no means agreeable to human nature, which chooses the beaten track, rather than the uncultivated desert If, after a long trial, any could be made to read and understand the bible, I expected to be recompensed for all my toil. A serious difficulty arose, lest suitable assistants could not be obtained: yet all these difficulties Divine providence has overcome, and what at first I accounted a task, is now one of my greatest enjoyments. I hope I shall not say too much of my own feelings on this subject, if I assert, that I rejoice to see Sunday arrive that I may meet my sable band We have now six or seven assistants, who teach every Sabbath In my absence brother Welch enters with avidity upon the labours of superintendent. After hearing the lessons, a short discourse is given, and the school is closed with prayer, when they all kneel and pay a devout attention

Several persons are known to be under deep exercise of mind, and many more are thoughtful. Every week I have some call on me to hear religious instruction. Our week day school has commenced a second quarter upon a more extended scale, and which promises to be a source of some profit, to lessen the expense of the mission. A large room has been rented for a school and meeting room, on the hill which overlooks the town, and is a most delightful situation for a summer academy.

Our school consists of two departments—1 A public school, or academy, in which all the branches of a common education, and even some of the higher branches are taught. The prices of tuition are 5 and 6 dollars per quarter. In this department are about thirty scholars, from respectable families; some of whom are French catholics —The 2d department is a free school. It is designed for the present to embrace ten poor French children, seven of whom have already entered. I have two French scholars; a boy eleven years, and a girl seven years, who commenced this quarter without knowing a letter of the alphabet They have attended twelve days and a half, and they now read in words of two syllables with surprising facility, besides repeating the Lord's prayer and the first commandment. I teach them the plain simple truths of the christian religion. Our object now is to get as many French children in our school as possible One female Catholic is under serious impressions. She is a steady attendant on our meetings.

By reviewing our school arrangement you will perceive, that in both the week and Sunday schools we have about 130. By mutual arrangements all the school departments are under my sole care as superintendent. The whole management of the week day schools is performed by me, with no other assistance at present than my oldest son. A course of scientific lectures are delivered to the school every Friday, P. M. when the public generally are invited to attend. The composition of these, the concern of all the schools, domestic affairs, together with public duties on the Sabbath, leave not a moment's time to spare. Brother Welch is likewise employed. Though there are trials of various kinds connected with my situation, I would not exchange it for any place in the middle or eastern states. My most ardent desire is to live and die a missionary to the destitute. I feel confident, from a variety of providential incidents, that this village is the very place where we ought to be, though a greater expense will be incurred than if we were farther interior. All that appears wanting to commence operations further back, or even among the Indians, is, *more missionaries.*

While such a field for constant activity and immediate usefulness is fast opening, we cannot think of leaving St. Louis for uncertain prospects. Mrs. Peck expects shortly to commence a Sunday school for adult females, in our dwelling house. As soon as sister Welch regains her health she will probably assist. Our subscription for the meeting house has increased to a little more than three thousand dollars; a sum nearly half sufficient to build. We have concluded a bargain for a lot of ground in the most central part of the village, 40 by 80 feet, for six hundred dollars. It is a corner lot, and is an excellent site to erect a house 40 by 60, with apartments, and a cellar under the whole, as it is on the brow of the hill. These rooms will either be rented, or used for school and vestry. We expect to commence building soon. The whole, when finished, will be the sole property of the Baptist Society of St. Louis.

Governor Clark, since his return from the states, has been made acquainted with us, and our object here. He pledges all the aid in his power to forward our pursuits. As a proof of this he has presented us the use of a large garden adjoining my dwelling, for the season. Several gentlemen of respectability and influence have lately taken an interest in the service in which we are engaged. On the whole, we are under every obligation of gratitude to the Father of Mercies, for the great blessings with which we are favoured, and the success that has hitherto followed.

The state of society and morals in St. Louis is fast improving. Almost every day I hear it observed, that things have altered for the better within six months past. Even since our communication of January 20th, a great change has taken place with regard to the Sabbath.

As I have filled my sheet, and the watch is crying *twelve o'clock,* I must close, with sentiments of unfeigned respect.

From Mr. Welch to the Corresponding Secretary, dated June 20, 1818.

On the 21st of May I started on a tour up the country about one hundred miles, having been solicited by some scattered brethren in that quarter to visit them and assist in the constitution of a church. Passing up on the north side of the Missouri, preaching every day, some time was spent in the vicinity of Marthas-ville, where arrangements have been made for the constitution of a church in October next

While in this quarter, according to previous intimation to the Board, I crossed the river to visit a small village of Shawnee Indians, situated about twenty miles from the Missouri, on a branch of the Merimek, and though it was my wish to reach the village if possible before they had finished planting their corn and departed on their summer hunt, yet it was my disappointment to arrive a few days after the greater part of them had left for the woods.

While there, I had some conversation with Fish, their white chief, and a Mr. James Rogers, (who is a half breed and son of their former chief) on the subject of religion and the education of their children, both of whom, and indeed the most of this little band can, though imperfectly, speak and understand the English language. They expressed some degree of willingness to have their children taught to read, but owing to the absence of most of the men, nothing decisive could be done; and in fact I was unable myself to decide, without first receiving an answer from the Board relative to the support of Indian youth while obtaining an education. Rogers being a half breed, and possessed of more information than the common Indians, cannot be given as a correct specimen of the state of religious improvement among them, but believing, sir, that every thing of the kind will be interesting to the Board, as well as yourself, I take the liberty of introducing a part of the conversation had on the subject of religion, as taken from my journal.

Welch. Do you know who made you?

Rogers. God Almighty made every body.

W. Dont you believe you will die?

R. Surely.

W. What do you think becomes of men when they die?

R. Good men will go to God Almighty, and bad men will go to hell.

W. Do you ever pray?

R. Yes. I never eat but I always pray.

Since I returned, Lewis, the brother of James Rogers, together with Fish, their chief, has been in this place, with whom brother Peck and myself had an interview on the same subject, which promises a happy issue, owing to the influence of Lewis Rogers, who reads tolerably well.

After my visit to the Indian village, I returned to the north side of the river, pursuing a line of appointments up to Coat's Prairie, and on the 31st of May constituted the "Salem Baptist Church," of nine members, five of whom are pious, prudent male members, and one of them a deacon of old standing in the state of Tennessee. There are several others in the neighbourhood, who no doubt will join them soon, not being informed in time of the intended constitution. You can best perceive the great increase of population, as well as an omen of what God intends to do in this western world, when I remark that, from information, not more than two years ago there was not a single family living nearer than ten miles of the place where this truly promising little body have pitched their tent. May it soon become a thousand.

Previously to my departure from home I was permitted the honour of receiving the *peace pipe,* at a council held by his excellency governor Clark, with eight chiefs of the Sioux tribe of Indians, who live twelve or fifteen hundred miles up the Missouri. Soon after my return, seeing one of them pass, I beckoned him in, and gave him, with some other small presents, an English and a French copy of the bible, pointing upward, to let him know that they came from *above*. In a few hours after he left me he returned with the great chief, one other chief, and his squaw; and I hope the Board will pardon me when I take the liberty again of introducing an extract from my journal.

"This was truly an interesting time, and as though Providence had ordered it, a young man walked in from a neighbouring family, who very politely acted as an interpreter.

"Soon after they came in, I gave the other two French bibles only, not having any more of the English edition to distribute. Upon the reception of these I commenced conversation as follows:

"*Welch*. When do you expect to go home?

Indian. In about eight days.

W. I expect to come away up that way some time.

I. When?

W. I cannot tell exactly.

I. Do you expect to come up where we live?

W. Not so far up as that, but may-be about Chariton, and you must come down to see me.

I. Yes.

W. I wrote my name in those books, that you may know me again when you come to see me. They are the words of the Great Spirit.*

I. I'll keep it.

W. If you could get some person to read that book, and do what it tells you, it will make you happy.

I. I came down here some time ago, and wanted some white man to talk good talk to me, but I went away home again without it, but now I find one good man to talk good talk, and (laying his hand on his breast) now I am glad.

W. If you will get some body to read that book, and mind what it tells you, it will make you happy all your life time, and make you glad when you die.

I. Yes, (rising and giving me his hand apparently with tears in his eyes) I'll tell my nation when I go home. Some white men talk to me, I call them *brother*, but I call you *father*, you talk good talk to me.

W. I love you, and hope the "Father of Life" may make your path smooth as you go home, and you find all your nation well.

I. Yes. What is your name?

W. Welch.

I. Welch, Welch, Welch! I'll tell my nation when I go home, that I found one white man to talk of the Father of Life, this is good talk, this is what I wanted to hear.

W. I love you, and all the Indians, and want to make them happy, and I want you to love the white men, and not do them any harm.

I. Yes, father, I love you.

W. May-be when I come and live away up the Missouri, you can send me many

---

* I found their name for the Deity was the *Father of Life*.

of your little boys to learn to read that book, for they are the words of the "Father of Life."

I. Yes, may-be

W. You will come and see me again before you go home?

J. Yes"

Since I recorded the above I have had frequent and interesting visits from them, and in fact, I have been quite pleased in my intercourse with the Indian character, and have on all occasions found them disposed to treat me in a friendly manner, and were it not for intrigue, and the introduction of so much minné-wàka, or whiskey, among them—possessed with equal advantages and improvement, there is no doubt they would manifest equal attachment to humanity and justice.

The bibles which I have given them, it is hoped will be useful, though it may be many days hence, and even should they be under the necessity of getting others to read to them · and having understood that they contain the words of the great Wà-kùndà, or "Father of Life," they will be preserved with the most jealous safety, from grandfather to son

Notwithstanding the length of my letter, I cannot deny myself the pleasure of informing the Board, that on the 7th of June, at 9 o'clock in the morning, we again assembled on the shores of this western Jordan, to witness the solemnities of christian baptism, and after repairing to the school room, our present place of worship, and receiving a valuable member by letter, a brother Floyde, from England, our little church in cordial union surrounded again the table of our common Lord At four o'clock in the afternoon a sermon was delivered on the spot where our meeting house is now erecting, and a collection taken to aid the building

---

LOUISIANA.

From Mr. Ranaldson to the Agent of the Board, dated St Francisville, April 23, 1818

HAVING the satisfaction to acknowledge the receipt of your letter from Richmond of the 19th ultimo, I address to you the following communications.

In my last to the Secretary I stated our need of at least six missionaries, without designating the ground of labour. The Board is aware, no doubt, that the whole of Louisiana is important missionary ground! Yet there are situations more important and more eligible than others. Among these I still regard the city of New Orleans as a place of greater magnitude than any other in the western world. The Rev. Mr. Larned, an eloquent Presbyterian, is now settled in that city. Brother Davis is sent by the Mississippi Society to labour among the poor, and the coloured people Still there is room for another.

It is very desirable to have a missionary stationed at Alexandria, on Red river. It has a population of six or seven hundred, and is daily growing into importance. The country around is extremely fertile, and is settling fast. It is all missionary ground, in fact, through Rapides, Ouachitta, and Natchitoches, whither the rapid tide of emigration is flowing. Opelousas and Atakapas, equally destitute of the gospel, present a large and interesting missionary field for several labourers' The eastern parishes of West Florida, though thinly inhabited, should not be omitted. There are several places in the Mississippi state, which deserve particular attention. The baptist church in Natchez is without a minister. Port Gibson, Pinckneyville, and Woodville, have need of schools, and each of these beautiful villages is supported by the most respectable and wealthy population in the state. The latter has recently followed the noble example of the merchants of St. Francisville, as respects the observation of the Lord's day, by a cessation from business. May the influence of this precedent be felt throughout the two states. For we have deeply to bewail the profanation of the Sabbath, a practice awfully destructive to all moral, religious, and political virtue!

The places designated should, in my humble opinion, be immediately supplied, if practicable, by active, zealous, and indefatigable missionaries, capable of conducting schools. The religious education of children in the country, is of so great importance, that I regard schools as one of the primary objects of a devout missionary. The state of literature is no less deplorable, than that of morality and religion. Though there are many learned and enterprising men in the country, yet there are few good schools, and too frequently they are conducted by men of dissolute morals and corrupt principles. Some of the sons and daughters of affluence are sent from home to receive their education; others remain in ignorance, or, what is still worse, are taught to drink in, with a superficial education, deep draughts of infidelity, which often lead to profligacy of manners. That system which is best adapted to Indian reform, will be found most effectual in the reformation of the civilized. A disposition to promote learning prevails much in our country: and parents who are even regardless of religion themselves, wish the gospel ministry for the benefit of their children, and would, on this account, give a liberal encouragement. A missionary would soon be able to support himself by teaching and preaching at either of the places above-mentioned. At least he might calculate on receiving something like $1500 a year.

My expenses have been much curtailed since I left the city, owing to the hospitality of this people, and particularly to the kindness of colonel Collins and family, to whose house we were directed in mercy, where we were greatly refreshed, and most cordially and gratuitously entertained for several months. He is senator of the parish, and both he and wife are members of our church. Besides the contributions and kind attention we received in New Orleans, I cannot forbear to mention in particular the generosity of my physician, (Dr. Flood), who attended me in all my sickness, and in the sickness of my family, without a charge.

I was offered in this neighbourhood, by two gentlemen, a donation of land, worth about $2000. But in order to be settled in a more useful situation, I have purchased a lot of five acres, with some improvements, one mile from the town. This situation is pleasant, and extremely eligible for a school, as well as for my ministerial labours. A cluster of agreeable families gives it the appearance of a village, and it is properly styled "Society Hill." Land in this vicinity is worth $50 per acre, and for my small lot I have to give $1150. Five hundred of this is paid by the contributions of the inhabitants. Am now repairing my dwelling, and fitting up a schoolhouse. I intend opening the school as soon as I can procure a well qualified teacher. The whole of my time cannot be devoted to the instruction of children, for my poor labours in this extensive harvest, are as a drop of a bucket. But I sometimes have the assistance of my excellent brother Cooper, from the Mississippi state. I have found in him an affectionate counsellor, a man of sterling sense, whose real worth cannot be duly appreciated in the churches and in the association

The moral reformation among us is matter of joy. As the spring opens, the prospects seem to revive around us in the Lord's vineyard. The tender plants begin to bud and to blossom! A few young converts sing, and the voice of the turtle is faintly heard in our land! The note is strange in Louisiana, but, oh! 'tis music, 'tis divine melody to our ears, and to the ear of angels! Two or three are ready for the ordinance of baptism; which duty, with its pleasures, is anticipated the first Lord's day in May, at my house, where we have water sufficient. Several are still inquiring with tears in their eyes, &c. the Saviour of sinners. May they soon find him in mercy! Pray for us, and for them.

Our town is rapidly increasing in business, numbers, wealth, and respectability. The love of matrimony is gaining ascendency over the habits of bachelor life, and marriage is esteemed honourable in all. The number of families in the village has, perhaps, doubled itself since August last, by marriage and emigration! We hope to build a house for public worship, which will cost 8 or $10,000. The judge of the parish gives a choice lot and $100 for this object. Others subscribe from 25 to $300. The subscription is now in circulation. A branch bank will soon be established here, which will probably facilitate the work.

The people seem disposed to receive the gospel. Their religious tenets are not yet formed. They are not very tenacious of educational prejudices. The inquisition is abolished. There is no burning zeal for catholicism. "The fire is gone into all the world," said a catholic priest, "but has not yet come to New Orleans." There is easy access to the catholic mind. I have been allowed to pray, exhort, and preach in their houses, and they manifest friendship. Among the protestants of the two states, the baptists are the most numerous. Learning and talents should be added to pious numbers, for the more able defence of the gospel. I hope it may be found expedient for you to visit this country. Perhaps there is no section of the United States, or of the world, which needs your labours more than this. Much may be done for missions—great things can be done, I trust, for education. Come and see! and may the Spirit of Elijah's God accompany you! Help us continually with your prayers. I desire that my short life should be devoted to the glorious cause of evangelical missions.*

From Mr M'Coy, near Vincennes, May 7th, 1818.

It is both my duty and my happiness to inform the Board, at their next quarterly meeting, in addition to what I have already communicated, what I have been doing, and what success has attended my labours since I have been under their patronage.

In my excursions I have listened attentively for the bleatings of the sheep of Christ scattered in this lonely wilderness through which my path has led me. I

* At a late meeting of the Board, Mr *Samuel Eastman*, a young brother of promising talents and great devotedness to the cause of missions, was appointed a missionary to the countries where brother Ranaldson has so successfully laboured.

have not only heard, but formed an acquaintance with many, some of whom were collected and formed into a church, (called White River church,) in the northern part of Gibson county, Indiana, on the 21st of February; and on Feb 25, in Pike county, I baptised a man in White river, who had followed me ten miles for the purpose. The same day sundry baptists, and our new convert among them, were constituted a church (Highbank). This was a most blessed time; all hearts were warm, and mine almost gladdened to enthusiasm, to observe the solitude of the desert suddenly beguiled by the joys of heaven. When I state, that in this neighbourhood, where, on the 8th of February, I delivered the first sermon ever heard from a baptist in the place, the hopeful appearances of religion have still been increasing, I fancy that I can almost hear the Board saying, Glory to God! In constituting these churches, I was careful to obtain the approbation of other churches. On the 23d and 24th of this month, I expect to attend the constitution of a church in Sullivan county; here also there are very encouraging appearances of a revival of religion. scarcely a countenance is seen in time of preaching, which does not express deep affection of mind, while some dear christians, like Elijah, seem to have a table in the wilderness, spread with the choicest fruit of the heavenly hills. In no part of the field of my labours have I had more reason to lament the want of religious sensation, than that in which my family resides, until a few days past. Three sermons which I have lately preached, seem to have been attended with a power which I am sure does not belong to me.

But these interesting scenes have not diverted my attention from my unhappy fellow beings who wander in the wilderness, without a friend to say "this is the way, walk ye in it." O, God! my heart must be insensible as steel, not to feel affected with the piteous cries of the wretched, hungry, naked infant, swung to the back of its degraded mother in a blanket, both alike doomed to nameless miseries. I cannot refrain from tears while I write. Last Sabbath, which was a day of feasting to my soul, in going from one preaching place to another, I passed about forty, of different ages, from the hoary sire to the infant at the breast. I felt—ah! how shall I describe what I felt!—your kindred feelings will better tell you what I felt, than this poor trembling hand of mine can do.

Since my last I have secured the friendship of major Chunn, commander at fort Harrison, and others, who have given me leave to use their names as friends to our benevolent enterprise. Major Chunn is placed in a situation which affords him an opportunity of doing us much service, as he is almost daily conversant with the Indians. Several Indians have said that they would send their children to school, provided one should be established near them, but it has been thought adviseable to wait the result of a council before we proceed to decisive measures. I had taken much pains to collect information, digest measures, and make preparation for the meeting of the Indians, and the prospects which were daily opening, were animating beyond any thing I had anticipated, when, to my great mortification, the business was brought to a stand by the death of the agent, general Thomas Posey, formerly governor of Indiana, the excellent and warm friend of our mission. The meeting of the Indians is necessarily delayed, until government can fill the vacancy occasioned by his death.

The Board, I presume, is apprized that many difficulties attend the introduction of the gospel among these northwestern Indians, whose minds and manners are of the most uncultivated nature, that will not be realized in respect to the southern Indians, on whom a visible impression of civilization has already been made. Here they have room to recede, as the settlements of the whites advance, for which reason they remain wild. I am fully persuaded, that a procedure different from any thing that has been attempted heretofore, will be necessary to ensure success. Something must be done to inspire them with a love of property, more than they at present possess. The possession of property will not only check their wanderings, but teach them the advantage of education. A number of Indians at different times have been educated "in the midst of white population, industry, economy, and refinement," who, on returning home, associated with a people who possessed but few motives to industry, and who imagined that they were as economical and as much refined, as any people on earth, and even as much disposed to adhere inflexibly to their notions of refinement, as the writer of this does to his; of course, the learned Indian found no use for his education, commerce being in a train that rendered his education useless, while his friends lamented that he was ruined, as he knew so little about hunting, trapping, &c. Much the same may be said in regard to religious instruction. from a principle which I will venture to call a principle of politeness, they will give as decent attention to an address on the subject of civilization or religion, as ever congress did to the president's message, and by their "whooh" approve of all that is said in respect to the advantages of both, when, in return, if you please, they will let you know the advantages attending their manners and customs. Some person must reside near them, where he may contract a familiar acquaintance with them, converse with them frequently, set them an example of industry, and take advantage of their hunger and cold in a winter storm, so that their privations shall subserve their best interests. Let the unhappy creatures sometimes realize the comforts of a warm room on a stormy night, let them be taught by actual experience, as well as by persuasive arguments, the great advantages to be derived from cattle, hogs, &c.

I hope my plan will not be alarming, upon the supposition that it will be expensive. On the frontier a very little attention to cattle and hogs, would more than supply a considerable mission establishment, and this attention would make a happy impression on the red children in the school. In a similar way could domestic economy be impressed on the females in the school, and on their mothers at home.

It is with deference to the wisdom of the Board, that I express my opinions on this subject. I shall invariably adhere to their instructions; and when they shall be of so general a nature as to leave things discretionary with myself, I shall be happy to avail myself of that information which experience in Indian affairs will enable my good friends to afford me.

I would suggest to the Board the propriety of associating another missionary with their unworthy servant in this great work; should they think proper to do so, let them try to obtain one a little better qualified than the one already in their employ. In addition to the endearing graces and indispensable qualifications of meekness and patience, let their missionary possess an education that will confer a dignity on the establishment.

What I have said with regard to an associate, is not merely the effusion of a heart which seldom finds a brother bosom, in which to breathe its plaintive air; but the result of deliberate reflection, and a full conviction that one is needed and I hope that the Board will not think my request superfluous, when they reflect on the opening prospects which are inviting vigorous efforts in missionary labour in this field, which is so extensive, that it is impossible for one person to cultivate it. Although I have travelled more than 1,900 miles since the 17th of last October, and besides attending church meetings, &c. have preached more than one hundred sermons, yet I have not been able to preach one sermon in Edwards, Davis, or Dubois counties, the last of which was formerly part of Pike county. In less than three weeks, I expect to have the sole charge of five churches, which are situated as follows: from White River church to High Bank is twenty miles, thence to Wabash twenty-four, thence to Maria twelve, thence to Prairie creek forty, from Prairie creek to White river church is seventy miles. This extensive route lies through an immense population, all destitute of preaching by our ministers. There are also two or three places where I think churches might in a little time be formed, but there is none to blow the trumpet to "assemble them." Now if I attend to preaching to these people, the Indians must be neglected, and if I attend to the Indians, "with whom shall I leave these few sheep in the wilderness?" Should I be so happy as to embrace a brother in this work, it would be my wish to form a family establishment, where, while one of us would be on a preaching tour, the other could be a father to his children, and could attend closely to the ultimate object of the mission. I am very desirous to hear from the Board something on this subject.

CHEROKEE INDIANS.

From Mr. Posey to the Corresponding Secretary, dated Haywood county, North Carolina, June 1, 1818.

ANOTHER three months of my time having expired, I herewith send you a brief account of my procedure in the service of the Board, by making extracts from my journal.

Monday, December 1, 1817.—Took my start, and preached that day and night on Scott's creek and Tuckasiegy. Next day went to Indian Dick's, held a long conversation with him about religion, civilization, and education. Found him anxious to have his children educated, but entirely ignorant of the necessity, advantages, and nature of religion. The two following days preached at Tillanoo-ry and Caneyfork.

Saturday 6.—Reached home, and continued in the neighbourhood of Richland, Fine's creek, and Jonathan's creek, and at Locust-oldfields, where, with brother Byers, I administered the Lord's supper, baptised one, and in these bounds preached eight sermons.

Friday 19.—Started again for the nation, but was prevented by ice from going further than Scott's creek and Caneyfork, at both of which I preached, and landed at home on Tuesday 23.

Wednesday 24.—Started into Buncombe county, and spent the balance of the month in a visit among my relations and friends; preached three times, and reached home just in time to finish the year in the embraces of my family.

1818. New-year's day.—Preached at Waynesville on "Ebenezer."

Sabbath 4.—Preached at Hyatt's meeting house, and baptised one, went into Buncombe county, and

Thursday 8.—Preached a funeral sermon on Swannanoa river.

Friday 9.—Attended a meeting of the managers of the Asheville Bible Society, at Asheville.

Saturday 10, and the day following—attended church meeting at Lof, preached both days, and with the help of brother Byers ordained brother Stephen White a minister, and brother Jonathan Osburne a deacon, in said church.

Monday 12.—Started for the nation, accompanied by brother White. Preached that day on Scott's creek, and the two following days we travelled through the nation. He preached each night, and I made a number of statements to the whites and Indians relative to my work among them.

Thursday 15.—We got into the vicinity of South Carolina, but had a number of natives of the Cherokees, who had went on to hear us preach. All of them could understand English.

Friday 16.—We continued further into the district of Pendleton, South Carolina, and continued together until the afternoon of Wednesday 21, at which time we parted: he continued on towards Georgia, and I continued winding along towards the nation, and preaching. In this circuit I formed a happy acquaintance with the Rev. Andrew Brown, of the presbyterian order, who has preached a number of years in Pendleton, and appears to have the Redeemer's cause at heart. At one of his preaching places I had the honour of preaching a missionary sermon to a numerous congregation of presbyterians and baptists. I also had the pleasure of being in company with some of our own brethren in the ministry; and finally, I had the distress of seeing a large population next to the mountains, almost as destitute as the Indians. Here and there a poor destitute baptist, and the ministers' hands so bound that they cannot travel to supply them. O, for labourers, and a disposition in the people to loose them and let them go!

Against Sabbath 25—I had with tears of mingled sorrow and joy left the white inhabitants, and this day preached in the nation to a number of whites who had come from the settlements, and some who lived in the nation, and also to Indians, half breeds, quarteroons, and negroes. It would be impossible to describe the sensations of mind that I had this day. My very soul was absorbed, as it were, in deep contemplation and fervent prayer, that God would put to his helping hand, and compel them to come in that his house might be filled.

The three following days were spent in travelling through Eastatory, Tessenty, Cowee, and Dick's Town, arranging business for schools, and conversing on religion, education, &c.

Thursday 29.—Landed at home, and preached six times in the settlements of Richland, Pigeon river, and Pine's creek, in the course of two weeks—the weather being extremely cold.

Friday, Feb 13.—Preached on Scott's creek. Next evening on Caney fork, and next day at Tillanoocy.

Monday 16.—Visited the school at Tillanoocy, and went on to Sugartown.

Tuesday 17.—Went to Eastatory, visited the school there, and preached in the evening to the scattered whites at Ned Tucker's, and then to the Indians through Tucker.

Wednesday 18—got to Tessenty, and next day to Cowee, held a talk in the evening at the house of a white man through Dick (commonly called Richard Walker) an Indian who speaks very good English, and through him next day held a general talk, with a number of Indians at an Indian house in Cowee town, in which I stated, in the plainest manner, their ignorance and disadvantages; and the necessity of education, religion, &c. after which I travelled along a very difficult way until dark, took up at an Indian's house, who did not speak any English; my lodging was on the dirt floor with a deer-skin or two, my own blanket and great coat, in a very open house, and alone, while the family were in their hot house: and after spending almost a sleepless night, on

Saturday 21—I had to travel probably 16 miles, and preached on Socoa

Sabbath 22 —Preached at the middle of the day on Oconylufty, and in the afternoon back on Socoa, and on Monday got home

Thursday night, 26 —Preached in my own neighbourhood, and attended church meeting on Saturday and Sabbath, at Hyatts' meeting-house, preached both days, and administered the Lord's supper on Sabbath with brother Byers.

Saturday, March 7—and the day following, preached at Locust-oldfields.

Thursday 12—Went into Buncombe, preached at Homony meeting-house, and went to Asheville, and on Friday finished my letter to the Board, and attended church meeting on Saturday at Newfound meeting-house, and preached.

Sabbath 15 —Preached again at Newfound, and in the evening on my way home, preached in the same neighbourhood, landed home on Monday.

Thursday 19 —Started a journey of something over four weeks, in the following manner: preached that night on Scott's creek, and next day at Tillanoocy. Saturday 21, travelled through a vast mountain to Sugar town, thence to Tessenty Sabbath, 22, preached in the far edge of the nation next to South Carolina.

Monday 23 —Entered Pendleton District, and spent eight days and several nights, preaching to crowded and attentive congregations, mostly of baptists and presbyterians, both of which appeared generally anxious to support the mission My dear friend the Rev Mr Brown (as named before) as well as the Rev. Isaiah Stephens, of the baptist order, had encouraged the business in their congregations I obtained in those parts several contributions for the education of the Indians, and some for my own support.

Tuesday 31.—Crossed Tuguls into Georgia, and preached that day at Carnesville (Franklin court-house) and the next evening in that neighbourhood.

Thursday, April 2.—Travelled on towards Jackson, and on Friday preached at Jackson court-house, where I met with an aged ministering brother (Thomas Johnson) who has been like a father to the churches for a number of years With him I had the pleasure of staying and preaching for five days in his bounds, and he accompanied me into the nation, where we parted on Wednesday 8th. This man and three others were appointed by the *Sarepta Mission Society*, to preach in that part of the nation lying next to Georgia, for one year. I then continued preaching every day on my way towards my own side of the nation, there being a number of natives and whites all along up the Chatahoochy river, until on Sabbath evening I preached at Edward Tucker's, and then had the sermon interpreted by Tucker.

Monday 13.—Tucker went on with me and interpreted a sermon at Tessenty;

and Tuesday at Cowee; here I saw upwards of twenty Indians in school, improving smartly, and had the attention of a number to a lengthy discourse.

Wednesday 15.—In the evening preached among the whites in the bounds of the Big-bear's town on Tuckasiegy; Thursday 16, on Socoa, Friday, on Jonathan creek, and then home, having tried to preach thirty-six times on my journey

Sabbath 19.—Preached on Pigeon river; Tuesday 21, at night, on Richland, Wednesday 22, and Wednesday night, and Thursday, on Scott's creek, and visited the school in Dickstown.—Friday 24, in my own neighbourhood.

Saturday 25—Preached and attended church meeting at Crabtree, and on Sabbath 26, preached at the same place.

Thursday 29—Went into Buncombe, Friday, preached on Swannanoa, and met the managers of the *Bible Society;* Saturday and Sabbath attended church meetings, and preached at Cane creek meeting-house; had the pleasure of seeing the brethren and friends unitedly agree to do something for the support of schools among the Cherokees, from thence I went to visit my relations on French Broad, and landed at home on Wednesday 6th of May.

Saturday, May 9—Attended church meeting at Lof, and preached that day and next, and baptised a man and his wife in Pigeon river, and on Sabbath evening preached in my own neighbourhood.

Sabbath 17—Preached at Waynesville with brother Byers.

Tuesday 19—Travelled over the mountain to Caneytork, and preached that day and night, Wednesday, at Tillanoocy, Thursday, on Tuckasiegy, at night on Scott's creek, Friday in the lower settlement on Tuckasiegy, Saturday, on Oconeylufty, Sabbath, on Socoa, Monday, on Jonathan's creek, and then home

Sabbath 31—At Waynesville with brother Byers

Thus, with very little comment, I have given a kind of view of my six months' travels and labours I can only say the Lord has been gracious to me, and I humbly trust he will bless the means of his appointment in this dark, remote, and destitute part of his vineyard.

ORIGIN OF SUNDAY SCHOOLS.

THE name of Robert Raikes, esq. of Gloucester, England, as the founder of sabbath schools, will be had in everlasting remembrance. On him has already come the blessing of thousands ready to perish.

The following interesting account of the origin of the first school is from the pen of Mr. Lancaster, to whom it was communicated by Mr. Raikes, when far advanced in life. "He said," observes Mr L. "about the year 1782 he had taken a garden, and wanted a gardener. He went to the outskirts of the city of Gloucester to hire one. The man he went to hire was from home; and while waiting for the man's return, he was greatly disturbed by a troop of wretched noisy boys, who interrupted him while conversing with the man's wife on the business he came about. Full of that compassion, which a christian only can feel and enjoy, he anxiously inquired the cause of those children being thus miserably neglected and depraved. The answer he received exhibited a true specimen of the wretched state of *tens of thousands* of the youth of Britain at that moment. Would to heaven it did not exhibit a picture of the state of tens of thousands of her youth at the present moment! Youth yet unbefriended—yet neglected—solitary—mentally poor—" as sheep on the mountains without a shepherd!" as fatherless children! who, did they know their own wretchedness—could they plead their own poverty, individually would say, help me! oh, my christian friends! for I am poor and needy, and *no man* careth for my soul!

"The answer he received was, 'oh, sir, if you were here on a Sunday, you would pity them indeed,—they are then much more numerous, and an hundred times worse, it is a very hell upon earth WE CANNOT READ OUR BIBLE IN PLACE FOR THEM'—It was this affecting answer which moved every feeling within him! He immediately asked, 'can nothing be done for these poor children? Is there any body near that will take them to school on Sunday?' He was answered, there was a person who kept school in the lane who perhaps might do it The wretchedness of the poor children, objects of christian pity and active benevolence, deeply interested him. The feelings of his heart spoke aloud, and told him this was not a time to trifle—to merely pity to say, be ye warmed and be ye clothed, and leave them unsheltered and cold —The novelty of an undertaking, which was likely to draw, and which has drawn, the eyes of multitudes towards him, naturally struck a reflective mind with its due weight.

"He made a solemn pause, to consider the step he was about to take. On his decision at that moment rested an opening for one of the highest blessings ever extended to the youth of any nation. Happy for Britain, her guardian angel was near. Procrastination, that 'thief of time,' was not admitted for an instant The humble diffidence of this worthy, pious christian, was not suffered to discourage him

"At this important moment (according to his own relation) the word '*TRY*' was so powerfully impressed on his mind as to decide him at once to action. I have heard of seeing things with 'the mind's eye,' and with him, this encouraging stimulating call to christian duty, seemed to be sounded in the ear of his soul Obedient to the impulse, he went and entered into treaty with the school-mistress to take a number of these poor destitute children, and here was the foundation stone of a mighty—a glorious superstructure.—*Here was the first sabbath school Britain ever saw* —Surely the sun that shone that day, arose in double lustre, and its rays have already extended their light into 'the dark places of the earth, which are full of the habitations of cruelty' That morning was an harbinger of many sabbaths for Britain, and the approaching day, when the groaning creation shall be at rest—and the 'earth enjoy her sabbaths again'

"Important consequences depended upon this interesting moment Two years had elapsed from the commencement of the first school. On retiring to rest one evening, he began to consider that his schools had now been fully tried, and that it was time for the public good that they should be made generally known. On this, instead of going to bed, he directly wrote a paragraph, and had it inserted in his newspaper, the Gloucester Journal It was copied into many other papers, and in consequence he had applications from all parts of the empire To a letter from the north, most earnestly pressing on the subject, he wrote an interesting answer, which was published The result of this publication was, that the dormant zeal of many was called into action The mode was simple, the expense moderate, the advantages grand and striking The establishment of such schools proceeded throughout the nation with the rapidity of lightning

Through the exertions of several public spirited gentlemen in the metropolis, a public meeting was held on the 7th of September, 1785, and an institution formed bearing the title of "A society for the support and encouragement of Sunday schools in the different counties of England." This establishment was exceedingly beneficial to the growing cause. The committee of this society soon engaged the co-operation of episcopal authority. "Among the dignitaries of the church, who patronized the plan, the bishops of Salisbury and Landaff, and the deans of Canterbury and Lincoln, obtained a conspicuous place, by their zeal and talents." Other distinguished characters did not hesitate to give the whole weight of their influence in favour of this good institution. Thus, notwithstanding the opposition which was made to the early efforts of Mr. Raikes, notwithstanding he was told, that it was folly to begin with children, and that he should begin by reforming the higher classes of society, &c. the work went forward, bearing down all opposition. To the cavils and contempt that were cast upon him, in consequence of his attention to the lower classes of society, he triumphantly replied, "the poor have the gospel preached to them."

Before his death, which took place in 1811, he had accounts of the establishment of similar schools in various parts of the country, comprehending no less than THREE HUNDRED THOUSAND CHILDREN.

"Well might he say," observes Lancaster, "to one who loves the sound of his name, and will cherish his memory, *I can never pass by the spot where the word TRY came so powerfully into my mind, without lifting up my hands and heart to heaven, in gratitude to God, for having put such a thought into my heart.*"

The friends of religion in Scotland, formed themselves into a society, called the Edinburgh Gratis Sabbath school society, the sole object of which was to promote the *religious instruction of youth*, by erecting, supporting, and conducting sabbath evening schools, in Edinburgh and its neighbourhood.

A society at Aberdeen, formed at the same time, and upon the same plan, has been alike prosperous and useful. Similar societies were soon after formed at Paisley and Glasgow, and still later at Greenock, Perth, and many other places. The system now prevails generally in the south of Scotland, and even in the highlands and islands.

'Wales, at a very early period in the history of Sunday schools, entered with eagerness into the scheme, and adorned her romantic and picturesque valleys with numerous asylums for the instruction of the poor. And here it is but justice to the Sunday school Institution, to assert its claims to the high honour of giving birth to the most noble and efficient society ever formed by man, or blessed by God, for promoting the interests of genuine christianity. Every reader will anticipate the name of the British and Foreign Bible Society. The honour of giving rise to this mighty combination of wealth, of zeal, and talents, is better worth contending for, than the highest place in the roll of monarchs, conquerers, or philosophers.

'By means of Sunday school education in Wales, the number of readers increased far beyond the supply of Welsh bibles to be obtained. This induced the indefatigable Mr. Charles of Bala, to undertake a journey to London, for the purpose of soliciting a private subscription from his friends, to defray the expense of printing an edition of Welsh bibles. In the course of conversation on this subject, at a committee meeting of the Religious Tract Society, a thought came into the mind of the Rev. Joseph Hughes, a thought which darted as one of the brightest beams from the fountain of light and life above, and for which millions will have reason to bless his name, that a little more exertion than was requisite for supplying Wales with the scriptures, might found an institution which should go on increasing its funds, and extending its operations, till not only the British dominions, but the whole world should be furnished with the word of God. Such was the origin of a society which is the glory of our age. I need not trace it further than just to say, that the plan was warmly embraced by the gentlemen present, and steps were immediately taken to give it efficiency. My object in adverting to this society was to show its pedigree, and to claim it as the offspring of the Sunday school Institution. The cause which originated still supports it, for in most cases a Sunday school teacher must be the forerunner of a bible.

So great was the progress of Sunday schools in Wales, that in three years 177 schools were established, containing more than 8000 children.

The Sunday school system was introduced into Ireland in 1793, its progress, however, was not rapid, until the formation of the Hibernian Sunday school Society in Dublin, in 1809. This society met with liberal patronage from the higher classes of protestants, and has been happily successful in its labours among the indigent and superstitious catholics. In April, 1815, there were upwards of 252 schools, containing more than 25000 children, under the care of this institution. Since that time the number of schools has been greatly augmented.

Besides the above-mentioned, and an association in Dublin formed in 1811, for the purpose of promoting the establishment of Sunday schools in Dublin and its vicinity, there are several Sunday school societies in other parts of Ireland, particularly one in Belfast, and one in Hillsborough.

Through the exertions of the society for the support and encouragement of Sunday schools throughout the British dominions, Sunday schools have been established in several of the West India Islands, in the Island of Cape Breton, in Nova Scotia, at the Cape of Good Hope, and in many other places.

"In tracing the growth of the Sunday school Institution," says Mr James, "it would be an unpardonable omission to pass by in silence that noble ramification of it, the instruction of ADULTS. A few years ago, had any one proposed such a design, a thousand voices would have exclaimed, in a strain somewhat similar to that of the wondering and doubting Nicodemus, "How can a man be taught when he is old?" BUT THIS IS THE AGE OF A DARING AND RESTLESS BENEVOLENCE, WHICH NO EXERTIONS CAN WEARY, AND NO DIFFICULTIES CAN APPAL. The first scion was planted by Mr. Charles, upon the mountains of Wales, in the summer of 1811. "God prepared room before it, and caused it to take deep root; the hills were covered with the shadow of it, and the boughs thereof were like goodly cedars."

"The account of his commencement and success, shall be given in his own words.—

"My maxim has been for many years past, to aim at great things, but if I cannot accomplish great things, to do what I can, and be thankful for the least success; and still to follow on without being discouraged at the day of small things, or by unexpected reverses. For many years I have laid it down as a maxim to guide me, never to give up a place in despair of success. If one way does not succeed, new means must be tried; and if I see no increase this year, perhaps I may the next. I almost wish to blot out the word *impossible* from my vocabulary, and obliterate it from the minds of my brethren. We had no particular school for the instruction of adults *exclusively*, till the summer of 1811, but many attended the Sunday schools with the children, in different parts of the country, previous to that time. What induced me first to think of establishing such an institution, was the aversion I found in the adults to associate with the children in their schools. The first attempt succeeded wonderfully, and far beyond my most sanguine expectations. The report of the success of this school soon spread over the country, and in many places the illiterate adults began to *call* for instruction. In one county, after a public address had been delivered to them on the subject, the adult poor, even the *aged*, flocked to the Sunday school in crowds, *and the shopkeepers could not immediately supply them with an adequate number of spectacles*. Our schools, in general, are kept in our chapels, in some districts, where there are no chapels, farmers, in the summer time, lend their barns. The adults and children are sometimes in the same room, but placed in different parts of it. *When their attention is gained and fixed, they soon learn, their age makes no difference if they are able, by the help of glasses, to see the letters.*

"Soon after this time, as if the plan had been carried in the bosom of the Severn, and from thence received by the Avon, it appeared in the city of Bristol. The individual destined to the high honour of establishing it there, was a man of obscure and humble origin. The rays of spiritual light do not always strike first on the tops of the highest mountains. Men in less elevated stations have often been employed as the almoners of Divine bounty. At the second anniversary of the Bristol Auxiliary Bible Society, among other intelligence communicated to the meeting, a letter from Keynsham was read, which contained the following sentence:—" We have been necessarily obliged to omit a great number of poor inhabitants, who could not read, and therefore are not likely to be benefited by the possession of a bible." This statement reached the heart of an individual present, by the name of William Smith. To be deprived of the inspired volume by an inability to peruse it, appeared to him worse than for a man to be dying of the plague, through ignorance of the way of applying a remedy, which in itself was within his reach. His benevolent mind meditated upon their situation. He longed to relieve them, but scarcely dared to hope that the case admitted of relief. In this dilemma he consulted Stephen Prust, esq. a respectable merchant in the city, whose name stands high in the long list of Bristol philanthropists. The object of his inquiry was to ascertain whether it were possible to instruct the ignorant part of the adult poor to read. It is of immense importance, that when the seed of benevolence begins to germinate, it should be cherished by the genial influence of a kindly atmosphere, a nipping frost, at that critical juncture, would cause it to perish in its bud. In the advice, the patronage, and support of Mr. Prust, the scheme of Smith met the sunshine which it wanted. He slept not a *second* night upon his plan, after he had received the promise of his generous friend to assist him in the undertaking, before he commenced his exertions. As he was employed the next day in collecting subscriptions for the Bible Association, whenever he met with persons who could not read, he asked them if they would like to learn, provided a school should be opened. Many embraced the offer with expressions of pleasure, and their names were taken down. Two rooms were immediately obtained, and the work of instruction commenced. So little could the ardour of Smith endure delay, that in nineteen days after he had disclosed his mind to Mr. Prust, the school was opened with eleven men and ten women. The number rapidly increased, till, a few weeks after, some active friends to the cause of religion and humanity, met the founder of the new institution, and formed themselves into a society, bearing the title of AN INSTITUTION FOR INSTRUCTING ADULT PERSONS TO READ THE HOLY SCRIPTURES. The society continued to attract the attention and engage the support of christians of all denominations, and at length received a most valuable accession in the active co-operation of Thomas Pole, M D. a physician in connexion with the society of Friends. Within the period of two years, this society admitted one thousand five hundred and eight scholars, exclusive of two hundred and seventy-six, which were taught by schools belonging to several dissenting congregations.

"Before we pass on from the successful results of William Smith's exertions in Bristol, it should be stated, that although his commencement was subsequent to Mr. Charles' labours in Wales, he had no knowledge at the time of his precursor's noble career the Fountain of all Good, thus causing this stream of his mercy to break forth in two distinct places, and almost simultaneously

"It was not likely that this new light, kindled by Charles and Smith, would remain long unobserved. It was seen and admired from afar The generous and noble-spirited benefactors in different parts of the kingdom, who are ever watching for new methods of benefiting their species, hailed the beaming signal with delight, and like the eastern Magi, followed its direction, and flocked to the brightness of its rising Schools multiplied every where, till, at the present time, they are to be found in almost every considerable town in this country.

"Only one more triumph of this mighty scheme remains to be recorded; but that is a splendid one no less than the invasion of ASIA—and its establishment, amidst the temples and the gods of that part of the world, which may be denominated the METROPOLIS OF IDOLATRY THE FIRST SUNDAY SCHOOL IN ASIA was established by the Wesleyan missionaries in Ceylon, June 4, 1815.

"Messrs Harwood and Clough, two of the Wesleyan missionaries to the island of Ceylon, thus report the commencement of this good work, in a quarter of the globe to which the christian patriot turns with a heart burning with the thirst of holy conquest, and an eye sparkling with most benevolent hope"

"We have the pleasure to inform you, that, through the great kindness of the Hon. Robert Boyd, member of council, and commissioner of revenue, we have the use of the *theatre* for our Sunday school, and a better place could not have been chosen, it being so very central and commodious. We have quite a train of native children now in our school"

"Thus widely and rapidly, to the present time, has this institution multiplied its funds, its objects, and its conquests It is scarcely possible, even to hazard a conjecture upon the number of the children and adults, which are every sabbath under the sound of instruction throughout the world Perhaps, if we were to state them at considerably upwards of a MILLION, we should not at all exceed the aggregate. What a reflection for the moralist and the christian, the patriot and the philanthropist ! What a wide and lovely scene for an enlightened and generous imagination to range over ! A million of scholars, collected perhaps by fifty thousand teachers, in mighty circles round the fountain of celestial truth, to cleanse from the eyes of their understanding the scales of ignorance and vice!"

BIBLE INTELLIGENCE.

OF those numerous societies and institutions for promoting the cause of religion, whose anniversary meetings have lately been held, we can at present only advert briefly to a few.

The tenth Report of the Bible Society of Philadelphia, presents an encouraging account of the state and exertions, and prospects of this parent institution. It announces the reviving of the Bible Associations in the neighbouring districts, and the design of employing an agent, soon as a suitable person can be obtained, for the purpose of organizing county auxiliary Bible Societies throughout the state of Pennsylvania. "In order to accelerate so desirable an event, a circular letter, and a form of constitution for such societies, have been circulated through the state, as generally as possible."

The second annual Report of the American Bible Society exhibits a spirit of vigorous exertion, and a degree of prosperity, which must be gratifying to all who know the worth of the bible, and the wants of our fellow-men. We rejoice that, "while using their endeavours that *the word of the Lord may have free course and be glorified* throughout the United States, and especially in the parts where there is an incredibly swarming population, the Board have not been unmindful of their *brethren of the woods*. The condition of these natives, divided from us by their language, their manners, their ignorance, their degradation—by every thing which distinguishes savage from civilized man—too often by the fraud and other injuries of the whites, addresses us a mute, but piercing expostulation, for that help which they can obtain only in very small portions from any other quarter."

"The managers," proceeds the Report, "have taken up this matter with a view to ascertain what is practicable in itself, and can be accomplished by the society. Two modes present the only alternative, either to teach them English, as the medium of their access to the bible, or to translate it for their use into the vernacular tongue. The former has its advantages. It would put into their hands the *same* translation from one end of the continent to the other, and that derived immediately from the originals, instead of being translated from a translation, as must in a considerable degree be the case if the bible be rendered into Indian. It would tend to break down the great barrier to friendly intercourse between them and the whites of a better disposition than they are accustomed to see. It would facilitate the introduction of useful arts, and the exchange of their roving for a settled life. Having, moreover, no letters, it is not easy to embody their speech in sounds of the English alphabet, and no successful attempt has yet been made to simplify their language, when written, by the invention of original characters.

"But these advantages are counterbalanced. In common with all other nations, the Indians are strongly attached to their mother tongue. They will not submit to the pain of learning another, without such a thirst for knowledge as no savages possess. You must either convince them of its necessity by instructing them in the things of God through an interpreter, or their children must acquire it imperceptibly from their familiarity with the white settlements around them. Experience shows the first to be an herculean task; and the question will always recur—*Why the worship of God is not as acceptable in Indian as in English?* The second cannot take place but upon a small scale; it is a very slow process, the labor strength is weakened with its acceleration, the young people are in danger of learning vice as fast as they learn English; the tribe is ruined when it is able to understand you, and your end is defeated. Besides, as the propagation of our language must keep pace with the extension of our frontier, we shall not readily gain admittance far beyond the line of the worst examples that can be set before them; and it will prove, not an encouragement, but a hinderance to their embracing christianity. Their repugnance also to the whites, which in this situation must every day grow more inveterate, from feeling themselves continually pushed off their grounds, will keep alive their prejudices, will kindle their resentments, and render them not very friendly to *the white man's talk*. Indians speaking to their brother Indians, " in the tongue wherein every one was born, the wonderful works of God," bid fair to carry the gospel from the Mississippi to the Pacific, and from Canada to the Gulf of Mexico, while the English preacher is wasting his life in penetrating a few miles into their own country."

Here the deep solicitude which we feel for the poor aborigines, compels us to acknowledge, that we are not satisfied with the arguments employed to prove that the advantages of teaching them English, as the medium of their access to the bible, are counterbalanced.

We apprehend that, in the case of any civilized nation, there is much more to create and preserve an attachment to the mother tongue, than there is in the case of the Indians. The German, for instance, has in his language a multitude of dear and venerated writings. He has works of taste, and records of the exploits of his ancestors. He remembers too, that his own is the language in which the renowned reformers thought, and often wrote. He has the precious oracles of God, with their phraseology familiar to him, and at the same time, venerable and sacred. Or at least he has the prescribed services of his church, or in his earliest years he has learned what he considers most valuable in religion and in civilization, through the medium of his own language. He finds in it all the terms which he needs; and besides, he labours under no conviction of inferiority, in any respect, to his English neighbours.

But, on the other hand, the Indian, as we find him in the forest, has none, or almost none of these strong ties to bind him to his scanty and uncultivated dialect. His oral traditions, having never been reduced to any precise form, can pass most readily, with all their attractions, into English. His war song may indeed be thought an exception. But that will cease to be repeated, and consequently will be soon forgotten, when the tomahawk and scalping knife are buried, and his attention is called, not to scenes of savage slaughter, but to the melting strains of the gospel, and to the arts of peace. As he has no written language, he has no choice writings to lose with his mother tongue,—no literature—no elaborate record of ancient times—no revered Luther—no volume of Divine inspiration,—and no favourite mode of expressing his views of the christian faith and worship. He finds that the true religion and civilization present to him many terms for which he has no corresponding words in his own language. He cannot but see the superiority of a civilized, christian people, and he powerfully influenced by it to imitate them when they kindly become his instructers, and strive to impart to him the blessings which they enjoy.

But admit that, "in common with all other nations, the Indians are strongly attached to their mother tongue,"—we are not prepared to conclude they cannot be induced to learn another. Have not multitudes of them already become acquainted with our language? Do not their children make rapid progress in acquiring it, whenever they are allowed the advantages of instruction? Doubtless some must be instructed in the things of God through an interpreter, and many of their children will acquire our language imperceptibly from their familiarity with the white settlements around them. But is this all that can be done? We are confident that it is not.—Let English schools be introduced among the Indians as generally as possible. Let them be furnished with pious, faithful teachers, and be placed under the superintendence of evangelic, patient, devoted missionaries. Let special pains at the same time be taken to improve the religious state of their white neighbours, and promote a virtuous and friendly intercourse with them. Let also our national government (and that of Great Britain too,) proceed to act in the same noble spirit that has been manifested by the heads of department and the Indian agency, with regard to promoting, among the natives, useful learning and civilization. In a word, let us adopt, and, as fast as possible, pursue among all the tribes, a course similar to that which the Rev. Cyrus Kingsbury is, at this moment, with the most encouraging success, pursuing at Chickamaugah, among the Cherokees. Then our language, extending from one of their nations to another, will open a broad and common channel, in which may flow to the inhabitants of the wilderness all the blessings of the gospel, and all the treasures of our learning and useful arts. It will form a tie which will bind the scattered remnants of these dwindling tribes one to another, and all to us, and save them from impending calamities, and utter extermination, to which, in their present state, they are hastening. Deny them our language, and insuperable obstacles are continued in the way of their improvement.—Deny them our language, and we must, to give them a single book, make several *written* languages for them; to prepare which, and the requisite translations of the bible, with any tolerable degree of accuracy, would be a work of much labour and expense; and then to learn one of these written languages so as to understand a translation, would cost the natives nearly as much time and pains as to learn the English. Missionaries and teachers must continue, age after age, to labour under peculiar disadvantages. And though they would probably meet with some success, yet their usefulness must always be circumscribed within very narrow limits,—with the melancholy prospect that, after the lapse of a few more years, the little flocks which they have gathered with so much care, will waste away, and disappear from the face of the earth.

But notwithstanding these remarks, which we have thought it our duty to make, we highly approve of what the managers have done to supply with translated portions of the bible, those natives who have been taught to read in their own language.

It is with much satisfaction that we lay before our readers the concluding part of the Report.

During the past year the Board have received from England 700 *Gaelic*, 200 *German*, and 500 *Welsh* bibles, bought of the British and Foreign Bible Society, for the purpose of supplying the wants of foreigners in this country who speak those languages. 399 copies of the Gaelic bible have been sent to Fayetteville, in North-Carolina, agreeably to a request made to that effect by the Fayetteville

Bible Society. One German bible has been sold. The remaining copies of that importation are still on hand.

During the same period there have been printed for the society about nineteen thousand bibles, chiefly of the *brevier type*, 12mo. making the total number printed to be 20,500.

Of the 1,050 copies of the *French bible* in sheets, presented last year to the Board by the New-York Bible Society, six hundred have been sent to the Louisiana Bible Society for *gratuitous* circulation among the French inhabitants in that region, and six copies have been delivered to an individual going to Mobile, for *gratuitous* distribution in that place.

Of the *stereotype plates for the French bible*, to be sent out by the British and Foreign Bible Society, only those of the *Old Testament* have been as yet received. The remainder are expected shortly.

In addition to the scriptures in the French language above-mentioned, the Board have made, since the last anniversary, the following donations of bibles in English, viz.

In June 1817, 100 copies of the brevier bible were sent to the Steuben County Bible Society, and one hundred to the Essex County Bible Society, for the destitute inhabitants on the frontiers of the state of New-York; in July, one hundred to St. Louis, Missouri Territory; in September one hundred to the Saratoga Bible Society, and fifty to the Bible Society of Adams and its vicinity, in Massachusetts; in November, sixty-five to the United States' ship the John Adams, for its crew, and 100 to the Female Bible Society of Wilkesbarre, in Pennsylvania; in December, 250 to the Marine Bible Society of New-York, for the supply of seamen from all quarters frequenting the neighbouring ports, and in January last, 50 copies to the African Bible Society. making in all 1,521 bibles gratuitously circulated by the society in the course of the past year. Many more would have been distributed in the same manner during that period, had not the means of printing for the society been so limited, by the want of sufficient accommodations, as scarcely to enable the Board, besides making the above grants of bibles, to supply the increasing calls of auxiliary and other societies desirous of purchasing them. The enlargement of its printing establishment, and the continuation of the public bounty, will, it is hoped, place the managers in a situation, during the coming year, to make a more ample distribution of the scriptures in destitute parts of the land.

Extract of a letter from a gentleman in London to his friend in this city, dated May 16, 1818.

It will give you pleasure to hear that the annual meeting of the British and Foreign Bible Society, held the 6th inst. was not less interesting than on former occasions; indeed some circumstances tended to give it additional interest.—An increase of 6000*l.* to its funds in the course of the past year, was a pleasing feature, affording evidence that this important object does not lose ground in the public estimation. The increased exertions and growing success of the female auxiliaries were very animating. What has been done at Liverpool is without parallel, the ladies having divided the town into upwards of 300 districts, and by this subdivision of labour, 5000 visits to the habitations of the poor are paid in a single day The improvement of mind and manners which has been produced, in a very short period, by such acts of kindness and attention, is in many districts very striking; and thus the ground is prepared for receiving the good seed. I am gratified in mentioning that Mr. Rush was present on this occasion; he accepted the invitation in the most cordial manner, and being requested to take a part in the business of the day, did it in a manner that made a pleasing impression on all present, indeed it added much to the interest of the day to observe the representative of the United States, and lord Gambier who was our negociator at Ghent, seated on the same bench at this feast of christian love the feelings excited on the occasion were such as we may delight to cherish, and can review without a sting.

The proceedings of the day shall be forwarded you by an early opportunity, and will be perused with satisfaction, as well as the Report of the Committee for the past year. The rapid progress which is making, in every quarter, in the spread of divine truth, and the remarkable instances in which opposition is overruled to promote the great object, afford indubitable evidence that the work is of God. To him be all the praise

---

Extracts from the Fourteenth Annual Report of the British and Foreign Bible Society, just received.

In conformity with the plan adopted in preceding Reports, your committee will pursue a course as nearly geographical as circumstances will allow, selecting from the mass of their materials, what may be most likely to interest the members at large.

Commencing with the *United Netherlands Bible Society*, your committee have to express their satisfaction at the vigour and cordiality with which the several establishments throughout the kingdom, (52 in number,) under this common designation, have prosecuted their benevolent object. The funds from various sources, within the first year, amounted to 33,763 florins, (nearly 3,500*l*.) and the issue of Bibles and Testaments to 4,578. Among the objects in which this Association is engaged, one is, an edition of the Malaya bible in the Arabic character.

The *Hanover Bible Society*, with its branches, has proceeded in its work of distributing the scriptures, among the protestants and catholics.

The *Brunswick Bible Society* has acquired considerable support. His serene highness, the duke Augustus, added to the sanction of his patronage, a donation of 100 rix dollars in gold, and, under these, and other favourable auspices, auxiliary societies have been formed in Greene, Lunsen, and Gundesheim.

The *Prussian Bible Society*, under the patronage of his Prussian majesty, consisting of the *Central Society* at Berlin, and various branches and auxiliaries in different parts of the kingdom, exhibits a gratifying spectacle to the eye of the christian philanthropist.

The *Central Society* in Prussia, in its third year, distributed 6000 German bibles. The large edition of 11,000 copies will soon be completed: after which, another edition of 10,000 must be immediately undertaken, as the deficiency is said to be still very great.

The *Hambro'-Altona, Lubeck,* and *Bremen Bible Societies*, are pursuing, within their respective spheres, the object of their institution.

The progress made by the *Bible Society* in the free city of Frankfort on the Maine, is truly gratifying, and has drawn from the emperor of Russia a strong testimony of his commendation and friendship.

The influence of this society has extended to many of the neighbouring parts: and the demand for the scriptures has increased, in a degree which has surprised, and, from the narrowness of their means, even embarrassed, the managers of the institution. "My room," says the secretary, "was often, on Sundays in particular, so crowded with people, that I was obliged to confine myself to one of the corners of it."

These applicants were, chiefly, day-labourers from Fulda, Hesse-Cassel, Bavaria, &c.

In the principal *Bible Societies* of Switzerland, the zeal so often commended continues to operate, and progress is making in each of them, though in different degrees, towards the attainment of the common object.

France and Italy have borne a part, though in very different proportions, in the great work of distributing the holy scriptures.

Of the protestant New Testament by Osterwald, and the catholic by Maitre de Sacy, stereotyped at Paris, many thousand copies have been dispersed in various parts of France. At Montauban, a large edition of the protestant bible, by Martin, is printing, under the direction of a very respectable committee: of the bible undertaken by the *Bible Society* at Strasburg, the New Testament is finished, and now in circulation, and the Old Testament is in progress; and, in general, it appears, that an increased desire is manifested in France to possess and peruse the holy scriptures. Your committee think it due to the late Rev. Henry Oberlin, of Waldbach, in Alsace, to bear their testimony to that zeal by which he was urged to sacrifice his valuable life, in exertions for distributing the holy scriptures among his countrymen.

In Italy, editions of the catholic New Testament of Martini, without note or comment, have been printed both at Turin and Naples and many channels have been found, through which copies could be circulated without impediment, and with the prospect of being very thankfully received.

In the Mediterranean, a *Bible Society* was formed, in May last, at Malta, under the designation of the *Malta Bible Society*. This active institution (for the encouragement of which your committee voted 500*l*.) has opened a correspondence with places of considerable importance, and is using every exertion to render its advantageous position conducive to the dissemination of the scriptures along the shores of the Mediterranean, and even in the interior of Asia.

The *Danish Bible Society* at Copenhagen, formed under the sanction of his Danish majesty, has been occupied during the past year, in printing the edition of 10,000 copies of the Danish Bible, with 5000 extra New Testaments, towards which your society had contributed 500*l*.

The *Icelandic Bible Society*, encouraged by the grant of 500*l* has made judicious arrangements for increasing its funds, and facilitating its operations.

The *Swedish National Bible Society* at Stockholm, continues its most active exertions for the promotion of that end to which the common efforts are directed—the distribution of the holy scriptures. In pursuit of this design, it is aided, not only by the patronage of his Swedish majesty, and the personal influence of the first members of the government, particularly of his excellency count Rosenblad, but also by the prelates and the parochial clergy of the realm.

Your committee now proceed to Russia, and here they feel equally at a loss to express their astonishment at the prodigious operations, in furtherance of the general cause, which are going forward in that extensive empire, and to exhibit any thing like an adequate representation of them.

Fostered by the paternal care of his imperial majesty Alexander, the *Russian Bible Society* has, in the course of the past year, enlarged very considerably the field of its exertions, and strengthened itself by various newly-formed and promising auxiliaries, in different parts of the empire. The following are the principal stations which they respectively occupy:—Penza, Kostroma, Tobolsk, Kief, Orel, Vladimer, Irkutsk, Kazan, Simbirsk, Pskoff, Minsk, Bialastock, Grodno, Posen, Bessarabia, Tahanrog, Tscherkask, and Twer.

Of all the auxiliary societies, that at Moscow is (as from the rank of this ancient capital might be expected) the most splendid and efficient, and, as well in the zeal of its supporters, as in the scale of its operations, is inferior only to the parent society at St. Petersburg.

"I consider" (said the emperor, in his address to the *Moscow Bible Society*) "the establishment of Bible societies in Russia, in most parts of Europe, and in other quarters of the globe, and the very great progress these institutions have made in disseminating the word of God, not merely among christians, but also among heathens and mahomedans, as a peculiar display of the mercy and grace of God to the human race. On this account, I have taken upon myself the denomination of a member of the *Russian Bible Society*, and will render it every possible assistance, in order that the beneficent light of revelation may be shed among all nations subject to my sceptre."

In the East, the object of the institution continues to be prosecuted with great zeal and diligence, by its several auxiliary societies and agents, in that interesting portion of the world.

At the head of these stands the corresponding committee at Calcutta.

In addition to the grants annually made to this committee, of 2000*l*., (one moiety of which is appropriated to the translations going forward by the baptist missionaries at Serampore,) 1000*l*. have been voted, for the special purpose of aiding the printing and distribution of the Chinese scriptures, translated by Dr. Marshman. And further, with a view to afford a more effectual encouragement to the translation and circulation of the scriptures in India, the corresponding committee have been authorized to appropriate the sum of 500*l*. to the first thousand copies of every approved translation of the New Testament into any dialect of India, in which no translation has previously existed. The resolution on which this procedure has been adopted, was prompted by the zeal and liberality of William Hay esq. of Leeds, and other respectable individuals, who, struck with the proposal of the baptist missionaries at Serampore, to execute 26 versions on those moderate terms, and desirous to excite increased attention to this subject, presented the society with the sum of *fourteen hundred and seventy-five pounds*, as an offering from certain "friends to the translation of the scriptures into the vernacular dialects of India."

The number of copies issued by the *British and Foreign Bible Society* to subscribers, &c. at cost and reduced prices, from the 31st of March, 1817, to the same period in 1818, is 89,795 Bibles, and 104,306 Testaments, making, with those circulated at the society's expense, from different presses on the continent, the total issued by the *British and Foreign Bible Society*, in somewhat less than thirteen years, more than TWO MILLIONS of bibles and testaments.

A new era appears to have commenced, and all things seem to be working together for the universal propagation of the gospel. Whether the accomplishment of this object is near or remote; whether it is to gladden the eyes of those who now labour, or is reserved for those who are to come after them, is a consideration which may be left to the disposal, as it is known only to the prescience of Him, in whose hands are the times and the seasons which regulate the events of his kingdom. Grateful for the past, and confident of the future, the members of the *British and Foreign Bible Society*, and all who co-operate with them in every part of the world, may securely commit the issue of their cause to the Author of the scriptures, while, in the devout strains of holy writ, they implore his continued benediction upon it.

"*Let thy work appear unto thy servants, and thy glory unto their children: and let the beauty of the Lord our God be upon us; and establish thou the work of our hands upon us, yea, the work of our hands establish thou it.*"—Psalm xc. 16, 17

The following impressive remarks are taken from the address of the Merchant-Seamen's Auxiliary Bible Society in London.

"LET not the peculiarity of their situation, (that is, of seafaring men,) and of their manner of life, be forgotten. They are necessarily deprived of many advantages of instruction enjoyed by persons who live regularly on shore. Once at sea, a seaman has no choice of associates: he is fixed to his shipmates, and thus for the most part secluded from any society but that of the profane and dissolute. The privilege of resorting with their families to the house of God, to listen to his word, and of uniting with the congregation of christian worshippers in the services of prayer and praise, is in a great measure unknown to them. The sun of the Sabbath generally arises to their view from beneath the same waste of waters with the light of a common day, and their thoughts and duties seem to merge in the single object of guiding their vessel through the deep. It has been calculated, that one half or two thirds of a sailor's life, is thus spent on the ocean and that, of the remainder, one half is passed in foreign harbours, where no christian instruction can in general be obtained. Under these unfavourable circumstances, it is scarcely to be expected, that during the fragment of his time which he passes in his own land, the means of instruction, even if offered to him, should be eagerly embraced. In point of fact, they are generally neglected, and for this neglect, those who are even slightly acquainted with the force of habit, and the common principles of our nature, will not find it difficult to account. The seaman remains, therefore, for the most part, as ignorant of the things which accompany salvation, as if the will of God had never been revealed to man—and even the hardships of a seafaring life, and the thousand perils peculiarly incident to his profession, instead of awakening his mind to serious reflection, too often produce in him, from the want of christian instruction, a contrary effect, and lead him to dedicate almost every moment of his time, while on shore, to the most sordid, and debasing, and ruinous indulgences

"With respect to some of the disadvantages which have been enumerated, it is obvious that we cannot remove them: they belong of necessity to a seafaring life. But then these evils are not without the means of alleviation. Sailors often have at sea much time for reading. By the general diffusion of education, many of them are qualified thus to employ their time; and the disposition either to read for themselves, or to listen to others, is very prevalent among them. Unhappily the few books to which they have access are often of the worst description. But may not their leisure hours, and their inclination for reading, be converted to a better account? Is it impossible to give a more profitable direction to their minds? Will they have no curiosity, if the means be afforded, to learn something of that God whose path is in the great waters, and whose wonders they behold in the deep? Is there nothing to interest them in the representation of their own state, and of the awful eternity to which they are hastening? Will they turn a deaf ear to the history of the Redeemer, to the hopes and promises, the invitations and threatenings, which involve their present peace and everlasting welfare? Is not the seaman, then, formed by the same Hand with ourselves? Is he not capable of being moved by the same feelings and affections? Does the volume of Divine Truth appeal so forcibly to all other men; and is he alone, by some law of creation, or by some hard condition of his lot, to be regarded as excluded from the common range of his Maker's bounty, and as inaccessible to the influence of his word and Spirit? With the evidence before us of Pitcairn's island—an island far removed from European civilization—where the descendants of a British seaman who was happily possessed of a bible, trained, by means of that blessed book, in the fear and love of God, are now exhibiting an example of piety which might well put even Britain to the blush;—with such an example before us, can we doubt for one moment that the word of God is still capable, under every variety of circumstance and situation, of answering the high and ennobling purposes for which it was given to mankind?

"That sacred volume, it is the object of this address to provide for the seamen who are employed in navigating our commercial marine And should it succeed in that object, it may be reasonably hoped, of numbers among them, that, through the blessings of its Divine Author, the bible may become their companion and guide through life; their consolation and support in every danger,—the standard, as it were, under which they sail, the anchor by which they hold amid the storms of this world, and the compass to direct them to that haven where perils will no longer beset their course, nor disturb their enjoyment of rest and tranquillity for ever.

VALUABLE ETHIOPIC MANUSCRIPT

TO open an intercourse with the ancient church of Abyssinia, in order to revive its primitive intelligence and zeal, was one of the important objects which the Church Missionary Society had in view in establishing its representatives in the Mediterranean. On Mr. Connor's joining Mr Jowett, a journey will be undertaken, as soon as practicable, to Egypt; one purpose of which will be, to open, with the aid of the British consul at Cairo, Mr. Salt, and through the patriarch of Alexandria, a communication with Abyssinia.

We extract a passage from the instructions delivered to Mr Connor, at a special meeting on the 28th of October, which will introduce to our readers the description of a valuable Ethiopic manuscript, lately come into the society's possession.

Speaking of the Abyssinian church, it is said—" That most ancient christian church lays a strong claim to our special regard. Surrounded, and continually encroached on, by mohammedan zeal, it seems to stretch out its imploring arms for our aid. It possesses the holy scriptures in an ancient and pure version; but the copies of these scriptures, in the gradual decay of the church, have become rare, scattered, and mutilated. No object can present itself to the christian world, of greater interest, or of more probable influence on that whole church and nation, than the communication to them, in rich abundance, of copies of that Divine word which they still reverence and love, but of which there is now among them a grievous deficiency. The good providence of God has lately brought into the society's possession a MS. of peculiar value. It contains a perfect copy of the first eight books of the Old Testament, in Ethiopic. The committee have offered to the British and Foreign Bible Society the use of this invaluable MS. in order to print from it an edition of this portion of scripture; and Mr. Lee has tendered his able services to edit this work. Other portions of the Ethiopic scriptures are unexpectedly discovering themselves, and, by the blessing of God on your researches through the medium of Egypt, we doubt not but that, at no great distance of time, the Abyssinian church will be revived and restored by the multiplication of copies of the Divine word "

Mr. Lee, the orientalist, has given the following statement respecting Ethiopic MSS. in general, and particularly that which is come into the society's possession

" It is remarkable," he says, " that notwithstanding the great repute of the Ethiopic version among the learned in Europe, for more than two hundred years, the far greater part of the bible has never appeared in print. It is probable, indeed, that Ludolf, the great Ethiopic scholar and grammarian, would have printed many portions, and perhaps the whole of the Old Testament, had sufficient encouragement been afforded him. but, in those times, neither the love of letters, nor the superior desire of giving the waters of life freely, had obtained an ascendency over the minds of men, sufficient to bring to light so valuable a portion of the sacred scriptures. Still we are much indebted to Ludolf and his excellent contemporaries, both for the portions of scripture which they did print, and for the elementary books which they left behind them. Much, however, remains to be done, in this very interesting department of literature, which has now, for more than a hundred years, scarcely been so much as named, much less inquired into.

"The first portions of the Ethiopic scriptures that appeared in print, were the Psalms, and the Songs of Solomon; edited, at Rome, by John Potken, A. D. 1513. In 1548 the New Testament was also printed at Rome, by some Abyssinian priests, and was afterwards reprinted in the London Polyglott; but, as the MSS used in the Roman edition were old and mutilated, the editors restored such chasms as appeared in the text, by translation from the Latin Vulgate. These editions, therefore, are not of much value, as they do not present faithful copies of the ancient Ethiopic text. About the middle of the seventeenth century appeared in print, the book of Ruth, the prophecies of Joel, Jonah, Zephaniah, and Malachi; the Song of Moses, that of Hannah (1 Sam. ii.), the Prayers of Hezekiah, Manasseh, Jonah, Azariah, and the Three Children; Isaiah; Habakkuk; the Hymns of the Virgin Mary, Zachariah, and Simeon, and the first four chapters of Genesis. In 1815, the British and Foreign Bible Society published a reprint of Ludolf's Psalter. This is the whole of the Ethiopic scriptures hitherto printed. It does not seem necessary here to enumerate all the reprints of the above portions of the Ethiopic bible.

"By the help of the invaluable MS. which has come into the society's possession, we hope, through the blessing of God on our endeavours, to add something to the very scanty stock above enumerated, and, what is far better, to multiply copies of the word of God, for the benefit of the churches in Abyssinia. This MS. contains the first eight books of the Old Testament, written on vellum, in a bold and masterly hand, in two columns on each page. The length of the page is that of a large quarto: the width is not quite so great. The volume contains 285 folios, of which the text covers 281, very accurately written, and in high preservation. On the first page is written, in Ethiopic, the invocation usually found in the books of the eastern christians: 'In the name of the Father, and of the Son, and of the Holy Ghost.' Then follows an account of the contents of the book, written in Latin by some former possessor, and a date, A D 1696. 20 September. On the reverse of the first folio is found a table, not unlike the tables of genealogy in some of our old English bibles, which seems to be intended to show the hours appointed for certain prayers. Then follows the book of Genesis, as translated from the Greek of the Septuagint. On the reverse of the third folio is the following inscription, in Arabic: 'The poor Ribea, the son of Elias, wrote it. O wine! to which nothing can be assimilated, either in reality or appearance; of which our Lord said, having the cup in his hand, and giving thanks, "This is my blood for the salvation of men."' Folios 7 and 8 have been supplied, in paper, by a more modern hand. On the reverse of folio 8 is a very humble attempt at drawing, in the figure of a person apparently in prayer, accompanied by an inscription, in Ethiopic, at the side of the figure: 'In the prayers of Moses and Aaron, to * Abraham, Isaac and Jacob, am I, thy servant, O Lord, presented in the power of the Trinity, a weak, infirm and defiled sinner. Let them implore Christ.' Under the drawing, in Ethiopic. 'In the same manner, every slayer that shall slay Cain,

* As this inscription, which occurs on the supplied leaves, savours of the errours of the Romish church, it was probably written by some Abyssinian catholic. The inscriptions of Isaac, the writer of the MS though mutilated, and sometimes obscure, seem free from these errours. The figure of St. Peter, mentioned below, was probably traced by the same hand.

will I repay in this, and, as he slew, so shall he be slain.' On the reverse of folio 98, at the end of the book of Exodus, are two figures, somewhat similar, but rather better drawn, and seemingly by the writer of the MS.; and in another place or two, there are marginal ornaments. At the end of Deuteronomy is this inscription in Ethiopic 'The repetition of the law, which God spake to Moses. Numbered 5070 (words.) Intercede for your slave Isaac.' At the end of the volume. 'Pray for those who laboured in this book, and for your slave Isaac, who gave this to Jerusalem, the holy.' Then follows an inscription, in Arabic 'In the name of the Father, and of the Son, and of the Holy Ghost, one God. O Lord, save thy people from every evil! O our God, Jesus Christ, the Speaker to men! O holy people, remember your slave Isaac, the poor. God shall remember you in the mercies of this book. Pray, if God be willing, that I may be permitted to see your face. And pray for me, the sinner. Pardon my sins, O Lord! and let my body be buried in Mount Sion.' Then follow other inscriptions in Ethiopic, from which it appears, that the book was written at Axuma, the ancient capital of Ethiopia, and that it was sent by Isaac to the Abyssinians residing in Jerusalem. No date appears in the MS. itself. It is, probably, about 300 years old. On the reverse of folio 235, is a drawing, intended to represent Andrew the apostle, with the book of the Gospels in one hand, and the keys in the other. Some less ingenious draftsman, however, has, by means of the transparency of the vellum, traced out this figure on the first page of this folio, and given the name of Peter to his humble representation. He has thus succeeded in assigning to St. Peter the first place, and also in bestowing on him the keys. Against this picture of Peter is placed his age, 120 years."

We trust that, at no distant period, we shall see, by the researches and endeavours of the Church Missionary and Bible Societies, the whole or the greater part of the Ethiopic scriptures issue from the press. The Church Missionary Society is directing its further inquiries to this end, and Mr Lee has prepared himself to edit the work: while the British and Foreign Bible Society is taking measures to print it in the most acceptable form.

[CHRISTIAN OBSERVER, January, 1818.

STATE OF RELIGION

Extract of a letter from Benjamin Stout esquire, Lexington, March 4, 1818

IN some of the churches of our connexion we hear of great revivals, to wit. in Madison, Mercer, Lincoln, Scott, Woodford, Gallatin, Bourbon, Clark, and other counties Some of them are indeed astonishingly great. Brother Vardeman, of course, is all activity and life, and constantly visiting those places, for, as he says himself, he lives best in the fire—not the fire of contention, but of divine love, &c. You know his character.

From Rev John Peck, Cazenovia, (N. Y.) May 23, 1818.

THE Lord is still good unto us. He is yet carrying on his glorious work in our country. This town yet shares in the divine blessing. A number, of late, have been bowed to his mild sceptre, and acknowledged his right of government, by submitting to his commands. The towns of Mentz, Smithfield, Bristol, and Lisle, God has visited in showers of divine blessings, and numerous other places have not been forgotten, but have received a share in the cup of blessings

From Rev. Silas Shelburne, Pleasant Grove, Lunenburg county, Va.

It is with pleasure I can inform you the good work of the Lord seems yet to be progressing in this vicinity. There are very considerable additions in these churches (Reedy creek,) and in Bluestone. Some addition is made at every church meeting. I expect to baptise a goodly number at our next season.

From Rev. David Barrow, Montgomery county, Ky. May 5, 1818.

There has, for several months past, been a very considerable revival of religion in the neighbourhood of Winchester, reaching up into our parts, embracing three churches of the North District Association, to each of which there have been, and still are making very considerable additions; the principal instruments in the work, appear to be elders Jeremiah Vardeman and George Boone. This is in Clarke and Montgomery counties. There is, or rather has been, a great work going on, all the winter past, in Paris, Bourbon county, under the presbyterians and methodists. They have been lately visited by elder Vardeman. The work still goes on, and numbers have been and still are coming to baptism.

From Rev. Absalom Graves, Boone county, Kentucky, April 20, 1818.

I must not omit giving you some account of the gracious work of the Lord in our section of the western country. It commenced in Gallatin, the county on the Ohio immediately below Boone, some time early last summer. The churches called the Twins, White's Run, M'Cools Bottom, Ten Miles, and Craig's Creek, have shared largely of this heavenly shower. The three first mentioned churches belong to the Franklin Association, and the two last to the North Bend. I have been much among them, and have no doubt of its being in reality the work of the Lord. I suppose, from the best calculation I can make, there has been baptised in these five churches, between six and seven hundred persons, and principally of the youth. Bless the Lord, O my soul, and all that is within me praise his dear name! This glorious work has reached us at Bullittsburgh. It began to make its appearance soon after our Association in September last, but there was not much ingathering until about christmas. We had meetings through the winter almost every night in the week; no weather was so cold, wet, or dark, as to prevent a crowded assembly. We have had frequently to break the ice, of considerable thickness, in order to administer the ordinance, yet none have received an injury by it. About the coldest weather we had in the winter, we baptised 34 in one day, without intermission. We have baptised in the whole, at Bullittsburgh, since the revival began, about 157. Also, our neighbouring sister church Middle Creek, has enjoyed a blessed refreshing season, which began about the time it did at Bullittsburgh. They have baptised about 100. In both these churches a great portion of the converts are of the youth—some only of about 11 or 12 years of age. When we view the great change and alteration here, we may truly say, "The Lord hath done great things for us, whereof we are glad." At this time there is a great work in several churches of our Association on Licking; as great, perhaps, as any we ever had an account of. I have had late accounts from the Great Crossings, from Mercer, Fayette, Clarke, Mason and Montgomery counties, of precious revivals there May the great Head of the church prosper his cause, till the earth be filled with his knowledge!

The " Narrative of the state of religion within the bounds of the general assembly of the Presbyterian church; and of the general associations of Connecticut, New Hampshire, Massachusetts Proper, and of the general convention of Vermont, during the last year," presents many pleasing facts and important considerations. We have room to insert only the following paragraphs.

"The General Assembly feel thankful that they can, without being charged with enthusiasm, say, *the interests of the Redeemer's kingdom have advanced throughout their bounds.* It is true the number of revivals is not so great as in some former years, but the fruits of these revivals remain in their beauty and usefulness to gladden our hearts. They who have been called into the church from the world, adorn the doctrine of God our Saviour. This we consider as a subject of congratulation and praise, for it is an indubitable truth, that on the consistent deportment of professors of religion, under the Divine blessing, depends the successful recommendation of its claims to the world "Let your light, (such is Christ's command,) so shine before men, that they, seeing your good works, may glorify your Father who is in heaven." " We therefore exhort you, brethren, partakers of the heavenly calling, that you walk worthy of your high vocation." Whilst you earnestly and perseveringly seek for the salvation of sinners, do not neglect your own growth in grace and the knowledge of the Lord Jesus. The age in which we live is correctly denominated THE AGE OF ACTION. So numerous are the associations for promoting the cause of truth, and so assiduous are the exertions of its friends to ensure success, that more than ordinary diligence is necessary to take heed to ourselves. There is a splendour which this universal and increasing action in the church reflects upon individual character, that may so far dazzle the spiritual perception, and taint the spiritual taste, as to give the adversary a real advantage over those very persons who are attacking his kingdom, and circumscribing his power. Be much engaged in your closets, examining the state of your own hearts, and the nature of your motives. Do still more for God in the world than you ever have done; but connect with this an increasing attention to your personal sanctification. Forget not that it is indispensably requisite for you to cultivate purity of intellect, as well as purity of affection. No attention to the latter will, or can compensate for neglect of the former Such neglect has in too many instances already, in different parts, caused a conformity of conduct to the maxims of the world. It is not sufficient for the professed believer to keep within the established rules of conducting social business, or the statute laws of the land; he must, in spirit and in deportment, do unto others as he would wish to be done by himself, under similar circumstances. His morality must be CHRISTIAN morality, the legitimate fruit of his actual union with Him who is " holy, harmless, undefiled, separate from sinners, and made higher than the heavens." Remember that " the kingdom of God is not meat and drink, but righteousness, peace, and joy in the Holy

Ghost: for he that in these things serveth Christ, is acceptable to God, and approved of men."

"In the bounds of the general associations of Connecticut, Massachusetts, and New Hampshire, and the general convention of Vermont, nothing has occurred of special importance since the last report. The churches are reaping the fruits of past revivals; the cause of religion is advancing, error and vice are losing ground."

MISCELLANEA.

Mr. Ward of Serampore, in his interesting "View of the History, Literature, and Religion of the Hindoos," has given a large number of scripture illustrations, derived from Hindoo manners and customs. The following are a specimen.

Genesis xliii. 34. "And he sent messes unto them from before him." This is the method among the Hindoos; the dishes are not placed on the table, but messes are sent to each individual by the master of the feast, or by his substitute.

Genesis xlv. 22. "To all of them he gave changes of raiment." At the close of a feast, the Hindoos, among other presents to the guests, commonly give new garments; a Hindoo garment is merely a piece of cloth, requiring no work of the tailor.

Exodus iii. 5. "Put off thy shoes from off thy feet, for the place whereon thou standest is holy ground." The natives of Bengal never go into their own houses, nor into the houses of others, with their shoes on, but always leave them at the door. It would be a great affront not to attend to this mark of respect in visiting, and to enter a temple without pulling off the shoes, would be an unpardonable offence.

Numbers xxii. 6. "Come now, I pray thee, curse me this people, for they are too powerful for me." Many accounts are related in the Hindoo writings, of kings employing sages to curse their enemies when too powerful for them.

Judges iv. 5. "And she dwelt under the palm-tree of Deborah." It is common for Hindoos to plant trees in the name of themselves and friends; some religious mendicants live for a considerable time under trees.

Psalm lxiii. 10. "They shall be a portion for foxes." This passage appears obscure; but give it the probable reading—*they shall be a portion for jackals*—and then the anathema becomes plain and striking to a Hindoo, in whose country the disgusting sight of jackals devouring human bodies may be seen every day. So ravenous are these animals, that they frequently steal infants as they lie by the breast of their mother, and sick persons who lie friendless in the street, or by the side of the Ganges, are sometimes devoured alive by these animals in the night. I have heard of persons, in a state of intoxication, being thus devoured as they lay in the streets of Calcutta.

Proverbs xi. 21. "Though hand join in hand." The Hindoos sometimes ratify an engagement by one person's laying his right hand on the hand of another.

Ecclesiastes ix. 8. "Let thy garments be always white." This comparison loses all its force in Europe; but in India, where white cotton is the dress of all the inhabitants, and where the beauty of garments consists, not in their shape, but in their being clean and white, the exhortation becomes strikingly proper.

Isaiah xviii. 2. "To a nation whose land the rivers have spoiled." In some parts of Bengal, whole villages are every now and then swept away by the Ganges when it changes its course. This river frequently runs over districts, from which a few years before it was several miles distant.

Isaiah xxxvii. 29. "I will put my hook in thy nose." The cow, the tame buffalo, the bear, &c. in this country, are frequently seen with a ring in their noses, through which a cord is drawn, and the beast guided by it, as the horse by the bit and bridle.

Isaiah lx. 4. "Thy daughters shall be nursed at thy side." The practice of carrying children astride on the hips, is as common here as carrying them in the arms in Europe.

Jeremiah xiv. 4. "Because the ground is chapt, for there was no rain in the earth." The cracks in the earth, before the descent of the rains, are in some places a cubit wide, and deep enough to receive the greater part of the human body.

Jeremiah xliv. 17. "To pour out drin-kofferings to the queen of heaven." The hindoos pour out water to the sun three times a day, and to the moon at the time of worshipping this satellite.

Amos v. 19. "Leaned his hand on the wall, and the serpent bit him." Snakes are very frequently found in old unplastered walls, built of bricks and clay; nor are fatal accidents uncommon in such houses, as well as in those built with mud only.

Nahum ii. 10. "The faces of them all gather blackness." Sickness often makes a great change in the countenances of the hindoos; so that a person who was rather fair when in health, becomes nearly black by sickness.

Matthew vi. 2. "When thou doest thine alms, do not sound a trumpet before thee." The mussulmans, who, in the ostentation, bigotry, and cruelty of their character, strongly resemble the pharisees, at their festival of the muhurum, erect stages in the public streets; and, by the sound of a trumpet, call the poor to receive alms of rice and other kinds of food.

Matthew vi. 5. "They love to pray standing in the synagogues, and in the corners of the streets." Both hindoos and mussulmans offer their devotions in the most public places; as, at the landing places of rivers, in the public streets, and on the roofs of boats, without the least modesty or effort at concealment.

Matthew vii. 26 "Shall be likened unto a foolish man, which built his house upon the sand," &c. The fishermen in Bengal build their huts in the dry season on the beds of sand from which the river has retired. When the rains set in, which they often do very suddenly, accompanied with violent northwest winds, and the waters pour down in torrents from the mountains, a fine illustration is given of our Lord's parable· "the rains descended, the floods came, and the winds blew, and beat upon that house, and it fell." In one night multitudes of these huts are frequently swept away, and the place where they stood is the next morning undiscoverable.

Mark xiv. 14. "Good man of the house." A hindoo woman never calls her husband by his name, but frequently speaks of him as the "man of the house."

John viii. 6. "Jesus stooped down, and with his finger wrote on the ground." Schools for children are frequently held under trees in Bengal, and the children who are beginning to learn, write the letters of the alphabet in the dust. This saves pens, ink, and paper.

Acts xxii. 3. "Brought up at the feet of Gamaliel." This is a term of respect used by the apostle towards his preceptor. Similar forms of speech are very common amongst the hindoos, as, "I learnt this at my father's feet," instead of saying, I learnt it of my father. "I was taught at the feet of such a teacher." "My teacher's feet say so."

Revelation xiii. 15. "He had power to give life to the image." The bramhuns, by repeating incantations, profess to give eyes and a soul to an image before it is worshipped.

It was well observed by an old writer, "A child of God falling into sin, is like a child falling into water; he will cry aloud for succour, that he may not be drowned. But a child of the devil falling into sin, is like a fish falling into water; he swims and sports in it, as in his element."

The honourable judge Tilghman, in his eulogium in commemoration of Dr Caspar Wistar, mentions the following fact to the honour of the deceased professor.

"When a youth at Edinburgh, his friend, Dr. Charles Stewart, made him a present of a neat edition of the bible in two small volumes. These he carefully preserved to the day of his death; and it was his custom, when he travelled, always to take one of them with him. The circumstance was well known to his children, the eldest of whom frequently accompanied him in his excursions, and could not fail to impress on their tender minds, a veneration for the book which their father so highly prized."

Mr. Burkitt on Philippians i. 29, has the following remark: "Angels glorify Christ by doing, but not by suffering. I doubt not but had the angels bodies of flesh, as saints have, they would be glad to lay their necks on the block, as saints do—but this is the peculiar privilege of believers, *unto you it is given, and not to them.*"

Mr. Trapp on the text "I and my father are one," adds, "both for nature and essence, and for one consent both in will and working. Out of the harbour of Goodwin's Sands (near the coast of Kent) the pilot cannot make forth, they say, unless he so steer his ship that he bring two steeples, which stand off, so even in his sight, that they may seem to be but one,—so is it here."

It is the highest madness for any one to pretend himself to be the head of the church, as the pope doth, unless he assume to himself to be head of all the angels in heaven, for they all belong to the *same church* with the saints here below. And therefore, when mention is made of the headship of Christ, they are expressly placed in the same subjection to him. Ephes. i. 20—23. *Owen.*

OBITUARY.

MRS. ELEANOR RICHARDS.

Mrs. Richards was born on the 22d day of October, 1761, in the parish of St Martins, London, and departed this life on the 27th June, 1818, at four o'clock, P. M. in the 57th year of her age.

She was the subject of divine grace, we have reason to hope, at an early period of life; her step-father, being a very pious man, frequently took her to private prayer meetings, from which she received her first convictions. The Rev. Dr. Conyers, who officiated at St Paul's church, Deptford, where she was brought up, opened at his own expense, a place for public worship on week day evenings, where she often attended, and was edified and encouraged; particularly from a sermon, which she frequently mentioned, from the 1st Corinthians, xv. 24th to 28th verse inclusive. "Then cometh the end," &c.

She was in the habit of attending more generally at the independent meeting house at Deptford, under the care of the Rev. Mr Barker, until her departure for this country. On her arrival here, she was pleased with the preaching of the Rev. Mr. Ustick, then pastor of the first baptist church in this city, and attended there till the house in Sansom street was erected, when she worshipped there and occasionally at the Rev Mr. Skinner's, as often as her health would permit. Under the labours of the pastor of that church and of the Rev. Mr. Skinner, she was often edified, and her heart enlarged and encouraged in Zion's ways, from the pulpit. She often brought home part of the sermon, and repeated it to her children, urging on them, with tears in her eyes, the importance of religion, and a preparation for another and better world, through the merits of a precious Redeemer. Her faith in Christ was fervent and strong to the last. She often said he was her refuge and salvation. She was a kind friend to the poor. Her heart was the seat of sympathy and affection in the extreme, indeed it might be said, the poorer the object, the more welcome. One instance of her mildness, among many others, occurring only on the Saturday previous to her death, we will relate. Her children being around her, and conversing a little harshly on the dissipation of a young man, who they knew was injuring himself and his family; she mildly said, "My dear, our dear Redeemer when upon earth never used harsh language to the vilest creature; his language was meekness and kindness, and we ought to follow his blessed pattern."

During her last sickness, one of her children (brother Richards, deacon of the church) asked her frequently if he should pray with her. She replied, "Oh, yes, do my dear;" and several times during the four days she laid ill, to inquiries how her mind was, she uniformly answered, "comfortable." She had some idea previous to this sickness, of making a public profession by baptism, and said to her daughter, "what would you think if I were to be baptised, my dear?" To which her daughter replied, "I should be pleased, mother." Her conversation of late, was more and more about Jesus and her soul's everlasting happiness. On the Saturday morning, the day on which she expired, a little before 5 o'clock, one of her children asked her how she was? She said, "much the same." Perceiving large cold drops of sweat upon her, he said, how is your mind, my dear mother? "Happy," she replied, "Thy kingdom come in my heart, dear Lord, and prepare me to meet thee." Are you relying on Christ for salvation? "He is my rock," she said. "I have desired of late to live to his praise." May the Lord bless you and comfort your heart, my dear mother. "Yes," she replied, "and may the Almighty pour his blessing on your head."

About two hours before she departed, one of her children said to her, My dear mother, are you willing to die? "Perfectly so," she replied. Are you willing to leave your children and all your concerns in the hands of God? "Yes," she said. Where is your trust for life eternal? "In Christ alone," she replied. My dear mother, has God, for Christ's sake, taken away from you the sting of death? "Yes," she answered. A friend by the bed-side, repeated this verse:

"Jesus can make a dying bed
"Feel soft as downy pillows are,
"While on his breast I lean my head,
"And breathe my life out sweetly there."

She said, "Oh! yes." A very near friend weeping by her bed-side, said to her, Are you happy? "Yes," she replied, "if you dont fret." About half an hour before her death one of her children engaged in prayer, when she appeared evidently occupied in the solemn service; and in a few minutes after, fell asleep in Jesus, without a sigh or groan, or the movement of a feature. So quiet and easy did she expire, that, though looking at her, it was a minute or two before we knew she was really gone.

"Her Maker kiss'd her soul away,
"And laid her flesh to rest."

Thus departed one of the kindest and tenderest of mothers, and the sincerest of friends. Each in the room involuntarily exclaimed, Oh! that I may die the death of the righteous, and that my last end may be like *hers!*

MRS. BUCKNALL.

The two subsequent letters, communicating the triumphant decease of Mrs. Bucknall, wife of Mr Benjamin Bucknall, of Baltimore, will be read with interest. The first is written by her son-in-law, the second by a niece.

Agreeably to your desire, I furnish you with a few of our deceased mother's dying expressions, in the hope that they may be usefully improved, at least in the private circle, if not publicly.

Her conversation throughout her last illness was strikingly characteristic of her predominant graces, which, in my feeble judgment, were meekness and patience. When sensible of the inroads of the last enemy, she betrayed no alarm, but encountered him with calm intrepidity. When I spake to her of maintaining her confidence in the intercession and faithfulness of her Redeemer, she expressed no uneasy doubt of her interest in his merits, but said, "'Tis no time now to cast away my confidence, I know whom I have believed." Once reading several verses of Watts on the Canticles, and among others,

> "The voice of my beloved sounds,
> "Over the rocks and rising grounds,"

suddenly she closed the book, observing, "Oh! if I continue reading these hymns, my soul will be all on fire, as in times past!"

One day, while in extreme agony, I said to her, "The Lord's presence, I trust, shines upon your path." She replied, "He doth not spurn me." Presently she spake of internal conflicts, and of the confusion of mind arising from the violence of the pain in her head, "but as to my dependence," said she, "that continues fixed on the *Rock*."

Another time I said to her "God is our refuge and strength, a very present help in trouble, therefore will we not fear?" After a pause, she replied, "What! a professor of the name of Christ, and *fear* death! and where is his terror? where is his sting?"

Humbly reflecting on herself as an unprofitable servant, she added, "Indeed I am not a bit too good, nor good enough. Oh! I am ashamed!" Soon after she said, "I long to be at home, singing the praises of the Lamb that has loved me and washed me," &c. I said, "Why you are singing now" Upon which she seemed reanimated, and folding her arms with vehemence, cried out, "Oh! I long to embrace Jesus in my arms, I long to put my foot on the top of the hill—there on a green and flowery mount." She repeated the verse "Jesus can make a dying bed," &c. and

> "Then shall I see, and hear, and know,
> "All I desired or wished below"

"I am going," she said, "into port under a press of sail." Her last words in my hearing, were,

> "I long for evening to undress"

During the indisposition of my beloved aunt, which from the first commencement of her confinement to her chamber, was about 14 or 15 days, in the short period of which I frequently visited her, she appeared sensible of her approaching dissolution, and often spoke of it with the greatest familiarity, composure and delight. On the Wednesday previous to her departure, I, in company with sister Ebsworth sat up with her. It was a season not easily to be forgotten. About midnight her bodily agitation was great, which made her very restless; nevertheless her soul appeared much engaged in prayer. She frequently inquired after her dear family. I endeavoured to pacify her by telling her they had retired to rest for a little while, being much fatigued with their labours and constant watchings. She looked up and anxiously asked, "Could they not *watch* with me one hour?" Our Lord's reply was given· "The spirit was willing, but the flesh was weak." A short time after we thought we perceived a visible change in her countenance. The family were called. She appeared very anxious to converse with us, but owing to her extreme debility, was unable, though she expressed both by signs and looks that her confidence in the Lord was *unshaken*. Many precious promises contained in the sacred oracles of truth, for the solace of believers, as well as some sweet verses from Watt's Psalms and Hymns were quoted, which appeared to strengthen and confirm her hope. About half past five in the morning she requested to be propped up with pillows; which was immediately done, as we thought, to bid us a *final adieu*. But the Lord, for ever blessed be his name, intended otherwise, we had a brighter scene to witness. After she had recovered her breath, superior strength appeared to be given. She broke out with such heavenly joy and rapture, that her feeble frame for a time appeared to sink under it. She turned her eyes to her partner, who stood weeping by her bed-side, and confidently exclaimed, "It is all well, it is all well, *well for ever*. What have I been doing all this time? *doubt* my safety in Christ! I should dishonour my God to do it for a moment." Turning herself to me, she cried out, "Cousin Sarah, this is faith." I replied, Yes, *strong faith*; God himself is faithful. "Fear not," she said, "I shall meet you in glory." I repeated that verse, as being suitable,

"Sweet to rejoice in lively hope,
"That when my change shall come,
"Angels shall hover round my bed,
"And waft my spirit home."

She stretched out her feeble arms, and with holy rapture exclaimed, "I can sing myself away to everlasting bliss. Oh! help me to praise him. Oh! help me to praise him. My breath, while I live, shall be *all praise*." Uncle observed to her, My dear, you appear firm. With emphasis she replied, "*Firm as a rock*. Christ Jesus and his precious blood, is *all*, my only plea." She then repeated those lines, and clasped her hands,

"Jesus, lover of my soul,
"Let me to thy bosom fly," &c.

She continued in this happy frame of mind to the last. On Friday evening, which was the last interview I had with this dear saint, as I entered the room, she looked very pitiful at me and said, "I am here yet." I replied, Still lingering on these mortal shores. "Yes," she said, "one night more." Her brother Rooker observed to her, You will, sister, have a glorious interview by and by with our kindred, who are gone before, and the heavenly host. She appeared overcome with the animating thought, and above all that she should see Jesus. "Yes," she said, "I shall have done with this vile body, this dust and ashes; no more pain and sorrow, for 'God himself shall wipe away all tears from all faces.'" She repeated those lines,

"And can he have taught me to trust in his name,
"And thus far have brought me to put me to shame?"

"No, no, I cannot doubt. This shall be my song, 'Unto him that loved me and washed me in his own blood, be all the glory.'" She would frequently tell us, and strive to impress it as much as possible on our minds, that it was all of grace from the beginning to the end. She totally disclaimed every merit of her own. "for, alas!" said she, "I merit everlasting punishment. I am nothing. Christ is all." She observed to one of her children the day before she died, "To-morrow I shall be singing praises in heaven, you on earth." Her daughter replied, No mother, if that be the case *we* shall not sing. She said, "Remember, my child, you are not to sorrow as those who have no hope. Only prepare to follow me." On Saturday morning, at half past 6 o'clock, the happy spirit took its flight. May we not exclaim—"Let me die the death of the righteous, and my last end be like hers."

POETRY.

The Sunday School Teacher.

Hail! day of the Lord, in thy brightness ascending!
The latter day, glory divinely portending;
The darkness and shadows have fled far away,
The bosoms of multitudes welcome thy sway.
I haste to the temple where thousands assemble,
Where saints are rejoicing, where enemies tremble;
Thrice happy the bands of young children to see,
And point the poor little ones, SAVIOUR, to THEE.

Hail! day of suspension from 'toiling and spinning,'
A prize is displayed worth contesting and winning,
Let manhood with joy in the labour engage,
And mingle in classes with spectacled age:
The bible—the bible's a life-giving treasure,
A fountain of wisdom, of virtue, of pleasure!
It offers a balm from LIFE's loveliest tree,
And points the adult and the aged to THEE.

Talk of colour no more, 'tis but skin-deep impression,
The blessings of grace are for *human* possession,
Comprehensive, the gospel's beneficent plan
Contemplates the sablest complexion as *man;*
Ethiopia's sons, Ethiopia's daughters,
Are welcomed to drink evangelical waters!
Since the mandate Divine bids the fetter'd be free,
I'll point the poor African, SAVIOUR, to THEE.

See the red men diffused through our westernmost regions,
Now pining away—*once* existing in legions,
Inquiring the path to "THE FATHER OF LIFE,"
All eager to terminate sorrow and strife:
Let the tomahawk sleep, and the bow and the quiver
From the foot of mount Zion effuses a river
Can bear all offence to oblivion's sea,
And waft the poor Indian, SAVIOUR, to THEE.

How blessed the men, who with heathen are toiling!
Though mortals may frown, the Redeemer is smiling,
O'er the glooms of Hindostan and shades of Rangoon,
Salvation shall shine all refulgent and soon:
GREAT SAVIOUR! succeed the increasing translations,
Let the charter of grace be perused by all nations;
And with eyes beaming transport, thy messengers see
Converted idolaters bending to THEE!

A dying Infant to a weeping Mother.

Fondest parent, cease to weep,
 Nor wish thy babe to stay;
Oh! let her gently sleep
   Her life away.

Soon as first I saw the light,
 My cries denoted pain;
Why then retard my flight?
   To die is gain.

Nought but sorrow have I known,
 Though few my wants have been;
I feel in every groan
   The pangs of sin.

Jesus loves the infant race,
 And clasps them to his breast,
To die in his embrace
   Is to be blest.

Then, fond mother, hush thy sighs,
 Nor wish me longer here;
Let not a murmur rise,
   Nor shed a tear.

Far beyond these lower skies,
 I fly from sin and death,
Where loud hosannas rise
   On every breath!

Thither, oh! my mother, come,
 And join the heavenly choir;
There we shall be at home,
   And never tire.

Cease thy weeping, then, be still,
 And learn thy God to trust;
Bow to his sovereign will,
   And own him just.

NORRISTOWN.   T. D. M.

THE LATTER DAY LUMINARY;

BY A COMMITTEE

OF

THE BAPTIST BOARD OF FOREIGN MISSIONS FOR THE UNITED STATES.

Vol. I.   NOVEMBER, 1818.   No. V.

BIOGRAPHY.

REV JOHN SUTCLIFF, A. M. OF OLNEY.

IN our last we presented to our readers the outline of the life of the excellent Fuller. In missionary exertion Mr. Sutcliff was his faithful, affectionate, and zealous associate. We had thought of drawing the outlines of the character of this valuable servant of Jesus Christ; but on a re-perusal of the sermon of Dr. Fuller, on his death, we are persuaded we cannot edify or entertain our readers better than by making extracts from that judicious and pathetic publication. The sermon, entitled " The Principles and Prospects of a Servant of Christ," was delivered June 28, 1814, from the passage which Mr. S. had himself selected, in Jude, 20, 21. " But ye, beloved, building up yourselves on your most holy faith, praying in the Holy Ghost, keep yourselves in the love of God, looking for the mercy of our Lord Jesus Christ unto eternal life."

Discoursing on the subject—Dr. F.

I. Offers "A FEW REMARKS ON THE PRINCIPLES WHICH ARE HERE SUGGESTED TO US AS CONSTITUTING TRUE RELIGION." These are

1st. " True evangelical religion is here represented as a building, the foundation of which is laid in the faith of Christ."

2d. " That religion which has its foundation in the faith of Christ will increase by praying in the Holy Ghost."

3d. "By means of building on our most holy faith and praying in the Holy Ghost, we "keep ourselves in the love of God." The love of God is here to be understood, not of his love to us, but ours to him; as when our Lord told the unbelieving Jews that they had not *the love of God* in them."

4th. "When we have done all, in looking for eternal life we must keep our eye singly and solely on the mercy of our Lord Jesus Christ."

II. Exhibits "THE PROSPECTS WHICH THESE PRINCIPLES FURNISH AS TO A BLESSED HEREAFTER." These embrace

— "an immediate reception into the presence of God and the spirits of just men made perfect."

— probably a joyous view of "the glorious progress of Christ's kingdom in this world."

— other streams of mercy for which we are directed to look, consist in "the dead being raised and the living changed," together with "the last judgment."

"After this nothing remains, but that ETERNAL LIFE into which, as into an ocean, all these streams of mercy flow."

The sermon is able, tender and impressive. We are not disposed to offer criticism on its contents, and if we were, the present article is not the place. The subsequent extracts delineate the life of the amiable Sutcliff.

I am aware that some great and good men have imposed silence on these occasions. Without impeaching their motives, I take the liberty to differ from them. It is true, that for sinful creatures, as we all are, to heap encomiums on one another, is vain and sinful: yet we may err on the other hand, by concealing what the grace of God has done for us. In this view one may on occasion speak of himself, as did the apostle Paul; and if so, why not of another? David did not withhold a tribute of affection to the memory of his brother Jonathan. Nor did Luke conceal the fruits of faith and love which had appeared in Dorcas. She might have left an injunction that at her decease nothing should be said of her: but the widows *must* weep, and show the garments which she had made for the poor in her lifetime. It is not for us to suppress the feelings of nature, and still less those of grace.

Our deceased brother was born near Halifax in Yorkshire, on the 9th of August 1752, O. S. His parents were both of them pious characters, and remarkable for their strict attention to the instruction and government of their children. Of course he would be taught the good and the right way from his childhood. It does not appear, however, that he was "made wise unto salvation through faith in Christ Jesus," till about the sixteenth or seventeenth year of his age. This was under the ministry of his revered friend and father Mr. John Fawcett, pastor of the church meeting at Hepden Bridge. Of this church he became a member on May the 28th, 1769. Being of a serious and studious turn of mind, he appeared to his friends to possess gifts suited to the ministry, and which was proposed to his consideration. The proposal met with his own wishes, and being desirous of obtaining all the instruction he could, he went in January, 1772, to the Bristol academy, then under the care of Messrs. Hugh and Caleb Evans. Of his conduct in this situation, it is sufficient to say, that it procured him the esteem of his tutors to the end of their lives.

In 1774 he left the academy, and after stopping a short time at different places, in July 1775 he came to Olney. It was in the spring of the following year, when the association was held at Olney, that my acquaintance with him commenced; and from that day to this all that I have known of him has tended to endear him to me.

He had a largeness of heart that led him to expect much from the promises of God to the church in the latter days. *It was on his motion, I believe, that the association at Nottingham, in the spring of 1784, agreed to set apart an hour on the evening of the first Monday in every month for social prayer for the success of the gospel, and to invite Christians of other denominations to unite with them in it.*

In all the conversations between the years 1787 and 1792, which led on to the formation of the *Baptist Missionary Society*, and in all the meetings for fasting and prayer, both before and after it was formed, he bore a part. In 1789 he republished President Edwards's Humble Attempt to promote Explicit Agreement and Visible Union of God's People in Extraordinary Prayer for the Revival of Religion. How much this publication contributed to that tone of feeling which in the end determined five or six individuals to venture, though with many fears and misgivings, on an undertaking of such magnitude, I cannot say; but it doubtless had a very considerable influence on it.

In April, 1791, there was a double lecture at Clipstone, and both the sermons, one of which was delivered by brother Sutcliff, bore upon the meditated mission to the heathen. His subject was, Jealousy for God, from 1 Kings xix. 10. After public worship, Mr. Carey, perceiving the impression that the sermons had made, entreated that something might be resolved on before we parted. Nothing, however, was done, but to request brother Carey to revise and print his Inquiry into the Obligations of Christians to use Means for the Conversion of the Heathens. The sermons also were printed at the request of those who heard them.

From the formation of the Society in the autumn of 1792, to the day of his death, our brother's heart and hands have been in the work. On all occasions, and in every way, he was ready to assist to the utmost of his power.

In 1796 he married Miss Jane Johnson, who was previously a member of his church. This connexion appears to have added much to his comfort. For eighteen years they lived together as fellow-helpers to each other in the ways of God: and their separation has been but short. The tomb that received his remains has since been opened to receive her's. He died on the 22d of June, and she on the 8d of September following, possessing the same good hope, through grace, which supported him. A sermon was preached at her interment, by Mr. Geard of Hitchen, from Romans v. 2. "By whom also we have access by faith into this grace wherein we stand, and rejoice in hope of the glory of God."

Mr. Sutcliff had been in a declining state of health for several years past. On the 3d of March, being on a visit at London, he was seized, about the middle of the night, with a violent pain across his breast and arms, attended with great difficulty of breathing. This was succeeded by a dropsy, which in about three months issued in his death.

Two or three times during his affliction I rode over to see him. The first time he had thoughts of recovering; but whatever were his thoughts as to this, it seemed to make no difference as to his peace of mind. The last time I visited him was in my way to the annual meeting in London, on the 19th of June. Expecting to see his face no more, I said on taking leave, "I wish you, my dear brother, an abundant entrance into the everlasting kingdom of our Lord Jesus Christ!" At this he hesitated; not as doubting his entrance into the kingdom, but as questioning whether the term abundant were applicable to him. "That," said he, "is more than I expect. I think I understand the connexion and import of those words—Add to your faith virtue—give diligence to make your calling and election sure—for *so* an entrance shall be ministered unto you *abundantly*—I think the idea is that of a ship coming into harbour, with a fair gale, and a full tide—If I may but reach the heavenly shore, though it be on a board or broken piece of the ship, I shall be satisfied."

The following letter received from his brother, Mr. Daniel Sutcliff, who was with him the last month, will furnish a more particular account of the state of his mind, than I am able to give from my own knowledge.

"From the commencement of his illness I found by his letters that his mind was in general calm and peaceful. 'All,' said he, 'is in the hands of a wise and gracious God. We are the Lord's servants, and he has a right to dispose of us as he pleases, and to lay us aside at any time.' Nearly a month before his end I went to see him—to see 'the chamber where the good man dies.'

"His mind was generally calm and happy; though as to strong consolation he said he had it not When something was mentioned of what he had done in promoting the cause of Christ, he replied with emotion, 'I look upon it all as nothing: I must enter heaven on the same footing as the converted thief, and shall be glad to take a seat by his side.'

"His evidences for heaven, he said, were a consciousness that he had come to Jesus; and that he felt a union of heart with him, his people, and his cause; and Jesus had said, *Where I am, there shall my friends be.* The heaven that he hoped for, and which he had in no small degree anticipated, was, union and communion with Christ and his people. He said, 'The idea of being for ever separated from him appears to me more dreadful than being plunged into nonexistence, or than the greatest possible torture.'

"He often intimated that his views of divine things were far more vivid and impressive than they had ever been before. He had a greater sense of the depravity of the human heart, and of the exceeding sinfulness of sin as consisting in disaffection to the character and government of God, than at any former period of his life. He had, he said, an inexpressibly greater sense of the importance of ministers having correct views of the import of the gospel message, and of their stating and urging the same on their hearers, than he had ever had before. He was ready to think if he could communicate his present views and feelings, they must produce a much greater effect than his preaching had ordinarily done. 'If I were able to preach again,' said he, 'I should say things which I never said before—but God has no need of me: he can raise up men to say them better than I could say them.' He would sometimes say, 'Ministers will never do much good till they begin to *pull sinners out of the fire!*'

"To Mrs. Sutcliff he said, '.My love, I commit you to Jesus. I can trust you with him Our separation will not be long; and I think I shall often be with you Read frequently the book of Psalms, and be much in prayer. I am sorry I have not spent more time in prayer.' At another time he said, 'I wish I had conversed more with the divine promises: I believe I should have found the advantage of it now.' Others of his expressions were, 'Flesh and heart fail—All the powers of body and mind are going to pieces—'Shortly this prison of my clay, must be dissolved and fall'—Why is his chariot so long a coming? I go to Jesus: let me go—depart in peace—I have seen thy salvation.'

"A day or two before he died, he said, 'If any thing be said of me, let the last word be, As I have loved you, see that ye love one another.'

"On the 22d of June, about five in the afternoon, an alteration took place: he began to throw up blood. On perceiving this, he said, 'It is all over: this cannot be borne long.' Mr. Welsh of Newbury being present, said, 'You are prepared for the issue.' He replied, 'I think I am: go and pray for me.' About half an hour before his departure, he said, 'Lord Jesus, receive my spirit—It is come—perhaps a few minutes more—heart and flesh fail—but God—That God is the strength of his people is a truth that I now see as I never saw it in my life.' These were the last words he could be heard to speak.

"Life, take thy chance; but, O, for such a death!"

Mr. Daniel Sutcliff adds the following lines, as having been frequently repeated in his illness.

> We walk a narrow path, and rough,
>   And we are tired and weak,
> But soon we shall have rest enough,
>   In those blest courts we seek.
>
> Soon in the chariot of a cloud,
>   By flaming angels borne,
> I shall mount up the milky way,
>   And back to God return.
>
> I have tasted Canaan's grapes,
>   And now I long to go,
> To where my Lord his vineyard keeps,
>   And where the clusters grow!

In saying a few things relative to his character, talents, temper, &c. I would not knowingly deviate in the smallest degree from truth. He possessed the three cardinal virtues, integrity, benevolence, and prudence, in no ordinary degree. To state this is proof sufficient to every one who knew him. He was economical, for the sake of enabling himself to give to them that needed. The cause of God lay near his heart. He denied himself of many things, that he might contribute towards promoting it. It was from a willingness to instruct his younger brethren whose minds were towards the mission, that at the request of the Society he took several of them under his care: and in all that he has done for them and others, I am persuaded he saved nothing; but gave his time and talents for the public good.

I have heard him sigh under troubles; but never remember to have seen him weep but for joy, or from sympathy. On his reading or hearing the communications from the East, containing accounts of the success of the gospel, the tears would flow freely from his eyes.

His talents were less splendid than useful. He had not much brilliancy of imagination, but considerable strength of mind, with a judgment greatly improved by application. It was once remarked of him in my hearing, by a person who had known him from his youth, to this effect—'That man is an example of what may be accomplished by diligence and perseverance. When young, he was no more than the rest of us; but by reading and thinking he has accumulated a stock of mental riches which few of us possess.' He would not very frequently surprise us with new or original thoughts; but neither would he shock us with any think devious from truth or good sense. Good Mr. Hall of Arnsby, having heard him soon after his coming to Olney, said familiarly to me, "brother Sutcliff is a safe man: you never need fear that he will say or do an improper thing."

He particularly excelled in practical judgment. When a question of this nature came before him, he would take a comprehensive view of its bearings, and form his opinion with so much precision as seldom to have occasion to change it. His thoughts on these occasions were prompt, but he was slow in uttering them. He generally took time to turn the subject over, and to digest his answer. If he saw others too hasty for coming to a decision, he would pleasantly say, "Let us consult the town-clerk of Ephesus, and do nothing rashly." I have thought for many years, that amongst our ministers, Abraham Booth was the first counsellor, and John Sutcliff the second. His advice in conducting the mission was of great importance, and the loss of it must be seriously felt.

It has been said that his temper was naturally irritable, and that he with difficulty bore opposition: yet that such was the overbearing influence of religion in his heart, that few were aware of it. If it were so, he must have furnished a rare example of the truth of the wise man's remark, "Better is he that ruleth his spirit, than he that taketh a city." Whatever might have been his natural temper, it is certain that mildness and patience and gentleness were prominent features in his character. One of the students who was with him, said he never saw him lose his temper but once, and then he immediately retired into his study. It was observed by one of his brethren in the ministry, at an association, that the promise of Christ, that they who learned of him who was meek and lowly in heart should find rest unto their souls, was more extensively fulfilled in Mr. Sutcliff than in most christians. He was " swift to hear, slow to speak, slow to wrath." Thus it was that he exemplified the exhortation of the apostle, " Giving no offence, that the ministry be not blamed."

There was a gentleness in his reproofs that distinguished them. He would rather put the question for consideration, than make a direct attack upon a principle or practice I have heard him repeat Mr. Henry's note on Prov. xxv. 15. with approbation—" We say, Hard words break no bones; but it seems that soft ones do." A flint may be broken on a cushion, when no impression could be made on it upon an unyielding substance A young man, who came to be under his care, discovering a considerable portion of self-sufficiency, he gave him a book to read on Self-knowledge.

He is said never to have hastily formed his friendships and acquaintances, and therefore rarely had reason to repent of his connexions; while every year's continued intimacy drew them nearer to him; so that he seldom lost his friends—but his friends have lost him!

He had a great thirst for reading, which not only led him to accumulate one of the best libraries in this part of the country, but to endeavour to draw his people into a habit of reading.

Allowing for a partiality common to men, his judgment of characters was generally correct. Nor was it less candid than correct: he appreciated the good, and if required to speak of the evil, it was with reluctance. His eye was a faithful index to his mind; penetrating, but benignant. His character had much of the decisive, without any thing conceited or overbearing.

In his person he was above the ordinary stature, being nearly six feet high. In the earlier stages of life he was thin; but during the last twenty years he gathered flesh, though never so much as to feel it any inconvenience to him. His countenance was grave, but cheerful; and his company always interesting.

THE WALDENSES, THE MISSIONARIES OF THE DARK AGES.

THIS distinguished and evangelic body of men, have long occupied a most interesting place in ecclesiastical history. Amid the darkness of the middle ages, and the corruptions of papal heresy, they were the salt of the earth, the light of the world. Their memory deserves to be cherished with veneration, and their history developed with assiduous care. They are the fathers of the Reformation, and, according to Beza, the seed of the most ancient christian church. Scultetus declares that their churches had continued down in succession from apostolic times. In the preface to the first French bible that ever was printed, they state, that they had ever possessed the scriptures, since the apostolic age, and through successive generations had preserved, in well-written manuscripts, the whole of Divine revelation. Eusebius speaks, in terms of high respect, of churches and martyrs under Antonius Verres, A. D. 179, in those very parts of France where the Waldenses chiefly flourished.

This wonderful people were known by various appellations. Sometimes they were designated by names indicating opprobrium and sarcasm; as, the *Cathari*, or puritans; the *Fratracilli*, or little brethren; the *Humiliati*, or humble men; *Paternes*, because, refusing to worship the host, it was asserted they worshipped only the Father; *Manichees*, because they denied that papal authority was the source of civil magistracy, &c &c. Their name *Waldenses*, could not, as Mosheim intimates, have been derived from Waldo, a citizen of Lyons; for they bore the title more than two centuries before Waldo's time. In his *Histoire des Hommes illustres*, Beza affirms that they were so called from their abode in the vallies and straiter parts of the Alps, where they had for a long time retired, being the relics of the pure primitive churches. They were called *Albigenses*, from *Albi*, a city in Languedoc, and for a similar geographical reason, they bore the names of *Arletenses*, *Picards*, and *Lombards*. The popular appellation of *Lollards* was probably derived from Walter Lollard, one of their eminent *barbes*. A prison in London whither they were sent, is said to be known to the present time, by the name of the Lollard's-Tower.

It may seem unnatural and absurd to derive the character of men from the testimony of enemies. And yet such was the purity and eminence of the Waldenses, that those who sought their extirpation were compelled to acknowledge their moral worth. Rainerius, an inquisitor, declares, that they live uprightly before men, and put their trust in God for all things: and when he states how these, whom he calls heretics, may be detected, he observes, they may be known by their *manners*, which are composed and modest, and by their *words*, for they avoid scurrility, detraction, levity and falsehood. Bernard Girard in his history of France (book 10th) observes, that the Waldenses have been charged with things of which they were never guilty. Very remarkable are the words of Jacob de Riberia, secretary to the king of France, in his Collections of Tholouse. "In so great honour was the sect of these men, that they were exempted from all charges and impositions, and obtained more benefit by the wills and testaments of the dead, than the priests: a man would not hurt his enemy, should he meet him upon his way, accompanied with one of these heretics; insomuch that the safety of all men seemed to consist in their protection."

The means, by which they maintained and diffused the truth of God, were numerous; but are chiefly reducible to three, the instruction of youth, the improving of ministerial abilities, and the influence the persecutions and martyrdoms they suffered produced on the hearts of thousands.

Into the knowledge of the holy scriptures their children were introduced by means of catechisms, committing large portions of the bible to memory, and the constant use of parental instruction. Every family was a college for spiritual information, and a chapel for frequent and fervent prayer. Mothers taught their babes to lisp the name of the blessed Jesus. Fox, in his Martyrology, asserts, that Vessember in his oration concerning the Waldenses, declares that the bishop of Cavaillon during the great persecution of Merindal in Provence, first sent a monk to convert them, who returned and declared that he had profited more in the knowledge of the scriptures by the interview, than he had ever done before. The disappointed bishop sent a number of young monks among them to confound them by subtle questions; but one of them declared on his return that he had learned more from the little catechized children among the Waldenses, than he had from the disputations in divinity which he had heard among the most eminent Parisian divines. The bishop, dissatisfied, sent for the little children, and "caused them to be interrogated in the presence of a great assembly, and to question one another, which was done with that grace and gravity and understanding that was marvellous to hear, to the confounding *the doctors* and *learned men* then present."

Their preachers were called *barbes*, from their wearing their beards. Such as did not travel, as missionaries, to propagate the gospel in distant countries, were employed in the vallies in instructing youth who were called to the work of the ministry. The studies of the young men embraced grammar, logic, moral philosophy and divinity. Many added to these pursuits an extensive acquaintance with clinical medicine and surgery, becoming at once skilful physicians for both the body and soul of man. Some of them promoted the mechanical arts, in imitation of Christ, who was a carpenter, and of Paul who was a maker of tents. Bucer represents their *college* as consisting of men excelling in gravity and prudence; and Bucer informs us that, besides the labours of the Sabbath, the pastors all the week carried the light of evangelic truth into the surrounding villages, preaching also in the fields to the keepers of the flocks. *In the month of September* they had a general meeting or association to consider the interests of the church of Christ.

It is a maxim long established, that persecution ever ultimately advances the cause it attempts to destroy. On the column of sufferers, of martyrs for the cause of Christ, the name Waldenses will ever stand high, and shine with deserved effulgence. Artifice was employed to detect and destroy these invaluable men. Persons were sent out by the Roman authority, among whom were Francis, Dominic and Benedict, who were commissioned to affect their plainness and simplicity, and thus to gain upon or confront them. These insidious opposers were *sainted* for their labours, and became the originators of the orders of Franciscan, Dominican and Benedictine friars. This policy not succeeding, pope Innocent sent out legates and inquisitors, and afterwards a crusade of armed men. Some of them, by these cruel measures, were scattered abroad; but as is observed by Dr. Usher, "as the persecution about Stephen by that dispersion proved much for the furtherance of the gospel in other parts of the world, so was it here; for those that were not fit for the war, went up and down, with more freedom into most parts of Europe; insomuch that Æneas Sylvius, afterwards pope Pius the second, confesses, *nec ullis vel Romanorum pontificum decretis, vel Christianorum armis deleri potuiss'*; neither the decrees of Roman pontiffs, nor the armies of Christians, could blot out their existence. The sufferings of the Waldenses in Dauphine, in Piedmont, in Bohemia, in Germany, in France, in Poland, in Flanders, in England, in Italy, in the Lesser Asia, were almost incredible. They were despised, abandoned, anathematized, imprisoned, dragged to death with horses, stoned, burned, beheaded and drowned: but they overcame by the blood of the Lamb, and by the word of his testimony. Their doctrine arose like the ethereal sun. Wickliffe and Calvin, and Luther and Zuinglius, and a thousand others, caught the celestial fire. The church of Christ in the present age has greater reason, than at first may appear, to bless God for the purity, fortitude, wisdom, heavenly-mindedness, and missionary ardour of THE WALDENSES. Their views on the subject of baptism are amply detailed by the learned and laborious Henry D'Anvers.

In the days of Edward II. and III. of England, the Waldenses bore the name of Lollards, for a reason already assigned. The great reformer Wickliffe, as has been suggested, was of their number. The testimony given to this excellent man by the University of Oxford, as it does honour to his memory, and may serve to illustrate the Waldensian character, shall close the present outlines.

" THAT the special good will and care we bear to John Wickliffe, some time child of this university, moving and stirring in us, we do with one mind, voice and testimony, witness all his conditions and doings throughout his whole life to have been most sincere and commendable; whose honest manners and conditions, profoundness of learning, and most redolent renown and fame, we desire the more earnestly to be notified and known to all the faithful, for that we understand the maturity and ripeness of his conversation, his diligent labours and travels to tend to the praise of God, the help and safeguard of others, and the profit of the church:

" WHEREFORE, we signify by these presents, that his conversation, even from his youth, unto the time of his death, was so praise-worthy and honest, that never at any time was there any spot or suspicion notified of him; but in his answering, reading, preaching and determining, he behaved himself laudably, and is a stout and valiant champion of the faith, vanquishing by the force of the scriptures all such (friars) who by their wilful begging blasphemed and slander Christ's religion, &c. And who, amongst all the rest of the University had written in logic, philosophy, divinity, morals, and the speculative art, *without peer.*

" The knowledge of all which we desire to testify and deliver forth, to the intent that the fame and renown of this doctor may be more evident, and had in reputation among them into whose hands these present letters-testimonial shall come.

" *In witness whereof,* we have caused these our letters-testimonial to be sealed with our common seal at Oxford, in our Convocation house, the 5th of October, in the year of our Lord, 1406."

REFLECTIONS ON WEALTH.

THE extravagant anxiety of the Spaniards, on the discovery of America, for the obtaining of gold and the detection of mines, may appear as dishonourable and mean, as it was to the natives ridiculous and surprising. And yet, who perceives not that on the acquisition of wealth, mankind are every where fixing their desires. For this the mechanic labours, the merchant projects the voyages of his vessels, the tradesman rises up early and sits up late, and even science herself lags on the pinions of discovery, unless she behold herself as " the wings of a dove covered with silver, and her feathers with yellow gold."

Riches, alas! are often amassed by the arts of oppression, extortion and deceit. Thus acquired, the blessing of heaven cannot rest upon them. The wise man assures us that " treasures of wickedness profit nothing," and that " the getting of treasures by a lying tongue, is a vanity tossed to and fro by them that seek death." Or, to use the elegant similitude of the prophet Jeremiah, " As the partridge sitteth on eggs and hatcheth them not; so he that getteth riches, and not by right, shall leave them in the midst of his days, and at his end shall be a fool."

The fair and virtuous path to earthly possessions is an honest and laborious industry. " The hand of the diligent maketh rich." " He that tilleth his land shall be satisfied with bread." " Seest thou a man diligent in his business? he shall stand before kings, he shall not stand before mean men."

But admitting that possessions are honourably attained, that they have descended from virtuous ancestors, or have resulted from our own frugality and toils, which have been succeeded by the blessing of heaven, what are they at best? They are no demonstrations of the favour of Jehovah. A prophet tells us " the ungodly prosper in the world; they increase in riches." " Go to now," saith the apostle James, " ye rich men, weep and howl, for your miseries that shall come upon you." Wealth exposes men to peculiar dangers and sorrows Agur wisely foresaw its injurious tendency, when entreating God to give him not riches, he assigns his reason, " Lest I be full and deny thee, and say, who is the Lord?" It is not only true as the Preacher states, that " the abundance of the rich will not suffer him to sleep," but it is equally true as observed by our Lord, that " the care of this world and the deceitfulness of riches, choke the word," and the hearer " becometh unfruitful." The influence of wealth in inciting to carnal indulgence, is justly exposed by an apostle, when, addressing rich men, he says, "Ye have lived in pleasure on earth, and been wanton; ye have nourished your hearts, as in a day of slaughter;" and equally does he expose the tendency of riches to produce pride and oppression, when he adds, "Ye have condemned and killed the just, and he doth not resist you."

Under circumstances the most favourable, it must not be forgotten, that riches are vain and uncertain. How many are there who heap up riches, and know not "who shall gather them!" God said to a certain rich man, "Fool! this night thy soul shall be required of thee, then whose shall those things be which thou hast provided?" A thousand unanticipated occurrences may remove man from his riches, or riches from man. As to the result, it is of little moment whether they or he take wing and fly away.

Where God has conferred abundance of this world's goods, it is the duty, and will be the honour of the possessor, as a faithful steward to occupy until the Master come. The advice given by Paul to Timothy was solemn and salutary, "Charge them that are rich in this world, that they be not high-minded, nor trust in uncertain riches; but in the living God, who giveth us richly all things to enjoy; that they do good, that they be rich in good works, ready to distribute, willing to communicate." Never was there a time in which the sons of wealth had a more favourable opportunity than at the present for making appropriations of their substance in ways serviceable to men, and glorifying to God. Numerous youth require to be assisted in their studies for the christian ministry! Missions demand support! Bible and Tract societies are every where crying aloud ' *men and brethren help!*' Many of the rich who are on the way to the kingdom of heaven, have done much by donations, and promise much in their bequests; but the field for renewed exertion is vast, and its necessities importunate. Should this paper fall into the hands of wealthy professors, let them solemnly consider at what a price their redemption has been obtained! how large a debt of gratitude remains undischarged! the certainty that their donations will be applied to the noblest purposes, and the short time that remains for their acting well in the service of the Son of God!

Above all, happy the men, who have "treasure in heaven," and who when *they fail* shall be welcomed, by crowds of pious poor and regenerated heathen, to whose best interests they have contributed, "into everlasting habitations."

A FATHER'S BEST WISHES FOR THE WELFARE OF HIS SON, EXEMPLIFIED IN THE PRAYER OF JACOB.

"God Almighty bless thee."—*Genesis* xxviii. 3.

THE suppliant was a patriarch, accustomed to prayer, and to whom, in answer to the voice of supplication, children had been granted. He was an old man. He had lived one hundred and thirty-seven years, at least; yet still felt all the glow of paternal love. It is not in the power of age to diminish the ardours of natural affection.

The son, for whom he prayed, was young; and youth, more perhaps than any other period of life, is alike exposed to temptation and favourable to pious impressions. This son was about to leave a father's house, and was on the eve of marriage. His father could not expect long to live, and yet was assured, from the inspirations of heaven, that his son, Jacob, should have a numerous progeny; for whose welfare Isaac must have felt an interest, similar to the interest for his immediate descendant.

The object he addresses is God Almighty; a name by which Jehovah, in the first ages of the world, was especially designated. Gen. xvii. 1. Exod. vi. 3. This heavenly Friend, though he cannot do any thing in itself impossible, contrary to his perfections or subversive of his purposes, yet, it is evident from the creation, from scripture, and from the groundwork of redemption, possesses the attribute of ALMIGHTINESS; an attribute at once incommunicable, boundless, and everlasting. The blessing of this omnipotent God involves in it his holy approbation, with all the gifts and graces a creature can enjoy. It can make us "blessed in the city, and blessed in the field." Thus saith the Lord, "Fear not, O Jacob, my servant, and thou Jesurun whom I have chosen: for I will pour water upon him that is thirsty, and floods upon the dry ground: I will pour my spirit upon thy seed, and my blessing upon thine offspring And they shall spring up as among the grass, and as willows by the water-courses." Dr. Owen considers the language of God to Abraham, "blessing I will bless thee," as purporting, 'I will do so *without fail;* I will do so *greatly*, without measure and *eternally*, without end,' and observes, that ' Abraham was the first person in the world, after our first parents, to whom the promise of the Messiah, as the offspring of the promise, was confirmed.'

The best wish of the patriarch was as submissive as it was comprehensive and ardent. It is as if he had said, I ask not for thee, my son, riches and honour; I ask not freedom from afflictions or length of days. The blessing I implore on thy behalf can sustain under poverty and reproach; it can sanctify accumulated distresses; it can sway thy life, and soothe an expiring hour; it can compensate for the absence of a tender father and a weeping mother; it can reconcile thee to the novelties and privations of the country of thy ancestors, it can inspire devotion in thy heart, render thy example propitious to thousands, and open before thee the portals of paradise—" God Almighty bless thee."

The prayer was answered. It may be considered as truly " a prophecy" as a prayer. He *shall* bless thee. The young man saw the same evening a vision of the ladder at Bethel. He wrestled afterwards with God, and prevailed. One of his sons saved a whole nation from destruction by famine, and from the loins of another the divine Messiah sprung.

Let parents offer for their children the supplication of Isaac, for the mercy of " God Almighty" endureth for ever!

TO THE EDITORS OF THE LATTER DAY LUMINARY.

THE celebrated Grotius having demonstrated the truth of the christian religion by proofs of the existence and character of Jesus, his doctrine, his miracles, his resurrection, the excellency of the gospel, and the rapidity and extent of its first propagation; has a short section which he denominates *an answer to those who require more and stronger arguments*. I have often admired it, and should be happy to see it in the Luminary.

Very respectfully,

A SUBSCRIBER.

" SI quis allatis hactenus argumentis," &c.—If there be any who is not satisfied with the arguments hitherto adduced for the truth of the christian religion, but desires more powerful ones; he ought to know, that different things must have different kinds of proof; one in mathematics, another in the properties of bodies, another in doubtful matters, and another in matters of fact. And we are to abide by that, whose testimonies are void of all suspicion: which, if it be not admitted, not only all history is of no further use, and a great part of medicine; but all that natural affection, which is betwixt parents and children, is lost, who can be known no other way. It is the will of God, that those things which he would have us believe, so that faith should be accepted from us as obedience, should not so evidently appear, as those things we perceive by our senses, and by demonstration; but only so far as is sufficient to procure the belief, and persuade a man of the thing, who is not obstinately bent against it: so that the gospel is, as it were, *a touch-stone, to try men's honest dispositions by.* For since those arguments, which we have brought, have gained the assent of so many good and wise men; it is very manifest, that the cause of infidelity in others, is not from the want of proof, but from hence, that they would not have that seem true, which contradicts their passions and affections. It is a hard thing for them lightly to esteem honours and other advantages; which they must do, if they would receive what is related concerning Christ, and for that reason think themselves bound to obey the precepts of Christ. And this is to be discovered by this one consideration, that they receive many other historical relations as true, the truth of which is established only upon authorities, of which there are no marks remaining at this time, as there is in the history of Christ; partly by the confession of the Jews, which are now left; partly by the congregations of Christians, every where to be found; for which there must of necessity have been some cause. And since the long continuance of the christian religion, and the propagation of it so far, cannot be attributed to any human power, it follows, that it must be attributed to miracles: or if any one should deny it to have been done by miracles; this very thing, that it should without a miracle gather so much strength and power, ought to be looked upon as greater than any miracle.

INSTITUTION

FOR PIOUS YOUNG MEN CALLED TO THE GOSPEL MINISTRY.

A MEETING of the Baptist Board of Foreign Missions was held at the city of New York, in August last, one of the principal objects of which was to consult on the best measures to promote an institution for improving the education of pious young men who are called to the gospel ministry.

Communications from distant members of the Board who were unable to attend, and from other much esteemed individuals, were read, and intelligence and observations were received from brethren present, feeling a deep interest in the undertaking. A committee, consisting of Drs. Baldwin, Staughton, and Allison, the Hon. Judge Tallmadge, and the Rev. Mr. M'Laughlin, was then appointed to take the subject into particular consideration; and they reported as follows:

I. That, whereas the Baptist Education Society of Philadelphia have proffered to co-operate with the Board, and have generously undertaken to support a Professor, the Rev. Ira Chase, as it is represented to this committee by Mr Chase, for at least one year, in order that the service of education may advance, until such time as competent and distinct funds shall be received for the purpose of establishing a theological institution under the charge of the Board,—Resolved, That they deserve the thanks of the Board, and of the religious community.

II. Resolved, That the offices of the Principal and of the Professor being considered by them as merely temporary, the thanks of the Board are tendered to the persons who were appointed to those places, for their readiness to carry on the business of instruction for the present year, until the Board shall have fully organized the institution contemplated.

III. Resolved, That effective measures ought now to be adopted by this Board, for the attainment of such competent and distinct funds as will enable them to organize the Institution, and assume the responsibility for expenses.

IV. Resolved, the United States being divided into three sections—the first embracing New York and the States east of the Hudson—the second the Atlantic States from New Jersey to Georgia inclusive—the third, the remaining States and Territories of the Union, That two persons be appointed by the Board to solicit in each of said sections, and receive contributions towards funds for an Institution which may have the united support of the whole Baptist denomination in the United States, to be under the control of the General Convention, and its Board; and that a suitable remuneration be made to such persons for their services, out of any monies distinctly received for Education purposes.

V. Resolved, That the Baptist churches throughout the United States, be respectfully requested to put forth their efforts to assist the Board in consummating the plan of education, particularly by forming auxiliary societies, by having an annual contribution towards the object, by appointing committees to solicit subscriptions and donations, and by assisting the persons that may be appointed to visit them from the Board.

VI. Resolved, That the Associations be also requested to adopt such measures as to them shall appear most proper, to give immediate effect to the designs of the Board in relation to this subject.

VII. Resolved, That the Plan hereto annexed, for the organization and government of the aforesaid Institution, be published, for the consideration of the ministers and churches of the Baptist denomination in the United States; and that, if any thing of special importance occurs to them in relation to it, either in the aggregate or in the detail, they be requested to forward their sentiments before the annual meeting of the Board, on the last Wednesday of April next.

VIII. Resolved, That, provided competent and distinct funds shall, by that time, have been obtained; which, from various intelligence, the Board have full confidence will be the case, so far at least as to enable them to arrange a system of education, they will at that meeting proceed to adopt a plan, and to locate and organize the Institution.

IX. Resolved, That an Address be made by the Board to the Associations and Churches, setting forth the nature and importance of the Institution, and the necessity of immediate and active exertions to promote it, as deeply connected with the glory of God, and the spiritual welfare of thousands.

X. Resolved, That such students from Baptist churches, as shall, during the approaching fall and winter, apply for admission to the advantages of instruction, and shall be approved by the Board, be received, to such an extent of number as shall be judged proper, and that from education funds already obtained, or that shall be obtained hereafter, the expenses of their sustenance shall be met by the Board, so far as it shall be found that the cases of individuals require.

The Report was accepted unanimously. The reverend brethren ELISHA CUSHMAN of Connecticut, and JONATHAN GOING of Massachusetts, were appointed the Soliciting Committee for the *first* section; LEWIS LEONARD of New York, and RICHARD DABBS of Virginia, for the *second;* and CHARLES G. SOMERS of New York, and WILLIAM WARDER of Kentucky, for the *third.*

In pursuance of the tenth resolution contained in the preceding Report, a committee was appointed to make the necessary arrangements for the accommodation of students, in the most economical way that they shall find to be practicable. Another committee was appointed to prepare an Address to accompany the Plan of the Institution as reported by the first mentioned committee; and it was resolved, unanimously, that the proceedings of this meeting, so far as they relate to the subject of education, be published in the American Baptist Magazine, and in the Latter Day Luminary.

PROPOSED PLAN OF THE INSTITUTION.

IMPRESSED with the importance of an extended course of education to the pious minister of the gospel, but aware, at the same time, that, owing to difference of age and circumstances, all who are called to the ministry, and can devote some time to preparatory studies, cannot spend in them the same number of years,—the Board intrusted by the General Convention of the Baptist denomination in the United States, with the instituting of a seminary devoted to the service of our Lord, in helping to cultivate the talents which he commits to those whom he calls to labour in the word and doctrine, have thought it their duty to give it such an organization as to afford suitable instruction both to graduates of colleges, and to others possessing those qualifications which are hereafter required.

The Institution is to be open for the admission of those persons only who give evidence of their possessing genuine piety, with suitable gifts and attainments, and of their being influenced by proper motives in wishing to pursue theological studies, and who, moreover, present certificates from the churches of which they are members, approving of their devoting themselves to the work of the ministry.

Those who have received a collegiate or a liberal education, are to enter immediately upon a theological course, embracing the various branches in the departments of Biblical Literature, of Divinity, of Ecclesiastical History, and of Sacred Rhetoric. Provision is to be made for the instruction of students in this course two years; and they are to be divided accordingly into two classes—the *Junior* and the *Senior.*

Other candidates for admission, except in extraordinary cases, will be expected to have pursued their studies so far at least as to be acquainted with English Grammar and common Arithmetic, and possess so much knowledge of the Latin and Greek languages, as to be able to translate from the original, with facility, the Works of Virgil, the Select Orations of Cicero, and the Four Evangelists

Upon being admitted, they are to commence a course embracing those academical studies which are the most important to a person preparing for the ministry; and, having provision made for their instruction in this course two years, they are to be divided into two classes—the *First-year* and the *Second-year*—and then be in readiness to enter the *Junior*.

At an early period, they are also to devote some of their attention to those subjects which particularly belong to them as students of the Bible, and candidates for the ministry. They likewise, as also and especially those in the two higher classes, are to begin, at an early period, to exercise their gifts in public speaking, and continue to do it, so often, and in such places, as in the judgment of the Professors, it shall, in the case of each individual, be expedient and most conducive to his improvement.

In the mean time, the state and exigencies of the Baptist denomination are to be regarded, and the term of residence at the Institution is to be shortened or protracted, as, in the judgment of the Faculty and of the Board, the cases of individuals and the interests of religion shall seem to require.

Candidates, after a satisfactory examination and probationary residence, are to be admitted by the Faculty, upon subscribing the following declaration and promise · "I declare it to be my conviction that it is my duty to devote myself to the work of the gospel ministry; and, relying on the aid of Divine grace, I solemnly promise, that, so long as I shall be a member of this Institution, I will endeavour to make use of its advantages in a faithful and christian manner; to pay due respect and obedience to the Guardians, Professors, and Teachers, and to conduct myself towards my fellow-students as brethren, and toward all men as becomes the Gospel of Christ."

While the students are thus with meekness and diligence, to strive for the acquisition of useful learning, to read the best human treatises, and to receive instruction from human teachers, ' *it is required above all, that they make the* BIBLE *the object of their most attentive, diligent, and prayerful study.*'

The Professors, including the Principal, in this Institution, are to be men of piety and learning, members of a Baptist church, and advocates for that system of evangelical doctrine, which maintains that it is "God who hath saved us, and called us with an holy calling, not according to our works, but according to his own purpose and grace, which was given us in Christ Jesus before the world began." They are also to be ordained ministers of the gospel, but this requisite is not to be indispensable with regard to those who are employed chiefly in the academical course; and they are to be considered as constituting a Faculty for the regulation and government of the Institution, according to such by-laws as may be approved by the Board, and not inconsistent with the constitution and acts of the General Convention.

They and such other instructors as it shall be found expedient to elect, are to be appointed by the Board; and whenever there is to be a choice of a Principal or Professor, notice is to be given by the Corresponding Secretary to all the members of the Board, three months at least before the time of election.

In the department of Biblical Literature, it will be the duty of the Professor to aid the students in the acquisition of a radical and adequate knowledge of the sacred Scriptures in the original languages, to guide them to correct principles of interpretation, and bring to their assistance in endeavouring to understand the various parts of the Bible, all those helps which may be derived from an acquaintance with Jewish customs and Oriental literature; to give lectures on the formation, preservation, and transmission of the sacred volume; on the languages in which the Bible was originally written; on the Septuagint version of the Old Testament, and on the peculiarities of the language and style of the New Testament, resulting from this version and other causes; on the history, character, and use of the ancient versions and manuscripts of the Old Testament, and of the New; on the canons of biblical criticism, on the canonical authority of the several books of the sacred code; on the Apocryphal books, on modern translations of the Bible, more particularly on the history and character of our English version, and also on the various readings and difficult passages in the sacred writings.

In the department of Divinity, it will be the duty of the acting Professor to demonstrate the existence, attributes, and providence of God, to discuss the soul's immortality and future state, as deducible from the light of nature and reason, to enforce the obligations of man to his Maker, resulting from the divine perfections and his own rational nature; to inculcate the great duties of life, flowing from the mutual relations of man to man, to deduce and delineate the several personal virtues, to intersperse the whole with remarks on the coincidence between the dictates of reason and the doctrines of revelation, and on the necessity of a revelation, notwithstanding such coincidence. But while he is thus required to give a view of *natural* theology, his grand object and business will be to unfold the system of *Christian* theology, contained in the sacred scriptures. It will be his duty to give lectures on divine revelation, on the inspiration and truth of the Old and of the New Testament, as proved by miracles, internal evidence, fulfilment of prophecies, and historic facts; on the nature, interpretation, and use of prophecy, on the great doctrines and duties of the Christian religion, together with the objections made to them by unbelievers, and the refutation of such objections. more particularly on the revealed character of God, as Father, Son, and Holy Ghost; on the fall of man, and the depravity of human nature, on the covenant of grace; on the character, offices, atonement, and mediation of Jesus Christ; on the character and offices of the Holy Spirit; on the Scripture doctrines of regeneration, justification, and sanctification; on evangelical repentance, faith, and obedience; on the nature and necessity of true virtue or gospel holiness; on the future state, the immortality of the soul, the resurrection of the body, and the eternity of future rewards and punishments, as revealed in the gospel; and on the positive institutions of Christianity

It will be the duty of the Professors to have frequent recitations and other appropriate exercises in the different branches of study; to devote their time and talents to accelerating the progress of their pupils in the acquisition of those attainments which shall be most conducive to their usefulness in the gospel ministry; to guard them against error, to guide them in their inquiries after truth, to communicate instruction adapted to their different capacities and attainments; to point out the course of study to be pursued, with the approbation of the Board; to furnish the students with a list of such books as may be perused by them with the greatest profit, to assist them in studying the Bible and other writings to the best advantage, to animate their pursuits by frequent inquiries and examinations relative to their progress in books and knowledge, to assign them proper subjects for their first compositions, and suggest a proper manner of treating them; to devote special attention to the improvement of their style and delivery, favouring them with free and affectionate remarks on their productions and their public speaking, to watch over their health with paternal solicitude; to teach them how they may distribute and employ their time to the greatest advantage, to give them friendly advice respecting their intercourse with persons in various stations and circumstances;—above all, to confer with them freely and frequently on those subjects, and to take those measures which are best calculated to promote their growth in grace, and warm their hearts with love to God and the souls of men.

All funds that may be received by the Board for the purpose of education, are to be kept at all times distinct from the mission funds, which, as the constitution adopted by the General Convention requires, are never to be resorted to in the least for the support of this institution.

Nothing is to be charged to any student for tuition, room-rent, or use of library; but should a student, or his parent or guardian, be disposed to contribute any sum for the benefit of the Institution, it will be gratefully received, and go into the general education fund.

Special care is ever to be taken that suitable boarding be provided for the students, at as low a price as may be practicable, and that all the affairs of the Institution be conducted with the strictest economy.

After affording a reasonable compensation to the instructors, and defraying the other necessary charges of the Institution, the education funds which may be intrusted to the disposal of the Board, are to be applied, as far as circumstances will permit, to defray or diminish the expenses for the sustenance of such students of the Baptist denomination, as may need pecuniary assistance. Students of other denominations, while nothing is charged for tuition, room-rent, or use of library, will be expected to pay such sums for their sustenance, as the Board may judge equal to the expense it incurs.

No money is to be drawn from the funds without a distinct appropriation for the purpose by the Board or by the Convention, and a written order from the proper officer.

A Report is to be laid before the Board by the treasurer at each of their annual meetings, and at such other times as shall be required, exhibiting the amount of funds belonging to the Institution, the several parts which constitute that amount, and a detail of receipts and expenditures for the preceding year, together with the suggestion of suitable ways and means of securing and increasing the funds; and a fair and minute statement of the whole, notwithstanding the exact but more summary accounts that may be published in the annual Reports of the Board, is to be furnished by him for the inspection of the General Convention, at each session of that body.

A sacred regard is at all times to be paid to the intentions and directions of donors and testators, with respect to monies or other property given or bequeathed to the Institution. And whoever shall, by donation or bequest, contribute for its general objects, or establish a fund for the support of a Professor or Professors, or for the maintenance of a scholar or scholars, or for any special purpose, due care is to be taken to perpetuate, in a proper manner, a grateful remembrance of their names and their favours.

Such measures are to be adopted, speedily as possible, for obtaining a library, procuring suitable buildings, and providing instruction, boarding, and other conveniences for the students, as the wants of the Institution may require, *and the funds devoted to this object permit,*—it being remembered that the Board, as acting under the authority of the Convention, can proceed in this work of benevolence, and assume the responsibility for expenses, no faster than " competent and distinct funds shall have been received for the purpose."

ADDRESS OF THE BOARD.

The Baptist Board of Foreign Missions for the United States, convened at the city of New York, August 10, A D 1818, to their brethren of the Baptist denomination, and to all who pray for the coming of the kingdom of God, present their affectionate Salutations.

WHILE our first and unremitted attention has been devoted to missions, that part of our duty which relates to aiding in their education, 'pious young men, who in the judgment of the churches of which they are members, and of the Board, possess gifts and graces suited to the gospel ministry,' has not been forgotten. Providence has seemed to smile on the design of the General Convention. The aid proffered by the Baptist Education Society of Philadelphia having enabled us to make a beginning in this department, without resorting at all to the mission funds, further delay appeared, at the last annual meeting of the Board, to be unwarrantable. It was judged incumbent on us, as faithful servants of the Convention, and of our common Lord, to employ the talent committed to us,—to commence an institution with such means as we had, and, relying on the favour of Him who has all hearts in his hand, appeal to the liberality of our brethren and of the christian public for more ample funds.

An ardent desire to render this Institution extensively and permanently useful, and to adopt the best measures for accomplishing a purpose in which the welfare of the churches and the prosperity of missions, are so deeply concerned, has at this time called us together from different parts of the Union. The counsel of others also has been sought, and the guidance of Divine wisdom implored. It has been a most interesting season. Past ages have risen to view, and shown the rocks on which various denominations of professed Christians have dashed. The history of our own has furnished many important lessons. Our present flourishing state, contrasted with the scenes of peculiar difficulties and trials through which our predecessors have passed, has called loudly for a grateful return, worthy of our superior privileges and increased means, worthy of the part assigned us to act as the friends of truth and holiness at this eventful period, and worthy of the commencement of that glorious day which is dawning upon the world. A spirit of love and union has prevailed at our meeting, and a disposition been felt to sacrifice local interests to the general good.

The results of our deliberations are exhibited in the preceding pages.

We wish to have it distinctly understood, that we have no desire to draw off the attention of our friends from literary institutions in those sections of the country where they respectively reside. A proper regard to them will, we believe, tend much to promote the objects and facilitate the operations of a general school sacred to the gospel ministry ; and for other reasons also, we shall ever rejoice to see our brethren taking an interest in them, patronizing and guarding them. Under the direction of devout and faithful instructors, it has been fully shown that they can be nurseries of piety as well as of learning; and some of them have, within a few years past, experienced the gracious effusions of the Holy Spirit. It certainly would be wrong to abandon them unnecessarily to the management of the irreligious, and leave the most interesting collections of sprightly, ardent youths, at the most critical period of their existence, without any restraint from the exemplary conduct and the influence of pious fellow-students. Discreet, decided Christians, enjoying the paternal care and counsels of instructors decidedly christian, can do much more than we are always aware of, for the cause of religion and the eternal welfare of their companions in study. Most fervently do we wish the salt of divine grace to be cast into the fountains of literature and science, that the streams which flow from them may be pure and salutary. Aside, therefore, from all other favouring considerations, we cannot but deem it very desirable that our young brethren, in cases where it is practicable, be encouraged to avail themselves of the opportunities which they may have of obtaining a liberal education before they come to the theological Institution.

At the same time, we wish to have it also distinctly understood, that we believe many ought to preach, who ought not to spend so long a period in preparatory study, and, indeed, that as there are at present, so there always will be, many useful and able ministers who never enjoyed the advantages of any public institution whatever. But there are many also, who, though they have not time for laying so broad a foundation as their younger brethren, yet can devote a few years to those studies and exercises which are the most directly calculated to promote their future usefulness. In extending encouragement to such, as well as to others, we have been influenced by a view of the actual dealings of God with his people, and have endeavoured to make such an arrangement as shall fall in with the dispensations of his mercy, and meet with his approbation. The candid and judicious, we trust, will not be displeased at our attempt to observe a medium between two dangerous extremes—making colleges *every thing*, and making them *nothing*.

Upon becoming acquainted with the objects and plan of this Institution, some of the wealthy, it is hoped, will not forget the high privilege which they enjoy of being able to contribute largely to its funds, nor lose, at last, the large reward of good and faithful stewards. They who have been intrusted with less of the goods of this world, need not be reminded that 'it is accepted according to that a man hath'

Education societies, in addition to those which are already in existence, will, we doubt not, be formed in most of the States, with the design of assisting suitable young men while at the Institution, and if necessary, while making the various degrees of preparation for entering it, that may be judged expedient in the cases of different individuals. The churches are, moreover, affectionately requested to make annually a public collection for the purpose.

While many of the students, doubtless, will need pecuniary assistance, some, it is to be expected, will be able to support themselves, and will most cheerfully do it. Others will as readily do all they can.

Parents, religious parents especially, we hope will not be unmindful of the peculiar obligations under which the mercy of God has laid them, to do all in their power for the assistance of their sons who give indications of its being their duty to become preachers of the gospel. Say not, dear brethren, that you cannot spare them yet.—What if they should be taken away by death? Their minds are the most susceptible of improvement while *young*. And if the work of the ministry is before them, they have no time to lose unnecessarily from the pursuit of those studies which may conduce to their future usefulness. You freely acknowledge that all you have is the Lord's. Whenever for the prosperity of his kingdom, he calls upon you for a part of that which you are intrusted with, you will not, you cannot refuse to deal it out even to a stranger. With what readiness, then, will you obey the call, when he allows you the distinguished privilege of contributing most directly to his cause by dealing out his silver and gold to your own children! You may live to see the happy fruits of your exertions; but should you not, it will be no subject of regret, when your stewardship is closed, and you are experiencing the realities of the future world, that you have done what you could to increase the talents of those whom you have left on earth, engaged in winning souls to Christ.

We commend the Institution to God, and, under Him, to the churches, to the ministers of his word, and to all the friends of religion.

Brethren of our denomination! we look to you for support, with peculiar claims and special confidence. And while you that are able extend your bounty, we entreat that no one withhold his *prayers*. If any of you have fears with respect to the undertaking, pray that your fears may not be realized, but that the Lord may indeed make it a rich blessing. If you approve of the plan, pray also that he may crown it with abundant success, and ever grant to all concerned in it much wisdom and grace.

We deem it unnecessary, at the present time, to expatiate on the utility of sanctified learning in Ministers of the Gospel at home, and in Missionaries abroad, or to direct your attention to the fields white already for the harvest, or to show the duty of employing the means in our power, as well as praying the Lord of the harvest to send forth labourers. You have, we trust, long since felt the importance of these subjects. The way is now open for our combined exertions. Whatever seminaries there may be among us in any part of our land, we cannot forbear to express our strong confidence that *this* will be considered, not as a rival, but as a common friend, encouraged and strengthened by the co-operation of them all. In a central part of the Union, and under the control of the Convention, a general theological Institution, supported by our united energies, must possess signal advantages for the diffusion of its blessings and the preservation of its purity. It must be viewed with a common interest by our churches throughout America, and, in its operation, tend, constantly, to strengthen the ties of love and harmony which already bind them together.

We are, in sincerity and affection,

Your brethren and servants for Christ's sake.

Signed by order of the Board.

THOMAS BALDWIN, *President*.

HORATIO G. JONES, *Recording Secretary*.

MISSIONARY INTELLIGENCE.

MISSION TO BURMAH.

From Mr. Judson to the Cor. Secretary, dated Rangoon, December 24, 1817.

AN opportunity of going direct to Chittagong, and thence back to Rangoon, in the same vessel—an opportunity which has never occurred since I have been in this place, and may probably not occur again for years—has induced me to suspend the dictionary, three-fourths of which is now completed, and take passage to Chittagong. It is a passage of ten or twelve days; and the vessel expects to be absent from Rangoon between two and three months. The expense of the undertaking, in addition to the regular expenditure of the mission, will be only two hundred and sixty rupees.

You are, no doubt, acquainted with the circumstance, that Mr. De Bruyn, the missionary at Chittagong, has baptised several of the Mugs, who are, I believe, a sort of connecting link between the Bengalees and the Arracaners, a tribe of Burmans. It is said that, among the converts, there are a few Arracaners; and, I believe, there is at least one real Burman. It has long been my desire to visit these people, in hope of being the means of promoting their spiritual instruction, and also of improving myself in that kind of religious dialect, which is, perhaps, better acquired from intercourse with converted natives, than in any other way.

My prime object, however, and that on which we have all set our hearts, and made a particular subject of prayer to God, is, to find some convert, acquainted with the Burman language, who will be persuaded to accompany me to Rangoon. If this purpose could be effected, we trust, that with the blessing of God, it would be essentially beneficial to the mission, and greatly facilitate the communication of divine truth.

I expect to embark this afternoon, and shall get out of the river in a day or two. Brother Hough and family and Mrs. Judson remain as usual.

I cannot but hope, on my return, to have the pleasure of being welcomed by the brethren whom we are now beginning to expect. May He who controls the winds and the waves bring us all together in peace!

STATION AT ST. LOUIS.

From Mr. Peck to the Cor. Sec., dated St Louis, August 3, 1818.

SINCE my last letter, which, I believe, brought up our history to the 27th of June, I have been on an itinerating mission in the country. My route was first directed to Bonhomme, where I preached, and visited two schools, thence to St. Charles, Wood's Fort, and Upper Cuivre, to Ramsey's Creek. The latter place lies about 100 miles N.W. of St. Louis, and 6 or 8 miles from the Mississippi. A small church was constituted here last spring, and a man by the name of Riddle preaches. In this route I made it an object to visit all the schools I found in my way. I hope Divine Providence will favour us, that we may soon fix a station in the country where we may educate persons for teachers.

We have occasional additions to our church. Dr. Cunningham, from New York, recently joined us, and I expect to baptise one or two coloured persons shortly.

August 13.—To say the harvest is great here, is only repeating what is said of every destitute region. To say it is immense, unbounded, and that this is the very crisis to enter it, is not saying too much. A fair prospect begins to open into the Indian country; and nothing but the *want of missionaries*, and school teachers, and the *want of funds*, prevent immediate effort.

Had my situation possibly admitted, (which might have been possible if another labourer had been here,) one of the best opportunities presents this day for an exploratory mission through immense tribes of savages, and that with apparent safety. A gentleman arrived here from New Madrid, a few days since, by the name of Tanner, who professes religion, is a baptist, sometimes preaches, and is an intelligent man. He has a brother among the Chippeways of the northwest—absent 27 years—seen last winter by lord Selkirk, and who wishes to get back to his native country. Lord Selkirk wrote to his relatives respecting his situation, and Mr Tanner has set off to find him. He has the governor's protection, and assistance; goes this day with the public stores to Prairie Du Chien, thence up the St Peters, on to Red river and Selkirk's colony, and expects to return next spring by the way of those nations which border on the Missouri, and through the Mandan villages, down the Missouri home. Did circumstances possibly admit, I believe I should leave my family, and accompany him.

However, to make the best of this providence, I have given him a kind of mission, or agency, and a list of instructions from the Western Mission Society, to do what he can amongst the Indians—hold councils—find out their dispositions to receive missionaries, schools, &c. and make communications to us; so that we have a sort of itinerating missionary now travelling amongst the Indians in the interior. Nothing is wanting to establish schools in the country, and even in two or three places amongst local tribes of Indians, but suitable teachers. I feel more and more impressed with the necessity of fixing a station in the interior (perhaps at Boon's Lick, or Chariton) where living is cheap, and where by a school we may educate young men for instructors of others.

Religion appears to be in reality gaining ground in St. Louis. Our meeting house is well under way. The brick work will be done in 7 or 8 days. Hitherto the building committee have been enabled to meet their demands.

The African Sunday school still continues, and occasional conversions take place among the Africans.

From Mr Peck, St. Louis, July 16, 1818, *to the Rev John Peck, (member of the Board) Cazenovia, N. Y.*

"I have lately returned from a tour into the interior, during which I visited several schools. But suitable teachers are very much wanted in this country.

In a little time we mean to adopt a school system after the model of our brethren in India. O, how do I wish that some of our pious young brethren of the north, might find it in their hearts to visit this land of darkness, in the capacity of teachers! If any in the circle of your acquaintance would be disposed to venture this way, with sufficient credentials of their qualifications to teach a common English school, they may readily find employment. We might now set up fifty schools in different parts of the country, if we had teachers.

"Our African Sunday school proves a valuable institution. I trust that a number of souls are already delivered from the dominion of sin, who, in the "illimitable circles" of endless existence, will look back on the Sabbath school, where the Holy Spirit first led them to see themselves bound in the chains of sin, and directed their hearts to the Son of God. Every Sunday brings forth some new case of conviction among these children of Ham. Nor is the blessed work confined to the people of colour. A number of conversions have taken place among the whites in this village.

"I have had repeated interviews with Indians of different tribes, particularly with a band of the Yanktons, a branch of the Sioux (pronounced *Soo*) nation. They came from more than 1000 miles up the Missouri. Brother Welch and myself, held a formal council with them a few weeks ago, relative to their receiving missionaries, schoolmasters, &c. They were quite friendly, and professed great willingness to receive teachers, saying, if their grandfather (the president) should send us, their children must attend school. Three chiefs of this band called on my school one day, and tarried an hour or two. They were quite interested in hearing the scholars read. Since that, they have frequently called at my house, and by picking up a few words of their language, and by signs, I have been able to converse with them on common subjects. They are quite different in manners, behaviour, and language, from the northern Indians. They believe in one God, who created both red and white men, who governs the world, to whom we are amenable for our conduct, and who is the author of all good. They call him *Waū-kūndā*, or the *Father of Life*. They readily understood that we were *Wau-kunda's* children, and sent by him to teach me how to worship him. They professed themselves dark—said the cloud hung over them—but that if we came amongst them, Wau-kunda would bless them, and cause the sun to shine—that they believed we were *Wash-tā*, i. e. good—and that Wau-kunda would bless us.

"A band of the Pawnees have visited St. Louis this season, about which I have collected the following information. The Pawnees live in the upper country, betwixt the Missouri and the Arkansas, and as high up as the river Platte. It has been denied by historians that the aborigines of North America ever offered *human* sacrifices; but that the Pawnees do, is now past all doubt. They worship the planet Venus, which in their language they call "the great star," and to secure the favour of which they offer human sacrifices. These are generally prisoners taken in war. There is now in St. Louis a Spanish boy, about 10 years of age, whom they took prisoner last year, and were about to offer him. He was ransomed by M. Lisa, a citizen of this town and a trader amongst them, who brought him to this place. Some time ago, this sanguinary band took a Pado woman prisoner, and devoted her to the sacrifice. As she was pregnant, the diabolical rite was put off till after her delivery. As soon as she recovered from child-birth, she stole a horse and made her escape. Being obliged to leave her babe in the hands of these bloody idolaters, it was immediately transfixed to a sharp pole, and in this situation offered to their god!

"Christian! canst thou read this affecting story, and not exert thyself to the utmost to send the gospel and the blessings of civilization to these western idolaters? Parents! Mothers! Do you love your children? Does the artless smile—the playful gestures of your infant offspring, cause the thrill of joy to expand your bosoms? And will you hear of the miserable degraded situation of the aborigines of your country, and not provide the means to send missionaries amongst them? Will you refuse your prayers for their relief?

"There are three bands of the Pawnee nation, residing but a few miles apart. They are distinguished by the French traders, and others, into *Repu'lican*, *Loup*, or *Wolf*, and *Bigstep* Pawnees. The Wolf Pawnees are the only band who offer human sacrifices to the god they worship. Their *priests* are about forty in number, and their power over the minds of these infatuated people is unlimited. Their chief, or king, who was in St. Louis a few days since, reigns with despotic sway. Notwithstanding their sanguinary character, and superstitious idolatry, they are an interesting race of beings. Their language is soft and melodious, and their minds appear susceptible of refinement and sensibility. The commissioners on Indian affairs in this place, had a treaty of peace with this nation soon after their arrival, which gave one of their chiefs, styled "the Warrior," the opportunity of a display of Indian eloquence, much to the satisfaction and amusement of his auditors. As the Pawnees never before had much intercourse with the Americans, it is to be hoped the introduction they have had, will leave on their minds just impressions of the blessings of civilization.

"O, my dear brother, pray for us. Forget not to pray that the cloud may remove from over the minds of the Sioux, and that the blood-stained Pawnees may no longer immolate their fellow beings on the altars of a false deity—but that the light of salvation may reach these 'dark parts of the earth that are full of the habitations of cruelty.'

"As ever, yours, &c. J. M. PECK."

INSTRUCTIONS OF THE BOARD TO MR EASTMAN.

PHILADELPHIA, *October* 2, 1818.

DEAR BROTHER,

CALLED as you have been to the important office of a missionary of the Cross, agreeably to the custom of the Board of Foreign Missions, under whose patronage you go forth, they present you with a few general instructions, which they hope may contribute to your assistance and comfort.

As you are about to labour in a sphere corresponding with that occupied by our beloved brother, Rev. Mr Ranaldson, the Board wishes you to consider the substance of the instructions given to him as directed to yourself, and trust that the same fervours of holy zeal and unwearied exertion which he has so pleasingly discovered, will be found in you. In him, and in our worthy brother Dr. Cooper, you will find affectionate friends and able counsellors.

In the regions of the Mississippi state, and in Louisiana, where the gospel is rarely preach'd, you will perceive an important field of action, which we wish you, in the name of the Lord Jesus, to endeavour to occupy; but still the Board wish you to have an eye directed, as far as may be, to the Indians in the west. Visit them when you can, and communicate all you can collect relative to their local situation, and the probable openings for doing good among them. The inhabitants of the United States are debtors to those unhappy and untaught wanderers; and the christian community feel their obligation to contribute to the discharge of the debt. The American baptists, in common with their brethren of other denominations, are anxious to convince the *natives* that the Son of Man came not to destroy men's lives, but to save them.

We hope you will be enabled " to walk in wisdom," and that the presence of the Redeemer, and the influences of his good Spirit, will afford you consolation and guidance. We shall be happy to hear from you often, and hope you may have tidings to communicate that will impart evangelic pleasure to our hearts, and to the hearts of thousands.

By order of the Board,

WM. STAUGHTON, *Cor. Sec'ry.*

GENERAL MISSIONARY INTELLIGENCE.

Letter from Mr. William Pearce to the Rev James Hinton, of Oxford, England, dated Serampore, January, 1818.

AS a vessel is about to sail direct to Liverpool, I embrace with pleasure the opportunity it affords me of conversing with an absent, though not forgotten friend.

The brethren have not been unmindful that your annual meeting is in June, and that you will then wish the latest intelligence you can obtain. But as I am confident that, should the review of the mission which they hoped to have forwarded by this vessel, reach you in time, the memoir of the translations will be certainly too late, I have gleaned the following particulars respecting them for your gratification. In giving you these sketches, I have preserved the order pursued in the memoir for 1815, to which I beg leave to refer you.

In the memoir, the whole of the scriptures in the Ooriya were represented to have been printed. I have now the pleasure of informing you, that a new edition of the New Testament, of 4000 copies, has been some little time begun, and the printing advanced to the middle of Matthew.

In the Bengalee, in which of course the version will be now as accurate as the brethren can expect ever to make it, and in which the opportunities for distribution are becoming daily more extensive, we have commenced a new edition of 5000 copies of the whole scriptures, in a new and much reduced type, reduced by brother Lawson, when he resided at Serampore By means of this alteration we shall be able to comprise the whole bible in one large octavo volume of 850 pages, which has hitherto occupied five volumes of 800 pages each. The brethren intend to print 5000 additional testaments, forming a thin volume of about 180 pages.

In the Sungskrit, the Latin of the East, and intelligible to almost all the learned men throughout Hindoosthan, the historical books have been completed, and the printing advanced to the middle of Jeremiah. We therefore expect to complete this volume within the next three months, and shall then have printed the whole of the scriptures in that language.

The Hindee bible is still further advanced; and we fully expect that within a month the last part will be ready for distribution. We shall then have printed the first edition of the whole scriptures, with a second edition of the New Testament

In the Mahratta, the historical books have been printed off, since the last memoir, and the Hagiographia advanced to the middle of Proverbs

In the Sikh, the Pentateuch is just completed, and the historical books begun

In the Chinese, we have just completed the Pentateuch, and are now proceeding with a second edition of the New Testament

In the Telinga, the New Testament is printed as far as the Thessalonians: and we hope to have finished the volume ere this reaches you

In the Pushtoo testament, the printing is advanced as far as the 1st of Peter; and in the Assam and Wutch, to the Romans, while in the Bruj Bhassa, although a delay has arisen in consequence of the distance of brother Chamberlain's station, who was superintending the version, we are preparing to proceed with the printing as before

In the Kurnata we have finished Mark and are proceeding with Luke, while in the Kunkuna, the Mooltanee, the Sindhee, the Kashmere, the Bikaneer, the Nepal, the Ooduypore, the Marwar, the Juypore, and the Khassee, not much progress in the printing has been made since the last Report, access to them in many cases being difficult, and their prosecution interfering with the supply of countries more extensive and more easy of approach As soon, however, as the Hindee and Sungskrit versions are completed, it is the intention of the brethren to proceed with them; while the return of brother Carapeit, as hereafter mentioned, afforded a most favourable opportunity of distributing the Gospel of St Matthew, already printed, in four of these languages.

Although the printing of the Serampore translations, has been in some degree retarded, by the printing of several elementary works for the Bengalee schools, as well as of the Roman Malay and Armenian bibles, for the Calcutta Auxiliary Bible Society, (a cause not much to be regretted,) you will be pleased to hear, that they were never proceeding with more rapidity than at present The office now furnishes our venerable editor, Dr. Carey, independently of the Chinese proofs it forwards to Dr Marshman, with twelve proofs per week on an average.

You will be gratified to hear, that our opportunities of distributing the scriptures, when printed, are becoming more extensive. Our much esteemed brother C. C. Aratoon, being desirous to return to Surat, to fetch his family, left us November last, intending to proceed up the river as far as Agra, (four months journey,) to supply the different stations in his way, with scriptures and tracts, and then to cross the country to his late station. The last letter we received from him, was dated Benares, and he had then in his journey, distributed himself, or left for distribution at the different stations through which he passed, (including Cutwa, Berhampore, Moorshedabad, Monghir, Patna, Digah, and Benares,) no less than 10,250 books or pamphlets, of which a large proportion were volumes of the scriptures, in Bengalee, Persian, Hindee, Sungskrit, Kashmere, Mahratta, Arabic, Sikh, Bulochee, Bruj Bhassa, and Chinese. The brethren wish him to proceed overland to Surat, distributing in his way, the gospels they have printed in the Jypore, Oodipore, Bikaneer, and Marwar languages. The countries in which these are spoken, could not be traversed by an European with safety, though we hope that our brother, being an Armenian, may pass through them without much difficulty; the universal engagement of his countrymen in commerce being his passport. We are chiefly deficient in means of circulating the Ooriya, Kurnata, Telinga, and Mahratta scriptures, and anxiously desire that you could send out one or two brethren to occupy a station near Balasore or Cuttak, by means of whose labours, the scriptures in these languages, now printing or printed, may obtain an extensive circulation.

With respect to the distribution of the Chinese, we have lately sent a box of scriptures to Java; and hope, that we may be able to distribute, with advantage, many more than we have yet done on that island, as brother Robinson complains that our supply has been hitherto too scanty. The late unsettled state of Amboyna has prevented our supplying Jabez Carey with any very lately, but as tranquillity is now nearly restored, we shall not neglect that quarter. We expect likewise every day two American missionaries, proceeding to Rangoon, to assist our brethren there. By them we shall likewise send a supply of Chinese, as we hope that, independent of the Chinese who visit Rangoon and its neighbourhood, one of our brethren may be stationed in one of the Chinese provinces of the Burman empire, in which case a regular supply will be indispensably necessary.

I entertain great hopes that the review of the mission will reach you in time, and shall therefore say very little on the subject. We heard yesterday the melancholy intelligence, that Mrs Moore of Digah was dead. Brother Moore, with whom we affectionately sympathize, being unwell, was gone to Buxar for advice, and had not returned when the event happened. At Benares, brother Smith is successful. He has baptised a brahman, and hopes, very shortly, to baptise three more inquirers. At Cutwa, *this year*, brother W. Carey has baptised four, and in Bheerbhoom, where Mr. Hart is now stationed to superintend schools, three more. The Bengalee schools prosper,——no less than 7000 children were under instruction, at the close of the year, in schools superintended by the brethren, and 5000 more in schools supported by government and the Church Missionary Society. Much machinery is in operation to destroy the outward obstacles to the spread of the gospel, but we want, too, those influences of the Spirit of God, which shall effectually convince " the world of sin," and incline them heartily to embrace the Saviour, as the only " hope set before them."

As to myself, I have abundance of employment, and that of the most useful kind. Alas! that it is so often engaged in with so little desire after the divine approbation and concern for the divine glory! I can claim no merit for coming here. I hoped to be kindly treated, and to have food and raiment, with an employment more agreeable to that desire of being useful which God in mercy had given me. I have found them all. Freed from embarrassment in temporal affairs, with a snug habitation and affectionate wife, surrounded by, and engaged with the most devoted of men in the best of causes, what sacrifices have I made? I recollect the privations with which those who preceded me had to struggle, and trace in them the operations of that simple love to the Saviour's cause, of which

I have given no pledge. Pray for me, that I may possess the spirit of a missionary and a martyr.

I am advancing, though not rapidly, in the knowledge of Bengalee, which I very much like, and in which I hope, ere long, to talk to the Hindoos, with fluency, of the only Saviour.

Brother Judson is, we understand, gone to Chittagong to obtain a Mug Christian as an itinerant. He will be grieved to find poor De Bruyn in the silent tomb. Mr Ward intends, next month, to take a tour to visit the different stations, and ascertain their wants and prospects. He will probably be absent two months. We anticipate much good as likely to result from his visit.

Extract of a letter from Mr. John Lawson, dated Calcutta, Oct. 6, 1817

At present an epidemic disease is ravaging the whole country. The natives are dying by hundreds and thousands. I heard last week, that a friend of ours in the interior of the country, had stated in a letter, that in his neighbourhood, within the compass of a small district, as many as nineteen thousand persons had died in two days. Whole villages are deserted; the poor inhabitants thinking they shall be safer in some other place, but every place seems to be alike. The disease is a bowel complaint, (cholera morbus,) which generally carries the patient off in twenty-four hours, sometimes in two or three hours. I mention all this to show you what a dangerous country we live in, and how it becomes us to be always ready for death.

Mr Lawson adds, the cause is attributed to the extreme wetness of the season.

Extract of a letter from the Rev. Mr Fisher, at Murut, to the Rev. Mr. Thomason, at Calcutta, dated Murut, May 6, 1817.

I am more and more convinced that the inhabitants of India are nearly inaccessible to us in their present state, (I mean with a view to their conversion,) from the gross ignorance and want of common rudimental instruction, which prevails among them; and the great means which India appears to be in want of at present, is a systematic plan of education, universally, patiently, and industriously to be acted upon throughout the whole of our territories. Only let the population have the power to read our scriptures, and we have done them a kindness, the benefit of which nothing can deprive them of. The Bible may do its own work: that it *can* do so has been repeatedly proved, in spite of the melancholy forebodings, and sensitive jealousies of the adversaries to its distribution.

Take an instance, my dear brother, which I think so well calculated to cheer our spirits. You know that Anund Messee is now baptised. I shall send you his history in the next packet. We have every reason to believe in the sincerity of his Christian profession, and we hope for many beneficial results from his real ability and consistent life. The other day he asked my permission to leave his little school at M——, to go over, for a few days, to Delhi; which was the more readily granted, as he still entertains hopes of bringing his wife over to the acceptance of the salvation of the gospel, as well as his brother and sisters.

During his stay at Delhi, a report was in circulation that a number of strangers had assembled together (nobody knew why,) in a grove near the imperial city, and were busily employed, apparently in friendly conversation, and in reading some book in their possession, which induced them to renounce their *cast*, to bind themselves to love and associate with one another, to intermarry only among their own sect, and to lead a strict and holy life.

This account filled Anund with great anxiety to ascertain who and what they were; and he instantly set off for the grove which had been pointed out as the place of rendezvous. He found about 500 people, men, women, and children, seated under the shade of the trees, and employed, as had been related to him, in reading and conversation. He went up to an elderly-looking man, and accosted him, and the following conversation passed.

'Friend, pray who are all these people, and whence come they?' 'We are poor and lowly, and we read and love this book.' *Anund* 'What is that book?' 'The book of God' *Anund.* 'Let me look at it, if you please.' Anund, on opening it, perceived it to be the gospel of our Lord, translated into the Hindoosthanee tongue, many copies of which seemed to be in the possession of the party; some printed, others written by themselves from the printed ones.

Anund pointed to the name of Jesus, and asked 'Who is that?' 'That is God; he gave us this book' *Anund* 'Where did you obtain it?' 'An angel from heaven gave it me at Hurdwar-Fair.' *Anund* 'An angel?' 'Yes to us he was God's angel; but he was a man, a learned pundit.' (Doubtless these translated gospels must have been the books distributed five or six years ago at Hurdwar by the missionary) 'The written copies we wrote ourselves, having no other means of obtaining the blessed Word.' 'These books,' said Anund, 'teach the religion of the European sahibs. It is their book, and they printed it in our language for our use.' 'Ah, no,' replied the stranger, 'that cannot be, for they eat flesh.' 'Jesus Christ,' said Anund, 'teaches that it does not signify what a man eats or drinks Eating is nothing before God; and not that which entereth into a man's mouth defileth him, but that which cometh out of the mouth, this defileth a man for vile things come forth from the heart, and out of the heart proceedeth evil thoughts, murders, adulteries, fornication, thefts, &c these are the things that defile.' 'That is true, but how can it be the European book, when we believe that it was God's gift to us at Hurdwar-Fair?' *Anund* 'God gave it long ago to the sahibs, and they sent it to us.' I find, from Anund, that these Testaments were circulated at Hurdwar (I believe by Mr Chamberlain,) and falling into the hands of different people, resident in different but neighbouring villages, they were found to be interesting records, and well worth the attention of the people.

A public reader appears to have been selected by themselves in each of the villages, for the express purpose of reading the miraculous book, and their evenings have been habitually spent in this blessed employment, crowds gathering together to hear God's book. The ignorance and simplicity of many was very striking. Never having heard of a printed book before, its very appearance was to them miraculous.

A great stir was created by the gradually increasing information hourly obtained, and all united to acknowledge the superiority of the doctrine of the Holy Book to every thing they had hitherto heard or known. An indifference to the distinction of cast soon manifested itself; and the interference and tyrannical authority of their brahmins became more offensive and contemptible. At last, it was determined to separate themselves from the rest of their Hindoo brethren, and establish a party of their own, choosing out four or five who could read the best, to be public teachers from this newly acquired book. The numbers daily and rapidly increased, especially amongst the poor, which at last suggested the idea of convoking a public meeting of all their congenial associates, to ascertain how many accepted their new doctrine. The large grove near Delhi seemed a convenient spot, and this interesting group had now all met for this very purpose, when Anund's visit took place.

They seemed to have no particular form of congregational worship, but each individual made daily and diligent use of the Lord's prayer. Anund asked them why they were all dressed in white? 'The people of God should wear white garments,' was the reply, 'as a sign that they are clean, and rid of their sins.' Anund observed, 'You ought to be baptised in the name of the Father, Son, and Holy Ghost. Come to M; there is a Christian padree there, and he will show you what you ought to do.' They answered, 'Now we must go home to the harvest; but as we mean to meet once a year, perhaps the next year we may come to M.'

In consequence of this, I have deemed it adviseable to send Anund to make all possible inquiry respecting these promising blossoms of hope, and trust to be enabled ere long to give you still more gratifying information.

Extract of a letter from Mr. Chater, dated Columbo, November 18, 1817.

I GLADLY embrace the present opportunity of writing you information of the present state of this mission. I am happy to have it in my power to inform you, that, painful as some circumstances have been, our prospects are, on the whole, brighter than at any former period. You will rejoice to hear, that the new translation of the New Testament was completed by the same time that it would have been by the justly lamented Mr Tolfrey. It was ready to present to the Columbo Auxiliary Bible Society, at their annual meeting in August. We had entertained hopes of accomplishing a small portion of the Old Testament by the end of the present year, but that period is now near, and we have scarcely entered upon the work. It was found necessary to introduce into the new translation many words not in common use. In order to remove this difficulty, it was thought proper to prepare a glossary to accompany the translation, which, though it will be a small work in bulk, requires considerable labour to prepare it, and we shall not do more than complete it by the end of this year.

On the first sabbath in October we opened a new place of worship at the Grand Pass, where we keep our Cingalese school, and where, for a long time we have preached in the Cingalese, and occasionally in the Portuguese language. On the day it was opened, we had a double lecture, both morning and evening. I preached in the morning in Cingalese, and brother Siers in Portuguese; in the evening, *vice versa*. My morning text was, Ps cxxii. 1. Evening, Matt. xviii.

20. Brother Siers's morning text was, Exod. iii. 5. Evening, 1 Sam. iii. 12. On that day I preached the word of life in three different languages. The meeting-house, which contains about 200, was well filled in the evening; in the morning, the congregation was small. This place is intended, almost exclusively, for Cingalese worship. It is in the most favourable situation for collecting a Cingalese congregation that perhaps could be found in Columbo. Some attend it, who, except when they were christened, never entered a place of worship before. We have better prospects of collecting a little congregation than we have ever had, and it is owing principally to our having built a decent place in which they can assemble. We have at present, however, no conversions to relate—the case of Theophilus excepted I have not witnessed a single instance in which it appears to me that a Cingalese has felt the convincing, consoling, renewing, and sanctifying power of the word of God. Theophilus, you will recollect, is the Boodhist priest, whom I hope God has saved, and called with a holy calling At present, I am sorry to say, he is very unwell; I fear we shall soon lose him.

In our Pettah meeting-house we have worship, at present, in the Portuguese language only. Brother Siers has, for some time past, preached there at the hour, on the sabbath evenings, that I do in the Fort; and though he began with a very small number, they have increased to a little congregation. Preaching in English has, of late, been very thinly attended; but we may hope to witness different scenes to those we lately have done, in this respect also. A part of his majesty's 83d regiment, which has been long expected here to relieve the 73d, is now arrived. I have already become acquainted with one of the officers, who is a gentleman from Warwickshire, my native county. Both himself and his lady are seriously inclined, and , says he will do all in his power to influence the men to attend preaching. In the 1st battalion, the arrival of which is daily expected, it is reported there are many pious men already. May we have the happiness to witness their increase! As I think the society will be glad, at all times, to know how their missionaries fill up their time, I send the following account of the manner in which brother Siers and myself go through the week. Sabbath morning, one preaches at the Grand Pass, in Cingalese, the other, in the Fort, in Portuguese, alternately. These two places of worship are more than two miles distant one from the other. Sabbath evening, I preach in the Fort, in English, and brother Siers in the Pettah. Monday forenoon, I visit the Cingalese school, sing a hymn, give an exhortation to the children in Portuguese, which brother Siers turns into Cingalese, pray with them in the same manner, and inspect the progress they have made during the week; after which, we examine a sheet or two of Mr. Siers's translation of the New Testament into the Portuguese of Ceylon, in which he has advanced to the middle of Luke. In the evening, we hold a prayer meeting in the Fort meeting-house, in English and Portuguese; on which occasion we deliver a short exhortation in both languages Tuesdays I spend at home in translating, reading, or composing Cingalese; in the evening, hold an experience-meeting for members of the church and others who manifest any real concern to seek the salvation of their souls; and whose conduct is, at the same time, strictly moral. Wednesdays, Thursdays, and Fridays, I spend the forenoon, from 10 to 1, at the translating room. Wednesday, half past 2, *p. m.* I preach in the garrison hospital; in the evening, either in

Portuguese at the Pettah, or in Cingalese at the Grand Pass and while I am preaching at one place, brother Siers is preaching at the other. Friday evening, we preach alternately in the Fort, in Portuguese. Saturday forenoons, we go in turns to the leprous hospital, and preach in Cingalese and Portuguese to the miserable objects at that place. They are miserable looking figures indeed: some of them have lost all their fingers, some their toes, and part of their feet; others have their faces frightfully disfigured. However, they have souls. But, till brother Siers, some time ago, proposed to go and preach to them, these poor creatures had just cause for the complaint, "No man careth for my soul." They appear to be the most attentive of any of the little companies to whom we preach; and we entertain a hope, that we shall have some seals to our ministry from among them. From this statement you will perceive, that though our congregations are small, we have a considerable number of them to supply. Should it be the will of our gracious God, several of them may soon increase a little one may become a thousand, and a small one a strong nation. That this may be the case, a few are constantly offering up prayers and supplications to that God who is able to do exceeding abundantly above all that we ask or think. In this, I have no doubt you unite with us. Allow me to entreat you to abound in it more and more. Brethren, pray for us, that we may witness a gracious out-pouring of the Holy Spirit (without which all our efforts will be unavailing,) that the gospel may have free course and be glorified, even as it is with you.

I will conclude this long letter with a sad, yet pleasing event. On Lord's day, the last of November, we lost Theophilus, the only Cingalese member of our church. His affliction was not long, but for a short time his pains were extremely severe. He continued, to the last, the same steadfast, upright character he had ever been from the time of his conversion. He had no ecstasies, but manifested an unshaken trust in God, under his sharpest affliction, and appeared to endure his pains with much patience. The last time I saw him, I asked him if he was afraid of death? he said, "No, he was afraid of his pains, but he had no fear of death." Being asked why he did not fear death? his answer was, "My trust is in the grace of our Lord Jesus Christ, therefore I do not fear death." On Monday morning, myself, and the members of the church, with the exception of one, followed his remains to the place of interment. A few of our Cingalese friends, and some of the school-boys, also accompanied us. Brother Siers spoke a little in Cingalese at the grave. We sung a verse or two of Dr. Watts's hymn, "Why do we mourn departing friends," and brother Siers concluded, with a prayer in Cingalese. Short has been the race of this our first, and at present, I fear, only convert, from among the Cingalese. But, I trust he has so run, that he has obtained, and that he will be found among those, of whom I may have to say another day, "Here, Lord, am I, and the children thou hast given me."

Extract of a letter from Mr. Siers, dated Columbo, December 16, 1817.

I BEG leave to inform you, that I intended to have written to the society long before this, had it not been for the various exercises of mind which prevented its accomplishment. The idea of writing to the society, especially when considering myself an illiterate native, a foreigner and stranger to European languages, to perform such a task, the thought of it made me, as it were, to blush and hide for shame. However, on considering the state and nature of true Christians, that it is far from them to sport at others' infirmities, but rather to pity and forbear one another, encouraged me, in some measure, to perform this duty; hence, to remove (as it seems) the still remaining doubts and fears, Providence directed the ship Alexander safely at anchor, with the precious gift from the society to me! truly, a clearer manifestation of Christian love and charity I cannot expect; consequently, however imperfect the language might be, I cannot forbear writing a few lines to the society, acknowledging, in the deepest sense, my sincerest thanks for the invaluable present of books voted to me: indeed, it is more than a cup of cold water given to a thirsty soul. I panted for them. May He, therefore, who abounds, yea, more than abounds, in all the riches of glory, reward you jointly as a society, and severally as his stewards, both temporal and eternal blessings. As it pleased the society to regard me in my low estate, I beg leave also to introduce myself to the honourable society as one of the unworthiest of your household; and, as such, I may be enabled by you, in future, to acquit myself in the important duty, till I shall cease the ploughing. I imagine you would be happy, or rather anxious, to know something of my present sphere of life. I shall most gladly inform, but briefly, for I do not doubt but brother Chater might have communicated it, therefore I shall state in short.

I attend every day, from ten in the morning till two in the afternoon, to school at the Grand Pass, little less than a mile's distance from my house. We have, at present, upwards of 50 pupils, of different descriptions, class, and age; amongst whom, there are four proper Malabar heathens, three of them born at and come from Kandy, with their parents; King's Cast, the father, is called royal teacher—Gooroo Ithajah. The languages taught are English and Cingalese. I preach five times in the week, both in Cingalese and Portuguese, in turns with brother C. at four different places in the Fort, Pettah, Grand Pass, and at the Lepers' hospital. I have some humble hopes of a work of grace in one or two of the poor women; they were all ignorant of true Christianity, previous to our going there. At present the three first-mentioned places of worship are attended by thirty to forty, and forty to fifty. The work of conversion is scarcely seen. O Lord, make bare thine arm to the saving of Columbian souls! The Portuguese preaching is much esteemed by most: my translation of the bible into vulgar Portuguese is very slowly going on, for want of more time, still, however, it has advanced to Luke. I humbly hope, should Providence spare me in health and strength, with his blessing, to bring it in more forwardness. It bears the approbation of the common people. O, that they be those poor, and this gospel such as our Redeemer termed! The gospel of Matthew is nearly revised by brother C. and myself. I am sorry he has no more time to spare, his hands and head are full of business. Besides regular turns with me, he preaches four or five times in English. His studying Cingalese, translating the bible, attending the family and mission affairs, I am led to fear, should there be a trying providence on either of us, much more on him, humanly spoken, the little that has been raised must be decayed. Therefore, dear fathers and brethren, allow me to beg of you to send over to us some plain missionaries, to help in the cause of the Lord. Lastly, as the society had the kind attention towards me, in favouring with an invaluable present of books to help me forward; permit me to petition to you for a few, but much-wanted books: viz. a Concordance, a Theological Dictionary, a Dutch and English, and English and Dutch, a Portuguese and English, and English and Portuguese, and a Pronouncing Dictionary—the two last but one are greatly wanted to help me in translating. I stand highly indebted to the society for all I have and enjoy; and will, till the last moment, acknowledge it, and endeavour to discharge myself as such an one, ever making mention at a throne of grace, praying to pour down his blessings on you copiously. I entreat you for an interest in your prayers on us, as a church, and on me and my poor labours.

Mr. Chater adds, in a P.S.—Brother Siers solicited me to put his letter into better English, but I thought it would be more gratifying to you to see him in his own dress. In general, I believe, you will understand his meaning.

Extract of a letter from Rev. J. Ivimey to Dr. Staughton, dated

London, August 30, 1818.

My dear Sir,

I have received several articles from you, for which I thank you. I hope the "Luminary" will become the mean of diffusing light throughout every part of your Union. We had a meeting of the committee of the Baptist Missionary Society last week at Birmingham. Great unanimity prevailed, and I hope the resolutions adopted will have a healing tendency.

The Society for Ireland is well supported. We are now expending about 1600*l.* annually. We have never had any funds to depend upon, but God has raised up friends as we have needed support. Our treasurer has never yet advanced a shilling. The Irish gentry begin to discover the advantage of the society, and in many instances contribute one half the masters' salary. The prejudices against teaching the Irish languages begin to wear away. The Bible Society has just completed the New Testament in the ancient Irish character. The Homily and Prayer Book Society are preparing the Common Prayer Book by printing the old Irish in one column and English in another. Mr. Charles Grant, junior, an excellent man, of Christian sentiments and feelings, is just appointed chief secretary, which is an event auguring well for the spiritual and temporal circumstances of Ireland, and especially for the native inhabitants of Connaught and Munster, who might for ages have said, "No man careth for our souls." I should think that there are persons from Ireland who have risen to opulence in the United States, who would cheerfully contribute towards education in the native Irish language, and circulating the scriptures among that superstitious people. Could you not propose, through your "Luminary," for a society to be formed among such persons as an auxiliary to ours? The same waters that wash your shores, flow upon the shores where many of our schools are established. It would be a pleasing feeling to consider those waves as conveying across the Atlantic the bounty of Irish-Americans, and returning the gratitude of Irish children to their kind benefactors.

Your affectionate and obliged brother,

JOSEPH IVIMEY.

Extract of a letter from the Rev. T. Roberts of Bristol, to Mr. Ivimey, dated Hague (Holland) June, 1818.

I PREACHED in Rotterdam twice, on the Lord's day, in the Scotch church, which Mr. Angus procured for me, by introducing me to the clergyman. The congregations were small, but very attentive. I have made particular inquiries concerning our denomination in this country. I am perfectly astonished at the indifference of the English baptists to this body of people—they are upwards of 30,000 in number, very rich, and powerful; their ministers very learned, of various sentiments—some evangelical, others sadly degenerated. I have no doubt but much good might be done, at a little expense, if our denomination would exert themselves. I feel persuaded, that, by prudent management, under a divine blessing, this immense body of Dutch baptists might be brought into the field of missionary exertions, might again have the ordinance of baptism restored to its original purity, and, eventually, be evangelized to the profession of the truth as it is in Jesus.

BURNING OF TWO WOMEN

LAST Thursday week, a *sutee*, or female sacrifice by burning, no less remarkable on account of the firmness displayed by the victims, than from some extrinsic circumstances, took place at Kalee-Ghat. The victims of superstition, in the present instance, were the two wives of Neeloo, a physician and inhabitant of Shobhabazar, the first aged twenty-three, and the second only seventeen. By a regulation of government, before any sacrifice of this nature can take place, notice must be given to the police; and we are informed, that the officers attached to the police establishment of the twenty-four purgunnahs, with a laudable humanity, employed many endeavours to turn the misguided from their fatal determination. Their persuasions, however, being utterly disregarded, it was suggested, we believe, by Ram-Mohun-Raya, that in the actual mode in which females are burnt on the funeral pile of their husbands, there had been a wide departure from the method prescribed by the books of the Hindoos, and that the correction of this irregularity, in the present instance, might not only lead to the saving the immediate victims, but also of many others on future occasions. According to the usual method, it seems, previous to the fire being lighted, the females lay themselves down beside the corpse, when such a quantity of wood and other combustible materials are immediately heaped upon them, that if, in the agony inflicted by the flames, they should be desirous of retracting, it is utterly beyond their power so to do. This is probably a mere invention of the brahmans to deprive their victims of all free agency; but, if we are rightly instructed, the shastra explicitly directs that fire shall first be applied to the fuel on which the corpse is laid, and while it is in a state of ignition, the wife shall go, if she pleases, and lay herself down upon it. Agreeably to this view of the law, we understand that it was determined, that the wives of Neeloo should have the full benefit of this latter mode of sacrifice. The brahmans were prevailed on to give their consent. It is with pain, however, that we are obliged to add, that the hopes entertained from the experiment, in respect to a change of determination on the part of the victims, were altogether disappointed. The flames had no sooner began to rise, than the elder female deliberately walked into the midst of them, and quickly afterwards the younger followed her example, but previously, with great animation, addressed herself to the by-standers in words to this effect—" You have just seen my husband's first wife perform the duty incumbent on her, and you will now see me follow her example. Henceforward I pray do not attempt to prevent hindoo women from burning, otherwise our curse will be upon you." We are informed that this young woman then flung herself into the flames, apparently with the same unconcern as she had been accustomed to plunge into the Hoogly river, in order to perform her morning ablutions and devotions We have heard of several respectable and intelligent natives openly testifying their abhorrence of the cruel ritual of the sutee, and it is probable that a similar sentiment prevails in the minds of many others, though prudence may induce them to conceal it. *From the Oriental Star, published in Calcutta.*

SETTING APART OF MISSIONARIES.

On Thursday, July 30, a public meeting was held at the Baptist meeting-house, Badcox lane, Frome, (England) for the purpose of setting apart Messrs Christopher Kitching, and Thomas Godden, as missionaries to Jamaica.

A number of friends having collected from the surrounding country, early in the day, there was a service at 11, A. M when Mr Saffery, of Salisbury, delivered a serious and appropriate discourse, founded on Luke xiii. 28, 29, 30. " There shall be weeping and gnashing of teeth, when ye shall see Abraham, and Isaac, and Jacob, and all the prophets, in the kingdom of God, and you yourselves thrust out. And they shall come from the east, and from the west, and from the north, and from the south, and shall sit down in the kingdom of God. And, behold, there are last which shall be first, and there are first which shall be last." From this interesting passage, the preacher took occasion to remark, the stability of the kingdom of Christ, notwithstanding all opposition—the vast increase which it should ultimately receive—and the solid happiness enjoyed by all its faithful subjects He concluded by observing, that the language of the text was calculated to check presumption—to counteract a spirit of despondency—and encourage exertion, in the cause of Christ. Prayer was offered, before sermon, by Mr. Dyer, of Reading; and, at the close, by Mr. March, of Frome.

The evening service began at half-past five, and at that early hour, this spacious place of worship was completely filled After singing "O'er the gloomy hills of darkness," Mr. James Coultart, lately compelled by ill health to leave Jamaica, for a season, read the scriptures, and engaged in prayer Mr. Saffery introduced the special business of the evening, by noticing the obligations of Christians to propagate the gospel, and the general inattention to this duty which prevailed for ages. This led him to glance at the missionary exertions, which have distinguished the present day, and to apprize the audience of the immediate sphere, which the missionaries before them were intended to occupy. Here, he introduced various interesting particulars, respecting the state of the negroes, in Jamaica; and mentioned, that Mr. Coultart's visit to England was not merely for the recovery of his health This, through the kindness of Provdence, had been, in some measure, attained; but, ere he returned to Jamaica, he was exceedingly desirous of assistance, towards erecting a chapel in the city of Kingston, for his numerous and increasing black congregation. In concluding, Mr. Saffery called on Mr Kitching, to give some account of the manner in which he had been led to devote himself to the service of Christ, as a missionary; and, to mention what those doctrines were, on which he meant to insist in the course of his future ministry. These questions were subsequently addressed to M.. Godden, and were answered by each, in a manner highly satisfactory to the numerous congregation.

Mr. Kitching, it appeared, had been reclaimed from a course of vice and folly, through the instrumentality of a worthy minister of the Independent denomination, in the north of England. Under the auspices of this valuable friend, he was preparing to enter into connexion with the London Missionary Society, when his attention was arrested, by the account given in the Evangelical Magazine, of the alteration of sentiment, in Messrs. Judson and Rice, on the subject of believers' baptism. This induced him to pause, and finally, he was led to adopt the same views, soon after which he offered himself to the Baptist Missionary Society, and was sent to Bradford Academy, where he has been, for a considerable time, pursuing his studies under the direction of Dr. Steadman.

Mr. Godden stated, that, early in life, he had entered into the royal navy, and for several years experienced the usual vicissitudes attending that profession. His career was terminated, by a captivity of eight years duration, at Arras, in France, where he sustained great hardships, and saw many brave companions around him, sink under the pressure of their sufferings. Here, however, it pleased Him who is wonderful in counsel and excellent in working, to deliver him from a yet more degrading captivity, and, in the best sense, to make him free indeed. This joyful change was effected, by means of a fellow-prisoner, who was accustomed to speak to them the words of salvation. Released, at length, by the conclusion of the war, he returned to his own country, united himself to the Baptist church, at Newbury, and was soon after called by them to the work of the ministry.

At the close of Mr. Godden's address, the ordination prayer was offered, with much solemnity and pathos, by Mr. Saunders, the minister of the place; and Dr. Ryland proceeded to give the charge, from the words of our Lord, to his disciples, recorded in Matt. x. 16. "Behold, I send you forth as sheep in the midst of wolves: be ye therefore wise as serpents, and harmless as doves." After briefly adverting to the history of the text, the Dr. remarked, how difficult it would be to reconcile such language as this, with the denial of original depravity; and then suggested to his younger brethren, that the words contained a striking picture of the difficulties to which they were exposed, and the dangers they would have to encounter—an express reference to the authority under which they acted—and suitable admonition, as to the course they were to adopt, in prosecuting the labours of their office. Under each of these heads, much judicious advice was offered, in a manner truly paternal and, at the close of his discourse, the Dr earnestly besought the friends of Christ present, to aid the missionaries, by their prayers, in the arduous undertaking to which they were now devoted.

Mr. Tidman, an Independent minister, lately removed from Salisbury to Frome, closed the highly interesting service, in prayer.

ARRIVAL OF THE MISSIONARIES.

Information has been received and communicated to us by brother Sharp, that brethren Colman and Wheelock, with their wives have arrived safely at Calcutta. Their passage, though not a quick, was a pleasant one. It is a most pleasing consideration, that, while on the mighty waters, it was the pleasure of the Lord to give them six or seven of the seamen as seals to their ministry. The whole crew were so wrought upon, as to render them, on their arrival at the desired haven, *men wondered at*. Thanks to the Head of the Church for these early fruits of the labours of these worthy men! May a harvest of blessings succeed on their arrival at Rangoon! Let this intelligence animate the joys, the prayers, the labours, and the expectations of all who are looking for the Messiah's universal reign!

BIBLE SOCIETIES.

ELOQUENCE can never be impressive, unless its theme be great and interesting. It may amuse, under other circumstances, but it can fire neither the speaker nor the hearer. Sublime description can exist only when a sublime object is to be described. A subject really important in its nature, and momentous in its bearings, operates like the sun; it warms, it illumines. Of this Moses was sensible, when he said, "Give ear, O ye heavens, and I will speak, and hear, O earth, the words of my mouth. My doctrine shall drop as the rain, my speech shall distil as the dew, as the small rain upon the tender herb, and as the showers upon the grass——BECAUSE I will publish the NAME of the LORD."

The objects Bible Societies embrace are of the first importance. They offer, gratuitously, a volume which delineates the Divine character, the miseries of man, the condescensions of the Mediator, and the happiness of the saint, in traces more striking, more correct, and more influential, than can be found in any human production. Addresses have been multiplied, during the last ten or fifteen years, on this subject, both on the eastern and western continents. Something new, and, what is of more importance, something peculiarly affecting and solemn, is found in almost every one of them. We have perused, with peculiar satisfaction, a judicious and eloquent address, delivered before the New Jersey Bible Society in August last, by the Rev. Dr. Wharton, of Burlington, New Jersey. We should be happy to insert the whole, but must content ourselves with presenting to our readers the following extracts:

FROM THE CHRISTIAN HERALD.

"Mr. President—It is with great diffidence that I rise to address you before this respectable assembly. It would indeed be presumption in me to flatter myself, that whatever I can say respecting the design, the excellence, and the advantages of Bible institutions, should add new feelings to the high and sacred estimation in which they are now held. The pious acclamations with which the establishment of these societies has been welcomed by the voice of Christendom, and the astonishing, I had almost said the miraculous success, which has attended their operations, are sufficient evidence of the deep, and I trust lasting impression, which their importance has made, upon the public mind and the hearts of their members.

"In viewing the rise and progress, and in looking forward to the probable issue of these associations, the only danger is, lest the mind should be carried beyond the bound of temperate exultation; or, recollecting the ages that are past, should experience too painful a sensation that this blessed work has been so long deferred. But, Sir, as from many other distressing recollections, so from this also, may spring up fresh motives for exertion. When we behold with the eye of pity, the manifold and awful calamities which, from the early days of Christianity, have grievously afflicted and debased its professors, leaving them little more than a name, when we strive to account for the numerous and destructive heresies, the disgusting immoralities, the puerile hallucinations, and the contemptible superstitions, which in many ages of the church have obscured the splendour of her doctrines, the purity of her morals, and the rationality of her worship; we do not immediately perceive that *these mighty evils sprang, principally, either from the difficulties in procuring, or from withholding from the general use, the volume of revelation* True indeed it is, that, within the four first centuries of the christian era, the gospel had been preached to all the civilized world Beyond the frozen Caucasus its standard had been erected on the plains of Persia, and its votaries established themselves on the shores of Hindostan. From Egypt it had penetrated beyond the sources of the Nile; and Nubia and Abyssinia had been gladdened with the tidings of salvation. The southern shores of the Mediterranean had beheld very flourishing churches rising over the ruins of idolatry, and the western provinces of the empire having submitted to the gentle yoke of Christianity, the victorious eagles of Rome had at last crouched to the banners of the Cross."

"Death, the fatal principle of destruction to other societies, serves only to multiply the number of Christians· until at length the generality of men open their eyes to the light, the temples are forsaken, sacrifices cease to be offered, marble and bronze are no longer divinities, and JESUS. by a kind of triumph totally unprecedented, and peculiar to himself, converts his bitter enemies into worshippers of his name."

"Now, Sir, I trust it will readily be admitted, that after the miraculous powers had been withdrawn from the church, her astonishing triumph over a flagitious and idolatrous world could only be attributed, under Providence, to the faithful labours of her ministers, *and a constant appeal to the law and the testimony contained in the scriptures.* As long as this continued, so long was she assailed in vain by hosts of heretics, rabbies, and subtle philosophists. The calumnies of Trypho, the plausibilities of Platonism, the powerful weapons of extensive erudition and refined ridicule, wielded by Celsus, Porphyry, and Julian, fell harmless at her feet, while cased in the heavenly panoply of the written word. Secure in this impenetrable armour, she defied the fiery darts of her wicked or deluded assailants. When heresies began to abound, and the mystery of iniquity began already to work, 'heaven taught champions arose, and knew where to find weapons to combat the threatening monsters.' 'The apostles,' says Ireneus, '*preached* the gospel, but afterwards delivered it to us in the *scriptures*, to be the foundation and pillar of our faith.'—' I do not follow men,' says Justin Martyr, in his controversy with Trypho the Jew, ' or human doctrines, but I follow God, and what he taught.'—And the great defender of the Trinity, the illustrious Athanasius, when confuting the gentiles, lays it down as a principle, that *' the holy and divinely inspired scriptures suffice for our instruction in all truth.'*

"Sir, nothing would be more easy than to produce a multitude of citations from the primitive fathers, all tending to declare the sufficiency, perspicuity, and potency of the scriptures, in defending and elucidating the doctrines of salvation. 'All things,' says one of them, ' are clear and perspicuous, and nothing contradictory can be found in the scriptures.' 'The scripture,' says another, ' expounds itself, and does not suffer the reader to err.' 'Whatever,' says another, ' has no authority from the scriptures, is despised as easily as it is alleged.' In a word, the great doctor of grace, St. Austin, with his usual force and accuracy, thus sums up the only method by which the church in his day maintained the purity of the faith. 'Let no one say this is true, because this or that person has wrought such and such miracles, or because some are heard who pray at the monuments (*ad memorias*) of the martyrs, or because such and such things happen there, or because he or she has seen such a vision when awake, or dreamed while asleep. Away with these fictions of lying men, or prodigies of deceitful spirits. Insist on their showing you some manifest testimonies from the *canonical books*. Remember the saying of our Lord, *they have Moses and the prophets.*'

"Thus it was, Sir, that the church was nourished, propagated, and defended, in her primitive days. The BIBLE was the charter of her rights, and the umpire of her decisions. To this she always appealed, and never appealed in vain."

"Among the reformed churches, even down to our days, great has been the scarcity of the holy scriptures. Editions indeed, of the bible, have been multiplied throughout Christendom, and have found their way to the libraries of public institutions, and of opulent individuals; but, like the five barley loaves, what were they among so many millions of famishing multitudes? Nothing but a similar miraculous multiplication of the bread of life could supply their urgent wants; and this, blessed be God, we have lived to witness; and in this, through his mercy, we are permitted to partake. We have seen, and have united with, a society of fellow-christians, which, like ' another angel flying through the midst of heaven,' not content to possess the everlasting gospel itself, was raised up at the time appointed by the inscrutable and immutable decrees of Providence, working all things according to his own will, ' to preach it to every nation, and kindred, and tongue, and people.'

"Great, Mr. President, though unmerited, is the privilege conferred upon us, of sharing in the labours and glory of this heavenly undertaking. Let us duly appreciate it, by discarding all minor considerations, and by concentrating all the scattered forces of our christian community to the beating down of the kingdom of satan, sin, and death. Let our messengers of salvation go forth, with the bible in their hands, and its spirit in their hearts, and let the grand experiments be repeated in this latter age of the world, whether the word of GOD, circulated among the heathen and nominal christians, and faithfully preached by those who are duly sent, may not induce *those* to believe and *these* to repent. Whether, if Paul shall plant, or Apollos water, the Holy Spirit will not give the increase, through the *only infallible communication* ever vouchsafed to mankind.

"Sir, I have offered these few remarks under the impression, that a recollection of the past evils which attended the ignorance of the scriptures, may prove an additional stimulus, in the bosom of every Christian, to obviate their recurrence, and to ensure success to the most godlike association which the world ever witnessed,—by the united, zealous, and persevering exertions of all their members on this western continent."

STATE OF RELIGION IN ICELAND, 1814.

IN regard to sentiment and style of preaching, the Icelandic clergy may be divided into two classes, those of the old, and such as are of the new school. The former professes to receive the bible as an authoritative and obligatory revelation of the will of God, and bow with reverence to its decisions. They do not exalt human reason to be the arbiter of what ought, and what ought not, to be embraced as dogmas of faith, but, conscious of their ignorance and proneness to errour, they consider it at once their duty and their privilege, to believe whatever God has been pleased to communicate in his word. Accordingly, in their sermons, they insist on the grand distinguishing doctrines of Christianity - the total depravity and helplessness of man; the eternal divinity, and vicarious atonement of the Son of God; the personality and saving operations of the Holy Spirit; the necessity of regeneration, and holiness of life; and the eternity of future punishment. I had an opportunity of meeting with many of these men in the course of my travels, and some of them, whom I heard from the pulpit, convinced me, that they were themselves deeply penetrated with a sense of the importance of those truths which they were engaged in preaching to others, that they had entered the ministry from no worldly motive, but were actuated by a sincere desire to advance the spiritual reign of their divine Master, and promote the best interests of their fellow men, and that they were living under an habitual impression of that solemn account which all, who have taken upon them the charge of souls, will have to give to the chief Shepherd at the day of final decision. They are men who are dead to the world, and devoted in heart and life to the service of their Redeemer. Their private walk exhibits the genuine tendency of the holy doctrines they teach, and their public discourses are earnest, energetic, animated, pointed, and faithful.

Such of the clergy as are of the new school, the number of whom is happily not very great, treat divine things in quite a different manner. Instead of drawing the matter of their sermons from the scriptures, they gather it from the writings of heathen philosophers: and the morality found in these authors, which, at the best, is but dry and insipid, absolutely freezes when transplanted into Iceland. The divine inspiration of the bible is discarded, and all the cardinal and fundamental points of the christian faith are either entirely omitted, or, when they are brought forward, it is only with a view to turn them into ridicule. The influence of such socinian and semi-deistical principles on the individuals who propagate them, is abundantly manifest. They are entirely men of the world. The awful realities of an approaching eternity have made no suitable impression on their minds; and levity, callousness, and indifference, mark the whole of their conduct. Nor are the effects resulting from the dissemination of their tenets, on such as imbibe them less visible and injurious. Their minds become imbued with scepticism and infidelity; every vestige of religion disappears, and immorality of one description or another generally occupies its place.

In their general habits and dispositions, the Icelanders are a very moral and religious people. They are carefully instructed in the principles of Christianity, at an early period of life, and regularly attend to the public and private exercises of devotion. Instances of immorality are in a great measure confined to such as frequent the fishing places, where they are often idle for days together; and where such as have made proficiency in wickedness, use every effort to ensnare and corrupt their young and inexperienced companions. In passing through the island, my stay at any particular place was too short to admit of my ascertaining the true state of vital and practical religion among its inhabitants; yet, making every allowance for the proneness of men to content themselves with a mere external form of godliness, and granting that there is often a correct moral deportment, without a single particle of love to God in the heart, I cannot but indulge the conviction, that in a country where the principles of revealed truth are so clearly and so generally known, and where the tone of morals is so high, there must be many whose minds have been savingly impressed with divine things, and who have experienced the gospel to be the "power of God unto salvation." The greatest number of these individuals are, in all probability, known only to God, having little or no intercourse with each other, and their situation may not unfitly be compared to that of the generality of real Christians in Scotland, about 30 or 40 years ago, where none of those institutions existed which now draw them together, make them acquainted with each other, and stimulate them to greater zeal and diligence in the service of their blessed Redeemer.

It may appear strange, that such a degree of religious knowledge should exist in a country where, of late years, few have had immediate access to the holy scriptures; but it is accounted for, by the circumstance, that almost every family is in possession of a volume of excellent sermons, written by bishop Vidalin of Skalholdt, about the beginning of the last century, which contains a great deal of scripture illustration, and that numerous passages from the sacred writings are produced in proof of the doctrines taught in the Icelandic catechism. The scarcity of bibles was severely felt. Numbers had been using every possible exertion, for a long series of years, to procure a copy of the sacred volume, but without effect. The poverty of the inhabitants was such, that they could not print a new edition themselves; they did not know to what quarter to apply for aid, and many began to apprehend that the word of the Lord would become extinct among them; and especially, that their posterity would be left destitute of this inestimable boon. But here foreign benevolence came most opportunely to their aid. The plentiful supply of the scriptures sent them by the British and Foreign Bible Society, and other friends to the best interests of humanity, was most joyfully and gratefully received: and while the Icelanders are now diligently employed in perusing the records of eternal life, their ardent prayers are ascending to heaven, for the present and eternal happiness of their spiritual benefactors. *Henderson's Journal in Iceland.*

MISCELLANEA.

THE cartilages in the vertebræ of the back yield considerably to the pressure of the body, in an erect posture, and expand themselves in the night when persons lie down. Hence arises a very singular phenomenon, but a very true one; which is, that a man is considerably taller in the morning after the expansion of these cartilages, during the absence of the pressure for several hours, than at night, when they have been pressed down all the day.

The Rev. Mr. Wasse seems to have examined this difference more strictly than any other person. He found that several persons, enlisted as soldiers, in a morning, had been discharged for want of height, on their being measured again before the officers in the evening, and on this occasion measured several other people, and found the difference, in many cases, to be not less than an inch. This gentleman observed in himself, that fixing a bar of iron where he just reached it with his head on first getting up in the morning, he could lose nearly half an inch in an hour, or less, if he employed that time in rolling his garden, or any other exercise of that laborious kind. He observed also, that riding often took off the height very suddenly; and what was more particular, that in sitting close to study five or six hours without any motion, he lost often a whole inch in height. The height once lost is not to be recovered again that day, not even by the use of the cold bath——a night's lying down alone can restore it.

This difference in height takes place only in the human species, as they are the only creatures who walk erect, and throw the pressure of their whole weight upon the spine. This gentleman measured horses both before and after riding, and could find no difference even after the longest journeys.

Philosophical Transact. No. 383.

Who, on contemplating this peculiar economy of the human system, can forbear exclaiming, with the devout Psalmist, that we are, indeed, "*fearfully and wonderfully made!*" But there is another reflection, neither less interesting, nor less useful. David was not only a devout man, but an enlightened philosopher; and we find him ever giving to his philosophical contemplations a pious and devotional direction. Hence, in the same psalm in which the exclamation above referred to occurs, we perceive him deeply penetrated with an impressive sense of the all-surrounding presence, and the omniscience of the Deity, and while he is humbled, he is animated with sentiments of adoration and joy. "I will praise thee; for *I am fearfully and wonderfully made!* How precious also are thy thoughts unto me, O God! how great is the sum of them!" It is, therefore, not genuine philosophy, but "*science, falsely so called,*" which leads the mind into the fogs of scepticism, the night of infidelity, or the blackness of atheism!

THE heart propels a weight of 51 pounds, with a velocity by which it may run through 149 feet in a minute; and this 4800 times in an hour.

Haller, *Prim Lin. Physiol.* cxxiii.

Ought not this prodigious power of the heart to awaken astonishment, while it serves to deepen every impression of reverence and awe in the presence of HIM whose "works" are "marvellous," who "is glorious in holiness, fearful in praises, doing wonders!"

COLONIZATION OF FREE PEOPLE OF COLOUR IN AFRICA.

We have received the "*twelfth Report of the directors of the African Institution, read at the Annual general meeting, held on the 9th day of April*, 1818." This valuable document is replete with the most interesting information, extracts from which, we regret to say, must be deferred to a future opportunity. So, too, in relation to the *American Colonization Society*, we are compelled to postpone what it would afford much satisfaction here to introduce.

In referring, however, to this subject, attracting, as it could not but do, the attention of an enlightened public, we cannot abstain from recording our unfeigned regret, which we are sure will mingle with the regrets of thousands, for the decease of the Rev. Samuel J. Mills.

Mr. Mills, and his worthy colleague, the Rev. Mr. Burgess, had been to Africa under commission from the American Colonization Society, to promote the objects of that benevolent institution. He died at sea, on his way back to the United States; but the fruits of his evangelical exertions in favour of the best interests of mankind, will live, it is believed, till time itself shall expire! We hope to be able to place the character of this excellent man, in a more conspicuous light, in an obituary article preparing for the next number of the Luminary.

Mr. Burgess has returned safely back to America. The novel and peculiarly interesting expedition on which himself and his deceased brother were sent, will probably produce an excitement in the public mind, that will be followed with blessings to unborn generations.

ORDINATIONS.

September 29th, 1818, the Rev. Samuel Eastman was ordained to the work of the ministry, as a missionary to the states of Mississippi and Louisiana, by prayer and imposition of the hands of the presbytery, in the meeting-house of the baptist church in Sansom-street. The Rev. Ira Chase offered the introductory prayer, Rev. John P. Peckworth preached the sermon, from 1 Cor. ix. 16. *For necessity is laid upon me; yea, woe is unto me, if I preach not the gospel.* Rev. James M'Laughlin proposed the usual questions; Rev. Richard Proudfoot made the ordination prayer, and presented the bible; Dr. Staughton delivered an affectionate charge from 2 Timothy iv. 5. *Do the work of an evangelist.* The services were solemn, appropriate, and interesting.

On Friday evening, the 16th of October last, in the meeting-house of the baptist church in Sansom-street, Philadelphia, the Rev. Daniel M'Cay, about to depart for the state of Mississippi, was ordained to the full office of the christian ministry. The introductory prayer was offered by the Rev. Richard Proudfoot. The Rev. Jacob Grigg preached an appropriate discourse from Acts xx. 24. *But none of these things move me.* The usual questions on the occasion were proposed by Dr. Staughton. Ordination prayer by the Rev. William Strawbridge. The Rev. Ira Chase, after a short and impressive address, presented the bible, and welcoming him as a fellow-labourer in the gospel ministry, gave the right hand of fellowship. The rest of the officiating ministers tendered the same pledge of christian regard. Dr. Staughton followed with a very interesting charge, from Matthew iv. 19. *Follow me, and I will make you fishers of men.*

POETRY.

The Missionary Conflict.

Herald of salvation, say,
Whither dost thou bend thy way?
Wherefore thus prefer to roam,
Far from friends and native home?

What if sickness lay thee low!
Who will then assuage thy wo?
Who support thine aching head?
Who the tear of pity shed?

Herald! stop and meditate,
Ere, alas! it be too late;
Sure it is not duty's call,
Thus to quit thy friends, thy all—

Ah! 'tis nature's voice I hear,
Oft she whispers in my ear.
Thus she tempts me day by day;
Thus would lead my soul astray.

Oft she prompts me to despair,
Fills my heart with anxious care;
Raises unbelief within,
And provokes my soul to sin.

But, when Jesus points the way,
Shall his servants not obey?
Let the fiercest trials come,
These but fit us for our home.

What if sorrow, toil, and care,
Make the gospel-herald's fare!
Jesus gives him joys to know,
Sends a balm for every wo.

If his Spirit still be nigh,
This can hush the rising sigh,
Grace can make our trials prove,
Angels sent on wings of love.

Soon the angry strife will cease,
Death will bring a sweet release;
Then, in yonder climes of bliss,
Christ will call the herald, his.

There with joy will he review,
All his toilsome journey through;
Perfect bliss shall fill his soul,
While eternal ages roll   T

Acrostic.

Repent and live, the Gospel cries,
Eternal Wisdom says, be wise;
Lean not to earth, nor put thy trust
In man, nor toil for senseless dust.
Go sinner seek the Saviour's face,
Implore his mercy, ask his grace,
On him rely, till time shall end,
Nor fear to trust in such a friend.   D

Parting Stanzas.

Saviour, ere we hence depart,
Touch the sinner's flinty heart,
'Tis thy gracious power alone,
Can dissolve the heart of stone.

Heavenly parent, hear our prayer,
Guard us with a father's care,
And when death shall close our eyes,
Let us praise Thee in the skies.   M.

Erratum.—Page 245, line 8th from top, for Hagiographia, read Hagiographa.

Note.—Pages 243 and 244 occur twice, owing to the introducing of some additional matter at that place, after striking off the form.

THE LATTER DAY LUMINARY;

BY A COMMITTEE

OF

THE BAPTIST BOARD OF FOREIGN MISSIONS FOR THE UNITED STATES.

Vol. I.   FEBRUARY, 1819.   No. VI.

COMMUNICATIONS.

THE CHARACTER OF THE APOSTLES.

AN apostle is one who is commissioned to execute the will of another, in the character of a representative or delegate. The name is applied to Epaphroditus, who was sent a messenger (αποστολον) from the Philippians, to supply the necessities of Paul. The brethren who accompanied Titus are called the messengers (αποστολοι) of the churches The name sometimes refers to an ordinary minister of the gospel. Romans xvi. 7. " Andronicus and Junia" were " of note among the apostles." In Acts xiv. 14. Barnabas as well as Paul is called an apostle. The same title is given him by Clemens of Alexandria. All the seventy disciples are termed apostles by Tertullian.

In one passage, Hebrews iii. 1. Christ himself is denominated an apostle. He was sent of the Father. The Spirit of God was upon him. He gave gifts unto men, confirmed his doctrine by signs and wonders, and was faithful to him that appointed him.

In the primitive age men arose who surreptitiously assumed the character we are contemplating. They were found in the church at Corinth, (2 epist. xi. 12.) " deceitful workers, transforming themselves into the apostles of Christ." To the church at Ephesus this commendation is given, Rev. ii. 2. " Thou hast tried them which say they are apostles, and are not, and hast found them liars."

Commonly the term is applied to the twelve disciples whom Jesus chose to accompany him in his ministry on earth, and to make known to the nations his glorious gospel after his ascension to heaven. In this sense it is used in the New Testament upwards of fifty times. A few general observations deserve attention.

1. They were men *called* to office by the Redeemer himself. Their names are introduced in Matt. x. 2. Mark iii. 13. and Luke vi. 13 &c. In the choice the Saviour displayed his sovereignty. "He called unto him whom he would." The names of the apostles are given by each of these three evangelists, to exhibit the honour conferred upon them, and to secure the churches against the arts of imposture. "Now the names of the twelve apostles are these. The first Simon, who is called Peter, and Andrew his brother. James the son of Zebedee, and John his brother, Philip, and Bartholomew; Thomas, and Matthew the publican; James the son of Alpheus, and Lebbeus, whose surname was Thaddeus; Simon the Canaanite, and Judas Iscariot, who also betrayed him." The choice was made after our Lord had "continued all night in prayer to God." It took place on the summit of a mountain. After their election "they went into an house," where the Lord gave them a commission to "go to the lost sheep of the house of Israel." Of these men, Matthew and James the son of Alpheus, were publicans; Simon, Andrew, James the son of Zebedee, and John, were fishermen. Probably the rest of the apostles were of this latter occupation.

In addition to these excellent men, who, except Judas, that afterwards deserted them, were persons of solid sense, real piety, and active zeal Saul of Tarsus was chosen, with a view to the salvation of the gentiles, of whom he is called "the apostle." His education and talents qualified him for vindicating evangelical truth before heathen philosophers and priests, magistrates and sovereigns. To him the Lord Jesus said, Acts xxvi. 16. "I have appeared to thee, for this purpose, to make thee a minister and a witness, both of these things which thou hast seen, and of those things in the which I will appear unto thee; delivering thee from the people, and from the gentiles, to whom I now send thee." To the call of apostleship, Paul often lays his modest, but unequivocal claim. He introduces his epistles to the churches at Rome and at Corinth, with the words, "Paul, called to be an apostle," (or κλητος αποστολ⊙, a called apostle) To the churches at Ephesus and Colosse, he declares himself "an apostle of Jesus Christ, by the will of God." To Timothy he presents himself as "an apostle of Jesus Christ, by the commandment of God our Saviour, and Lord Jesus Christ." And having mentioned himself to the same evangelist as an ordained preacher and *apostle,* he adds, " I speak the truth in Christ; I lie not." He opens his address to the churches in Galatia with the assurance that he was an apostle, " not of men, neither by man, but by Jesus Christ, and God the Father, who raised him from the dead."

2. The *number* of the apostles was small. It was at first limited to twelve, perhaps in allusion to the patriarchs and tribes of Israel. This idea carries with it, to say the least, an air of probability, from the language of our Lord, Matt. xix. 28, ye shall sit on twelve thrones, judging the twelve tribes of Israel. See also Luke xxii. 30.—In the book of the Revelation of John, chap. xxi. 14. where a description is given of the heavenly Jerusalem, we are informed that " the wall of the city had twelve foundations, and in them the names of the twelve apostles of the Lamb." Such allusions were common under the economy of the Old Testament. Thus, Exodus xxiv. 4. Moses builded an altar under the hill, and twelve pillars, according to the twelve tribes of Israel.—In the days of Joshua, chap. iv. 8. " the children of Israel took up twelve stones out of the midst of Jordan, according to the number of the tribes of the children of Israel." Perhaps this arrangement was made to intimate that the apostles of Christ were worthy of patriarchal esteem; or perhaps it was done in a way of accommodation to Jewish feeling. When, however, the Jews rejected the gospel, the number was disregarded, and a new apostle raised up.

3. With the exception of Judas, in whose place Matthias was elected, they all appear to have been *real converts.* They were called disciples before their election to office. Our Lord says, " Ye are clean, but not all," alluding obviously to Judas Iscariot. Hence they are termed, Eph. iii. 5. " holy apostles," and, as we have seen, " apostles of the Lamb."

4 For the services they were to render in the world, and in the church of Christ, they were carefully *trained.* They were taught by their heavenly master how to pray. His public instructions were expounded to them in private. The natural ambition of the human heart was checked by the exhibition of a little child as their pattern, and especially by the example of their Lord himself. As a judicious general, agreeably to the manner adopted by Washington, often accustoms his men to skirmishing before they enter on the toils and dangers of a general battle, so our Lord sent out his disciples on minor expeditions, " two by two," before he commissioned them " to become witnesses of himself, not only in Judea and Samaria, but unto the uttermost parts of the earth." He breathed on them, and said, " Receive ye the Holy Ghost," and assured them of his presence " to the end of the world."

5. Something like diversity of *rank* is observable among the apostles. Paul informs us, Gal. ii. 9. that " James, Cephas, and John, seemed to be pillars." Such an idea seems implied 2 Corinthians xi. 5. where Paul says, " I suppose I was not behind the very chiefest apostles," and in the same epistle, chap. xii. 11. " In nothing am I behind the very chiefest apostles, though I be nothing." This superiority certainly involved in it nothing of a *papal* description. In fact, the friends of the church of Rome will find it a difficult task to reconcile these assertions of Paul, with their supposed supremacy of Peter.— Whether some of the apostles seemed chief, because of superiority in natural talent, in holy zeal, or in extended usefulness; or whether because their acts were more particularly delineated by Luke; or whether, because some, as Paul, James, Peter, John and Jude, were inspired to write new-testament scripture ; it is certain the apostles, in relation to the churches, affected no proud superiority : nor was any thing of the kind suspected by the brethren. When a difficulty existed in the church at Antioch relative to circumcision, they determined to send a deputation " to Jerusalem, to the *apostles* and *elders*, about this question " " When they were come to Jerusalem, they were received of the *apostles* and *elders*," " and the *apostles* and *elders* came to consider of this matter " And when the subject had undergone a full discussion, " it pleased the *apostles* and *elders*, *with the whole church*, to send chosen men of their company to Antioch, &c. See Acts xv. verses 2. 4. 22, 23 and xvi. 4.—Apostles themselves, with all their official eminence, obviously considered the independence of the churches of Christ as sacred and inviolable.

6. Certain *qualifications* appear to have been necessary to form the apostolic character. Paul speaks of " the seal" of an apostleship, 2 Cor. ix. 2. and of the " signs of an apostle," 2 Cor xii. 12. It seems to have been a requisite in an apostle, that he should have seen the Lord, 2 Cor. ix. 1 ; that he should have been able to perform miracles; to speak with tongues; and, especially, to convey spiritual gifts : which last prerogative was peculiar to the apostles. These miraculous powers were derived from the Son of God himself, and plainly demonstrate his proper divinity. Arnobius, who flourished at the beginning of the fourth century, in his treatise " Adversus gentes," makes a forcible appeal to heathen Rome, with this interesting idea before him; " alicuine mortalium Jupiter ille capitolinus hujusmodi potestatem dedit?" *Did your boasted Jupiter impart to any one such a power?* Moses and Elijah had the spirit of the Lord, but to another they could not communicate it. Num. xi. 2. Kings xi This was reserved for the divine Redeemer.

7. The apostles were men *inspired* of God. Their writings have a claim on our veneration and devout acceptance. They felt themselves, as men blest with a divine afflatus, standing on similar ground with the ancient patriarchs, see Jude, verse 12. compared with verse 17, and with the ancient prophets—See also Ephesians ii. 20. iii. 5. and 2 Peter iii. 1, 2. The words in this latter passage are remarkable—" I stir up your pure minds by way of remembrance: that ye may be mindful of the *words* which were spoken before by *the holy prophets*, and of *the commandment of us*, the *apostles of the Lord and Saviour.*" They spoke and acted under an entire persuasion that they were the subjects of inspiration, see 1 Cor ii 11. and vii. 40. 1 Thess. iv. 8. Each apostle who was engaged in writing, was prepared to say, as did Paul to the Corinthians, " If any man think himself to be a prophet, or spiritual, let him acknowledge that the things that I write unto you are the commandments of the Lord "—The apostles use language respecting themselves, as is evident from the introduction of their epistles, more forcible than any the prophets ever employed Peter places the writings of Paul on the same eminence with " the other scriptures," 2 epistle iii. 15, &c. The apostles gave charge that their epistles should be read; and pronounced a curse on the man that should dare to add to their words, or take away from them. Rev. xxii. 18, 19. The fathers, who cautiously distinguished between spurious and genuine productions, admitted without hesitation, the authority which the apostles claimed, as due to their writings; writings which, in the mercy of God, are preserved to us as a most precious and copious part of the oracles of heaven.

THE APOSTLES WERE MISSIONARIES.

DEPLORABLE, indeed, was the state of the world when the apostles, in the name of the Lord Jesus, commenced their holy labours. The nations were sunk in the depths of idolatry the most gross, and of superstition the most abominable. The gods they professed to adore, varying in power and office, and restricted to particular elements or nations, were exhibited in lights too human, too fallen, to secure from degradation and neglect the common dictates of morality. Mysteries were cherished too obscene for description. The heavenly orbs and departed heroes were worshipped with extravagant honours, and the absurd religion of pagan Rome was spread through the nations which her arms had vanquished. Religious observances, if they deserve the name, originated in the policy of states, as with the

Egyptians and Persians; or in an appetite for war, as with the Celts, the Germans, the Britons, and the Goths. If into the popular mythology a supreme deity were admitted, his character was dishonoured by his committing the foulest offences, and his authority ever considered as controllable by an eternal *necessity*.

For removing these evils the efforts of philosophers were feeble and unavailing. If occasionally they presented sublime ideas, more frequently they offered notions too subtile for general comprehension, or too absurd to secure belief. Some doubted whether gods existed at all; others supposed the doctrine of the immortality of the soul a fable, and a third class represented it as uncertain whether vice or virtue were more favourable to the best interests of man. The philosophers themselves were corrupted; and it were as vain to expect that corruption would purify itself, as that a fountain should rise higher than its source.

But " after that, in the wisdom of God, the world by wisdom knew not God, it pleased God by the foolishness of preaching to save them that believe." The apostles went forth without wealth, without arts, without influence. Sustained by divine qualifications, by the force of truth, and by the spirit of Christ, they accomplished wonders which in the history of our race are without a parallel. Unassuming in their manners, plain in their attire, with the idiom of Galilee, they were sent as sheep into a forest of wolves. The prejudices of the Jew, the craft of the heathen priesthood, the policy of rulers, and the bigotry of the people, were in array against them. It is said that in the arsenal of Bremen there are twelve pieces of cannon which are called the twelve apostles, as if to insinuate that by such means men are to be convinced. But the apostle of Christ knew nothing of weapons that are carnal. They employed such only as are mighty through God. To their hearers they could promise no earthly emoluments and honours. Contempt, persecution, confiscation, banishment, martyrdom, attended an acceptance of the gospel. Yet modest, fearless, incessantly they pursued their course, gloriously turning the world upside down, until Rome, the arbitress of the nations, bowed to the doctrine of the Cross. They preached the gospel on the very soil which had been stained by the blood of their master; entered the largest cities, disputed with the most insidious and malignant adversaries, and loved not their lives even unto the death.

Little more than a century had passed when Justin Martyr declared, "there is not a nation, either of Greek or barbarian, or of any other name, even of those who wander in tribes and live in tents, amongst whom prayers and thanksgivings are not offered to the Father and

Creator of the universe, by the name of the crucified Jesus." Tertullian, who succeeded Justin, says, " We were but of yesterday, and we have filled your cities, islands, towns and boroughs, the camp, the senate, and the forum." This victory of holy truth was the more surprising, inasmuch as the apostles and their fellow christians were every where calumniated. They were represented as enemies to government. Earthquakes, pestilences, calamities of any kind, were ever charged on them, and considered as indicating the anger of the gods that such monsters as Christians were permitted to live. Because they worshipped without temples, images, priests, and sacrifices, they were contemplated as a *class of atheists*, and such as killed them imagined themselves rendering a public service.

Had Mahomet, with his followers, been called to conflict with difficulties such as the apostles surmounted, his religion could never have prevailed. It must have been blasted in its bud. With all the advantages which family connexions, riches, assuasive manners, and courtly policy supplied him, only fourteen followers were the fruit of the first three years of his mission. The labour of seven years scarcely augmented his disciples to the number of a hundred. Perceiving no possibility of advancing his religion and reputation by the tedious process of persuasion, in the thirteenth year of his mission he declared that he had received an order from heaven to propagate the doctrines of the Koran by the terrours of the sword. To these he had recourse, and his system spread in proportion to his victories. To become Christians, was to become exposed to " deaths oft,"—to become a Mahomedan, was to avoid them.

In a succeeding number we propose following the apostles in their missionary tours.

TO THE EDITORS OF THE LATTER DAY LUMINARY.

Not many days ago an old German book fell into my hands, entitled Der Weg des Lebens, oder Kurtze und einfältige Unterweisung von der Natur und Eigenschafften der wahren Kraft der Gottseeligkeit—*The Way of Life; or a short and simple exposition on the nature and properties of the true power of Godliness.* The work was written originally by Salden, a divine of the city of Delft, in Holland; the same, it is presumed, who was afterwards of Utrecht, the minister of the church at the Hague, and author of several valuable treatises, as Otia Theologica, Concionator Sacer, De Libris variorum, eorumque usu, &c. It was translated, and printed at Amsterdam in the year 1667, for the purpose, as the translator informs us, of rousing the fallen piety of Germany. It seems to have been the production of a mind deeply imbued with evangelical sentiment, and much concerned for the souls of men. Presuming that your readers will listen with interest to a voice of piety and faithfulness, issuing from the age and the country in which this book was written, I have been induced to render into English, and send you a part of the 5th chapter. T.

THE INTERNAL PRINCIPLE OF HOLINESS.

WE come now to consider the internal principle from which a holy life must proceed. The good works of the truly pious, do, indeed, for the most part, spring forth outwardly; but the roots are concealed deep in the heart. There the tree is planted which produces the lovely fruit.

We will here only point out briefly what, and how necessary, this internal principle is, since all our goodness must arise from it, in order to be acceptable to God. It is

A gift bestowed through divine grace, by which a man, chiefly from internal hatred of sin, forsakes it, and from an internal inclination to holiness, earnestly endeavours to observe all spiritual good.

The internal cause is termed a gift bestowed through grace, rather than an act, to indicate that a person *may* be really pious, although he is not, at all times, excited to good works; when only the root,[*] the internal principle, remains constantly with him, as is often exemplified when a man off his guard, is assailed by temptation.

This internal principle is said to be in a man, that is, in the regenerate, and whether we say in his understanding, will, and affections, or in him, it comes to the same thing: It is imparted to the whole man by the sanctifying Spirit.[†]

It is added that, in virtue of this principle, he forsakes his iniquities from an internal aversion, and a hatred of them; that is, not only from fear of hell, or incited and constrained by the promises and threats of men, which arise from without, but because there is internally, in his heart, something which strives against and rejects the commission of sin.

It is stated that he observes spiritual good, from internal inclination to holiness,—not from any outward view which might present to him some advantage, but from an inward propensity which accords with what is right, and urges and impels him to it for its own sake. The regenerate and the unregenerate are often excited to the same good deed, the unregenerate, however, are prompted to it by outward advan-

---

[*] Matt. xiii. 11. [†] 1 Cor. vi. 20.

tage, honour, or worldly favour, but the regenerate by an internal love to God, and to every duty which he has commanded us to perform.*

Here it is to be remembered also, that we speak not of every kind of good, whether natural, or relating merely to outward morality, or to those amiable qualities which, among men, are good and valuable, but which may spring from a sort of natural instinct, and sense of what is becoming and unbecoming; † but here regard is had only to that which is spiritually good, and can be acceptable to God.

It is moreover affirmed, in the definition, that the pious do right, *chiefly* from hatred of sin and an internal inclination to holiness, in order to indicate that our meaning is not as if no outward causes ought to excite us to godliness, and as if no regard may ever be had to our spiritual nor bodily welfare, nor to the good opinion of others, nor to chastisement for sin; but we wish to show that these outward considerations must not be the only, nor the principal reasons why we lead a holy life. Those *principal* reasons must spring from something internal; but, at the same time, others may exist as *subordinate* ones, for God often excites by promises.

Permit us now to remark, that in the really pious, the forsaking of evil and the doing of good must spring, not from an outward motive, but from an internal spiritual principle.

This is clear from the apostle when he terms it an *inward man* and a *law of the mind*.‡ And this was the promise of God: "a new heart also will I give you, and a new spirit will I put within you."§

The view which we have presented must tend to the conviction of many of the apparently pious, who, because they have attended seriously to some external duties, and have not involved themselves in sins so grossly as others, often flatter themselves that they have attained to a high degree of holiness, while yet they have done all without having the requisite internal principle by which they should be excited and impelled. Such persons miserably deceive themselves, for the source of our regard to virtue, as may here be seen, must be not so much without, as within us. O that the following classes of men would lay this to heart!

1. Those who forsake sins, not from an internal loathing or hatred of them, but from some outward deterring considerations.

Many preserve a decorum in their language, because they are restrained from profaneness by the presence of a pious man. Many pay their debts because it would be dangerous to neglect it. Many

---

* Deut. vii. 9. † Rom. ii. 14, 15.
‡ Rom. vii. 22, 23. § Ezek. xxxvi. 26.

contribute for charitable purposes, not from conscience, but from shame of refusing. So also with regard to contentions and fighting, it is not the love of peace, nor a forgiving disposition, but the *penalty*, that often keeps the dagger in its sheath. And there is reason to believe that a thousand times more sinful acts are forsaken through fear of hell than through hatred of sin. But they who refrain from wickedness for no other reason than that they may not be eternally miserable, have not a genuine conversion, even though their deportment be irreproachable, for there is required not only an external forsaking, but a hearty loathing of what is sinful *

2. Those who, from an internal disrelish, forsake *some* sins but not *all*.

A man, from his natural constitution and habits, may not be inclined to some particular vices; and along with these he may also avoid many others, not because he has no internal disposition for them, but because they would be destructive of his reputation, or otherwise injurious, or because no occasion may have called forth his disposition. This goodness cannot be genuine: for while the man has an internal disrelish for some sins, and not for all, it is evident that he does not hate any of them *as sins*, but only so far as they are injurious to him, or as his circumstances have not prompted him to the commission of them Suicide is an awful crime; for which, however, all men by nature have in their hearts an abhorrence, but all men are not therefore truly pious. To commit an outrage upon one's self, in a less degree, is also a great sin, and yet the worst being in the universe has in himself a disrelish for it, because it is not to be supposed that he seeks his own hurt; but no man will therefore acknowledge him for a genuine Christian. Let no one then, although in this manner, from an internal principle, he avoids some sins, flatter himself that on this account he is to be reckoned among the children of God; for it affords no certainty of grace in any one. It may arise from terrour of natural conscience, and many other causes.

3. Those who break off from every vice, and maintain a religious course, but do it for the sake of external advantages.

Surely it is to be regretted that the precious and worthy Saviour cannot be valued so high as the vain things of this world. Reader! examine thyself diligently, whether thou belong to the class of which we are speaking If such be the fact, thou art no voluntary servant of the Lord, but only a hireling. While it is for the sake of gain and reward that thou followest him, thou dost not *give* him thy heart—thou *sellest* it.

---

* Rom. xiv. 9. Ps. cxix 163

4. Those who lead a religious life, not indeed for the sake of securing earthly benefits, which they profess to consider worthless, but for the sake of gaining heaven.

Many when they are asked why they lament and confess their sins, give alms, or perform other duties, betray their sad mistake when they reply, it is because they seek for heaven, and regard their happiness there. We will not say that the promise of heaven should afford us no excitement to godliness; but it is not this alone that must excite us. There must be something more powerful and of a higher character, namely, love and esteem of God, who is worthy in himself and for his own sake, to be served.* They, therefore, who do good, merely for the sake of heaven, and have no other object than their own eternal welfare, are in this respect no better than those of the preceding class; since they for their labour charge God not less than those, but much more, requiring of him heaven, while those perhaps are satisfied with a handful of earth.

TO THE EDITORS OF THE LATTER DAY LUMINARY.

The following piece is respectfully submitted to your disposal, with the hope, that, should it be judged worthy of publication, it will not be altogether useless to some of the young, engaged in the pursuit of science, into whose hands it may fall. T.

RELIGION NOT A HINDERANCE TO THE STUDENT.

TO deter men from a serious and timely attention to religion, every expedient has been tried which subtilty could devise. Every passion has been enlisted. All the corrupt propensities of human nature have been flattered and caressed. And, as if our evil inclinations were not sufficient, resort has been had to representations the most palpably erroneous. It has been asserted that religion tends to impede the student's progress in science and literature.

This assertion, coming as it does from those who claim for themselves all the light of reason and philosophy, is well calculated to influence the youth of brilliant talents. He contemplates with delight and admiration, the characters of those whose genius has thrown around them a dazzling lustre. High above the region of moral and political fluctuations, he sees them enthroned on the esteem of the world, and crowned with garlands, which, amidst the frost of a thousand winters, perpetually blossom and flourish. He discovers in that exalted station, many a vacancy yet to be filled. Encouraged by promising

* Eph. i. 4. Heb. vi. 10. Rom xiii. 10. Eph. vi. 5. 7 2 Cor v. 2.

abilities, and impelled by an ardent desire of commanding the admiration of his cotemporaries, and the applause and homage of posterity, he sighs for literary eminence. He resolves to make every exertion to gain some envied seat among the illustrious objects of his veneration. But when he thinks of his duty to God, and his obligation to obey the gospel, he is told that religion would blast his fairest hopes; that it is hostile to rational investigation; that it distracts the attention from scientific pursuits; and that it robs genius of its splendour.

Illiberal and erroneous as this account of Christianity must appear to every candid inquirer, it has had many supporters. It has been too much believed, and, among a certain class of persons, its influence has been great and lamentable.

So far, however, is religion from discouraging philosophical inquiry, that she holds out to it the strongest and most noble incentives. Which, we would ask, has the greatest inducement to investigation, he who views the operations of the material system as the contrivance of infinite wisdom and benevolence, or he who sees in that system no design, no superintending Providence, nothing but a huge mass of matter thrown together by chance, put in motion by chance, and by chance liable every moment to stop its movements, or to revert to primitive chaos, or to sink into non existence? What person has not stronger incitements to analyze the powers, and trace the workings of a mind destined to immortality, than to perplex himself concerning any number of mere animal instincts which are soon to perish for ever? Who would not deem it more important to establish rules for the regulation of beings on whose present conduct depends eternal bliss or endless wo, than of creatures the consequences of whose actions can be, at most, but temporary? Religion, it is true, never attempts to teach earthly science. Her object is infinitely more grand and important. But she appeals to reason for proof of her divine origin. Many truths, indeed, she discloses, which human sagacity could never have ascertained. But in every declaration of hers, which is not absolutely *above* their province, reason and conscience echo to her voice.

Should it, at length, be admitted, that the scriptures are not at variance with the language of enlightened reason, still the votary of science is told that a devout and scrupulous attention to their injunctions, will so divert him from his studies as to be detrimental to his progress.

To prove the erroneousness of this opinion we might only point to those men who have the most enlarged the boundaries of human knowledge, and ask, were they not disciples of Christ? But, without adverting to those brightest luminaries that ever shone upon the regions of science, we are willing to rest our arguments upon the natural effect which true religion has upon the mind. To say nothing of its preventing all those excessive gratifications of the senses, which are fatal alike to health of body and vigour of intellect, what is its immediate effect upon those corroding anxieties and restless passions which distract the thoughts? It subjects them to the dominion of reason. By moulding the will to a cordial acquiescence in the Divine government, it tranquillizes the soul, and prepares it for the most complicated and abstruse investigations. Since frequent relaxation from study is absolutely necessary, the time requisite to be spent in religious exercises, is by no means lost. Such exercises, by calling off the mind from all perplexing subjects, and diffusing over it a dignified serenity, enable the Christian to resume his studies with fresh vigour and delight. His motives to diligent exertion must certainly be more powerful than any which can actuate the irreligious. The present world, viewed by itself, he indeed looks upon as vain and transitory. But considered as the place allotted to prepare for an endless state of existence, it rises in his estimation to unspeakable importance. Every day is big with everlasting consequences. He feels himself urged to activity by the most tremendous considerations, while he hears as the voice of God, " Whatsoever thy hand findeth to do, do it with thy might." He is sensible of duties devolving upon him which are intimately connected with the dearest temporal, as well as with the eternal interests of himself and of his fellow men. Emoluments and fame, alluring as they are in themselves, he regards only as affording him the means of becoming extensively useful, and of gaining more noble objects. What others view as the ultimate reward of their labours, are with him inferior considerations, compared with the great object of his pursuits. He looks beyond the wreath that entwines the brow of the learned. He looks beyond the wealth and the applause of the world. He elevates his thoughts to the grandeur of his destiny, and seeks the approbation of his almighty Redeemer.

If, then, it appears that religion is not hostile, but friendly to scientific research, and that, instead of diverting the student from his pursuits, it is admirably adapted to purify and strengthen his mind, and excite him to industry, we have now only to inquire into the justness of the charge that it robs genius of its splendour.

The effect here alleged, it is easy to perceive, must be produced either by diminishing the range of thought, or by blunting the sensibilities of the soul. The first supposition is too palpably absurd to be seriously maintained. Religion presents scenes too grand for imagination to grasp. It furnishes ideas which not only fill, but expand and exalt the sublimest conceptions, and will continue to expand and exalt them for ever. It adds immensity to our prospects, and infinity to our existence. It is also so far from tending to blunt the sensibilities of the soul, that it has precisely the contrary effect. By its influence the obdurate heart is softened, and the tenderest sympathies are awakened. Friends and companions, and the whole human species, appear more important in the scale of being; and, of course, the social and benevolent affections become more ardent. The mind is prepared for enjoying, in the highest degree, all the pleasures of taste. The works of nature, by being associated with 'the first good and the first fair,' appear with new beauties and peculiar charms. The passions, divested of all that is hateful, are not destroyed, but directed to proper objects; and, gathering strength from whatever is beautiful, affecting, or sublime, they greatly conduce to that ardour of feeling and glow of devotion, which never fail to exalt the natural powers of genius.

Examples in confirmation of these remarks, were it necessary, might be adduced; for they are innumerable. Many of them must be familiar to every well-informed and reflecting mind. A vast multitude rise at once to the view, eminent for religious devotion, and for splendour of talents. When this is remembered in connexion with the fact that the whole number of real Christians has ever been very small, in comparison with the millions that have been of a different character, who does not perceive an evidence of the ennobling nature of genuine piety? And, with the considerations before us which have now been presented, who can doubt, that, whenever we find Christians of but inferior parts or attainments, we ought to ascribe their inferiority to some other cause than the tendency of religion?

REVIEW OF NEW PUBLICATIONS.

The Conversion of the World: or the Claims of Six Hundred Millions, and the Ability and Duty of the Churches respecting them Second edition. Andover: printed for the American Board of Commissioners for Foreign Missions. Flagg & Gould. 1818. pp. 94.

THE *conversion of the world* is an object which cannot fail of being dear to the heart of every Christian; for he perceives how needful it is, and he believes the declarations of his Bible. Even in the darkest days that ever hung over the church, it was a theme of delightful anticipation to the prayerful and devout. The distant prospect, seen only by the eye of faith, served to support them under their trials, and animate them in their labours. But could those holy men, for a moment, have been brought forward to the present period, and been allowed to see the way prepared, by a long series of mighty political concussions, for the general spread of the gospel,—the facility with which religious information may now be communicated,—the channels now open for the combination of christian efforts,—the light which has already been diffused,—and the success which has already attended the commencement of exertions, with what zeal would they have been inflamed! It would surely have been a matter of astonishment to them, had they found the great body of professed Christians, at such an hour, we will not say, doing *nothing*, but doing only *little* towards obeying the command of their LORD.

With the advantages which we possess, and the motives which are placed before us, it were reasonable to expect that, at this late period, we would not withhold the requisite exertions for sending the gospel to *every creature;* that we would not content ourselves with having sent it to a few individuals, or a few provinces, and defer the glorious work of evangelizing all the nations to a distant age,—without such an excuse as will bear examination when we, and the millions whom we leave destitute of all the temporal blessings of Christianity, and ignorant of the only way of eternal life, shall appear before our common Judge. We would not be understood as limiting the Almighty. While we maintain that it is only through Jesus Christ that any of the human family are ever saved, we do not deny that the pardoning mercy of God may, in some instances, be manifested to individuals in a land where the gospel has never been proclaimed. But from what we know of heathen nations, as well as from the holy scriptures, we have the utmost reason to consider such instances as rare. Every candid, reflecting mind, must acknowledge that it should be our concern, not to determine in what cases the omniscient Ruler may bestow his grace without the ordinary means, but to employ the means which he has been pleased to establish and reveal to us for the salvation of men. He might justly have left us all to the consequences of our sins. Most manifestly he had a right to choose the time and the method of granting what no one could demand. He has ordained the *Gospel* 'the power of God unto salvation to every one that believeth;' and he has committed it to us with the command that it be preached among all nations. If now any are neglected, the fault is ours—not HIS.

Under impressions like these, the little work whose title is placed at the head of this article, has been perused by us with a lively interest.

It possesses special claims to our regard. It is not the project of idle theorists, but of men who, in an eminent degree, are acting upon their own principles, and wearing out their lives in the cause for which they plead. It is the joint production of the Rev. Messrs *Gordon Hall* and *Samuel Newell*, American missionaries at Bombay, in India; and it is addressed to the American churches and Christians, without reference to any particular denomination. It consists of four Parts. The first maintains the following proposition: "*It is the duty of the churches to send forth preachers of the gospel in such numbers as to furnish the means of instruction and salvation to the whole world.*"

The authors commence thus:

"How comprehensive and how rational is that petition in the Lord's prayer, 'Thy kingdom come, thy will be done, on earth as it is in heaven' What more could the most exalted piety ask? what more could the most enlarged benevolence desire? It includes the glory of God and the best good of all men. For when God shall reign on earth as he does in heaven, then will he appear in his glory, and then will there be peace on earth, good will among men But at present how deplorable is the condition of mankind, and how is the God of heaven dishonoured in this revolted world! Idolatry and superstition prevail over the greatest part of the human race The fairest portions of the globe are covered with Egyptian darkness, filled with wretchedness, and polluted with crimes

"The gospel of Christ is the remedy, which the wisdom and mercy of God have provided for the disorders of our fallen world. It is a sovereign remedy Wherever it has yet prevailed, it has visibly meliorated the condition of men It has rescued whole nations from the gross ignorance, and the cruel rites of idolatry, and it has purified great multitudes of successive generations, from the pollutions of sin, and prepared them for the holy society of heaven. How desirable it is that the benign influence of this religion should be extended over all the nations of the earth! How desirable that the renovating and saving power of the gospel should be experienced as extensively as the ravages of sin have been spread in our world!

"To this end the Son of God was born; for this end he lived, and died, and revived, and rose from the dead. Having commanded his apostles to go and teach all nations, he ascended to heaven, there to reign till all the earth should be subjected to his authority. But though such is the benevolent design of the gospel; though in condescending to be born, the Saviour designed to destroy the works of the devil, and to recover all the nations of the earth from idolatry, sin, and wretchedness; it is a melancholy fact, that nearly eighteen hundred years have passed away since his gospel was first promulgated by himself and his apostles, and yet a small proportion only of the human race have received the heavenly message How shall we account for this fact? If Christianity is from heaven, why is it not the religion of the world? If it is the only remedy for the miseries under which the human race have groaned for six thousand years—if Jesus Christ is the only name under heaven given among men by which they can be saved—why do not all men every where invoke that sacred name?

"The answer to these inquiries will readily occur to every reflecting mind 'How shall they call on him, in whom they have not *believed?*—and how shall they believe in him of whom they have not *heard?*—and how shall they hear without a *preacher?*—and how shall they preach except they be *sent?*' Has the gospel been preached to all nations? We know it has not. We have then a satisfactory reason why all nations have not believed and obeyed the gospel We might as reasonably expect the harvest without sowing the seed, as look for the conversion of the world without first preaching the gospel to all nations.

"In the scripture as now cited, we are plainly taught that the gospel is to be propagated in the world, not by miraculous power, but in the ordinary way of instruction;—that the particular method of instruction which God has ordained for the conversion of the world is preaching,—*and that it is the duty of Christians to send forth preachers of the gospel in such numbers as to furnish the means of instruction and salvation to the whole world*

"That the gospel is to be propagated by instruction will be readily admitted by all. But there may be some diversity of opinion as to the kind of instruction to be pursued; whether it should be the education of children in the principles of Christianity, or the distribution of the Scriptures, or what is emphatically called the preaching of the word. Some may be disposed to place a greater dependance on one of these methods, and some on another. They are all doubtless the legitimate means of disseminating the gospel, and will each produce the greatest effect when they all proceed together, and are duly proportioned to each other. But every attentive reader of the word of God must be convinced that the greater stress is there placed on preaching. When our Lord commanded that his kingdom should be established in all the world, the means which he pointed out for effecting the object was *preaching* the gospel to every creature; and St. Paul tells us, that when the world by *wisdom* knew not God, it pleased God by the *foolishness of preaching* to save them that believe. It is fully implied in the declaration, that God has been pleased to *appoint* what the wisdom of this world esteems folly, viz. *the preaching of the gospel, as the grand instrument and means* of salvation in all ages, even to the end of the Christian dispensation." p. 5—7.

In a subsequent paragraph it is added:

"Preachers are wanted, in the first place, to call the attention of the ignorant and careless heathen to the word of God;—secondly, to direct his mind to such parts of the sacred volume as are best adapted to his capacity and circumstances;—thirdly, to make explanations where the sense is not obvious, and finally, to enforce the truths of Scripture by argument and persuasion. Without Christian teachers, an indiscriminate distribution of the Bible in heathen and Mahometan countries would be but little better than throwing it away. Some solitary instances of conversion there have been in heathen and Mahometan lands, which were occasioned by reading the Bible only—*but there is no instance on record of a nation being evangelized by the Bible without the preaching of the gospel*

"Bibles should by all means be circulated extensively among the heathen, but ministers of the gospel should be sent along with them. Thousands of Bibles may be sent with every preacher of the gospel, but they should not be sent alone. Sending teachers without the Bible was the errour of the church of Rome; let it not be the errour of Protestants to send the Bible without preachers." p 8.

The view which is here presented appears to us such a one as the apostles would have approved. The case of the eunuch mentioned in the eighth chapter of the Acts, will doubtless be recollected by our readers as affording a happy illustration; and many others of a similar kind, that have occurred in modern times, were it necessary, might be adduced.

The authors proceed to another topic.—

"If christian teachers are to be sent forth, it is obvious that the christian churches must send them. We cannot suppose that the *world* will take up the business of propagating the religion of Christ, or that ministers are to expect a special commission from heaven directing them to go to the heathen, nor can we suppose that individuals will, of their own accord, and at their own discretion, go and preach to the heathen, if they should do this, they would not answer the description which the apostle gives of christian missionaries, viz persons that are *sent*.

"As to the number of preachers, the same reasons which prove the duty of sending one, equally prove the duty of sending as many as are requisite to fulfil the command of Christ, to preach the gospel to every creature." p. 9.

It is obvious, from other parts of the pamphlet, that the authors, in speaking here of the duty of Christians, would not be understood as overlooking our ability. They would not be understood as maintaining that we should erect a vast edifice instantly; but that the same reasons which make it our duty to lay one stone, make it our duty to *complete* the edifice with all the rapidity in our power.—They proceed to observe:

"If we send half a dozen missionaries to a country where there are as many millions of souls, we are too apt to imagine that we have discharged our duty to that country—we have sent them the gospel. The fact however is, we have only sent the gospel to a few individuals in that nation. The great body of the people never hear of our missionaries or the religion they teach. The thing that Christ commands is to preach the gospel to every creature,—not merely to a few individuals in every nation.

"Let us not deceive ourselves by general expressions and vague notions. Let us look at the simple fact. The missionary goes to some part of the heathen world,—he selects a town or village, the best adapted to his object, and there he fixes his residence. When he has learned the language of the people, he begins to preach to the inhabitants of the place where he resides, and he makes occasional excursions to the distance of forty or fifty miles around him. If he is such a man as Brainerd or Swartz, perhaps, in a populous country some hundred thousands may occasionally hear his voice in the course of his ministry; but his labours are principally confined to a few thousand.

"That the number of missionaries at present employed in preaching the gospel among unevangelized nations is nothing like an adequate supply, will be evident from a moment's attention to the following general survey.

"Let the population of the globe be computed at eight hundred millions.

Asia	500,000,000
Africa	90,000,000
Europe	180,000,000
America	30,000,000
Total	800,000,000

"The number who bear the Christian name throughout the whole world may be ascertained with a sufficient degree of accuracy for the present purpose.

"Europe, we know, contains the greatest part of the Christian population of the globe. After deducting about three millions of Mahometans, we may allow the whole remaining population of that quarter of the globe to be Christian, in a very general acceptation of that term.

"In the United States of America there are about eight millions that may also be reckoned Christians. The Christian population of the European possessions in North and South America is not accurately determined, but it probably is not far from ten millions. If we include Abyssinia in the list of Christian nations, we may allow about three millions of Christians for the continent of Africa.

"The late Rev. H. Martyn, one of the English chaplains in Bengal, computed the Christians of all denominations in India and Ceylon at nine hundred thousand. If we allow one hundred thousand more for the islands in the Indian Ocean, and one million for Western Asia, we shall have a total in the whole of Asia, of two millions.

"According to the foregoing estimate the Christian population of the world will stand as follows:

In Asia	2,000,000
Africa	3,000,000
Europe	177,000,000
America	18,000,000
In all the world	200,000,000

"This amount, deducted from the whole population of the earth, leaves us six hundred millions of the human race, to whom Christ has not yet been preached. If this calculation is at all correct, it demonstrates the melancholy fact, that in eighteen hundred years only about one-fourth part of the world has been evangelized, and that, if the progress of the gospel should be no more rapid in future, than it has been hitherto, it will not be spread through the world in five thousand years to come. How distressing must this prospect be to every benevolent mind, to all who have been taught to say from the heart, ' *Thy kingdom come*' Let us hope, however, and let us pray, that God in mercy to our miserable and guilty world, may cut short the reign of sin, and speedily establish the holy and peaceful kingdom of his Son over all the earth." p 9—11.

In answer to the inquiry, "What exertions is the church of Christ now making for the advancement of the kingdom of her Lord?" it is replied:

"The number of missionaries actually labouring for the conversion of six hundred millions of people is only about three hundred and fifty in all the world, that is, one preacher of the gospel to one million seven hundred thousand souls.

"The following is a pretty accurate list of all the missionaries in the world, who have been sent by the churches in Europe and America to preach the gospel to the heathen not including native missionaries, or persons converted from heathenism, now preachers of the gospel

1 ASIA.

Danish missionaries in India	7
Baptist missionaries, Do	20
From the London Missionary Society, in India and China	22
From Do. in the islands of Otaheite and Eimeo	16
Wesleyan Methodist missionaries in India	6
From the Church Missionary Society in India	10
From the American Board of Commissioners for Foreign Missions, Do.	9
From the American Baptist Board of Foreign Missions, Do.	4
From the Edinburgh Missionary Society, in Russian Asia	6
United Brethren in Do.	2
Total in Asia	102

2. AFRICA.

The United Brethren have	21
The London Missionary Society	30
The Church Missionary Society	8
Wesleyan Methodists	2
Total in Africa	61

3. AMERICA.

In the West Indies, Wesleyan Methodists	40
The London Society	5
Baptist Society, (England)	3
The United Brethren have in the West Indies	63
Do South America	15
Do. Greenland	19
Do. Labrador	28
Do. Canada and United States	10
American Board of Commissioners &c to the Aborigines	4
Other missionaries from different societies	7
Total in America	194

America	194
Africa	61
Asia	102
Total in the world	357

"Six hundred millions of the human race who want the gospel, and less than four hundred missionaries to impart it to them! It is thus, O ye disciples of Jesus, that you repay the debt of gratitude, which you owe to your Redeemer! He died for you and all mankind. He called you by his grace, delivered you from sin and hell, restored you to God, and inspired you with the blessed hope of everlasting life. Now he calls you to his service, and requires that henceforth you should live, not to yourselves, but to him, who loved you and gave himself for you, and washed you from your sins in his own blood. He confers upon you the singular honour the high privilege of going as heralds before him into all the world, to proclaim his approaching reign, and call the nations to repentance. And is it so, that among the millions that bear the Saviour's name, only three or four hundred can be found who are willing to accept of this service? It cannot be. There are, there must be, if the gospel is not a fable, if religion is not a dream, there must be thousands, in different parts of the Christian world, who are ready, whenever the churches shall call them forth, to embark for any part of the world, to spend their lives in preaching the gospel to the heathen, who are ready and willing 'to endure all things for the elect's sake, that they also may obtain the salvation that is in Christ Jesus with eternal glory.'" p. 12—14.

Allowing only one missionary to every twenty thousand souls in heathen countries, the writers state the claims of the different quarters of the globe as follows:

Heathen population in		Number of missionaries required.
Asia	498,000,000	24,900
Africa	87,000,000	4,350
Europe	3,000,000	150
America	12,000,000	600
Total	600,000,000	30,000." p. 15.

As a reason why the number is rated so low they add:

"We may observe that one foreign missionary to twenty thousand souls may be considered a tolerable supply, because that, wherever the gospel is preached and its power experienced, native preachers will be raised up on the spot to aid the missionaries, and ultimately to take the work off their hands.

"The Danish missionaries on the Coromandel coast have raised up many native preachers, who have adorned the Christian profession, and have been able ministers of the New Testament

"The Baptist missionaries in India have, at the present time, about fifty preachers in their connexion, who have been converted and raised up in the country. They are of various descriptions, Europeans, halfcasts, Portuguese, Armenians, and converted Hindoos. The number of country preachers in this mission is double the number of the missionaries sent from England. As the work advances, the proportion of country preachers will probably increase." p. 16.

The second Part of the publication before us, maintains that

"*The churches are able to furnish the requisite number of missionaries for evangelizing all nations.*"

The authors take it for granted, that, in all Christendom, there are not less than 30,000 suitable young men who might be called to this work. They assign one-fourth to the American churches, and three-fourths to the European. They reckon the number of churches in America four thousand,—which, doubtless, is a very low estimate, and the whole number of communicants six hundred thousand. And they propose that each church, possessing on an average, according to the calculation, a hundred and fifty members, furnish one missionary, and have him in readiness to enter the field in seven years, that time being allowed for his preparatory studies. Then, the American churches furnishing 4,000, and the European 12,000, the whole number furnished every seven years would be 16,000. And, even supposing that one-third of them die, or leave the work in seven years from the time of entering it, two-thirds in fourteen, and the whole in twenty-one, still, it is stated, that from accurate calculation, it appears there would be at the end of fourteen years, more than 26,000, and at the end of twenty-one years, more than 30,000, actually in the field.

"Here then," observe the authors, "is a plan, which, if entered upon immediately, and executed with fidelity, would, in less than twenty-one years, furnish such a number of missionaries as would be, in a good degree, a supply for evangelizing the whole world! Yes, this whole supply of labourers, vast as it may seem, might be furnished in so short a time that many who are now exhorted to aid the object, might live to see it fully accomplished. And what would they see? They would behold thirty thousand ambassadors of Christ, scattered over the face of the whole earth, preaching the word of life to every creature. What would this be but the millennium, that long expected day, when 'the way of the Lord shall be known upon earth, and his saving health among all nations.' and when, 'from the rising of the sun even unto the going down of the same, the name of Jehovah shall be great among the gentiles, and in every place incense shall be offered to his name, and a pure offering.' O glorious day! and glorious that work which is to usher it in!" p. 18, 19.

In subsequent paragraphs, the writers, proceeding to a more particular calculation, introduce it thus:

"It is granted that there are suitable men enough, if they were disposed to go, and if the churches were able to send them to the work. Now there are three ways in which Christians might furnish the requisite pecuniary aid, without depriving themselves of their ease, their comforts, or the increase of their wealth. These are *first*, a trifling increase of their industry; *secondly*, a very little more frugality and self-denial, in their manner of living; and *thirdly*, by appropriating a small part of their annual income to the object.

"The *first* of these resources would be abundantly sufficient for preparing the missionaries, in the first instance, for the field. But can it be necessary to say a single word to show, that one hundred and fifty Christians, with hearts glowing with gratitude for their own redemption, and animated with desires and hopes of extending the same redemption to others, and for this purpose conscientiously uniting in the support of *one* youth,—can a single word be necessary to show that they would find it an easy task?

"Should each individual of the hundred and fifty, add that little to his accustomed diligence in business, which would in the course of a year gain him one dollar, that would amount to one hundred and fifty dollars annually in each church. This sum, in ordinary cases, would be a comfortable support for a young man training up in that rigid economy and self-denial which the missionary life demands." p. 20.

It is suggested, and certainly it ought not to be forgotten, that if some churches are poor, and cannot do so much, others are rich, and can do more. Besides, some of the persons called to this work, would be able to support themselves in preparing for it, and some might be prepared in a shorter time than seven years.

Neither ought it to be forgotten that, in the calculation, no account is made of assistance from any who are not members of churches. But many generous individuals of this description, did professed Christians but move forward, would, no doubt, contribute largely for the object; so that the burden upon the churches would be much, very much alleviated. This remark, our readers will perceive, is applicable also to the calculation for meeting other expenses, to which the authors proceed:

"Three ways have been mentioned by which Christians may raise money for the support of missions. The first of these has been considered as devoted to the preparation of the missionaries for their work, and the avails of the other two may be appropriated to their subsequent support.

"Let therefore the inquiry now be made, how much money, for the support of missions, might Christians annually raise, *first* by a little more frugality and self denial in their mode of living? and *secondly*, by consecrating a small part of their annual income to the object?

"Frugality and self-denial in the mode of living, are here considered in application to decoration of buildings, to dress, servants, and equipage, sugars, teas, wines, liquors, and other luxuries, and also to amusements. Millions are annually expended on these things, and they are carried to that extent which causes not only an immense waste of money, but which is also injurious both to soul and body. So generally is this the case, that there is scarcely a family, nay, scarcely an individual, in the country, who, by a little pious frugality and self-denial in the use of these costly luxuries, might not thereby annually save a considerable sum, and at the same time find it for his real comfort and benefit in the present life. And if his faith for a moment transports him forward to the day of judgment, what does he behold? At the right hand of God he sees a vast multitude, collected from the ends of the earth. How came they there? He now learns, that while himself was upon the earth, he, with many others, conscientiously moderated their use of the elegancies and luxuries of life, and employed these pious savings in sending abroad that gospel, by which this multitude believed in Christ and have entered into life.

"Can such, he exclaims, can such be the fruits of those little, momentary self-denials which were made, while in the flesh! O, blessed self-denials! and blessed be that grace which disposed me to make them! How infinitely does this object transcend, in magnitude, the abolition of the slave trade, an object for which so many thousands of all ranks in England cheerfully abandoned, 'as a moral duty,' the use of luxuries to which they had always been accustomed!

"But with all the claims of this object on the one hand, and the great number of articles of living, in which expense might so easily be saved on the other, suppose that each individual Christian, on an average, saves, in the course of a year, no more than two dollars for the missionary treasury this alone, the number of Christians being 600,000, would give an annual sum of 1,200,000 dollars for the support of missionaries in the field." p. 22—24.

Reckoning the annual income of each Christian, on an average, at twenty dollars, or that he gains this sum yearly above what he expends, the authors propose that he devote one-tenth of it to the missionary cause. The amount thus raised would also be 1,200,000 dollars. This, added to the sum before provided, would give annually for the support of missionaries, 2,400,000 dollars, an amount abundantly sufficient: It

—"would give to each of the four thousand missionaries, who would be in the field the first seven years, an annual salary of six hundred dollars. It would give more than three hundred and fifty dollars to each of the six thousand six hundred and sixty-seven, who would be in the field in the second seven years, and it would give annually three hundred and twenty dollars to each of the seven thousand five hundred missionaries, which is that part of the whole thirty thousand which falls to the share of the American churches." p. 25

With regard to the sufficiency of the sum, the authors observe:

"In the *first* place, it may well be hoped, that the smallest salary just stated, which the annual missionary revenue gives even to the whole number of missionaries, would, on an average, be equal to their support. This may be hoped, for two reasons. And *first*, because many missionaries would go to those places, where living is so simple and cheap, and where the highest success of their mission would require them so far to labour as agriculturists, mechanics, and artisans, or as teachers and translators, as almost entirely to support themselves. The difference by which their support would fall short of the average salary, being appropriated to the maintenance of missionaries in more expensive stations, would, probably, make the average sum of three hundred and twenty dollars to each man, sufficient for the support of the whole.

"The *second* reason for supposing that this sum may be sufficient, is the probability that, as yet, the best system of economy, in the management of Protestant missions, has not been adopted. It will always be a solemn duty, to seek the most economical methods of conducting missions. And while we inquire whether the churches are willing to contribute according to the self-denying spirit of the gospel, it becomes us also to inquire whether missionaries are willing to labour in the same self-denying spirit. No doubt, the deeper the churches drink of the cup of self-denial at home, the more effectually their missionaries abroad will imbibe the same heavenly spirit.

"Were that spirit, which excited, animated and comforted the apostles and first Christians, in their unequalled self-denials, labours and sufferings, were that same spirit now duly to pervade the churches, what wonders it would soon produce both among missionaries in the field and their patrons at home! How would the latter rejoice to give 'the half of their goods!' And how eagerly would the former go forth and preach the word of life, though they should be obliged to labour with their own hands, and receive from others but little, or nothing, for their support!

"How cheerfully would all unite in doing this, if there were no other way of sending the great salvation through the world! And how pure, how exalted would be their consolation from the reflection, that in all they do and suffer in this cause, they are only treading in the footsteps of apostles and martyrs, of primitive Christians, and of the Saviour himself! As a motive for giving, what a noble pattern do Christians behold in the first believers under the gospel! and as an example for missionaries in their labours, what do they not behold in the poverty, the toils, and the self-denials of Jesus and his apostles!'" p. 25, 26.

"It is maintained, however, that the missionary's usefulness will generally be in a great measure proportionate to the pecuniary aid, which he receives in prosecuting the various methods of advancing christian knowledge among the ignorant.

"Again, to show that the missionary revenue, as before estimated, would prove an adequate support for the number of missionaries, we may consider, that from the time the plan is adopted, seven years are allowed for the preparation of the first four thousand missionaries, consequently, none of the annual income of 2,400,000 dollars, for the support of missionaries in the field, would be expended during these seven years, but would go on accumulating, and might be funded for future use. Besides, after the first four thousand enter the field, for the seven following years the income would exceed the salaries of the missionaries, and still farther increase the fund in reserve.

"But what is still more, from the commencement of the work, to the time when the final number of missionaries to be supported would be in the field, is twenty-one years. And this is about the period in which the population of the country doubles. If then the number of the pious should increase only in proportion to the general increase of the population, their number would be doubled also, and consequently, those resources for the support of missions, which have been named, would every way be doubled.

"In these calculations, no account has been made of legacies, private donations, or public contributions. Might it not reasonably be supposed, that these would add very considerable to the missionary funds? Nor has any calculation been made on the ground of *faith!* Ought not this to be done? Did Christians set their hearts on the conversion of the whole world, and humbly and earnestly exert themselves to accomplish it, would not a blessing from Heaven come upon them? Would not He, who loves Zion with an everlasting love;—He, who sends forth his sun, and his rain, and causes the earth to yield her increase;—He, who holds the winds in his fists, and breaks or preserves the ships of Tarshish as he pleases; would He not bless them in their basket and in their store, and cause their wealth to come in like a flowing stream? If there were in his people a heart to build up Jerusalem, the beloved city of God, would He not bestow on them abundant means for doing it? Ought not his people to cultivate a faith in Him, as strong as this? Indeed, if such a faith is not absolutely required of us, what can be the meaning of such promises as these?—'There is that scattereth and yet increaseth. The liberal soul shall be made fat, and he that watereth shall be watered also himself.' Yea, when the common acclamation among the churches is, 'Let the people praise Thee, O God! let all the people praise Thee. O, let the nations be glad, and sing for joy.' And when, with a corresponding zeal, they strive to make his way known upon earth, and 'his saving health among all nations' 'Then shall the earth yield her increase; and God, even our own God, shall bless us.'

"It should also be considered, that this great demand for missionaries from foreign countries, must not be contemplated as a permanent demand. So far as Christianity gains a footing in any country, in the same degree will that country furnish its own ministers and the means of their support. It costs the heathen nations more to support idolatry than it would to support Christianity. Consequently, as fast as they become converted they will be abundantly able to support the Christian religion among them, independent of foreign aid. Hence, when Christians enter fully into the great work of evangelizing the world, duly trusting in God for the success of their exertions, they may anticipate the time, as near at hand, when those pecuniary resources of the heathen, which have been so long prostituted to the support of their senseless idols, will be consecrated to the support of the holy religion of Jesus, and when the burden, which now lies upon the Christian churches, will thus happily be removed." p. 27—29.

According to the very highest calculation which the authors have presented, our readers will perceive that the annual sum required of each professed Christian, on an average, (the deficiency of the poor being supplied by the abundance of the rich,) is only five, or at most six dollars, for completing the whole work. They will also perceive that this sum would, in fact, be more than sufficient at the commencement, and would be constantly decreasing as the work advances; that the calculation, too, has been made upon supposition that nothing is received from any but members of churches, and yet, that, should the whole burden fall upon these, they might easily sustain it, would each add so much to his accustomed industry as to gain one dollar annually, diminish so much from needless expenses in living as to save two dollars, and devote, besides, only one-tenth part of his income, or of the increase of his property.

This sum, a small one indeed, in comparison with the vast magnitude and the infinite importance of the work, would, as we have already intimated, be more than sufficient. Suppose, therefore, we deduct from it two dollars, the part to be derived from the third source. The whole amount still furnished for the support of missionaries actually sent forth, would be 1,200,000 dollars annually. A small part only of this would be needed for immediate use. The remainder would be secured as a fund, increasing and in readiness, and do much towards the support of the four thousand and their successors, who, according to the calculation, might be prepared to enter upon their labours after the first seven years.

Having followed our authors thus far in the general estimates which they have given, we cannot forbear now to call the attention of the Baptist churches in particular to this momentous subject. We are far from believing that the conversion of the world is to be accomplished by 'an arm of flesh,' or by human wisdom. We know it is the energies of the Holy Spirit that must rouse the people of God to prayer and exertions, that must excite and impel the future heralds of salvation to the sacred work, and that must make their labours effectual. But we know, too, that exertion is the duty of Christians; and were they, with becoming reliance on God, to perform what devolves upon them for the extension of the Redeemer's kingdom, we have no reason to fear that the part which he has reserved to himself will be neglected. In this age of wonders, with the Saviour's commission in our hands, and his promise before us, it is for us to "expect great things, and attempt great things."

There are of the Baptist denomination in the United States, not less than 2680 churches, containing at the lowest estimate, about 180,000 members,—nearly one-third of the members allowed by our authors, in the preceding calculations, to the churches of all the denominations. But, considering that our wealth does not bear an equal proportion to our numbers, let it be supposed that only one-fourth part of what devolves upon the American churches belongs to the Baptists—and we hope our brethren will not be willing to have a less share in the glorious work of evangelizing the world—then one thousand suitable persons are to be furnished by our denomination for the missionary field in the first seven years. The number would be supplied in the first instance, were only one to be selected and called forth from every 180 members. And they, with their successors, would be supported, both in their preparatory studies and in their future labours, were each member, on an average, to contribute annually two dollars, one for the former object, and one for the latter. Indeed, according to the calculation which we have made, the sum falls somewhat short of this, it lacking more of one dollar for the former object than exceeding it for the latter; but, that the estimate may not be too small, and for the sake of conveniency, we say *two dollars*.

Now suppose each member, in the course of the year, to gain by a little additional industry, fifty cents, suppose him to save by dispensing with a few useless, not to say pernicious luxuries, one dollar, and, reckoning his income only ten dollars, suppose him to raise by devoting only a twentieth part of it, fifty cents more....How easily, in most cases, might this be done! The burden of the poor might be and ought to be lightened, and in some instances entirely sustained, by those members who are capable of doing more than is here proposed, "that there may be equality." (2 Cor. viii. 14.)

Besides, we may safely reckon that for every communicant there are among us three other persons at least, who are willing and equally able to assist in supporting the missionary cause. The average sum, then, required of each member, is in fact reduced to fifty cents! Can our churches hesitate for a moment? May not the work be commenced immediately? and commenced without exhausting the resources of our brethren or of our friends, or diverting them materially from other benevolent objects? Is not the way already open for prosecuting the grand enterprise, with a vigour and rapidity that shall wake the slumbering world from the sleep of ages?

To the churches it belongs to move forward. It is for them to implore the guidance and blessing of the Lord. It is for them to seek out and call forth the messengers of salvation; and we respectfully submit to them, whether it would not be wise for each church to consider how much of the requisite sum is required of her, and to feel herself bound to see it furnished either by herself, or by missionary and education societies formed in her neighbourhood; and to take such measures as shall be deemed most expedient and scriptural, for leading each of her members to feel the delightful and sacred obligation of supplying, according to his ability, the proposed sum, and inducing his friends to do the same.

After the calculations which we have just presented, the following paragraphs from our authors, must come home to the conscience with double force.

"Is it possible to persuade Christians to do so much for the universal praise of their Redeemer, and the salvation of all nations? Or will they reply by saying, 'True, the conversion of the world is an object infinitely great and important, to effect it would bring everlasting glory to God, and both temporal and eternal felicity to an innumerable multitude of immortal beings it is an object above all others desirable and dear to our hearts; we earnestly long to see it accomplished, nd it is our daily and most fervent prayer; that it may soon be done

But it is certain that we cannot obey the Divine injunction: we cannot furnish the means necessary for accomplishing this work, without either adding something to our industry, without being more careful and sparing in our manner of living, or retarding the increase of our wealth, and very likely the completion of the work would oblige us to deny ourselves in all these three ways. Now, can any one suppose, that it is our duty to suffer all this, and to sacrifice so much merely for the sake of glorifying Christ, by publishing his redeeming love among all nations for their salvation? Monstrous impiety! Who that pretends to be a Christian would not shudder to find such a thought in his heart! But monstrous as such language may seem, by what better plea can Christians excuse themselves, for so long neglecting to send the glad tidings of the gospel throughout the earth? What else is the language of their present neglect of this duty?

"Let Christians again and again, consider how very light the burden is which is laid on each individual, and on each church; and which is not to be increased throughout the whole progress of the work. Let them consider with what a trifling exertion they might raise the sum, and still be left in the possession of their ease, their comforts, and an increase of their abundance.

"This great demand for missionaries, if hastily glanced at in the gross, may appear wild and visionary, but if deliberately viewed in the detail, can any thing appear more reasonable? Can any thing be more obvious than the *duty* and the *ability* of the churches to fulfil it? Is not the whole a sober, moderate calculation? The great secret lies in persuading every Christian to do his part in the work. And how *easily*, how *soon* might this be done, would every one, whose office it is to plead the cause of God among the churches, faithfully and perseveringly urge upon the consciences of his people, the claims which their crucified Redeemer, and their perishing fellow men, have upon their liberality and their exertions, and the infinite privilege of becoming co-workers with Christ, in building up his everlasting kingdom!

"Yes, the whole calculation is a moderate one. Let the churches examine and deliberate: let Christians in their conferences, their families, and their closets, scrutinize every part of it. And let each one inquire solemnly with himself, whether he might not, in the three ways which have been mentioned, raise his annual contribution, without any material variation of his ease, his comforts, or the increase of his fortune." p. 30—32.

The remaining Parts of the pamphlet contain much interesting matter. They are executed with ability, and in the spirit which the subject inspires. But we fear we have already trespassed upon the patience of our readers.

(*To be continued.*)

Address to the American Society for Colonizing the Free People of Colour of the United States. Read at a special meeting, in the City of Washington, November 21st, 1818. Washington: Davis and Force. 1818. pp. 56.

FEW subjects are more worthy the attention at once of the philosopher, the statesman, and the Christian, than the one presented in the address before us,—the proposed planting of colonies in Africa. The causes which have led to an undertaking so grand and benevolent, as well as the practicability of accomplishing it, and the consequences which will probably follow, suggest numerous themes for profound reflection. The devout philanthropist casts a mournful eye upon the past; but while he surveys the present, and anticipates the future, he rejoices in the light which begins to beam upon the mysterious ways of Providence.

For ourselves, we look to the operations of the American Colonization Society as promising incalculable benefits to the people of colour among us, and to their kindred on the continent of Africa, and, at the same time, as promoting the true interest of our own country, and *gradually* removing, what we all feel to be one of our foulest stains and sorest evils. The more the plan is examined and understood, the more, we are confident, it will be approved. Whatever difference of opinion there may be respecting the right, in any case, of retaining persons in servitude, we trust our readers will meet as the common friends of Africans and of African colonization. We are aware that, on some points, allowance ought to be made for peculiarity of situation. We can easily conceive that what would be proper and a duty in some circumstances, would in others be very wrong. It is certain that the laws of Christianity, adapted to men in every situation, command the servant to be obedient and faithful, the master to be kind, ' knowing that he also has a master in heaven,'— and all of us (forgiving on the one hand, and repairing as far as possible on the other, past injuries,) to seek the good of our fellow-men, as, were our conditions exchanged, we would require them to seek ours.

Contemplating the subject with these sentiments, we have been not a little gratified with the perusal of the publication to which we now have the pleasure of directing the attention of our readers. Mr. Burgess, the author, it will be recollected, was one of the gentlemen commissioned by the society to explore some of the western parts of Africa for the purpose of obtaining definite information relative to the country. Upon returning to America, he met his patrons, and laid before them this address, not as a final report of the mission in which he had been engaged, but as containing " some general views and particular statements, which may properly introduce further communications." It affords evidence of much reflection, and of accurate and extensive research. It gives a brief, but highly interesting view of the actual state of western Africa,—the stations occupied by Europeans on the coast and on neighbouring islands, its capes and rivers, its soil and climate, its inhabitants, its productions, and its trade.

Respecting the government of the country, the following extract will not be unacceptable.

"The African nations along the western coast are divided into small, independent kingdoms and republics. The form of government has for its basis the patriarchal; but in different places, it verges towards the two extremes of a pure democracy or a military despotism. Each town has its head-man or governor. Several of these towns and head-men profess allegiance to one particular head-man, usually venerable for age, whom they address as king and father. Thus, by a subordination, nominal rather than real, a whole people look up to one man as their father and king. Tribute is not common, whether from the people to their head-man, or from the subordinate head-men to the king. The nominal king often has much less physical force in his town or towns, than many of the subordinate head-men. What, in some measure, supplies the place of a regular tribute, is the universal practice of giving presents. When a stranger wishes to trade with them, settle among them, or pass though their territories, he takes a present in his hand and makes his addresses to the head-man, in the presence of the people.—When one head-man visits another, whether on business or for friendly intercourse, he usually takes a small present.—When a person brings a suit into public council, he lays a present before the head-man, even if his poverty allows him to bring only a few cola nuts. In all cases the amount of the present depends on the generosity of the individual, but it is expected to be proportional to his rank, wealth, or the importance of his business. All business is discussed in the assembly of the people. The king or head-man presides; the elders and princes speak according to age and rank. Most of the head-men have one or more domestic attendants, but very few on the whole coast, have any kind of military guard." p. 18, 19.

On another topic we present a few paragraphs, as they exhibit facts of too important and serious a nature to be read without exciting a desire to see some vigorous measure adopted for the benefit of degraded Africa.

"These three centuries past, no trade to Africa in gold, ivory, ebony, diewoods, ship-timber, gums, and wax, has been so regularly or extensively prosecuted, as that in the lives and bodies of men. The influence of this trade on the population, on the state of agriculture and the arts, and on the social relations and moral dispositions of the people, is too obvious to escape notice. Thousands are reduced to hundreds, towns to villages, villages to a few solitary cottages. In many places, where towns once stood, instead of solitary cottages, the visiter will only see vacant spaces overgrown with wild grass, while the banana, plantain, orange, and lime trees stand around, and near, too, are the sacred *pullom* trees, erect and stately, under which these poor pagans were accustomed to howl for the dead, and deprecate the displeasure of malignant spirits.

"Not only is the population diminished, but any progress in agriculture and the manufactures is checked. It is proverbial, that necessity gives a spur to invention. While, therefore, they have depended on foreign supplies of cloths and other articles of necessity or convenience, which Europeans were happy to afford them in exchange for slaves, they have neglected the culture of cotton, coffee, the indigo plant, and the sugar cane, and have actually forgotten much of their knowledge in the manufactures and the arts which they formerly possessed. It is a convincing testimony of this, that as one advances into the interior, the towns are larger, the houses are better constructed, rice and cotton are cultivated in greater quantities, and cloths are manufactured and died with more taste and skill.

"It is hardly necessary to say that this trade has weakened the social affections, and depraved the morals of the people. Parents and children have been rudely dissevered. From motives of gain husbands have sometimes sold their wives, and fathers their children. The articles of merchandise introduced have ever been contaminating, and the conduct of slave traders, seldom distinguished for chastity or temperance, have laid no strong or salutary restraints on the less instructed pagans.

"Before this traffic was abolished, the annual exportation from the western coast alone, was between eighty and one hundred thousand: the last and the present year, when it is abolished by Denmark, Holland, France, Great Britain, and the United States, the annual exportation does not fall short of thirty or thirty-five thousand." p. 10—12.

The reasons which the author urges as properly inducing to the settlement of colonies in Africa from the free people of colour in our own country, must, we think, commend themselves to the good sense of all candid inquirers. To lay before our readers the main sources of argument, we select from the address, a few additional paragraphs.

"Leaving to the private hours of every good man considerations of a religious nature, arising from our obligations to diminish the sufferings of men and to diffuse the heavenly light of sacred scripture and leaving, respectfully, to the legislators of this country, considerations of a political nature, arising from a mature reflection on the different casts or classes of the people, the improbability of their speedy amalgamation, and the inconvenience to both parties in their present state,——— (not to add, what is out of my province, and, in some respects, the least of my solicitude amidst weightier thoughts, the diminution of the poor rates in some of the large cities, the improvement of the system of agriculture in several of the States, the extension of the honourable commerce of the country, and the possible future importation of all the productions of the West and East Indies, from settlements made in Africa under the parental care of the American government, ———. I shall confine myself to two or three considerations of a general nature, leading to the same conclusion. And I feel a confidence that it is only justice to the character of the American society and the dispositions of the American people, to dwell on the following as the most persuasive and acceptable. The more complete abolition of the slave trade, the elevation of the character of the free people of colour in this country, and the improvement of the condition of the African tribes who may come within our influence." p. 24, 25.

"According to existing laws, the trade is now illegal north of the equator, and in 1823, will be illegal on the whole coast. But what are laws without penalties? What are penalties, if not inflicted? None but British ships attempt to make captures under the abolition laws, and they have no right to board a ship under the Danish, French, or American flag.* All present laws may therefore continue in force, and the slave trade go on indefinitely.

"A colonization of the free people of colour of the United States in Africa will operate, in several ways, directly against this trade. It will take away its grand temptation with the native princes and people by introducing those articles of foreign produce and manufacture, to which they have become accustomed, and have few means of obtaining, except by the sale of slaves. It may lead some of our vessels to engage in an honourable trade along the coast. It may be found convenient that some of our armed ships should occasionally visit stations on that continent. The people of colour themselves, taught in the school of experience, will surely exert their influence by persuasion, example and instruction, to effect its ruin. Though a single colony could not look far up or down the coast, yet a few colonies like Sierra Leone would do much to guard the coast. Colonization may be regarded as one principal means, by which this scourge of Africa will be destroyed, this blot of humanity washed away, for ever.

---

* To elucidate the author's statement, we take the liberty of subjoining a note.—In treaties which have recently been concluded with Great Britain by Portugal, Spain, and the Netherlands, it is *mutually* agreed that, under certain circumstances, the vessels of one nation, having on board slaves acquired by an illicit traffic, may be detained by the armed ships of another, and brought for trial before the tribunals constituted for that purpose. A similar arrangement has not yet been made by France, Denmark, nor the United States.—See *Twelfth Report of the African Institution.*

"The elevation of the character of the free people of colour, who are now in this country, is another inducement to their colonization in Africa.—They have not here a fair opportunity to show themselves men. Their minds are, in some degree, shackled from childhood. They have not the same motives to improvement, nor the same encouragement to honourable exertion, as others born in this land. Their debasement and subordination can afford us no pleasure. The principal ground of their inferiority is acknowledged to be a matter of prejudice. But the time when colour will not be a ground of prejudice in this country, is not near. A distinction, then, painful and injurious to them, and no source of pleasure to us, will for a long period be inseparable from their residence with us. Having in some sense been accessory to this state of things, we ought to be willing, and are willing, to assist some of them to change their condition. If they shall desire no change, when they know all that may be known on this subject, our business will be at an end. We shall have the credit of having, at least, designed well." p. 26—28.

"Another inducement to a colonization of our free people of colour in Africa, is the improvement of the condition of those African nations who may come within the circle of our influence. These children of nature, hospitable and kind, attentive to the stranger, and respectful to the aged, are taught by education to be timid and suspicious, and allured by appetite to theft and plunder. Growing up in ease and plenty, they are usually tall and erect, remarkably free from personal deformities, and unshackled with abjectness of spirit. With the richest fruits, and all the crude materials for happy subsistence and wealth, they live in comparative poverty and meanness. Having few wants, and those easily supplied, they waste their time in indolence, sleeping by day, and dancing by night. The constructing their cottages and canoes, the manufacture of cloth and mats, the culture of rice, maize, yams, and cassada, the boiling of salt and palm-oil, and the gathering of honey, ivory, and dye woods, are a summary of their useful labours. They do every thing to great disadvantage. The plough, spinning-wheel, loom, a machine for cleaning rice, and mills for sawing wood and grinding corn, would be of inestimable service. Their criminal code, in some particulars, is grossly absurd, and their superstitions dark and gloomy. Their homage is paid to devils. Though they sometimes speak with contempt of 'white man's fashion,' they would have few objections to adopt the English language, habits of dress, arts, and manufactures. They would be particularly gratified to have their children taught to read and write. Any improvement in their general and moral state, will, most probably, be slow and gradual; but no means to civilize and instruct will be so sure as colonization, and no agents so acceptable and efficient as their own brethren and children, if men of intelligence and character, like some of the people of colour in this country." p. 29, 30.

The author has obligingly appended to the address a body of valuable Extracts from works relating to Africa, adapted to show that the proposed colonization "is practicable and safe—that lands are attainable, and that the natural resources and productions of the country are rich, various, and abundant." He has also added a brief account of Sierra Leone, as to its extent, population, religion, schools, history, &c.

We hope the pamphlet will be extensively circulated; and we hope too, that a gentleman so eminently qualified, as we know the author to be, by his various attainments, his enlarged and elevated views, and his having imbibed so much of the spirit which animated his late colleague, will be induced to continue in the service of the Society, till many a colony, flourishing as that of Sierra Leone, shall have arisen on the western coast of Africa.

A new era seems about to commence in the history of the people of colour. A brilliant prospect is before them. And, in the ample field which we trust they are soon to enter, there will be needed, more than ever, all the piety and talent among them that can be called into action. Happy it is for Africa that many of her children in this land are to be numbered among the pious, that not a few are prepared already for important stations, and that increasing attention has of late been paid, in many places, to the instruction of the young.

Still there is room for more exertions, and no time is to be lost. Momentous and lasting consequences will follow from the character of the first colonists.

At a period like the present, we trust our readers generally, and the churches and individuals of our denomination in particular, will be awake to the importance of this subject....Is there a family among the people of colour, growing up in ignorance and vice? Let its members be taught to read and revere the word of God. Who can calculate what may be the happy effects in Africa fifty years hence? Is there a youth of amiable disposition and promising talents? Let him be encouraged to enrich his mind with various knowledge. Who can tell how useful he may be, or how responsible a station he may occupy in Africa? But, above all, is there a young Christian brother who has gifts for the gospel ministry, and whose heart longs for the salvation of his countrymen? Let him be called forth, and allowed the means of cultivating those gifts. Let him be aided in pursuing such studies as, with the blessing of God, will conduce most to his usefulness, and prepare him to teach others. Who can compute the good he may be the means of doing in Africa?—in the colonies, and, through them, among the millions of the native inhabitants?

Other denominations are becoming active in preparations of the kind we are recommending, and our brethren in Massachusetts are beginning to perform their part. But there is, we trust, *much* to be done. We have many African churches, and many persons of colour in other churches, and it must be that there are many who, when the wide fields of Africa are thrown open to them, ready for the harvest, will feel as the apostle to the Gentiles felt: "necessity is laid upon me; yea, woe is unto me if I preach not the gospel." Should the scheme of colonization be prosecuted, as it probably will be, a fairer opportunity could not be imagined for introducing Christianity and spreading it among the numerous tribes of natives. It will be recollected by many of our readers that about two years ago, an African Society auxiliary to the Baptist Board of Foreign Missions*

---

* See the Third Annual Report, p. 180.

was formed in Richmond, Virginia, for the express purpose of contributing to the support of a future mission in Africa. If the way should now be opened, we cannot doubt that many, who have thus begun the work of benevolence, would rejoice to go themselves, with thousands of others, and carry the gospel to their kindred. What country to them can be more desirable than the land of their ancestors? Would any prefer the kingdom or the republic of Hayti? The Roman Catholic is the established religion, and the whole island is a camp, harassed with alarms, and liable every day to become a field of slaughter. That country is not, indeed, to be overlooked by the philanthropist; but then it should be remembered that St. Domingo is only an *island*, while Africa is a *continent*.

We cannot, perhaps, close this article better than by publishing, from manuscript copies which we have been allowed to take, the following letters sent by people of colour at Sierra Leone to their friends in America. The writers, we are assured, are men of reputation and piety. One of them, John Kizell, a preacher in connexion with the Baptist church in that colony, accompanied the commissioners, and performed the part of an interpreter, in their tour to the Sherbro and their interviews with the native kings and head-men of the country.

SIERRA LEONE, 18th *May*, 1818.

TO THE BRETHREN GENERALLY.

I WRITE these few lines to all at large. I am surprised to hear from brother John Kizell, that he has seen a letter of your publication, in which you oppose the colonizing in Africa;—you oppose the coming to a land which your fathers went from. You may be rich, but do you think you will be respected as the real Americans? Do you not know that the land where you are is not your own? Do you not know that you are strangers in that land? Your fathers were carried into that land to increase strangers' treasures, but God has turned it all to good, that you may bring the gospel into your country.

When will you become a nation, if you refuse to come? If you say you refuse to come, I will say to you in the words of Mordecai to Esther,—" Think not with thyself that thou shalt escape in the king's house, more than all the Jews. For if thou altogether holdest thy peace at this time, then shall there enlargement and deliverance arise to the Jews from another place, but thou and thy father's house shall be destroyed."—Think not that you will dwell in fine houses, and feed on the best, and live easy. If you refuse to come and deliver Africa out of darkness, God will send deliverance from another quarter. Who knows, Mr R— A—, but God has made you a minister to train up young men to be ministers in Africa? I do not speak this to you alone, but to all the brother preachers, for the Lord commands you, saying, " Go ye into all the world, and preach the gospel to every creature," and you do refuse to go,—only standing and preaching there in America, where there are thousands of ministers, and let the devil have power over your country, and your relations. "He that knows his master's will, and does it not, shall be beaten with many stripes." Will you have the goodness to tell me your objections to settling a colony in Africa to enlighten the Africans at large? The country is a good country. It only wants cultivation, and the gospel in it. The people are a very kind speaking people.

Sir, when I set my foot on the African shore, I had only seven and sixpence sterling,—now, notwithstanding all my sickness, I am master of a hundred pounds sterling. I think if I had had something to have begun with, I should have had about four or five thousand.

SAMUEL WILSON.

SIERRA LEONE, 19th May, 1818.

DEARLY BELOVED BRETHREN,

I EMBRACE this favourable opportunity to inform you that God has prepared a place for you all that desire to come to your mother country. The land that is prepared for you is like the land of Canaan, abounding in honey and fruits, fish and oysters, wild fowls and wild hogs. The land is a good land, and then it has a good sea port for vessels to come into.

Dear brethren, I hope it will be for the glory of God, and the salvation of Africa. you may also improve your talents to the glory of God, and to your own satisfaction. Dear brethren, I wish to remove the dark cloud from your minds concerning Africa. The people are good-tempered and kind. The only thing that Africa wants is the knowledge of God. But, sirs, if you had seen the glory of God displayed as I have, this dark cloud would give way from all your minds in a moment. The greatest experience that I ever heard in this world, was given by a captive man. It is impossible for any man to tell more about Jesus Christ than this man did. He is equal to Paul when he was caught up into the third heavens. This man has been from his native place about two years. I hope, dear friends, the Lord has blessed my labours to the conversion of some souls, within these two years, since I have been in Africa. Remember, dear sirs, that you, like Joseph, have been sold from your birth right; but though Joseph became lord over Egypt, yet he charged his brethren when they should leave Egypt to carry his bones with them. Which of you is lord over America, that you do not want to come to your birth-right? It is the will of God for you to come into the possessions of your ancestors. The name of the place is called Sherbro, about one hundred and thirty miles from here. You cannot enjoy yourselves in America as free men. Though there are many good men in America, yet their laws are not in your favour. Perhaps one will say, Why not? I answer, because you are captives in a strange land. This I say, there is no man of colour that can say he is not ashamed in America. To tell the truth, I was once in a church where the first thing I saw was a writing in large letters, "Negroes' Seats." This made me ashamed.

Dear brethren, fear not to come, if the Lord will. When you come out, I hope to be with you, and more besides me, by the permission of God. Dear friends, let this be printed, if you please.

I remain your sincere friend,

PERRY LOCKE.

SIERRA LEONE, 21st *May*, 1818.

DEAR FRIENDS AND BRETHREN,

"A PEOPLE scattered and peeled,"—"a nation meted out and trodden under foot"—We who now write unto you are your brethren, who have once laboured under the same trouble as a great many of you now do, but, thanks be to God, through Jesus Christ our Lord, he has delivered from all that trouble. We must know, brethren, all that has befallen us is of God for our good, that we may bring the gospel into our country. We were not left in darkness as our countrymen were. Brethren, you know the land of Canaan was given to Abraham and to his seed, so Africa was given to our forefathers and to their children. Brethren, you know that Joseph was sold into a strange land wrongfully by his brethren, and, dear friends, you know many of you were sold wrongfully into a strange land.—and you have increased in the land where you are. Word was sent by God unto the children of Israel for them to return into the land of Canaan, and you have the same word sent unto you to return into your own land. The hand of God is in this business. The children of Israel brought the ark of God into their land, and you will bring the gospel into your land. The Levites were set apart among them, and you will have young men set apart among you. Now let us follow the word of God.—The prophet says, " ye have sold yourselves for naught, and ye shall be redeemed without money." Again, in another place, " I will give this people favour in the sight of them, and they will let you go."—It is God who has put it into the hearts of these good men to assist you back to your country. Look back, and see if ever such a thing was done as you now see. Be ye thankful to them in America, and be not fearful to come to Africa, which is your country by right. If any of you think it proper not to come, and say it is well with you,—you must remember your brethren who are yet in slavery. They must be set free as yourselves. How shall they be made free, if not by your good behaviour and by coming to get a place ready to receive them ? Though you are free, that is not your country. Africa, not America, is your country and your home. Africa is a good country. You will have no trouble to raise your children, when all things are plenty.—you will have no want of warm clothing,—you will have no need of fire-wood, for we have it in abundance, and here you will be looked upon like the blessed creatures of the Almighty God, and that bad opinion and contempt which our white brethren harbour, will be quite done away, and the whole of us will become a large and wonderful nation. We will forget all our former troubles when we return to the land from which our forefathers came. The whole of you will have your own lands and houses, when you cultivate the land (in which a few horses would be an assistance,) you will be supplied with rice, yams, cassada, plantains, fowls, wild-hogs, deer, ducks, goats, sheep, cattle, fish in abundance, and many other articles, good running water, large oysters. In truth, the whole country would be happy if they had only the gospel in it, to improve the minds of the people. We have travelled up into the country, and have found it to be a very good land, and the inhabitants of it to be a very kind sort of people to strangers. We hope, dear brethren, that you all will bring the gospel into this land in its purity and spirit, that the Lord may bless our prosperity. Brethren, the men-stealers are all driven out of the country,* so we have nothing to fear from that

---

* The neighbourhood of Sierra Leone.——ED

quarter. Brethren, we recommend to your approbation, Samuel J Mills, and Ebenezer Burgess, two worthy ministers whom the good people of America have sent out to seek a place for you. They are men worthy of the station they hold, full of Christian love and piety. We are eye-witnesses of their labour for the people. You will therefore please to believe their assertions concerning this great work which the Lord has begun, and we hope will finish with speed. Now, brethren, we commend you to the grace of our Lord Jesus Christ, and the love of God the Father. Amen.

(Signed)

John Kizell,	Peter Mitchell,
Wm. Martin,	Perry Locke,
Geo. Davis,	Thos Williams,
Geo. Lewis,	John Kizell, Jr
Robt. Robertson,	Pompey Rutledge.
Samuel Wilson,	

MISSIONARY INTELLIGENCE.

MISSION TO BURMAH.

From Mr. Hough to the Cor. Secretary, dated Rangoon, May 4, 1818.

ON the 25th December brother Judson left us for Chittagong. Lest his letter to you, written just previous to his departure, may not have reached you, I will mention the reasons inducing to that undertaking. We had understood by the monthly circular letters, printed at Serampore, that some Burmans at Chittagong had received the word of life; that one had began to preach, and that every month some appeared to inquire after the truth, and concerning Christ. It was thought, if we could obtain a Burman, having a spiritual discernment of Christian truth, capable of telling his countrymen, in their own tongue, the wonderful works of God, it would be an important acquisition, and an additional help in opening a way for the introduction of the gospel here. It was also believed, that the reciprocal advantages resulting from brother Judson's spending a few weeks with converted Burmans, in conversation and preaching, would be an object worthy attainment. Add to these the consideration, that brother Judson's health was very imperfect, and it appeared proper to take some steps to regain it; towards which object, a change of scenery, habits, and circumstances, might largely contribute —these were the main reasons, which induced him to take a passage in a vessel bound directly to and from Chittagong.

Previous to his departure we had felt that the affairs of the mission had arrived at such a state, as to render it both prudent and necessary to make them more public, and to enter, as far as our capacity would enable us, upon a general publication of the gospel, endeavouring, with humble trust, to cast ourselves upon the mercy and protection of our Lord, and to feel prepared for those trials which appeared, at least, within the bounds of probability We looked around us, and often consulted together, on the plan most eligible to adopt, at the same time watching the intimations of Divine Providence. Our situation was like that of a vessel at sea, caught in variable winds, the seamen standing with their hands upon the ropes, ready to shift their sails to the first favourable breeze.

On the 25th December brother Judson left us. On the first of January an arrival from Calcutta brought us a letter, informing, that Mr. De Bruyn, the Baptist missionary at Chittagong, had been murdered, in a most daring manner, by one of the baptized Burmans! This afflicting event was related in such a way as to leave us in little doubt that the murderer was the very person who, we had hoped, would accompany brother Judson back to Rangoon. This is to be received as one of those mysteries of the Divine government, which we are only permitted to contemplate at a distance, and which may serve to confirm us in the truth, that whatever hopes we may place on such unstable beings as men, may perish.

We all continue in health, though a dreadful mortality has prevailed here for about five weeks, and carried off multitudes, yet God has continued the voice of health in our habitation.

Tell brother Rice I love him as a friend to the Burman mission, and am decided in my opinion that his is the path of duty. The Lord send him prosperity.

STATION AT ST. LOUIS.

From Mr. Peck to the Cor. Secretary, dated St. Louis, October 6, 1818.

FOR two days past my time has been occupied with Indians affairs. This day a treaty of peace and amity was concluded between the Cherokees and their allies, and the Osages, who have been at war more than a year. As this event appears to have some bearing towards Indian missions, it may be necessary to particularize. The war commenced in consequence of depredations committed by the Osages, on the Cherokees, Arkansas, Delawares, Shawnees, &c. The Cherokees having the superiority over the Osages from their civilized habits, gained a decided advantage, took some prisoners, and brought them to just and equitable terms. The Osages have agreed to relinquish all right to their hunting grounds south of the Arkansas, to the Cherokees, as a reparation for injuries done, while the latter agree to deliver up all prisoners in their possession.

The Cherokees appeared in council clad in decent and comfortable garments, mostly of their own manufacture. Their chief is an old man, and nearly blind, but a man of a sound judgment and great penetration. To convince the Osages of his unwillingness to continue the war, he said—" War is disagreeable to me and my people. It is better to be at peace. In war we lose our friends—our children. Let us live in peace. Look at us Cherokees. See, here is our own manufacture which we wear this day. This we have from following the advice of our father, the President. It is better to labour than to be at war. You see proof of this in our appearance this day. I have followed the advice of general government for a long time. I wish these people to do so. Let them hunt; let them become civilized, provide their own clothing, and lay the tomahawk down. Do not get scalps; scalps will do you no good they fetch no money."

Like their brethren on the east of the Mississippi, the Cherokees on the Arkansas are making advances towards civilization. They cultivate the ground, raise cattle, horses, hogs, &c. make butter, manufacture clothing, and perform several mechanical arts. As Rev. Mr. Ficklin, agent from the Kentucky Mission Society is now at my house, and as he is exerting himself to get Indians to go into Kentucky, we obtained an early interview with two of them, who arrived a few days before the rest of the deputation from their tribe. They have come to my house several times. One can speak tolerable English. To him, and through him, we made known our object in regard to the Indians, and read and interpreted from the Annual Report and Luminary, whatever related to Indian missions. They were much pleased, and were inquisitive. I gave them a brief outline of the Christian religion. The creation of man and the origin of evil were quite interesting. I told them the way of man's recovery. One was affected. His name is George Duvaul. The other inquired the cause of thunder, and said the Cherokees supposed it was a sensible being, because it would strike the tree or any other object with such exactness. I gave him an illustration of it, at which both seemed pleased. This evening after council I invited Mr. Rogers with five others to supper. Mr. R. is one of the interpreters, and a man of information.

After supper the evening was spent in friendly chat, and much information relative to our mission communicated. Their polite and refined manners would have made them interesting in the circles of your city. It will be recollected these are the best informed and most civilized of their nation; but their situation not only proves the practicability of Indian reform, but that even a little money and small efforts, if rightly directed, will do wonders. To-morrow brother Ficklin and myself are to meet the band, and hold a formal council in presence of the old chief, on the subject of schools and a mission amongst them, &c. I need not add, we anticipate a favourable answer. Major Lewis, their agent, is disposed to promote our object.

The settlements of the Cherokees are dispersed for 30 miles on the Arkansas, and a little more than 300 miles from St. Louis. They are about 25 miles from the main road leading from St. Louis through the St. Francois settlements, by Lawrence Court-house on to the Red river country, Oupalousas, Natchitoches, and the extensive and very important missionary fields which Mr. Ranaldson so importunately presses upon the Board in his letter published in the fourth number of the Luminary. If my feeble influence would strengthen brother Ranaldson's plea in favour of immediate efforts in the Red river country, it should be exerted. Within a few days past I have received exact information of that country. There are many Baptist professors scattered through those regions, but not a single minister of our society. Emigration is rapidly flowing into that country. From the St. Francois settlement, in the western parts of St. Genevieve county, the people are flocking to Red river. Others are coming from the States to fill their places. With one of our brethren lives a Spaniard, an intelligent young man, and a native of San Antonio, in the province of Texas. From him I have learnt a very interesting account of the state of things in that quarter. They have schools, but under bad regulations. The people can read, though poorly, and he saw before he left the country, three or four Spanish bibles, which were read with eagerness. They came by the way of New Orleans.

On the mode of Indian missions, what brother M'Coy says in his letter, published in the fourth number of the Luminary on the importance of setting them an example of industry, and impressing on them *the value of property,* is so very important, and so exactly expresses my views of the subject, that I beg leave to refer the Board to that letter as a precious treasure of information. In every advance I have made in a knowledge of Indian habits, my mind has been forcibly impressed with this truth. I have seen the want of it in our Indian conferences. I have seen it while entering their wigwams. One very important means, therefore, to get at them, and teach them religion, is, *by example*, to show them the value of property, of labour, and of industrious habits. No arguments, I presume, are necessary to support this position. The success of the Moravians, of Vanderkemp, Kircherer, and others, among the Hottentots, are demonstrations. Indeed this, instead of increasing, will lessen the expense, after the first year, as the missionaries and school teachers would raise their own provisions, and make their own clothing. Qualifications and habits for husbandry and mechanical arts ought, therefore, to be sought after in the appointment of missionaries for the Indian department, rather than splendid attainments in literature.

From Mr. Peck to the Cor. Sec., dated St. Louis, October 9, 1818.

'Since the first of September, I have travelled about 400 miles, on two occasions. The first tour originated from a mistake I made about the time and place of the Bethel association. I passed on to Herculaneum, from hence up the Plattin on to Hazel run, to Big river settlement, to Murphy's settlement, Cook's settlement, Main La Motte, to St. Michael and the settlements on the St. Francois. Here I formed an acquaintance with Rev. Mr. Farrar, who preaches to Providence church on the St. Francois, which brother Welch constituted in 1814. Though I missed the object of my journey, my time and expense do not seem lost. There was an unseen hand that guided me this way. Besides preaching in several settlements, and from house to house, (as this is a mode of operation which in this country will do more real good than mere public meetings,) I visited several schools, and learned the wants of the people, their wish to encourage schools, and the great necessity of devising some plan to form them into districts, and supply them with suitable teachers. A scheme which in part unfolded itself to my mind last fall while coming up the river, before my sickness, now more fully evolved; and I saw not only the want of it, but the prospect of speedy success, and in such a way as would not hinder our usefulness as missionaries, or our exertions amongst the Indians, but promote them. But this was not the main object attained in this journey. Near St Michaels I found a little band of Muskogee or Creek Indians, who with a principal chief emigrated to this country some years ago. These Indians can speak French as well as their own language, and two or three can talk a little English. They are poor, but do not wander abroad. Some poor French families live with them. I immediately began to look about for a school teacher, as here was a door opening. As I was obliged to return next day, I engaged brother Farrar to hold a " *talk* " with them, and let me know if they would receive instruction. Returning home I preached in Cook's settlement, Murphy's settlement, attended meeting on Big river with a Methodist circuit rider, and was overtaken with a violent storm, and was obliged to spend two days on Sandy creek at esquire Johnson's, where I was hospitably entertained.

Sep. 25. I again started for the Bethel association, through St. Genevieve, crossed the Saline, passed through Bois Brule bottom, and reached the association at brother Duval's Saturday night, where I preached that evening on missions.

The association took up the business, resolved to correspond with the Board, entered into the spirit of missions, schools, Indian missions, &c.

From brother Farrar I learned that the Muskogees were not merely willing but desirous to be instructed, and that some poor French children wished to attend with them. And will the God of missions, thought I, thus open the way for an Indian school, and not provide a teacher? While ruminating on the subject, and inquiring amongst the brethren, I found an old pious brother by the name of James James, who observed, that if no better could be found he was almost disposed to offer, observing at the same time, he felt it in his heart to do something to promote the cause of Christ. Upon inquiring I found he had in his younger days taught school—that his wife was pious and industrious, and could assist the squaws, and that they had no family but a little grand-daughter, and lived near the Indians, and had not much property of their own to look after. Thus far all appeared well. I engaged to be there the first week in November, and get the school into operation. The result I will let you know. This place is 100 miles a little west of south from St Louis, and directly on the road to the Cherokees.

To-morrow I attend the Illinois association, 16 miles east of this place, where I shall propose the subject of missions, education, &c. and in two weeks the Missouri association, above St. Charles.

From Mr Peck to the Cor. Secretary, dated St. Louis, December 7th, 1818.

By my last communication, accompanying a constitution of the "United Society for the spread of the Gospel and common Schools," you have learned the pursuit in which I have been engaged. Having completed my tour in the counties south of this, and being about to start for the settlements north of the Missouri, I deem it proper to apprize the Board of the encouragement presented the infant society which I am attempting to promote.

On Nov 3d, I left St. Louis, passed through Herculaneum, St. Genevieve, and the Barrens, where I had several opportunities of explaining to individuals the objects of the society. I reached the vicinity of Jackson in season to attend the quarterly meeting of the Bethel association. Here I was happy to find some worthy brethren, whose hearts had been touched with the spirit of missions. Saturday and Sabbath were spent here, during which time opportunity presented to plead the cause of missions, and a collection of $32 37½ cents was received. Considering this as the first effort, and in a land where never before a missionary sermon was preached, or money raised for such a purpose, I could not hesitate to acknowledge the fostering hand of God. At the same time, I enjoyed the pleasure of receiving several annual subscribers for the "United Society," &c. and of forming the "*Cape Girardeau Mite Society Auxiliary,*" &c. which promises to grow into a useful institution.

Nov. 10th Passing through the town of Cape Girardeau, I preached at 12 o'clock to a small but solemn assembly, and from thence eight miles further, where I preached in the evening, and aided in forming the "*Tywappity Mite Society Aux* iliary," &c. Returning to Jackson the next evening, where a sermon was delivered at the house of hon. R. S. Thomas, and the "*Jackson Female Mite Society Auxiliary,*" &c was formed. This society, consisting, when organized, of 17 amiable ladies, presents the encouraging hope, that, as it is the first female institution ever formed west of the Mississippi, it may prove the forerunner of many more.

Leaving Jackson I proceeded towards the interior, and spent the following Sabbath with the Providence church near St Michael, St. Genevieve county, where a small collection was received. Tuesday following, brought me to Cook's settlement, where I had the satisfaction of seeing formed the "*Liberty Mite Society Auxiliary,*" &c and $30 subscribed to its funds in a few moments. Returning to the vicinity of St Michael on Thursday, Nov. 19th, the "*St. Michael Mite Society Auxiliary,*" &c. was organized. While in this region, the idea passed my mind to attempt something for such ministers as are already preaching to churches, or settlements around. Accordingly I drafted a subscription paper on the behalf of Rev Mr Farrar, which I proposed for circulation. The success attending the first attempt not only taught me the practicability of the object, but that similar measures might be pursued elsewhere with similar results.

It was near this that I had intended to set up an Indian school, as mentioned to the Board in a former communication. But as some of the Indians had already moved to the waters of Black river, and others contemplated going next season, it was thought best to suspend the design for the present, and attempt it next season in the settlements to which they have removed, and where it is hoped they will obtain from government a permanent residence.

Nov 21st and 22d, were spent in the settlements down and on the west side of St Francois. Here is a small church, and a preacher by the name of Street. Returning over a very rough broken country, it was not without considerable exertion I was enabled to reach my appointment in Doe-run settlement, where I preached on Monday evening. Here are several professors, and a church will probably be constituted next spring. The next day brought me to Bellevue, where I spent two days, preached three times, and left arrangements to form an auxiliary society next season.

Returning towards St Louis I preached in Herculaneum on Friday evening, where the state of things present the encouraging prospect of an auxiliary society at some future time. Going from thence to Gravois, where I preached the following Sabbath, I had the misfortune to lose my path, and for hours the following evening and night I was compelled to wander over hills and gullies, through thickets and brambles, till at last a kind Providence brought me to the place of destination. In Gravois, ten miles from St. Louis, there are some favourable indications of seriousness, and it is hoped one or two instances of conversion.

Sabbath evening, Dec 6th, I embraced the invitation of some of the members of the legislature now sitting, and preached a missionary sermon in their hall to a large and respectable assembly, from whom was received in collection $26 75 cts. This was the first attempt to collect for the mission in St. Louis. In reviewing this tour I find much cause of gratitude for the encouragement afforded the mission, and feel confident that God, the Parent of all mercies, will give success to the infant society which we have been enabled to form.

In this journey I spent 27 days, travelled 466 miles, preached 24 sermons, assisted in forming five auxiliary societies, left constitutions for three others to be formed next spring, attended three church meetings, one communion season, was present at one baptizing, visited all the schools in my rout, besides calling on families as I passed along, with a view to religious instruction, and in various ways endeavoured to promote the general objects of the society. Considering the vast increase of population in this territory, (estimated by the legislature at more than 100,000 souls,) the almost unlimited field, especially in the southwest, towards the Red river country, and the impossibility of two missionaries and a few local preachers even visiting all these extensive settlements, much less affording any thing like occasional supplies, the Board will forcibly realize the importance of additional missionaries in this extensive harvest. The necessity of this will be more readily felt when it is understood, that the funds of the " United Society" will soon be competent to employ one or two itinerating missionaries at least a part of the year, and no suitable persons who can be spared are yet found to enter their service.

We have formerly intimated to the Board, that Charaton, up the Missouri, has presented a favourable position, but a more extended acquaintance with the interior, has given rise to two objections against the upper settlements on the Missouri —

1st. A number of ministers are already in those settlements, and from the state of society, soil, and local advantages, that people are more likely to receive the gospel from the emigration of ministers than other parts.

2d. The country south and southwest of St. Louis, embraced in St. Genevieve, New Madrid, and Lawrence counties, and the vast regions on the Arkansas, White and Wachita rivers, are not only entirely destitute, but present a probability of remaining so for some time to come. Also, the Cherokees, Piankishaws, Quappaws, Peorias, and other Indians removing from east of the Mississippi, are settling in regions west of this, and are the most likely first to receive the gospel. To whatever part we may be directed, I hope we shall follow the leadings of Divine Providence.

From Mr. Welch to the Cor. Sec., dated St. Louis, November 1, 1818.

According to previous intimation to the Board I left St Louis on the 22d of June, on a missionary tour down the Territory below, passing through Herculaneum, St. Genevieve, and Cape Girardeau, a distance of about 120 miles, visiting and preaching to the destitute neighbourhoods that intervene.

About the middle of July I passed over into Illinois, and thus on to Kentucky, for the purpose of visiting some of the associations. The particular object in view was to make collections for the erection of our meeting house in this place, as well as for missionary purposes. The object of my visits from place to place was rendered less auspicious by the almost universal exertion among the Baptist churches in that part of the state for building large houses for public worship, seven or eight of which are now erecting, while others are receiving enlargement and repair. Although my success was thus circumscribed, yet it was matter of rejoicing to see the prosperity of the churches through this interesting portion of our country. Agreeably to their wonted liberality, in the space of about ten weeks, the time actually devoted to this service, they put into my hands the sum of 430 dollars, besides my expenses. I take the liberty of mentioning the names of Rev. Messrs. Jeremiah Vardeman and Walter Warder, to whose influence much of my success is indebted.

On the 28th of August it was my satisfaction to aid in the formation of " The Female Missionary Society of Richmond auxiliary to the Madison Missionary Society of Kentucky." It will be understood by the Board that the Madison Society was constituted last fall, and stands connected with the general body. A similar pleasure was enjoyed, on the 11th of September, in the constitution of "The Female Missionary Society of Lexington auxiliary to the Baptist Board of Foreign Missions for the United States." By the kindness of the " Preserver of men" I arrived in St Louis again on the 15th of October, and found all the mission family well.

Agreeably to arrangements made last spring, I attended, on the 23d of October, the formation of the " Friendship Baptist Church," constituted on the north side of the Missouri, about 60 miles above this village, and at the place where old Col Daniel Boon now lives On this occasion the same number of disciples as was called to accompany the Saviour while on earth, manifested a desire to enjoy the privileges pertaining to the people of God in a church relation A sermon was delivered from Psalm cxxxiii 1. " Behold how good and how pleasant it is for brethren to dwell together in unity;" and after the church covenant and articles of faith were read, &c the right hand of fellowship was offered, and the blessing of God solicited, that it might " flourish as the vine, and shoot forth its branches like Lebanon."

This is truly a destitute region of country. The harvest is great, and the labourers are few, pray ye, therefore, that the Lord of the harvest would send forth more labourers into his vineyard.

The 24th and two following days were spent at the meeting of the Missouri association on Femme Osage, 15 miles below, in the bend of the river; at the close of which was formed the " United Society for the promotion of the Gospel and common Schools, both among the whites and Indians "

An United Society for the Spread of the Gospel.

AGREEABLY to the recommendations of the Bethel, Illinois, and Missouri Baptist Associations, a respectable number of professors of religion and other persons, met at Femme Osage, St. Charles county, to form a missionary society.

Rev. Messrs Peck, Welch, Badgley, Jones and Craig, were appointed to provide a constitution, which was presented, read article by article, and adopted.

The following persons were elected managers for the ensuing year. Rev Messrs. David Badgley, Wm Jones, T R. Musick, T P Green, J. P. Edwards, Wm Thorp, Bethuel Riggs, J. M Peck, J E. Welch, and Messrs John Jacoby, Cumberland James, Thomas Smith, and Wm Biggs, Esq

Adjourned to meet at the Illinois association, Looking Glass prairie, Illinois, the Friday before the 2d Lord's day in October, 1819.

The managers present proceeded to elect Mr. John Jacoby treasurer, Rev. James E Welch secretary.

Resolved, That Rev. J. M. Peck be agent and superintendent, and authorized to obtain subscribers, collect monies, originate auxiliary societies, establish schools, and promote the general objects of the society.

WYANDOT, SANDUSKY INDIANS, &c.

From Rev. Henry George to the Cor. Sec. dated Owl Creek, Oct. 21, 1818

AFTER informing you the cause why I did not write to you sooner, I shall let you know what success I have had among the Indians. The cause of my not going to them sooner was, when I came home they were, the most of them, out in the wilderness hunting, and after they returned they went to St. Mary's to form a treaty. Being partly acquainted with the nature of their business, I knew when they would again return. I left home last Monday week, and preached at Radnor twice, where, when a missionary under the Domestic Mission Society, I was an instrument of baptizing several, and of constituting a church. I went from thence to the bounds of the Indian lands, and preached among the white people where the gospel was never preached before. I then went to Upper Sandusky, to the Indian agent, who received me in the most friendly manner. I showed him my commission as a missionary. He sent to the Indian chiefs to inform the Indians, (and to come themselves to the council house on last Lord's day,) that there was a missionary going to preach for them, who was sent by the Baptist Board of Foreign Missions. He readily promised to interpret for me. According to our appointment we went to the council house, and found many of the Indians assembled together singing praises to God.

There is a man of colour that has been some time among them, exhorting them to turn to the Lord, who came from Marietta. He is a methodist by profession. I believe his exhortations have been made a peculiar blessing, and will open the way for the preaching of the gospel among them. Mr Walker, the Indian agent, informed me that he (the coloured man) has been very faithful in exhorting them. Mr. Walker having informed the chiefs, &c. that I was the missionary, they received me in the most friendly manner, and requested me to preach. I opened the meeting by singing. Seven or eight of the Stockbridge Indians were there, who were going to White river to live. They are all professors of religion, and are congregationalists. They all had Dr. Watts' books, and sung three parts in music as correctly as any I ever heard. We sung the 92d psalm. I then prayed, and preached from Mark xvi. 15, 16. Mr Walker interpreted. I closed by singing, and the man of colour prayed, and made some short observations on my sermon, and closed by a hymn. I do firmly believe that our meeting was blessed with the presence of God, and his word was attended with the Holy Ghost sent down from heaven. I have no doubt in my mind that a mission is opened among them already.

After the meeting was closed, one of the chiefs made a speech on the necessity of religion, and repentance towards God, &c. the particular heads are as follows:

1. That the word of God had come to them in many ways, and that there is an evil day at hand.

2. Now let us repent, and have compassion on ourselves, and hearken to God in his word.

3. If we repent we shall escape in that terrible day when God shall call to his bar all the sons and daughters of men that have been, that are, and that shall exist, to judge them according to their works.

4. If they would turn to God with all their hearts, and repent, they should be happy in heaven with God for ever.

5. The nature of repentance. You must quit every evil practice, and pray to God to give a will to repent; then, in his time, he will enable you. I have been warned, said he, in dreams, &c. concerning these things.

He spoke about an hour with the greatest solemnity. We have a meeting to begin next Friday at 12 o'clock. It is to continue till Monday. They are going to invite the tribes of Indians to meet. The chiefs gave orders to the young Indians to make benches for seats. I believe that if there were an English school among them it would be of great use.

Dear brother, I rejoice that the Lord, by his providence, has brought a poor unworthy dust, such as I am, near 4000 miles from my native country, to preach the unsearchable riches of Christ among the ancient idolatrous gentiles of America. This I am resolved to do as long as I am supported by the Lord and his people. Dear brother, pray for me without ceasing.

From Rev. Henry George to the Cor. Sec. dated Owl Creek, Dec. 14, 1818.

I HAVE this opportunity to write the following lines, being as I am the spared monument of God's mercy, to inform you what the Lord has done by his precious gospel among the Indians. I wrote to you concerning the prospect and success I had at the beginning of my mission among them. I have been twice out with them since, about three weeks each time. We had a meeting that continued three days and three nights, with the greater part of the Wyandot and some of the Delaware tribes, preaching, praying and singing the most part of the time, I believe that I have witnessed that the Lord was amongst us.

I went down the river to the Seneca tribe; but, for want of an interpreter, could do nothing among them. From thence I went to Lower Sandusky, and preached three times among the whites. The Lord has been visiting them with a sore, mortal disorder. Thirty two or three were buried there this fall. It is a place almost without the preaching of the gospel. I passed from this down the bay, preaching almost daily, and up the Huron river through Richland county, &c. a country near the Indian lands, where I found some scattered Baptists and others in great need of a gospel ministry. When I had done preaching where I could conveniently have an open door, I returned home and tarried a few days.

I again went to Upper Sandusky, and preached to the Indians on the Lord's day. Mr. Walker, the agent, was my interpreter. We appointed a meeting on the day following, for the Indians to come together, to tell the exercises of their minds. They attended at ten o'clock. When they told their experience, I found, to my great satisfaction, there were many hopefully converted to the Lord. One old squaw brought A LITTLE IDOL, which she declared had been worshipped in her family by her father, mother, &c, but she said she had found that there are no blessings can proceed from any but God—no salvation but by Christ.

I went from Upper Sandusky to the Mohawk Indians, at a place called Honey Creek, where I found some religious Indians belonging to the church of England, who had the New Testament translated into their language, the Common Prayer Book, and the Psalms in metre. They sung and went to prayer morning and evening. The old Indian I stayed with was a preacher. He treated me with kindness and brotherly love, but I could not preach for want of an interpreter. I went from thence to Lower Sandusky, and preached there three times, and called the professors together to form a religious society, and every Lord's day to read and pray and sing the praises of God. I travelled thence nearly the same route as before, and preached almost every day until I returned home.

This, dear brother, is the sketch of the success of my mission. If the Lord preserve my life and health, I am going out this week to the Indians again. We have appointed another meeting, to last two days. Many, in relating their experience, informed us that they had found great benefit from the three days' meeting which we before held there. The Lord has been pleased, I hope and believe, to begin a good work among the aborigines of our country. Pray for me, that I may be made an instrument to do much good in the western wilderness of America. If I can meet with a safe opportunity, I will send to Philadelphia the idol which was given to me by the squaw.

GENERAL MISSIONARY INTELLIGENCE.

Extracts of letters from Rev. Wm. Ward to Rev. Dr. Staughton, dated

SERAMPORE, *December* 13, 1817.

I SEE that the Lord is still blessing America with those saving influences which we here so much need. Ah! if divine services here were but attended with those awakening impressions which are felt in America, how blessed we should be; but, alas! we still preach to stocks and stones. It is true we cannot give those discourses which are filled with pathos, flowing from feelings all expanding under the subject discussed; our discourses are dry, through the want of the power of speaking a foreign tongue with fluency; not that I would confine Divine influence to human eloquence, God can work by a ram's horn, and make the walls of Jericho fall; still, however, he is the God of means.

You will see by the Circulars that additions are made from the kingdom of darkness; but it is like cutting down two or three trees in the midst of your immense forests, it seems to tell for nothing. Pray for us, especially in reference to the outpouring of Divine influences. Vain is the help of man. We doubt not but the cause of missions is the cause of God; and that a faithful missionary is a co-worker with God, and hence there can be nothing to fear about success, since he is associated with infinite power, wisdom, and benevolence. So far, therefore, as we are faithful men, we need not give way to fear. "the cause is God's." Still, however, we may fail to do good, by not pursuing such means as God approves. The cause and means must therefore both be good. I have been looking at the means we have hitherto adopted, and I hope in substance they are such as may be accepted of God, and receive his almighty sanction. We print and distribute his word, he has said "My word shall not return unto me void." We promote the preaching of the word, and he has taught us, that "by the foolishness of preaching he saves them who believe." We set up schools to instruct the youth, and our blessed Lord surely sanctioned this step when he said, "Suffer the little children to come unto me, and forbid them not, for of such is the kingdom of heaven." We encourage the native and country converts to do all that they are capable of, because they have the language naturally, and they can endure the climate, and become familiar with their hearers. We hope here also we are in the path of duty. Further, we distribute tracts, and send them in all directions, to meet the case of the illiterate and those of little leisure; and we have in these tracts endeavoured to give them the gospel, rather than any thing of doubtful interpretation. This part of our work we think is also amongst legitimate means. If then we have God's smile and promised co-operation, and the weapons of our warfare be not carnal, they must and will be mighty, through God, to the pulling down of the strong holds of idolatry.

Your brethren at Rangoon, I hope, are doing well. My family are returned from England; but though Mrs. Ward's constitution appears strengthened, the disorder does not appear to be eradicated.

Brother Carey has thus far gone through the latter end of the year with good health. Sister Marshman is still complaining, with symptoms of an affection of the liver, but labours zealously in a large school of females.

I have just had a letter from brother Smith, a country born missionary, lately gone to Benares, the Athens of India, in which he informs us that he has baptized a bramhŭn in the Ganges there. And thus this holy place, too holy to be considered as a part of the earth, and where all who die immediately become shivŭs, (the god Shivŭ,) is at length beginning to feel (should this baptized bramhŭn be a real convert) those influences which will make it the residence of the GOD of the whole world.

SERAMPORE, *May* 11, 1818.

Brethren and Sisters Wheelock and Colman, have been very pleasant guests at the mission house. They are going in a few days, to do, I hope, great good in the empire of Bouddhism. I hope, through your missionaries, we shall have a complete development of their system of philosophy and mythology. They should be urged to bend their minds to this. The work will cost them years of labour, but it will be as much missionary work as any they can do, except the very act of snatching sinners as brands from the burnings.

I hope our beloved friends now going to Rangoon, will write to you of our affairs here. We are pushing on. We are now in a merciful state of health. All around us announces *His* coming to bless the heathen.

Extract of a letter from Mrs. Rowe to Mrs. E——, dated Dinapore, near Patna, June 13, 1818.

THE glorious day of the Lord is apparently approaching. He has given a measure of his Spirit to the European part of society in this dark land, in stimulating them, not only to all good works in late institutions for the promotion of knowledge and morality at large, but in forming domestic missionary societies, which they term branch and auxiliary to the society in England.

The barriers to knowledge and religion among the natives, are crumbling away. The religion of the Gospel is, to my view, naturally exemplified in the PEEPLE tree of this country, which shoots its tendrils into the interstices of walls, and there growing to an immense size, take fresh root, and send out fresh arms, until it bursts asunder the most formidable structures. This I beheld in the golden mosque at Gaur, which had become a covert for owls, bats, and wild beasts. Thus shall the glorious gospel undermine and fracture the firmest structures of human errour.

I know not what to say about the missionaries and ourselves, more than I have said before. The senior brethren at Serampore, are going on as usual in point of labours. Dr Carey has just recovered of a bilious attack, and Mr Ward also. The females there are pretty well, I believe.

The united junior brethren at Calcutta, are advancing in their missionary operations, having lately formed a missionary society auxiliary to the parent society in England. Dinapore has co-operated with them, in the formation of a branch society. Native schools at Calcutta are doing well, and meet public countenance. The number of natives increase who inquire the way of salvation. Our native brethren make frequent excursions into the villages around.

DOMESTIC INTELLIGENCE, REVIVALS, &c.

Extract of a letter from Rev Joy Handy, dated Fredonia, August 3, 1818

I HAVE just received a letter from elder Andrews, who lives on the Purchase. He informs me God is now doing wonders for His people in the second church in Middlebury, so called on our Minutes. "Such a sight," he observes, "I never saw before. Youth pleading with youth, as though eternal happiness or misery turned on the present moment. The first awakened and brought out was a little girl, about 14 or 15 years old. She felt such uncommon concern for others, that she ran from house to house to exhort her mates. The effect was wonderful. Her sister and brother soon brought out meetings that set up the work now spreading. O, his people will be gathered in, whether in Philadelphia or Middlebury'

Extract of a letter from Rev John Young, dated Greenup county, Kentucky, November 29, 1818.

THANK the Lord, since the year 1780 the gospel has spread with our population. Last fall, being up Missouri, I found a Baptist association far above St. Louis, the bounds of it two hundred miles higher up. Missions for Indians ought to be amongst them; teachers for their children ought to be with them. May the King of our salvation point the way.

Extract of a letter from Rev Mr. Sheppard, dated Salem, N. J. Dec 12, 1818.

I HAVE lately had the pleasure of seeing the cause of religion flourish in a branch of Salem church and congregation. A few years since, a kind friend, not a member with us, gave to the Baptist society in the vicinity of Canton, a handsome building lot of ground. The society and its friends have built a decent house for the worship of the Lord. It has the advantage of convenient place for baptizing, quite near

On the 12th of November, agreeably to appointment, a numerous assembly met Brother Smalley delivered a sermon from 1 Pet. ii. 3, 4 Dismissory letters from the churches of Cohansey and Salem, and a church covenant were read. The latter, together with our Confession of Faith, were adopted, and after the usual questions were asked, thirty one brethren and sisters were constituted a regular, separate, independent gospel church of the Lord Jesus. The right hand of fellowship was affectionately tendered. I then delivered a charge to the newly organized church, from 1 Tim iii. 15. Deep interest and solemnity were visible through all the exercises of the day.

From Rev A Waller to the Cor. Sec. dated Prospect Hill, Va. Sep. 14, 1818.

THE Goshen Association having closed its session for the present year, I feel it my duty to give you the earliest information respecting our proceedings.

Our meeting was a very pleasant one indeed, and the intelligence from a part of our churches was of the most pleasing kind. There have been added to our number since the last association by baptism, 612 persons. Of these 407 were received in the congregations which I attend We have enjoyed a little Pentecost. The work of grace still goes on amongst us This day I baptized 17, and expect in a very few days to be again employed in the precious work of baptizing

As soon as our Minutes are printed I will send you a copy, according to the order of our association Two missionary societies have recently been formed in my congregations. I hope they promise usefulness in the cause of our Master.

From Rev E Ferris to the Cor. Sec. dated Lawrenceburg, Sep. 28, 1818.

THE Lord has graciously revived his work in many churches in our vicinity, since brother Rice visited us at Cedar Grove, where the association was held last year. A glorious work began in the spring, which was carried on with that solemnity and order that becomes the gospel. Before the association, upwards of sixty had been baptized. A similar work commenced more recently at Lick creek, higher up, on White water, where upward of 40 were baptized; and in the small county of Boon, on the Kentucky side, adjoining us, I think there have been as many as 500 baptized since the commencement of the present year, and I may add that, throughout the eastern part of this state, the cause of the baptists is much more prosperous than it has been at any former period A new association has been formed between us and Silver creek, called Lawery.

From Rev. Hosea Holcomb to the Cor. Sec. dated U District, S C Oct. 7, 1818.

I RETURNED last evening from the Bethel association, held in Spartanburg district, where we experienced such a season as we have not seen for many years. There was a large assembly, who, in general, appeared to be all attention Ministers preached with zeal and energy the words of eternal life; which, we think, was accompanied by the power of the Divine Spirit. Christians rejoiced exceedingly; and some professed to be delivered from the burden of sin which they had laboured under for some time, while numbers were brought to cry, "What shall we do to be saved?" Many were struck to the ground, and lay a while apparently dead. We hope this work was the great power of the Lord. however, time will evince whether it is or not. It appears the most like the great work in

1801, 2, and 3, of any I ever saw. There has been a considerable revival for some time in that vicinity, and a number have been added to some of the churches. The work continues to spread, and (if it be of the Lord) we pray that it may continue to spread far and wide over our large continent, that God's name may be glorified, and sinners saved.

From Rev. S. Pillsbury to the Cor. Sec. dated Hebron, N. H. Dec. 2, 1818

The Lord is pleased to visit us in the region where I dwell, with refreshing showers of grace. We have had a long and tedious winter, but, blessed be God, the spring is come at last. The work commenced in Groton, a town adjoining this, early last spring, in a congregational society. It soon made its appearance in this place. Backsliders have been reclaimed, and a number have been hopefully translated from nature's darkness into God's marvellous light. The association last September at Lime, was made a great blessing to that people. A reformation soon made its appearance, and the work, I hear, has been very powerful, and pretty extensive for the time. Within a few days I learn that an awakening has been begun in Dorchester, about eight or ten miles from where I dwell, and that appearances are very encouraging. I have heard of some other places in this region, where appearances are favourable. Surely this is the Lord's doing, and it is marvellous in our eyes!

From Rev. E. Montague to the Cor. Sec. dated Leveritt, Dec. 7, 1818

There is a good work of grace going on in a number of towns south of where I live. It began in Belchertown, by the means of the following providence. The Baptist church there being vacated, their ministering brother elder Pease, by consent having just removed, another brother, elder Thomas Marshall, was employed by a special providence, so that they were not destitute one Lord's day. But, oh! as two of the brethren were moving brother Marshall's goods, &c. the wagon by some means ran over the body, but especially the head of one of them, crushed his under jaw, and pressed out one of his eyes! He was taken up for dead; but, to the astonishment of all, is yet alive, in body and soul. His conversation, with brother Marshall's improvements, was the beginning of the work, which has spread into five or six towns.

From Mr. Wm. Polke to the Cor. Sec. dated Corydon, (Ia.) Jan. 1, 1819.

Brother M'Coy has done and is doing much in the cause of missions, by dispelling the gloom, so that I confidently hope Indiana will contribute something handsome to aid the cause. His amiable and unassuming manners, his fervent piety, his zeal in the cause of missions, and his perfect acquaintance with the manners of the western people, make him popular with all the pious of different denominations.

THEATRE AT ALBANY, N. Y.
TURNED INTO A BAPTIST MEETING HOUSE.

This edifice was erected in 1812, and opened January 18, 1813, for theatrical exhibitions. To the honour of Albany, and especially of its christian ministers, it was found that *there* the establishment could not procure to itself adequate support. In June, 1818, the Baptist brethren purchased the whole. The scenery, galleries, stage, recesses, &c. have been torn away, and arrangements made, alike neat and spacious, for the accommodation of a large christian assembly.

In a communication on the subject, the Rev. Mr. Bradley, pastor of the church, thus expresses himself:

"The singularity of the place obtained for public worship, and the constant endeavours of this church and society, and even young children, to pay for the building, and to fit it up conveniently, have inclined many to believe that the agency of Christ was in these transactions. The very man who superintended the erection of the theatre, superintended its disorganization. The very ministers who prayed and preached against its erection, have liberally aided us in pulling it down, and encouraged their people to give us assistance."

The house was opened for the worship of the Lord, January 1819, at 3 o'clock P. M. The first part of the 84th Psalm, L. M. was sung. Brother Bradley prayed: the Rev. President Nott, of Schenectady, read the 132d Psalm, from the pause. Brother Bradley preached from Psalm cxxxii. 8. *Arise, O Lord, into thy rest, thou and the ark of thy strength.* After elucidating his text, and deducing a few inferences, brother Bradley presented to the assembly a brief account of the rise, progress, and present condition of the church who were then entering their new place of worship. Brother Sommers prayed, and the exercises were closed by singing an ode composed for the occasion.

On the evening the congregation again assembled, when the Rev. President Nott delivered an eloquent and appropriate discourse from Psalm xxvii. 4. *One thing I have desired of the Lord, that will I seek after, that I may dwell in the house of the Lord all the days of my life, to behold the beauty of the Lord, and to inquire in his temple.* Brother Willey prayed. About 2000 persons attended, both in the afternoon and evening. The collections amounted to $356. The edifice is brick, 80 feet long and 54 feet wide.

The closing language of brother Bradley's address, every pious heart must feel pleasure in adopting.

"Take this house as thine, we beseech thee: furnish it with ministers after thy own heart; keep it from being destroyed, and fill it with thy presence, and the whole world with the knowledge of thy glory!"

MISCELLANEA.

A REASON of difference among Christians may be attributed to different feelings; or Christians giving way to be governed by feelings, instead of the bare written word of inspiration. There are the remains of depravity in the best of men, so long as they remain in this life, the fruit of which is SELFISHNESS. Perhaps nothing tends to widen the jarring interests of Zion more than this evil. *I feel so*, is often urged instead of all arguments, and is made to answer all ends, *I feel*, often serves as a comment on Scripture, *I feel*, prescribes rules for churches; *I feel*, perhaps too often, is the judge of ordinances. *I feel*, is often the ground of difficulty amongst brethren, even where the Scriptures themselves are silent. This mighty prince gives ground and rule for the forgiveness of faults; and, in short, he claims to hold the standard that weighs out rules for God's kingdom on high, and his footstool here below! Again, under the pretext of exalting the doctrine of the Cross above human learning, many have disapproved of the study of divinity with the aid of human instruction. By some it is thought that *ignorance* is a bright mark of honesty in a preacher, and is viewed as an eminent qualification and evidence of divinity. This pretext is by some urged in the place of ministerial support. For, say they, if the minister be called of God to preach, he need not study his sermons; he may labour all the week, and preach on the Lord's day; for the promise is, "Lo, I am with you." Brethren in the ministry, be exhorted not to carry unbeaten oil into the sanctuary of the Lord. Search out and set in order acceptable words. Be sure that you bind Isaac with cords on the altar, and if the Lord provide himself a lamb for a burnt offering at the important moment, receive it thankfully.

From the Letter of the Holland Purchase Baptist Association, 1818.

JOHN xiii. 34. "A new commandment I give unto you," &c. '*New*,' says Cradock—'1. because purged from the corrupt glosses of the pharisees, and, as it were, made *new* by Christ, because by him further extended and raised to a higher pitch. 2. Because pressed by a *new* example, even his own—*as I have loved you*. 3. *New*, because it is never to wax old, but to be always fresh in memory and practice. 4. *New*, because *newly* delivered and more plainly and openly set forth to the world; as a picture, done over with new colours, may be called a new picture.'—To which may be added *new*, because of its excellency—See Ps. xxxii. 3. Is. lxv. 17. Rev. ii. 17. and *new* because it relates not to men, or even to relations as such, but to the disciples of Christ in reference to each other. 1 John iii. 23.—1 Thess. iv. 9. 'Raphelius has the best *note*,' says Doddridge, 'I ever saw on the passage, though I think it hardly reaches the full spirit of it, in which he shows that Xenophon calls the laws of Lycurgus καινοτατοι νομοι, *very new laws*, several hundred years after they were made; because, though they had been commended by other nations, they had not been practised by them.'

WHEN Elymas was struck blind at Paphos, Sergius was astonished, we are told, at "THE DOCTRINE" of the Lord, and commenced a Christian from that hour. Acts xiii. 12. The expression is remarkable, but has a peculiar propriety. A mere historical believer would have been astonished at the miracle merely. Sergius, a true convert, who entered into the nature of the gospel by a spiritual perception, is astonished at "THE DOCTRINE." *Milner*

ERROR is no where stable or certain; but fluctuates, like the fabled isle of Delos, beyond the skill of men or devils to give it fixation. *Owen.*

CHRONOLOGI non magis congruunt quam horologia.
Chronologers no more agree than clocks. *Strigel.*

Riches are as a flock of birds. One cannot say they are his, because they sit on his bushes. for they take unto them wings, saith Solomon, and flee away.
Trappe.

The second epistle of John is the only epistle in the Scripture directed to a female

---

"The female sex, almost excluded from civil history, will appear more conspicuous in ecclesiastical. Less immersed in secular concerns, and less haughty and independent in spirit, they seem, in all ages, to have had their full proportion, or more than the other sex of the grace of the gospel" *Milner*

The following is part of an epitaph on *Thomas Tallis*, one of the greatest proficients in psalmody of the 16th century. He died 1585, and was buried at Greenwich, in Kent.

> " Enterred here doth ly a worthy wyght,
> Who for long tyme in music bore the bell ;
> His name to shew was Thomas Tallis hight,
> In honest vertuous lyff he did excell.
> As he dyd live, so also dyd he dy
> In mild and quyet sort, O happy man '
> To God ful oft for mercy dyd he cry,
> *Wherefore he lyves, let deth do what he can.*

OBITUARY.

Elizabeth Lovlas Jones, was born 25 years and about 7 months ago, in the town of Redruth, county of Cornwall, England. She was a subject of Divine impressions from a very early period of her life, as she could scarcely recollect a time when she had not the fear of God before her eyes. This may be owing, under the agency of the Holy Spirit, to the precepts and example of her parents, who were both eminently pious.

About eight weeks ago, the disorder which had almost as early as her arrival in America, taken a fatal grasp of her constitution, and finally terminated her life, began to put forth more formidable and alarming symptoms. She then felt the necessity of a clearer sense of the Divine favour, and expressed ardent desires for more holiness to qualify her for heaven. However, she possessed that hope which was the anchor of her soul, and her confidence was usually strong in the Redeemer; being assured that he who she knew had begun a good work in her soul would finally complete it. Often she sent up her petitions to God, for more grace, and often it was evident that he deigned to answer her prayers. When she was sometimes overtaken with spiritual darkness and doubts, she would complain of unfaithfulness to her Saviour, and would frequently say that she did not love him as she ought, or as she wished; and she considered her affliction as sent in mercy to stir her up to greater diligence in the divine life.

The disorder, which was of a pulmonary description, proceeded rapidly to its issue. When it was told her that the physicians considered her affliction incurable, and that it would, to all human appearance, soon ultimate in death, she was not in the least shocked or alarmed; but said, with a cheerful countenance, "My Father's will be done!"

There was one occasion on which she made some observations so peculiarly interesting, that they must not be unnoticed. On the evening of the 18th of last month, she had a severe paroxysm, and we feared that she would have expired in it. But, contrary to the expectation of every one present, she revived, and as soon as her voice returned, it was lifted in praise and thanksgiving to God. She seemed then to have obtained a fresh and full assurance of the Divine favour, and she was enabled to rejoice in the hope and in the prospect of eternal life. The following are some of her expressions. "Glory to God!—Blessed Jesus!" were the first words from her quivering lips. "I hoped I was going immediately to my Saviour, but he has thought proper to leave me a little longer in this world—this wilderness world. By and by I shall see him as he is,—face to face.—Blessed Saviour! O what glory! Then I shall be freed from this feeble, perishing body. Then I shall be exempt from pain, and sorrow, and every evil. Then I shall meet my dear friends who are gone before. Happy meeting! O how shall I sufficiently praise my God and Saviour for his amazing love to such a sinful worm as I! O that I had strength and a voice to praise him as I desire!" Then she called upon the nurse to assist her in praising God, and exhorted her to seek that religion, which, she observed, would support her under all the trials of life, and particularly in such a situation as, said she, I myself am now in. Being almost exhausted with speaking, she lay silent for a few minutes, and then resumed,—"But how can such a sinful creature as I, presume to hope for such happiness! How is it possible!" Her husband said, "My dear, our blessed Redeemer hath obtained this happiness for us; it is through his everlasting righteousness, and not by any merit of our own, that we obtain pardon, holiness, and heaven." "Yes," she replied, "*that* is all my trust. He, (the Redeemer,) He is my hope—my confidence is all in him!"

Many other of her subsequent observations are equally interesting; but our limits preclude an enlargement. As she drew nearer to her end, her confidence in her Redeemer seemed to increase. her soul was often elevated to the contemplation of heavenly bliss; and sometimes she appeared remarkably happy, which, even in her severest spasms, and when she was deprived of the power of speech, was manifest in the cheerfulness, composure, and serenity of her countenance. About ten minutes before she breathed her last, she was asked if she then felt the Divine presence to support her in such a trying hour. She answered with an emphasis that astonished all present—"*I know in whom I have trusted!*" which she repeated three times, and then asked "*if that was not enough!*"

In a few minutes after she breathed her happy spirit into the hands of Him who gave it, without a struggle, or a sigh, or a groan.

Her remains are interred in the cemetery of the Baptist church in Sansom street, of which church, since her residence in America, she has been an amiable member.

Philadelphia, December 13, 1818.

POETRY.

THE END OF AFFLICTION

THAT God, whose power, from nothing, all things made,
Who spoke, and swift the light his call obey'd,
Looks from his lofty throne beyond the sky,
And downward casts an ever-watchful eye,
The meanest sparrow falls not to the ground,
Nor dies an insect in creation's round
Without his sovereign will, his firm decree;
Nought can his power elude, his notice flee
And will that God, who guards the meanest form,
The creeping reptile, and the insect worm,
Despise immortals, pass his children by,
Nor deign to hear the virtuous sufferer cry?
Ah, no! indulge no more the impious thought,
Nor stain his glory with so foul a blot,
Believe his word, that word is ever sure,
His truth, through endless years, shall still endure.
Our sorrows, wisely viewed, shall work for good,
And thus afford our souls substantial food,
Affliction's furnace fits us for the skies,
And tears are changed for bliss that never dies.
'Tis thus the cottage, veiled in silent wo,
Where sighs and tears in sad profusion flow,
Is better far for souls of heavenly birth,
Than all the joys that gild the house of mirth,
'Tis here the soul in converse sweet with God,
Bows to his will, and owns the chastening rod,
Perceives its glory tarnished by the fall,
And, prostrate, crowns IMMANUEL Lord of all.

M

ON THE DEATH OF A CHILD

To Mrs. P———.

'TIS DONE! Behold the happy spirit soar
To the blest realms where death shall be no more,
Where infants, saved by Jesus' wondrous grace,
Ever behold his Father's beauteous face
"Why weepest thou?" the angels said to one,
Who mourned the death of God's beloved Son,
The words to thee may be repeated now,
Then tell me if thou canst, "Why weepest thou?"
What if thy Lord, mysterious as just,
Has laid another infant in the dust?

What though he chose to take thy darling boy,
And disappoint again thy earthly joy?
Yet bow in meekness to the gilded rod,
Scourging may bring thee nearer to thy God.
Let this console thee 'mid repeated woes,
Thou hast a Father whom thou canst not lose,
"A Friend that closer than a brother" keeps;
A Guide, a GOD, that "slumbers not, nor sleeps,"
Who form'd all things; "in whom we live and move,"
Himself the fount of everlasting love!.....
An elder Brother, also, in the skies,
Whose pleading voice for all his ransomed cries.
(Behold the channel where all mercies flow,)
"Father, forgive, they know not what they do!"
"Why weepest thou?" Oh may these prospects rise
In bright array before thy tearful eyes!
Viewing Jehovah's love, mayst thou "be still,"
And learn to *bear*, as well as *do* his will!
How short, and yet how weary is the way
That leads us to the plains of endless day,
That grace which saves "through faith, the gift of God,"
Alone supports us in the chequer'd road,
Views the "reserved inheritance," the lands,
The river, tree, "the house not made with hands."
Though "dark" her vision of the heavenly place,
It urges us with joy, "to run the race,"
Oh! may we "look to Jesus" as we go,
To speed our passage from the plain below;
Unspeakable the bliss! at length to rise,
And "be for ever with him" in the skies.
May God assist us *now*, as also *then*,
T' ascribe *all* glory to his name—*Amen!*   H. M. P.

THE MISSIONARY.

From friends beloved, and from the happy home
   Where life's first blush in peaceful splendour rose,
O'er oceans vast or distant wilds to roam,
   The self-devoted missionary goes.

His breast no mercenary views control;
   No earthly principle usurps a part;—
The day-spring from on high has fired his soul;
   The God of glory shined into his heart.

These rays celestial light his lonely way,
   As Israel once the trackless desert trod,
And all his powers, with glowing zeal, display
   The grace and mercy of his Saviour God.   C.

THE LATTER DAY LUMINARY;

BY A COMMITTEE

OF

THE BAPTIST BOARD OF FOREIGN MISSIONS FOR THE UNITED STATES.

Vol. I   MAY, 1819.   No. VII.

BIOGRAPHY.

TO THE EDITORS OF THE LATTER DAY LUMINARY.

BELIEVING that biographical sketches of men eminent for piety are productive of happy effects, I take the liberty of transmitting to you the enclosed for publication in the Luminary, if you shall deem it sufficiently interesting to entitle it to a place in so valuable a repository. The subject, ROBERT POLK, Esq. was my intimate friend; and in his death I have sustained an irreparable loss. The facts are collected by one who knew him well, and from a source that may be confidently relied upon. Most of them were within my own knowledge. If departed excellence demands the tribute of a tear, the triumphs of his death alleviate the mourner's wo.

His letter to me before he made a public profession of religion, was designed for a candid disclosure of his views upon that subject, when his diffidence would not yet permit him to *speak* with unreserved freedom. Its length is too great for publication in a work devoted to miscellaneous purposes, and an abstract only is communicated. His relation before the church was substantially the same, with the addition of clearer manifestations of his interest in the atoning blood of Christ.

O. B. BROWN.

WASHINGTON, March, 1819.

ROBERT POLK, ESQ.

Robert Polk was born in the city of Philadelphia, on the 9th of December, 1788. He was remarkably delicate from his infancy, and little hope was entertained by his parents that he would be raised to manhood. At four years of age he discovered a fondness for books. and at the age of five could read remarkably well. In his tenth year he was placed under the care of the Rev. Mr. Samuel Knox, (now president of the Baltimore college,) who then was principal of an academy at Fredericktown, in Maryland, and celebrated for his distinguished qualifications as a classical teacher. Through the kind attentions of this gentleman, who soon discovered the talents of his pupil, he made rapid progress in the acquisition of the Latin and Greek languages, in which he became a proficient in a few years.

After the removal of his father to the seat of government, he prosecuted his studies with the ablest teacher in that place; and acquired such a fondness for the Greek, that when he made profession of religion, it was his daily practice to study the New Testament in that language.

In the year 1807 he commenced the study of the law, under the patronage of the honourable Gabriel Duvall; and in 1810, after undergoing the usual examination by the judges of the circuit court for the District of Columbia, he was admitted to practise as an attorney. He did not, however, appear to be fond of the profession of the law: and after the establishment of the office of the commissioner of the revenue in 1814, he was appointed principal clerk in that office; in which station he continued until his death in 1818.

Besides the arduous duties in which he was engaged for several years, such was his love of study, and habits of industry, that he made a complete digest of the laws of Congress, down to the year 1817, besides writing a number of essays on law and politics.

By the appointment of the mayor and council of the city of Washington, and at their special request, he delivered an oration on the 4th of July, 1810, before the President of the United States, the heads of department, and a numerous concourse of citizens. His performance on this occasion, both for the sentiments which were advanced, and the language in which they were clothed, received the marked approbation of the President.

In the spring of 1811, he married a lady of respectability in the state of Virginia, by whom he had four children.

Having for several years had his mind exercised on the subject of religion, he addressed the following letter to the Rev. Obadiah B.

Brown, with a view of laying before him the state of his mind on that subject, preparatory to becoming a member of the church under his pastoral charge.

WASHINGTON CITY, May 20th, 1817.

DEAR SIR,

Having long laboured under much darkness of mind, respecting my views of the gospel of salvation, which has been promulgated to the world in the name of Jesus Christ our Lord, and in the truth of which, in common with my fellow men, I am deeply interested; I have concluded that it might be advantageous to me, to lay before you a sketch of the past exercises of my mind on this, the most important of all subjects.

It would seem to be a position not liable to doubt or controversy, that a system which professes to have God for its Author, salvation for its end, and truth for its matter, must be entitled to the most serious consideration of those to whom it is addressed. Of such a character is the gospel of Christ. It merits, therefore, the profound attention of every human being. No man can be justified in disbelieving or rejecting this gospel, until, after a serious investigation, he shall be satisfied that its claims to a divine origin are unfounded. And whether such would be the result of his inquiries cannot, surely, be an unimportant question.

I do not recollect any period of my life at which I was wholly insensible to the importance of religion. Having been religiously educated from my infancy, by a father whose precepts and example were continually before me, and having been accustomed to a regular attendance on the external duties of Christianity, my religious impressions were coeval with my earliest recollections. But these were transient and fleeting, and had no permanent effect on my mind, except, perhaps, to restrain me from the practice of some of the grosser vices familiar to youth. As I grew up, my mind became much engaged in literary and political inquiries,—to which I was prompted both by my love of reading, and my expectation of their determining my future lot in life. For some years my thoughts were almost exclusively directed to such subjects, and I became indifferent or unconcerned in regard to my eternal welfare. But about my twentieth year, my attention began to be recalled to it, and religious inquiries and metaphysical discussions were the subjects which engaged my reflections. The Christian religion appeared to me a fit subject for the exercise of my reasoning faculties, and I determined to believe no more of it than should be reconcileable to reason. In this spirit of mind, without ever imploring the guidance of the Author of all wisdom, I undertook to subject this divine system to the test by which ordinary questions are tried and determined, and to frame for myself a set of tenets which might satisfy my understanding, without affecting my heart. The result was such as might have been expected. All the various forms under which the religion of Jesus has been assailed by infidels and philosophers, presented themselves to my mind in succession. The divine origin of the scriptures—the fallen state of man —the divinity of Christ—the necessity of a Mediator—the endless punishment of any portion of mankind,—were all questions on which I doubted or disbelieved. But, although the arguments against these doctrines presented themselves under the fair semblance of truth and reason, and for a while engaged my acquiescence, yet I could not satisfy myself, in such a degree, of their truth, as to rest on them with confidence the fate of my future being. I was disturbed with anxious and perplexing fears; and, although I saw and lamented the insufficiency of human reason to arrive at any satisfactory conclusion respecting them, I was not sensible of the necessity of a Divine instructer. Without looking to him for wisdom to guide and direct me in the path of truth, I wandered in a labyrinth of darkness,—unhappy at the present, and distressed about the future.

The reflections which occupied my mind, and prevented my settling down contented with any one of the systems of unbelief which alternately crossed me, were such as these: "What if I am mistaken! What if the doctrines generally believed among Christians should be true! I cannot be certain that they are not so, although I cannot reconcile them to my views of God and futurity, yet I know men, whom I esteem to be good men, who believe them, and who consider the belief of them essential to salvation, and I have read of others who, on their dying beds, and even in the midst of flames and torments, have borne witness to their truth. Can I disbelieve, or reject *such testimony?*—Where, on the other hand, can the Deist, the Socinian, or the Universalist produce such examples? What am I then to do? I cannot rest secure in my present sentiments, because all my reflections and inquiries have not assured me of their truth. I cannot risk eternity upon them." Thus, wearied and distressed in mind, not knowing what to believe, or what to rest on; about two years ago, I came to this conclusion, (I hope led by the Spirit of God,) "I will throw aside every set of doctrines which I have ever known taught among men, as being the essence of true religion. I will leave them out of view, and ascend to first principles. Reason assures me that there is a God. He must be infinite in all his attributes: that he must be the greatest, the wisest, and the best of beings. I will look to him, therefore, and I will beseech him to grant me wisdom, to preserve me from errour and delusion, and to guide me into the truth."

I had all along thought, that if I could settle down into the belief of a system of doctrine, I should find no difficulty in conforming to its practice. But I had never suspected or believed the deceitfulness of my own heart. But now I began to discover my errour, and to think there must be some radical defect in myself. In this state of perturbation, " to stop too fearful, and too faint to go," it occurred to me that the safest course I could take, would be to address myself to my Creator, and to beseech him to lead me by his holy Spirit in the way everlasting,—to lead me to the knowledge of him, the only true God, and of Jesus Christ whom he had sent. While in this frame of mind, I saw the publication of a new work announced in the papers, under the title of " Dissertations on the scriptural Doctrine of *Atonement and Sacrifice*," by William Magee, D D of the University of Dublin. Its title struck my attention. The doctrine of atonement for the sins of men, had long been a stumbling-block to me, as being inconsistent with my views of the mercy of God and the merit of man. I was desirous to see how it could be illustrated and established. I procured the book, and read it through with attention. I was convinced by his arguments, that the custom prevailing among all nations, in all ages, of offering up sacrifices for the expiation of sin, by shedding the blood of innocent animals, could not have had its origin from human reason—that it must be ascribed to the traditionary remains of a divine revelation, and that it shadowed forth the GREAT SACRIFICE which was once to be offered for sin. I was hence led to see that, in all ages, mankind had considered themselves unworthy to approach the Deity, except through the medium of an atoning sacrifice, which was designed to avert the punishment of their offences, and to propitiate the object of their worship. I perceived the errour under which I had so long laboured, and the *necessity of a Mediator* between God and sinful man. I saw that the scriptures clearly exhibited Jesus as the mediator, and that God would not accept the person or worship of any mortal who did not come to him in the name of JESUS CHRIST,—that man was in a fallen state— that his moral powers were so depraved he could not, of himself, render any acceptable service to a BEING OF INFINITE PURITY:—and that, without the shedding of blood, there was no remission. I perceived that all the different modes of unbelief which I had embraced, were, in reality, only refuges of lies, for me to escape from the obligation of that sincere obedience and worship which I owed to God:

that under them I had, in fact, (though then unknown to myself,) been disguising my aversion to the service of God, and my unwillingness to *feel* and *acknowledge* myself a depraved and sinful creature.

I looked around me, and found that no where, either among families or individuals, was the name of the Lord invoked, or his worship set up, except among those who professed to *rely upon Jesus Christ* as the only medium of access to him: as the only name by which God could, or would, be approached by sinful men. I determined that I would go among these people, that I would attend their social meetings for prayer, and other devotional exercises. I have accordingly attended to this and other means of grace for some months past, and have reason to bless God, that my mind has thereby been strengthened and established in the faith of the gospel, and is now, I trust, firmly fixed on Jesus Christ, the Rock of Ages: in whom is all my hope, and all my joy.

With sincere respect and esteem, I am yours,

ROBERT POLK.

Rev. OBADIAH B BROWN, Pastor
of the Baptist church, Washington city.

The substance of the foregoing letter was related by him before the church, in communicating his experience, and upon satisfactory evidence of his interest in the atoning blood of Christ, he was baptized, and by unanimous consent admitted a member of the First Baptist Church, on Lord's day, August 10th, 1817.

Added to the natural weakness of his constitution, the close confinement and laborious duties of his station, as principal clerk in the office of the commissioner of the revenue, brought on a general debility of system, under which he languished for about eighteen months. On the 1st of June, 1818, he found himself obliged to retire from public business, with a hope that travelling, and attending some springs in Virginia, would restore him. But he was able to go no further than to the residence of his brother-in-law, in Frederick county, Virginia. Here he continued, able to use but little exercise, and, notwithstanding every personal kindness and attention by his friends, and the best medical advice the neighbourhood afforded, on the 21st of July he was taken ill, and confined to his bed. His system was too far gone to be restored, and he died on the 31st of July, 1818.

The following letter, written to his father, will show, at the time, the state of his mind, when his health and life were in a critical situation.

Robert Polk, Esq.

BELLEGROVE, *June* 18th, 1818.

MY DEAR FATHER,

I would have written you before this time to inform you of our safe arrival at this place, had I not been in hopes that, by deferring it, I might be able to give you an account of some change for the better in my health; but I do not, as yet, perceive any amendment whatever in the state of it. My breast continues to be very much affected; and although I expectorate a little, it is insufficient to free me from the oppressive load under which I labour.

Amidst these troubles and afflictions which oppress my "outward man," it will be some satisfaction to you to know, that I am enabled more fully and confidently to look to that blood which *cleanses from all sin*. The person, the character, the offices of the divine Redeemer, are, I trust, becoming more and more precious to me. I see him to be just that infinite, almighty, compassionate Saviour which I need; and, having nothing to plead for my acceptance but his infinite merits, I would throw myself upon his divine mercy as a miserable lost sinner. I could wish, above all things, if it be his holy will, that I might be delivered entirely from the bondage and pollution of sin, and that I might run the way of his commandments with an enlarged heart. Whether I live or die, I trust that I shall be enabled to confide in him:—knowing that he is able to save to the *uttermost* all that come unto God by him; and I do earnestly beg, my dear father, that you will supplicate him, in my behalf, to grant me all the grace I need, and to keep me in the way everlasting.

I remain your affectionate son,
ROBERT POLK

Mr. CHARLES P. POLK, Washington city

He had for some time anticipated and been prepared for death During his confinement, although in great pain from the affection of his breast, yet not a murmur escaped his lips. He conversed with his wife and friends in the most serene manner. He had lived in the utmost affection and harmony with her, was remarkably fond of his children, and expressed an entire confidence in the providence and promises of a gracious God towards them.

A few days before his death, he said he knew, from his feelings, that he could not survive but a short time; and requested that all the family might be invited into the room. When they had assembled, after affectionately acknowledging the kindness they had all shown him, he addressed them in the following language: " My friends, you behold in me a monument of the power of the Christian religion, you see how weak I am in body, and how much I suffer. but, blessed be God, my soul is full of the love of Christ; by faith I see Jesus, my Redeemer, who bled and died for my sins, and I am sure, that through his merits, I shall enjoy everlasting happiness beyond the grave. Glory inexpressible fills my soul, and I shall soon be where I shall sing glory, glory, glory for ever."

Just before he expired, he requested the favour of a servant man who waited on him, to adjust his arms and legs for death, as he was no longer able to move himself. He then breathed out his spirit into the hands of Him who gave it, without a sigh or groan.

During his confinement he was visited several times by the Rev. William Buck, a baptist minister in the neighbourhood, who expressed great satisfaction at his conversations, and who preached his funeral sermon at the time of his interment.

We shall close this sketch with the obituary notice that was written by an intimate friend of his, and published in the "National Intelligencer" of August 6th, 1818.

Died on Friday, the 31st ult. in Frederick county, Va. on a visit for his health, ROBERT POLK, Esq. chief clerk in the office of Internal Revenue, in the 30th year of his age. Such a rare combination of intelligence and meekness, of learning and humility, as were united in the character of the amiable deceased, is very seldom witnessed His unaffected piety, and conciliating deportment, had greatly endeared him to the church with which he stood connected, and to the numerous circle of friends, to whom his memory will be ever dear His widowed companion and fatherless children, have experienced a loss which no earthly boon can compensate; but, for himself, the event is unquestionably most happy; he has exchanged a world of sin and sorrow for that happy state " where the wicked cease from troubling, and the weary are for ever at rest."

MEMORIA JUSTI BENEDICTA.

COMMUNICATIONS.

APOSTOLIC MISSION TOURS.

THE principal, and indeed the only authentic source, from which we can derive intelligence on the subject before us, is the New Testament, and particularly the Acts of the Apostles. We will collect what information we are able, relative to the journeyings of those holy men, with the exception of Paul, whose travels will be contemplated in a future number of this work.

After the success which had attended the sermons of PETER, on the day of Pentecost, and on the healing of a cripple, and after various persecutions endured for the truth's sake, this apostle, accompanied by his associate John, went from Jerusalem to Samaria to lay hands on such as had believed under the ministry of Philip. This appears to have been the first apostolic tour. They "testified and preached the word of the Lord," and, as they "returned to Jerusalem," they "preached the gospel in many villages of the Samaritans." Samaria, Galilee, and Judea, about the year 39 or 40, being in a state of tranquillity, Peter performed a journey through many parts of these territories, diffusing the knowledge of his Lord. At Lydda he healed Eneas, who had kept his bed eight years with the palsy. Such was the effect of this miracle, attended no doubt with the preaching of the apostle, that " all that dwelt in Lydda and Saron turned to the Lord." Thence he passed to Joppa, where he raised from the dead a most benevolent female of the name of Dorcas. The miracle " was known throughout all Joppa, and many believed in the Lord." At this latter station he was requested by Cornelius, a pious centurion of Cæsarea, and directed by a vision from heaven, to visit his family. He cheerfully accompanied the messengers who came to invite him, and at Cæsarea saw a door of faith opened to the gentiles. Returned to Jerusalem, he gave to his astonished brethren an account of the circumstances of his mission. "When they heard these things they held their peace, and glorified God, saying, Then hath God also to the gentiles granted repentance unto life." From this period the wall of partition was broken down, and the fact obvious, that there is neither Jew nor Greek—but that all are one in Christ Jesus. After the memorable council at Jerusalem, we find him at Antioch, conversing familiarly with the Gentile converts. From this time we know little more of this apostle than what is stated by Eusebius, that " coming to Rome, he was crucified with his head downward, having himself desired it might be in that manner;" and by Jerom, who concludes his article on Peter by saying, " he was buried at Rome, in the Vatican, near the triumphal way, and is in veneration all over the world."

No record is extant of the mission tours of JOHN, the apostle and evangelist, with the exception of that to Samaria in company with Peter. It is probable he continued a long time in Jerusalem, where he is found at the time of the council, Acts xv. About the 14th year of Domitian he was banished to the isle of Patmos, at which place he is supposed to have continued until the commencement of the reign of

Nerva. His zeal in the ministry appears to have procured his exileship. "I John was in the isle of Patmos, for the word of God, and for the testimony of Jesus Christ." It is, by ecclesiastical historians generally, admitted, that in the later periods of his life he resided in the lesser Asia, particularly at Ephesus, where, at the advanced age of a hundred years, he died.

For what reasons infinite wisdom has seen fit to leave the actions of many of the disciples unrecorded in the sacred pages, it is not our province to determine. The conjecture of Dr. Cave is probable, that "a particular relation of the acts of so many apostles, done in so many several countries, might have swelled the holy volumes to too great a bulk, and rendered them less serviceable and accommodated to the ordinary use of Christians." The ancients affirm, that the apostles agreed among themselves, or, as some say, determined by solemn lot, into what countries each should travel.

It is generally supposed that ANDREW passed through the regions of Galatia and Bythinia, taught the inhospitable inhabitants of the shores of the Euxine, and then penetrated into the solitudes of Scythia. The Greeks represent him as the founder of a christian church at Constantinople.

JAMES *the elder* is said to have preached to the tribes that were scattered abroad. Sanctius and others contend, that he first preached the gospel in Spain.* The probability is that James restricted his zealous labours to the city Jerusalem, where he died, the first apostolic martyr, being beheaded from motives of hatred or policy, by Herod Agrippa. Acts xii. 1.

PHILIP is supposed to have laboured in upper Asia, south of the Euxine and Hellespont. Theodoret says he preached in the two Phrygias, and Eusebius that he was buried at Hierapolis.

BARTHOLOMEW, it is highly probable, was the same with Nathaniel, his name Bartholomew being constantly appended to Philip's after the call to the apostleship, as was the name Nathaniel before. This servant of Christ is said to have preached in India, leaving among the natives a copy of the gospel by Matthew. On his passage thither, and on his return, mention is made of his publishing the doctrine of the cross through Arabia Felix and Persia. Probably he also visited Lycaonia, and died a martyr to the truth, at Albanople, in the greater Armenia.

Chrysostom mentions that THOMAS preached to the Ethiopians, Parthians, Persians and Medes. Several of the fathers state that he

* Dr Cave says, "what became of James after our Saviour's ascension, we have no certain account from sacred or ecclesiastical stories."

published the divine word in Ethiopia and the East Indies. The Thomæans, or Christians of St. Thomas, found in Cochin and on the Malabar and Coromandel coast, according to tradition, received the gospel from this apostle.

It is generally imagined that MATTHEW preached and suffered martyrdom among the Persians or Parthians, but nothing approaching certainty can be collected.

SIMON, who by Luke (chap. vi 15. Acts i. 13.) is called Zelotes, perhaps from his ardour in receiving and propagating the gospel of the Redeemer, is said by some to have journeyed through Egypt and Cyrenaica, Mauritania and Lybia. Others state that he preached in Britain, and afterwards sealed his testimony with his blood, at Sunir in Persia. The Greeks are of opinion that he was the bridegroom at the marriage of Cana. The particulars of his life are very imperfectly known No mention is made of him by the evangelists after his investiture with the apostolic office.

Nothing satisfactory is recorded by ecclesiastical historians and others, concerning JUDE, the same who is surnamed Thaddeus or Lebbeus, and called the Lord's brother, Matt. xiii. 55. The modern Greeks affirm that the field of his labours was Mesopotamia; others refer them to Armenia and Persia A writer quoted by Eusebius, describes him as put to death at Berytus, and there honourably interred.

JAMES, who was probably called *the less* because of the inferiority of his stature, seems to have lived and died in Jerusalem. His integrity of character procured him the title of THE JUST. Hegesippus, as quoted by Eusebius, ascribes his death to his public testimony that " Jesus, the Son of man, is now seated at the right hand of the supreme Majesty, as the Son of GOD, and must one day come borne on the clouds of heaven " Many of the Jews attribute the overthrow of their city to the murder of this excellent man.

The Greeks believe that MATTHIAS, who was chosen in the room of Iscariot, preached and died at Colchis.

From the whole we may remark, that the voice of antiquity, while it is uncertain in many instances as to the sphere of apostolic labours, is agreed in admitting that they were extensive. Mosheim himself observes, that " the distance of time, and the want of records, leave us at a loss with respect to many interesting circumstances of the peregrinations of the apostles," but admits that, having finished their work at Jerusalem, they " travelled over a great part of the known world, and in a short time planted a vast number of churches among the gentiles " Let the servants of Christ in later ages, imitate these holy men, and like them possess a readiness of spirit *to labour*, *to suffer*, and, if required, *to die* in the best of causes

THE INFLUENCES OF THE SPIRIT OF GOD NECESSARY TO MISSIONARY SUCCESS.

[Communicated by Rev. Mr. WARD, Missionary, Serampore.]

I PRESUME that none of those to whom these pages are addressed, entertains any doubts whether the influences of the Spirit are bestowed on men or not. The effects of Peter's sermon, on the day of Pentecost, fully prove the fact. In the close of that account it is said, "And *the Lord added* to the church daily such as should be saved." It is said of Barnabas (Acts xi. 24.) that "he was full of the Holy Ghost and of faith: and much people was added to the Lord." The preaching of the cross is called (1 Cor. i. 18.) the *power of God* to those who are saved; and in 1 Thes. i. 6. the apostle says, "Our gospel came not unto you in word only, but in *power*." When to these passages of scripture are added the effects of the preaching of the gospel by Brainerd, Whitfield, and many others in England and America, the fact will be established beyond all doubt, that setting aside all natural impressions on the passions, the Holy Spirit does give power and efficacy to the preaching and other modes of making known the divine word, so as to "give testimony to the word of his grace," and that he carries it to the hearts of men as in "the demonstration of the spirit and with power." Hence, also, in the work of conversion, (John iii. 5.) the Holy Spirit and the word (under the term water) are united by our Lord himself, and the necessity of a holy birth by these two agents, is there expressly insisted upon as a qualification for heaven.

The account which Brainerd gives of the change wrought under his preaching and catechizing upon the hearts of the savage *Indians*, is too remarkable to be omitted. Speaking of the Indians, he says, "God was pleased to give the primary gospel truths such a powerful effect upon their minds, that their lives were quickly reformed." Again, "When these truths were felt at heart, there was no vice unreformed, no external duty neglected. Drunkenness, the darling vice, was broken off. The same might be said of all other vicious practices. The reformation was general, and all springing from the internal influence of divine truth upon their hearts." "It is now nearly a year since the beginning of this gracious out-pouring of the divine Spirit among them." I will only quote a few more of Brainerd's own words on this subject: "There was much visible concern in the assembly, and I doubt not but a divine influence accompanied what was spoken to the hearts of many. Five or six of the strangers appeared to be considerably awakened. and in particular one very rugged young man, who seemed as if nothing would move him, was now brought to tremble like the jailor, and weep for a long time."—"The pagans that were awakened, seemed at once to put off their savage roughness, and became sociable, orderly, and humane."

President Edwards adds, at the close of the account of the life of Brainerd—"The foregoing account of Mr. Brainerd's life may afford matter of conviction that there is indeed such a thing as true *experimental religion*, arising from immediate divine influences, supernaturally enlightening and convincing the mind, and powerfully impressing, quickening, sanctifying, and governing the heart." The president then gives proof of this from Brainerd's life, and from the effects of those truths which he believed and preached to the Indians, in which summary we have these words relative to the Indians: "And this example and these endeavours were attended with most happy fruits and effects on others, in humanizing, civilizing, wonderfully reforming and transforming some of the most brutish savages, idle, immoral, drunkards, murderers, gross idolaters, and wizards; bringing them to permanent sobriety, diligence, devotion, honesty, conscientiousness, and charity."

Respecting the power of the word on the hearts of the *Africans*, thus speaks the right Rev. Bishop and Chancellor Pontoppidan, relative to those in the Danish West India islands. "Among the negro slaves, even of the most wild and barbarous nations, who, in their own country seemed to have quite lost all humanity, one may meet with very many instances of a sincere and abiding conversion to Christ; that is to say, a conversion to his mind, and the following of his example."

The state of the *Greenlanders* before conversion is thus described by Crantz: "They were not only heedless, volatile, and trifling under the instruction, but if the brethren tarried longer than one night with them, they used every means to entice them to a conformity to their wanton dissolute ways. And when this did not succeed, but the brethren retained, in all circumstances, their seriousness and sobriety, then they tried to tire them out by mocking and mimicking their reading, singing and praying, with all kinds of antics, or by accompanying it with their drumming and odious howling. They took occasion from their outward poverty to ridicule them with all manner of cutting sarcasms, which the brethren had by this time learned to understand, as well as their significant looks and gestures. And if they replied, that they did not stay there for the sake of outward advantages, and good eating and drinking, but for the sake of their souls, to teach them the will of God, then they retorted with a taunting jeer: *Illivse ajokar saromarpisigut!* 'Fine fellows, indeed, to be our teachers! We know very well that you yourselves are ignorant, and must learn your lessons of others.' The brethren bore such rudeness and mockery with calmness and serenity. But when the savages perceived that they could effect nothing this way neither, they insulted and abused their persons. They pelted them with stones out of sport, climbed up their shoulders, took their things and shattered them to pieces, and tried to spoil their boat, or to drive it out to sea. Nay, one night the brethren heard a noise on the outside of their tent, and perceived that some body was striving to pull aside the curtains of the tent which they had fastened with a couple of pins. They went out to see who it was, and there they beheld a number of Greenlanders gathered about the tent, some with their naked knives in their hands; nor could they drive them away till they threatened them with their fire-arms. The brethren supposed at that time that they only came to cut their tent-skins to pieces; but some years after, when some of the Greenlanders in these parts were converted, they were informed, that they had conspired against their lives, in hopes that the other Europeans would not think it worth their while to revenge the death of such poor despised people."

"Any one who had known the heathen, had seen the little benefit from the great pains hitherto taken with them, and considered that one after another had abandoned all hope of the conversion of these infidels, while some thought they would never be converted till they saw miracles wrought, as in the apostles' days, (and this the Greenlanders expected and demanded of their instructors), one that considered this, I say, would not so much wonder at the past unfruitfulness of these young beginners, as at their steadfast perseverance in the midst of nothing but distress, difficulties, and impediments internally and externally, and that they never desponded of the conversion of these poor creatures amidst all seeming impossibilities. Hitherto they had not seen the least trace of an abiding blessing and impression from the truths that had been held forth unto them. The Greenlanders that came from a distance, were stupid, ignorant, and void of reflection; and the little they could tell them at a short visit, even if it was heard with some impression, died away presently in their perpetual wanderings. Those who lived constantly at Ball's river, and had been instructed so many years, were not grown better, but most of them worse, they were disgusted, tired, and hardened against the truth. They resolved to hear no more without a present, for they would be paid even for lending their ears. As long as they were told any kind of news, they hearkened with pleasure; they could also bear to hear some little histories out of the bible, and the miracles of our Saviour and his apostles. But if the missionaries wished to give them right ideas of the nature and attributes of God, of the fall and the corruption of the soul, of God's wrath against sin, of the necessity of an atonement, of faith in Jesus, of the means of grace, of the cure and sanctification of the ruined soul and body, of the example of Christ, and of eternal happiness or misery; they were sleepy, said Yes to all, but slunk away presently. Or else they showed their dislike openly, and began to talk of their seal catching; or excused themselves, that they could not understand and comprehend it. 'Show us the God you describe, (said they,) then we will believe in him and serve him. You represent him too sublime and incomprehensible, how shall we come at him? Neither will he trouble himself about us. We have invoked him when we had nothing to eat, or when we have been sick, but it is as if he would not hear us. We think what you say of him is not true. Or, if you know him better than we, then do you by your prayers obtain for us sufficient food, a healthy body, and a dry house, and that is all we desire or want. Our soul is healthy already; and nothing is wanting, if we have but a sound body, and enough to eat. You are another sort of folk than we; in your country, people may perhaps have diseased souls, and indeed we see instances enough in those that come here, that they are good for nothing; they may stand in need of a Saviour and of a physician for the soul. Your heaven, and your spiritual joys and felicities may be good enough for you, but this would be too tedious for us. We must have seals, fishes, and birds. Our souls can no more subsist without them, than our bodies. We shall not find these in your heaven, therefore we will leave your heaven to you and the worthless part of the Greenlanders; but as for us, we will go down to *Torngarsuk*, there we shall find an exuberance of every thing without any trouble.'"

Such was the state of these people immediately preceding their conversion. Let us now see the wonderful effects of divine influence on their dispositions and characters.

'*June 2d.* Many of the southlanders that went by here, visited us. John Beck was just writing out fair, part of a translation of the evangelists. The savages wanted very much to know what was contained in that book. He read something of it to them, and took that opportunity to enter into a discourse with them. At the same time, he read out of the New Testament the history of our Saviour's conflict on the Mount of Olives, and of his bloody sweat. Then the Lord opened the heart of one of them whose name was *Kaiarnak*, and he stepped up to the table, and said with a loud, earnest, and affecting voice: How was that? tell me that once more; I would fain be saved too. Some of them laid their hands upon their mouths, as is customary among them when they are struck with wonder.* In short, there was such an agitation and stirring among them, as we had never seen before.'

The moral effects of these impressions on the characters of the Greenlanders are too well known to need farther mention. They have excited the admiration of the whole christian world. And thus adds Crantz, respecting the Greenlanders: " What men have contributed to this blessed work, is a small matter. It is the Spirit of the Lord, that gave power to the word; called, gathered, and enlightened these poor heathens by the gospel, and hitherto has kept them with Jesus Christ in the only true faith."

In the year 1816, as had often been the case before, divine influences were enjoyed by many persons in North America. Whole congregations were sometimes deeply affected, and the persons thus impressed were often persons of liberal education, some of whom had been long under the influence of deism, and had the strongest aversion to the doctrine of divine influence on the heart. Many students at colleges were thus impressed, and by their future actions testified, that, by these influences, their dispositions and characters had undergone a most important and interesting change.

TO THE EDITORS OF THE LATTER DAY LUMINARY.

The distinction in the following passage appears just and striking Your inserting it in your publication will oblige a subscriber.   O.

THE KINGDOM OF THE STONE AND THE KINGDOM OF THE MOUNTAIN.

" AS the fourth kingdom of the Roman empire was represented in a two-fold state, first strong and flourishing, ' with legs of iron,' and then weakened and divided, ' with feet and toes, part of iron and of clay;' so this fifth kingdom, or kingdom of Christ, is described likewise in two states, which Mr. Mede rightly distinguished by the names of *Regnum Lapidis*, the kingdom of the stone, and *Regnum Montis*, the kingdom of the mountain: the first when the stone was cut out of the mountain without hands, the second when it became itself a mountain, and filled the whole earth. The stone was ' cut out of the mountain without hands,' the kingdom of Christ was set up first, while the Ro-

---

* This is exactly what the Hindoos do in moments of surprise.

man empire was in its full strength, with 'legs of iron.' The Roman empire was afterwards divided into ten lesser kingdoms, the remains of which are subsisting at present.

"The image is still standing upon [as to] his feet and toes of iron and clay; the kingdom of Christ is *yet* 'a stone of stumbling and a rock of offence; but the stone will one day smite the image upon the feet and toes, and destroy it utterly, and will itself become a great mountain, and fill the whole earth: or, in other words, Rev. xi. 15. "the kingdoms of this world shall become the kingdoms of our Lord, and of his Christ, and he shall reign for ever and ever." We have, therefore, seen the kingdom of the stone, but we have not yet seen the kingdom of the mountain. Some parts of this prophecy still remain to be fulfilled: but the exact completion of the other parts will not suffer us to doubt of the accomplishment of the rest also in due season."—*Bishop Newton.*

OBSERVATIONS ON JOHN XX 17.

"*TOUCH me not, for I am not yet ascended to my Father.*"—— Our translation of this text labours under two serious inconveniences.

1. It supposes that the body of Christ was intangible, or that to touch it was improper. Mr. Burder has introduced into his Bible a print, taken from a painting by Lauri, in which our Lord is portrayed starting away from Mary, to elude her touch. On the contrary, he said to Thomas, " Reach hither thy hand, and thrust it into my side," and to all the disciples, " Handle me and see, for a spirit hath not flesh and blood, as ye see me have." As the women went to announce to the disciples the resurrection of their Lord, " Jesus met them, saying, All hail! And they came, *and held him by the feet,* and worshipped him."

2. The above translation seems to convey the idea that the body of Christ will be more susceptible of touch in heaven than on earth; " touch me not, for I have not yet ascended;" but surely nothing in the sacred writings warrants such a thought.

The word ἅπτομαι means not simply to *touch*: it signifies also to *lay hold of,* to *embrace,* to *cling to.* Washing, *wiping, kissing, anointing* the feet of Christ, are all expressed by the word ἅπτεται. Matt. vii. 39. " This man, if he were a prophet, would have known who or what manner of woman this is that *toucheth* him, for she is a sinner."— Knatchbull, in his annotations, says, " The old Latin, not willing an argument should be drawn from the words next following, that he would not be touched, doth prudently and very rightly include them in a parenthesis, and so corrects *Noli me tangere* with *Vade autem ad fratres meos,* &c. Meddle not with me, (for I am not yet ascended to my father,) but go unto my brethren, &c." Dr. Doddridge renders Μη μου απτου, *Do not embrace me;* and Mr. Charles Thompson, still better, *Cling not to me.*

With such a translation the passage becomes lucid, beautiful, and affecting. Embrace me not, cling not to me, hang not about me, Mary! I see thy attachment, thy veneration, thy transport! Don't think I am going immediately to leave thee, and that thou shalt never see thy Lord on earth again "I am not yet ascended to my Father," nor shall I ascend, until I have had frequent interviews with my beloved disciples. Stay not, Mary; relieve their anxieties. Fly with the tidings. Tell them I am risen. Say to them, "I ascend to my Father and your Father,—to my God and your God!"

How interesting a display is here of the ardour of pious affection, the compassion and care of the Redeemer, and the duty of his servants to forego their personal consolation for the sake of doing good!

INSTRUCTIONS TO BE OBSERVED CONCERNING PRAYER,
BY JOHN BRADFORD, MARTYR PUBLISHED A. D. 1633.

THERE be nine things that pertain to the knowledge of true prayer.

1. To know what prayer is.
2. How many sorts of prayer there be.
3. The necessity of prayer.
4. To whom we ought to pray
5. By whom we must pray.
6. Where to pray.
7. What to pray.
8. The excellency of prayer.
9. What we must do, that our prayers may be heard.

1. *What prayer is.*

Prayer is a simple, unfeigned, humble, and ardent opening of the heart before God, wherein we either ask things needful, or give thanks for benefits received. Paul, in the first to Timothy, chap. 2. calleth it by four sundry names in one sentence, to wit: prayer, supplication, intercession, and thanksgiving: in Latin, *deprecatio, obsecratio, intercessio, & gratiarum actio.* Whereof the first is for the avoiding and preventing of evil; the second is an earnest and fervent calling upon

God for any thing; the third is an intercession for other: the fourth is a praising of God for things received.

2. *There be two manner of ways how we should pray.*

First, publicly, and that is called common prayer, where the people are assembled together: pray all with one heart and mind. And privately, as when men pray alone, and that is called private prayer: and how both these two are allowed before God, the scripture beareth testimony by the example of all the holy men and women before and after Christ.

3. *The necessity of prayer.*

There be four things that provoke us to pray: First, the commandment of God: Secondly, sin in us, which driveth us of necessity to God for succour, life and mercy: Thirdly, our weak nature (being unable to do any good) requireth prayer to strengthen it, even as a house requireth principal pillars for the upholding of it: Fourthly, the subtility of the enemy (who privily lurketh in the inward parts, waiting to overthrow us, even in those things which we think to be best done) stirreth us vehemently thereunto.

4. *To whom we ought to pray.*

Three things do necessarily pertain to him that must be prayed unto. First, that he have such ears as may hear all the world at once. Secondly, that he is in all places at once: Thirdly, that he hath such power, that he is able to help; and such mercy, that he will deliver, that is, none but God.

5. *By whom we should pray.*

Christ only is the way, by whom we have free access unto the Father, and from whom our prayers are accepted, (our infirmities notwithstanding,) without whom all our prayers are abominable.

6. *Where to pray.*

As touching the place where we should pray, seeing all places are one, there is none forbidden; only the common prayer must be made in what place soever the congregation of Christ doth assemble.

7. *What to pray.*

What to pray, lyeth in the necessity of every man: and forasmuch as we need both spiritual and corporal things, we may boldly ask them both. For as to ask spiritual gifts is profitable, and is commanded: so to ask corporal, is necessary and allowed.

8. *Of the excellency of prayer.*

The worthiness of prayer consisteth in two things; in the dignity of the commander who is God, the fountain of all goodness, who also commandeth only good things: and in the effect that followeth it, which is the obtaining of whatsoever we desire faithfully, according to the will of God.

9. *What to do that we may be heard.*

First, we must put off our own righteousness. pride, and estimation of ourselves, and put on Christ with his righteousness: Secondly, an earnest faith and fervent love, with the laying aside of all rancour, malice and envy, is required: Finally, true repentance knitteth up the knot; for in it are contained all the virtues before named.

REVIEW OF NEW PUBLICATIONS.

The Conversion of the World: or the Claims of Six Hundred Millions, and the Ability and Duty of the Churches respecting them. Second edition. Andover: printed for the American Board of Commissioners for Foreign Missions. Flagg & Gould. 1818. pp. 94.

(Concluded.)

WHEN from Eden our first parents were ejected,

"The world was all before them, where to fix
"Their place of rest, and Providence their guide."

Over so small a portion of the earth has Christianity thrown its sacred rays, that "the world" may, in a manner, be conceived as "all before" the missionaries of evangelic truth. Providence has, in many instances, been their faithful guide. It is the province, nevertheless, of piety and wisdom, to survey the wide and extended wilderness, and fix on those spots which promise to the hand of cultivation the largest success. Our authors justly observe, that

"Until there shall be a sufficient number of missionaries to supply all parts of the world, it will be our duty to select the most important places first. To do this requires much information and much reflection." p. 33.

They add:

"The Moravians, while they have set a pattern to all other Christians for zeal, and patience, and perseverance, seem to have erred in many instances in the choice of their fields of labour. They have in general chosen the two extremes of heat and cold, and have sent great numbers of missionaries to thinly peopled countries; while many of the finest climates and most populous regions of the globe have in the mean time lain quite neglected. There is no part of the world, from the pinching cold of the frigid zone, to the burning plains of the equator, to which missionaries must not, ultimately, go; but while almost the whole world lies before us unoccupied, we ought not to choose the less eligible, in preference to the more eligible places." p. 33.

While, in this attachment of mistake to the direction of the labours of the Moravians, we on the whole concur, we are not surprised at the course they have pursued. When, at the coronation of Christian the Sixth at Copenhagen, count Zinzendorff found that the Danish government had resolved to abandon the mission in Greenland, the sight of two converted natives of the country soliciting assistance, was too powerful to be disregarded; as was also the importunity of a person of colour, referring to a sister of his at St. Thomas, who often besought the Lord to send some teacher who might show her the way of salvation. Considering the limited extent of their field of operation, the success of the Moravians has scarcely been exceeded by any subsequent missions.

In contemplating the range for missionary attempt, it has been customary to exhibit men in reference to their different religions, whether Jewish, Mahometan, or Pagan; or in relation to the state of society, as civilized or savage. In the interesting production before us, the authors, pursuing the THIRD part of their design, which is to present *a brief view of some of the most important openings for the extension of the Redeemer's kingdom*, attend to distributions strictly geographical.

"Without attempting to determine precisely what places are the most important, as fields for missionary exertions, we may mention the following as interesting, and worthy the immediate attention of the christian public.

"*First*, the northern and western parts of the continent of Asia.

"From the Indus to the Mediterranean, and from the gulf of Ormuz to the Caspian sea, there is not a single protestant missionary. Within these limits there are probably fifty or sixty millions of people, destitute of the gospel, immersed in gross ignorance, and led away by the delusions of Mahomet. Scattered over these regions are not less than a million of Armenian, Syrian and Greek christians, in general destitute of the Bible, destitute of spiritual light and life, and on the whole but little better in any respect than their mahometan masters. What a field for the benevolent exertions of enlightened Christians! How much good might be effected by endeavouring to revive pure religion and christian knowledge in these eastern churches, venerable for their antiquity, their situation, and their origin.

"Siberia, Tartary, and the northern parts of China, form another immense theatre for missionary operations, a field as yet unexplored and uncultivated.

"All these regions merit particular attention at the present moment, because Providence seems to be preparing the way for the dissemination of the gospel in this quarter of the world. In proof of this remark we may mention three facts *first*, the recent translation of the New Testament into Persian and Turkish,—*secondly*, the reprinting of the Armenian Bible both in India and Russia, and the effort that appears to be making in Armenia for the revival of oriental learning, and the introduction of the arts and improvements of the west,—*thirdly*, the foundation of Bible societies in different parts of the Russian empire." p. 33, 34.

After detailing much important matter in confirmation of these facts, our authors present the

"SECOND FIELD. The eastern coast of Africa, including Egypt, Abyssinia, and the island of Madagascar, presents another extensive and interesting field, for the propagation of the gospel. This important field, like the one just mentioned, lies at present entirely neglected. No missionary has yet been established in any of these countries. Dr. Vander Kemp projected a mission to Madagascar, but was called home by his divine Master before he had time to carry it into effect.

"There are several circumstances which call the attention of Christians to these regions of pagan and mahometan darkness. The eastern coast of Africa and the island of Madagascar have long been the scene of the vile traffic in human beings, which has lately been abolished by most of the civilized nations of the world. Christians have now an opportunity of repairing, in some degree, the wrongs they have done the poor Africans for centuries past. They have formerly torn them away from their friends and native land, and carried them into slavery,—instead of any longer approaching their shores in slave ships, armed with hostile weapons, and furnished with the instruments of bondage, they may send them the peaceful message of the gospel, and impart to them that liberty with which Christ has made them free. De la Goa Bay, Sofala, Mosambique, Quiloa, and Melinda, on this coast, are places well known to the commercial world. Some of them are populous and healthy. The Portuguese have an establishment at Mosambique, and carry on a constant trade between that place and Goa. From Goa and also from the Isle of France missionaries may find conveyance to most of the places on the eastern coast of Africa and to the island of Madagascar. Between Madagascar and the Isle of France the communication is constant, as the English at the Mauritius receive all their supplies of cattle from Madagascar." p. 45, 46.

The relative situation of Abyssinia, surrounded with Egypt, Nubia, Sennaar, Arabia, and the African tribes, is justly represented as highly important. The consideration that in this country, supposed to consist of three millions of inhabitants, the christian religion has existed ever since the fourth century, is calculated to encourage exertion.

The THIRD FIELD

"The Burman empire, and the other neighbouring countries on the eastern peninsula, and the great and populous islands in the Indian ocean, present another extensive field for the propagation of Christianity, and demand very earnest attention." p. 49.

They add:

"This is an ample field, and calls for a large supply of labourers; especially when we view it in connexion with the adjacent countries of Siam, Malacca, Cambodia, Cochin China, and Tonquin, to which no protestant missionary has ever been sent.

"The great islands of Sumatra and Borneo are also without a single missionary, wholly destitute of christian instruction. In Java and the Moluccas, where the Dutch formerly had settlements, there are many nominal Christians of the protestant persuasion. The Malay language is almost universally spoken among these islanders, and the Malay scriptures, many years ago translated by the Dutch, are now reprinting at Serampore, both under the direction of the Calcutta Auxiliary Bible Society. Java and the Moluccas are now restored to the Dutch, and will probably be open to missionaries. The Americans carry on a considerable trade with Java, and on this account we might conveniently send out a number of missionaries to that island. A mission established there might branch out into the neighbouring islands, as Providence should open the door. It is said there are a hundred thousand Chinese in Java. Might it not be well to send a special mission to them with a view to raise up among them preachers to be sent back to China?" p. 49, 50.

The following fact ought, surely, to lie with weight on every friend of the gospel of Christ.

"India has been the seat of a christian and protestant mission for more than a hundred years, and within twenty years past the number of missionaries and missionary establishments has been considerably increased,—but yet there is room! There is not even now a missionary to a million of souls" p. 51

The FOURTH FIELD is the continent of America, north and south; an attention to which devolves, with propriety, on American christians.

Part IV. of the production before us states, that *in this work there are many difficulties to admonish, but none to discourage.*

"The obstacles and discouragements to the missionary work, which are proper here to be mentioned, may all be comprised under the three following heads.
"1 The mortality and defection of missionaries
"2 The obstacles to their entering the field.
"3. The opposition which they may meet with after they enter upon their work" p 57, 58.

These difficulties are diminished, or obviated, by various weighty remarks. Under the *third* class of obstacles, the following fact is well worthy to be remembered.

"No heathen or mahometan government, has ever sent from the field a single *protestant* missionary, nor can they with propriety be said to have opposed them, but on the contrary they have often greatly encouraged and patronized them! Happy would it be could the same be said of *christian* governments." p. 64.

The advantages that must result from pursuing the great object of evangelizing the heathen, is urged by several considerations:—as, that such exertions would tend to promote religion among the churches at home, and impart strength and encouragement to missionaries already in the field The state of the Christians who are found in the midst or in the vicinity of pagans and mahommedans, the provision made for supplying almost all nations with the bible, and the ease with which the churches might send out the requisite number of missionaries, are pressed with affection and force upon the public attention.

"O ye blood-bought churches of Christ, let the cry among you be, "Whom shall we send, and who will go for us as our messengers to the heathen?" And O, ye pious youth, in Christ's strength let the echo among you be, "Here are we, send us" Most happy, most blessed will be the individual, the church, the nation, who shall be earliest, longest, and most faithful in this glorious work And may the God of all grace mercifully bestow this greatest of all blessings upon America, her churches, and her youth AMEN." p. 81.

We have read this pamphlet with no ordinary interest. If it possess not the eloquence of Melville Horne, it discovers a passion of soul for the universal diffusion of the kingdom of Christ, equally ardent and active. It completely destroys the objection that the ability of Christians to fill the earth with missionaries is too circumscribed, and manifests a boldness of conception, an originality and perfection of plan, and a concern for the eternal salvation of men, which, it is hoped, will produce an impression that shall be retained for years to come.

A Discourse on the Duty and Advantages of Improving our Baptism. By John Stanford, M. A. New York: Gray & Co. pp. 24.

FROM an advertisement on the reverse of the title page, we learn that "the substance of this discourse was delivered to the church under the pastoral care of the Rev. Archibald Maclay, after the baptism of nine persons. It was afterwards enlarged, and is now published by request." The sermon is founded on Galatians iii. 27. "For as many of you as have been baptized into Christ, have put on Christ." Its design is to show "the ability of BELIEVERS, and of a CHURCH, to improve the subject of their baptism." After a neat and instructive exposition of the text, Mr. S proceeds to state in what "the competency of a Christian to improve his baptism" consists "This arises from his active REASON, his personal FAITH, and his ardent LOVE TO CHRIST." Under the head of personal faith the author remarks, that

"This faith is not the production of nature or of art, neither does it merely affect the mind, but, like the vital fluid in the animal body, which animates all its parts, it actuates all the powers and faculties of the soul" p 8.

The "important purposes for which" individual believers "may and ought to realize and obtain advantages" from their baptism, are, "the increase of humility, the enlivening of the affections, the maintaining of a christian profession, promoting holiness in life, and invigorating the hope of a glorious resurrection from the dead." Having in a pleasing and striking manner, illustrated these ideas, the author adds:

"I shall claim your attention a few more minutes to show you, that a CHURCH, as such, may likewise improve the ordinance of baptism, for the purposes of maintaining and enlivening their union in the faith and fellowship of the gospel

"On this subject Paul wrote an animated epistle to the church at Ephesus, beseeching them to *walk worthy of the vocation wherewith they were called, with all lowliness and meekness, with long-suffering, forbearing one another in love, endeavouring to keep the unity of the spirit in the bond of peace* And, to stimulate them to this holy union, and to these important practices, he named SEVEN UNITS as so many reasons, comprising the chief doctrines of the gospel. There is said he, ONE *body and* ONE *spirit, even as ye are called in* ONE *hope of your calling;* ONE *Lord,* ONE *faith,* ONE *baptism,* ONE *God and Father of all, who is above all, and through all, and in you all* (Eph iv 1—6) To the church at Corinth, he wrote with the same design *As the body is* ONE, *and hath many members, and all the members of that* ONE *body being many, are* ONE *body so also is Christ For by* ONE *Spirit are we all baptized into* ONE *body, whether we be Jews or Gentiles, whether we be bound or free, and have been all made to drink into* ONE *Spirit. For the body is not* ONE *member, but many* (1 Cor. xii 12—14) The sum of these addresses, may be thus stated. Christ in his person, and with the Father, are ONE The church in Christ, though of many members, are ONE. And although its various members have their different faculties and offices, analogous to the human body, as the eye, the ear, the hand, the feet, the head yet all have their proper places and uses in the ONE body, as God, to the pleasure of his grace hath set them for the beauty and benefit of the whole. The unity of this body, is admirably expressed by ONE baptism. ONE element of water; ONE Christ; ONE profession of the gospel; consequently, the solemn and frequent recollection and improvement of this ONE baptism, is, in the highest degree, calculated to promote unity, peace, order, and happiness among the respective members of a gospel church.—In addition to these reflections for the use of churches, I am disposed to say, that MINISTERS too, besides their christian character, may, and ought to improve their baptism. What obligations are they under to their Lord for putting them into his service, and granting them his supports, and success in their labours? Paul could not forget the memorable time when he was baptized by Ananias, and straightway preached Christ in the synagogues, that he is the Son of God. In his after days, the recollection of it served as an incitement to newness and vigour of life, and to maintain the honour of his Lord in every department of his ministry. And, as ministers, I am persuaded, that we also may reflect upon our baptism for the most valuable purposes, and especially to promote a happy ministerial union among ourselves, as well as with the people of our respective charges." p. 18—20.

The discourse concludes with a solemn address to such as "may have been in the habit of attending the administration of baptism for no other purposes than to gratify a vain curiosity, or to indulge their ridicule." Those who differ from the author, as to his views of the rite, are addressed in a tone candid and affectionate; and the newly baptized persons are reminded of their privileges and their obligations.

"What enemies may hereafter assail you; forget not, that your greatest foes lie within your own breasts. Bishop Hall, in his contemplations on the baptism of your Lord, very justly says, "No sooner was he led up out of the water of baptism, than he was led into the fire of temptation." In your measure, you must expect the same, for the disciple is not above his Lord." p. 23—24.

We have seldom seen a discourse, of equal length, more replete with judicious, practical and pious ideas. We hope its circulation and its utility in the churches of Christ, will be extensive.

A Drop of Mercy from the Bright Cloud of Righteousness: containing, I. A View of the state of Religion in the congregations at Waller's, County Line, and Bethany, prior to the late Revival. II. A Narrative of the commencement and progress of the revivals in those churches for five months. III. Four Letters on the subject of experimental and practical Religion. IV. Some Remarks on the regular support of Gospel ministers. By A. Waller, of Spottsylvania county, Virginia. Richmond: W. W. Gray, pp. 48.

ACCOUNTS of the revival of religion are among the most desirable and precious of magazine materials. The work before us contains delightful intelligence relative to the progress of the Mediator's kingdom. The title, we confess, is fanciful. It is of a description with the quaint and curious names which, a century and a half ago, the pious authors of the times were accustomed to adopt. The figure of "a drop" falling from a "bright cloud," we cannot think a happy one. The contents, however, abundantly compensate for this trivial errour.

We had often heard that the labours of our worthy brethren, the Rev. Isaac Hodgen and the Rev. Walter Warder, were greatly blessed in Virginia on their return from the Baptist Convention in Philadelphia, in May, 1817. A pleasing detail of particulars are here given. Our author states,

"In the middle of wheat harvest the ministers before named came among us, in the spirit and power of the Lord Jesus, and afterwards preached in rotation four or five times, with all the simplicity of apostolic zeal, and great success, to vast crowds of people. The first sermon, however, of Hodgen, was a master piece (at least) to me. It was on these words "He that goeth forth and weepeth, bearing precious seed, shall doubtless come again rejoicing, bringing his sheaves with him." I never saw his face before, but he told me all my faults, and sweetly described all my sorrows and my joys." p. 9.

Our author proceeds, in a plain and affecting manner, to relate the exercises of his own heart.

"Several pious ministers who frequented the meetings of the Kentucky brethren, informed me that they could not feel any engagedness in the work, which seemed to be bursting forth under the ministry of those preachers. This tended very much to strengthen my excuses in secret before a throne of grace, and I tried to believe that no sacrifices were required of me in the work, except the faithful discharge of my stated labours in the Lord's vineyard. But I tried in vain! My distress of mind continued to increase, from an inward conviction that I was disposed to roll in the lap of domestic indolence, while the great harvest of souls was ripening for the active labourer all around me; until I became fearful it would settle down in a fixed melancholy. Sometimes I would endeavour to divert my mind by the conversation of a loving wife, and the innocent prattle of our children, but my efforts were ineffectual. I was in the frequent habit of retiring into a grove of pines, (where are deposited the remains of many of my relatives, together with two of my own children,) for the purpose of prayer; and having one cloudy morning felt more than common distress in mind, concerning my own situation, as to my unwillingness to forsake all for Christ, and rush into the great harvest of souls, I entered my usual retreat for the solemn purpose of seeking communion with God. The lowering clouds, the thick cluster of pines, as also the graves of the sleeping dust, seemed greatly to increase the spirit of devotion; my very soul was lifted in strong cries to the throne of mercy for divine instruction concerning the way of duty. While I was thus engaged, the thought struck me with great force indeed, that the souls of my dear departed children, (near whose graves I was then kneeling,) were at that moment in glory, singing the praises of the Lamb of God, who died for the redemption of lost sinners! and that I was surely a most ungrateful wretch, to feel unwilling to spend and be spent in the cause of Christ! I am unable to describe my feelings at that moment. I wept under a sense of God's goodness, and my own ingratitude —nay more, I fell on my face, and cried out, O Lord! send me, and I will go, I will forsake all for Christ, and try to spend my latest breath in exhorting sinners to repent and turn to God!" p. 10, 11.

The revivals have chiefly taken place "in the congregations at Waller's, County Line, and Bethany." Of the emotions of the author at a monthly meeting at Waller's, the reader may form an estimate from the following language.

"It would require the pen of an angel to describe the sensations of joy and gratitude which filled my own soul, when meeting the broken hearted sinner at a throne of mercy on the floor, after sermon. I had long since been watching for the coming of the Master, by fervent prayers and humble groans; and now to behold numbers upon their knees, crying out, What shall we do to be saved? produced in my enraptured mind, a foretaste of those immortal pleasures which bloom in the paradise of God." p. 13, 14.

He adds:

"In the early part of October, the bright cloud of mercy began to extend its wings over the congregation at Bethany, and on the third Lord's day, in the morning, I commenced the precious work of baptizing among those people, fifteen persons were on that day added to the church. The revival had now become general in the three churches, and having none to help me, I was almost exhausted in the fatigues and labours of the vineyard, as well as in continual watchings by night and by day. But the great Head in Zion was with me, and supported my feeble frame beyond conception, so that the months of September and October were to me at least upon mount Tabor; in which I preached over forty discourses, and baptized one hundred and forty five persons." p. 14.

We regret that our limits forbid more extensive extracts. The following will afford a specimen of the numerous cases the pamphlet contains:

"A young gentleman of liberal principles, who had spent a morning in light and sarcastic conversation with a carnal neighbour on the subject of the revival of religion, on his return home stated that he was suddenly seized with such an awful sense of his lost state, and the omnipresence of God, that he was brought upon his knees to beg for mercy, through a crucified Saviour, and from this period he became an attendant on public worship, a penitent and broken hearted sinner, and finally he obtained a full assurance of pardon for sin, and has since become a zealous member of the church which he once despised.

"Two christian friends entered into covenant that they would unite in fervent supplications before the throne of grace in behalf of a thoughtless acquaintance, for whom they entertained great personal respect, and to their great joy and surprise, in about three weeks afterwards the gentleman came to meeting—was struck to the heart with the power of conviction for sin, together with his lady. They have both since become members of the County Line church. It was truly a melting sight to behold him leading the partner of his earthly joys down into the watery tomb, while tears of sweet contrition for sin, and humble gratitude to God for his pardoning love, through a divine Redeemer, were rolling in pearly drops down his manly cheeks." p. 19.

"The last (among the many wonderful circumstances which have transpired) that we shall notice is the case of the author's own relatives. My parents were among the first fruits of the Spirit under the ministry of the noted Samuel Harris, justly styled the apostle of the Virginia baptists. They became members of the baptist church about fifty years past, prior to their marriage several years. They have lived to raise five sons and one daughter, all of whom they have the satisfaction to see happily married, and settled in comfortable circumstances. I was their first born, and I have often remembered, with humble gratitude to God, my happy lot to be born of such parents. They used to converse with their children about the great things of eternity, from the earliest dawn of reason, and, as soon as we could read, the holy bible was put into our hands, and occasionally they would make us read, and then explain the contents (of what we read) to us, especially on the Sabbath day. Our father was, from my earliest remembrance, very punctual in the observance of family worship, which made a gradual and deep religious impression on my mind. About the commencement of my fourteenth year, I obtained a hope of an interest in the merits of our blessed Redeemer, and in a few days after I entered my fifteenth year, became a member of the baptist church. Shortly after the pastor of our church baptized a younger brother in our family, and in the lapse of years I had baptized two more of my brothers, and our sister, together with my own wife, as also the husband of our sister prior to their marriage. In our late revival the heavenly drops of divine mercy came down again in rich profusion upon our highly favoured family, and the last of my brothers four sisters-in-law, three nieces and a nephew, the youngest not thirteen years, have bowed to the sceptre of King Jesus. Our aged parents, at the advanced age of over threescore and ten, are in good health, and full of piety and good works—waiting for a gentle dismission, and the earnest hope of a glorious immortality, and a place at the right hand of God, where are pleasures for ever more." p. 20, 21.

The letters " on the subject of experimental and practical religion" and " the remarks on the regular support of gospel ministers," are judicious and interesting. We are much pleased with the evidences he adduces of " a renewed mind,"—such as love to God, love to Christians, self loathing, distress for the sins of thought, an earnest desire for the salvation of others, a forgiving spirit, and a spirit of inquiry concerning the way of duty.

In an Appendix to the work, the author, whose zeal and piety call for holy emulation, has the following observations.

" In looking over my papers, I find that the unbelieving wives of *seventeen* brethren, and the husbands of *five* sisters, have become the subjects of divine mercy in the revival. Thirteen cases have occurred in which both husband and wife entered the baptismal tomb. O, how delightful the prospect, for the heads of families to be united in the cause of ' 's king' .

" Since the commencement of the revival, the author has baptized about four hundred, (May 2d,) and including the additions made to the sister churches of Gold Mine, Mount Hermon, and Little River, together with the additions elsewhere in neighbouring churches, we conclude, that at least *six hundred souls* have professed to obtain the pardon of sin since the visit of elders Hodgen and Warder, on their way from the missionary Convention. What a glorious display of divine mercy in favour of the missionary cause is this! The zeal of Bible and Missionary societies, we humbly hope, will continue to increase, until the knowledge of God shall cover the earth as the waters do the fountains of the great deep." p. 47, 48.

To the preceding accounts we have the pleasure of adding extracts of

A letter from Mr. Hodgen, dated January 18, 1819, addressed to his intimate friend and brother, Mr. J. K. H. of this city

" I shall rejoice your heart by giving you a short account of my labours since I wrote last. In the month of September last I received a letter from Logan county, Kentucky, signed by upwards of forty persons, in which they expressed an anxiety that I would visit them, and preach two or three weeks in that section. Hoping the Lord had put it into their hearts to invite me, I accordingly went in October, praying the angel of the Lord of Hosts to go before. I arrived on an evening of their stated weekly meeting, and was invited to preach. While I was engaged in prayer (I trust I speak with humility,) the Spirit of the Lord was upon me, and before I closed the whole assembly were bathed in tears. I then addressed them from these words, "Repent ye, therefore, and be converted, that your sins may be blotted out, when the times of refreshing shall come, from the presence of the Lord." The effect was great, and nearly all came forward to join in prayer. I continued with them ten days. Many old saints rejoiced, and many poor sinners were made to mourn for sin, and some few found pardon. I baptized three; one of whom, I think, will preach the gospel. Three were baptized a few days before I arrived. I returned home about one hundred miles, but could not rest in spirit. I visited them again in November. During my absence the Lord brought many souls to the knowledge of the truth, and upwards of fifty were baptized. I stayed with them four weeks, preaching day and night, and baptized fifty-five. Twenty-five were baptized by other brethren, I think, since the revival commenced in October. About one hundred and fifty have been baptized on profession of faith in Jesus. The work is still increasing and spreading, and the ministers of Jesus are alive to the cause. O may it spread to the ends of the earth, and all flesh see the salvation of God. I have often felt, lately, if I was a young man and not encumbered with a large family, that I would like to be a missionary, should the Lord say Go, and the brethren let me. My soul longs for the salvation of souls. O the worth of one soul! I had rather be the means of saving one sinner, than to possess the world.'"

FOREIGN INTELLIGENCE.

WORKS IN THE SERAMPORE PRESS.

Extract of a letter from Mr. Ward to Dr. S. dated Calcutta, Sept. 14, 1818.

THE following list of works now in the press, will, perhaps, give as good an idea of the state of things here, as any thing I could send you.

The New Testament in Bengalee, translated by Mr. Ellerton.
  Do. in the Assam, do by Dr Carey.
  Do. in the Sungskrit, by do. (second edition.)
  Do. in the Telinga, by do.
  Do. in the Kornata, by do.
  Do. in the Wutch or Ootch, by do.
  Do in the Nepaul, by do.
  Do. in the Marwar, by do.
  Do. in the Oojein, by do.
  Do. in the Bhugulkhund, by do.
  Do. in the Bundulkhund, by do.
  Do. in the Dukshina Sind, by do.
  Do. in the Kashmere, by do.
  Do. in the Jumboo, by do.
  Do. in the Mujud, by do.
  Do. in the Harotee, by do
  Do. in the Huriana, by do.
  Do in the Bunoj, by do.
The Prophetical Books, in Hindee, by do (just finished.)
  Do. in the Mahratta, by do.
The Pentateuch, in the Shunkun, by do.
The Historical Books, in the Shikh or Punjabee, by do.
  Do. in the Pushtoo or Affghan, by do.

The New Testament, in the Bruj Bhasa, by brother Chamberlain
The Poetical Books, in the Chinese, by brother Marshman
The Gospel by Luke,* in do. do.
The Pentateuch,† in Bengalee, by Dr Carey.
The Gospel of Matthew, in the Malay (Roman character) by brother Robinson.
The Pentateuch, in the Malay (Arabic character) by the Rev. Mr. Hutchings, for the Calcutta Auxiliary Society.
The Sungskrit Dictionary, second edition.
A Sungskrit Grammar, edited by J Marshman, jun.
     Do. by Tara Chaud, a christian hindoo, with a Bengalese translation
Baxter's Call to the Unconverted, in the Malay, translated by Jabez Carey.
Bunyan's Pilgrim's Progress, in Bengalee, translated by F Carey.
Goldsmith's History of England, in Bengalee, translated by do. for the School Book Society of Calcutta.
Bengalee Dictionary, by Dr. Carey, in 2 volumes 4to.
The Ramayuna, in Sungskrit. 4th volume, by Drs Carey and Marshman
The Sankyu Pruvachuna Bhashya, a hindoo philosophical work in Sungskrit, edited by Dr. Carey.
An English translation of do by do.
A Bengalese translation of do. by Ramjay Turkalunkar
The Flora Indiana, a botanical work, in several volumes, edited by Dr Carey.
The Book of Common Prayer, in Tamul, printing for Gen Brownrigg, governor of Ceylon.
Bengalese Hymns, about 300 pages.
The Friend of India, a magazine or monthly publication in English
Monthly Letters to the Society from all the Stations
Sumachar Durpuna, a Bengalese monthly newspaper, by Mr. John Marshman
The Dig Dursuna, a Bengalese monthly magazine, by do.
An Astronomical School Book in Sungskrit, by do.
     Do. in Bengalee, by do
Spelling Tables for Schools, by do.
Scientific Copy Books, by do
The Happy Deaths, a work translated into the Bengalese.

We are beginning a Sungskrit College, for the instruction of christian and other Hindoo youth, that by this means we may spread through the country European science and the principles of Christianity.

FROM THE BAPTIST MAGAZINE, LONDON.

Extract of a letter from the Rev J. Chamberlain to Mr. Ivimey, dated Monghyr, April 1, 1818.

WELL, you will say, what prospects have you? What have you been doing?—What shall I say? I will tell you all I can. In last November, my family and I went to Diggah, to meet our dear friend Mrs. W. from Agra, who came all that way (400 miles) to follow her Lord in his appointed way. Then I had the hap-

---

* This will complete the New Testament.
† In small type, to get the whole Bible in one volume.

piness to baptize a person, whom I can look upon as the fruit of my former labours. A letter from her, received to day, says, that she 'went on her way rejoicing' all the way home again, and in her journey distributed about 700 gospels and pamphlets amongst the people in the towns and villages by the river side. I rejoice in this, as my work is thus carried on by others, while I am engaged in another department.

"On the 27th of December, (1817,) Glory be to God, Hingham Misser, a native, was baptized in the Ganges, just below our house. His conversion and baptism have made a great stir among the natives. On the day he was baptized, some said, '*Monghyr's Ka nak Kata gye:*' i. e. 'Monghyr's nose is cut off.' By which expressive phrase, great disgrace is intended. Hingham Misser is a Brahman, of very respectable cast and connexions. He had been employed as a reader of the scriptures for more than twelve months, during which time he had shown such an attachment to Christianity, as to separate himself from all his connexions. He was visited by illness for some months, during which time none of his relations cared for him none called to see him. On his recovering, he was enabled to make a profession of his faith in Christ, before many witnesses: to do which, he has left a wife and five or six children, and his home. Two lads, his eldest sons, saw him baptized in the river as though they saw him burned, and they have not spoken to him since they may be twelve or fourteen years of age. To one of them the father sent a pair of shoes, which he threw away with contempt. The relations unite to support the family, and many others unite with them to preserve the whole from becoming Christians. I suspect, however, that this will not last long the benevolence of a native is seldom a perennial stream. Of all the professions of Christianity, which have been in this country, few have been attended with such triumphant circumstances as this has been. Hingham Misser is a very meek man, very humble, very diligent, and of a good understanding in the scriptures; he is daily employed in the instruction of the people here, amongst whom he boldly declares his profession, and meets with more attention than in his circumstances could have been expected. Brindabun, our aged native brother, has been greatly encouraged by this instance of Divine favour. He is now gone to Diggah, in company with Nygunsookh, a young man who was baptized about a fortnight ago. He was sent by the brethren from Diggah for instruction, and remained here upwards of two months he was originally from Joypore. We have one inquirer whom Brindabun and Nygunsookh brought from a party of pilgrims; he has shaved himself, and appears very hopeful. Another young man appears to be on the Lord's side, but his fear of his father and mother prevents his coming forward. An European Lady has, I hope, been brought to discover her sinfulness, and the excellency of the Saviour, by a visit to Monghyr, which Providence brought about. She is mother-in law to sister P. She appears to be brought from the state of mind of the boasting pharisee, to that of the contrite publican. Brother Capt P. is not yet returned from the Cape, to which he went on account of the state of his health. We were rejoiced to hear from you, respecting brother Buck, as we had been very anxious on his account. Our sister Moore has been removed by death, and our brother Moore is in deep distress, and has been afflicted with a fever for a long time. I regret that I have to impart no welcome tidings respecting myself: I have been labouring under a cold ever since I left Diggah, and from the beginning of this year have been almost laid up. For a whole month I did nothing. My cough, which is very severe, is attended with asthma, and what will be the termination of my complaint is at present very dubious. I am much debilitated in body, and do very little. I delight in the work of translations, and have my heart set upon the completion of two versions for the work of God. But my heart fails me. If my cough continues, what can I do? Pray for me, for I hope I shall not be beyond the reach of prayer when you get this. Peace and good will be to Ireland, and to France, and the Isles of the sea.

INTELLIGENCE RESPECTING PERSIA.

The Rev. Deocar Schmid, a missionary from the Church Missionary Society, in a late communication, dated Madras, October 5, 1817, has mentioned a conversation he lately had with an Armenian bishop from Jerusalem. After stating a few particulars respecting the present state of Jerusalem, he observes — "But by far the most remarkable things which I heard is, that there is a number of about 80,000 persons in Persia, called Sophis, who, about ten or twelve years ago, openly renounced Mahomedanism, abolished circumcision, established separate places of worship, and adopted a peculiar dress to distinguish themselves from Mahomedans. They are said to speak highly of Christ, to revere the scriptures and, on the whole, as the vicar expressed it, 'to come into the Christian way.' They would receive copies of the Bible, and especially of the New Testament, with the greatest joy and gratitude, and would support with the greatest zeal all attempts to enlighten the Persian nation. They have their most learned teachers in Shiraz. They have a book in the Persian language containing their religious principles, which the vicar promised to procure me for my perusal.

"Are these not wonderful accounts? Are these not mighty calls to be diligent in the work of the Lord?"

TOLERATION IN PERSIA.

It is well known that the Mahometans profess to believe that Jesus Christ is a great prophet, that he performed miracles; that he ascended up into heaven, and that he will judge the world. They in general, however, treat Christians with great contumely and cruelty. We are happy to hear that the prince royal of Persia is attempting to protect the Christians in that kingdom. He has lately assembled at Tauris, a city of Persia, containing about 200,000 inhabitants, a divan, composed of the Sheickal-Sellum, (or head of faith, an office answering to that of mufti in Turkey,) and the principal doctors of the law, and proposed the following questions for their determination. 1. Was Jesus Christ a true prophet sent from God? 2. Are the laws contained in the Gospel just? 3. Is it lawful to blaspheme these laws? The first two questions were answered in the affirmative, the last, in the negative. These decisions have received a legal form. The prince royal has in consequence punished one of his domestics for insulting a Christian.

TRIUMPH OF RELIGIOUS LIBERTY IN FRANCE.

A cause involving questions of the highest interest to our Protestant brethren in France, has just been decided in the superior court of criminal justice. The mayor of the little town of Lourmarin, had ordered the inhabitants to cover the fronts of their houses with tapestry, in those streets through which the idolatrous mass was to pass, at what is called the "Feast of God." The police of Gap fined monsieur Roman, a protestant, six franks, for refusing to obey the mayor's edict. M. Roman appealed to the Court of Cassation. The question was, "Can a citizen be compelled to hang out tapestry on the front of his house, while the external ceremonies of the Catholic worship are performing?" On this question the counsellors for M. Roman delivered the most correct sentiments upon the subject; declaring, that "all the constituted authorities had proclaimed the principle of religious freedom; and had completely separated questions of religion from those connected with civil and political rights." "The court, after a long deliberation, pronounced a judgment, said to be most *strongly worded*, by which it annulled the judgment complained of, and decided that the municipal authorities have no right to make a rule for constraining citizens to cover the fronts of their houses on occasions of religious ceremonies." Comparing the above decision with the spirit manifested towards the protestants in France only three years since, we consider it a subject for congratulation to all who love our Lord Jesus Christ in sincerity, as the triumph of reason and religion over superstition and idolatry.

DUTCH MENNONITES.

Extract of a letter, dated April 2, 1818, from Mr. W. H. Angues, residing with Mons. Maumers, Pasteur Reforme.

Among other good men here is a minister, who is a Dutch baptist, or Mennonite, and has the character of being a pious and learned man. It is greatly his wish to promote an acquaintance with the English baptists for which purpose he would be glad to open a correspondence with any intelligent person in London, or elsewhere, of that denomination, to interchange communications on the state of religion, &c. This co-operation might extensively promote objects of a public nature for the spread of truth. His name is Mr. Mascaart, and he being a respectable man, and desirous of doing good, I have thought of making an effort through him to recommend the Baptist mission, and some other benevolent objects, to the churches in the Mennonite connexion, (which, throug' Holland, I learn, are both opulent and numerous, particularly in Friesland,) and also to the German baptists. I wish you, therefore, to forward some copies of Fuller's Abridgment of the Baptist Mission, Ivimey's History of the Baptists, and any other publications you deem suitable to the design of making this object fully known. Mr. Mascaart informs me, that he has had for some time in MS a General History of the Baptists, in his own writing but has not yet had an opportunity of printing it. He further states, that most of the literary journals throughout Holland are conducted by ministers of the Mennonite persuasion.

FROM THE AMERICAN BAPTIST MAGAZINE.

CONVERSION OF THE SAILORS.

The account in your last Number of the interesting scenes which transpired on board the ship in which the missionaries sailed to India, has no doubt filled many hearts with joy. I must confess while reading this account to my family, such powerful emotions were awakened in my breast, that I found it difficult to proceed. Feelings of delight, of gratitude, and of astonishment, compelled me repeatedly to pause. The reflection that our dear brethren did not forget their missionary character, afforded me almost as much satisfaction as the success which attended their pious and faithful labours. There was one consideration, however, which caused me to "rejoice with trembling"—the probability that some of these hopeful converts might make "shipwreck of faith and a good conscience" before their return to America. I was fearful lest some of them should be drifted from their course by the fatal current of sin, and thus perish on those shoals and quicksands which endanger our passage to eternity. For ever blessed be the Lord, there is reason to believe they have escaped these evils. With Christ for their captain, the scriptures for their compass, the hope of the gospel as their anchor, and the Holy Spirit to waft them forward, they seem to be steering to the port of endless rest.

As soon as I heard of the arrival of the Independence, I went on board. I was almost afraid to make inquiry of the officers, concerning the conduct of the men, lest my trembling apprehensions should be realized. It gave me however the greatest satisfaction to be informed, both by the captain and first mate, that the sailors had conducted with the greatest propriety. I observed to the first mate, we had received intelligence that several of the crew had become very serious on their voyage to Calcutta, and I wished to know from him whether their deportment on their passage home had been such as becomes religious men. He unhesitatingly assured me it had. Having ascertained this pleasing fact, I gave them all an invitation to call on me, that I might hear from their own lips "what the Lord had done for their souls."

The first evening after this invitation, only one of them visited me, the others being unavoidably engaged. From him I received a very pleasing and satisfactory account of his conversion to God. It would occupy too much of your Magazine to give a detail of the exercises of his mind. Suffice it to say, that N. from being a notorious swearer, and a lover of pleasure more than a lover of God, displays the meekness and humility of a disciple of Christ. O, said he, "never did I go such a voyage before! it is frequently the case that sailors are picking up a quarrel, swearing at one another, and sometimes fighting; but we were all like a band of brothers trying to please one another. I never was in a ship where we knocked off the work so pleasantly and so cheerfully. There was no such thing as swearing all the way home. Such of our shipmates as had no religion did not swear in our hearing." While attending to his artless story, the words of Watts occurred to my mind with peculiar force:

> Lions and beasts of savage name,
> Put on the nature of the lamb;
> While the wild world esteem it strange,
> Gaze, and admire, and hate the change.

On a succeeding evening three others came to converse with me. It was really a feast to hear these weather-beaten mariners relate their experience with the simplicity of little children. One of them, a Scotchman by birth, said, "the day before he shipped on board the Independence he was very low in his mind, and endeavoured to remove it by intoxication," but, as might be expected, the momentary excitement produced by the liquor left him still more depressed. His convictions of sin however were not very deep, or permanent, till the missionaries commenced their ministerial labours. Then he had a view of his lost condition. He saw that he was exposed to the tremendous storm of divine wrath. He observed, "he felt so bad that he thought he could not possibly live." At first he supposed he could do much himself. Said he, "I thought I could knock off swearing, and knock off drunkenness, but I soon found I could do nothing of myself." He was at last brought to hope in the mercy of God through our Lord Jesus Christ.

The Norwegian, who was taught by one of the missionaries to read, gave a very affecting account of the dealings of the Lord to his soul. His broken language gave a peculiar charm to the story of his life, and especially of his return to God. Said he, "for some time I did not tink of dese tings at all. I made sport of dem, and to't it all foolishness. One day Mr. Wheelock, he talk to me, to turn from my evil ways, but in my inside I laughed t him. Afterward my conscience pricked me, I to't dere was someting in religion. Den I felt so bad I could'nt help crying. I felt sush a load of guilt on my conscience, I did'nt know what to do. After dis I had sin-sorrow, and prayed to de Lord he would have mercy on me." This poor man saw that salvation could be obtained only through the blood of Christ. But I can do no justice to the childlike manner in which he spake of divine things; I shall therefore forbear any further description of his conversation.

S. F. another of the sailors, has had a good education, and is an amiable young man. Having sat under the ministry of the gospel in England, his habits, previous to his becoming truly serious, were more correct than is usual among seafaring men. I trust he will be an ornament to a christian profession. There are two or three others whom I have not seen, but of whom their brethren speak well.

It will be gratifying to the friends of missions to be informed, that three of the sailors, of their own accord, have each presented three dollars to aid the funds of the Baptist Foreign Mission Society. When the rest return to town they will probably do the same, as they unanimously agreed, while at sea, to present their mites to the Society.

I have been thus particular in my account of these men for the satisfaction of your numerous readers. They may rely on the above as a plain statement of facts. I have introduced no colouring in the representation for the sake of giving effect. What is here recorded will leave an impression far short of that which would be felt in a personal interview with them.

Perhaps it would be improper to close this communication without a few brief reflections.

1. We learn what great good may be done by missionaries when they possess the spirit of their station. Had our brethren contented themselves with the idea that they were sent as missionaries to Burmah, and had no special duty to

perform till they arrived there, we should probably have heard nothing of the conversion of the sailors. To their honour be it stated, they commenced their labours on board the vessel as early after their embarkation as possible. They not only preached on deck, by the kind and cheerful permission of the captain, but embraced opportunities of conversing with the crew in the forecastle, and while one was engaged in teaching a poor foreigner to read the English language, the other was performing the same kind office for another foreigner. While pursuing these works of love, the Holy Spirit descended as a monitor, and as a comforter. Such were the effects which followed, the sailors as well as the missionaries exclaimed, "that instead of the ship being a floating prison, it was a floating heaven."

2. We are taught by this interesting event the efficacy of prayer.

No one present at the prayer meeting, when the missionaries were commended to the protection of the Lord, can easily forget the solemn services of that evening. There was a remarkable spirit of devotion. And while the missionaries were prayed for, the officers and men were not forgotten. There is reason to believe that the prayer of faith was heard. A sceptic may smile at this remark, but Christians who believe that God has made it their duty to pray, and that he answers prayer, will give it the importance it deserves.

3. Let us be encouraged to hope that our missionary brethren will be succeeded in their labours. A recollection of what the Lord has done, should inspire us with confidence in him to future success. The conduct of our brethren on board the ship is a pledge that they will enter on their labours with zeal, and persevere in them with faithfulness and constancy. The same power which accompanied their ministrations on the water, can with the greatest ease subdue the hearts of Burmans to the truth. May we not indulge the hope that this power will be exerted, till we hear that Gaudma has fallen, and his votaries have become the humble followers of the Son of God!

4. I cannot dismiss this paper without entreating Christians to remember these converted sailors at a throne of grace. O! pray for them, that they may be kept by the power of God through faith unto salvation. Perhaps few men are placed in more trying circumstances than they are. Compelled by their calling to be with men of no religion, and exposed to their sneers and scoffs, they will greatly need the ballast of divine grace to enable them steadily to keep on their way. O! pray for them, that out of the fulness of Christ they may receive, and grace for grace. There are many other evils unavoidably connected with a seafaring life, which must be detrimental to the spiritual growth of the Christian. Among these may be enumerated, absence from the means of grace—the time which is spent in ports where the gospel is not preached—the situation of sailors as strangers who have few or none to watch over them, to admonish or console them, even in places where evangelical truth is proclaimed. A consideration of all these circumstances should excite the sympathy and prayer of all who love the Lord Jesus Christ.

May the Lord keep them from falling, and grant them an abundant entrance into his heavenly kingdom. In whatever part of the world they may terminate the voyage of life, it is my earnest prayer that each of them may have the triumphant feelings so beautifully expressed in the lines of Henry Kirk White,

Now safely moor'd, my perils o'er,
I'll sing, first in night's diadem,
For ever, and for evermore,
The Star—the Star of Bethlehem

EUMENES.

MORE INFORMATION RELATIVE TO THE CONVERSION OF SAILORS.

In the ship Edward, lately arrived at Philadelphia, are several seamen who have recently, and for the most part on ship-board, been converted to God. One of them was baptized by brother Lawson at Calcutta, the Lord's day preceding the time of the vessel's sailing. They appear to be men of deep experience, and are communicative, intelligent and amiable. They have been introduced into several pious families in this city, where their religious converse and modest deportment have left a most pleasing impression. The officers of the vessel bear testimony to their exemplary conversation on board. It is impossible to converse with them without observing the softening, sanctifying and elevating nature of the gospel of the Son of God. The prophecy is surely accomplishing—"The abundance of the seas shall be converted unto thee."

DOMESTIC INTELLIGENCE, REVIVALS, &c.

THE Rev. Joshua Bradley of Albany, N. Y. has just published a book containing a concise account of the several revivals of religion which have taken place in the United States since the year 1815.—From this interesting work, we select the following articles.

TROY. Since the commencement of 1815, there have been received into the communion of the Presbyterian church, two hundred and sixty—into the Baptist 225—and into the Methodist 320—and a number into the Episcopalian communion. These were the fruits of those astonishing influences experienced in this small city.

The present revival commenced its visibility on the second Lord's day evening in January 1819, after the usual religious services were closed in the Methodist church, a few young people tarried to sing after the congregation was dismissed. A preacher who was raised up in this city, being present on a visit, observed one of the number affected, and after some conversation with this young person, who requested him to pray, a number came to the altar, and the Spirit descended and spread its influences upon that people, until near two hundred have joined the church.

In relating their experiences, they profess to have been seriously impressed from different periods of time, none probably exceeding a year.

The danger of procrastination, and particularly as it procures hardness of heart, has been faithfully proclaimed in their ears, and the Spirit has set the word home to their hearts. Almost the whole of that congregation exhibit signs of great seriousness.

The work is now increasing among all the denominations in the city. Upon the fourth of February, Rev. Mr. Sommer observes, that he had conversed with thirty-five since the 26th of January, who have felt the powerful influences of grace. Some of them have been approved by the standing committee of the church, as suitable candidates for the ordinances.

The means, by which it has been the pleasure of Jehovah to originate and carry on the work among his people have been as various, as the application has been sovereign. Several of the converts are scholars in the Sabbath school, and some of them date their first impressions from the affectionate exhortations of their pious teachers; while others make mention of the preaching of the everlasting gospel as the instrument of their conversion to God.

Rev. J Coe, D. D. observes, that it seems almost too much to expect a general revival, in so short a time since the other But that we ought not to limit a God of boundless mercy. He works like himself. Many little children, and some young people, and others further advanced in life, appear to be solemnly impressed That very considerable divine influence is diffused among his congregation, in awakening and convincing them of their guilt and danger But where this will issue God only knows, and time must determine. They rejoice with trembling. Yet may they with an holy pleasure look up and utter the language of Isaiah, *Who are these that fly as a cloud, and as doves to their windows?*

ALBANY. Since the commencement of 1815, a divine influence has been exerted in this city, and the gates of our Zion have been thronged with anxious sinners and joyful converts But the cloud that hung over the city of Troy, fraught with divine compassion, passed around us, only letting here and there a few drops fall to refresh and cheer this thirsty hill of God.

In 1816, the truly pious of all denominations, had their expectations greatly raised, and were daily expecting a copious shower of grace they could even hear the thunder of God's power, and see some who had been careless seeking a refuge for their Christless souls yet He who governs the universe, *and will have mercy upon whom he will have mercy*, has not come down with such overwhelming influences, as upon some other cities.

His Spirit seems to have been hovering over us, and though often grieved with our hardness of heart and malconduct, yet being slow to anger and abundant in mercy, has not withdrawn from us, nor given us over to work out our eternal condemnation.

In the summer of 1816 a revival began in the Baptist society, and about forty professed to cherish hopes in a Saviour's merits, and thirty-five joined the church.

In the spring of 1817, the Spirit descended again, and a considerable number were brought into the light and liberty of the gospel. It continued its gentle influences for more than fourteen months: in which time the society increased, backsliders were brought to remember their first love, to confess their sins, and move on in fellowship with his people, and many converts have been added to our communion. In June 1818, we purchased the Albany theatre, and fitted it up for a place of public worship, and opened it on the first day of January 1819 Thus this church and congregation, by the benevolent assistance of their fellow citizens, and public benefactors, have been instrumental in one short season, of sweeping away and burying for ever, one of the proudest ensigns of unhallowed ambition, that was ever exhibited upon the banks of the Hudson This event has been ominous of millennial achievements, of national regeneration, and of the redemption of the world.

Upon the very day this house was opened the Spirit descended, and his regenerating influences were felt, and one soul at least, heard the voice of Christ speaking within his troubled mind, saying, *Son, be of good cheer, thy sins are forgiven thee.*

It is now a most solemn time in this city. Let a stranger enter any congregation within this metropolis, and look over the crowds that seat themselves to hear the word, and he will see a more than usual attention and anxiety among them to know the things of the kingdom of heaven. And in some congregations he will hear sighs, and behold hundreds in tears, before a sermon is closed.

There are but a few congregations out of the eleven established in this city, but what (according to my best knowledge, obtained from the pastors of the churches, and my daily observation,) feel more or less this heavenly dew.

I find every minister labouring under the same embarrassment with myself, when interrogated concerning the work in his congregation. We cannot tell how many are labouring and heavy laden under a sense of their sins. About two weeks since I knew of only four or five in my congregation who were under very deep distress of mind, and now a large number are willing to own that they have been under awakenings for some time. Almost every day some new cases appear, and some soul is made willing to be saved, entirely by grace abounding through the blood of Jesus.

For many months I have discovered a solemn and gradual work among the Presbyterian congregations, and an earnestness in their preachers for the reviving presence and power of Christ, that led me to believe, that the reign of heaven was approaching.

Since the commencement of 1815, one hundred and thirty-one have been added to the first Presbyterian church, upon examination, and to the other, considerable additions have been made. To the Baptist more than one hundred, and many by letters to all the churches. Many candidates are examined, and are now coming before the churches in this city. At our next communion, we expect to receive accessions that will gladden the hearts of the righteous, and swell the songs of angels in heaven. Surely we can say, *The Lord is merciful and gracious, slow to anger, and plenteous in mercy. He will not always chide, neither will he keep his anger for ever. As far as the east is from the west; so far hath he removed our transgressions from us. Bless the Lord, all ye his hosts; ye ministers of his who do his pleasure. Bless the Lord, O my soul.*

To the Editors, dated New York, February 9, 1819.

Hoping it will be interesting to your readers, I present you a brief account of the revival of religion under my ministerial charge. In December, 1816, " The Bethel Baptist Church" of this city gave me an invitation to become their pastor, but my health at that time being extremely feeble, and having just before received invitations to settle with other churches, one of which was " the Second Baptist Church" in the city of Washington, where the prospect was flattering, for these and other reasons my mind was not determined, until May 1817, to accept the invitation of the Bethel church; and on the 27th of the same month I was ordained their pastor. From the blessing of the Lord upon my previous labours, by this time the congregation had greatly increased. The Lord not only blessed his word for the comfort and edification of his saints, but also to the conversion of sinners unto God through Jesus Christ our Lord, so that a number of both sexes, and of different ages, were with great solicitude inquiring the way to Zion.

On the second Lord's day in June I baptized five, and the same day they were added to the church. A few weeks after this, when the attention of the congregation was interesting, it pleased the Lord to lay me on a sick-bed with a typhus fever, so severely that many of my friends were apprehensive I should not recover. In this sickness I hope the Lord was pleased to teach me many valuable lessons, for my future usefulness; and in eight weeks from my first confinement, he was pleased so far to restore my health as to enable me to resume my public labours. My first sermon was from Psalm 116. 7. "I was brought low, and he helped me." The place was crowded with attentive hearers, and I never saw an assembly more generally affected. Many have since dated their convictions of sin, and others their conversion to God, from under that discourse. The number of converts became so great that on the second Lord's day in September, which was as soon as I was able to go into the water, I baptized twenty-one persons. It was a solemn time, long to be remembered. It was supposed there could not be less than six or seven thousand spectators, and when the weather has been favourable, I apprehend quite as many have since, frequently, attended the administration of the ordinance.

It would extend my letter too far to enumerate all the particulars attending this revival. The Lord still continues to pour out the spirit of his grace upon us. At the time of my taking charge of this church, there were about seventy members, many of which were in an unsettled state; but now they are not only united, but in the space of seventeen months three hundred added. The Lord grant that they may prove plants of his right hand's planting. Perhaps a larger proportion of these are heads of families, than what is usual in times of a revival. I apprehend more than one half; and about one third of the whole are males. It is the opinion of our christian friends, of different religious denominations, that this has been the greatest increase that has ever been to any one church in this city in the same space of time. May it prove as a few drops before a more copious shower! Our congregations, at present are large and solemn. When I first came to this church our place of worship was small, only 36 by 40 feet, but the congregation much smaller in proportion, consisting of not more than forty or fifty hearers, on the first Lord's day; but they continued to increase, so that on the eighth Lord's day the house was thronged.

The church now thought it necessary to enlarge the building. To accomplish this object a subscription book was circulated; but owing to my illness, and during my confinement, the congregation growing much less, the preparations for enlarging were delayed till a few weeks after my recovery. I have often thought it remarkable, that notwithstanding my recess of labour the people were favoured with preaching from ministers superior in talents to my own, yet the congregation was reduced to less than half the number; this teacheth us that "the Lord's ways are not as our ways," and that he maketh use of such means as seemeth good in his sight, that the "excellency of the power may be of God, and not of us."

I cannot but remark, that during this revival it hath pleased the Lord to bless the administration of his ordinances, in a peculiar manner, and especially the ordinance of baptism, for the conviction and conversion of sinners. I cannot say how many were first brought to see their guilty and lost condition, while attending to the address, to the prayer, or to the singing at the water side, and perhaps still more when seeing the ordinance administered. Others likewise on such occasions have been made to rejoice in the Lord Jesus, and to fix their hope in his mercy. Hence to me it appears evident that the Holy Spirit comes down in our day, as well as in past ages, if not in "the shape of a dove," yet with his enlightening, convincing, and sanctifying influences. Surely these things, connected with the scriptures, should convince such professed Christians as either neglect or reject the ordinance of baptism, that in this they are incorrect, and especially such as by their hard speeches pour contempt upon it. But if they do not discover the beauty and glory of this institution, which is thus honoured by God, our prayer is, that from the word and spirit they may see it their duty, as well as their privilege, to practise the ordinances as they were first delivered to the saints

Because we read of two households being baptized, many are disposed to infer that there must have been some infants; but I have the pleasure to say, that during this revival I have baptized three if not four whole households, and they all gave evidence of repentance towards God and faith in our Lord Jesus Christ.

My labours are so numerous that I am often bowed down with fatigue, but hope I can say, I am never tired of the work of the Lord.

Our place of worship has been enlarged, making it now 36 by 70 feet, and yet it is not sufficient to receive the people who are anxious to attend. We have constant preaching three times every Lord's day, the ordinances every month, and through the most of the last fall, baptism every two weeks. On every Monday afternoon and evening, I receive inquirers after the way to Zion. These seasons have often been blessed to their souls. Tuesday evenings we have service in the place of worship, and preaching on Thursday evenings. Wednesday evenings I preach in the outskirts of the city, on Friday evening attend church meeting, to examine candidates for baptism and communion. By these services, together with visiting the sick, attending funerals, and other ministerial duties, you may readily perceive that my time is fully employed. Were it not that I perceive that by preaching in various sections of the city there have been, and still are, instances of conviction and conversion among the hearers, I should be disposed to relinquish some of my labours. but I hope the love of Christ, and the salvation of souls, still prompt me to persevere. During this revival it hath pleased the Lord to call two of our young brethren of promising talents to the work of the ministry, viz. John Smitzer, and Thomas B. Stevenson. They have both been *licensed* by the church. Mr. Smitzer is receiving the benefits of the Baptist Theological Seminary in this city.

On the 29th of October last, our brother Sullivan Bijotat, who had been a licensed preacher from this church for many years, was solemnly set apart to the work of an evangelist. May the God of all grace confirm his health, and make him useful in the cause of Christ.

Although our present place of worship is computed to hold a thousand people, it is believed as many more are anxious to have admittance to hear the word, but cannot. We therefore contemplate, in the fear of the Lord, to erect a stone building, 70 by 85 feet. When this plan was proposed to the church, there was the same evening nearly four thousand dollars subscribed as a donation, by a number of the members, to promote the object, and soon after the subscriptions amounted to between five and six thousand dollars. The whole building finished is estimated with the land to cost from twenty to twenty five thousand dollars.

Our people having experienced such inexpressible blessings by the means of the glorious gospel, and feeling greatly concerned for those who are destitute of the same, were led on the 10th of June last to form a Domestic Missionary Society, to send the good news of salvation to such as "are perishing for lack of vision." To promote this object, one hundred dollars was collected by contribution, and three hundred subscribed. Soon after a Youth's Missionary Society was formed auxiliary to this; and although there are two other Baptist Youth's Missionary Societies in this city, it is pleasing to observe, that about one hundred and fifty have joined themselves to this new society.

From this statement of the Lord's gracious dealings with us, we do with solemn reverence ascribe the whole glory to his most blessed name! And while you rejoice with us for the rich showers of mercy we have already received, we earnestly beg your prayers, that the Lord may still continue the blessings of his love and grace upon us.

These from your affectionate brother and fellow labourer in the gospel.

JOHNSON CHASE.

THE DEVIL WORSHIPPED.

Extracts of a letter from Edward Tanner, Esq. to J. M. Peck, of St. Louis, dated New Madrid county, Missouri, January 1st, 1819

"AS I expect to be in St. Louis in the spring, when I can give you a more particular description of the people and country through which I passed, I shall give you only some general information at this time, of the inhabitants I visited, both Indians and whites, with which I was conversant. I am much indebted to the army for the attention and polite treatment I received at all the posts I passed, particularly Michilimackinac. The officers of that post, as also Detroit and Fort Wayne, opened their purses liberally for my expenses. As to the northern tribes of Indians, there is so much resemblance in their religious manners and customs, and the frequent opportunities you may enjoy of an acquaintance with such as annually visit St. Louis, that you may form a general idea of them. Some few particulars I will mention.

"Almost every Indian has a skin of some small animal which he keeps constantly about him, and in which he carries his medicine, and other little necessaries. If he finds a pretty stone, or any other little curiosity, he puts it in this bag, and should he on that day experience any extraordinary deliverance, or good luck, it is attributed to the curious article, and ever after he pays it religious adoration. The Indians generally worship the 'Great Spirit,' as they call him, but they also worship the devil, the sun, moon, planets, fire, earth, water, their hands, feet, &c. &c.

"Their worship is performed by offering sacrifices, smoking, dancing, singing, praying, and various other exercises. I was present at a ceremony of worship paid to the devil, by a party of the Winnebagoes. After descending Fox river, about 100 yards below the outlet, or lower end of the Ox lake, it receives a tributary stream called 'Devil river.' With me were two Winnebagoes, and one half breed Mynominey, who spoke French, by whose means I conversed. Arriving within about 200 yards of Devil river, the Indians laid down their paddles, and began to speak something like a prayer, after which they sung, and as the canoe passed the mouth of the stream where the evil spirit is supposed to reside, they strewed over the water coloured hair, feathers, tobacco, &c.

"The Sack Indians live on Rock river, about four miles from its junction with the Mississippi. They have one town or village, and are about 1000 strong. They have two village or civil chiefs, who take cognizance of all domestic concerns, and two war chiefs, who head their warriors. Their warriors are divided into two classes, of 400 each. The first composed of all those who have performed any extraordinary feats of valour, the other of the ordinary warriors, besides which they have about 200 old men and boys, able to bear arms in case of any emergency. They encourage marriages with other tribes, and give decided preference to foreigners. By this policy they have increased in a few years from a small band to what they are now. The Aioways live on the west side of the Mississippi, and up some of the small streams. They have about 400 warriors, and are in alliance with the Sacks. The Foxes are scattered along the Mississippi to Prairie Du Chien. They have four villages, the chief of which is at De Bukee's lead mines, where they work, but to little profit.

"The Winnebagoes live on the Ouisconsin and Fox rivers, have a number of small villages or places of resort in summer. They are in alliance with the Sioux of the Mississippi, and told me if the Sioux went to war they would join them. They are about 700 strong. The Mynominies live on the west side of Green bay, and are about 800 strong—have considerable intercourse with the inhabitants living at Green bay, where about 70 families reside. These are chiefly French traders who have married Indian wives, exclusive of the fort, which contains a garrison of four companies of troops."

MISCELLANEA.

THE NAME JESUS.

THE reverence due to this holy name, I conceive, hath been the occasion, that though it was a common name among the Jews, yet it is otherwise among us Christians. The names of the greatest apostles and of the blessed Virgin mother are in familiar use among us, but *who ever presumed to name his son after the Son of God.*

Dr. Newton.

When there was a greater scarcity of cattle than there is at present, it might be a good political reason to enjoin the eating of fish in *Lent*, for the preservation and increase of cattle, and for the encouragement of the fishing trade, and this is the reason assigned in the statutes of Edward the VIth, but I believe no other good reason, either natural or religious, can be assigned for this usage.

Dr. Newton.

God made the animals all *after their kind*. Not only of divers shapes, but of divers natures, food, and fashions. Some to be tame about the house, others to be wild in the fields. Some living upon grass and herbs, others upon flesh. Some bold and others timorous. Some for man's service, and not his sustenance, as *the horse*, others for his sustenance, and not service, as *the sheep*; others for both, as the *ox*, and some for neither, as the *wild beasts*. In all which appears the manifold wisdom of the Creator.

Henry.

In the 12th year of his age, Jesus went up with Joseph and Mary to Jerusalem, at the Passover time, Luke ii. 42. The reason of our Lord's coming up at that time is probably thought to have been in order to his being examined by the Jewish doctors in the temple, that he might be admitted to the eating of the next Passover, according to the custom of the Jews, whose usual admission to the Passover was at thirteen years of age.

Dr. Wells.

The book of the Apocalypse may be considered as a PROPHET, continued in the church of God, uttering predictions relative to all times which have their successive fulfilment as ages roll on. And thus it stands in the Christian church, in the place of the SUCCESSION OF PROPHETS in the Jewish church; and by this special economy PROPHECY IS STILL CONTINUED, IS ALWAYS SPEAKING; and yet a succession of prophets rendered unnecessary.

Dr Clark.

There is a period, I am persuaded, in which the gospel is destined to make glorious progress, according to Rev. xi. 15. and xiv. 6. (which are synchronical,) while yet the vials are pouring out, (as chap. xvii.) and the enemies of Christ opposing it with all their might. The Word of God going forth upon a white horse, (chap xix.) is before the millennium, and the opposition made to his progress will bring on what, in chap. xiv. is called the harvest and vintage, and in chap xix is described as the last battle prior to the millennium. Be of good courage, my dear brethren, we shall overcome through the blood of the Lamb, and by the word of our testimony.

The period between the sounding of the seventh angel and the millennium, is like the reign of David, whom the Lord prospered whithersoever he went; but then it was *in the face of opposition*. The millennium, on the other hand, will be as the reign of Solomon, who had *rest round about* given him from all his enemies.—Thus Satan will then be *bound*; and the beast and false prophet *gone into perdition*. This is emphatically the Messiah's rest, which will be glorious, Isa. xi. We may not expect to see the latter, but we may the former; and surely it will be enough for us to follow him that rideth on a white horse, or to rank among the armies of heaven in so glorious a warfare.

Fuller.

OBITUARY.

ON Monday, the 23d of March, about 2 o'clock P M departed this life, Mrs. Furman, late wife of the Rev. Dr. Furman of Charleston, S C In all the social relations, as a wife, a mother, and a friend, she discovered a sweetness of disposition, mingled with sobriety of judgment, that will long be remembered. She has left a husband, a numerous band of children, and a large circle of affectionate acquaintances, shedding the tears which nature and the remembrance of her worth unavoidably prompt. Herself has no doubt ascended to the bosom of that divine Redeemer whose name she had glorified by an unblemished profession, and the extension of whose kingdom was among the dearest wishes of her heart. The Hon Judge Tallmadge, who communicated the above intelligence, says, "Our dear and excellent friend, Mrs. Furman, in her long and painful sickness, manifested a patient waiting and a serene faith, worthy of her vocation She has given to the world a practical exhibition of the power of grace, and of the excellence of her hopes."

CAPTAIN PAUL TITCOMB.

It is with feelings of regret we announce to our readers the death of this excellent man Though our acquaintance with him was not so intimate as to enable us to give a minute history of his life, yet we cannot deny ourselves the mournful pleasure of paying this respectful and affectionate tribute to his memory.

Mr. Titcomb was a member of the congregational church at Newburyport under the pastoral care of Rev. Daniel Dana, D. D. He maintained an honourable christian profession, and evinced a noble superiority over those sectarian feelings which have so often kept pious men asunder from each other. He loved, and treated as brethren, all who seemed to bear the image of his blessed Lord

By the interposition of a kind Providence, Mr. T. was induced to accept the office of supercargo of the ship Independence. When he was informed that we were desirous of sending Messrs. Colman and Wheelock, with their wives in that vessel, he expressed peculiar gratification. His knowledge of a sea life, and of what was suitable for missionaries destined for India, qualified him to assist us in making preparation for their outfit. He used his influence to obtain a passage for them as cheap as possible; and after our brethren had commenced their voyage, the same influence was employed, in promoting their comfort, respectability and usefulness. We recollect these facts with sensations of gratitude. If his valuable life had been spared we should have made our grateful acknowledgments to him in person, but as we are denied this pleasure, we will perpetuate the remembrance of his kind acts in the pages of our Magazine.

It has often been said, "If you would know a man's religious character you must travel with him in the stage, or sail with him on the ocean; there he will unbend himself, and you may know what he is." If this be any criterion, we must pronounce that our departed friend was an eminently pious man. Our missionary brethren speak of him in their journals, with affection and gratitude. In one place they say, "brother Titcomb related his christian experience; we enjoyed a refreshing season." In another extract it is stated, "brother Titcomb met with us for prayer." After his death the first mate observed, " he had seen many who professed religion, but he never knew a man who lived up to his profession so much as Capt. Titcomb."

After his arrival at Calcutta, Mr. Titcomb was afflicted with the bilious fever, this left him in a very weak state. It was a matter of doubt whether he would recover, but his physician advised his return in the Independence. When he was first sensible that his dissolution was at hand, he was severely tried in his mind. The idea that he should never see his dear wife and beloved children again, was very distressing; but he was assisted to rise above these feelings, and resign them to the care of Him " who is the widow's God, and the Father of the fatherless." At his request, the officers and crew assembled in the cabin a short time before he died, when he affectionately and earnestly exhorted them to forsake their wicked ways, and seek an interest in Christ. He enjoyed sweet peace of mind, and looked forward to his departure with calm and joyous hope. The last word he was heard to utter was—Alleluia! He died July 30th, 1818, and was committed to the deep with all the respect which circumstances would admit, where his mortal part will remain till " the sea shall give up its dead."

May the disconsolate widow seek refuge in God, and her fatherless children find in him an almighty Friend. Under the great loss she has sustained, religion allows her to sorrow—but not like those who have no hope. We trust she will suppress every repining thought, and dry up her tears while she calls to recollection his pious life, his tranquil death, his joyful transition to the abodes of bliss.

There is something delightfully solemn in the contemplation of such a death. To see a dying man in the cabin of a ship, ten thousand miles from home, calmly committing to God the wife of his youth, and the pledges of their mutual love—addressing the officers and sailors on the importance of religion—declaring that it is this which supports him in the hour of dissolution—and then expiring, with the song of heaven—Alleluia—on his lips, is a scene, which, while it makes infidels tremble, confirms the faith of the believer, and awakens in his bosom admiration and gratitude for that gospel which brings life and immortality to light.

We shall conclude this obituary of our departed friend with the lines of Fanch, which we think are peculiarly descriptive of his abundant entrance " into the everlasting kingdom of our Lord and Saviour Jesus Christ."

" Now safe arrives the heavenly mariner;
The battering storm, the hurricane of life,
All dies away in one eternal calm.
With joy divine full glowing in his breast,
He gains, he gains the port of everlasting rest."

[From the American Baptist Magazine.

Happy in the Lord died Mrs. RHODA G PAUL, of Philadelphia, who, on Lord's day, July 18th, 1818, was committed to the grave, in hope of a joyful resurrection.

Her complaint was a consumption. During her sickness she was much supported by the grace of the Lord Jesus and towards the close of her exercises appeared impatient of sleeping, and anxious to be ever awake, that she might enjoy the presence of her Lord and Redeemer. Some plain but pious lines were repeated to her, which she said exactly described her feelings. For three successive mornings her heart was much comforted with the words brought home to her mind, "And the word was made flesh," &c. Several ministers of the gospel waited on her, and had much pleasure from her resigned and pious conversation. She took a most affectionate leave of her husband, her adopted child, her sister, and several very beloved and attentive friends, whose kindness she mentioned with heartfelt gratitude. She begged her husband to prepare to meet her in the kingdom of heaven. At her desire the 23d chapter of Job was read to her, and afforded her much comfort. She was much employed in praying to the Lord, and praising his holy name. Seeing her sister much affected, she said, "O don't do so! I thought you were better prepared for this! There is no cause for sorrow. I want no consolation. I desire to praise the all-wise, all-powerful, great and glorious God! O what condescension, that the Lord should stoop so low as to speak to such a sinful creature as I! Lord, stand by me, and send some guardian angel to convey my spirit from this world of tears! Come down, blessed Saviour, thyself, and take me!"

She cried, "O Jordan! O Jordan!" She was asked, Do you find it hard to cross the stream? "O no! O no! it has no terrour to me. He will not forsake me! 'Those that thou gavest me I have kept, and none of them is lost.' I long to hear thee say, Come ye blessed," &c. Addressing the friends round her dying bed, she cried—"O ye handmaidens, if you won't have this Jesus for your friend you must perish! Weep not for me, but for yourselves!" She then asked to be laid down. Her request was complied with, and she immediately fell asleep.

POETRY.

HYMN.

"*Israel did eat manna forty years.*"—Exodus xvi. 35.

WHEN Israel through the desert went,
  A sandy dangerous way:
The Lord abundant manna sent,
  To feed them day by day.

'Twas food ambrosial, small and round;
  Of pearly, snowy white,
Wide it bestrew'd the dewy ground,
  And blest the Hebrews' sight.

But richer food his grace prepares
  To sinners when they cry:
Who Christ the hidden manna shares,
  Shall never, never die.

Faith can in Jesu's flesh discern
  Refreshment for the mind.
Approach my soul the golden urn,
  For gentiles seek and find.

'Tis uncorrupted, angels' food,
  'Tis daily, freely giv'n;
'Tis all my soul on earth calls good,
  And all she hopes in heaven.

MILLENNIUM.

Hark, the seventh angel loud proclaims,
—While through the air his vial streams,—
'Tis done.' away with shields and swords,
The peaceful kingdoms are the Lord's.

With numerous crowns he rides on high,
His name recorded on his thigh;
Chain'd in black shades let Satan roar,
He shall deceive the earth no more.

The sun no more remits his rays,
But steady shines with sevenfold blaze;
The moon, her softer journeys run,
Reveals the radiance of the sun.

Open the heavenly temple stands,
The ark appears, not made with hands;
The vail that once all faces bound,
Lies rent and scatter'd on the ground.

See, from the dust the Church arise,
Drest with the beauties of the skies;
With songs the bride moves on to taste
The pleasures of the marriage feast.

Mountains and hills their transport join,
Clap their glad hands and pour their wine
Creation feels divine release,
Her pains, her groans, her travail cease.

Well pleas'd from his eternal throne
The King of kings looks mildly down,
Perfumes the universal song,
And bids the ages roll along.

THE LATTER DAY LUMINARY;

BY A COMMITTEE

OF

THE BAPTIST BOARD OF FOREIGN MISSIONS FOR THE UNITED STATES.

THIS NUMBER CONTAINS
THE FIFTH ANNUAL REPORT OF THE BOARD.

Vol. I.   MAY, 1819   No. VIII.

ADDRESS.

THE Baptist Board of Foreign Missions for the United States, grateful for the support and encouragement which they have experienced in the discharge of their official duties, have again the pleasure of presenting the annual Address required by the Constitution of the Convention.

They are happy in the reflection that the events of another year serve to confirm the expectations and increase the joy of the thousands who are *waiting for the consolation* of the latter day, and who, from the signs of the times, have concluded that the promised period cannot be distant. The ardour of the supporters of Bible Institutions discovers no indication of abatement, while endeavours to teach the young, the adult and the aged, to read for themselves the charter of salvation, have been employed and made useful, to an extent not exceeded, they believe, in any year since the introduction of Christianity. That zeal for the Lord of Hosts which has recently translated the scriptures into most of the languages of the earth, is still engaged. It presents to the world an example sought in vain in the history of the spread of false religious systems. What efforts were ever made by the disciples of Zoroaster, of Brumha, or of Mahomet to translate their sacred volumes into other languages? They had still remained in their native Chinese, Sungskrit and Arabic obscurity, had not the industry of Christians brought them forth to the light. It is, probably, to be resolved into the wrong idea formed by the Jew, that the smiles of heaven were to be confined to his own nation, that no more attention was paid to translating the Old Testament. It is well known the Septuagint version is to be ascribed to the literary ambition of Ptolemy, and not to the desire of Hebrews for the diffusion of the scriptures. But the time has arrived when the friends of Christ, not fearing the universal investigation of a volume which they are conscious is the record of God, and persuaded that it conveys to a dying world the words of eternal life, are using means to send it unto all people, nations and languages, that dwell in all the earth. Missionaries in lands remote are explaining to the heathen its sacred contents; and where, in the movement of a mysterious Providence, death diminishes their number, fresh servants of the Lord approach to perpetuate the work. Prophecy is illustrated and established by its glorious accomplishment, and the prayers of the saints are increasingly answered and encouraged. The Sun of Zion has risen which shall no more go down.

The Board have reason for gratitude for the mercies that have been extended to the mission at Rangoon. The gospel by Matthew has been translated by Mr. Judson, and printed by Mr. Hough in Burman, and a few tracts, designed to explain the principles of the gospel, have been published in the same language. Messrs. Colman and Wheelock, with their wives, have safely arrived at their destination. The circumstance that their pious conversation and example were rendered instrumental to the conversion of several of the ship's company, offers encouragement to future missionaries, and furnishes, we trust, a token of the success that shall crown their future labours. Experience has proved that the climate of Burmah is not unfriendly to health, while its population, and its proximity to China, Siam, and other mission fields, display the importance of the station. Difficulties, nevertheless, must be expected. The manners of the Burmans are fierce and untractable, and their attachment to their idolatries blindly ardent. The recent military measures in the hither India, have created a spirit of jealousy among them, and induced the suspicion that white men are emissaries. The Board would be ready to conclude that the stay of the brethren in Burmah depended on the caprice of the emperor, were they not satisfied that the hearts of kings are in the hands of the Lord. The design of the late expedition of M:

Judson, undertaken with a view of obtaining a convert from among the *Mugs* to assist in the mission, is fully approved by the Board, and will, they have no doubt, meet the approbation of all the friends of Zion. The disappointments attendant on the voyage were such as no human prudence could foresee. They affectionately sympathize with their brother under the trial he has experienced, and pray that, as the means of surmounting every obstruction, himself and his associates may be favoured with an abundant " supply of the Spirit of Jesus Christ."

The Board has viewed with satisfaction the labours of their missionary brethren Peck and Welch at St. Louis. A baptist church has been formed there, which is gradually increasing. A new place of worship, in a pleasant and conspicuous part of the town, has been erected. It is already in part paid for. The church at Salem, Massachusetts, has generously aided the attempt by presenting the sum of one hundred and seventy-three dollars. It is hoped the benevolence of other churches and brethren will assist in extinguishing the remaining incumbrance. The brethren there have done much in opening and encouraging schools, in seeking acquaintance with Indian chiefs, and ascertaining the circumstances of the tribes scattered through the territories. They have travelled in various directions, preaching the everlasting gospel, animated with the expectation that the Lord will make the wilderness of the west " like Eden, and her desert like the garden of the Lord: joy and gladness shall be found therein, thansgiving, and the voice of melody."

The high expense of living at St. Louis has produced regret and difficulty. The brethren have proposed that one of them remove to St. Charles, a neighbouring situation, where subsistence can be procured on easier terms, and the prospect of establishing a permanent school is fair and inviting. The Board have approved the measure, and recommended its adoption.

The assiduous and self-denying labours of their missionary the Rev. Isaac M'Coy, in the Illinois state, have imparted the liveliest pleasure. He has shown himself willing to forego the conveniences of a settled country, and to share, with the hope of diminishing, the afflictions of an uncivilized state of society. He is ready to live and die among the aborigines, if he may but be the means of teaching them the way to heaven through the knowledge of the Lord Jesus. He had put up a plain building for his family, and as a place where the Indians might receive religious instruction. Since which he has found encouragement to settle on lands belonging to the United States, under circumstances which promise a greater sphere of usefulness.

The Board are of opinion the change proposed is desirable, and the more so, as the disposal of the building he has erected will probably more than remunerate the original cost. The nearness of the new site for missionary exertions to the brethren in the Missouri territory, will enable them to strengthen each other's hands.

The labours of the Rev. Humphrey Posey among the Cherokees, have been zealous, and marked with holy prudence. His schools have been well attended. A temporary suspension of them has arisen, chiefly owing to the unsettled state of the nation; the question being as yet undecided whether they will continue to occupy the soil of their fathers, or retire farther westward.

The Sandusky Indians, during the year past, have been repeatedly visited by Rev. Henry George, of Owl Creek, Ohio, who has expressed much satisfaction at observing their solemn attention.

The Rev. Mr. Eastman has begun his labours in the vicinity of Natchez and St. Francisville. He feels himself greatly encouraged. May the blessing of the Lord accompany his endeavours.

Among the occurrences which have recently taken place west of the mountains, the Board has witnessed, with no ordinary satisfaction, the removal of a misapprehension on the part of their brethren of the Kentucky Baptist Mission Society. It has been the general opinion of the Board, that the reformation and spiritual welfare of the Indians, would be best promoted by missionaries opening schools and preaching the gospel in the vicinity of the tent and wigwam. The Kentucky brethren were in favour of sending for Indian youth from the wilderness, and educating them in Kentucky. The Board sincerely wished them success. They were far from supposing that because the settling of missionaries in the bosom of the tribes seemed most promising, that this consideration ought to preclude attempts at instructing, in any way, the children of the aborigines; but to assist that Society in its endeavours, by appropriating any of the funds intrusted to their management, it was believed their responsibilities would not warrant. At a period when it became, for several reasons, peculiarly desirable that the sentiments both of the Board and of the Society should be understood in the clearest manner, the Rev. Mr Rice, agent of the Board, was at the Great Crossings. The exposition of mutual views which then took place, terminated in a manner most pleasing and satisfactory. The Society voted itself an auxiliary to the Board, and the Board engaged to appropriate its funds to such objects, only, as the Society shall designate, and in every way to facilitate, to the utmost of their power, a common design. Such mutual and affectionate harmony among fellow-labourers in the service of the Son of God, is sweet as the ointment of Aaron, and refreshing as the dews of Hermon.

To the plans that are in operation for colonizing a part of the world that has for ages been sunk in ignorance, bondage and affliction, the Board wishes the most ample success. It cannot reasonably be supposed that numerous bands of men, in possession of the knowledge of useful arts, and especially of the word of life, can settle on African shores without meliorating the state of society. Such a course must tend to elevate the character of the people of colour to that point which shall open before them the advantages, and excite the habits, of self-government and industry. The Christian will surely discover in the National Colonization Society, a new and encouraging presage of the spread of the kingdom of Christ, and cheerfully wait the fulfilment of the prophecy, "From beyond the rivers of Ethiopia my suppliants, even the daughter of my dispersed, shall bring mine offering."

A communication has been received from the Rev. O. B Brown, of Washington city, stating that there are two coloured brethren of the church at Richmond, of good moral character, of ardent piety, and possessing talents for the ministry that have been tried for several years, and are much approved. They are willing to leave America, and attempt, on the soil of their forefathers, to preach the unsearchable riches of Christ. In the fall, it is expected, they will have an opportunity of going out in a vessel which will sail under the sanction of the President of the United States. They wish to place themselves under the direction of the Baptist Board of Missions, not so much for the sake of funds,—for these they in a good degree possess,—as for the purpose of receiving such counsel and information as the Convention or its Board may be able, time after time, to communicate, and to enjoy the assurances of their affection and co-operation. The Board have taken those brethren under their patronage, and encouraged them to spend the interval between the present time and their sailing, in improving their minds to the utmost practicable extent. The recommendation of the Convention to the people of colour to form and encourage mission societies, has been the means of exciting the zeal of these brethren to seek a home on Afric's coasts.

Various communications have been received on the subject of the Institution connected with the Board, for affording education to such pious youth as shall have been approved by the churches as candidates for the ministry. Some parts of the Plan proposed for consideration are objected to, particularly in reference to the qualifications for a pupil's entering, which are thought discouraging, because too high This, and any other objections that may offer, will become the subject of deliberation at the meeting of the Convention in April next, to which period the adoption of a plan, and the organizing the Institution, are laid over. It will be gratifying at that time to know the wishes of the churches and brethren generally, as they will, no doubt, be attentively regarded. In the mean time the young brethren, now in Philadelphia, will continue to be boarded and instructed, as during the past year, from funds wholly distinct from those collected for missionary purposes.

The Board feel it their duty to state, that they are increasingly gratified with the active services of their agent, the Rev. Mr. Rice. They pray that his health and life may be continued, and that the God of Abraham may be his shield and his exceeding great reward. He is affectionately commended to public attention and respect.

Brethren, it is our happiness to live in an age when the *cause* of Christ is pressed on the attention of his people by the most reviving considerations. To each of us He is saying, "It is good that thou shouldest take hold of this; yea, also from this withdraw not thine hand." In the days of Nehemiah, when the wall about Jerusalem was building, it is mentioned, to the reproach of the nobles of Tekoa, that "they put not their necks to the work of the Lord." Others, however, as if incited by their inaction to greater assiduity, applied themselves vigorously to the sacred task. Several rulers of Jerusalem and neighbouring cities, engaged in the work, and the men of Jericho and of Gibeon, of Mizpah and Zanoah joined them. "Goldsmiths, apothecaries, merchants" united their labours. Pious ladies were also employed. "Shallum, the son of Halosheth, the ruler of the half part of Jerusalem," repaired, "he and his DAUGHTERS." To the prompt and generous endeavours of females the friends of missions are under the strongest obligations. It is believed that their amiable exertions, so far from abating, increase. Of the female engaged as was Priscilla and others, in the service of the Lord Jesus, it may be said, "strength and honour are her clothing, and she shall rejoice in time to come."

It is recorded of Baruch, the son of Zabbai, that he "earnestly repaired." *Earnestly* to engage in advancing the kingdom of Immanuel, in diffusing the oracles of truth, in lessening the miseries of man, and expending time and talent in the service of Him who has redeemed us to God by his blood, is a most solemn duty. Work is placed before us, and requires to be executed with all the MIGHT that can be commanded,—while the eye of faith is directed for a blessing to the aim and promise of the LORD.

TO THE CORRESPONDING SECRETARY OF THE BAPTIST BOARD OF FOREIGN MISSIONS FOR THE UNITED STATES.

Baltimore, (Md.) April 28, 1819.

DEAR SIR,

TO systematize and extend the circulation of the *Latter Day Luminary*, as connected with completing arrangements for a regular intercourse between the Board and all the Baptist Associations, Mission Societies, and Churches throughout our country; and to collect funds for aiding the various endeavours of the Board relative to missions, foreign and domestic, and to an Institution designed to improve the education of persons called to the work of the christian ministry, as connected with placing these subjects in a just light before the public, have occupied my attention and employed my efforts another year.

Measures having been adopted at the annual meeting of the Board last April, to give immediate scope to the education design recommended by the Convention, also, resolutions entered into encouraging an effort to provide a special fund ultimately for the support of a Secretary of the Board, but for the present, for his support, as occupied partly in the instruction of the young men in the Institution, and partly in editing the *Luminary*, for which services no compensation had been provided—my attention was immediately and solemnly called to these objects. In May and June, I had the satisfaction of visiting the Chowan Association, in North-Carolina, the General Meeting of Correspondence of Virginia, held at Lynchburg, and the Portsmouth Association in Norfolk, and experienced no small gratification in perceiving so much of a disposition in favour to a general Theological Institution. Considerable sums for this object, and for the special fund before mentioned, by collections, donations, and subscriptions—principally subscriptions, and these chiefly for the special fund—were obtained.

It had been concluded to have a meeting of the Board in Philadelphia, in July, for the particular purpose of giving vigour, enlargement, and effect to the plan of the Theological Institution.—The measures to be pursued by me, were, of course, conformed to that calculation; the meeting, however, was postponed until August, and held in New-York. In consequence of this, the course it had been my intention to pursue, was materially changed;—it became necessary to make a hasty excursion into a part of Virginia, on the concerns of the *Luminary*, Mission Societies, &c. in that quarter, at considerable expense, and with but little pecuniary advantage; and, for the balance of the year, my path led in a direction where much less aid to the funds was to be expected than had been justly calculated on in the range at first designed to be pursued. These disadvantages, however, it is hoped, may have been more than counterbalanced in the benefits yet to arise from developments and results, for which foundation was laid at that meeting in New-York.

In the fall I made a tour through New-York state, and a corner of Vermont, visiting the Madison, Cayuga, Ontario, Vermont and Rensellærville Associations in my way. An excellent zeal for the prosperity of Zion was manifested by the worthy people through this beautiful section of our country. A number of gold necklaces, and many gold rings, were thrown into the collections for missionary and education purposes.

Afterwards, passing again through New-York state, I visited the western country, meeting every where with more or less of a disposition to patronize the objects of the Board.

Connected with this tour an event occurred, which signally displayed the hand of the Almighty in favour of the cause of missions, and which ought not to be contemplated without feelings of devout and fervent gratitude. For some time, as need not be concealed, the proceedings of the Kentucky Mission Society, owing, as it appears, to a misapprehension of the views of the Board, had worn an aspect tending to produce a partial division of the Baptist interest in our country in missionary operations; and the enemies of this glorious cause, for a moment seemed confident of success. Arriving, however, providentially, in Kentucky, just at the moment a specially called meeting of that Society was about to dissolve all connexion with the general Board, I afforded me very particular satisfaction to be able to furnish such an explanation of your views and measures as has resulted in a perfectly good understanding between the parties concerned, and placed the Indian school in Kentucky under your patronage and management. A more full account of this matter, it will occur to your recollection, was furnished in my letter of the 1st of February.

To complete the arranging of this momentous concern, so auspicious to the preservation of the union and co-operation of the great body of the American Baptists in the missionary scheme, and to accomplish other important objects, it was necessary for me to make another excursion. From this, as is known to you, Sir, I have but just returned; and it is particularly gratifying to state, that your Superintending Committee to manage the Indian school above referred to, consisting of Cols. James Johnson and Richard M. Johnson, the Rev Messrs. Jeremiah Vardeman, Jacob Creath, Silas M. Noel, James Suggett, John H. Ficklin, Thomas Henderson, and Samuel Trott

B S Chambers, Esq. and Mr. Craig, have organized themselves, and zealously entered on the duties connected with a prosecution of the object of their trust. Already have buildings been erected for the accommodation of the young Indians, and a valuable instructor engaged to teach them. Already eight of those children of the forest,—Lewis Rogers, a young chief, probably about twenty years old, with Maria his wife—Henry Rogers, nephew of Lewis, near seven years old—Franky Craig, a little girl—Wm Thompson Suggett, nineteen years old—James Suggett, fifteen—John Ficklin Fish and Paschal Fish, about 6 or 7 years old, sons of the principal chief of the tribe,—belong to the Institution, and more may be had, in proportion as the benevolence of the community shall supply the Board with the means of doing them good.

The School, indeed, wears a most promising aspect; the harmonious arrangements which have secured to it the patronage of the Board, are highly gratifying to many, and much may be expected from the zeal and talents of your Superintending Committee.

In relation to the *Latter Day Luminary*, with the circulating of which, the Agency allotted me by the Board has so much concern, involving a great deal of labour and responsibility, it is gratifying to state that near eight thousand are now called for, and it was thought best to print at least ten thousand of each of the numbers of the present year. It was to be expected in the outset of so extensive an undertaking, on the novel plan, too, of transmitting the work free of charge to the subscribers in all parts of the country, that no small difficulty must be experienced. In some instances a failure of the seasonable conveyance of the publication has induced subscribers to withdraw, but, wherever attentive, active persons have been found to engage in the business, it has succeeded well, and the difficulties yet to be encountered, it is believed, will be, in a good measure, surmounted by the end of this year. Be assured, no exertion shall be spared, on my part, to render the circulation perfectly systematic, and as expeditious as practicable; so that subscribers, every where, may calculate on receiving the *Luminary* with as much regularity and despatch as the nature of the case will admit.

Considering the state of things in a pecuniary view, the expenses unavoidably attending the commencement of a work on so large a scale, and the necessity of re-printing all the numbers of the last year, much profit on the first *half* volume cannot have been anticipated. At the termination of this year, however, with the completion of the first volume, the Board may reasonably expect of me to report a satisfactory result in a pecuniary sense, and I flatter myself they will not be disappointed. Conformably with your instructions, I have engaged several persons in different parts of the country to assist in the business of circulating the *Luminary*, and have authorized and requested them, as circumstances shall encourage, to solicit aid, by collections, donations, subscriptions, &c for promoting the objects of the Board, while, at the same time, they will be performing, substantially, the service of domestic missionaries. The benefits of this part of the general plan, it is confidently believed, will be realized in due time, and will not be unimportant.

It must be obvious to every one, that the necessity of travelling near ten thousand miles within the narrow circle of a year, in order to combine the distant points, and arrange the general system, could not but incur heavy expenditures, while it would very much abridge both time and opportunity for obtaining, either by public collections or private donations, pecuniary assistance to the cause. I experience great satisfaction, therefore, in being able to announce the approach of that state and operation of the business, which will require less of toilsome journeying, while it promises more of direct advantage to the missionary concern.

The general circulation of the *Luminary* will render unnecessary the publishing of so large a number of the Annual Report for distribution among the Associations and Mission Societies. In addition to ten thousand converted into a number of the *Luminary*, the striking off of one thousand, simply in the shape of Report, will furnish a sufficiency for indiscriminate, general, and individual use

The Institution connected with the Board for improving the education of persons called to the christian ministry, is an object most deeply interesting to the whole denomination, and should attract general and solemn attention. From all that has fallen within my observation and hearing, an impressive conviction rests upon my mind, that something efficient ought to be done! This is affectingly called for by the deplorable paucity of *able and faithful ministers of the new testament;* and anxiously expected by a jealous, a watchful, and a liberal public!

Misapprehensions exist with many, in relation to the plan of education published after the meeting of the Board in New-York last August, which it is important should be corrected; and such modifications of the plan should be adopted as shall be acceptable to the denomination at large. These modifications, as I am convinced by many observations heard the past year, and conceive it my duty to state to you, must embrace the idea of affording, in some instances, improvement in the english language, composition, and theology, without going through a regular classical course. With something of this nature introduced into the plan, there is no doubt with me, that an impression, which appears to be already gaining ground, in favour of a general Institution, will be strengthened and extended; while, it is to be hoped, the Institutions set up in different parts of our country, having the same object in view, may pursue a course conducive to its enlargement, elevation, and success.

At the Vermont Association, I had the pleasure of meeting with Elder Jonathan Going of Massachusetts. After much consideration, we agreed on a general model for *Female Charitable Societies*, having special regard to the education object, as connected with that of missions. On this model some societies have been formed already, and many more might be. Societies, also, particularly for aiding the Theological Institution, might easily be originated, and put into operation in many places. Several Mission Societies have been formed during the past year, and others are in contemplation.

The great and benevolent cause, then, to which the attention of the Board is so solemnly called, and zealously directed, appears to be successfully advancing, and offers additional evidences and pledges, with each revolving year, that it will move onward, all opposition notwithstanding, to its triumphant consummation.

Permit me, in the conclusion, to record a tribute of exalted gratitude to that Divine Goodness which has accompanied my various and extended journeyings, shielded me from danger, preserved my health, and strewed my path with consolation during another year.

With sentiments of profound respect, suffer me to subscribe myself, sincerely and affectionately,

Your Agent,

LUTHER RICE.

Rev. Dr. STAUGHTON, Cor. Sec. &c. &c.

SUBSTANCE OF THE MINUTES OF THE BOARD,

From the time of the Annual Meeting, 1818, to the present time

JUNE 2.—*At a called meeting of the Board, Philadelphia*—Elder Henry George of Ohio was appointed a missionary to the Indians at Upper and Lower Sandusky, in the service of the Board, for three months, compensation at the rate of $500 per annum.

JUNE 25.—*At a called meeting of the Board, Philadelphia*—It was agreed that the meeting to be held in July be postponed until the first Thursday in August, and be held in New-York, for the purpose of meeting delegates from education as well as mission societies at the northward and eastward.

July 10—*At an adjourned meeting of the Board, Philadelphia*—It was agreed that brother Samuel Eastman be appointed a missionary to the state of Louisiana, and that the Corresponding Secretary draw up a letter of instructions to him, and that $500 per annum be appropriated for his support.

The Corresponding Secretary presented to the Board a copy of the gospel of Matthew in the BURMAN LANGUAGE, also a catechism and tract,—all from *the mission press at Rangoon.*

The Corresponding Secretary informed that the Philadelphia Bible Society had presented to the Board fifty Bibles and one hundred New Testaments for distribution in the Missouri Territory, whereupon it was

Resolved, unanimously, That the thanks of the Board be presented to the Philadelphia Bible Society for the above-mentioned donation.

Dr. Staughton and Mr Curwen were appointed a committee to procure Dr Rees's Cyclopædia for the use of our missionaries in Rangoon.

AUGUST 7th, New-York.—*Agreeably to adjournment the Board met.*

Various communications were received from different parts of the United States, on the subject of establishing a general Institution connected with the Board, for improving the education of persons called to the ministry. These, mostly, were of an encouraging nature, whereupon resolutions were adopted which have been published already in the fifth number of the *Luminary*, the object of which was to give effect to the education design, and to prepare the way, by the collecting of funds, for the complete organization of the Institution the ensuing spring.

A plan of the course of study to be pursued in the Institution, was also published, *for the consideration* of the churches and brethren throughout our country.

It was resolved that $100 be paid towards the education of brother Colman, missionary to Burmah.

Resolved, unanimously, That the thanks of the Board be presented to their friends in New-York, for the kind and affectionate reception given this body.

OCTOBER 2, Philadelphia.—*Agreeably to notice the Board met.*

Dr Staughton, Dr. Allison, Elder Jones, and Professor Chase, were appointed a committee to solicit the donation of books, for the purpose of forming a library for the use of the Theological Institution.

Ordered, that $35 be paid for 500 of Dr Baldwin's sermon preached before the Convention in May 1817.

Resolved, unanimously, That the thanks of the Board be presented to Dr David J Davis of this city, for his kind offer to instruct any of our students in the science of medicine gratuitously.

A statement of accounts from the Rev. Missionary Brethren at Serampore was received, for which the Board acknowledge their obligations.

An interesting letter was received from J. Jennings, Esq one of the Indian agents.

OCTOBER 12, Philadelphia.—*The Board met pursuant to notice.*

A letter from J Jennings, Esq and one from Thomas L M'Kenny, Esq on the subject of Indian concerns, were presented. Also two letters from Elder Isaac M'Coy, missionary. These were heard by the Board with much interest.

Voted, That fifty dollars be paid for the purchase of medical books and instruments for the use of our missionary, Mr. Price.

Resolved, That $250 be transmitted to our missionary Elder Humphrey Posey.

OCTOBER 19, Philadelphia.—*The Board met agreeably to adjournment.*

Resolved, That $100 be afforded brother Daniel M'Call, to enable him to commence his ministerial labours in Louisiana, which, from the solemn impression resting on his mind of its being his duty to go to that quarter, they cannot but hope will be useful.

OCTOBER 26, Philadelphia—*The Board met pursuant to adjournment*

Communications were received from the Rev Isaac M'Coy, relative to his prospects and plans of usefulness among the Indians, he requests the aid of a fellow labourer in that quarter. The Board regret that they do not know a brother of the description he mentions to send out as an assistant missionary, but will look for one.

A communication was received from the Rev J. M. Peck, St Louis, detailing the pecuniary concerns of that mission Resolved, that $500 be appropriated for the use of our missionaries at St Louis

Resolved, That the Rev Messrs Bradley of Albany, Davis of Boston, Dossey of South Carolina, and Vardeman of Kentucky, be requested to use their influence in favour of the general interests of the Board, and particularly, if circumstances will permit, that they aid in the collecting of funds for the Theological Institution.

DECEMBER 7, Philadelphia.—*The Board met according to notice*

Several communications were laid over to a future meeting

Resolved, That $125 be appropriated for the use of brother Price, missionary, for clothing and contingences.

1819. FEBRUARY 1, Philadelphia—*The Board of Missions met.*

A communication was received from brother Rice, Agent of the Board, enclosing a communication from the Kentucky Mission Society, requesting the Board to take under its patronage and management, the domestic Indian School in Kentucky, set on foot by that Society, and pledging themselves, in case their request be granted, as an auxiliary to the Board. The request was cheerfully complied with, and the Board instructed their Agent, Mr. Rice, on his return to that quarter to convey their answer to the communication from the Kentucky Mission Society, and to pay over $500 for the use of said Indian School.

A Committee to superintend the above-mentioned Indian School in Kentucky, was appointed, consisting of Cols James Johnson and Richard M. Johnson, the Rev Messrs. Jeremiah Vardeman, Jacob Creath, Silas M Noel, James Suggett, John H Ficklin, Thomas Henderson and Samuel Trott, B. S Chambers, Esq. and Mr Craig.

Resolved, unanimously, That the thanks of the Board be presented to the Rev Mr. Ficklin for his past services to the Indians —The Board sincerely hope he will be able to continue his exertions in instructing the unlearned inhabitants of the western forests.

Resolved, unanimously, That a letter of condolence be addressed to Mrs. Titcomb, sympathizing with her for the loss of her excellent husband, supercargo of the vessel which conveyed our missionaries to India, who died on his voyage homeward.

Resolved, unanimously, That a letter be addressed to captain Bangs, expressive of the high sense the Board entertain of his kindness to our missionaries on their passage to India.

A letter from the Rev PHILIP MILLEDOLER, D D Corresponding Secretary of "The United Foreign Missionary Society," was communicated by our Corresponding Secretary, conveying the friendly sentiments of that body in relation to this, and wishing a correspondence. The Board cordially reciprocate these sentiments, and will be happy to correspond with that Society, interchange Reports, and in every way contribute to the great work of spreading the kingdom of the Mediator.

FEBRUARY 8, Philadelphia.—*The Board met agreeably to adjournment.*

A memorial to Congress on the subject of Indian reform was read, and adopted, and ordered to be sent to Col. Richard M. Johnson, requesting him to lay the same before that honourable body, which service he had the kindness to fulfil.

Ordered, that $25 be paid for medical books, &c. for brother Price.

MARCH 29, Philadelphia.—*The Board met agreeably to notice.*

A communication was received from our Agent, Mr. Rice, relative to the Indian School in Kentucky.

Resolved, That our brother Ficklin proceed to the Indian tribes, should the Superintending Committee think it best, with a view to obtain more young Indians to enter the School.

Resolved, That the thanks of the Board be presented to Col. James Johnson, for his generous offer to convey Mr. Ficklin to the west, and himself and the young Indians from the wilderness back to Kentucky, free of charge.

MEETING OF THE BOARD IN BALTIMORE, APRIL 28, 1819.

The Board entered on business. Our Agent, Mr. Rice, was invited to a seat, as were also brethren Brown, Reis, Walker, Davis, Chase, Richards and Osborne.

Numerous communications were laid before the Board.

The brethren Allison, Staughton, Jones, Peckworth, and Cauldwell, were appointed a committee in relation to the Eastern mission. Brethren M'Laughlin, Healey, Curwen, and Bradley, in relation to the Western missions.

Brethren Curwen and Bradley were appointed a committee to examine the Treasurer's accounts, and also the accounts of the Agent.

Brethren Allison, Healey, and Jones, were appointed a committee on the subject of the Theological Institution. Brethren Staughton, M'Laughlin, and Curwen, on the subject of an African mission.

Brethren Staughton, Allison and Peckworth, were appointed a committee on the general communication from the Agent,—and also on a communication from Mr. Joshua Kidwell of Tennessee.

The committee on the Eastern mission reported,

1. That in their opinion the sum of $3000 should be appropriated for the support of our missionaries at Rangoon, and that the same be forwarded, as soon as convenient, to the care of brethren Carey, Marshman and Ward, Serampore.

2. *Resolved,* That the Board highly approve of the object of brother Judson's journey to Chittagong, in quest of a native to assist in the mission, and sympathize with him in the dangers to which he was exposed on his passage.

3. *Resolved,* That the conduct of Mrs. Judson in returning to the mission-house at Rangoon, (*see Mr. Judson's letter,*) under circumstances so unpropitious, and though disaster menaced her, meets the distinguished approbation of the Board.

4. *Resolved,* That the Board entertains a high sense of the kindness of the Rev. Mr. Thompson, chaplain, and of the Rev. Mr Loveless, missionary, for the

hospitality and friendship manifested to our missionary, Mr. Judson, when, in the providence of God, he was unexpectedly borne to Madras.

5. *Resolved,* That the Board, while they sympathize with our missionaries in Burmah under the trials they are called to endure, and offer their prayers to the Supreme Head of the Church, for their support and guidance, have full confidence in their piety and discretion in conducting the concerns of the mission, and the more so from the advantages that the experience of brother Judson can supply.

The report was adopted unanimously.

The Committee on the Western missions reported that they had attentively considered the voluminous communications referred to their inspection. In relation to the mission at St. Louis—Your Committee cannot refrain from expressing their high sense of the laborious exertions and persevering fortitude of the missionaries there. Five churches, one Mission Society, one Bible Society, four Mite Societies, and several schools, constituted through their instrumentality, are the grateful fruits, resulting, by the blessing of the God of heaven, from their toils, and claim for them the affectionate commendation of the Board. Your missionaries, for reasons stated at large in their letter of March 4th, are of opinion that another station should be taken at St Charles, where their principal school might, with much advantage to the mission, be established. Presuming, from their intimate acquaintance with the various circumstances which form the data of their calculations, and from their long and serious consideration of the subject, that their decisions are such as experience would prove to be highly advantageous and favourable to the best wishes of the Board, your Committee respectfully submit the following resolutions.

1. Resolved, that $200 be appropriated for the purchase of a site for a mission house in or near the town of St Charles.

2. Resolved, that $400 be appropriated for the purchase of a few acres of land near the town of St Charles, for the use of said establishment.

The Committee also recommended that Mr. John Buttolph, provided his testimonials should prove satisfactory to the Board, be appointed to the Western mission, in connexion with the brethren Peck and Welch.

Application having been made by Mr. Peck in favour of Mr. Edward Tanner, as a western missionary, resolved that attention be paid to his case.—This is encouraged by the peculiar circumstances of his brother, who is acquainted with several Indian languages, and whose aid, most probably, may be obtained.

In relation to the schools among the Cherokees, under the management of Elder Humphrey Posey, the Committee observe, that, owing to the unsettled state of the tribe, having it in contemplation to remove beyond the Mississippi, the schools have been broken up. In case, however, they do not remove, it is recommended that brother Posey be requested to continue his labours among them, and re-establish schools.

The plans and proceedings of Elder M'Coy in relation to the Indians in the Illinois state, appear to be prosperous and promising, claim the approbation of the Board, and should be followed up with steady energetic support.

The mission to the Wyandot and Sandusky Indians it is thought adviseable, for the present, to discontinue.

The report of the Committee was unanimously accepted.

The Committee on the subject of the African mission reported

That the communication from the Rev. Obadiah B Brown of Washington city, and those from Mr. Crane of Richmond, Va. were important and highly satisfactory. In their opinion a most auspicious opening, in Divine Providence, invites and sanctions the undertaking of a mission to Africa, the land of servility, darkness, and moral misery. They are pleased with the characters of Collin Teague and Lot Carey, licensed preachers of colour in the Baptist church at Richmond, Va. and are happy to find them willing to go out as missionaries of the Cross. They recommend, therefore, that those coloured brethren be accepted by the Board as missionaries under their care, and that they be sent out in the fall in a vessel which the President of the United States is about sending to the western coast of Africa, or in one which the Colonization Society shall send; and that these brethren be encouraged to improve their minds to the utmost, before they sail,—and, should it be necessary, that the Board afford them pecuniary aid for this purpose. The report was unanimously adopted.

The following note from Professor CHASE was communicated by the Corresponding Secretary.

BALTIMORE, *April* 29, 1819.

REV. AND VERY DEAR SIR,

I NEED not inform you with what painful emotions I announce to the Board that I must retire, for the present, from the labours in which I have had the happiness of being associated with you. It has become my duty to make a vigorous effort for regaining and confirming my health. At the same time, it is impossible for me to be unmindful of objects so dear to my heart as those of the seminary and of missions.

In these circumstances I have looked around me, with no small degree of anxiety, in order to ascertain what particular course I ought to pursue, and permit me to state that a visit to Europe has presented itself to my mind in such a light as to appear worthy of very serious consideration. Among the purposes which it affords the prospect of accomplishing, some that have seemed the most obvious and important, are, to procure books for the library of the Institution—books which must be had, and which cannot be obtained in this country, except at extremely high prices; to learn the state of our baptist brethren in Germany, and other countries on the European continent, to open a friendly correspondence with them, and to prepare the way for their taking an active part in those great exertions for the spread of evangelic truth, which the present condition of the world demands.

Should the Board judge these objects worthy of their patronage, and should it, after further consultation with my physician, be deemed expedient, I am willing to embark personally in the undertaking. The only request which I would make, and one which I now respectfully submit to them is, that, provided I can obtain the means of defraying the necessary expenses without having recourse to their treasury, they will *authorize me to go in their name.* Whatever may be the result, it is my ardent desire that the enterprise, should it be entered upon, assume such an attitude that I may not be the means of impeding the operations of the Board in what they have already begun, nor of impairing, for a moment, the confidence of any portion of our brethren.

In closing this communication it would be extreme ingratitude were I to cast a cloud over the fair prospect, which I am permitted to enjoy, of confirmed health, and in view of what *may* await me, I cannot but advert to the animating consideration that the objects which the Board are cherishing have a PATRON whose wisdom and resources are infinite, and that whenever he removes individuals from his service, it is a very easy thing for him to call forth other and better instruments. Yours, dear sir,

With much respect and affection,

IRA CHASE.

Rev. Wm. Staughton, D. D. Cor Sec. &c

This letter was referred to the Committee on the subject of the Theological Institution.

The Committee appointed on the subject of the Institution for educating young men approved by the churches as candidates for the gospel ministry, reported

That as the Board, in August last, at a large and special meeting, presented to the churches and brethren of our denomination a Plan for their perusal and consideration; as the members who then attended were more numerous than at the present meeting, and as several members of the Board, who had designed being now present, have, in the providence of God, been prevented, particularly brother Semple of Virginia, by personal indisposition, and brother Cone of Alexandria, by domestic, your Committee are of opinion, that it is inexpedient to enter, at the present session, into any discussion of the parts of said Plan, but that it be referred to the serious review of the Convention at their meeting in Philadelphia in April next.

That to said meeting be referred the communications from brethren Semple, Mercer, Posey, the Committee of the churches of the Charleston Association, signed by the Rev. Dr. Furman, &c. &c.; when, any difference of opinion relative to the previous qualifications of the students, the period of their continuance, the location of the Seminary, the permanent appointment of the necessary officers, &c will, without doubt, engage the attentive consideration of the Convention.

That as the low state of health of the worthy and much esteemed Professor of Languages and Biblical Literature, compels him, for a while, to retire from the labours of instruction, a circumstance which the committee deeply deplores, and which, they trust, the God of mercy will soon remove, a suitable character be sought to fill, for a time, his important station.

That the Rev. Dr. Staughton be respectfully and affectionately requested to continue his services in the Institution.

That a young brother of the name of Robinson, residing at Pittsburg, and a member of the church in that place, be encouraged to come to Philadelphia, agreeably to his request, and prosecute his studies.

That the Corresponding Secretary be requested to write to Mr. James M'Aboy, who has applied for advice relative to his education, who is in a sphere of considerable usefulness, and is also acquiring the Latin and Greek Languages, and state that it is the opinion of the Board, that he appears called by Divine Providence, to pursue his studies in his present situation.

The Committee beg leave to mention, that the officers of the Institution have succeeded in obtaining upwards of THREE HUNDRED volumes towards a library, besides $53 60 in money, of which last sum $18 45 have been expended in books, as per the following account.

BOOKS PURCHASED FOR THE INSTITUTION

Beattie's Works, 10 vols.	$4 75	Williams' History of Vermont, 2 vols.	$1 20
Ellicott's Journal,	1 50	Staughton's Virgil, 3 copies,	6 00
Clarke's Holy Land, 3 vols.	1 25	Adams' Latin Grammar, 5 copies,	3 75 ——18 45

They recommend that the thanks of the Board be tendered them for these services, and that they be requested to continue similar endeavours.

The above report was read over by sections, and unanimously adopted.

The following is the answer of the Board to the note of Professor Chase

DEAR SIR,

Your communication of the 29th has been duly received, and laid before the Board of Missions

Assure yourself, Sir, of the sympathies of the Board under your present indisposition, and their fervent wishes for your speedy and perfect restoration.

The plan you have conceived of visiting Europe, with a view of accomplishing several important objects, they have seriously considered. How far the voyage would contribute to the restoration of your health, they are not able to conjecture. They have, however, long considered an exposition of the circumstances of the German Baptists, the cultivating an intercourse with them, and bringing their latent energies into extensive action, occurrences greatly to be desired, and they have no doubt, from the knowledge you possess of the German language, and from the deep interest your heart has taken in this service, that you would be able to accomplish something of importance. The judicious purchase of books useful for the Institution, would, without question, be aided by a European visit. The principal difficulties that the Board experience, result from the impracticability of appropriating any of the mission funds to the object of visiting the Baptists in Germany, and the present insufficiency of Education funds for effecting purchases to any material extent.

Should you, Sir, on your own foundation, or from funds drawn from other sources, enter on a voyage to Europe, the Board will, with pleasure, supply any credentials you may deem expedient, and be pleased to recognize you as a Professor of the Institution, their friend and their brother. As soon as a kind Providence shall conduct you to convalescence, they will be happy in your resuming, without delay, the labours of your Professorship.

In offering this communication, I cannot deny myself the pleasure of expressing my cheerful recollections of the mutual aim and harmony that have attended our endeavours since we have mutually laboured in the Institution, and to renew the assurances of my most affectionate regards.

I am, dear Sir, your affectionate friend and brother,

WM. STAUGHTON, *Cor. Sec.*

The committee on the communication from brother Rice, reported:

That said communication is highly satisfactory; the concerns of the *Luminary* appear prosperous, and the state of things in general, in relation to the objects of the Board, exhibits a favourable aspect. The suggestions relative to the Theological Institution, they need not here remark upon, as that subject is before the Board and the churches, and will be, no doubt, fully discussed at the time of the next Convention. They cannot close, however, without observing that they consider the labours of brother Rice the past year, deserving the thanks of the Board, and of the friends of the Kingdom of the Son of God, in general.

The report of the committee was unanimously adopted

Communications from brethren Cushman, Sommers and Davis, appointed to collect funds for the Institution designed for improving the education of the ministry, were received.

Mr. Cushman expresses regret that indisposition rendered it impracticable for him to fulfil the service to the extent he had designed. He obtained some aid to the object; expended about 7 dollars travelling, which, with his time, he tenders to the Board.

Mr. Sommers succeeded in constituting a Society for this purpose at White Creek, where he collected $9 07—subscriptions collected, $3 50—amount of subscriptions in this Society at present, say about $50 per annum. Another Society in Hudson, where the collection amounted to $ 7 90—subscriptions paid $ 5 50—annual subscriptions, $ 23 50—donations from different individuals, $ 35 18. Another Society in Shaftsbury, where the collection after sermon was $14 05—annual subscriptions $ 14. Whole amount collected $ 75 20½—Annual subscription $ 87 50. In the conclusion he observes, "I have travelled 230 miles in eleven days, and expended for horse hire, turnpikes, &c. ten dollars which the Board will oblige me by accepting"

Mr. Davis collected $196 28¼. His expenses amounted to $ 27 56¼,—of which, he accepted only $ 16 56, and gives his time without compensation.

Communications of a very satisfactory nature were received from the Rev Thomas Henderson, Clerk of the Superintending Committee for the management of the Indian school in Kentucky. The Board highly appreciate the zeal of their western brethren for the reformation of the Aborigines of our country, and rejoice that the school consecrated to this benevolent purpose, offers a prospect so animating to their hopes. They are well pleased with the accounts rendered, as taken from the *cash book* of the Committee.

Resolved, unanimously, That the thanks of this Board be presented to their brethren and friends in Baltimore, for their hospitable and affectionate attentions during its session in this city.

In the evening of the following Sabbath a missionary sermon was delivered by the Rev. Dr. Staughton, in the meeting house of the First Baptist Church in Baltimore, and at the same time by the Rev. Mr. Peckworth in the Baptist meeting house at the Point. In both places collections were taken.

NOTE ON THE FOLLOWING TABLES.

Besides the following table of 140 associations, may be mentioned the *Sabbatarian General Conference*, having, as by the latest minutes of that body which have come to hand, 10 churches, 11 ministers, and 1934 members. There are also many unassociated churches in our country, and many who deviate in some less important respects from those things which distinguish and characterize the main body of the baptists in the United States. The Rev. Mr. Willey, Corresponding Secretary of the Shaftsbury association, has furnished the following statement of those, of the description just referred to, in that quarter:

"There are within the bounds of this association, and belonging to no other, *ten* baptist churches of our faith and order, containing about 785 members. I have taken considerable pains, and give the number nearly, if not quite accurate. *Seven* ordained ministers not on minutes. Also there are *three* baptist churches called open or free communion, containing 355 members and *two* ministers. Also, *two* seventh day baptist churches, containing 250 members."

From this it should seem that a considerable aggregate of unassociated churches would be found in the United States, enough undoubtedly, to swell the main body of the denomination, united, generally speaking, in the same distinguishing views, to considerably more than 200,000 members.

Mr Willey is entitled to our grateful thanks for furnishing the above statement, *and it is earnestly requested,* that all the Corresponding Secretaries of the Associations, and those to whom Circulars for the Associations are sent, will be equally particular in their communications on the subject.

TABLE OF ASSOCIATIONS.

Associations.	Sts.	C.	M	Bap	Tot	Correspondents.	Times of Meetings.	Places of Meeting.
Bowdoinham	Me.	39	31	292	2317	Thomas Francis, Leeds, Kennebec co	1 Wed. 22 Septembr	Bloomfield.
Lincoln	Me	50	32	128	3737	Phinheas Pilsbury, Nobleboro, Lin co	3 Wed. 15 Septembr	Thornton, Lincoln co
Cumberland	Me.	20	26	92	2020	John Tripp, Hebron, Cumberland co	Wed. af. 4 Wd. Sept	Paris, Oxford county
New Hamp.	N. H.	21	26	101	1960	Timothy Hudson, York co. Me.	2 Wed. 9 June	Cornish, York co. M
Meredith	N H	11	1	19	1103	Stephen Pillsbury, Hebron, Grafton co	2 Wed 8 Septemb	Conway
Dublin	N H	10	14	75	932	John Parkhurst, N Ipswich, Hills. co.	3 Wed. 20 October	Swansey, Cheshire co
Shaftsbury	Vt	31	23	291	3474	Eliji T. Hedey, Lansingh Rens. co N Y	1 Wed. 2 June	Pittstown.
Woodstock	Vt	23	24	166	2199	Gen Ab Forbes Windsor, Windsor co	Last Wed 29 Sept	Rockingham, Windr.
Vermont	V.	21	15	100	1903	Jno. Conant Esq. Brandon, Rutland c	First Wed 8 Octobr	Addison, Addison co.
Fairfield	Vt	10	6	61	856	Roszell Mears, George, Franklin co.	1st Wed. 25 Aug	Milton, Chittenden co
Barre	Vt	13	6	19	435	L. Huntington, Braint co, Orange co.	3 Wed. 13 Septem.	Bethel, L. Village,
Danville	Vt	10	5	77	409	Daniel Mason, Craftsbury, Orleans co	3 Wed 18 June	Craftsbury, Orleans c
Leyden	Ms.	28	24	182	2514	Elijah Montague Leverett, Franklin co.	2 Wed 15 October	Wendell.
Stubridge	Ms.	20	28	68	1031	Thos. McGregory, Shrewsbury.	Last Wed. 25 Aug	Monson, Hampden co.
Boston	Ms.	30	25	184	3073	Lucius Bolles, Salem, Essex county.	3 Wed. 15 Septr	Beverly, Essex co.
Westfield	Ms.	11	9	56	814	E. Arnold, Esq. Westfield, Hamp. co.	First Wed 1 Sept	Middlefield, Hamps.
Warren	R. I	30	36	191	4680	Nathan Wickerman, Esq. Providence	Tu af 1 Wd. 7 Spt	3 Church in Middleb
Yearly Meet	R. I	17	14		4752	Philip Slade, Swasey, Bristol co Ms	Fd b 2 Sab. 10 Sep.	Last min. not in hand
New London	Ct.	16	23		2041	Jna Goodwin, Mansfield, Wind. co	3 Tues. 29 October	Last min. not in hand
Stonington Un.	Ct.	16	14	5	2850	Roswell Burrows, Groton, N. Lon. co	W. if. 3 Sab. 23 June	2 Ch. N Stonington.
Hartford	Ct.	20	20	115	2126	Elisha Cushman, Hartford, Hart co	1 Wed. 6 October	Amenia, Dutch. co Vt
New York	N. Y.	25	20		1775	William Parkinson, New York city.	Last Wd 26 May	Last min. not in hand
Warwick	N. Y	17	11	74	1172	Aaron Perkins, near Newburg.	2 Wed. 9 June	Clinton, Dutchess co
Otsego	N. Y.	34	19	191	2321	C. Douglass, Whitestown, Oneida co	1 Wed. 1 September	Western.
Chemung	N. Y	16	12	71	833	Thos. Smiley, White Deer, Lycoming. co.	4 Wed. 6 October	Smithfield.
Renssclerv.	N. Y	19	18	64	1602	Dea. Hiland Hill, Catskill, Green co.	1 Wed. 6 October	Worcester, Otsego co
Cayuga	N. Y.	27	17	242	3277	Elkanah Comstock, Auburn	3 Wed. 15 Septem	Throopsville, Cay. co
Essex	N. Y	9	5	15	508	Samuel Churchill, Elizabethtown	3 Wed. 20 October	Brookfield.
Saratoga	N. Y	24	22	200	3700	Edward Barber, Greenwich, Wash. co	Last Wed 30 June	Bap. m. h. Edinburgh
Black River	N Y	17	15	184	1103	E Osgood, Naples in Henderson, Jef. co.	2 Wed. 9 June	Denmark, Lewis co.
Madison	N Y	44	36	562	4806	John Peck, N. Woodstock, Madison co.	2 Wed. 8 Septembr.	Sherburne, Chenan
Lake George	N. Y.	5	3	43	292	John Lee Chester, Warren county.	3 Wed 15 Septem.	Chester, Warren co.
Union	N. Y.	15	8	246	1042	Job Foss, Dover, Dutchess county.	1 Wed. 1 Septemb	Patterson, Putnam co
Franklin	N Y	21	13	101	2002	John Bostwick, Hartwich Otsego co	3 Wed 16 June	Near Lisbon, Otsego
Holland Pur	N. Y.	20	9	137	995	Joy Handy, Fredonia, Chatauque co.	2 Wed 9 June	Hamburg, Niagara co.
St. Lawrence	N. Y	5	4		80	Jon. Payne, Gouverneur, St. Law. co.	3 Wed. 19 January,	Cow Marsh.
Ontario	N. Y	30	21	269	2480	Soln Goodale Bristol, Ontario county	4 Wed. 22 Septemb	Avon, Ontario county
Hudson Riv.	N. Y.	6	8	124	1352	I. Leonard, Poughkeepsie, Dutch co	1 Wed 4 August,	Mt. Pleasant, W. Ch
Genessee	N Y	11	7	88	633	Elv Stone, Caledonia, Genessee co.	Last Wed. 29 Septr	Sweden, Genessee co
New Jersey	N J	24	15	106	1286	Joseph Sheppard, Salem, Salem county	1 Tues. 7 Sept tr.	Cohansey, Cumb. co
Philadelphia	Pa.	23	38	301	2828	Joshua P. Slack, Holmesburg, Pa.	1 Tues 5 October	3 Bap. Ch. Philadelp
Redstone	Pa.	31	21	96	1127	Jas. Latop, Mt. Pleasant, Westmd. co	Fd. b. 1 Sab. 3 Sept	Horse Shoe
Abington	Pa	4	3	12	280	John Miller, Abington, Luzerne co.	1 Wed 1 Septembr.	Last min. not rec'd
Delaware	De	6	8	2	535	Samuel R Green, Wilmington Del	Sat. b. 1 Sab 5 June,	Cow Marsh.
Salisbury	Md.	14	5	20	100	Stephens Woolford, Ish. Cr. Dor co.	Fd. bf. 4 Sab. 22 Oct.	Broad Creek.
Baltimore	Md.	20	20		1206	Spencer H. Cone, Alexandria,	Th b 3 Sab. 13 May	Alexandria, D. C.
Ketockton	Va	38	14		2382	Thornton Stringfellow, Fauquer co.	Thur. b 3 Sb 12Aug	Last min. not in hand
Strawberry	Va.	21	5			John S. Lee, Lynchburg, Va.	this associa. holds	two sessions a year
Dover	Va.	44	30			John Bryce, Richmond, Va	2 Saturday 9 Oct.	Last min. not in hand
Middle Dist	Va	8	8			Benjamin Watkins, Powhatan county	Last Sat. 26 August	Tomahawk m h Chu
Roanoke	Va.	30	16		2810	J Jenkins, n Grasty's store, Pittsyla. co.	As year before.	Last min. not rec'd
Portsmouth	Va.	20	13	170	2260	James Mitchell, Norfolk, Va.	Sat. bf. 2 Sab 8 May	Racc. Swamp m h S
Albemarle	Va.	11	11			Martin Dawson, n. Warren Albem. co	As year before.	Last min. not rec'd
Goshen	Va.	26	1			Absalom Waller, Spottsylvania co.	As year before.	Last min. not rec'd
Shiloh	Va.	21	13		1625	Richd. T Tutt Esq Culpeper county,	Fd bf. 1 Sat. 3 Sept	F. T. m. h. Culpeper
New River	Va.	7	5		325	Jesse Jones, Montgomery county.	3 Sat 21 August,	Salem m h Montgy
Mayo	Va	15	14			Benjn. Jewel, Rockingham co. N C.	As year before.	Last min. not in hand
Appomattox	Va	15	1			Rachel Dabbs, n. Keysville Charlo co	Sat. bf. 1 Sab. 1 May	Last min. not in hand
Meherrin	Va.	16		208	1018	Dea J. Saunders, n Percival's, Bruns. c.	Sat bf 4 Sab 24 Au	Foun Cr. m h Grai
Union	Va.	20	1	152	1522	Joshua Heckman, n Morgantown, Va.	Fd. bf It Sab 28 Ag	Prickett's Cr. Mon.
Green Brier	Va	5	1	2	147	Josiah Osborne Lewsb. Green B. co	Fd b 2 Sab. 10 Sept.	Mann's m h Monroe
Accomack	Va	6	1	8	778	Wm. Costen, L. Northampton, N. co.	Sat. b. 3 Sab 14 Aug	Hunger's m h North
Washington	Va	15	6	23	533	Elv Gillingwaters, Esq. Washington co.	2 Frid. 10 Septem.	Last min. not rec'd
Teass Valley	Va.	13	6	20	382	John Young, near Greenupsburg, Ky.	Sat. bf 4 Sab. 21 Ag	Falls of Cole River.
Sandy Creek	N. C	14	11		704	Robt. T. Daniel, n. Pittsboro' Chatm c	4 Sat. 23 October	Last min. not rec'd
Kehukee	N. C.	18		41	1634	Jesse Read, n Halifax, Halifax county,	Sat. b. 1 Sab. 2 Oct.	Deep Cr. m h Halif.
Yadkin	N C	17	8		508	Thos Wright, Esq. Hamptonville, S. c.	1 Sat. 2 October	Flat Rock, Surrey
Flat River	N. C	11	6		1108	Elisha Battle Oxford, Granville co.	Sat bf. 3 Sab.16 Oct	Last min. not in hand
Neuse	N. C	22	6	21	937	Wm P. Biddle, n. Newbern, Craven co	Sat. b 3 Sab. 16 Oct.	Foisnot, Edgecomb
Mountain	N. C.	14	12		783	Reuben Coffey, n. Ft. Defiance, Wilkes c	4 Sat. 28 August	Lewis Fork m h Wi

ociations	S's	C	M	Bap	Tot	Correspondents	Times of Meetings	Places of meetings
e Fent	N. C	2			1476	Charles M'Allister, Esq. n. Fayette	Sat. b. 1 Sab. Aug. 31	Last min. not received
an	N. C	29			2013	George Outlaw, Esq. Bertie county	Sat. b. 1 Sab. 21 May	Last minutes mislaid
try Line	N. C	11	11	27	807	G. Roberts, n. Brown's Store, Caswell c.	3 Sat. 21 Aug 1st	Deep Creek m. h.
igh	N. C	18	8	16	707	John Purify, near Raleigh	Fri b. 1 Sab. 24 Sep	Smithfield, Johnson co.
ch Broad	N. C	19	12	43	615	James Whitaker, Esq. Buncombe co.	Sat. b. 1 Sab 21 Aug	Cane Cr. Buncomb co
Dee	N. C	10	7		637	John Culpeper, n. Allenton, Montg. c.	Sat. b. 3 Sab. 16 Oct	Last m. not c. to hand
rleston	C	31	22	296	3093	Wood Furman, Esq. Charleston	Sat. b. 1 Sab. 6 Nov	Mechanicks Durl. D.
h l	S. C	36	21		2159	St. M Creary Beckmaville Ches. dis.	Sat. b. 1 Sab. 2 Oct	Last m. not c. to hand
d River	S. C	27	16	11	1563	Wm Lancaster, Esq. Mt. Astrea S. L.	Frid. b. 1 Sab. 15 Oct	Head of Tyga
ur	S. C	28	24	31	1095	James Crowther, Abbeville District	Sat b. 2 Sab. Aug	Big Creek m. house.
efield	S. C	4	13		2445	Joseph Key, Edgefield District	Sat. b. 3 Sab. 18 Sep	Last m. not c. to hand
nah	C	10	7	24	665	Jesse Lewallen, Lane's cr. Anson co.	Sat. b. 3 Sab. 18 Sep	M. Branch An. c. N. C.
rgia	Geo	38	23	56	2767	Jesse Mercer, Powelton, Hancock co.	Sat. b. 1 Sab. 9 Oct	Kiokee, Columbia co.
daziah	Geo	36	20	8	2028	Charles I. Jenkins Esq. n. Louisville	Sat. b. 1 Sab. 25 Sep	Buk Camp Burk co
pta	Geo	37	19	14	1014	Isham Goss, Oglethorpe county	Sat. b. 1 Sab. 23 Oct	Grovelevel m. h. I. c.
annah R	Geo	33	9		771	Wm. T. Brantly, Beaufort, S. C.	Sat. b. 1 Sab. 23 Oct	Last m. not c. to hand
nulgee	Geo	39	2		2111	Francis Flournoy, Madison Morg. co	Sat. b. 1 Sab. 1 Sep	Last m. not c. to hand
ucer	Geo	19	11		681	Irch. Taylor, Esq. n. Hartford Pul. co	Sat. b. 2 Sab. 11 Sep	Last m. not c. to hand
lmont	Geo	6	1		106	Wilson Conner, Sarepiah church	Sat. b. 2 Sab. 9 Oct	Last m. not c. to hand
bury	Geo					Charles O'Screven, Sunbury	Sat. b. 2 Sab. 13 Nov	Last m. not c. to hand
t River	Ala.	22	16		1213	Willis Hopwood, n. Shelbyv. Bed. c. T	Sat. b. 1 Sab. 3 Oct	Last m. not c. to hand
b	Ala.	6	3	4	169	Jesse Denson, Oaktuppa, Wash. co	Fri b. 2 Sab. 12 Nov	Salem Wayne co Mis.
ssippi	Mis.	40	18	48	1352	Wm. Snodgrass, Esq. Natchez, Ad. co.	Sat. b. 3 Sab. 16 Oct	Hepzibah 1ch co. L.
ston	Ten.	18	10		1085	Jona Mulkey, Buffalo Ridge Wash c	2d Frid. 13 August.	Last m. not c. to hand
nessee	Ten	29	41		1675	West Walker, n. Knoxville, Knox co.	1st Sat. 2 October	Last m. not c. to hand
sberland	Ten.	14	9	25	665	Garner M'Connico, near Franklin	Sat. b. 3 Sab. 18 Sep	Rutherford cr. c. M. c.
l River	Ten.	24	22		1095	Sugg Fort, Port Royal Montgomery c.	Sat. b. 2 Sab. 7 Aug	Last m. not c. to hand
River	Ten.	11	12		1412	Hardy Holeman, Lincoln county	2d Sat. 11 September	Last m. not c. to hand
ord	Ten	35	22	91	2318	R. C. Foster, Esq. near Nashville	Sat b 1 Sab. Au. 31 Jul	Providence, Ruthf. co.
s Fork	Ten	11	12		472	George Dawson, Esq. Sparta, White c.	4th Sat 25 Sept	Last m. not c. to hand
y One	Ten.	15	15		886	Garner M Connico, near Franklin	Sat. b. 1 Sab. 4 Sep	min. not yet obtained
horn	Ky.	30	12		720	Jeremiah Vardeman, near Lexington	2d Sat. 14 August	Last minutes mislaid
m	Ky.	10	11	157	1654	Gen Joseph Lewis Bardstown	4th Frid. 24 Sept	Nolin. m. h. Hardin co.
ys Creek	Ky.	18	16	40	1202	Wm. Goodloe, Esq. near Richmond	4th Sat. 26 August	V Fork, m. h. Mn. co
cken	Ky.	14	12	143	1102	Walter Warder, May's Lick, Mason c	1st Sat. 4 Sept.	I Branch, m. h. Ma. co.
en River	Ky.	20	10	36	1071	Michael W Hall, Esq. n. Glasgow	Frid. b. 4 Sat. 23 July	Dover, m. h. Barren c.
th Bend	Ky.	16	11	61	1453	Absalom Graves, Boone co.	4th Frid. 24 Sept	Dry cr. Campbell co.
thDistrict	Ky.	21	19	284	1500	Jas Mason, Esq. n. Mount Sterling	4th Sat. 24 July	Spencers. m. h. M. c.
th Dist.	Ky.	20	10	320	1126	Wm. Starman Perrysville, Mercy co	3d Sat 21 August	Fork m h Garard c.
g Run	Ky.	31	26	340	2070	George Waller, Shelby county	1st Friday 3 Sept.	not mentioned in min.
sel s Cr.	Ky.	18	14	36	991	John Chandler near Campbellsville	Fri. b 3 Sat. 17 Sep	Union m. h. Adair co
ckton's V	Ky.	15	8		76	Wm. Wood, Esq. Stockton Val Cam c	3d Sat. 21 August	List m. not c. to hand
ncipat	Ky.	7	6		213	David Barrow, m. at Mt S rling	Sat. b. 2 Sab. 11 Sep	List m. not c. to hand
king	Ky.	22	7	126	932	Ambrose Dudley, n. Lexington	2 Sat. 11 Sept.	Bryans Fayette co.
th River	Ky.	18	13		720	Thos. Paschall, Esq. Somerset, Pul. c	1st Sat. 4 Sept.	List m. not c. to hand
per River	Ky.	25	18	17	976	Dr. Edward Collins, Logan county	Sat. b 4 Sab. 21 Aug	S. Point m. h. Logan c.
ue River	Ky.	31	20	14	1246	Thomas Ross, n. Dover, Stuart c. T	Sat. b 3 Sab. 11 Au	Lit. River Christian c.
ung Spi	Ky.	12	10		359	Samuel Hanna, Buffalo Shoal, Floyd c.	1st Sat 2 October	Last m. not c. to hand
ion	Ky.	9	4	87	416	Archelaus Vanhook, Esq. Cynthiana	4th Frid. 27 Aug	P Creek, Harrison co.
aklin	Ky.	12	10		1083	John Scott n Ghent, Gallatin co	1st Frid. 6 August	List minutes mislaid
th Union	Ky.	9	6	12	260	Peter Engle, Esq. Barbourville	Frid. b. 4 S. 24 Sep	L. Camp, m. h. Knox c.
hen	Ky.	18	9	12	512	James H. L. Moorman Breckenridge c	2d Frid. 8 Oct.	Concord, Grayson co.
um	Ohio	19	13	59	817	John Mason, n. Centreville, Montg. c	Sat. b. 2 Sab. 11 Sep	Springfield Hamtn c.
oto	Ohio	15	11	40	540	Samuel Comer, near Lancaster	Sat. b. 1 Sab. 9 Sep	Union, m. h. Pick. co.
ver	Ohio	19	13	37	692	Thomas Hand, Wooster, Wayne c	Thu. b. 1 Sab. 19 Au	New-Lisbon, Col. co.
ught Cr	Ohio	5	3		97	Thomas Lloyd, near West Union	Fri. b. 4 Sab. 20 Aug	Straight Creek m. h.
skingum	Ohio	19	10	58	630	Jacob Drake, Delaware, Delaware c	Thu. b. 1 Sab. 19 Au	Salt cr. Muskingum c.
l River	Ohio	18	9	65	507	John Thomas, Urbanna	Fri. b. 3 Sab. 13 Aug	Honey Creek, m. house
le Miami	Ohio	8	6	65	411	James Jones Indian Hill, Hamilton co.	Sat. b. 1 Sab. 1 Sep	R Bottom Hamtn co
ad River	Ohio	7	5		218	Azariah Hanks, New-Lisbon	2d Weds. 8 Sept	Madison, Geauga co
le Creek	Ohio	3			107	Dea. Elijah R. Dunn, Decatur, Ada c.	Sat. b. 1 Sab. 2 Oct	Decatur, Adams co.
ambus	Ohio					Jacob Drake, Delaware, Delaware co.	the mo. of the ass.	not yet obtained
ash	Ind	4	8	9	303	Isaac M'Coy, near Vincennes	Sat. b. 1 Sab. 2 Oct	B River m. h. Posey c
te Water	Ind	18	12		608	Ezra Ferris, Lawrenceburg, Dearb c	Fri. b. 2 Sab. 13 Aug	List m. no c. to hand
er Creek	Ind	14	12	107	513	Rice G M'Coy, Charleston, Clark co	4th Sat 28 August	M. Pleasant J. Jean c.
a River	Ind.	24	15	27	769	James M Coy, Esq. Salem, Indiana	2d Sat 11 Sept.	Union, m. h. Wash. c.
nois	I.	7	5	9	169	David Badgley, Ogles cr. St. Clair co	Frid. b. 2 Sab. 8 Oct	Looking Glass Pr. m. h.
ssouri	M. T	9	6		183	Jas. E. Welch, St. Louis, Missouri T.	Sat. b. 1 Sab. 2 Oct	Feefees cr m. h.
nel	M. T	8	8	27	260	Thos. P. Green, n. Jackson C G. co.	Sat. b. 4 Sab 25 Sep	Bellevieres. c. h. W. c.
Pleasant	M. T	5	6	15	161	Wm Thorp, Mt Pleasant, Howard co	2 Sat 11 September	Mt Zion Howard co.

0 associations—2700 churches—about 2000 ministers. baptized 9612 in 104 associations; probably, in all of them, 13000: returned, as per minutes of 131 associations 182,393: in all not less than 195,000, besides the large ber of unassociated churches.

BAPTIST BOARD OF FOREIGN MISSIONS IN ACCOUNT WITH J. CAULDWELL, ESQ. THEIR TREASURER.   *Dr.*

1818.		D	C
May 4	To counterfeit note,	5	00
June 8	cash on act. of Rev. I. M'Coy, missionary,	230	87
16	purchase of six per cents (250)	260	00
18	expense in forwarding Luminary	1	40
	loss on foreign paper		90
20	dollars for translations	1000	00
	premium, commission and sundry expense	45	86
29	counterfeit note	5	00
July 3	cash Messrs Welch and Peck	237	37
22	S. F. Bradford for Rees's Cyclopædia	170	00
24	cash for 7,500 U S six per cent 2½ ad.	7706	25
	commission ‡	19	26
Aug. 11	cash for education of Rev. J. Colman	100	00
11	draft in favour of Rev. H G. Jones	194	00
11	cash on act. of Rev I. M'Coy (mis)	125	00
Sept 25	do on acct. of Mr Eastman (mis)	250	00
Oct 15	do H. Posey, missionary	250	00
15	do J Price student in medicine	50	00
19	do on acct. of annual sermon	35	00
23	do Daniel M'Call	100	00
Nov 26	do. Rev H. Posey (mis)	80	00
26	do. Messrs. Peck and Welch	500	00
Dec. 9	do Jonathan Price student in medicine	125	00
1819—Feb. 11	cash for 2000 N Y. state stock, commission, &c	2025	05
Mar. 12	do Mr J. Price student in medicine	25	00
17	discount on Charleston paper	1	60
Apr. 6	cash Rev Henry George, (mis)	125	00
9	do for 2000 N Y state stock commission	1974	92
16	do refunded to Mrs Rowe (late White)	200	00
16	postage	7	53
May 1	balance due the Board	1581	91
		$ 17431	92

1818	CONTRA,	*Cr.*	
May 4	By balance due the Board	3292	61
4	Mrs Nash, Tolland female cent society for translation	18	00
9	S Law, Esq Sunbury, Ga. F. M S.	135	00
May 13	By Samuel Payne, Esq. Hamilton, Madison co F. M. S.	230	00
13	do. do. Masonic Society, Delphi, 44, Transn	10	00
16	Rev. M. Bolles, Mr F Wildman, Danbury, Conn.	3	34
	do. do. Mr. A Osborn, Patterson, N. J.		50
	do. do. a collection,	5	00
	Cayuga Baptist Foreign Mission Society,	150	00
19	Rev. J H Brouner, Mount Pleasant Cent Society,	20	00
26	E Harrington, Saratoga and Washington, N. York F. M. S.	100	00
	sale of Luminaries,	1	60
28	Rev A. Sha, Ontario and Holland Purchase Association,	88	00
June 1	L. Pierce, Esq Plymouth and Bristol, Ms F. Mis. Soc.	120	00
5	R. H. Kemball, Haverhill. (Mass)	45	00
10	E. Secomb, Esq. Salem, (Mass.) Foreign Mission Society,	100	00
	do do. South Berwick Female (for translations) Bible Soc.	30	33
12	Lincoln & Co Hebron, N. H. F. Mission Society,	55	00
16	Mrs. P. M Handy, Pomfret Female Mission Society,	12	00
	Rev. Jesse Mercer, Powelton, (Ga) Foreign Mission Society,	120	00
June 25	I. Loring, Esq Boston Foreign Mission Society,	200	00
30	Rev. B Sears, Franklin (New York) Association,	100	00
July 2	Interest of Stock,	225	73
	Reimbursement of New York State Stock,	5000	00
	L. Pierce, Esq. Plymouth county and vicinity, (Mass.)	100	00

Fifth Annual Report of the Board. 391

Date		Description	D.	C.
July 15	By	Rev C. Douglas, Utica, New York, Foreign Mission Society,	96	10
16		E. Cole, Worcester co. and vicinity, (Mass) F. Mis Society,	100	00
23		R. Lupardus, treasurer of Brunswick F. Mission Society,	100	00
Aug 4		Elder Willey, treasurer of Shaftsbury Association,	100	00
6		Rev Mr. M'Laughlin, Bapt Jun Mis Society, Philadelphia,	100	00
8		T. Skelding, Esq. from Elder Harrington, Washington and Saratoga Societies,	220	00
10		Rev. L Rice, on account of balance as per Annual Report, page 210,	1563	15
11		I Conant, Esq. Brandon, Vt F Mission Society,	100	00
Sept. 14		D. Chapman, Warren, R.I Female Mite Society,	10	00
		Rev. W. T. Brantly, Beaufort, S C Foreign Mis Society,	120	00
28		B. H. Pitman, Female African Good Intent Society, Newport, R. I.	15	00
Oct. 5		October Quarter Interest, United States' Stock,	254	23
		Mrs. Withington, from the Fayette & Mulberry st F M S.	203	84
8		Rev. E. Harrington, (Thos. Skelding, esq) Washington and Saratoga Societies,	52	00
		Mrs. S. Vanderpool, New Ark Female Mission Society,	50	00
19		E. Arnold, Westfield, Massachusetts Association,	37	64
22		James Loring, Esq Boston Foreign Mission Society,	488	93
		do. do. for Western Mission,	18	94
		do. do. for Translations,	16	79
		do. do. for Heathen Schools,	25	34
30		Rev. C. Douglas, Utica Foreign Mission Society,	154	56
Nov. 3		Female Mission Society, Attleborough, for translations,	37	39
9		Rev L Austin, Lyden Foreign Mission Society,	63	00
		R Burrows, Stonington Union Association, Con.	10	00
17		Rev A. Sha, Ontario Foreign Mission Society,	65	00
27		Rev. J Handy, Holland Purchase Association,	24	00
Decr. 17		Gen. A. Forbes, Windsor Union Society, Vermont and N H.	300	00
		do. do. Barre Baptist Association,	34	50
18		Rev. William Hill, Saybrook, a donation,	10	00
19		M. Harris, esq. Cumberland co F. Mission Society,	90	00
		do. do. Baptist Society, Sumner, Oxford co.	17	00
1819—Jany. 2		United States' January Quarter Interest,	284	23
5		Bank Dividends,	9	00
15		Rev. B Bates, Bristol and Newport Mission Society,	36	00
Feb. 6		D. Adams, Esq. Charleston (S C) Foreign Mission Society,	971	06
24		Rev. Jesse Mercer, Georgia Association,	100	00
Ma. 12		Dr Furman, from Joshua Scott, Edgfield, S. C. Association,	167	00
		do. do. from Rev. S M'Creary, Chester District, S. C	132	00
29		E. Secomb, Esq. Salem, Mass Foreign Mission Society,	120	00
		Mrs D. Gregory, Stratfield, Con. Female Mite Society,	40	00
Apl 1		United States April Quarter Interest,	284	23
19		Rev S Pillsbury, Meredith Association, N. Hamp.	60	00
26		Thos Shields, Esq. from various sources,	310	00
29		Rev. O B. Brown, Washington F. Mission Society,	100	00
		Wm. Wilson, Esq Baltimore, do. do	100	00
30		A donation from Mr. Fleming, by Mr. Healy,	8	88
		Rev. J. P. Peckworth, Southwark, Philadelphia,	100	00
			17431	92
		Balance due the Board,	1581	91

The Committee appointed to examine the Treasurer's accounts, report, that having attended to the same, and compared it with the vouchers exhibited, they find it correct, and that there remains in his hands a balance of fifteen hundred eighty one dollars ninety-one cents. That there is also, as appears by a certificate of Messrs. M'Clay and Williams, dated April 20, 1819, twenty one thousand two hundred and forty-nine dollars fifty-four cents, in public stock.

JOHN BRADLEY,
GEORGE F. CURWEN.

Baltimore, May 1, 1819

MONIES RECEIVED BY THE AGENT OF THE BOARD FROM MAY 1, 1818, ONWARD TO MAY 1, 1819, INCLUSIVE.

1818.   D. C
May   By Elder Augustus Bolles, for Annual Reports, (omitted last year by mistake)   3 90
 1-15 By various societies and individuals—see 4th An Rep. p 211, or 3d No Lum p 143   730 00
      By same, 5 25, El. Slack, 2, a lady 1 40 ; another, 1, cash 87 cts. *secretary fund*, 13 52
 14 19 By Miss Peale 15, Mr Ford, Mr Egleton, and Mr Compton 1 dol. each for *sec. fund*, 18 00
 20-22 By F Rutter, Ky 10, J. Foster, Ten 10, Gen Swift 10, another 1, cash 6 cts. *do.*   31 06
 23   By collection at the Chowan Association, North Carolina,   35 00
      By Thomas Brownrigg, Esq. Treasurer of the Chowan Baptist Missionary Society,   100 00
      By the hand of the same, from the Edenton Female Missionary Society,   25 00
 24   By Enoch Sawyer, Esq Woodlawn, Camden co N C for the *secretary fund*,   1 00
 27   By J Wilson Esq Baltimore, 10 , Mr Rooker 5 , Mr Carnighan 5 25, cash 2 36 , *do*   22 61
 30   By a lady, 1 6—mother person 1 13, Winchester, Va for *secretary fund*,   2 19
June 1 By the Sedwick Seminary Female Mite Society, Winchester, Va   33 25
  2   By Thomas Buck 1—Mr. M'Coy, 1, near Front Royal, Va. for *secretary fund*,   2 00
  7   By M Almond 1—G Thomas 50 cents—W Grady, 12 cents, Lun. Va. for *sec fund*,   1 62
 1-6 By Mr Harrison, Harrisonburgh, 10 , Mr C Payne, Lynchburg, 5 , Mr Leftwich 5, *do*   20 00
  7   By collection in Presbyterian M. H. Lynchburg, Va. for *Theol. Institution*,   66 58
  8   By M S Lee, treasurer of the Lynchburgh Baptist Female Mite Society,   36 85
 8 10 By Montague 5 , Jennings 5 Carters—Dr. Flood, Buck co. 5 , Mrs Greenhow 1, *s. f.*   0 00
 10-11 By collection, Cartersville, 7 87, Goochland c. h Va 34 21, for *Theol. Institution*, 42 11
      By Mr Anderson 5—Mr. Bryce 5, Goochland, Va. for *secretary fund*,   10 00
 12   By Atinase. M Russell 10—Mr Faulcon 5—Mr. Fleet 5, for *Theological Institution*,   20 00
      By George Roper, 10—Elder William Leftwich 5, for missions,   15 00
 14   By coll in Cumberland st. Baptist m. h. Norfolk, Va. 15 , Mr. Cornelius's m.h. 20 60, 35 60
 15   By coll Portsmouth, 33 28, S. Whitehead, Esq. 10 , —— Wilson, Esq. 5 *Theol. Inst*   48 28
      By I Mitchell, coll Chowan Asso. 73 19 , Bowers 5 ; King 1 , *secretary fund*,   79 19
      By Norris 50 cts—Hudgins 5—Lugg 5—Holleman 5—Hoskins 5—Burghan 1, *do*   21 50
 16   By a gentleman, Norfolk, Va. 5—Darden 2—Griffin 50 cts.—Clinton, 2—Kello 1, *do*   10 50
      By Mrs Cox, 5 for missions—also 5, and El. Mitchell, per coll. 35 52, *Theol. Institution*, 45 52
 17   By Dr Branch 2—Morris 2—Dr. Mettauer 5—Tatum 2—W B Spooner, Esq 1, *sec f*   12 00
 18   By collection at Petersburgh, 13 21—a lady 2—others 1 13, for *Theological Institution*, 16 34
 19   By Mr Corling, 3—Mrs. E. Corling 3—Mrs. A. Corling 3—two ladies 50 cts each *s.f*   10 00
 22   By collection Bethany Spotsyl. co 24 65—Col. Todd 5 00, for *Theol Institution*,   29 65
 23   By collection, Wallers m. h. Spotsylvania co. 49 00—at Mrs. Andrews, 7 62, *do*.   50 62
 24   By collection, at Zion m. h. 19 00—Orange court house, 1 27, *do.*   18 17
      By Rogers 5—Chapman 5—Cave 1—Taylor 3—Campbell 2—Dr. Grymes 2, *sec. fund*,   18 00
 25   By collection m c h Fairfax, Culpeper co 33 09—at Oakley, 1 75, for *Theol. Inst.*   34 84
      By Betsey Stanley 50 cts.—Polly Abel 19 cts.—Catherine Stringfellow 6, for *Th. Ins.* 6 69
 26   By Mr Jennings 1—others after a narrative of going to India, 1 25, for *Theol. Inst.* 2 25
 27   By a few persons at the brick m. h. Culpeper co Va for *Theological Institution*,   2 15
      By Richard Rixy, Rock Spring, Fauquier co. Va. for *secretary fund*,   2 00
 28   By collection at Buck Marsh Frederick co 21 1—Battletown, 2 57, for *Theol. Ins.*   23 63
 29   By collection at Bethel Frederick co, Va. 41 01—at Front Royal, 6 22, *do*.   47 23
 30   By J Buck, Esq. Ft. Royal 5—W Buck 2—Middletown 4 97—Newtown 10 64, *do*   22 61
July 1 By the hand of Rev. Geo. C Sedwick, Winchester, Va for the *western mission*,   5 00
      By Rev Mr Wilton presbyterian, Charleston, Va. for *secretary fund*,   5 00
  2   By collection, Harpersferry, Va for the *Theological Institution*,   15 11
  3   By Hammond Welch Lisbon, Ann Arundel co Md for the *sec. fund*,   2 00
  5   By collection, Welsh Tract, for *Theological Institution*,   27 31
 10   By remittance from V. M. Mason Lexington, Va. to be added to a coll taken there   5 00
 18   By Absalom Dempsey, Fincastle Va. for the *sec. fund*,   1 00
 19-20 By coll. Salem, Bottetourt co. 13 77 , Mr. Dillard, 1 ; coll Liberty, 7 95, *Theol. Inst* 22 72
 23   By John Morrow, Esq. Cumberland co 10 , Hezekiah Ford, Felixville, 5 , *sec. fund*,   15 00
 24   By Col Francis Dancey, Petersburgh, 10 , Ashton Johnston, 5, *do.*   15 00
 26-27 By coll. at the Union Meeting, Beulah, 71 86 , near Louisa c. h. 35 82, *Theol. Inst.* 107 68
 31   By George Howard Esq Mount Sterling, Ky. for the *sec. fund*,   5 00
      By remittance from Josiah Penfield, Savannah, besides 12 50 *Luminary*, for missions, 17 50
      By remittance from the Roanoke Mission Society, by C. Payne, of Lynchburg Va.   100 00
Aug. 1 By remittance, from Wm. Lancaster, Esq. Spartanburgh Dis. S. C.   1 50
  9   By collection, in the Bap. m. h. Newark, N. J. cr. the East Jersey Mission Society,   18 00
 16   By collection, in baptist m. h. Marcus Hook, Pa. for missions,   10 00
 18   By Rev Thomas Roberts, from the Great Valley Baptist Female Mission Society,   100 00
      By collection, in the baptist m. h. Mount Holly, N J. for the *Theol. Inst.*   4 17
 24   By the hand of Deacon Allen, Burlington, N. J.   2 00
      By the hand of the same per collection, 4 30 ; Miss Craft, 3, *Theol. Institution*,   7 30
Sep. 2 By Colonel William Williams, North Carolina, for the *Secretary Fund*,   25 00

Fifth Annual Report of the Board.

1818.

Date	Description	D.	C.
Sept 6	By collection Bethany, Wayne county, Pa. for the *Theological Institution*,	11	09
10	By collection Fabius, Onondaga county, N. Y. for the *Theological Institution*,	9	68
	By a lady at Delphi, Onondaga county, N. Y. *personal*,		50
11	By collection, New Woodstock, Madison county, N. Y. for *Theological Institution*	8	69
	By a young lady, in addition to the above mentioned collection, a Hymn Book,		50
	By collection in the Presbyterian m. h. Cazenovia, for the *Theol. Institution*,	10	22
12	By Mr Nash, Shelburne, Chenango county, N. Y. for the *Secretary Fund*,		25
	By collection, Deruyter, Madison county, N. Y. for the *Theol. Inst.*	6	04
	By collection, Truxton, Chenango county, N. Y. for the *Theol. Inst.*	7	37
13	By collection baptist m. h. Homer, 15 19, presbyterian m. h. 6 50, Mrs. Treat 12,	21	81
14	By coll. presb. m. h. Skaneateles, 18 02; do. Onondaga, 2 92, for *Theol Inst.*	20	94
15	By collection, 9 m. e. Camillus, Onondaga co. N. Y. for do	6	14
	By coll. Elbridge 8 91. Monro, 5. his son, 2. ladies of the family 1. others 1 90,	18	81
16	By the Groton Female Mite Society, by Elder Andrews, 8 12. Elder Haines, 25 cts	8	37
17	By collection at the Cayuga Association, 34 28, Elder Jefferies, from a lady, 25 cts	34	53
	By collection in Auburn, Cayuga county, N. Y. for the *Theol. Inst.*	9	76
18	By do. in Brutus, 5 15, Julia Morley, 1 00, Throopsville, 4 09.	10	24
19	By do. Scipio, Poplar Ridge m. h. 8 32. first church Aurelius, 3 38	11	70
	By a few persons at Deacon Turner's after a narrative of my passage to India,		50
20	By coll. first ch. Scipio, 8 50. Anna Kelsey, 1, Sibyl Kelsey, 1. 2d ch. Aurelius, 3 88,	14	33
	By Treasurer of Young Ladies' and Gentlemens' Mission Society, Aurelius, N. Y.	15	27
21	By collection Seneca Falls, 3 7. Presb. m. h. Geneva, 8 14. Mrs Griffiths, 5	16	21
22	By collection, Canandaigua, 2 89; Bristol, 14 78	17	67
23	By Cornelius Treat, Esq. Mendon, Ontario county, N. Y. for Mr *Judson*,	1	00
	By several persons after narrative of passage to India,	1	87
24	By collection at the Ontario Association, 35 31. Palmyra, 6 16	41	57
	By several persons after narrative of passage to India, &c.	1	00
27	By collection, Sackett's Harbour, 15 6. afterwards, 5 00, *Theol Inst.*	20	06
	By do. West Soc. in Henderson, 12 72. Brick S. H. Ellisburg, 10. *and a gold necklace*,	22	72
	By several persons after a narrative of passage to India, &c.	1	26
28	By a lady, 1—another person, 25 cents—additional to the collection in Ellisburg,	1	25
29	By collection, Whitesboro', Oneida county, N. Y.	15	06
30	By collection, Westmld. N. Y. 14 23—little daughter of Eld. Philleo, 5 cts—young lady 50,	14	78
	By collection, Madison, 15 06—do. Eaton, 9 08—Madison county, N. Y.	24	14
	By a few persons after narrative of passage to India,		75
Oct 1	By coll. Hamilton, 18 2, *g ring* Madison, Con. Soc. 12 51, *g ring* Sangersfield, 12 21	42	75
2	By collection, Smithfield 10 55. Vernon, Presb. m. h. 20 56, *a gold necklace*,	31	11
3	By collection Schuyler, 21 56. Utica Presb. m. h. 17 58, *also a gold ring*,	39	14
4	By collection, Newport, 11 38. Fairfield, 7 65	19	03
	By Dr. Willoughby, Newport, for *secretary fund*,	1	00
8	By collection, Poultney, Vermont Association, for *Theol. Inst.* (half the collection)	12	50
	By a lady (*for she wishes the privilege of praying for the heathen*)		25
	By *two gold necklaces, a pair of gold ear-rings, two gold finger rings—next day another gold ring, a silver clasp, a pair of large gold ear-rings, two silver hooks*, and 25 cents by a young lady,——another gold necklace by Mrs. Doane, of Granville—Part of the collection and jewellery taken by me for the General Theological Institution, and part left with the Vermont Education Society. By two ladies add to the above, 25 cents for education, left with the Vermont Society, and 25 cents for missions—another person for missions, 40 cents—another 20 cents,	1	35
12	By collection, Lansingburg New York	15	19
	By Deacn. Silas Covel, Troy, N. Y. for *ser. fund* two ladies, *gold clasp & bracelets*,	2	00
13	By coll. Albany, 36. Mr Seymour 3. besides *four gold rings*,	39	00
15	By collection, Rensselaerville Asso. Lex. N. Y—*2 pair ear-rings, 2 gold finger rings*,	30	46
	By Miss. Soc. from F. M. Societies, payments by members of Soc. & *one gold ring*,	164	58
	By Noah Dimmick, Esq. for *Theological Institution*,	1	00
16	By collection, Windham, Green county, N. Y. 1 47—Mrs. Stillman 25 cents.	1	72
	By collection, Durham, N York, 2 19—hand of Elder Hervey, after 12 cents,	2	28
17	By collection, Durham, 2 62—Greenville, 3 41—Mr Reed after, 1,	7	03
18	By collection, Eld. Stuart's m h near Greenville, 8 64—Mrs Stuart, 13 cents,	8	77
	By collection, Cairo, Presbyterian meeting house, also, *a gold ring set in pearl*,	10	96
	By collection, Catskill, Presbyterian m h—13 50—Mrs. Field, after, 50 cents,	14	00
23	By Elder Hardy Holeman, Fayetteville, Lincoln county, Te. remitted,	5	00
26	By Elder Jehiel Fox, Chester, New York, remitted for missions,	10	00
28	By remittance from Rev. Joseph Shepperd, from Mr Elijah Smith,	1	00
Nov 2	By remittance from Elder J. Jones, Indian Hill, Hamilton co. for *domestic missions*,	41	00
5	By the hand of Mr. Woodson, from Mr. Lester, for the *Theological Institution*,	1	00
8	By collection, New Brunswick, N. J. for *Theol. Inst.* credit the E. J. Mission Society,	12	58
9	By collection in Newark, N. J. 6 72—a friend after, 25 cents for the *secretary fund*,	6	97
10	By collection in Mr. Chase's congregation, New York, for the *Theological Institution*,	14	21
	By Mr. Thompson, 10 00 for *secretary fund*—and 5 00 for *foreign missions*,	15	00

		D. C
1818		
Nov. 11	By a few persons at Mt. Pleasant, 32 cents—another, after, 50 cents, for *Theol Inst.*	82
12	By a few persons at Newburg, New York, for the *Theological Institution*,	56
13	By collection at Latintown, New York, for the *Theological Institution*,	4 49
14	By collection at Catskill, New York, for the *secretary fund*,	4 32
15	By collection, Presbyterian meeting house, Madison, Green county,	6 65
	By collection, Hudson, New York, *a gold necklace, a gold ring, a pair of gold ear rings,*	4 46
17	By Mr. Seymour, Albany, 2—another person, *a gold ring,* for the *secretary fund,*	2 00
	By collection in Waterford, Saratoga county, New York,	5 0
18	By collection in Troy, New York, for the *Theological Institution,*	9 25
	By General Thomas, Troy, New York, for the *secretary fund,*	5 00
19	By collection, Presbyterian m h Schenectady, N.Y for *Theol Inst.* another 45 cts.	15 95
20	By Dr. George Beal, Schenectady, for the *secretary fund,*	1 00
	By collection in Schoharrie, for the *Theological Institution,*	2 80
21	By collection, Cherry Valley, New York, for the *Theological Institution,*	12 00
22	By collection, Springfield, New York,	13 01
23	By a few persons at an evening meeting, at El. Phillico's, Clinton, N Y for *Theol Inst.*	3 24
24	By collection, Vernon New York, 3 10—by a lady next morning, 56 cents for *sec. fund,*	3 65
26	By coll. Fabius, 5 50 Pettit 1 Keeny 1 St John 1 Miss B 25 cts.. G.C. Pettit, 12cts do.	8 8
	By P. P. Roots, j. 6 cts. several persons after narrative of passage to India, 1 12 for do	1 18
27	By Elder Freeman, from a lady in Truxton,	1 00
	By collection, Pompey, 3 71—a lady 50 cts. another person after narrative, 50 cts for *s f*	4 21
28	By a few persons at Deacon Lawrence's, Marcellus, for *secretary fund,*	62
29	By collection, Skaneateles, in a school house, for missionary purposes,	4 55
	By a few persons, Auburn, Cayuga county, New York, for the *secretary fund,*	1 16
30	By two persons, Junius, New York,	50
Dec. 1	By a few persons, Gorham, 69 cents—Mr. Griffiths, Geneva, 5, for *sec. fund,*	5 69
2	By a few persons at Elder Goodale's, Bristol, Ontario county, New York, for *sec. fund,*	4 41
3	By a few persons at Col. Pearson's, Avon, 1 42—Col. Pearson 1, for *sec. fund,*	2 42
4	By a few persons, Caledonia, for *Theological Institution,*	1 2
5	By a few persons at Elder Bigelow's, 1 75 : another, 37 cents, for *sec. fund,*	2 12
6	By a few persons at Murray Four Corners, New York, for *secretary fund,*	1 44
7	By a few persons at Mr. Edmunds 45 cents—Mr. Edmunds 25 cts for *Theol. Inst.*	70
8	By a few persons at Lewiston N Y 1 06—Deau. Gray, 50 cents, for *Theol Institution,*	1 56
9	By two persons, Willoughby, Upper Canada,	50
10	By a few persons in Buffalo, New York, for *Theological Institution,*	1 73
11	By collection, Fredonia, Chetaugue county, New York, for *Theological Institution,*	7 83
12	By a person, Northeast, Erie county, Pennsylvania,	13
13	By collection, Erie, Erie county, Pa. 9 26—Mr. G after, 50 cts. *Theol. Institution,*	9 75
14	By a few persons at Dean Miller's, Springfield, Pennsylvania, for do.	1 1
15	By a few persons, Ashtabula, Ohio, for do	2 6
	By Wm. Gould, Esq. Conneaut, 1 12—Mr Smith, Ashtabula 1 for *secretary fund,*	2 12
16	By a few persons, Painesville, 2 22 Euclid, 2 78, for *Theological Institution,*	5 00
18	By collection, Tallmadge, 3 62—Mr Sackett, after, 1 25—Miss Granger, 17 cts for do	5 04
	By Mr. Benjamin Fenn, for foreign missions,	2 00
20	By collection, Wooster, Wayne county, Ohio, 10—Mr Patton, after, 94 cts. for *s. fund,*	10 4
23	By collection, Delaware, Ohio, for *s fund,* 5—by Elder Drake from Musk. Asso 48,	53 00
25	By Elder John Thomas, from Madriver Association for 1817 11 07—for 1818, 44 00,	55 07
	By a few persons after preaching at brother Morgan's house, O. for *Theol. Inst*	1 02
25	By collection at the house of brother Smith Mechanicksburg Ohio, for do	2 15
27	By collection, Covington, Campbell county, Ky. 9 06—Mary Gano, 1 do	10 06
28	By Mrs. Goforth 5—Mrs. Gano 3—Mr and Mrs Robins 3 for do.	11 00
	By the hand of the Rev. Mr Wilson, per collection in Presbyterian m h. Cincinnati,	55 00
	By Mrs Smith, treasurer of the Female M Society, Cincinnati.	27 00
31	By collection, Great Crossings, Ky 5 12—Col. J Johnson, 1—a lady 3, for *Theol Inst.*	18 12
1819 Jan. 3	By collection at Maj. Briscoe's, 7 75, at Perrysville, 2 87; for do.	10 62
5	By collection, Glasgow, Kentucky, for *Theological Institution,*	16 00
6	By a person after an evening meeting, near Mount Gilead, Ky. for *Theol. Inst.*	25
7	By collection, Springfield, Kentucky, for *Theol. Inst.*	13 25
8	By a few persons after an evening meeting at Elder Penny's Ky for *Theol. Inst.*	2 50
10	By collection, Presbyterian meeting house, Lexington, Ky. and given after, for do.	55 30
12	By collection, May's Lick, 10 88, J. Shotwell, *personal,* 1; for *Theol. Inst*	11 88
15	By collection, Chillicothe, Ohio, for *Theol. Inst.* 6; by a person for *Indian reform* 1;	7 00
17	By collec. Columbus, & given after, 46 65, Worthington, & given after, 13 14, for do.	59 79
	By Elder Drake, addition to the collection in Delaware, Ohio, for *sec. fund,*	3 00
30	By remittance from Elder Reuben Coffey, for missions,	11 50
Feb. 10	By Mrs. Holt, Bermuda 3—Mrs. Grant 3, annual subscrip—Mrs Scon 5, for *Theol Inst.*	11 00
17	By Female Society, Somerset, Pa. 5—collection 4 76—Mrs Ross, 1—Miss Stephens 1,	11 76
21	By collection in Pittsburg, and 50 cents given after for missionary purposes,	14 30
22	By collection, Philip's meeting house, Alleghany co. and given after, for *Theol. Inst.*	2 93
23	By collection, Washington, Pa. 13 54 ; by Dr. Leatherman, Canonsburg 5, for do.	18 54
24	By collection, Wheeling, 4 87 ; after by Mrs. Fawcett 1 ; Mr. Mix 1, do.	6 87

Fifth Annual Report of the Board. 395

		D. C.
1819.		
Febr. By collection, St. Clairsville, Ohio, for missionary purposes,		3 69
26 By collection, Morristown, Belmont co. Ohio, for missions,		4 67
28 By collection, in the Presby. m. h. Zanesville Oh. & 75 cents in Putnam, & 56 cts. after,		15 10
Mar. 4 By collection, Bainbridge, Ross co. Ohio, for missions,		1 69
5 By collection, Presbyterian m. h. Washington Ky. and given after for missions,		9 74
6 By a person after preaching at Ariett's 25 cents, another next morning 50 cents,		75
7 By collection, Millersburgh Ky. 15 35, Paris 12. for missions,		27 35
10 By collection taken in Frankfort, 10th January, for the *Indian School, Ky.*		111 00
12 By collection at Newport Campbell co. Ky. for missions,		5 62
14 By collection Round Bottom m. h. Hamilton co. O 1 50, Methodist m. h. Milford 2 44		3 94
15 By collection, Lebanon 13, with 75 cts. by Mrs. Collet, and 2 dols. by Miss Van Horne		15 87
17 By Elder Ferris, church at Lawrenceburg 3, church at Elkhorn, Wayne co. 2,		5 00
18 By collection Burlington Boone co. Ky. 10 44, Elder Absalom Graves 1,		11 44
21 By collection, Louisville, Ky. 25, Henry C. Hardin 5 · Elder Benjamin Allen, 1,		31 00
23 By collection, Shelbyville 13 32, by a lady 1, for *Theological Institution,*		14 32
27 By collection, Lebanon, Ky. 8 35—Issachar Pawling, o 82, *secretary fund,*		14 97
28 By collection, Campbellville 1 75, Greensburgh, 28 37, for missions,		30 12
31 By Bardstown society, *Indian reform,* 80 14—collection, 8 69,		88 83
Apr. 3 By Miss Martha Ayres, treasurer of the Lexington Fem. Mite Soc. for *Ind. reform.*		30 75
4 By cash for missions, David's Fork, Kentucky,		37
7 By the Washington Auxiliary Mission Society, Ky.		106 45
By El. Jesse Holton 2; collection, Maysville 13 65, George Corwine 1, for *Theo. Inst.*		16 65
11 By collection, and given afterwards, Granville, Ohio for missions,		12 72
14 By Rev. Mr. Wheeler, to be added to the amount sent on from the Redstone assoc.		3 50
20 By Rev. J. George Schmucker, York, Pa.		5 00
22 By Elder Job Foss, from the Union Association, N. Y.		15 75
By the hand of Dr. Staughton from R. M'Ginty, see of the Ocmulgee M Society,		300 00
By do. a donation for *Cor. Sec.* from Wm. Walker, Putnam co. Ga.		50 00
By do. from Deacon Jos. Saunders, from the Meherrin Association,		86 00
By do. from Rees Bayles, by John M'Allister, Esq. Jonesboro, Ten.		66 00
By do. from Mr. Comer, Secretary of the Scioto Association, Ohio,		26 50
By do. from Elder Josiah Osborne, Greenbrier Association, by Rev. R. Semple,		35 80
By do. from Elder Jacob Drake, Delaware, Ohio,		50 00
By do. from Beverly Caldwell, Virginia, by Mr. D. Brown,		100 00
By do. from General William Madison, from an Auxiliary Mission Society,		200 00
By do. from Rev. Robert M'Creary, 136, do. 91 from Hugh Slater, 20 50,		247 50
By do. from Edward Fowler, from Mission Society, Charlotte Va. 100; do. 100,		200 00
By do. from Wm. Clanahan, Esq. from the Madison Mission Society, Kentucky,		86 25
By do. from Joseph Morris, Olive Branch, Elk Creek, Ohio,		12 00
By do. from T. Buck, Esq. Ket. Asso. by H. Richardson, 20, do. by Dr. Warfield, 23 83,		43 83
By do. from Mrs. Allen, from the Burlington Female Mite Society,		100 00
By do. from Mrs. Staughton, from the Sansom Street Female Society,		235 45
By do. from Mrs. Eliza Collett, Lebanon, Ohio,		45 00
30 By account as per *cash book* of the Superintending Committee of Indian School Ky.		1138 27
By receipts in payment for the *Latter Day Luminary,*		2121 22
By subscription not yet paid for the *secretary fund,*		788 00
By subscriptions not yet paid for the *Theological Institution,*		75 00
Total,		10523 47
As designated for Mr. Judson, *personally,* 1—for Agent, 4,	5 00	
do for *Secretary Fund* 556 99 paid, besides 788 subscribed,	1344 99	
do. for *Theological Institution,* paid 1162 06, subscribed 75,	1237 06	
do for *Indian ref.* and *West. Miss.* besides *cash book* of Sup. Committee,	273 39	2860 44
Balance for missionary purposes,		7663 03
Paid over to the Treasurer, after the close of the annual meeting,		6267 52
From the sum total of the foregoing receipts,		10523 47
Deduct for *personal,* 5—*Secretary fund,* 1344 99—*Theol. Inst.* 1237 06—paid 6267 52,		8854 57
Will leave a balance of		1668 90
Accounts as rendered to the Board, to say, for travelling expenses,		399 26
Stage and steam-boat fares, ferries, gates, 393 69—postage, 97 87,		491 96
Horse hire, keeping, shoeing, 117 49—stationary, circulars, &c. 45 72,		163 28
Costs arising from issuing the *Luminary,* 2014 22—52 weeks service 416,		2430 22
Paid Elder I. M'Coy, missionary, 25 50—postage and stationary of *Cor. Sec.* 69 75,		95 25
Board and lodging, medical books, instruments, &c. for Mr Price, missionary,		227 50
Boarding, rent of *theol. students,* 364 15—clothing, wood, furniture, &c. 153 54,		499 69
Paid Sup. Committee of Indian School, Ky. 510—per *cash book* of Committee, 1138 27,		1648 27

The Committee appointed to examine the Agent's accounts, having attended to the same, report that they find them correct.

Philadelphia, May 10, 1819

JOHN BRADLEY, } Com.
GEORGE F. CURWEN,

Additional Items connected with the general Agency, circulation of the Luminary, Associations, Societies, &c. &c.

Elder Peter P. Roots, in the State of New-York, spent five weeks last Fall, in the service of the Board, to promote the circulation of the *Luminary* in that quarter. He visited more than twenty places, preached near forty times, scattered a number of subscription papers, and received—of a poor man in Broome, 3 certs at Jefferson, 70 cents; Worcester, 71 cents, collection at Milford, 5 31, of two persons at Manlius, 17 cents, a few persons at Salina, 64 cents, Mr. Avery, 20 cents; a person in Sherburn, 20 cents; at Oxford, 98 cents; a lady at Unadilla, 25 cents; collection at Franklin, 4 24; at Meredith, 1 50, in all $ 14 93.

The Rev. Samuel R. Green, the latter part of Winter, and early in the Spring, spent five weeks and five days, in the same kind of service, principally in New Jersey and Delaware. He rode upwards of five hundred miles, preached thirty four times, scattered subscription papers, and obtained subscribers for the *Luminary*, and received in Frankford, 4 16, in Trenton, 6 01, of the Female Mite Society of Trenton and Lamberton, 53 27, at Hightstown, 5 31, at Wilmington, 5 87, near Bethel Cross Roads, 12 32, at Laurel, 5 52, at Salisbury, 6 53, at Milford, 7 22, at Brinzion, 3 31, Smyrna, 6 43, George Walker, Esq. 1 25, in all $ 117 20; expenses incurred, $ 8 37.

In looking over the *minutes* of the associations, it is gratifying to mark the spirit of increasing zeal and liberality which they discover for advancing the empire of the Son of God. Several of them have recommended to the churches of which they are composed, the taking up of *three public collections, annually* one for *foreign*, and one for *domestic* missions, and one for the *education* of persons called to the work of the christian ministry. The Hudson River, Madison, Cayuga, Ontario, Vermont, and perhaps others, not observed in the haste of glancing through their minutes, have set this praiseworthy example.

The monies annually collected by the Associations for these and other objects, furnishes a happy demonstration of their activity and benevolence, and is the consecrated pledge of future great results. *Bowdoinham Association*, from female societies, churches and congregations, individuals, and collection at the session, 175 38, *Cumberland*, do do. 366 22, *New-Hampshire*, do do 65 14; *Meredith*, do do. 83 97, *Shaftsbury*, do. do 214 16, *Woodstock*, do do. 278 47, *Vermont*, do. do 241 93, *Fairfield*, do do. 30 76, *Danville*, do. do 74 92, *Leyden*, do. do 37 53; *Sturbridge*, do do. 12 83, *Boston*, do. do. 1138 43, *Westfield*, do do 36 72, *Warren*, do do 349 34, *Otsego*, do. do 151 64, *Chemung*, do do 16 25, *Rensselaerville*, do do 30 46; *Cayuga*, do. do. 34 28; *Saratoga*, do do. 27 60; *Black River*, do. do. 182 94; *Madison*, do. do. 142 89, *Lake George*, do do 10, *Union*, do do 15 75, *Franklin*, do do 166 93; *Holland Purchase*, do. do 35 82, *Ontario*, do do 167 28, *Hudson River*, do. do 95 41, *New Jersey*, do do 190 66, *Redstone*, do. do 222 03; *Delaware*, do. do 87 95, *Strawberry*, do do 30 25, *Middle District*, do do 42 00, *Portsmouth*, do do. 32 75, *Meherrin*, do. do. 26 07, *Neuse*, do. do. 36 00, *Mountain*, do. do 19 79, *Raleigh*, do do 17 34, *French Broad*, do do 19 59, *Charleston*, do do. 1599 89, *Moriah*, do. do. 22 52; *Georgia*, do. do 260 87; *Hephzibah*, do. do 226 68, *Mississippi*, do do. 130 63, *Cumberland*, do do. 15 00, *Concord*, do do 38 25; *Tate's Creek*, do do 4 00; *Bracken*, do do. 33 62; *North Bend*, do. do. 139 00, *Russell's Creek*, do. do. 15 75; *Little River*, do do. 34 37, *Miami*, do. do 68 00; *Scioto*, do do 25 50, *Muskingum*, do do. 48 50, *Mad River*, do do. 44 00, *Little Miami*, do. do. 41 00, *Missouri*, do do 20 75, *Bethel*, do. do. 37 50; *Mount Pleasant*, do. do. 16 88, *Hartford*, do. do. 83 81.

From this it appears that *fifty-eight* Associations, out of *one hundred and forty*, little more than *one third* of the whole number, have received the last year $7816 98, but some of these have no other object than printing their own minutes, and some small additional expenditures. *What, then, might not be accomplished, if all the associations possessed the same spirit of expanded, ardent benevolence, which some of them display?* Others, besides the ones here mentioned, are doing worthily, whose last minutes have not come to hand; and some, whose minutes have come to hand, have not reported all that they are attempting for the cause of Zion, and among them also are many mission societies, whose exertions and successes are not detailed in the association minutes.

How many *mission societies*, and *female mite societies*, have been formed the past year, cannot here be stated. An account of all of them in the United States, as nearly accurate as practicable, may be expected in the ensuing annual Report, after the meeting of the Convention, to be held in Philadelphia the last Wednesday in April next.

Several *education societies* have been originated, having special regard to the Theological Institution, connected with the Board. Besides those mentioned by Mr Sommers, see p 247, a *Female Education Society* has been constituted in the Sansom street church and congregation, which has already collected upwards of 200 dollars, besides various articles of clothing and of furniture, for the students and the Institution. And one also by the ladies of Lexington, Kentucky, with highly favourable prospects; and, perhaps, others, information of which has not yet been communicated.

MISSIONARY INTELLIGENCE.

MISSION TO BURMAH.

From Mr Judson to the Cor Secretary, dated Madras, May 28, 1818.

IN former letters I have stated my circumstances at the close of last year, and the reasons which induced me to leave Rangoon on a visit to Chittagong—particularly the prospect of a direct passage, and speedy return in the same ship, an opportunity of very rare occurrence in Rangoon

Since that time a series of unexpected providences have befallen me, which, though uninteresting in detail, must be briefly mentioned, in order to account for my present situation

When we left Rangoon, December 25th, we expected a passage of ten or twelve days At the expiration of a month, however, by reason of contrary winds, and the unmanageableness of the ship in the difficult navigation along the coast, we found ourselves still at a great distance from port; and the season being so far advanced, as to deprive us of the hope of more favourable winds, the captain and supercargo agreed on a change of the ship's destination, and made sail for Madras

Previous to leaving the coast, we put into Cheduba, a place under Burman government, for a supply of provisions. I was unable to go ashore, but took the opportunity of sending a tract by the boat. It happened to be conveyed directly to the governor, and he ordered it read in his presence. Soon after, when our captain had an audience, the governor inquired after the writer of the tract—who he was, and how long he had been in the country. The captain evaded some questions, for fear of detention, I suppose, and merely stated that the writer was a foreigner, who had resided in Rangoon about four years. "No," replied the governor, "that is not to be credited. You cannot make me believe that a foreigner, in so short a time, has learnt to write the language so well. It must have been written by some other person." The captain related this to me on his return—I felt particularly gratified by this testimony to the perspicuity of the style, and thought it not unworthy of mentioning, because it could not be suspected, as others which had been made to me personally, of having been a mere compliment.

The ship's destination was changed on the 26th of January. We retraced our course for a few days, and then stood to the westward. It was with the most bitter feelings, that I witnessed the entire failure of my undertaking, and saw the summits of the mountains of Arracan, the last indexes of my country, sinking in the horizon, and the ship stretching away to a distant part of India, which I had no wish to visit, and where I had no object to obtain. It was, however, some mitigation of my disappointment, that I should, in all probability, be able to return to Rangoon, and resume my missionary business much earlier, than if I had visited Chittagong. But even the consolation of this hope was not long allowed me. We had, indeed, a quick passage across the bay; but, on drawing near the Coromandel coast, the wind and current combined to prevent our further progress, and at the expiration of another month, having for a long time subsisted on nothing scarcely but rice and water, and being now reduced to very short allowance, we concluded to make sail for Masulipatam, a port north of Madras, which we doubted not we should be able to reach in a very few days. In this, again, we were disappointed, and through the unmanageableness of the ship, or the mismanagement of the captain, were detained at sea nearly another month. During this period, we were sometimes in great distress, deeming ourselves very fortunate, when able to get a bag of rice, or a few buckets of water from any native vessel which happened to pass. Once we sent the long boat to the shore, and obtained a considerable supply of water, which was a great relief. But of rice we could obtain no sufficient supply, and all other articles of provision were quite out of the question.

The low state to which I was at length reduced, occasioned a partial return of the disorder of my head and eyes, to which I was subject two years ago. This, with other circumstances united, left me no other source of consolation but resignation to the will of God, and an unreserved surrender of all to his care; and praised be his name, I found more consolation and happiness in communion with God, and in the enjoyments of religion, than I had ever found, in more prosperous circumstances.

Finally, we did reach Masulipatam, and I left the ship on the 18th of March, twelve weeks after embarking at Rangoon. I waited at Masuly a few days, until it was ascertained that the ship would unlade her cargo, and remain several months. And as there was no prospect, that season, of reaching Madras by sea, the only port on the coast where I could hope to find a vessel bound to Rangoon, I was under the necessity of taking a journey by land—distance about three hundred miles. I accordingly hired a palanquin and bearers, and arrived here the 8th of April. My first aim was, of course, the beach, and my first inquiry, a vessel bound to Rangoon. But my chapter of disappointments was not yet finished. No vessel had sailed for Rangoon this year, and such, it was understood, was the unsettled state of the Burman country, that none would probably venture for some time to come

Here I have remained ever since, under very trying circumstances. Have scarcely heard from Rangoon, since I left, or been able to transmit any intelligence thither, by a conveyance to be depended on. The weakness of my eyes prevents my application to study, or attempt at any exertion. I am making no progress in missionary work, I am distressed by the appalling recollection of the various business which was pressing on me at Rangoon, and made me very reluctant to leave home for the shortest time. Now, I have been detained twice as long as I anticipated, and have, withal, wholly failed in my undertaking. Where, my rebellious heart is ready to cry, where is the wisdom of all this? But it is wise, though blindness cannot apprehend. It is best, though unbelief is disposed to murmur. Be still, my soul, and know that He is God.

From the same to the Cor. Secretary, dated Rangoon, October 9, 1818.

My last was dated Madras, May 28, 1818. At that place I remained waiting for a conveyance to Rangoon, until the 20th of July, when I took passage on an English vessel, at one hundred and sixty-seven rupees. During my stay in Madras, I experienced great kindness and hospitality in the families of the Rev. Mr. Thomson, chaplain, and the Rev. Mr. Loveless, missionary, and received such proofs of Christian affection from many dear friends, as rendered parting with them very painful, though my detention in Madras had, in other respects, been almost insupportable. We anchored at the mouth of Rangoon river, on the 20th of August. The next morning, when the pilot came on board, I was overwhelmed with the intelligence, that, on account of the dangerous situation of affairs, the mission had been broken up, and that Mr Hough and family, and Mrs. Judson, had taken passage for Bengal. To my great relief, however, it was added, that, before the ship left the river, Mrs Judson's reluctance to leave the place, had so increased, as to force her back to the mission house alone, and further, that the ship, being found unfit for sea, was still detained. On my arrival, I found that brother Hough was inclined to pursue his original plan. His reasons, he will, doubtless, communicate to the Board. It is expected that the vessel will be ready for sea in about a fortnight.

The brethren Colman and Wheelock and their wives, arrived the 19th of September, about six weeks after my return. We had, I can truly say, a most joyful meeting. You have never seen them, or it would be unnecessary to add, that they are four *lovely* persons, in every sense of the word, and appear to have much of an humble prayerful spirit. Such being their interesting appearance, we regret more deeply to find, that the health of the brethren is so feeble. They have both had a slight return of bleeding at the lungs, an old complaint to which they were subject in America. May the Lord graciously restore and preserve them!

A few days after their arrival, I introduced them into the presence of the viceroy. He received us with marked attention, which, however, must be ascribed to the influence of a handsome present, which went before us. Though surrounded with many officers, he suspended all business for a time, examined the present, and condescended to make several inquiries. On being told, that the new teachers desired to take refuge in his glory, and remain in Rangoon, he replied, Let them stay, let them stay: and let your wife bring their wives, that I may see them all. We then made our obeisance and retired.

The examination which brother Hough sustained during my absence, and the persecution of the Roman Catholic padres, have made us feel more deeply than ever, the precarious situation of this mission, and the necessity of proceeding with the utmost caution. It was only through the favour of the viceroy, that the padres were allowed to remain here, when they arrived from Ava, under sentence of banishment. And it is only through his mediation, and the influence of large presents made to the king, that the order of banishment is reversed, if indeed it be reversed, a report not yet confirmed. One malicious intimation to the king, would occasion our banishment; and banishment, as the Burmans tell us, is no small thing,—being attended with confiscation of all property, and such various abuses, as would make us deem ourselves happy to escape with our lives.

Such a situation may appear somewhat alarming to a person accustomed to the liberty and safety of a free government. But, let us remember, that it has been the lot of the greater part of mankind to live under a despotic government, devoid of all security for life or property a single moment. Let us remember, that the Son of God chose to become incarnate under the most unprincipled and cruel despot that ever reigned. And, shall any disciple of Christ refuse to do a little service for his Saviour, under a government where his Saviour would not have refused to live and die for his soul? God forbid. Yet faith is sometimes weak—flesh and blood sometimes repine. O, for grace to strengthen faith, to animate hope, to elevate affection, to embolden the soul, to enable us to look danger and death in the face; still more, to behold, without repining, those most dear to us, suffering fears and pains, which we would gladly have redoubled on ourselves, if it would exonerate them.

We feel encouraged by the thought, that many of the dear children of God remember us at the mercy seat. To your prayers I desire once more to commend myself, the weakest, the most unqualified, the most unworthy, and the most unsuccessful of all missionaries.

MISSION TO AFRICA.

THE friends of human happiness will be gratified in marking the decisive tendency of some great proceedings of the present auspicious period in favour of the abused and subjugated population of the benighted land of Ham. To this country of debasement and misery, the Board have conceived it their duty to undertake a mission. Two coloured brethren of the baptist church in Richmond, Va. they feel pleasure in announcing to the public as suitable subjects of their patronage for this benign purpose. These brethren, it is expected, will sail in the fall for the land of their forefathers, to publish the gospel of peace and salvation, promoting, at the same time, the great and merciful designs of the American Colonization Society.

The reasons for commencing a mission of this nature, the Board cannot better suggest than by presenting to the public the following communication from the Rev. Mr. Brown to the Corresponding Secretary, dated,

Washington, April 1, 1819.

DEAR SIR,

A meeting of the Board of Managers of the Colonization Society, was held yesterday, and as one of the Board, I was present. The practicability of obtaining territory in Africa, of good soil and healthy climate, is no longer problematical A law of the last session of Congress, places it in the power of the executive to further the views of the Society; and the President has expressed his readiness to co-operate, so far as a fair construction of the legislative provisions of the government will justify.

The Rev. William Mead is elected agent of the Society, to reside at this place, and to travel abroad for the purpose of soliciting donations, &c. Mr. Mead is an episcopal clergyman, of liberal views, and a man of real piety. A committee is appointed to confer with him upon such measures as shall be best adapted to effect the object of the institution, and to select a suitable number of the descendants of Africa, who shall voluntarily offer, and shall give satisfactory testimonials of their moral character and industrious habits, to sail for Africa in October or November next, in a vessel to be sent by the Society, with an agent, who will procure the territory by purchase from the natives, and commence the settlement.

I have this morning received a letter from our brother William Crane, a very worthy and respectable member of the baptist church at Richmond, Va. some extracts from which I will here copy.

"*Richmond, March* 28, 1819.

"You will probably recollect, that I introduced you to two of our coloured brethren in this place, who are accustomed to speak in public; one named Collin Teague, the other Lot Carey. Ever since the missionary subject has been so much agitated in this country, these two brethren, associated with many others, have been wishing they could, in some way, aid their unhappy kindred in Africa; and I suppose you have heard of their having formed a missionary society for this sole purpose. Some letters published in No. VI. of the *Luminary*, have served to awaken them effectually. They are now determined to go themselves to Africa; and the only questions with them are, in what way will it be best for them to proceed? and what previous steps are requisite to be taken? They think it necessary to spend some time in study first. They both possess industry and abilities, such as, with the blessing of Providence, would soon make them rich. It is but two or three years since either of them enjoyed their freedom, and both have paid large sums for their families. They now possess but little, except a zealous wish to go and do what they can. Brother Lot has a wife, and several little children. He has a place a little below Richmond, that cost him $1500, but will probably not sell for more than $1000 at this time. Brother Collin has a wife, a son 14 years of age, and a daughter of 11, for whom he has paid $1300, and has scarcely any thing left. Both their wives are baptists; their children, amiable and docile, have been to school considerably; and I hope, if they go, will likewise be of service. Collin is a saddler and harness maker He had no early education. The little that he has gained, has been by chance and peace-meal. He has judgment, and as much keenness of penetration as almost any man. He can read, though he is not a good reader, and can write so as to make out a letter. The little knowledge he has of figures, has been gained by common calculations in business. Lot was brought up on a farm, and for a number of years has been chief manager among the labourers in the largest tobacco ware house in this city. He has charge of receiving, marking and shipping tobacco; and the circumstance that he receives $700 a-year wages may help you to form an estimate of the man. He reads better than Collin, and is in every respect a better scholar. They have been trying to preach about ten or eleven years, and are both about forty years of age.

"They would be glad to receive the patronage of some public body, and wish advice how to proceed. I had thought of addressing the Corresponding Secretary on their behalf, for the patronage of the American Baptist Mission Society, but again thought, that the Colonization Society might be pleased with taking them under their care, and that their mission might bear a more imposing aspect under the auspices of this society than it would with the baptists alone. But should they go under the Colonization Society, they would still feel themselves attached to the mission cause, and would wish some connexion with the general Board. We are desirous of your thoughts upon the subject. In a little time they can be ready to engage. They would go to Sierra Leone, but will submit that to the decision of their patrons. It would, I suppose, be somewhere between the tropics, on the western coast. Their object is to carry the tidings of salvation to the benighted Africans. They wish to be where their colour will be no disparagement to their usefulness. I suppose the funds of our African Mission Society here, after their next meeting, on Monday after Easter, will probably amount to $600, which I believe the society will be willing to appropriate to the aid of their brethren should they go. Brother Bryce will also write to you on this subject."

Thus, you will see, from the proceedings of the Colonization Society, compared with the above extract from the letter of brother Crane, a striking indication of the design of Divine Providence, to illuminate the dark regions of the sons of Ham. From the formation of the Colonization Society, I have been unshaken in the belief, that God designed it as a means of erecting the standard of the gospel upon the shores of Africa. We have followed the good example of our English brethren in Asia, and shall we not labour with them also for the fulfilment of that prediction, "Ethiopia shall soon stretch out her hands to God." I shall lose no time in laying the subject before the Committee appointed by the Board; and have no doubt but they will very readily receive, and convey these brethren to Africa. But the Colonization Society is not formed for missionary purposes; and it will not, probably, comport with the views of the Society, in furthering its object, to extend support to any denomination, under the character of missionaries. The course to be pursued, appears perfectly plain to my mind; but to attempt to mark out the plan, and recommend to the general Board of Missions, would not become me. I therefore submit the facts to you, as the organ of that Board, in the full conviction, that the proper measures will be adopted to embrace these favourable occasions for spreading the glad tidings. I hope it will become a subject of immediate deliberation with you, and I shall be happy to receive, as early as practicable, your views upon the subject. If you think any possible benefit could arise to the great cause, from my being in Baltimore at the meeting of the Board this month, tell me so, and I will be happy to be present, as it will not be attended with any great inconvenience. The arrangements effected betwixt our eastern and western brethren, are regarded as a propitious event. A general union of our denomination in America, and concentration of our resources, if wisely managed, will result in something great, and worthy the cause we profess. If the establishment of a mission in Africa, under such favourable auspices as the Colonization Society will present, shall meet the views of the general missionary Board, I have no doubt that it will find ample support, and prove the eternal salvation of thousands yet unborn. The Lord is opening the doors and bids us labour in his vineyard. O how inscrutable are the ways of God!

Man is torn from his kindred, and dragged by barbarous hands to a distant, unknown country, to wear the shackles of slavery among men of strange language and complexions, where no friendly hand can soothe his anguish, nor pitying eye mingle with his the tear of commiseration. But the mystery begins to unfold, and develop a design worthy of God. From these victims of oppression, whose cries are heard in heaven, God is raising up a seed to return to the land of their progenitors, bearing the gospel of salvation, and illuminating with beams of truth and mercy the regions of darkness. Our cup has too long been sweetened with their blood. It is time to begin the work of benevolence. The voice of mercy and of justice conspire to call us from indolence and cupidity.

I had forgotten to mention, that a government vessel will sail for Africa, and an agent from government to reside in Africa, at such place as the society shall procure, at the same time that the vessel of the society shall sail. For my own part, I have no great doubt of the success of the undertaking.

WITH peculiar satisfaction this opportunity is seized on to record, emphatically, an expression of profound regard for that exalted combination of talent and of benevolence, consecrated in THE AMERICAN COLONIZATION SOCIETY to the most noble of purposes. This Society, formed by distinguished citizens of the United States, in the second annual Report of its Board of Managers, furnishes the most convincing and happy presages and pledges of the dignified, useful and glorious career, which, in the allotments of Divine Providence, it seems destined to pursue. The Report and its valuable appendix, are replete with documents, and facts, and observations, and estimates, of the greatest interest and importance. In relation to a point of no common moment to the welfare of mankind, the Managers remark·

"In the distribution of free colonies along the coast of Africa frequented by the slave ships, and the employment of a suitable naval force to guard its peace, the Managers believe that the most efficient, if not the only adequate remedy, will be provided for enforcing the existing laws of the United States against the African slave trade.

"The Managers, sensibly impressed with the inefficacy of the present laws against this abominable traffic, and firmly persuaded that its entire abolition is essential to the success of the leading objects of the Society, offer no apology for having dwelt so long upon this branch of their report, nor for having enlarged its appendix, by the admission of several documents, that manifest the extent to which this cruel and iniquitous trade is still pursued by citizens of the United States.

"The numerous, respectable, and concurrent authorities, to which the Managers have resorted in their endeavour to acquire all the knowledge which is attainable of the western coast of Africa, have augmented their desire to liberate its artless, docile, and amiable inhabitants, from the chains of slavery and superstition, in which the oppression and ignorance of so many ages have fast bound them. In the climate, soil, productions, and general health of this much injured country, there is every inducement to a zealous prosecution of the experiment which the Society have begun.

"That a colony of the free people of colour of the United States may be planted and protected on the western coast of Africa, at little comparative expense, can no longer be questioned. Should it prosper in its future growth, the extent of the blessings to which that prosperity may lead, as regards the civilization of

Africa, the happiness of the free people of colour, and the reduction of the number of slaves in America, no human sagacity can either foresee or compute. It is the duty of man to obey the Divine will by labouring to achieve all the good within the compass of his limited capacity, and to trust, with humble but zealous confidence, for the success of his efforts in the superintending providence of God."

From the Journal of the lamented SAMUEL J. MILLS, who, with Mr Burgess, visited Africa as agent of the Society, as well as from the numerous other documents in the appendix, much valuable information may be derived. Just before leaving that quarter, Mr. Mills observes, dated,

"Sierra Leone, Monday, 18th May, 1818.

"I have now visited most of the villages in the colony. The population of the colony is nearly twelve thousand. The schools are in a flourishing state, accommodating nearly two thousand children. Each village has a superintendent, who is a clergyman or school master. Each village has a place of worship, where prayers are made, morning and evening, in the presence of the people. The Sabbath is observed through the colony. The governor is justly esteemed as a father and patron of the colony. He makes great exertions for its improvement.

"I am every day more convinced of the practicability and expediency of establishing American colonies on this coast."

It is much regretted that our limits will not allow more copious extracts to be introduced, and particularly the insertion entire of the luminous "*Report of the committee of the House of Representatives of the United States*" on this subject.

Already the benefits of the Society begin to be realized, and bleeding humanity, in some instances, is permitted to exchange the tears of grief and despair, for those of gratitude, and hope, and joy. The worthy Agent of the Board of Managers, the Rev WM MEAD, is now at the south, and has succeeded in making arrangements for the liberation of a number of those unhappy victims of cruelty, who were liable to be sold, under the regulations of the government of Georgia, on account of their having been introduced into that state contrary to the laws of the United States. If room for it could be allowed, it would be gratifying to present to our readers the whole of his interesting letter to the Secretary of the Society

MISSION TO ST. LOUIS.

Letter from Messrs Peck and Welch to the Cor. Sec. dated St Louis, Feb 18, 1819.

WE think it due the Board to inform them, that owing to the almost incredible expense attending the residence of *both* of our families in this village, we have been seriously contemplating for months, the propriety of removing one of them to the country, or some less expensive situation, or at least to one where the prospects of lessening our expense by our own individual exertions may appear more favourable

We have no intention of abandoning this, which we esteem one of the most important fields for missionary labour in this western world. This we could not do without betraying public confidence, and subjecting the little church with which we are connected, to pecuniary difficulties, in consequence of our attempts to build the Lord's house.

Brother Peck has been absent on itinerant and missionary service through different parts of the territory for four months, a few days excepted, and will start again this afternoon, with an expectation of being absent until the first of March.

We have reason to believe, that for the last two months there have been individuals in our little congregation who have felt the power of divine truth, and occasionally have manifested a strong desire to "see Jesus." Fathers and brothers, pray for us, that the gospel may have free course and be glorified. This is a very important era in the history of the western churches. A few years will effect much. Public lands are selling, and emigrants from almost every part of the world are settling. Each possessed of his own prejudices, we may rationally conclude that there is great diversity of opinion on the subject of religion.

At such a crisis as this, a few zealous and devoted men, with the blessing of God, may do much good. We feel the importance of working while it is day.

From the same to the Cor. Sec. dated St. Louis, March 4, 1819

THROUGH you, as the proper medium of communication, we desire to lay before the Board the following statement, exhibiting a brief review of our past efforts and the result, together with some outlines of that course which it appears to us ought to be pursued for some time to come.

Upon arriving in St. Louis, which was pointed out by the Board as the field where we should *commence* our labours, our first effort was to ascertain the state of things in its immediate vicinity, and to open a small school. A few weeks' residence in the place made us acquainted with several pious persons, professors of our denomination, with whom we soon associated in constituting a church. This took place February 8, 1818. Occupying our school room as a place of meeting, it soon appeared too small to contain the number who assembled to hear the gospel. This circumstance, together with the general desire of the public for a more commodious place, induced the church to attempt the erection of a meeting house. The subscription that was soon raised, fully justified the undertaking. Accordingly a lot was purchased, and contracts made with builders.

At the time these efforts commenced, some encouraging appearances presented in the conviction and conversion of several individuals.

The degraded situation of the Africans, and the importance of some exertion to deliver them from the thraldom of sin and guilt, induced us to open a Sunday school, which, though small at first, soon increased to a large number, so that at one period upwards of ninety were on the list. As the moral and religious improvement of these children of Ham was the object of the school, we soon had the satisfaction to see our labour was not in vain. Not only was a visible change produced in the morals of a number, but some were found under convictions for sin. Of these several have manifested a hope, who by their fruits evince their love to the Redeemer. Others are still anxiously inquiring, while some few, who at first appeared serious, have turned back.

Occasional excursions into the country gave us a knowledge of the low state of religion, and pointed out the necessity of some public exertion to induce the churches already existing in the country, and those persons friendly to the promotion of religion and literature, to enter into a system of efforts to disperse the light of the gospel through these dark regions. A plan was exhibited to three associations, which, after securing their approbation, was adopted as the constitution of the "United Society for the spread of the Gospel." Three objects are embraced in this institution,—the employment of itinerating missionaries, the promotion of common schools, and the education of pious men called to the work of the ministry, the moral and religious improvement of the Indians.

Though this society is in its infancy, and for some time to come its efforts must be very limited, yet we hope, by the blessing of God, it will become the herald of good news to multitudes ready to perish. Since its formation the labours of one of us have been directed to its promotion, while the other has devoted himself to the charge of our school and other concerns in St. Louis.

Besides the church in St. Louis four others have been constituted, all of which, though small, are in harmony, and we hope will increase.

In relation to our school department.—Our principal school in St. Louis has been a little fluctuating. Some part of the time the number has been large. In the fall and winter it has been more limited. Rent and other incidental expenses have prevented this pursuit from producing much real profit to defray our family expenses, though some avails have been realized. Motives of charity induced us to receive a few French children gratis last summer. Two other schools, partly through our efforts, have been established, the profits of which are enjoyed by the teachers as their compensation. One of 30 scholars in the settlement of Gravois, St. Louis county, taught by Mr. Shubael Marsh, the other in Montgomery county, of 14 scholars, by Mr. James Greenhalgh, son of the Rev. John Greenhalgh of Kentucky. These schools are under good regulations, and meet the approbation of the people.

In taking this retrospect of our past labours, it is necessary to exhibit the result of our inquiries relative to the Indians. No opportunity has been omitted nor pains lost in forming an acquaintance with such as came within our reach, or of acquiring information of those more distant. Interviews have been obtained and councils held with the "head men" of several nations who visited St. Louis during the last summer, and in most instances a disposition discovered itself to receive instruction and adopt habits of civilization. One of these tribes, partly through our friendly "*talks,*" embraced the proposals of the Kentucky Missionary Society, and placed eight of their number under that institution.

While adverting to the present state of mission concerns, our spirits do not flag, nor are our prospects obscured by any dark clouds. Though the meeting house in St. Louis is unfinished, and all our labours are so far from being completed, that we view them as just commencing, yet we are not disposed to relax our pursuits, or leave any part of what we have been enabled to begin for uncertain and more distant prospects. Some appearances of seriousness are discovered in our congregation, and a growing attention to public worship. On the whole we trust the same spirit which first put it into our hearts to labour for the promotion of the gospel will keep us from falling, and enable us to live and die missionaries of the Cross.

Having taken a cursory view of the course that has been pursued, we beg leave to lay before the Board the following outline as a plan, which we think best to be pursued for some time to come.

I. *In relation to the Indians.*

Although we feel no small desire to extend immediate relief to those benighted people, we are compelled to suspend any direct and enlarged efforts amongst

Indian tribes, till more means and more missionaries can be obtained to enter the harvest.

Unhappy differences have recently taken place between the settlers on Salt River and the adjacent country, and the Sacks and Aioways—murders have been committed, and the Indians have removed their old men, wives and children far interior, which indicates hostile intentions. This state of things precludes the possibility of exertions amongst them for the present.

The Indians on White and Black Rivers, in this territory, which have removed from Ohio, Indiana, and Illinois, are yet in an unsettled state. The Shawnees, Delawares, and other small bands nearer us, can, however, receive some attention with respect to schools, either directly from the Board, or by the means of the "United Society."

To ensure any great prospect of success our station must be fixed in the Indian country. But if one of us should immediately remove thither, some part of our labours already begun must be relinquished, and usefulness in the settlements greatly abridged; and the advantages anticipated in the formation of the "United Society" in a great degree lost.

II. *In relation to St. Louis.*

It appears expedient that one of us should remove with his family from this town, and establish a school or academy somewhere else. This can be done without breaking our compact, under the name of the "*Western Mission.*" It will ultimately save much expense, and the necessity of exertions in the surrounding country loudly calls for it.

III. *In relation to our school system.*

The great expense attendant on a school in St. Louis from the rent of rooms, &c.—the advantage of having a piece of land to cultivate—of erecting or procuring buildings to save rent in a literary institution—the advantage of receiving boarders at a moderate price from the country—of educating persons to become teachers—and particularly of an establishment where pious ministers may receive some education, whose situation or circumstances would not permit them to avail themselves of the important Theological Seminary established under the direction of the Board, and the impossibility of obtaining these advantages in St. Louis, induce us to think a removal of our main school is necessary, and we think the town of St. Charles is the best calculated to secure these objects.

This is a very healthy situation, and is a kind of central point from which communications may be made with most parts of this and the adjoining state of the Illinois. A very important field for missionary labour lies in every direction around it.

IV. *The particular course to be pursued.*

We submit to the Board whether it would not be expedient, and tend much to lessen the expense of this mission, if a SUM was appropriated for the special purpose of procuring a LOT on which to erect an academy and dwelling house, and to purchase from 20 to 50 arpents of land [an arpent is less than an acre] to be improved for family use. The great advantages of this will be more clearly seen when it is understood that rent, in about four years, would cover the expense of a small house, and that the rise of property in the same period would far exceed the most exorbitant interest from funds.

If we possessed a *lot,* improvements might be made at leisure, and from time to time, as the institution might be enabled to meet the expense.

With respect to the *amount*, the particulars we have stated will enable the Board to decide. It is supposed, however, that five or six hundred dollars for *that special object* would be sufficient.

It will be extremely desirable and proper that we have the opinion of the Board, on the several subjects which this communication lays before them.

From John Buttolph to the Cor. Secretary, dated Northeast, January 22, 1819.

IT is with diffidence of myself that I now attempt to address you at this important crisis of duty, assured, however, of your indulgence, I shall proceed to lay before you the subject of this communication.

It is four or five years since my mind was first roused in the cause of missions since, I have had at different times the most solemn impressions of duty, but have given them up, again and again, from the consideration of deficiencies in myself. In the year 1814, I was ordained an Evangelist, and spent the summer season in travelling. In my first tour I spent a few weeks in Massachusetts and Connecticut. In my second, I travelled to the west, visiting Shaftsbury, Otsego, Madison, Cayuga and Rensselaerville Associations—preached in the destitute places, and enjoyed peculiar satisfaction in feeding the sheep and lambs of Christ But the poor state of health that attended me, together with frequent speaking, rendered it necessary for me to relinquish an object that lay so near my heart.— On my return I engaged in teaching school, which had been my occupation for several years. While thus engaged, the destitute parts of the world would often come under my observation, and excited such sensations that I could hardly content myself but no opportunity offered, in which I might pursue, with hopes of success, the object I had in view. In 1816, at the request of the church in this place, I engaged in the pastoral duties of it, which is my present situation.

During this period I have had impressions of going to the destitute, and at different times the dealings of Providence greatly strengthened them on my mind; until last spring I did not express my views to any one. Then my mind had become so agitated with the subject, that not only duty, but my happiness urged the necessity of disclosing to some one my impressions. Having had an opportunity of acquaintance with the Rev. John M Peck, I addressed a letter to him, in which I gave a statement of my situation in his answer he laid before me the destitute territories west of the Mississippi, together with the success of the mission In our correspondence he has suggested the propriety of offering myself to the Board—in his last letter he stated that he should address the Board, and mention my name I hope he has not exaggerated in my favour, nor excited too high expectations of one who possesses so little. Should Providence still favour, at a suitable time, I should in a more full communication, proceed to offer myself to the Board as a candidate for the western mission. Relative to acquirements, I can only say, that excepting some knowledge of the languages, my education is nothing more than common.

INDIAN SCHOOL

Among the numerous plans which the inventive benevolence of the present times has put into operation for advancing human happiness, the INDIAN SCHOOL, established near the Great Crossings, Kentucky, it is believed, will not be one of the least efficient. The idea of educating Indian youth in the English language, in the midst of civilization and the blessings of an improved social condition, offers itself to view, not as the visionary dream of the imagination, but as the sober project of the understanding, calculated to produce the most substantial benefits to the aborigines of our country. The experiment is now making on a plan, it is conceived, somewhat different from any that has yet been tried—that of not merely educating the young natives in our own language, and in those general rudiments and elementary parts of learning, which are a sort of common possession in our improved state of society, but, at the same time, as an essential part of the system, in the arts, and the industry, and the economy of civilized life.— This design relies for success on the same active and exalted benevolence which has given it existence. For its enlargement and prosperity much will depend on the wisdom with which it shall be conducted, and the bounteousness of the charitable. Although objects which solicit the liberality of the public are greatly multiplied already, the Board cannot hesitate in making a distinct and solemn appeal to that liberality on behalf of this school in Kentucky for educating young Indians. Nor can they, for a moment, sustain the burden of a doubt, that an enlightened community will extend an ample patronage to this interesting object. *The liberal deviseth liberal things, and by liberal things shall he stand!*

The opening of the School offers a prospect in no common degree gratifying to the wishes of those who long for the arrival of the period when *the wilderness and solitary place shall be glad,* and when *the desert shall rejoice, and blossom as the rose.*

The following communications on this subject the Board find pleasure in presenting before the public.

From the Rev. Mr. Henderson, Clerk of the Superintending Committee of the Board, and Cor. Sec. of the Kentucky Mission Society, dated,

DEAR SIR,   *Great Crossings, Ky. April 22, 1819.*

AGREEABLY to an order of the Committee appointed by the general Board to superintend the Indian School in Kentucky, I hasten to lay before you documents and communications by which you will discover the state of affairs in this section of the country. Some time previous to the arrangements which have been so happily accomplished the past winter, the Rev. John H. Ficklin was appointed agent to visit several Indian tribes in Illinois and the Missouri Territory for the purpose of procuring some of their children to be educated in this state. His report is enclosed.

On the arrival of Mr. Ficklin with the young Indians, measures were adopted for building houses, and providing food and raiment for them, and also a teacher to take charge of the school—consequently several convenient houses were erected, and a teacher of good character employed.

The school had been in operation a short time when we received your communication by the hand of brother Rice, and is still progressing beyond our most sanguine expectations. Evidences abundantly multiply of practicability and success in this enterprising project of Indian reform. From the present flattering prospects we indulge strong hopes, that, with the patronage of the general Board, under the smiles of heaven, this will become a most flourishing institution.

The total amount of debt created in starting the establishment is $784 44, including compensation to agents, travelling expenses with the Indians to Kentucky, building houses, &c together with food and clothing sufficient for eight or nine months. About seven hundred dollars of this amount have been paid— That you may see the state of the funds, I send you an abstract from our cash book, and will also enclose you a copy of the proceedings of the Committee since its organization.

Under date of the 15th, Mr Henderson wrote again to say,

Since writing on the 12th inst in which I promised to furnish you with a copy of the proceedings of the committee, I find it will make too large a packet, and perhaps be of but little service.

Just permit me to observe that the committee shortly after its appointment had a meeting, and elected Col James Johnson, chairman, and myself, clerk

Every thing seems to harmonize extremely well. The Indian School excites a great deal of notice in this country.

I remain, most respectfully,
Your obedient servant,
THOMAS HENDERSON

Rev. Dr. WM. STAUGHTON, Cor. Sec &c. &c.

ABSTRACT FROM THE CASH BOOK OF SAID COMMITTEE.

Dr. CASH.	D	C	CONTRA.	D.	C.
March, 1819.			March, 1819		
24 To cash from Treasurer Ky. Mission Society,	200	00	24 By cash paid John H Ficklin,	200	00
To donation from North Bend Association,	70	63	By do. do.	70	63
To cash collected by Mr Clark,	41	12	By do. do.	49	12
To do. do.	8	00	By do. do.	320	00
To donation by the Rev. Mr. Rodgers,	5	00	By do. do.	111	00
To cash by Rev L. Rice, Agent of Gen. Board,	350	00	By do. paid Samuel Trott,	20	50
To do. do	139	00	By do. do.	133	49
To do. do. per collection in Frankfort,	111	00	By do. do.	46	00
To do. do from Treasurer K M Soc	204	53	By balance,	637	53
To do by Rev. S. Trott proceeds of bill sold,	230	00			
To do. received as per account,	165	00			
To do. received by hands of col. R. M. Johnson,	60	00			
To do. received by letter,	20	50			
To do received as per account,	133	49			
Total	1638	27		1638	27

[The report of Mr. Ficklin is necessarily deferred, for want of room, to a future number of the Luminary]

CHEROKEE INDIANS.

From Mr. Posey to the Cor Sec Waynesville, Haywood Co. (N C) March 11, 1819.

WITH some difficulty I attempt writing to you once more. There are so many subjects on which I wish to write, that to do justice to every one would fill a volume instead of a letter; but I must make a few words suffice on each subject. And first, in regard to my labours in the service of the Board:—

My time was generally spent in a similar manner as it was before I wrote in June last, which seems to render it unnecessary to go the general round in the way of a journal. In June and July, I took a tour through a considerable part of the nation, in which I attended a council between the Indians and governor M'Minn of Tennessee, relating to the exchange of their land here for land over the Mississippi. At this *talk*, I had the opportunity of conversing a good deal with Mr Charles Hicks, one of their principal chiefs, who is a man of considerable information, and I trust a real Christian. He and some other natives have been baptized by the Rev. Mr. Gambold, the Moravian missionary at Springplace.

I found a general anxiety prevailing among them for school establishments, as soon as they can know what part of their land will be occupied by them. This they have still hoped would soon be known, and now, I understand, Mr. Hicks has gone on to Congress it is probable on his return it can be determined.

Owing to this uncertainty, all my schools stopped, having continued only a quarter. A number of the poor young Indians made considerable advances, and they all, generally, are anxious for a continuance of schools immediately on the settlement of their affairs. I believe the schools all closed with the Indians holding the Board in great honour; and notwithstanding the many of bad white people among them, I never found that they once suspected me of any bad design. They always seemed to receive me as one sent by the Great Spirit to instruct them, &c and they are expecting me to attend to the fixing of schools whenever their business is settled. I humbly trust my travelling among them last year has not been in vain; and in compliance with the request of the Board, and my own feelings, I have in view to spend some time this spring amongst them. But I feel satisfied if they stay here it would be best to procure a missionary that would live in the nation, and my family is too large for this; and also, it would be too confining, as I have a natural turn for itinerancy. And again, when I was in the Missouri territory, I agreed to remove to that part, if the Lord will, but still intending to have something decisively done among the Cherokees, which I hoped could be done this summer. Whatever time I spend in the service of the Board, I will inform you, and any thing else relative to the Indians which may appear necessary.

I discontinued my missionary labours about the middle of September, and on the 26th of October started for Missouri, in which tour I travelled near two thousand miles, tried to preach forty-seven times, and landed at home precisely in three months. I was at St. Louis, but brother Peck was gone on a tour up the Missouri. I think highly of their procedure in that land of darkness, and hope the Lord will bless them there. The Baptists in the town appear much united. I had the pleasure of preaching, two nights in succession, to a little attentive band in their preaching room

Leaving this subject, I next take the liberty of dropping a word respecting the Institution for educating young men called to the ministry by our churches. I feel a great solicitude for its prosperity, and knowing the general tone of the brethren for a considerable distance, I use the freedom of saying, that I think, if there were less learning required of students before they are admitted, it would meet with more general approbation. In fact, I have heard no one speak of doing any thing towards it, on the present plan, as the qualifications for admission seem to put it out of the power of almost any in our parts, or for some hundred miles, to receive any benefit from the Institution. I hope, however, the Lord will guide you in wisdom and prudence, and, whatever the result may be, I trust it will redound to the glory of God.

MIAMI AND OTHER INDIANS.

From Mr. Isaac M'Coy to the Cor. Secretary, dated Maria, (Ia.) April 7, 1819.

In haste I write you a few lines, in hope they will be received before the close of the annual meeting of the Board. I am now on my way to Vincennes, on business of the mission, the most important of which relates to the acquisition of a more eligible spot for our mission establishment. The Secretary of War has granted me permission to settle among the Indians, provided they have no objection. There are two places which at this time appear inviting: one is a Miami reservation on the Wabash, about one hundred miles from our present residence, the other is at Prarie du-Chien, on the Mississippi. Since last December I have been endeavouring to obtain a settlement on the former, some of the advantages attending which are the following. 1st, It is a large reserve, say thirty miles square, which will afford tolerable room for operation. 2d, On it government will probably erect the two mills, and settle the two smiths, to which the Miamies are entitled by the conditions of the late treaty. And 3d, It is a central point, in relation to reservations made by the tribes. I have already made arrangements with the proper persons, for making a trial to obtain the consent of the Indians; the house and land which we at present occupy, can readily be sold at any time for more than they have cost us. The expense of moving will not be considerable, but we shall likely be obliged to settle on land to which we shall not have a permanent title; this, however, is the less to be lamented, in consequence of a hope that I may get an appointment in the superintendence of the mills, &c. which may contribute to the lessening of our expenses, and also facilitate our operations among the Indians. I need say nothing in regard to the expenses that will be incurred at such a station after the first year, since brother Peck has made such a judicious remark on the subject, which I have just now seen in the sixth number of the Luminary.

Now, sir, will it be proper, all things considered, to prosecute my present undertaking, or pursue a different course? This question is asked with an indescribable desire that the answer should be in the affirmative. Our greatest fears are, that the Board will not think the little good we are doing, and are likely to do, will justify the expense that will be incurred, which, however, we shall study to make as light as possible. Ever since we have been in the service of the Board, we have felt ourselves bound, under the strongest obligations, to observe a strict frugality. Permit us to live where we hope we may be most useful to the miserable Indians, and if there must be an abridgment of the support which we may deem necessary to carry our plans into effective operation, let it be of that which is given for our subsistence. I now feel as if I had rather subsist on the dried venison of the Indians, than be denied the means necessary to render the mission serviceable to them; but my resolution, in general, is too much like Peter's. It is my happiness, however, to believe that you pray for us, yea, we trust we are subjects of the intercession of One whose prayers are heard always.

We are in daily expectation of receiving the gladdening intelligence that another missionary is appointed to this station.—My accounts were forwarded to you two or three months ago.

From Mr. Samuel Eastman to the Cor. Sec. dated Natchez, March 23, 1819.

More than six months having elapsed since I commenced my endeavours under the patronage of the Board, I deem it my duty to give some account of the manner in which I have spent my time.

I left my parents and friends in New-Hampshire on the 8th of September, and commenced my journey to the state of Mississippi, according to your instructions, at which place, by the blessing of God, I arrived on the 22d of December. As most of my journey was performed in the stages and steam-boats, few opportunities of preaching on the way were offered me. While passing through Ohio and Kentucky, made some effort to collect money for the use of missions, and in some places the zeal of the people was displayed by liberal contributions.

Since my arrival at the place of my destination have spent my time in the city of Natchez, and in visiting the churches and destitute places in its vicinity, to the distance of thirty miles. Have also made one tour to Louisiana, during which had the pleasure of seeing our worthy brethren, Rev. Dr. Cooper and Rev. Mr. Rinaldson, to whom the Board was pleased to refer me for counsel and friendship.

I know of no remarkable religious intelligence to communicate to you. In many of the congregations which I visit, a solemn seriousness is depicted on each countenance during the time of service, and some inquire what they shall do to inherit eternal life. The churches are receiving gradual additions, backsliders are returning, and in some instances lukewarm professors are shaking off the slumber of carelessness.

It has, in most parts of the state, become disreputable openly to deny the divine origin of the Holy Bible. But the largest part of our population is constituted of those who are stout hearted against the power of truth. I trust you will not forget how much we stand in need of your supplications. The more I contemplate the condition of those who are afar off from God the more is my commiseration enlisted in their behalf. If well directed exertions to evangelize the world are vigorously pursued by every denomination of Christians, we ought to entertain no doubt but the Lord will, in due time, make these exertions effectual. In due time shall we behold the troops of hell relinquishing their unequal warfare, laying down the weapons of their rebellion, and enlisting under the banner of Immanuel. May the followers of Christ never grow faint or weary in their labour, until the triumphs of his cross shall be extended far and wide, and the whole earth be filled with his glory!

From William Polke to the Cor. Secretary, dated Bruceville, January 25, 1819.

Permit an entire personal stranger to express his satisfaction at the conduct of the Board, and its members individually, as far as has come to my knowledge, and, I may almost say that I am lost with wonder, love and praise, when contemplating the success of the missionary cause. You will see by the minutes of the Wabash Association, which some time past I transmitted to you, that there is some opposition to the cause of missions. But that opposition will, I firmly believe advance the cause, as truth has nothing to fear from investigation, and I find it has created an inquiry, as I discover by the increased demand for the "Latter Day L nary" in these parts I have advised brother M'Coy to visit as many of the Associations as practicable the ensuing summer, as I know from my acquaintance with him from his childhood, and my knowledge of his character among the baptists generally, in our neighbouring States, that no one can better aid the cause of missions in the frontier settlements, where it cannot be expected the majority of the people are well informed on the subject, and where, unfortunately, ill-founded prejudice exist against any thing like education but which gloom, I am happy to say, is vanishing before truth.

GENERAL STATE OF RELIGION.

ON this article our limits do not allow the scope we could wish. Accounts of particular revivals must be deferred to a future number of the *Luminary* Although the year past has not been peculiarly marked as a season of extensive outpourings of the Divine Spirit, very precious showers of mercy have, on various parts of our country, descended By the best estimates that can be made out from the information communicated in the minutes of the associations and letters of correspondents, not less than *thirteen thousand* have been baptized in our denomination the past year, on profession of their faith in the Son of GOD.

While, however, we have much cause for devout gratitude, we have also much for humiliation and prayer. A body numbering nearly *three thousand churches*, with more than *two hundred thousand* communicants, and only about *two thousand preachers*! Who shall supply the affecting wants of the *hundreds of thousands* connected with this body of professors! *Who will not pray the Lord of the harvest to send forth labourers!*

If we extend the calculation so as to embrace the whole population of our country, the result is still more distressful! and ought to arouse the supineness of the slothful, to encourage the beneficence of the opulent, and elicit the prayers and zeal of all who prefer Jerusalem above their chief joy Surely, the importance of Education Societies, as means of *stirring up the gift* which the Saviour has bestowed on those of his servants whom it is his pleasure to call into the ministry, can scarcely be too highly appreciated While various institutions of this nature are springing up in different parts of the United States, A GENERAL ONE. such as that designed by the Convention to be connected with the Board of missions, religiously claims immediate, decisive, energetic, abounding patronage.

THE fourth annual Report of the Baptist Society for promoting the Gospel in Ireland by establishing schools for teaching the native Irish, for itinerant preaching, &c. &c. is full of information of a most pleasing character.

It appears that "the Society has four men who are employed reading the Irish scriptures and inspecting the Irish schools, (in addition to a gentleman in Sligo, who has frequently visited the schools,) who are perfectly acquainted with the Irish language. These are men of well-informed minds and religious habits, whose hearts are yearning over the ignorance and superstition of their countrymen; and who are pursuing their useful labours in travelling through several counties; visiting the cabins of the poor, and, in some instances, the mansions of the rich"

These Irish leaders refer the society to a Mr. Henderson who was instructed to visit them. Mr. H observes in a letter to the secretary, "I have spent three

Lord's days in three different places, where there are about 120 inquirers, I hope not unprofitably to them or myself. It is delightful to have to say that many have, through the instrumentality of his own word, become the followers of our Lord Jesus Christ. It would have rejoiced the hearts of the Lord's people in England, (and surely in America too,) to have heard some poor ignorant Irish boors expatiating on the proofs contained in the 1st chap. of Ephesians, that salvation was without regard to any merit in man, but that it flowed from sovereign and predestinating grace. *One of them counted upon his fingers, while another was reading, 20 evidences of this doctrine in 18 verses of that chapter.*" The Rev Mr Dobney, of Wallingford, having been appointed by the Committee to visit Ireland, in order to unite with the Rev. Mr. West of Dublin, to visit the schools, and to collect for the Society, they had an opportunity of seeing some of the persons referred to, and are of opinion that " there are twenty persons in the neighbourhood of E. who appear to be brought to the knowledge of the Lord by reading the Scriptures." They say, "a place for preaching is freely offered by a Roman Catholic, and a church of twenty members will soon exist, all the fruit of reading the Scriptures." The Committee ardently hope that a pastor, able to preach in the Irish language, will also soon be provided for this church, which has been collected entirely from the native Irish."

The schools have more than doubled in number since the last meeting. The Irish gentry are gradually discovering the benefits that must result to the community from an educated peasantry. It appears that " the total number of the Society's schools (exclusive of the *Sunday schools*, of which there are several) is now 65; about 3860 children are generally instructed in them, excepting at those seasons of the year when the children are employed in planting or digging potatoes."

"In concluding their account of the schools, the Committee give the following quotations from a letter of one of the Inspectors " Going along the shores of the Atlantic for 50 miles, where your schools are planted, and perceiving some of the effects of the word of life manifest in young and old, it brought to my mind the chief scene of operation selected by Him who has all power and wisdom, where many of his works were performed 1800 years ago, and who from the sea coast chose his witnesses. The hope sprung up in my mind, from the earnest already given, that your Society would be the honoured instrument of once more causing *fishermen* to leave their boats and their nets and to go *every where preaching the word*. Already some of your teachers, and the four readers whom I have seen, are become decided witnesses —clerical opposition ceasing —doors for usefulness opening —may we not yet live to see effects produced such as were wrought of old, when *the word of God increased, and the number of disciples multiplied in Jerusalem greatly, and a great company of the priests were obedient to the faith!*"

Other denominations have experienced the past year, in numerous instances, the refreshing dews of heavenly grace. From their reports, narratives, &c we hope, in a future number, to find room for interesting extracts.

In foreign countries, although there is much discoverable of a melancholy and gloomy description, there is much also which cheers, delights, and animates the heart. If, indeed, we were to contemplate merely the *dark parts* of our own, and of the European states, and from these turn our eyes upon the abominations and miseries of the heathen nations, the survey becomes overwhelming. *Of one thousand millions of human beings inhabiting this globe, only two hundred and fifty millions are to be found in countries which have adopted the christian name!* and of these two hundred and fifty millions, *even a greater proportion as really devoid of genuine piety, as are the worshippers of Juggernaut, or such as sacrifice themselves to demons!*—Alas! Alas! " *the whole world lieth in wickedness!*"

From this frightful scene, foreboding the blackness of darkness for ever, we hasten to take refuge in the sanctuary of a Redeemer's mercy. Blessed be God! here we find ample relief.

A review of missionary operations tends to awaken anticipations most auspicious to the hopes and gratifying to the wishes of benevolence. From the domestic efforts of our own country, and those which are causing *the wilderness to rejoice*,—through all the range of the missionary stations in the South Sea Islands, in New Holland, among the Hottentots, and other nations of the interior of Africa, among the Laplanders, among the inhabitants of the burning climes of India, the eastern Islanders, and the Hindoos, and the Burmans, and the Chinese,—we behold increasing exertion, accompanied with growing success. These, with the extended operations and happy results of Sabbath schools, and the great CONCERT PRAYER MEETING,—these are the indications of Providence at which, coinciding with the predictions of the OMNISCIENT JEHOVAH, furnish at once the assurance and the pledge of the approach of that glorious scene which shall introduce to astonished and delighted mankind millennial splendour and joy. The *day spring from on high has visited the earth*, the *morning star is even now above the horizon*, THE LIGHT OF THE WORLD shall soon appear, *and all flesh shall see the salvation of God.*

BIBLE SOCIETIES, then, should not be past in silence, in making out an estimate of the moral condition and prospects of the human family. These have multiplied and are multiplying with astonishing rapidity, and are accomplishing indeed great things for the Zion of our God. The AMERICAN BIBLE SOCIETY already numbers *one hundred and ninety two* auxiliaries in her train; it has received during the last year little short of *forty three thousand dollars*, and has printed since the commencement of its operations, that is, in the short period of three years, more than *a hundred thousand* bibles and testaments. Its late anniversary is said to have been much more numerously attended than either of the preceding ones, and by persons of the highest respectability.

The great RUSSIAN BIBLE SOCIETY causes indeed the sacred *word to run and be glorified* among the rude tribes which make up the population of that vast empire, and is fast blessing the nations of the north with the knowledge of salvation; while the august BRITISH AND FOREIGN BIBLE SOCIETY, the parent of this consecrated family, moves on in her majestic and luminous career, animating by her powerful influences many European, Asiatic and American societies, and propelling, with her mighty energies, the machinery of that hallowed beneficence, which is communicating to a debased, a guilty, and a miserable world, the glorious gospel of the blessed God.

THE LATTER DAY LUMINARY;

BY A COMMITTEE

OF

THE BAPTIST BOARD OF FOREIGN MISSIONS FOR THE UNITED STATES.

Vol. I.   AUGUST, 1819.   No. IX.

COMMUNICATIONS.

MISSIONARY TOURS OF PAUL THE APOSTLE.

THIS distinguished servant of Christ was a descendant from the tribe of Benjamin. His native place was Tarsus in Cilicia, a city that in philosophy and the arts was the rival of Corinth and Athens. He was a pupil of Gamaliel, the most illustrious teacher of his age. When his education was completed, after the manner of the Jews, who thought every child must learn a trade, he was instructed in the art of making tents. As to his religious profession he was a Pharisee. His hatred to the gospel was cruel as the grave. On his way to Damascus, breathing out threatenings and slaughter against the disciples of the Lord, he was arrested by a vision of the Son of God, became a preacher of the faith he had endeavoured to destroy, and was in nothing behind the most eminent of the apostles. His writings form a considerable portion of New Testament scripture, and his history, detailed by the evangelist Luke, exhibits the manner in which the gospel was first preached to the nations, the difficulties it surmounted, the confirmation it received, and the surprising success it obtained.

In this eminent apostle "God was mighty towards the gentiles"— "to make them obedient by word and deed, through mighty signs and wonders by the power of the Spirit of God." From Jerusalem round about unto Illyricum, he preached the gospel of Christ. In

Rome also he planted the standard of the Cross; and, according to the sentiment of the ancients, engaged in the same sacred service in Spain and in Britain.

After the visit of Ananias to Saul at Damascus, the apostle straightway preached Christ in the synagogues there, Acts ix. 21 while all that heard him were amazed Shortly after he went into Arabia, where, during a residence of two years, by serious study, and by immediate revelations from the Son of God, he became qualified to fulfil the work of an apostle. From Arabia he returned to Damascus where " he confounded the Jews," proving that Jesus is the very Christ. Escaping a malicious contrivance to kill him, being let down the wall of the city by the disciples, through a window, in a basket, he hastened to Jerusalem, where for fifteen days he lodged with Peter. From this city he was ordered to depart by a vision of the Lord Jesus. The brethren conducted him to Cesarea Philippi, and to his native city Tarsus; thence he travelled into Syria and Cilicia, where he was favoured with those exalted visions described in his first epistle to the Corinthians. At Cilicia he was found by Barnabas, and brought to Antioch. Here the disciples were first called Christians, and here Agabus foretold the great dearth throughout the world which came to pass in the days of Claudius Cæsar. A seasonable and generous collection was made in the church at Antioch for the relief of the Judean brethren, and was conveyed by Barnabas and Saul to Jerusalem. On their return to Antioch these excellent men were separated, at the direction of the Spirit of the Lord, to a peculiar expedition. Affectionately and solemnly dismissed by their brethren, and accompanied by John Mark the son of the sister of Barnabas, they sailed for the island Cyprus, landed at Salamis on the eastern coast, they preached the gospel in the synagogues, and then crossing the island, arrived at Paphos, on the western coast, where Elymas was smitten with blindness, and Sergius Paulus was converted to the faith of the gospel. At this place the Hebrew name of Saul was changed to the Roman name Paulus, or Paul, as some have thought from his respect to Sergius Paulus, in the same manner as Josephus assumed the name of Flavius from his attachment to Vespasian.

Leaving Paphos, Paul and his associates passed by sea to Perga, a city in Pamphylia situated on the river Cestros. At this place Mark left them, and returned to Jerusalem. From Perga, Paul and Barnabas pursued their way to Antioch, the chief city of Pisidia. Here Paul delivered the charming sermon recorded Acts xiii. 16—47. Many were converted to the faith. The Jews in this place " contradicting and blaspheming," Paul said " Lo, we turn to the gentiles." and from that moment ceased to confine his ministrations to the Jews only Driven from Pisidia by the spirit of persecution, they went and preached the gospel at Iconium, the chief city of Lycaonia. The town still subsists, and from its ancient name is called Cogni.

Aware that the people of this city were about to use them despitefully, and to stone them, they fled to Lystra and Derbe, and to the countries around Lycaonia. At Lystra, Lois, Eunice and Timothy became converted. Here, on the cure of a lame man, Paul and Barnabas were about to be worshipped as gods. Here too, so inconstant is human applause, Paul underwent the same affliction which, in the days of his ignorance, he rejoiced to see the martyr Stephen endure. His body was dragged out of the city; but as the disciples stood round him he arose, perfectly restored. Surrounding cities were visited, churches were established, and bishops and deacons were ordained by prayer and fasting. At length they came to Atalia, a seaport in the vicinity of Perga, and sailed for Antioch in Syria.

To this city they had not long returned before a question was agitated on the subject of circumcision, which determined the church to send Paul and Barnabas, with certain other persons, to consult the apostles at Jerusalem. This journey was performed by land Phenicia and Samaria heard of the conversion of the gentiles, and the hearts of the brethren were filled with joy. Having obtained the wished for decision, they returned again to Antioch. Having taught and preached the word for a considerable time in this celebrated city, Paul proposed the desire of his heart to Barnabas, " Let us go again and visit our brethren in every city where we have preached the gospel, and see how they do." Barnabas consented, but wished Mark to accompany them. This measure Paul disapproved, on which Barnabas took Mark and sailed for Cyprus, and Paul chose Silas to be his future companion.

With his new associate he " went through Syria and Cilicia, confirming the churches " Having visited Derbe and Lystra, whence Paul took Timothy as an assistant, they passed through Phrygia and the country of Galatia and the lesser Mysia, and came to Troas Troas was a seaport from which travellers frequently took shipping to Europe. While tarrying here a man of Macedonia appeared to Paul in a vision of the night, inviting him to cross the sea and help his unhappy countrymen. Satisfied of the design of the vision, Paul and his companions, to whom at Troas Luke the evangelist was added, sailed direct for the island Samothrace, and thence to Neapolis, one of the seaports of Macedonia. Philippi being a leading city in Macedonia, thither these heralds of the Cross first directed their way. One of the most amiable of the primitive churches was planted and flourished in this city

Our limits forbid a detail of the adverse and prosperous events which attended these ancient missionaries, as they continued their successive course through Aphipolis, Apollonia, Thessalonica, Berea, Athens and Corinth. They are detailed at large in the Acts of the Apostles. On leaving Corinth he went with Aquila and Priscilla by sea to Ephesus, and thence to Jerusalem.

Having kept the passover, our apostle again visits the Syrian Antioch, traverses the country of Galatia and Phrygia, and passing the upper coasts arrives once more at Ephesus, where he staid a considerable time. From Ephesus he passed to Macedonia, and then journeyed westward as far as Illyricum on the gulf of Venice. Returning through Greece he preached the word of life in several of the islands of the Archipelago, and arrived again at Jerusalem, where the brethren received him with gladness.

Only a short time had the venerable man entered this degraded city, before a conspiracy was formed by the Jews to kill him. He was borne by night to Antipatris, and the day succeeding to Cæsarea, where he found his security connected with an appeal to Cæsar. It was resolved by Festus that Paul should be sent to Italy by sea, with other prisoners, who had probably appealed as did the apostle. Luke and Aristarchus resolved to accompany him and share his distresses. At Melita he was saved amid the horrours of shipwreck. From Melita he went by sea to Puteoli, and afterwards by land to Rome. At this metropolis of the Latin empire he dwelt two years in his own hired house, and received all that came unto him. At the expiration of this period it is conjectured that Paul was released, that he returned by sea to Judea, that he visited the churches in the lesser Asia and in Macedonia, and finally returned with Titus to Rome. As to these latter ideas a diversity of sentiment exists. Dr. Wells says, " By some, he (the apostle) is said to have returned into Greece and the parts of Asia, upon no other ground, as is probably conjectured, than a few intimations in his epistles that he designed to do so."

Chrysostom states that Paul, going to see a cupbearer and a concubine of Nero, was a means of the concubine's conversion, and that this circumstance excited the emperor's indignation and fired his resentment. It is generally asserted by christian writers, that Paul suffered martyrdom in the 12th year of Nero's reign, A. D. 66, and that two years after the emperor Nero assassinated himself.

THE CREATION.

TO become acquainted, in some good degree, with the *origin of things*, is gratifying to the speculative, and profitable to the pious mind. We find ourselves in the midst of a vast universe. Around us roll thousands of stars, or more probably of suns,—centres, perhaps, of other systems, equal in dimensions and grandeur with our own. The globe itself which we inhabit, though a mere floating atom compared with the immensity of creation, presents to the reflecting mind a stupendous scene. A body of between twenty and thirty thousand miles circumference, performing annually its journey round an orbit of at least one hundred and eighty-five millions of miles diameter, winding at the same time its diurnal rounds, and bearing along with it as it flies, its mountains and forests, its isles and its continents, its rivers and its oceans, millions of irrational animals, and millions of men, offers a display which excites awe by its vastness, and delight by its simplicity.

But the questions arise, How came this earth into being? What power gave birth to those innumerable orbs, which

———the clear concave of a winter's night
Pours on the eye or astronomic tube?

To have resort to the opinions and decisions of the heathen, whether enlightened by science or degraded by savageness, whether ancient or modern, is to enter the dominions of absurd conjecture. One philosopher declares the world never had a beginning, another that its origin results from a fortunate concurrence of kindred atoms. Lucretius describes animals as coming up from the ground like plants. Sanchoniatho insists that the first principle of the universe was air; that air produced mud, mud senseless animals, and these were the parents of men: while Anaximander cannot doubt but that men were engendered in the intestines of fishes.

From these we turn, and find in the Holy Scriptures a rational, succinct, and sublime description of the whole. The first sentence of the Bible conveys a mass of information. "In the beginning God created the heavens and the earth." "In the first page of this book," says Dr. Fuller, "a child may learn more in an hour, than all the philosophers in the world learned without it in a thousand ages." The author of this vast work is God. He produced the whole by the agency of his Word and his Spirit. No other cause is equal to it. *Nothing* could never have given birth to the creation, or to a being who might create. The raising of the vast fabric is uniformly attributed, in the sacred pages, to the divine Architect alone. He is called " the Creator of the ends of the earth." —" The moon and the stars are the work of his fingers. The sea is his, and he made it, and his hands formed the dry land. It is He that hath made *us*, and not we ourselves.' Surveying the exactness and harmony, the variety and sublimity, the beauties and mysteries of creation, we may, with Milton, sing,

> These are thy glorious works, Parent of Good!
> Almighty! Thine this universal frame,
> Thus wond'rous fair! Thyself how wond'rous, then,
> Unspeakable!

The detail of creation is intended not to gratify the impertinence of the curious, but to inform the humble and inquiring mind. It imparts all the information it is of importance that we possess, and there it ends. Written for the use of the inhabitants of this globe, it acquaints us but little with the formation of the heavenly bodies, and still less of the creation of angels. The primary acts of God in this great work appear to have been of a general nature, a chaos of darkness and a chaos of light preceding the formation of the earth and the orbs of heaven. " The earth was without form and void," without order and inhabitant, " and darkness was upon the face of the deep." " The Spirit of God moved," or brooded, as a bird over its nest, " upon the face of the waters."

The FIRST day was distinguished by the creation of light, and the dividing of the light from the darkness. Light, as it existed before the forming of the sun and moon, has been supposed to have appeared like the cloud in the wilderness, not however limited to one place, but revolving in a lucid body around the forming globe. Longinus, the renowned secretary of Zenobia, admires the manner in which Moses records this part of the Creator's work, and produces it as an instance of the real sublime. "God said, let there be light, and there was light." " He spake, and it was done; He commanded, and it stood fast." We are informed that " God saw the light that it was good:" good, because it supplies so fair an emblem of the Creator himself, and because it is the medium by which the earth is cherished, and its landscapes discovered. Of the value of light we may form some idea from the ecstasies of those who have recovered from a state of blindness. Mr. Boyle mentions a case of a young man who, restored to sight, was almost distracted with transport. On the contrary, Homer, Ossian, and other celebrated poets, have described the calamity of blindness in the most impressive terms. Milton thus deplores his affliction:

> "O loss of sight, of thee I most complain!
> —————————O worse than chains,
> Dungeon, or beggary, or decrepit age!
> Scarce half I seem to live, dead more than half!
> O dark, dark, dark, amid the blaze of noon
> Irrecoverably dark! total eclipse,
> Without all hope of day!
> O first-created beam, and thou great word,
> *Let there be light!* and light was over all,
> Why am I thus bereav'd thy prime decree?
> Thy sun to me is dark!"

"The evening and the morning were the first day." The Hebrews afterwards called a day an evening-morning, and the Greeks a night-day. With different nations their day is begun at different hours. The Jews continue to commence theirs with the evening, and the order of Jehovah in forming first the darkness, and afterwards the light, appears to justify their habit. Mr. Henry observes that "this was not only the first day of the world, but also the first day of the week. I observe it to the honour of that day, because in the resurrection of Christ, early in the morning of the first day of the week, as the light of the world, the new creation began. In him," he adds, "the day-spring from on high hath visited us; and happy are we, for ever happy, if that day-star arise in our hearts." It had been easy for God to have formed this universe in an instant. The six days he devoted to the work, provide us with an opportunity of distinctly and carefully contemplating the labours of each.

On the SECOND day the Lord made all that is discernible between the surface of the globe and the starry heavens. He said "Let there be a firmament in the midst of the waters, and let it divide the waters from the waters." By the firmament or expansion may be intended our atmosphere. Rising to the height of forty-five miles, and stretched all round the earth, it is the element of vegetable and animal life. By the different degrees of rarefaction and condensation it experiences, it produces the gentle zephyr, with its "silken wing," and the roaring storm which breaks the cedars and overturns the deep. This expanse is designed to "divide the waters from the waters," to separate the fountains and rivers, the lakes and oceans, from the clouds. Solomon, referring to this part of the work of the Creator, says, "He established the clouds above, he strengthened the fountains of the deep." Clouds are produced by an association of the vapours which are raised from the surface of the earth or ocean by the action of the sun. They continue their flight, until, becoming heavier than the sustaining air, they fall in fruitful and reviving showers

The Jews have a remark, more ingenious than convincing, that on the second day God created the devil and his angels, because the work of this day is not pronounced good: but the truth is, he made satan and his associates angels of light, and all very good. Their crimes alone transformed them into demons.

The THIRD day is memorable for the dividing of the land from the water, and for the production of vegetation. The land, which was before buried under the deep, now appears, and the congregated waters occupy an appointed place. To convey to our minds an idea of the infinite ease with which the ocean was placed in its vast bed, Jehovah says, alluding to a parent laying a babe to rest, " I made the cloud the garment thereof, and thick darkness a swathing band for it; and brake up for it my decreed *place*, and set bars and doors; and said, hitherto shalt thou come, and no further, and here shall thy proud waves be stayed." God called the dry land earth, and the gathering together of the waters called he seas. As yet the sea was without a living creature, and the land without a single plant. The earth was no more *without form*: it was the pleasure of God that it should remain no longer *void*. He said, " Let the earth bring forth grass, the herb yielding seed, and the fruit-tree yielding fruit after its kind, whose seed is in itself upon the earth, and it was so." Then was the soil

"With sudden greens and herbage crown'd,
And waters murmur'd all around;"

an instant and beautiful reverse of the preceding chaos. Flowers and shrubs, the grass and the grain, obdurate oaks, and impurpled vines, displayed their gay variety. From the expressions the herb yielding *seed*, and the fruit-tree *fruit*, it has been conjectured that time began its course at the period of our autumnal equinox.

The lights, or enlighteners, as the word imports, in the firmament of heaven, were formed on the FOURTH day. The greater lamp to rule the day, and the lesser to rule the night. The astronomer teaches that the moon, from its nearness to us, and the sun, from its real magnitude, being more than one hundred and fifty times larger than our earth, deserve to be called great lights. Of other heavenly bodies no more is said than he made " the stars also." The design and use of these orbs are stated merely in relation to man. They are for *signs*. Not for *astrological* ones, for such God commanded Israel not to regard, but for *ecclesiastical* signs: by these the Jews regulated their new moons, and other solemn feasts: for *miraculous* signs; the standing still of the sun and moon, and the retrograde course of the shadow on the dial of Ahaz, were to Joshua and Hezekiah assurances of victory and restoration. They were for *nautical* signs: before the discovery of the polarity of the magnetic needle, the seaman was guided over the waters by the sun and stars: for *agricultural* signs; the husbandman finds his interest connected with a careful discernment of the face of the sky. Sometimes they supply *portentous* signs. Our Lord foretold the overthrow of Jerusalem, by fearful sights and signs from heaven. They are " for seasons, for days, and for years." The approach of the sun toward his northern solstice produces, with us, *summer*, and towards the southern, *winter*. The revolution of the earth on its axis forms a *day*, the course of the moon round the earth a *month*, and the journey of both round the central sun, a *year*.

On the FIFTH day God said " Let the waters bring forth abundantly." On which fishes began to cleave the deep, and fowls the air. The desolate atmosphere and sea became replenished with inhabitants, whose generations are continued as well for the entertainment as the support of man.

The SIXTH and LAST day witnessed the birth of the cattle, the creeping thing, and the beast. These were formed from the earth, as were the fowl and the fishes from the water. God made them all after their kind. " Some to be tame about the house; others to be wild in the fields, some for man's service, and not his sustenance, as the horse: others for his sustenance, and not his service, as the sheep; others for both, as the ox, and some for neither, as the lions and wolves of the forest."

Last of all man was created. His formation is represented as the result of divine counsels. It was not said, " Let there be man," but " Let us make man." This noblest inhabitant of the world was fashioned after the image of God. His body is erect, and not prone like the beasts. His soul bears some resemblance to his Maker, in that it is spiritual, invisible, immortal. The likeness is seen in his station: he was a stranger to sorrow, and clothed with dominion " over the fish of the sea, and over the fowl of the air, and over every living thing that moveth upon the earth." From him the creatures received their names. Especially he bore the likeness of God in the rectitude and holiness of his nature. He was made of the dust of the ground, and is for this reason said to be " of the earth, earthy." When the beautiful statue was perfected, God breathed into it the breath of life, and man became a living soul. Adam was created with dispositions favourable to social intercourse. As perfect solitude must have been alike inconsistent with the design of God and the happiness of the man, from his side, as he lay sleeping, he formed the woman, to be the partner of his toils and the associate of his felicities. The goodness of God appears in his providing a world for man before he gave him birth. It is also a pleasing reflection that Christ Jesus has ascended to heaven to accomplish for his disciples what God did for our first parent—*the preparation of a place*. The process of the creation suggests a gradation in the value of life. First mere matter is formed—then vegetables—afterwards irrational animals—and finally men. To the beasts and fowls God gave every green herb for meat, and to man every herb and every fruit tree. Possibly before the fall neither herb nor fruit possessed poisonous qualities.

"Thus the heavens and the earth were finished, with all the host of them." The Supreme Architect, who, in the presence of the sons of the morning, laid the foundation, now brings forth the topmost stone. The great Creator, resting from his work on the seventh day, has sanctified it, and ordained its observance as a day of rest through the generations of time. It is our duty to keep holy one day in seven to God. Its violation, in this world or in a future, will be followed with tokens of his displeasure. Both man and beast find or ought to find it a day of rest, while its devotional exercises render it the fairest emblem of that everlasting Sabbath enjoyed by saints and seraphim in heaven.

EXTRACT

THERE is a limit, across which man cannot carry any one of his perceptions, and from the ulterior of which he cannot gather a single observation to guide or to inform him. While he keeps by the objects which are near, he can get the knowledge of them conveyed to his mind through the ministry of several of the senses. He can feel a substance that is within reach of his hand. He can smell a flower that is presented to him. He can taste the food that is before him. He can hear a sound of certain pitch and intensity; and, so much does this sense of hearing widen his intercourse with external nature, that, from the distance of miles, it can bring him in an occasional intimation.

But of all the tracks of conveyance which God has been pleased to open up between the mind of man, and the theatre by which he is surrounded, there is none by which he so multiplies his acquaintance with the rich and the varied creation on every side of him, as by the organ of the eye. It is this which gives to him his loftiest command over the scenery of nature. It is this by which so broad a range of observation is submitted to him. It is this which enables him, by the act of a single moment, to send an exploring look over the surface of an ample territory, to crowd his mind with the whole assembly of its objects, and to fill his vision with those countless hues which diversify and adorn it. It is this which carries him abroad over all that is sublime in the immensity of distance, which sets him, as it were, on an elevated platform, from whence he may cast a surveying glance over the arena of innumerable worlds, which spreads before him so mighty a province of contemplation, that the earth he inhabits, only appears to furnish him with the pedestal on which he may stand, and from which he may descry the wonders of all that magnificence which the Divinity has poured so abundantly around him. It is by the narrow outlet of the eye, that the mind of man takes its excursive flight over those golden tracks, where, in all the exhaustlessness of creative wealth, he scattered the suns, and the systems of astronomy. But, oh! how good a thing it is, and how becoming well, for the philosopher to be humble even amid the proudest march of human discovery, and the sublimest triumphs of the human understanding, when he thinks of that unscaled barrier, beyond which no power, either of eye or of telescope, shall ever carry him: when he thinks that on the other side of it, there is a height, and a depth, and a length, and a breadth, to which the whole of this concave and visible firmament dwindles into the insignificancy of an atom! And above all, how ready should he be to cast his every lofty imagination away from him, when he thinks of the God, who, on the simple foundation of his word, has reared the whole of this stately architecture, and by the force of his preserving hand, continues to uphold it, ay, and should the word again come out from him, that this earth shall pass away, and a portion of the heavens which are around it shall again fall back into the annihilation from which he at first summoned them, what an impressive rebuke does it bring on the swelling vanity of science, to think that the whole field of its most ambitious enterprises may be swept away altogether, and there remain before the eye of him who sitteth on the throne, an untravelled immensity, which he hath filled with innumerable splendours, and over the whole face of which he hath inscribed the evidence of his high attributes, in all their might, and in all their manifestation!

Dr. Chalmers.

THE IMPORTANCE OF HAVING DIVINE REVELATION COMMITTED TO WRITING.

IN the early ages of the world, when the life of man was in many instances protracted to nearly a thousand years, the necessity of a written declaration of the will of God was not so importunate as in following generations. Had some special revelation, for example, been made to Adam, and the same announced to the world by Abraham, the mediums through which such information had passed would be found to be so few as to impair, in but a small degree, the validity of the testimony. Abraham was cotemporary with Shem, Shem with Methuselah, and Methuselah with Adam. But when human life became abridged to seventy years, oral tradition must necessarily slide through too many individuals to secure to itself respect and confidence.

Important as is the art of writing in the circles of science, of friendship, and of commerce, it is not improbable that the divine Being permitted the discovery, and facilitated its improvement in the first instance, that it might become the channel of his will to man. The most ancient writings in the world are those of Moses, and the first laws ever uttered in writing were impressed on tablets of stone by the finger of Jehovah himself. Moses was commanded to write the institutes and history of his nation in a book. Future prophets had similar instructions. To each, as to Isaiah, Jehovah seemed to say, "Now go write it before them in a table, and note it in a book, that it may be for the time to come, for ever and ever."

The Lord Jesus, in the discharge of his prophetic function, wrote not any thing, but his apostles and other disciples, under the inspiration of the Spirit of God, at an early period composed the biography of their Master, and directed their invaluable epistles to the brethren and the churches that were scattered abroad. A written revelation depends not on the frail and uncertain recollection of mortals It precludes all those additions or suppressions which caprice, or malice, or interest might occasion. It presents not truth to the mind in parcels disconnected and mutilated, but as a perfect and harmonious whole. Like the ocean it distributes its riches through all the climes of the earth, and like the orb of day maintains its effulgence through every generation.

A written communication from heaven is highly valuable, for if it give the infidel a fair opportunity of raising objections, it affords the christian abundant means for refuting them. It is capable of being perused again and again, so that what is not comprehended at one reading, may be understood at another. This holy record will talk with the good man by the way, and be found a companion in solitude, a comforter in sorrow, a guide in perplexity, a clue that conducts to the gates of paradise.

Nations have found it absolutely requisite to commit their laws to writing. The institutors of false religions have adopted the same measure, probably in imitation of the true prophets of God. It is reasonable to conclude that the doctrines, and the duties, and the consolations of the gospel, designed not for a single nation, but for all the earth, should be communicated in a mode the most easy, plain, convincing and permanent, and such is writing.

If it be objected that errours may easily insinuate themselves into copies of the scripture which at first were perfectly correct, it may be answered, that such errours could not have found place before the christian era, for the Jews were such faithful guardians of the sacred deposite that they enumerated even the words and the letters of inspiration. To them were committed the oracles of God, and they kept them with a vigilance and jealousy which, while it illustrates the wisdom and faithfulness of Jehovah, deserves the grateful remembrance of the whole world. After the introduction of the gospel, interpolation would have been found impracticable, had it been attempted. The Jew would have watched the conduct of the Christian, and the Christian the Jew, while the different sects that arose in christendom would operate as a safe and constant check on each other.

As to the circumstance that the revealed will of God reaches thousands only through the channel of a translation, it will be remembered that this, though an unavoidable inconvenience, invalidates not the blessed testimony. Translations are usually made by pious, learned, and disinterested men. Besides, the originals are at hand, by which the correctness of any version of the scriptures may be tested.

We are not left to decipher the pleasure of our God from characters in rocks which time has defaced. It is not ours to search for it in memorials raised by the hand of pious gratitude. Bethels and Ebenezers may be removed, or perish. We have not to learn our religion from the vain traditions received from our fathers. The best of volumes is introduced into our hands, and the voice from heaven to us, as to Augustine, is, Tolle, lege; Take, read.

THE JEWS.

AT a period when the spread of the kingdom of the Redeemer is an object of universal concern among christians, every idea should be cherished, calculated to feed the hallowed flame. The exertions now in operation for the conversion of the Jews are vigorous and praise worthy. To that wonderful nation, professors of the gospel are under greater obligations than they may at first imagine. Our divine Lord taught the Samaritan woman that salvation is of the Jews. The Jewish history occupies a large portion of Divine revelation, and is a medium through which the depravity of the human heart and the attributes of Jehovah are disclosed to mankind. The passovers and pentecosts, the altars and victims, which exhibited in shadow the future character and excellencies of the gospel were all Jewish. Jewish priests and sovereigns supplied the fairest types of the great Messiah. Prophets almost exclusively were Jews. The Son of God, in human nature, was the descendant of a Jewess. Among Jews he fulfilled his ministry, and made choice of Jews to be his disciples, and to bear the tidings of salvation to the ends of the earth. The fall,—the diminishing,—the casting away of the Jews, has been "the riches of the gentiles, and the reconciling of the world;" what then shall "their fulness—the receiving of them be, but life from the dead?" The examples of meekness, piety, and fortitude, which are presented in the New Testament, are commonly deduced from the character of Jewish fathers, and the grand scenery of heaven itself in the Revelation of John, is laid in the Jewish metropolis and temple. The root of Jesse is now standing for an ensign of this people. Soon, we trust, shall he "assemble the outcasts of Israel, and gather together the dispersed of Judah from the four corners of the earth." Let gentiles, with pleasure expect, and with ardour facilitate, the approach of the glorious day.

CONVERSION OF THE JEWS.

THAT the descendants of *the father of the faithful* are not always to remain in unbelief, appears certain from the promises of God, and that the time of their conversion is near, appears in a great degree probable, from the present state and operations of Divine Providence. Under these impressions it is not a little gratifying to observe the efforts which christians are now making in relation to this scattered people. The committee of the "*London Society for promoting Christianity among the Jews,*" near the close of a very interesting Report, remark,

"ON a general view of the communications from abroad, the committee conclude: 1. That a spirit of religious inquiry is spreading itself among the Jews in various and widely distant parts of the globe; in Holland, in Germany, in Prussia, in Tartary, in India:— 2. That among considerable bodies of the Jewish nation, especially in the northern provinces of continental Europe, even where little of the genuine spirit of christian truth has yet begun to operate, circumstances have recently occurred, which indicate a general diminution of prejudice, and a gradual removal of those barriers which have hitherto precluded the friendly approach of christianity:—and, 3. That christians are every where beginning to take a more lively interest in the spiritual state of the Jews; that men of piety in opposite hemispheres, without any communication with each other, or with this society, have been excited, at one and the same time, to compassion and exertion in behalf of the scattered descendants of Abraham."

The committee justly ask, in conclusion, "Whence originate these simultaneous independent movements, but with Him from whom " all good counsels and all just works do proceed," and who, in the plenitude of his wisdom, and in the greatness of his condescension, sees fit to employ human agents in accomplishing the purposes of his goodness?"

ON THE STATE OF THE JEWS AT JERUSALEM,

Mr. Burckhardt thus writes.—"The Jews of Jerusalem are under seven chiefs, called procurators or deputies, who are nominated by the Jews themselves. These persons settle causes at law among their countrymen. A Jew, desirous of buying a hebrew New-Testament, did not venture to do so till he had shown it to one of the procurators. Their religious affairs, in general, are under the government of the rabbis, who had formerly the right of nominating the rabbis of the neighbouring towns; but, for about 20 years past, this practice has ceased.

"It is said that the total number of Jews amounts to 12,000: but this varies, as many of the Jews come to Jerusalem to stay only for a limited time. Among the Jews are many old men, as people advanced in age come from all parts of the world to die there, hoping to escape certain pains after death, which they suppose to be remitted to them who finish their days in the holy land."

MISSION TO JERUSALEM.

IN the course of the last autumn, the prudential committee of *the American Board of Commissioners for Foreign Missions*, determined, under the favour of Providence, to send a mission to western Asia, with a view to its ultimate establishment at Jerusalem. Two of the missionaries of the Board, the Rev. Levi Parsons and the Rev. Pliny Fisk, were assigned to that service.

No sooner was this mission announced, than it was hailed by the religious public as a most interesting effort, and one which might be the means, not only of conveying the Gospel to Jews and Mahomedans, but of awakening many among ourselves to the duties of the times. Let the hearts of Christians be intent on the contemplated mission; let their prayers ascend for a blessing upon it, and, it may be, that He, who has the hearts of all men under his control, will bestow upon it the marks of his gracious approbation, and make it the commencement of a great and glorious display of his grace

[PANOPLIST

THE CROISADES.

THE expeditions bearing the above denomination, were designed to recover Palestine from the possession of heretics and infidels The name was derived from the circumstance that the professed object was to rescue the cross of Christ from supposed dishonour, and because the soldiers wore on their shoulders consecrated crosses of various colours; the Italians preferring yellow, the Germans black, the Flemish green, the French red, and the English white.

Curiosity to see the country where the Lord Jesus lived and suffered; an idea that there was something meritorious in such a journey; an expectation that at the end of a thousand years from his resurrection, Christ would come again to judge the world; a sense of indignation that the holy land should be under the yoke of Mahometans, whose treatment of christian pilgrims was cruel and vexatious; and the immunities granted to those who assumed the cross, were among the considerations that gave rise to a crusading spirit. Nine successive invasions were attempted; but they brought little to the projectors and executors of so extravagant a plan, except defeat and mortification, misery and death.

New expeditions are now contemplated, not for the purposes of destruction, but salvation. No clangour of arms, no military policy is about to ensanguine the soil once trodden by the foot of the Prince of Peace. Missionaries of Christ, bearing the cross in the affections of the heart, and in their public addresses, are visiting the promised land. It is still the land of promise;—there the glorious Lord will be to thousands " a place of broad rivers and streams "

In the year 1095, pope Urban, in the presence of his cardinals and prelates, and of assembled thousands, from an elevated scaffold, recommended the recovery of Jerusalem and Judea. He was unable to proceed in his oration. The multitudes with one voice exclaimed, " *Deus vult—Deus vult.*"—" God wills it—God wills it." " It is indeed the will of God," replied the pope, " and let this memorable word, the inspiration surely of the Holy Spirit, be for ever adopted as your cry of battle, to animate the courage and devotions of the champions of Christ." It is unnecessary to observe how much the motto " *Deus vult,*" rescued as it now is from the follies of superstition, and the rage of resentment, ought to animate all who acknowledge Jesus their Lord, and who pray for the approach of his kingdom. The crusaders, after the efforts of two hundred years, were covered with disappointment and shame; the missionaries of Christ must ultimately succeed, for the God of salvation is on their side. The anticipation is perhaps as really sanctioned by the indications of the scripture, as it is animating and joyous, that in less than two hundred years, not only Judea, but all the earth, shall see the salvation of God.

JEWISH SCHOOL AT BOMBAY.

From the Rev. Gordon Hall to the Secretary of the Female Society of Boston and the vicinity, for the propagation of Christianity among the Jews,

DEAR MADAM,   Bombay, April 1, 1818.

IN behalf of my brethren of the Bombay mission, I have the happiness of acknowledging the receipt of your letter of Oct. 2, 1817, apprizing us of the appropriation of *one hundred dollars* by your society towards the support of the Jewish school under our care in Bombay. The money has been duly received through Mr. Evarts, for which we desire you will present our most cordial thanks to the society; assuring them that we feel a high pleasure at the formation of such a society, and that it will be our delight to apply the money already appropriated, or any other sums which they may see fit to appropriate, agreeably to their wishes.

We have much pleasure in stating, for the information of the society, that the Jewish school was commenced in May last. About forty Jewish boys soon entered it, and the number has continued, without essential variation, until now. The boys are from six to eighteen years of age. Some of them remain but a few months in the school, others a longer time.

Soon after the formation of the school, the ten commandments, and other moral precepts and lessons were given to the boys, all in the Mahratta language, which is best understood by them. A hymn also was given them, expressive of repentance for sin, faith in Christ as the only Saviour of sinners, praise to him, and a desire that all may know and praise him. More or less of these are daily read, and repeated in the school; and not unfrequently a number of the adult

Jews are present, who must receive some christian instruction from what they hear.

As soon as the gospel of Matthew and our religious tracts were printed, they were introduced into the school, and as yet there is no objection to any thing, which we have proposed to teach the boys We say *boys*, because in this country it is never expected that *girls* will be taught to read or write.

The school is instructed by a Jew about forty years of age, from *Choule*, a large town on the coast, twenty-five miles south from Bombay. But few among the Jews so well understand the Mahratta language as this man. His brother, from the same place, teaches the school which we have established among the outcasts of the Hindoos, called *Mhars*. It will be interesting to the society to know, that numbers of the Jews in Bombay have solicited and received copies of the gospel of Matthew, and that copies have also been sent to the Jews in Choule.

Though we see nothing particularly encouraging at present, still we indulge the hope, that we may live to see some of these branches, long ago broken off through unbelief, again grafted into the true olive.

The whole expense of this school, as now conducted, will be about 100 dollars a year, subject to some small additions for school books in future. Perhaps it may be the wish of your society to take the entire patronage of this interesting school. Any communication on this subject we shall receive with much pleasure.

That God may at all times direct, encourage and bless you in your every attempt to promote the knowledge of Christ, and the salvation of sinners, is our united and fervent prayer.

[PANOPLIST

WORTHY OF IMITATION

THE following communication has been published in the BOSTON RECORDER and in the WEEKLY RECORDER, and perhaps in other periodical papers. Some, at least, it is to be hoped, on reading pieces of this kind, will form the resolution to imitate the conduct which they describe, and if all would *go and do likewise*, no doubt they would promote their own happiness, besides conferring benefits on others. "*But do good and lend,—and great shall be your reward in heaven*" Nor is it difficult to point out the object to which such savings and donations may conveniently be applied The Board of Missions have an INDIAN SCHOOL in Kentucky, in which the children and youth of the natives are receiving education. It will not be difficult to furnish an estimate of the annual cost of the education of each, on an average; and many an individual could easily spare enough from luxury, or from gains, to defray annually the expense of educating one young Indian. Or, should it be preferred, such aid may be employed in supporting the schools established among the tribes. Or, to promote the same benevolent design in Burmah, for the missionaries there, as soon as practicable, will institute schools for the instruction of the youth Or, to mention one thing more, the Board have in charge *an Institution for promoting the education of the ministry* Young men who, in the judgment of the churches of which they are members, are called of God to this momentous service, are pursuing a course of preparatory study, the more fully to qualify them as *able ministers of the New Testament—workmen that need not to be ashamed, rightly dividing the word of truth* O how much sweeter and happier would be the reflection *in a dying hour* of having supported, out of love to Christ, if it were but one of his servants, through a course of education, that he might more beneficially employ his talents in edifying the church, or in preaching the gospel to the heathen, than the memory of expensive indulgences and useless finery! Ah, think of the estimate which these things will bear amid the scenes of the GREAT DAY!

EXTRACT—*Snuff and Segars*

Mr. Willis,—Some time last summer, being on a visit to a worthy family, which, by the will of God, had been reduced from affluence to straitened circumstances, and expatiating on the great things now doing in the world, for the spread of the Redeemer's kingdom, the good lady of the house expressed a wish to give her mite, but regretted that she had nothing to spare. I hinted, that we should not make a plea of poverty so long as we indulged in any one luxury, and that a mite, accompanied with the sacrifice of some sensual gratification, was more acceptable to God than whole burnt offerings and large donations from those who gave only what they enjoy, and of which they feel not the loss; and that if she gave to some pious use, the few shillings she expended for *snuff*, she could not tell what good it might do. I thought no more of it. But a few months afterwards, on another visit to the same house, I was astonished to find that the old lady had totally quitted the practice of taking snuff, of which she had been immoderately fond, and had resolved to appropriate the amount she had annually expended in that article to a pious use. What a sacrifice, considering the inveteracy of habits retained to old age! It is astonishing that I did not profit by the example: but this morning, while reading the Recorder, the event again occurred to my mind, and I could not help making the application to myself. By the blessing of God, my temporal circumstances and my wishes not being very far apart, what I give I do not feel, especially as I have no children, and therefore I make no *sacrifice* for the honour of God, or the good of man. But I am now resolved to practise by the good lady's example. I spend ten dollars a year for segars. I will quit the practice, and apply the money to a good use—I had so resolved—but to what use? Your paper (or God by your means) directs me. Twelve dollars a year will educate a heathen child. Be it so; I will add two dollars more to the segars. I have the means of an easy communication to Ceylon. Messrs. Meigs and Poor, shall educate a heathen youth at my expense. (I have just made the necessary arrangement.) He shall bear the name of good Mrs. ——— She shall not leave off her snuff for nothing. Perhaps it will be the means of raising another Obookiah. What a tree of righteousness from a grain of mustard seed! Perhaps this communication may induce others to do likewise. What a forest! Perhaps many, by these means educated, may be evangelists to their nations. How shall the wilderness rejoice and blossom as the rose! And then *eternity!* Oh, how much better the bare *perhaps*, than all the tobacco in the world!

[RECORDER

MISSIONARY INTELLIGENCE.—FOREIGN.

MISSION TO BURMAH

Extract of a letter from Mr Wheelock to his parents, dated

MY DEAR PARENTS,   Rangoon, October 7, 1818.

WE were detained at Calcutta four months, anxiously waiting for a passage to Rangoon. Our voyage to Rangoon, where we arrived the 19th Sept. was short and pleasant. The captain and his officers, though far from being serious, treated us politely; and we were furnished with every thing comfortable. At the mouth of the river, we were favoured with a note from brother Judson, informing us that brother Hough or himself would be ready to receive us at the wharf, or more properly, the landing place.—Judge of our feelings when we arrived before the town, which is to be, as we trust, our home on earth!—We were all soon landed, and in the company of our *dear* missionary friends. What a meeting was this! Never before did I experience such a joyful season. To behold our beloved brethren, and their companions, afforded me such pleasure as I cannot express! Indeed, the joy was mutual. We felt our souls united. After we had been searched by the officers of government, we, a happy missionary band, proceeded to the mission-house. Here we arrived about dark on Saturday evening. "Bless the Lord, O my soul, and all that is within me, bless his holy name!"

The mission-house is delightfully situated among the trees, about two miles from town. A large piece of ground is attached to it, containing a number of fruit trees. The house is large and commodious, well constructed for two families, so that at present brother Colman and myself have only one room each. We however are comfortably situated, as we live with brother Judson. We prefer *one* room in Rangoon, to *six* in Boston. We feel that we are *highly* blessed.

Shortly after our arrival, brother Judson, went with brother Colman and myself to introduce us to the viceroy. We found him in his garden house, surrounded with his officers of government. We took off our shoes before we came into his presence, (which is the same thing here as taking off the hat in America,) and then seated ourselves on a mat opposite him. He observed that we were not accustomed to the Burman mode of sitting, and said to brother Judson, "let them sit comfortable." We had brought with us from Calcutta, a small chest of carpenters' tools, for the use of the mission. The viceroy heard of it, and expressed a desire for it. As there never was one like it seen here before, it was a great curiosity. We carried it with us as a present, knowing that he must have it. Accordingly it was placed before him, and he arose himself, (a thing very uncommon on such occasions,) and opened it. He appeared much gratified with it, and called one of his artificers to examine it also. He inquired if we intended to remain here, and had brought our women? Mr Judson observed that we had, and that "we wished to take shelter beneath his glory." To which he answered, "Stay! stay!" and desired that Mrs Judson might come with our women. Business being entirely suspended, while we remained, he appeared to desire our departure. We therefore again paid him our respects, and retired, much gratified with the favour shown us, and which, we hope, through the overruling hand of our heavenly Father, will be continued.

The excessive heat of Bengal, combined with my exertions in private and public, considerably enervated my system. My extreme sea-sickness reduced me still lower. But after my arrival at Rangoon I forgot my weakness, and exerted myself *too much* in attending to our affairs, the difficulty of which can only be known by experience. And the Saturday evening following the evening of our arrival, after engaging in family worship, I was attacked with a slight return of raising blood. It was very unexpected and alarming at first. But in a few days I ceased to raise any more, and have now gained considerable strength in my lungs. Through divine mercy, I trust that I am getting better. Do you inquire, my dear parents, how I felt when thus afflicted? I did not feel as when in America. I thought that I had now certainly arrived in Burmah, and I felt less anxious about my sickness than formerly. I remembered that God had already gratified *one* of the *most ardent* desires of my soul; and, *at least*, I should have the great privilege of being *buried* in a heathen land—a privilege which I once feared I should never enjoy, and of which I am utterly unworthy. But my soul pitied the *poor* Burmans, and I longed, if it could consist with the will of God, to live a little while, that I might point them to "the Lamb of God." Blessed be his name that I have an encouraging prospect of returning health. I have a Burman teacher. I engaged him the 5th instant, and attempted to study, but was obliged to relinquish it. Harriet, however, employs him, and has now begun to read the Burman. I hope that, ere long, I shall be thus highly favoured.

From Mrs. Wheelock to a friend in the neighbourhood of Boston, dated Rangoon, October 23, 1818.

MY EVER DEAR MRS. B.

This country presents to the eye a scene truly picturesque and delightful. But instead of beholding houses dedicated to the worship of God, and being sur rounded by dear christian friends, a gloom is spread over it. our minds are filled with melancholy by viewing innumerable pagodas sacred to the memory of Guadama, and thousands who pay superstitious homage before them. Sometimes I can scarcely realize, that in a few months *so great* an alteration has been effected in my circumstances, prospects, and pursuits. It is not long, however, before I find myself awake to the certainty of it, and am, I trust, enabled to rejoice in all the privations, toils, and privileges, which result from so great a change. Though we have left the bosom of friendship and liberty, for that of enmity and despotism, we feel that God is not confined to places. Even here, amidst the darkness that covers the land, and gross darkness that covers the people, we are permitted to enjoy some sweet communications of his love; some seasons of refreshing from his presence, and to look forward to the time, when numbers of these captive souls will be liberated from their chains, and made kings and priests unto God

Our arrival at Rangoon apparently afforded much diversion to many of the Burmans. A sight of eight foreigners, and four of them newly arrived, was sufficient to collect most of the inhabitants together. Had you been a spectator of our meeting the dear friends here, I think you would have congratulated each of us. Brother Judson and brother Hough were waiting at the shore to receive us. After being searched at the custom house, they conducted us to the mission house, our long anticipated *home*. The situation is rural, and delightfully pleasant. I need not assure you that we experience the greatest possible gratification in enjoying the company of our friends, and that we daily offer unto God our thanksgivings, and praises, that we are brought to the heathen land. Our united desire is, to be useful to the souls of this perishing people. This is the object, the only object for which we left our native land. To accomplish this, we trust that we constantly have your prayers, and the prayers of all the dear people of God. "For Zion's sake" may christians not hold their peace; and for Jerusalem's sake may they not rest, "until the righteousness thereof go forth as brightness, and the salvation thereof as a lamp that burneth; until this desert shall rejoice, and blossom as the rose," and streams of living water, from the river of God, refresh this *parched* ground

Since our arrival, we have enjoyed the privilege of meeting around the sacramental board, and commemorating the dying love of our ascended Redeemer. And it was indeed a precious season. The Saviour's fruit was sweet to our taste, and his banner over us was love. In this benighted region, the ordinances of the gospel shine with redoubled lustre. Every thing around is calculated to inspire us with gratitude and love to our heavenly Father, and to incite us to activity in his blessed service.

From recent communications, you have probably received some information of the late difficulties here among the Roman catholic priests. Being represented to the king as spies for the English, they were instantly ordered out of the country. They however remain in Rangoon, through the favour of the present viceroy; and undoubtedly will continue to remain here, as their friends have collected a large sum of money, and sent it to the king with a petition. It is now generally understood that the order is countermanded, and will soon arrive here to the satisfaction of the petitioners. Had they been banished from the country, it is very likely that we should soon have been ordered away also. Under a tyrannical government, in a land filled with every abomination, among a people destitute of the common feelings of humanity, we feel ourselves safe only in the hands of God. An assurance in our own souls that he is indeed our father and our friend; that he regards this mission, and in his own time will bring some of these poor, deluded, superstitious Burmans to a saving acquaintance with himself, renders us happy in the midst of surrounding danger, and is a constant incentive to exertions for their eternal good. How inexpressibly happy should we be, if, within the narrow limits of our knowledge, there was one Burman whose heart had been regenerated, upon whose mind the celestial rays of the Sun of righteousness beamed, and whose thoughts and conversation were daily in heaven! Though we are wholly unacquainted with the manner, and the time in which God will display his glory in this part of the world, yet to him the precise way, the exact time is perfectly known. The period must arrive, when Jesus shall take to himself "the heathen for his inheritance, and the uttermost parts of the earth for his possession," when all nations shall worship him, and his name be adored from the rising to the setting sun. To persevere in the rugged path before us, we need a spirit of self denial, constant and large supplies of divine grace; great humility, and more ardent piety. That we may enjoy these invaluable blessings, permit me again to ask you to be importunate at the throne of mercy on our account, and be assured, though a fathomless expanse rolls between us, that you are daily remembered with much affection.

[AMERICAN BAPTIST MAGAZINE.]

Extract of a letter from the Rev. Dr. Carey, dated

MY DEAR BROTHER STAUGHTON,   Serampore, June 29, 1818.

It has long been my opinion that European brethren should be dispersed through all the country, so as to occupy each a circle of 100 miles or thereabouts diameter, in the centre of which the brother should reside, and would be able to journey from home fifty miles in every direction with tolerable ease. I recommend that native brethren, preachers, readers, &c. be stationed around him at convenient distances, to labour continually in preaching, reading the word, conversation, &c. and that the European brother superintend them, and strengthen their hands in the work. By this, or similar methods, for a general rule must admit of exceptions, a considerable degree of light may be spread through a wide extent of country by a few persons; and if a divine blessing accompany their labours, many souls may be converted. There are in Calcutta four of our brethren in the ministry, and two not in the ministry, but probably as active as those who are, besides two belonging to the London Society, and two evangelical clergymen.

Through divine mercy I am well. My dear wife enjoys but little health; she has from her youth been afflicted. Brethren Marshman and Ward are well; upon the whole the cause of our God prevails. The printing of the word of God goes forward as fast as so large and multifarious a work can be expected to go on. Schools meet with much support, and I trust are not the most ineffectual means of doing good to the people of this country. The natives of this country begin to become authors and publishers, and some periodical publications in the Bengalee language have been lately begun; these I consider as favourable circumstances.

Extract of a letter from the Junior brethren, dated

Calcutta, July 22, 1818.

In the Bengalee department we first mention schools, in which, indeed, at the date of our last letter, we hoped to have increased our exertions to a greater extent than we have yet been able to realize. It is our desire to enter pretty fully into exertions of this kind, which we shall do with the greatest confidence, a Mr Penny's intimate acquaintance with Mr Lancaster's system will enable us to apply, in the most efficient manner, the money with which we may be intrusted, while he and Mr Pearce are desirous of devoting to this object the whole of the time which remains from other engagements. Besides the two schools which we reported in our last communication, two new ones in populous parts of the city, for which we have taken ground, and are building houses, and one school under the superintendence of the brethren at Serampore, no other means of this kind are at present employed in connexion with the propagation of Christianity amongst the inhabitants of Calcutta.

We ought, however, never to forget that the preaching of the gospel is the means appointed by the Head of the church for the extension of his kingdom, and that which he has always honoured with the greatest success. In this part of missionary labour we are happy to say, that we have been enabled of late considerably to extend our efforts in the Bengalee. In two places of worship, the gospel is regularly preached once, and sometimes twice a week. Another, somewhat larger, which is in a state of considerable forwardness, we expect to occupy in the course of a fortnight; and as soon as ground, in eligible situations, can be obtained, we shall commence building three others. These, with our present number, will be quite sufficient to employ us, and to lead to such arrangements as will enable one, or another, to be amongst the Bengalees every day. Besides these daily services amongst the natives in Calcutta, Mr E Carey proposes, when the rains have ceased, to commence an annual itinerancy of two or three months continuance, through the province of Bengal, in different directions.

With respect to the success that has attended our labours amongst the natives, we cannot say much. It gives us, however, great pleasure to witness the spirit of hearing which has been excited, and the increasing attention which is given to the preaching of the gospel, so that in either of our places of worship we can always obtain a congregation of 50 or 60, generally upwards of 100, and sometimes approaching to 150 people, who, in most instances, listen with considerable attention, although in others there is a strong disposition to cavil and object. They generally afford, during the time they remain present, as serious an appearance as most English congregations. During the period of one service of two or three hours' continuance we have perhaps three perfectly different congregations, who are successively addressed by two, three, or four preachers. We have not, however, been entirely without encouragement.

In the English department we are still labouring with much the same success as when we last addressed you. Our congregation in the fort has gradually increased, and there are many pleasing appearances of the power of Divine grace in the 59th regiment. Our Calcutta Baptist Auxiliary Society will, we hope, ultimately be an efficient agent in accomplishing your benevolent plans in India. Its subscriptions at present amount to about 100 sicca rupees per month. This sum is small, it is true, and the Society itself has to struggle with difficulties, but we believe it is destined to live and to be a great blessing to the heathen around us. Two branch societies to this have been formed, one is amongst the heathen in Fort William; the other amongst the brethren of the 24th regiment at Dinapore. This last bids fair to be a flourishing one indeed.

GENERAL SURVEY OF BAPTIST MISSIONARY STATIONS.

THE following exhibition of the different stations under the direction of the English and Serampore brethren, taken from a recent Review of the Mission, cannot fail of gratifying our readers

AN idea having been formerly given of the geographical situation of the various stations and places where the gospel is made known, it may be best, perhaps, to follow the same order.

SERAMPORE, CALCUTTA *and its neighbourhood.* In this spot, which has been the scene of labour for twenty years, there is now an abundance of labourers, as nine have entered thereon since the last review; four brethren having arrived from Europe, three from the London, and two from the Church Missionary Society. This spot, therefore, twenty-four miles in length and about ten in breadth, at present enjoys the labours of fourteen brethren from Europe, besides those of three evangelical clergymen, who have the work of God as much at heart, and in mind and spirit are as really missionaries, as any of us. Of the nine of our own denomination, brethren Carey, Marshman, Ward, Randall and Pearce, are at Serampore,—and brethren Lawson, E. Carey, Yates and Penney, in Calcutta. In addition to these, there are, labouring in the same circle, a number of brethren raised up in the country, (the number of whom, blessed be God! is increasing every year,) who, from their superior knowledge of their vernacular tongue, their intimate acquaintance with the habits ideas of their countrymen, their being accustomed to the constant fatigue of walking in a climate congenial with their constitutions, and a variety of other circumstances, are far more adapted to the work of making known and explaining the gospel to small groups of their own countrymen, than Europeans, and have been generally more successful.

At CALCUTTA, preaching is continued in the chapel, four times on the Lord's day, as usual. The number of those who have been baptized at Calcutta since the last review, amounts to above ninety. Of these, the greater part have been soldiers from the fort, who have been added to the churches in their respective regiments the rest consist of catholics, nominal christians without any real religion, and natives. In this circle, about eight miles northwest of Calcutta, and about ten northeast of Serampore, lies Dum-Dum, a military station for the honourable company's regiment of artillery. Here, brethren Kymer, Hale, and Flatman, (the former baptized some time ago by brother Chamberlain, the two latter by brother Thompson,) being stationed for a season, about a year ago attempted to introduce the gospel among their countrymen. We therefore erected for them a mat place of worship, and some European brother has preached there, in general, every week. No less than nine have been baptized there in the course of the past year, of whom three belonged to this regiment of artillery, and the rest natives of India. The little church formed there consists of fourteen members

At BARRACKPORE, opposite Serampore, we have also had an opportunity of introducing the gospel, since the last review of the mission; and here also it has pleased God to bless the word, among both our own countrymen and those born in India. Of the former, several non-commissioned officers in the various native regiments occasionally stationed there, have opened their houses for worship, both on the Lord's day and in the days of the week. The effect has been, that in the past two years six or eight of our countrymen there, some of them considerably advanced in years, have, we trust, been brought savingly to the knowledge of the truth.

At SERAMPORE, the seat of so many years' labour, we are furnished with strong proofs of the truth of the necessity of that previous illumination, that general diffusion of knowledge, which, pervading the whole country, shall dispel its gross delusions, and free the mind from those fetters which even yet hold back the natives around from approaching sufficiently near the gospel to discern what it really contains. The whole number of persons baptized at Serampore since the last review is thirty-five.

About eight miles northwest of Serampore, at GUNDULPARA, our friend Tarachund now resides. This brother, ever since his baptism, (nearly five years,) has maintained a course of conduct highly honourable to the christian character, and has around him a number of intelligent young men, some of them brahmuns, who, attracted by the temper and spirit he manifests, as well as by his superior knowledge, voluntarily come to him for instruction; and with whom he meets and converses, at those seasons of leisure so amply afforded by an Asiatic life. These meetings are often prolonged till midnight, and tend exceedingly to diffuse abroad the light of the gospel.

JESSORE.—In this district the divine word seems to have taken root, although its progress is slow. The labours of brother Thomas, and of various native brethren, have not only spread a degree of general knowledge respecting the gospel, through many of its towns and villages; but have we trust been, in numerous instances, effectual to conversion—a goodly number having been baptized since the last review, and between twenty and thirty often sitting down at the Lord's table at one time.

Proceeding about a hundred miles further eastward, we come to DACCA, once the capital of Bengal. Here, since the last review, means have been found to introduce the light of divine revelation in a considerable degree. A school has been established for the instruction of those indigent children who bear the christian name, which has been encouraged beyond our expectation. The Jew Solomon, with his wife, long resident in Dacca, had heard the word of life from our friend who has established the school there for christian children; and, after counting the cost many months, both of them determined to make an open profession of faith in the promised Messiah, and were in consequence baptized by our friend.

A few miles from Dacca, there is a body of natives who have rejected entirely the laws of the brahmuns, and in a great measure the worship of the hindoo gods; but they still retain much of the prejudices respecting cast, and still more of those which connect sin with receiving certain kinds of food. Among these our native brethren have occasionally been, and some of them have visited our brethren at Dacca.

SILHET.—In the attempts which have been made to diffuse the rays of the gospel in this part, little has occurred of an encouraging nature. One of our brethren sent there, Bhagvat, died of a fever about eighteen months ago. His end was peaceful, and he had preserved the christian character unspotted to the time of his death, and was mentioned in terms of regard and esteem by the few European friends who knew him there. Brother Da Silva still remains there, and is well spoken of by those who are near.

CHITTAGONG.—At this station, scenes have occurred, since the last review, which have both filled us with joy and almost overwhelmed us with sorrow, scenes which have displayed the grace of the Saviour, and discovered alike the malice of the great enemy of the gospel, and the desperate malignity of the human heart. Bordering upon Chittagong is a large tract of country inhabited by the people termed Mugs, in reality natives of Arakan; who, in language, manners, and habits, assimilate with the Burmans, under whose government they were for many years; but, about twenty-four years ago, they voluntarily placed themselves under the British government. They have no cast, and are described, by a friend who lately travelled through a great part of their country, as being intelligent, and frank and kind in their manners. Some of these coming to Chittagong in the way of business, about two years ago, heard of our brother De Bruyn, then labouring among the inhabitants, and highly esteemed by them for his mild, inoffensive, and upright conduct. As some among them had acquired a sufficient knowledge of the language, they repaired to him to inquire what doctrine he was teaching. They soon heard sufficient to excite their attention. The news of a Saviour they communicated to their countrymen at home, and others soon came to hear the gospel. In a few months, two or three of them made an open profession of faith in Christ. The work advanced amidst all the opposition it met with from their own priests. More came forward and were baptized, and they at length pressed brother De Bruyn to come occasionally among them into their own country. This he did, and was welcomed in the most cordial manner. The work still went forward, more were added to the church, and the prospect of the gospel's spreading among these appeared brighter daily. Some of the baptized Mug brethren too, made a journey to Serampore, where they remained several weeks, and their conduct appeared fully to agree with the profession they had made of faith in Christ. The testimony also as to their walk and conversation, given by brethren Smith and William Carey, who both visited Chittagong, was highly favourable. And brother De Bruyn at length attempted to make arrangements for his spending great part of his time among these kind and inoffensive foreigners, of whom between sixty and seventy had now made a profession of faith in Christ.

The great enemy of souls, however, beheld with an evil eye, these attempts to rescue from his grasp those over whom he had so long tyrannized without opposition, and meditated a blow in a way little expected. Among those who came to brother De Bruyn for instruction, was a young man born at Rangoon, the son of a native of France and a Burman woman. This young man he had taken into his house, and treated as his own son, labouring to instruct him in the knowledge of christianity, in the hope of his being hereafter a useful instrument in making known the gospel. This young man, however, had latterly given him much concern by what he deemed improper conduct, and in the month of September last, some circumstance occurring, which, as far as we have been able to judge from the various accounts we have received, induced brother De Bruyn to reprove him with more severity than usual; satan, watching his opportunity, so inflamed the passions of this headstrong youth, that, seizing a knife, he plunged it into the side of his benefactor and friend; who, after languishing a day and a night, expired, not, however, before he had written to the judge of the court, excusing the rash deed of his murderer, and entreating that he might not be punished. His remains, captain M a friend residing there, informed us, were accompanied to the grave the next day by nearly all the European inhabitants, by whom he was held in high estimation, and who expressed the most feeling regret at his untimely end. Thus, about the fiftieth year of his age, were we suddenly deprived of a most useful as well as highly esteemed brother, who had patiently persevered in his work through evil report and good report, till it pleased God, at length, to crown his labours, beyond those of almost any brother yet engaged in the mission. Brother Peacock has since avowed his desire to go and settle there, and is ready to depart; so that we trust the Lord will yet provide for the continuance of his work among them.

Cutwa.—Here the word sown by the labours of brother Chamberlain, has since been watered by those of brother William Carey, jun. who has exerted himself much, both in journeying himself, and in sending out and watching over a considerable number of native brethren employed in the capacity of readers and itinerants. Ten have come forward since the date of the last review, and put on the Lord Jesus by being baptized in his name; of whom the far greater part have continued steadfast in the profession of the gospel, and two or three discover a desire to be useful to their own countrymen. Within these four months we have sent a brother of the name of Hart to the assistance of brother William Carey, that, by labouring under his immediate eye for a year or two, he may enter more thoroughly into the nature of missionary work, and be fitted to occupy a station alone.

Berhampore.—To this military station, where the 14th was for some time, and among whom the Lord was pleased to manifest his grace, a few brethren in the honourable company's European regiment are now removed, who have been called and formed into a church since the date of the last review. In this regiment a few were wrought upon at Berhampore, above two years ago, and brother Marshman, in a journey that way, having been previously informed of their state, and of their wish to put on the Lord Jesus by a public profession, after due examination baptized five soldiers belonging to that regiment, together with a native of Bengal, and afterwards formed them, with our brother Pran-krishna, into a church.

Moorshedabad.—About ten miles above Berhampore lies Moorshedabad, the capital of Bengal before the residence of the English government there raised Calcutta to that honour. This city contains an immense population. A strong desire has long been felt to introduce the light of the gospel there. An opportunity offered about sixteen months ago. Mr. J. W Ricketts, a young man brought up in Bengal, but afterwards stationed at Amboyna, where he was secretary to the English resident, and, when it was formed, became secretary to the Bible Society there, being awakened through our young brother Jabez Carey to a more deep and lively sense of his obligations to the Saviour, thought it his duty to return to Bengal, and labour for the salvation of his own countrymen. After being baptized at Serampore, and for some time instructed there in the doctrines of grace and the nature of missionary work, he agreed to go and attempt to realize his wish respecting his own countrymen, by labouring at Moorshedabad. Here he has obtained permission to erect a bungalow, and, assisted by a native brother, has begun to itinerate around him, and to open schools for the instruction of native children. His mild and steady deportment, and the deep acquaintance he appears to have with the divine word, give us reason to hope that, if such be the will of God, he will prove a useful labourer in the Lord's vineyard.

Malda.—At this place, or rather at English Bazar, a town near Malda, Krishna resides. Here he is employed in diffusing the knowledge of the gospel in the towns and villages near him, and he occasionally makes excursions to distant places, for the purpose of distributing tracts and parts of the scripture. Two of his countrymen have come forward, and in baptism openly confessed the Saviour of men, in the course of this past year.

Dinagepore.—At this place, although none have openly come forward lately to confess the Saviour, there are now several waiting for baptism, and christianity seems to be actually taking root, no less than twenty-two persons having rejected idolatry, and placed themselves under the sound of the gospel there, in the course of the past year. The number of those who have rejected idolatry and attend the word of God, including children, now amounts to between seventy and eighty.

The brethren add, "We have now taken a full view of the state of the mission in Bengal, and, though we find nothing perfect,—nothing that will bear a comparison with that maturity in doctrine and practice exhibited in the churches of God in Britain; yet, when we consider that, with the exception of one circle, all is the work of gifts raised up here, of whom the first made an open profession of christianity only seventeen years ago, there is abundant reason for future hope, and even now to say, What has God wrought in a heathen country in the course of these few years!"

HINDOOST'HAN.—In Hindoost'han there are, at present, three brethren from Europe; brethren Chamberlain, Moore, and Rowe: the other brethren there, are merely such as have been raised up in India since the commencement of the mission, like those already mentioned in the review of Bengal.

Monghir.—At this place, which is a station for invalids, brother Chamberlain settled about two years ago. In this period, the Lord has not left him without tokens of his blessing on his labours, both among the Europeans resident there, and among the natives. Of the former class of inhabitants, three have been baptized, among whom captain P. stands particularly eminent for zeal in the cause of God, combined with great solidity of judgment. Within these few weeks too, our brother has been so favoured as to baptize a native, the first fruits of his labour among the heathen in and around that place. May the Lord make this the forerunner of a copious harvest!

Patna.—At this place brother Thompson has continued to labour for these last three years, if we except the time employed in various journies into other parts of Hindoost'han, with the view of more widely diffusing the knowledge of the gospel. In one of these journies he baptized the brethren Flatman and Hale, at Benares; in another, certain brethren at Allahabad. In the course of the past year, among other journies, he has taken one as far as Lucknow.

At Gya, about two days' journey from Patna, to the northeast, resides, on his own estate, brother Fowles, which, as a native of India, he is entitled to hold. This comprises several villages, to the inhabitants of which, and to others around, he constantly makes known the word of life

DIGA.—At this place, the labours of our brethren Moore and Rowe have been greatly owned and blessed in these three years past, particularly in their ministrations to the brethren in the various regiments which have been from time to time stationed at Dinapore. Numerous letters, which we have seen, speak in the most affectionate manner of their labours among these brethren, and acknowledge, with gratitude, the profit and edification they derived from them. Nor have their labours among them been without fruit, as it relates to conversion. At Diga, and at Amowa, the number baptized has been considerable; we are unable to speak precisely, but in the different regiments which have been at Diga, the number added to the respective churches by baptism, chiefly by the labours of our brethren, considerably exceeds fifty.

BENARES.—To this celebrated city, the seat of Hindoo learning and superstition, we have long wished to send the light of the gospel, and brother William Smith, (called in Orissa under brother John Peter,) from his acquaintance with the Hindee, and his humble and godly deportment, appearing likely to be useful there, we sent him thither the latter end of the past year, who, after dispersing the word of life in numerous towns and villages on the road, in a journey of three months, arrived in the middle of February this year. Many seem to pay a degree of attention to the gospel, and one rich native, Juya-Narayuna-Ghosal, has visited our brother several times; and has professed a strong desire to renounce idolatry, of the evil of which he declares himself fully convinced, and to embrace the doctrine of the Saviour of the world. The Lord has been pleased to encourage our brother, by permitting him already to see the first fruits of his labours in this city, in the baptism of a brahmun, who put on the Lord Jesus, by a public profession.

ALLAHABAD.—To this large city, the capital of the province in which it stands, we, about eighteen months ago, desired brother Mackintosh to direct his attention, as we had reason to hope that our brethren of the Church Missionary Society would fully occupy Agra, where he then was. Since he has removed hither, the Lord has been pleased greatly to bless his labours

CAWNPORE.—At this large and important military station, the Lord has been pleased to introduce the gospel in a manner almost unexpected. While our brethren in the 66th regiment were lying there, in the latter end of the year 1816, his majesty's 24th regiment of light dragoons arrived, and our brethren put into their hands such books as were calculated to awaken them to a sense of their state. This, with the labours and conversation of the brethren, the Lord was pleased so to bless, that, in three months, twenty of them came forward, and were baptized in the name of the Lord Jesus. The 14th regiment was ordered there a few months afterwards, the 66th being ordered to St. Helena; and the Lord was pleased so to continue this display of his grace, that, in August this year, on the addition by baptism of seven to the 14th regiment, and of thirteen to our brethren in the light dragoons, the church in the 14th numbered thirty-six members in full communion, and the newly raised church in the light dragoons no less than thirty-seven; so graciously has the Lord been pleased to work in the course of about ten months.

In the other stations on the continent of India, where the gospel has been, in some degree made known, *Nagpore, Surat,* and *Orissa,* little has been effected beyond the general diffusion of light.

NAGPORE, at which one person has been baptized, has been in a state of alarm for some time, on account of the Pindaries, or predatory hordes, who have long been the terrour of this part of India. The Lord has preserved our much valued friend Moxon, with his family, however, in a way that demands our warmest gratitude. It is probable, that after peace and tranquillity shall have been restored, there will be a fairer field opened for missionary labour than before.

At SURAT, our brother Carapeit has laboured the greater part of his time since the last review; and numerous have been the conversations which he has held, from time to time, with men of various religions.

Relative to ORISSA, we are at present able to say but little. Brother Peters, with his family, in the beginning of the year, returned to Bengal, for a season, on account of his health. We therefore desired him to labour in Calcutta during his stay there, where he at present continues. His health, however, is now much improved.

OF THE ISLANDS.—The islands, if we include all into which the Lord has been pleased in any degree to cause his word to go forth, are, the *The Isle of France, Ceylon, Java, Penang* and *Amboyna.*

From our brethren in the ISLE OF FRANCE, we have heard but little since the last review: and we have reason to fear that they are in declining circumstances. Letters, however, from brethren Forder and Blatch tell us, that things around *them* are, on the whole, in a hopeful state, and that one or two had been added to them by baptism.

CEYLON.—In this island brethren Chater and Siers appear to have been steadily devoted to their work, each in his different sphere. Brother Chater has enlarged his sphere of usefulness, by preaching in the Portuguese language as spoken there, which is a valuable medium of communication to a large class of persons who bear the christian name. His labours in the Cingalese, too, are highly praiseworthy. His grammar in that language has been much approved, and his knowledge of the language has been found particularly useful in carrying forward the translation of the scriptures since the lamented death of the late Mr. Tolfrey. His labours in the pulpit, also, have not been without a blessing, particularly to our own countrymen. Of the exact number he has baptized in this period, we cannot speak with precision, as accounts from Ceylon are less regular than from the brethren in Bengal and Hindoost'han, but we think they amount to ten or twelve

JAVA.—In this island, much has been seen, and many changes have been experienced, since the date of the last review. Brother Robinson has been brought down to the gates of death by disease, but has been hitherto graciously preserved in life: but our highly esteemed and lamented brother Trowt has been removed, in the midst of his opening career of usefulness. His too close application to his studies so affected his constitution, as ultimately to cause him to fall a prey to a liver and bowel complaint, with which he had struggled nearly two years. Brother Trowt's labours served to encourage and invigorate brother Bruckner, whom he has left to follow in his footsteps, and to carry forward that translation of the sacred scriptures into the Javanese language, on which the heart of our brother was so fully fixed. Brother Bruckner steadily perseveres in his work, and has experienced much encouragement from the Europeans around him, and even from the baron Van der Capellan himself—his Netherland majesty's governor general in India.

Brother Robinson has met with much to encourage him in his work, as well as with things of a contrary nature. His labours have been owned of God, both in the English and Malay languages, he and brother Trowt having baptized nearly twenty, of different nations, since the date of the last review. Among these, one brother, Diering by name, is likely to prove as valuable a helper to him, as we have found in Carapeit, Thompson, Mackintosh, and others.

The arrival of brother and sister Phillips appears greatly to have encouraged brother Robinson. We rejoice therein; and we trust he will prove a most valuable helper to brother Bruckner, to join whom, at Samarang, we find he left Batavia two or three months ago.

Of PENANG we can say but little at present. it is the goodness of God alone that has given us a little handful there, under the direction of brother Sylvester, as has been mentioned already.

AMBOYNA.—In this island, a change has now taken place, relative to the government. The conduct of our brother Jabez Carey had, however, so effectually recommended him, that the new government have requested him to continue in his employment as superintendent of schools. As he is now well acquainted with the Malay language, we have reason to hope that he will ultimately become highly useful as a missionary, for which his desires are strong. It is to his labours that we are indebted for our much valued brother Ricketts, who may, therefore, be justly considered, the first fruits of the Amboyna mission.

DOMESTIC MISSIONARY INTELLIGENCE.

THE prospects in relation to *Indian reform* brighten daily. New developements are constantly occurring, and it is much to be hoped that the period is not remote, when the children of the forest shall enjoy the blessings of civilized man, become citizens in the American union, and experience the happiness resulting from an acquaintance with the gospel of the grace of God.

INDIAN SCHOOL IN KENTUCKY.

Report of Rev. Mr. FICKLIN, *after making a tour to the Indian country, and returning with eight of their youth, who are now receiving instruction near the Great Crossings, Scott County.*

AUGUST 20th, 1818, I set out for the Missouri and Illinois territories, accompanied by Mr. Eli Short. We passed .... parts of Kentucky. I occasionally preached and made .... About the 8th of September I arrived at a small village of .... ple creek, in the Missouri territory, but found considerable difficulty .... communications, for want of an interpreter. The Indians, however, at this place, received us kindly, and expressed some gratification that we had paid them a visit Although they were not willing to enter into any arrangement to send their children to be educated, yet they referred us to their principal chiefs at the West Prairie, and agreed to conform to their decision.

After tarrying about two days, we set out for the West Prairie to have an interview with the principal chiefs of that place, and arrived on the evening of the 13th At this place we were also kindly received The village consisted of about 30 lodges, some of which had the appearance of civilized life, compared with the state of wretchedness among other Indians Fortunately at this place I met with a man by the name of Laramee, a half blood, who speaks good English, and can both read and write He rendered me great service, from his intelligence, and great solicitude to have the Indians educated. I proposed to him my plans, which he highly approved The chief and principal men were convened, and my views and plans spread before them by Laramee. but as it is the universal custom of the Indians to defer giving immediate answers on any occasion, we adjourned until next morning, to meet at the chief's house.

Next morning, about 8 o'clock, we met again at the house of the old chief, and I received the following answers to the preceding interview, after Laramee had again spread our views and plans before them The chief replied that the thing was new to him, that nothing of the kind had ever before been proposed. He said he had thought on the subject all night; that he could not sleep for thinking about it. He said he did not wish to say No, and he was afraid to say Yes, too soon. He determined, however, to consult his people, and send me an answer in a few days.

From this place we proceeded to the Delaware town on the Foxescotoway, and arrived on the 19th. At this village we found about thirty families, all in a state of wretchedness. The prospects of procuring children were equally flattering, provided time could be given to consult their principal men Two leading characters among them agreed to accompany me to St. Louis, to consult governor Clark. We went by the way of Rogers town, and had an interview with the Indians of that village, and they promised to give an answer in three days. We stayed a few hours, and proceeded on our journey to St Louis, and arrived on the evening of the 27th Had an interview with governor Clark, and found him very solicitous to encourage our mission. About sixty of the Osage Indians had just arrived at St Louis The governor afforded every opportunity to converse with the Indians; made several speeches himself; introduced me to the principal agent, and was of great service in promoting the domestic missionary cause among the Indians at this place We had frequent interviews for the space of ten days, and I procured from them, in substance, the following answers. They let us know that their object in coming to St. Louis was to treat with their red brethren on the Arkansaw, that the subject was new, however they very much thanked us for our attention to poor Indians; that they would consult their people when they returned, and that if some good man would visit them next spring, they would send some children at all events

About the 3d of October a chief and fourteen men of the Cherokee nation arrived at this place; the same proposals were made to them, upon which I received the following answer from the chief, viz That they preferred having schools established among them, but as that was not consistent with our plan, they would, if any opportunity offered, send some of their children next summer. In all these interviews I feel under lasting obligations to governor Clark, for his uncommon zeal and activity to promote this good cause.

About this time a deputation, consisting of Fish and Rogers, arrived from Rogers town, with the answer they had promised me in three days after I left them, the result of which was, after some deliberation they had determined, if I should return that way, that they would send some of their children with me to Kentucky. I proceeded immediately to Rogers town, and made arrangements with them who had agreed to come to meet me at Patosi on the first of November, and I determined in the mean time to visit the Peyankeshaws on Black river. After much difficulty and fatigue I arrived within twenty miles of their village, where I was informed that they had all gone out to perform their winter hunt, consequently I returned, and appointed the Rev. Mr. F Redding and William Ficklin as agents to visit them next spring, make the proposals, and report to me the result.

I returned to Rogers village, and made the necessary arrangements for the children to come on to Kentucky. Having procured them some clothing, blankets, &c. I then proceeded to Patosi. On the 29th of October Lewis Rogers and the children arrived at Patosi, and after the necessary preparations, such as shoeing horses, &c we set out for Kentucky on the 2d of November. When we arrived at Kaskaskia, colonel Manair had just arrived from West Prairie, and informed me that the Indians had given him to understand, that if Lewis Rogers should approve of the plan, they would send their children, we proceeded from this place through almost insurmountable difficulties, hardships, and insults, through an inhospitable country, until we arrived in Kentucky. I arrived at home on the 22d.

INDIANS OF ILLINOIS

Extract of a letter from elder M'Coy to the Cor. Sec. dated

REV. AND DEAR BROTHER, Mission-house, May 13th, 1819.

Although we are not able to state any circumstances in particular, in relation to the red people who swarm around our house, that would be very interesting or encouraging, yet we have the happiness to believe that we are daily advancing in the work of Indian reform. They are much more friendly than when we first came hither, and have manifested a great partiality for us. While on a tour to Vincennes last month, on which I was absent eighteen days, they were almost daily at our house, and sometimes lodged here, and a few times some were intoxicated. No person was here to take care of our house, or to accommodate their uncouth manners, except my wife and a female companion. They might have robbed us of half our living, yet they universally behaved with as much decorum as if they had been taught the first principles of good breeding by the bible. About this time they stole a saddle and blanket from one of our neighbours, and refused to give them up, while the only offence which occurred at this place was by a young woman in taking a trifle of clothing, which we had not missed until next day, when two men returned it. This was a stronger expression of friendship for us, by the sensible ones, than if the thoughtless girl had not committed the crime. But, O! who can avoid dropping a tear over the degraded condition of a sprightly female youth, who wants only an opportunity of improving her mind, to make her feel a virtuous abhorrence of the prostration of the principles which ennoble a human being! They often amuse themselves, for hours at a time, with the pictures in Goldsmith's Natural History, and not unfrequently they examine other books, always carefully replacing them. Could we get things properly into operation, I conclude it would be serviceable to have books embellished with pictures suited to their taste and circumstances. I have employed a Wea for an interpreter, and am expecting him, with some others here, every hour. They will bring with them several children, some of whom we hope to persuade to continue with us; but we have been so often disappointed, that we are afraid to say much. About this time I expected to be on a tour in the Indian country, but I am waiting until some who have gone to Fort Harrison to receive an annuity, shall have dispersed.

In a late journey to Vincennes, I took with me our Indian boy, the only one that we have in our school, who is about eleven years old. By request he pronounced a speech on the subject of Indian reform, before the Bruceville Missionary Society, which presented him a bible. The next day the Bruceville Female Missionary Society made a similar request, which, being complied with, the society voted our little red orator a coat. Could the happy effects of such favours as these be generally appreciated, surely many ladies would acquire a name like Dorcas, which would be spoken of to their honour, when the reward of a better world would take place of happy sympathy, and the songs of the blessed, Indians not excepted, would render unheard the applause of men, and the grateful acknowledgments of the objects of benevolence. It is impossible for me to describe, or you to conceive, the deep impressions which even a small present, sent hundreds of miles, would make on the minds of these unhappy people, who, in a thousand ways, have been taught to consider themselves friendless.

I have the happiness to state that, since last summer, a gracious impulse, like the leaven in the meal, has been diffusing a fermentation in the churches of Maria and Prairie creek. Knowing how liable, from his peculiar situation, a missionary is to suffer his zeal to run away with hopeful appearances, I have been, hitherto, almost afraid to say any thing on the subject; but I think I may now venture to assert, that the Lord is evidently carrying on a blessed work of salvation in the neighbourhood of these two churches. Within a few weeks twenty-six have publicly declared what God hath done for their souls, and ten others that I have heard of, are singing the songs of grace, and will also be baptized the first opportunity. More than once have the congregations been melted into tears by the affecting acknowledgments of backsliders, and the sighs of the penitent have become familiar, though not the less affecting. O, brother, this heavenly change makes the writer sometimes almost imagine himself translated to another country. So much time is engrossed by religious conversation and devotional exercise, that nature is denied her ordinary and necessary repose. A few nights ago, in Bruceville, I arose, by request, out of my bed, to pray for two young people who said they were on the brink of eternal ruin, and knew not how to escape. The relations of a work of grace on the hearts of the converted, are of the most clear and satisfactory kind. No passionate fire is blown up to mislead, by its false light, the penitent inquirer, but "truth in the inward parts," revealed by the impressions of the Holy Ghost, imparts to these the solemnity of the grave, to those the ecstacies of heaven.

I live, you know, between the whites and Indians. If I except about twenty miles of white settlement adjoining our humble residence, I think I may safely say the fields are whitening on each side of us. O that God would send us a few more labourers! A zealous young preacher has lately joined Prairie creek church, and preaches occasionally at Maria, but believe me, sir, while the pomegranates begin to emit their odoriferous exhalations, humanly speaking, the vine must droop for want of the hand of cultivation.

CHEROKEE INDIANS.

Extract of a letter from elder Posey to the Cor. Sec. dated

EVER DEAR BROTHER, Ashville, May 9th, 1819.

I have now made a decisive trip into the Cherokee nation, and landed at home on Saturday last. I was with Mr Charles Hicks (their chief,) about five days ago, a great deal of the time by ourselves, which gave us a particular opportunity of conversing, so as to get into each other's views and feelings respecting missionary exertions in his nation; the result of which, and the impression it left on my mind, I shall briefly relate.

They have finished the late treaty, and keep a considerable scope of country in their usual form. They have given up twelve miles square, and three other valuable sections, to be sold to the highest bidder, and the money deposited in the hands of the President, to be by him laid out to the best advantage for educating their children. They wish every school to be an establishment, and the children principally to board at the place. They look to the religious societies for teachers, preachers, and farmers, as they have unanimously found out that christians are their only friends, whose examples they wish their rising generation to follow, and whose instructions they hope will prove a lasting blessing to their nation. The American Board of Commissioners, in conjunction with the United Brethren, and the Baptist Board, are the particular sources to which they look. The two former have one establishment each, and the wish is for the next to be conducted by the Baptist Board in a part of the nation called the Valley towns, contiguous to North Carolina, which is a very healthy, fertile place, and will be very populous. After acting almost the part of Jonah, I feel compelled to say, I humbly conceive it my duty still to labour amongst them, and therefore tender my services to take the charge of the institution, in conjunction with some faithful brother in the ministry, if practicable, and, any how, one who can teach on the Lancasterian plan, is a good scholar, and a real friend to the heathen. We will also have the privilege of selecting two farmers, one blacksmith and miller, which would enable us to go into the nation a constituted church; all but the two last would be considered the missionary family, and they would not be taken contrary to our wishes, therefore I call it six families. I have pledged myself for the Board, that they will see to the institution; and the wished for way is, that the Board recommend the teachers to the President, and let him grant them the privilege of establishing a school or schools in the Cherokee nation, by consent of the Indians. In October they hold a general council, at which I have promised to attend, or have some other person there, and when received by them, we will be permanently established. I expect, with a Divine blessing, to continue on, and spend the most of this summer in preaching, as usual, and arranging business for the removal into the nation; though, if the Board have otherwise determined, I hope they will let me know as soon as possible.

LETTER WRITTEN BY AN INDIAN FEMALE.

The following letter was written by a native Cherokee woman, the first known convert to christianity in that tribe, and a member of the church at Springplace, under the care of the Rev. John Gambold. It was addressed to a gentleman at the seat of government, whose benevolent regard for the Indians was known to the writer, and whose official duty makes him perpetually acquainted with the state of their affairs. As to the letter itself, it needs no recommendation from us. The heart that is not touched by its simple and powerful eloquence, would be unaffected by any thing which we could say. In copying the letter not a word was altered, omitted, inserted, or transposed.

HONOURED SIR, Mountjoy, January 15th, 1818.

You often write to my dear brother Gambold, and I hear that you are a true friend to the poor despised Indians. God bless and reward you for it, and grant you long life and happiness.

Now, as my uncle, Ch. Hicks, is gone to Washington, to plead our cause before our dear father the President, and make our distresses known, I take the liberty to write this to you. I wish you to be on my uncle's side, if I dare ask this favour; for we poor Indians feel very much humbled.

I really know if our friends there with you knew our situation, they would sincerely pity us. Oh, for the sake of God's love and mercy, pity us! If we do not get help from that quarter, we are undone.

Our neighbouring white people seem to aim at our destruction. They have not the fear of God before their eyes; they seem not to believe in a Saviour; they set wicked examples before the poor ignorant Indians; they insult our poor people, who bear it patiently. I cannot cease from weeping to our merciful Saviour to show mercy to us, and help from the hand of our oppressors. We are persuaded if our honoured father the President could see our great distress into which we are brought, he would weep over us, he would pity us, he would help us. Yet we live far off from him, and he cannot see us. Yet we constantly look from a distance to him for help, as poor helpless children look up to their father, crying to have pity on them.

Since I have experienced grace and mercy from my dear Saviour, and have become truly happy in him and with his children, it is my constant prayer, that my whole dear nation might enjoy the same blessings that I enjoy.

This grieves me more than I can tell, that at a time when there is a good prospect that many more will join the few who have embraced christianity, we shall be driven away from the land of our fathers, which is as dear to us as our own lives, from our improved farms, from our beloved teachers, into a land strange to us; yea, into savage life again. Dear Sir, I declare I would prefer death to such a life again.

I am in hopes, and many more with me, that our beloved father the President will certainly help his poor children, when he hears from my uncle our distressed situation. Yes, God the father of all mankind will incline his heart to consider our case and help us. Oh, Sir, I implore you, for the sake of the dear crucified Saviour, who shed his blood for the poor red as well as white people, continue to be our friend. Pray for us; plead for us; and the blessings of those who are ready to perish will come upon you, and the great Judge of all flesh will, at the great day of retribution, remember your kindness to our poor people.

[PANOPLIST

WYANDOTT INDIANS

Extract of a letter from elder Drake to the Cor. Sec. dated

RESPECTED BROTHER,   Delaware, May 26th, 1819.

Brother Evans called on me on the 18th to accompany him to Sandusky, for the purpose of informing ourselves more particularly of the situation of the Indians. The result has but confirmed the opinion I gave you in my last, and I should not have troubled you again on the same subject, but at the special request of brother Evans. That there has been a reformation among the Wyandots, much to their advantage, is confirmed by the united testimony of all who have examined for themselves, and it is also evident that Mr. Steward (a coloured man, possessing some Indian blood,) has been the principal, if not the sole cause, under God, of any religious impressions and attention to the concerns of their souls. This man possesses good talents, and some advantage from education, appears candid, and free; is a methodist, and has obtained the confidence of the Indians. He has therefore the advantage of strangers. And furthermore, the Methodists have not only given him license to preach, but have also made arrangements for supplying them with other preachers every three weeks, so that, agreeably to this calculation, our visit occurred at the same time with their appointment, in consequence of which brother Evans thought best for him to proceed on to Lower Sandusky, having obtained what information circumstances would allow, and left me to tarry with them through the meeting.

One of the chiefs introduced the meeting by exhorting the Indians to pay attention to what should be said, and expressed, as they did, much satisfaction that we had come to see them; after which brother Steward proceeded by singing and prayer, and a short exhortation, to open the way for the methodist preacher. After his discourse, and an exhortation and prayer by a brother methodist, who came with him, I was requested to preach. The Indians appeared well pleased, and I left them, and returned to Mr Walker's.

When we parted, brother Evans requested me to write immediately, and to say that he is fully of the opinion, that in the present situation of the Indians, it would not be adviseable to be at the expense of supporting a missionary to visit them, for the reasons above stated.

[Elders Drake and Evans had been requested by the Board to visit Sandusky, for the purpose of ascertaining the expediency of continuing the mission of elder George, or the propriety of relinquishing it.]

BIBLE SOCIETIES, &c.

THE BRITISH AND FOREIGN BIBLE SOCIETY.

THE anniversary meeting of this society was held in Freemason's hall. There were 2000 persons present. At 12 o'clock the right honourable lord Teignmouth took the chair, when the report was read. It detailed the number of Bible societies on the continent and in the Indies, &c. stated the number of bibles issued at cost and reduced prices, from the 31st of March, 1818, to the same period in 1819, was 123,247 bibles, and 136,784 testaments, making in the whole 260,031 copies, being an increase beyond the issues of the preceding year of 65,930 bibles and testaments, making, with those issued at the expense of the society, from various presses upon the continent, a total of more than TWO MILLION THREE HUNDRED THOUSAND

Professor Kieffier, from Paris, presented himself to the meeting, and, through the medium of an able address, which was read by the Rev D Wilson, informed the meeting, that the government of France had promised their utmost support to the Bible Societies in that country It is then stated that 9000 copies of the New Testament, printed in the Turkish language, from the royal press of France, had been sent to Turkey. Three of those testaments, which were exceedingly well printed and bound, and bearing the royal arms of France, were then presented to the meeting by the professor, who, aided by the advice of baron Sylvestre de Sacy, had inspected the edition The duke of Gloucester then moved the thanks of the meeting to the chairman, who made a suitable reply. The meeting shortly after broke up

BREMEN BIBLE SOCIETY.

The last report of the Bremen Bible Society contains a very gratifying letter from professor Leander Van Ess, the worthy Roman catholic preacher at Marlburg He continues his benevolent labours, and is unwearied and undaunted in distributing the holy scriptures Perhaps there is no person in Europe, who, amid many important engagements, conducts a more extensive correspondence He speaks with great fervency of the blessing of God, by which the influence of Bible societies has been such as to bring nearer together christians of different religious denominations. Giving an account of his present opportunities and difficulties he says *for a great door and effectual is opened unto me, and there are many adversaries* 1 Cor. xvi 9. And Mr Van Ess expresses his confidence in God, who is able to protect him against all his enemies. An increasing thirst after the *sincere milk of the word*, and an active desire to attend to the principles of unadulterated gospel, is observable in the Catholic church He concludes his letter in the apostolic request, with which every true christian will cheerfully comply: *Finally brethren, pray for us, that the word of the Lord may have free course and be glorified, even as it is with you.* 2 Thess. iii 1. The report states that in two years and a few months Mr Van Ess has distributed among the catholic brethren, 233,541 copies of his translation of the new testament, and among protestants, 5334 bibles and 2800 testaments.

BOSTON MARINE BIBLE SOCIETY.

Mr. Editor—Having noticed a statement in a late number of the Recorder, that there was no *Mariner's Bible Society* in Boston, and being moreover influenced by the address of Mr Ingersol to do something, I send two dollars, or in other words "two mites," to be deposited in the Recorder office, till such a society shall be established. While we dwell securely on land, the blood of our seamen's souls must not "be found in our skirts!" The time has come when "those who go down to the sea in ships, and do business in great waters" are to see the "wonderful works of God" in the redemption of their souls.

BOSTON RECORDER.

SCHOOLS FOR JEWISH CHILDREN IN LONDON.

The schools erected for the instruction of Jewish children on each side the Episcopal Jews Chapel, London, are rapidly advancing. The school for the boys is nearly completed, and that for the girls had received contributions to the amount of more than 650*l* sterling, as early as February. The concentration of the schools and chapel, is regarded as a most desirable object, on account of the saving produced to the society in rent, &c.—the monument thereby formed of national charity towards the Jewish people—and its effect in conciliating the attention of all who behold it, whether Jews or Gentiles. The society anticipates a call for assistance in the education of Jewish youth in foreign countries, at a period not far distant, and considers it highly expedient that the home establishment be put on a permanent footing.

EDUCATION OF HEATHEN CHILDREN.

It is stated in the Charleston Evangelical Intelligencer, that the ladies in that place have not been backward in imitating the good example of their sisters in Savannah. One hundred and seventy dollars have been raised, ($150 of it being an annual subscription,) for the support of a Charleston school in India.

The children of two of the Sabbath schools have begun to cast their little offerings into the treasury of the Lord. From one school, $18 have already been forwarded in behalf of Cherokee children. The other school will probably raise enough to support a school in India. A few ladies have raised $30 to begin the education of a child, to be named William Hollingshead.

Two benevolent ladies have appropriated $550, as a fund, the interest of which is to be annually paid for the support of a child in the mission family. By this means one child may be kept constantly in a course of christian education, and thus a succession of youths brought forward, some of whom there is reason to believe will become eminently useful. This we believe is the first example of the kind, but we flatter ourselves that it will not be the last. We trust these offerings are but the first fruits of a plentiful harvest. Could the inhabitants of this country enter into the feelings of missionaries who are surrounded by thousands of idolatrous children that might be educated at so cheap a rate, we are sure that pecuniary aid would not be wanting. This is a consideration to which we particularly invite the attention of our readers.

ASYLUM FOR THE DEAF AND DUMB.

The report of the directors of the Connecticut Asylum for the education of the Deaf and Dumb, lately published, exhibits a list of forty-seven pupils belonging to that institution at the commencement of the late vacation. The expenditures of the institution for the last year amounted to $20,543 32, of which sum $8,860 85, were expended in the purchase and repairs of the house and lands occupied by the institution, $3,283 67, for tuition, and $7,285 52 for boarding the pupils. The funds for the expenditure of the year were derived principally from the following sources, viz. from donations $7,528 48; paid by pupils $5,843 20; contributions from churches in Connecticut $2,646 12 and interest and dividend on stock $1,018 42. The funds of the institution are $12,345 Phoenix bank stock, cash on hand $2,423 48, besides real estate, and a township of land granted by Congress.

PEACE SOCIETIES.

Among the benign institutions which mark the peculiar character, and auspicious prospects of the present day, PEACE SOCIETIES begin to wear a conspicuous aspect. The *Massachusetts Peace Society*, formed in Boston, December, 1815, has, since December 10, 1817, distributed 8298 tracts of different kinds, a large proportion of which were copies of that excellent work " the Friend of Peace."

Nineteen peace societies have already been organized in the United States, and several others, it is expected, will soon be formed.

There are two independent Peace societies in London. *The Society for promoting permanent and universal Peace*, is strengthened by auxiliaries in different parts of the kingdom. May the period speedily arrive when " *Glory to God in the highest*" shall be the universal song, for " *peace on earth, and good will toward men!*"

COLONIZATION SOCIETIES.

It is gratifying to learn that the Rev. Wm Mead, Agent for the Board of Managers of *the American Society for Colonizing the free people of colour of the United States*, has succeeded in establishing auxiliary societies in Milledgeville, Augusta, and Savannah, Georgia, with the prospect of one in Bryan county, and the prospect also of similar ones being soon formed in Beaufort, Charleston, Georgetown, Columbia and Camden, in South Carolina,—Fayetteville, North Carolina, and several other places. An auxiliary Colonization Society was some time ago organized in Philadelphia, and one recently in Fredericksburg, Virginia.

EXTRACTS

From a narrative of the state of religion within the bounds of the General Assembly of the Presbyterian Church; and of the General Associations of Connecticut, New Hampshire, and Massachusetts Proper, during the last year

It cannot fail to cheer the heart of every friend to religion and morals, that, without an exception, the reports of the several presbyteries, represent the cause of evangelical truth, as attended with a gradual, but uniform success. On almost every section of our church, has God been pleased to bestow some refreshing showers of grace. And although it does not appear that he has, in any instance, displayed such wonders of mercy, as in some former years, yet we cannot but indulge the fond hope, that during the past year, the accessions to the church have, on the whole, been about as numerous as at any former period. The great and permanent interests of religion have, undoubtedly, during the last year, been more extensively secured and promoted than heretofore. But our heavenly Father has not suffered a whole year to pass over us, without imparting to us some rich tokens of his tender regard, by extending to some of our churches the *special* influences of the Holy Spirit. The congregations of Bloomfield, Pennfield, and Easa, of the Presbytery of Ontario—Prattsburgh, of the Presbytery of Bath—Ulysses, of the Presbytery of Geneva—Bridgwater, Vernon and Verone, of the Presbytery of Oneida—De Kalb, Russel, Blacklake, Stockholm and Hopkinton of the Presbytery of Champlain—Ralston, in the Presbytery of Albany—and Aurora of the Presbytery of Cayuga, have all of them been visited with more or less of the *special* influences of the Divine Spirit. In the middle, southern and western sections of our church, we notice as places that have been *specially* visited, West field, Jersey City, North Hardiston, Newfoundland, Stony Brook and Long Pond, in the Presbytery of Jersey—Columbia, in the Presbytery of New Castle—York and Chester, in the Presbytery of Concord—Huron, Florence, Bath and Atwater, in the Presbytery of Portage—Waterford, in the Presbytery of Erie—several congregations in the Presbytery of Union—and Braceville, Sharon and Geneva, in the Presbytery of Grand River. In Percipeny, in Jersey Presbytery, and in several congregations in the Presbytery of West Lexington, have been gathered, to a very pleasing extent, the fruits of past revivals.

The Assembly are happy to learn that Sabbath schools have been formed in unusual numbers, with the high promises of extensive usefulness, in almost all the Presbyteries within our bounds: and would earnestly recommend the organization of them in all parts of the United States. We advert with much satisfaction, to the schools of this kind established in the cities of New York and Philadelphia, in the former of which, from eight to ten thousand, and in the latter and its vicinity from twelve to fourteen thousand children are instructed on every Lord's day.

From the delegates from Connecticut, New Hampshire, and Massachusetts, we derive the pleasing intelligence that God is carrying on his work in these States with power and success. From fifteen hundred to two thousand persons are supposed to have been the hopeful subjects of special divine influence during the last year, in the counties of Hampshire, Franklin, Hamden and Worcester, in Massachusetts. In Dartmouth college fifty out of one hundred students are hopefully pious, and are prosecuting their studies with a view to the gospel ministry.

MISCELLANEOUS.

STATE OF RELIGION IN FRANCE.

Extract of a letter from Mr. Le Jeune to the Rev. Mr. Reis of Baltimore, dated London, October 19, 1818.

BELOVED BROTHER IN THE LORD JESUS CHRIST,

YOUR heart will rejoice with ours on hearing of the late favourable and pleasing accounts received from different parts of France. Eight or nine hundred schools on the Lancasterian plan are already established in different parts of the kingdom. A young minister is going about France and the Netherlands preaching the gospel. The last accounts from him (from Valenciennes) are very interesting. There are several protestant churches there and in the neighbourhood. Many catholics inquire after the way to Zion, and wish for the gospel preached to them. Some other persons are at this moment travelling in different parts, the south, &c. to inquire after the state of religion in those parts, especially where protestants are in great numbers, but they are, indeed, in great darkness there, as well as in your native place, (Paris.)

News has been received here lately, that above three thousand catholics under the Pyrenees have recently abandoned the Roman church.

A benevolent society has been just formed here under the name of the *Continental Society*, having for its object to support native preachers on the continent of Europe, and the distribution of the holy scriptures, and religious books and tracts.

BETHEL ASSOCIATION.

Extract of a letter from T. P. Green, Cor. Sec. of the Bethel Baptist Association, to the Cor. Sec. of the Board, dated

DEAR SIR,   Cape Girardeau Co. December 2, 1818.

WE, the scattered believers on this side the Mississippi, view with great pleasure the noble exertions of our brethren in different parts of the earth to spread the knowledge of our Lord and Saviour Jesus Christ, especially those of our beloved brethren of the Board, &c. And, with peculiar pleasure the Association resolved to open a correspondence with the Baptist Board of Foreign Missions, through you their Corresponding Secretary. Since the time of the Association the brethren of this part (permit me to add the females likewise) have evidenced that they do not intend to be idle spectators of so great a work, and not be helpers together in the Lord, by forming societies, &c. &c. an account of which I expect you will receive from brethren Welch and Peck, as the latter was principally engaged with us in this business.

Agreeably to appointment, I transmit to you copies of the minutes of this Association. It is, dear sir, with gratitude to God, that I view the lovers of the kingdom of Jesus, uniting in every part to spread the knowledge of the Lord. Does not the church begin to use her own language, predicted of her by the Prophet, "the place is too strait for me, give place, that I may dwell?" Is not Zion arising from the dust, and putting on her beautiful garments? Long has she lain, especially in America, apparently careless for the situation of the heathen. It appears to me that the Saviour hath once more said, "Arise, let us go,"—not to be betrayed, but to go forth conquering and to conquer.

LONG RUN ASSOCIATION, KENTUCKY.

Extract of a letter from elder Waller, Cor. Sec. of the Long Run Association, to the Cor. Sec. of the Board, dated

DEAR SIR,   Shelbyville, (Ky.) May 25th, 1819.

AT the meeting of the Long Run Association for 1818, the churches composing that body were advised to be prepared, at their next meeting, to make contributions for missionary purposes, to be especially appropriated to Indian reform, subject to the management of the general Board. If this arrangement should be carried into effect with energy, it will yield something considerable to the great work. We rejoice in the idea that our Lord is rapidly preparing the way for the introduction and manifestation of the spiritually glorious millennial reign of the Redeemer on earth. May he go forth conquering and to conquer, till the kingdoms of the world become the kingdom of our Lord and of his Christ. Even so come, Lord Jesus, come quickly. Amen.

AFFECTING ANECDOTE.

A pious young gentleman found some difficulty in comprehending this text of scripture,—"The meek shall inherit the earth." How shall the meek inherit the earth, he said to himself, they are the children of God, and the Lord's people are not well portioned in houses and lands; indeed they are generally poorer in the wealth of this world than those who live without God. One day as he was riding out and meditating on this subject, he heard the voice of some person speaking with much earnestness, and approaching a cottage from whence the sound proceeded, beheld an aged woman kneeling before a small table, on which were placed a cup of water and a morsel of bread. She raised her hands and eyes to heaven, and feelingly uttered, "O Lord, thou hast given me Jesus, and all this beside!" The inquirer here found the desired explanation, and retired, fully convinced that the poor of this world are heirs of the kingdom, and that having nothing, they possess all things.

"IF any where" in the epistle to the Hebrews, "as in the beginning of the first chapter, the style seems to swell in current above the ordinary banks of the New Testament, it is from the greatness and sublimity of the matter treated of, which was not capable of any other kind of expression." *Owen.*

ORDINATIONS.

ORDAINED, at Shapleigh, (Me.) on the 2d of September last, the Rev. JOHN CHADBOURN, to the pastoral care of the second Baptist church in that place. Introductory prayer by Rev. Zebedee Delano, sermon by Rev. Simon Lock, from 2 Cor. iv. 5., ordaining prayer by Rev. Henry Smith, charge by Rev. Gideon Cook, right hand of fellowship by Rev William Goding. After which a well adapted anthem was performed in handsome style, and the Rev. Mr Chadbourn concluded by prayer. The performances were all appropriate and solemn, to which a crowded audience listened with the deepest attention and interest.

IN the city of Washington on the 27th of Feb. 1819, the Hon. OLIVER C COMSTOCK, a member of congress, was ordained to the work of an evangelist. Dr. Comstock came to Washington as a delegate to the house of representatives in 1813. His mind had been, a short time previous to that period, seriously impressed with divine things, and after his arrival at the seat of government he occasionally attended the preaching of the Rev Obadiah B. Brown, pastor of the first Baptist church in that city. Under the ministry of Mr Brown his sentiments became settled as to the doctrine of grace, and being convinced of the divine authority of believers' baptism, he offered himself as a candidate, and was baptized by Mr Brown, during the succeeding session of congress, and was received a member of the church under his care. The church subsequently observing in him talents which they concluded would be useful in the ministry, gave him a call to the exercise of his gifts, and, in the winter session of 1818, licensed him to preach. Thus, on Lord's days and evenings, he was preaching the gospel, as a minister of Christ, whilst on week days he was serving his country, and discharging the trust reposed in him by his constituents, as a national legislator.

His ministry having been approved by the neighbouring churches, as well as that of which he was a member, it was thought proper that he should be ordained prior to his return home, and just before the close of the session of congress. The solemnities of the ordination commenced at half past 10 o'clock, A M in the Baptist meeting house of the first church, in presence of a large and solemn audience. The officiating ministers were, the Rev. B. Allison, D. D Rev O B. Brown and the Rev. S H. Cone. Dr Allison presided: the sermon was preached by Mr Cone, from 2 Tim iv. 5 *Do the work of an evangelist* Mr Brown asked the questions, and Dr. Allison gave the charge, and closed with the benediction A singular coincidence of circumstances took place in this ordination The subject of it was baptized and joined the church, called to the ministry, and ordained, whilst actually serving as a member of congress Of the ministers who ordained him the first named was the chaplain to congress, and the two others had been such previously.

On Saturday, the 29th of May, 1819, Rev SAMUEL R. GRIFFN was solemnly ordained to the pastorship of the first Baptist church in Wilmington, Delaware: The services were opened by the Rev Mr. Walker of Marcus Hook, with a sermon from 2 Cor. iv 5. *We preach not ourselves, but Christ Jesus the Lord; and ourselves your servants for Jesus' sake* Rev. Mr Ferrell, of Welsh Tract, proposed to the church and to the candidate the usual questions, and received from the latter an interesting account of the exercises of his mind in reference to the christian ministry. The ordination prayer was offered by Rev Mr Peckworth, who, together with brethren Ferrell, Rice, Walker, Staughton and Strawbridge, engaged in the imposition of hands, brother Peckworth gave the right hand of fellowship, and brother Rice presented the bible to the candidate, with an affectionate exhortation that its sacred contents might ever be the subject of his ministry. Dr. Staughton delivered the charge from 2 Timothy iv 5 *Watch thou in all things, endure afflictions, do the work of an evangelist, make full proof of thy ministry.* It was a time of refreshing from the presence of the Lord The common emotion of a large assembly appeared to say, "God is the Lord which hath showed us light bind the sacrifice with cords to the horns of the altar"

OBITUARY.

REV MR BROOK, OF BALTIMORE

THE Rev. Mr BROOK was a native of Stockport, in Cheshire, England His father was an independent minister of considerable repute in that place, and his mother also being a pious character, he received from them a religious education, and was brought up in the strictest morality and the observance of every religious duty. Their pious instructions, we have reason to believe, were not in vain in the Lord. The seed thus sown in early youth, began in riper years to spring up and bring forth fruit. He was made a subject of divine grace a few years previous to his emigration to this country; but, owing to his mind being very much exercised concerning baptism, not being able to determine respecting the mode, he did not make a public profession until after his arrival in America. He landed in Boston in the year 1805, and shortly after it pleased God to lead him in the "good old way" He was immersed, and joined the church in Charleston, under the pastoral care of the Rev Mr. Collier, and soon after entered into the ministry. He was a strenuous advocate for that doctrine which maintains the honour of the divine character, abases the sinner, and exalts the riches of free and sovereign grace; and during his last illness, more particularly, reaped the benefit of that blessed doctrine. He would frequently converse on the subject with pleasure. In the commencement of his last illness he entertained hopes of recovering, and agreeably to the advice of his physicians declined teaching youth and sailed to Boston; but finding himself little benefited, soon returned home Shortly afterward his disorder, which was of a pulmonary nature, began to put forth more alarming symptoms. Perceiving these he observed, "I cannot stand it long" but, not in the least alarmed at his approaching dissolution, he would speak of it with the greatest familiarity. The two weeks previous to his death, during which he was confined to his bed, he suffered considerably from his breast and cough together, but was very patient under all his sufferings His constant language was, "Thy will be done!"—"It is the Lord, let him do what seemeth him good!" His faith in Christ was strong to the last He often said, "My whole dependence is on the righteousness and atonement of Christ for acceptance," totally disclaiming all merit of his own Owing to an extreme hoarseness which he had towards the close of his illness, he was unable to converse much, but was very fond of hearing pious conversation He would say to his friends, "Although I cannot join with you in conversation, I can enjoy it" On Sunday, the day previous to his departure, a friend observed to him, 'You will not go out any more, Mr. Brook.' With emphasis he replied, "No! but I shall go in, into the kingdom." To inquiries how his mind was, he would answer, "Comfortable!" On Monday a sudden change took place· he found he was going, and requested some friends to be sent for whom he wished to see When they arrived, he calmly and affectionately took leave of them, and all that were in the room, and observed, "I am going, but I am not afraid of death!" In a few minutes after he was deprived of speech, but expressed, both by signs and looks, that his confidence in the Lord was unshaken In this situation he continued for about half an hour, and at 6 o'clock in the morning of the 29th of June, sweetly fell asleep

---

MRS. SOPHIA BRYCE

Died, on the 21st of April, 1819, aged 33 years, Mrs Sophia Bryce, the amiable wife of the Rev John Bryce, pastor of the Baptist church in the city of Richmond, after a lingering and painful illness of five months She sustained her great sufferings with Christian fortitude and resignation—not a murmur or impatient word escaped her She possessed a calm serenity of mind, which manifested the unshaken reliance which she had on him in whom she believed, and who was able to keep that which she had committed to his hands

A short time before her departure she told her afflicted husband that she knew she was dying, and that she felt resigned; but observed that, if it were the will of God, she wished to have a brighter assurance of her acceptance, that she might glorify him the more. To this she appeared to have an eye in all her conduct, and it was the last desire expressed by this faithful follower of Jesus, that God might be glorified.

She requested her husband to have her four children brought into her chamber, that she might join him in prayer for them; after which she took leave of them with affection, yet with composure. She mentioned to a relation that she had been considering to which of her friends she should leave her children; but that she had, at length, come to the determination to commit them to the Lord, who could take care of them, and who was her best friend: and expressed no other wish concerning them, except that they might be brought up in the fear of God. She retained her senses to the last; and when unable to speak, being asked if she felt Jesus precious, she gave *a sign* that she did, and shortly after fell asleep in the arms of the Saviour, to awake in his likeness, and inherit that blessedness possessed by all who die in the Lord. She rests from her labours, and her works have followed her.

In the death of Mrs Bryce her bereaved family sustains an irreparable loss; But they are consoled by the reflection that her's, in the event, is incalculable gain. Her friends and acquaintances lament the departure of an amiable and valuable associate—yet they mourn not for her, but for themselves, for the fruits of the Spirit, love, gentleness, meekness, goodness, and peace, shone so conspicuously in her, that a witness is left in each conscience that she has entered into the joy of her Lord. In her, the poor have lost a kind benefactress. Her liberal hand was, on every occasion, extended to their relief. As far as was in her power, and even beyond it, she was willing to minister to their wants, and, it is believed, often denied herself to supply their necessities. The church with which she had for many years been connected, deplores the loss of a valuable member, and her brethren sorrow that they shall see her face no more in this world, but are comforted by the cheering hope, that she is removed from the church militant to the church triumphant——for though

> An angel's arm can't snatch her from the grave,
> Legions of angels can't confine her there.

Nothing, perhaps, since the days of miracles, manifests more clearly the truth of Divine revelation, and is a greater confirmation of the scriptures, than the triumphant death of a real believer. In this solemn hour he realizes the promise. "I will never leave thee, nor forsake thee," and can say, "Though I walk through the valley of the shadow of death, I will fear no evil, for thou art with me." He is now a competent witness of the faithfulness of God, and that all his promises are "Yea and Amen" in Christ Jesus, who is his hope, which hope he finds an anchor to the soul, both sure and steadfast, while passing the Jordan of death, to that promised land, where, arrived in perfect safety, he receives the end of his faith,—the complete salvation of his soul.

> Death wounds to cure. We fall, we rise, we reign!
> Spring from our fetters,—fasten in the skies,
> Where blooming Eden withers in our sight!
> Death gives us more than was in Eden lost
> This king of terrours is the Prince of Peace

POETRY.

ON THE COMET,
NOW VISIBLE IN THE HEAVENS, JULY 10, 1819.

HAIL, wonderful stranger! with thousands I hail
Thy lunar-like orb, thy illustrious trail!
Say, why to our ether thy course thou hast run?—
To feed with new fires the diminishing sun?
Over nations in guilt to exhibit the rod?
Or invite to the high contemplation of GOD?
Dost thou range with the links which, let down from the throne,
Bind suns and their far-spreading systems in one?
Or, say, dost thou kindly descend to repair
With life-cheering virtues the regions of air?
Or wait'st thou the will of yon infinite Sire,
To shock earth to fragments, or whelm it in fire?
A Tycho, a Newton may measure thy course,
Determine thy fervours, and value thy force.
But, alas! to frail man 'tis not given to know,
What fields thou hast travers'd of sun-beam or snow!
Perhaps, when releas'd from this mansion of clay,
My soul may attend thy mysterious way,
With holy inhabitants pass through the sky,
And sing the loud praises of GOD as we fly!
Great FATHER! Thy wisdom, Thy goodness and pow'r,
Revealed in yon firmament, low I adore:
My dearest attachments to Thee I resign,
Since the GOD of Creation——of *Comets*, is mine!

PSALM XIX. 6.
His going forth is from the end of the heaven, and his circuit unto the ends of it.

As stars high scatter'd o'er the vault of night,
PROPHETS of old disclos'd a trembling light;
With fairer lustre JOHN approaches near,
As Phosphor, day's prophetic harbinger,
At length MESSIAH opes the orient skies,
Westward his mild, refulgent chariot flies,
Cheers the Pacific isles—sweeps o'er the main,
And now illumines eastern climes again.

THE LATTER DAY LUMINARY;

BY A COMMITTEE

OF

THE BAPTIST BOARD OF FOREIGN MISSIONS FOR THE UNITED STATES

VOL. I.   NOVEMBER, 1819.   No. X.

COMMUNICATIONS.

VARIOUS LIGHTS IN WHICH THE FUTURE GLORY OF THE CHURCH IS EXHIBITED.

IT has been the pleasure of God to represent, in his word, important truths and considerations, in diversified points of view. This circumstance enlarges the conceptions of the humble inquirer, and corresponds with the sublimity of divine subjects, which, from their nature, cannot be fully understood without such aids. Had our Lord represented himself merely under the idea of a rock, our minds had been led to contemplate his stability and duration; but still such ideas of his character had been wanting as are supplied by the figures of a vine or a fountain, a banner or a sun. Had he described his kingdom only by the parable of treasure hid in a field, or a merchant-man in search of goodly pearls, the mind had become impressed with the worth of the gospel, and the duty of seeking earnestly its blessings; but it required other parables to teach the effects of the publication of truth on the hearts of men,—the discrimination that shall be made between the righteous and the wicked, and the gradual and triumphant progress of knowledge and grace throughout the earth.

It would be a service of no ordinary value, were some pious person, whose industry, leisure, and taste qualify him for the task, to undertake a representation of the various lights in which the glories reserved for the church are portrayed; embracing every material display, from the commencement to the close of divine revelation. It would furnish the ministers of Christ with a rich diversity of topics for sermons, and tend to remove that deficiency of genius and original idea so frequently discoverable in missionary discourses. It would contribute to enlarge the views and animate the zeal of private Christians, as well as excite thankfulness of heart for the glorious things which are spoken of the city of our God.

As a specimen of the plan referred to, the subsequent selections are made from the prophecies of Isaiah. Every passage gives a distinct and encouraging view of the empire of Christ, and affords a separate theme for contemplation and pulpit exhibition. It is, perhaps, unnecessary to add, that the translation of bishop Lowth is here employed.

ASTRONOMICAL ALLUSIONS.

1. *Sun rise.*—Isaiah ix. 1 and lx. 1, 2, 3.
    The people that walked in darkness
    Have seen a great light;
    They that dwelled in the land of the shadow of death,
    Unto them hath the light shined.

    Arise, be thou enlightened; for thy light is come;
    And the glory of Jehovah is risen upon thee.
    For behold, darkness shall cover the earth;
    And a thick vapour the nations:
    But upon thee shall Jehovah arise,
    And his glory upon thee shall be conspicuous.
    And the nations shall walk in thy light;
    And kings in the brightness of thy sun-rising.

2. *The absence of the sun and moon.*—lx. 19.
    No longer shalt thou have the sun for a light by day;
    Nor by night shall the brightness of the moon enlighten thee:
    For Jehovah shall be to thee an everlasting light,
    And thy God shall be thy glory.

3. *The perpetual sun-shine of Divine favour.*—lx. 20.
    Thy sun shall no more go down;
    Neither shall thy moon wane:
    For Jehovah shall be thine everlasting light;
    And the days of thy mourning shall be ended.

4. *The lustre of the heavenly bodies increased.*—xxx. 26.
    And the light of the moon shall be as the light of the meridian sun,
    And the light of the meridian sun shall be sevenfold:

In the day when Jehovah shall bind up the breach of his
    people;
And shall heal the wound, which his stroke hath inflicted

JEWISH ALLUSIONS.

5. *Enlarging of a tabernacle.*—Isaiah liv. 2, 3.

Enlarge the place of thy tent:
And let the canopy of thy habitation be extended:
Spare not; lengthen thy cords,
And firmly fix thy stakes:
For on the right hand, and on the left, thou shalt burst forth
    with increase;
And thy seed shall inherit the nations;
And they shall inhabit the desolate cities.

6. *The pillar of cloud and fire.*—iv. 5, 6.

Then shall Jehovah create upon the station of mount Sion,
And upon all her holy assemblies,
A cloud by day, and smoke;
And the brightness of a flaming fire by night:
Yea, over all shall the Glory be a covering.
And a tabernacle it shall be, for shade by day from the heat;
And for a covert, and a refuge, from storm and rain.

7. *A feast.*—xxv. 6.

And Jehovah God of Hosts shall make
For all the peoples, in this mountain,
A feast of delicacies, a feast of old wines:
Of delicacies exquisitely rich, of old wines perfectly refined

8. *A blast, as of a trumpet.*—xxvii. 13.

And it shall come to pass in that day,
The great trumpet shall be sounded;
And those shall come, who were perishing in the land of
    Assyria;
And who were dispersed in the land of Egypt.
And they shall bow themselves down before Jehovah,
In the holy mountain, in Jerusalem

9. *The removal of a covering from the countenance.*—xxv. 7

And on this mountain shall he destroy
The covering, that covered the face of all the peoples,
And the vail, that was spread over all the nations.

10. *Proclamation of a jubilee.*—lxi. 1, 2.

The spirit of Jehovah is upon me,
Because Jehovah hath anointed me.

To publish glad tidings to the meek hath he sent me;
To bind up the broken hearted:
To proclaim to the captives freedom;
And to the bounden, perfect liberty:
To proclaim the year of acceptance with Jehovah;
And the day of vengeance of our God.

11. *A herald announcing peace.*—lii 7.

How beautiful appear on the mountains
The feet of the joyful messenger, of him that announceth peace!
Of the joyful messenger of good tidings: of him that announceth salvation!
Of him, that sayeth unto Sion, Thy God reigneth!

12. *Drying up of seas or rivers.*—xi. 15.

And Jehovah shall smite with a drought the tongue of the Egyptian sea;
And he shall shake his hand over the river with his vehement wind;
And he shall strike it into seven streams,
And make them pass over it dry-shod.

13. *Elevation of a standard.*—xi 12. and xlix. 22.

And he shall lift up a signal to the nations;
And he shall gather the outcasts of Israel,
And the dispersed of Judah shall he collect,
From the four extremities of the earth.

Thus saith the Lord Jehovah:
Behold, I will lift up my hand to the nations,
And to the peoples will I exalt my signal;
And they shall bring thy sons in their bosom,
And thy daughters shall be borne on their shoulder.

14. *Building an altar and a pillar.*—xix. 19, 20.

In that day there shall be an altar to Jehovah,
In the midst of the land of Egypt;
And a pillar by the border thereof to Jehovah;
And it shall be for a sign, and for a witness,
To Jehovah God of Hosts in the land of Egypt.

VEGETABLE ALLUSIONS.

15. *The flourishing of a branch or cion.*—Isaiah iv. 2. and xi. 1.

In that day shall the Branch of Jehovah
Become glorious and honourable,
And the produce of the land excellent and beautiful.

But there shall spring forth a rod from the trunk of Jesse;
And a cion from his roots shall become fruitful.

16. *The influence of dews and rains.*—xlv. 8.
Drop down, O ye heavens, the dew from above;
And let the clouds shower down righteousness·
Let the earth open her bosom, and let salvation produce her fruit;
And let justice push forth her bud together.

17. *Process of vegetation.*—lxi. 11.
Surely, as the earth pusheth forth her tender shoots;
And as a garden maketh her seed to germinate.
So shall the Lord Jehovah cause righteousness to spring forth;
And praise, in the presence of all the nations

18. *Wine latent in the cluster.*—lxv. 8.
As when one findeth a good grape in the cluster;
And sayeth: Destroy it not; for a blessing is in it:
So will I do for the sake of my servants.

19. *Change of produce.*—lv. 13.
Instead of the thorny bushes shall grow up the fir-tree;
And instead of the bramble shall grow up the myrtle.

ANIMAL ALLUSIONS.

20. *Safety from rapacious beasts*—Isaiah xxxv. 9.
No lion shall be there;
Nor shall the tyrant of the beasts come up thither

21. *The harmony and mildness of the animals.*—xi. 6, 7.
Then shall the wolf take up his abode with the lamb;
And the leopard shall lie down with the kid:
And the calf, and the young lion, and the fatling shall come together;
And a little child shall lead them.
And the heifer and the she-bear shall feed together;
Together shall their young ones lie down;
And the lion shall eat straw like the ox.

22. *Their abundance and willingness in the service of the Lord.*—lx. 6, 7.
An inundation of camels shall cover thee;
The dromedaries of Midian and Epha;
All of them from Saba shall come:
Gold and frankincense shall they bear;
And the praise of Jehovah shall they joyfully proclaim

All the flocks of Kedar shall be gathered unto thee;
Unto thee shall the rams of Nebaioth minister:
They shall ascend with acceptance on mine altar.

23. *Destruction of a serpent.*—xxvii. 1.
In that day shall Jehovah punish with his sword;
His well-tempered, and great, and strong sword;
Leviathan the rigid serpent,
And Leviathan the winding serpent:
And shall slay the monster, that is in the sea.

24. *Anxiety of birds at the cry of their young.*—xxxi. 5.
As the mother birds hovering over their young;
So shall Jehovah God of Hosts protect Jerusalem;
Protecting, and delivering; leaping forward, and rescuing her.

ALLUSION TO THE ARTS.

25. *The operation of a smith.*—Isaiah liv. 16, 17.
Behold, I have created the smith,
Who bloweth up the coals into a fire,
And produceth instruments according to his work;
And I have created the destroyer to lay waste.
Whatever weapon is formed against thee, it shall not prosper.

26. *Refining.*—i. 25.
And I will bring again mine hand over thee,
And I will purge in the furnace thy dross;
And I will remove all thine alloy.

27. *Thrashing.*—xli. 15.
Thou shalt thrash the mountains, and beat them small,
And reduce the hills to chaff.

28. *Improvement in materials for building.*—lx. 13. 17
The glory of Lebanon shall come unto thee;
The fir-tree, the pine, and the box together:
To adorn the place of my sanctuary;
Instead of brass, I will bring gold;
And instead of iron, I will bring silver;
And instead of wood, brass;
And instead of stones, iron.

29. *Making a public road.*—lxii. 10.
Pass ye, pass through the gates: prepare the way for the people!
Cast ye up, cast up the causey; clear it from the stones!

MIRACLES.

30. *Creation repeated.*—Isaiah li. 16. and lxv. 17.
    I have put my words in thy mouth;
    And with the shadow of my hand have I covered thee:
    To stretch out the heavens, and to lay the foundations of
        the earth;
    And to say unto Sion, Thou art my people.

    For behold, I create new heavens, and a new earth;
    And the former ones shall not be remembered,
    Neither shall they be brought to mind any more.

31. *A desert transformed into a paradise.*—xxxv. 1, 2. and li. 3
    The desert, and the waste, shall be glad;
    And the wilderness shall rejoice, and flourish:
    Like the rose shall it beautifully flourish.

    Thus therefore shall Jehovah console Sion;
    He shall console all her desolations:
    And he shall make her wilderness like Eden;
    And her desert like the garden of Jehovah.

PROMISCUOUS INTIMATIONS.

32. *There shall be an uniformity of speech.*—Isaiah xix. 18.
    In that day there shall be five cities in the land of Egypt,
    Speaking the language of Canaan,
    And swearing unto Jehovah God of Hosts:
    One of them shall be called the city of the Sun.

33. *An increase of veneration and possessions.*—xlv. 14.
    The wealth of Egypt, and the merchandise of Cush,
    And the Sabeans tall of stature,
    Shall come over to thee, and shall be thine:
    They shall follow thee; in chains shall they pass along;
    They shall bow down to thee, and in suppliant guise address
        thee:
    In thee alone is God,
    And there is no God besides whatever

34. *An elongation of life.*—lxv. 20. 22, 23.
    No more shall be there an infant short lived;
    Nor an old man who hath not fulfilled his days:
    For he, that dieth at an hundred years, shall die a boy.
    For as the days of a tree, shall be the days of my people.
    And they shall wear out the works of their own hands.

My chosen shall not labour in vain;
Neither shall they generate a short-lived race:
For they shall be a seed blessed of Jehovah;
They, and their offspring with them.

25. *A glorious cavalcade.*—lxvi. 20.
And they shall bring all your brethren,
From all the nations, for an oblation to Jehovah;
On horses, and in litters, and in counes;
On mules, and on dromedaries;
To my holy mountain Jerusalem, saith Jehovah.
Like as the sons of Israel brought the oblation,
In pure vessels, to the house of Jehovah

26. UNIVERSAL JOY.—xliv. 23.
Sing, O ye heavens, for Jehovah hath effected it;
Utter a joyful sound, O ye depths of the earth:
Burst forth into song, O ye mountains;
Thou, forest, and every tree therein!
For Jehovah hath redeemed Jacob;
And will be glorified in Israel.

COMPARISON BETWEEN THE NORTH AMERICANS AND THE ANCIENT GERMANS.

THE question relative to the origin of the Indians of our country, increases in interest, in proportion as means are employed for spreading among them the arts of civilized society, and the tidings of redemption by Jesus Christ. Whatever can tend to throw light on inquiry, cannot fail of proving acceptable. Dr. Robertson, in his "View of the Progress of Society in Europe," has contrasted the condition of the Indian tribes with the ancient inhabitants of Germany; and though he supposes the resemblance to have risen from the similitude of their political situation, he has little doubt but that Bochart and other philologists, would have pronounced with confidence, "that the Germans and Americans must be the same people." He states, as his own opinion, that "the resemblance between their condition is greater, perhaps, than any that history affords an opportunity of observing between any two races of uncivilized people."

The following is the amount of his observations, and may, at least, offer an assisting clue to future investigation.

1. The Americans subsist chiefly by hunting and fishing; some tribes neglect agriculture wholly,—when attended to, the labour is performed by the women. Subordination is scarcely known. The

children are generally left to educate themselves, and are in a state of wildness resembling the deserts they inhabit. It was so with the ancient Germans.

2. Civil authority is extremely feeble. The sachem or chief is elective, with a council of old men to assist him; but neither he nor they have much power. Their influence lies chiefly in persuasion, while the obedience of the people is altogether voluntary. Such were the circumstances of the ancient Germans.

3. War is entered upon, not by constraint, but by choice. When resolved on, a chief proposes himself as their leader. Volunteers may offer to fight under him, for none is compelled, but such as engage cannot recede, on pain of the total forfeiture of reputation, and perhaps of life Such was the habit of the Germans.

4 Those who follow any leader, expect to be treated with great attention and respect They always look for presents from him of great value, and he feels himself under obligation to comply with their wishes. The Germans did the same.

5. When an injury is received, the jurisdiction of the magistrate is usually disregarded, and the offended party proceeds to avenge himself of his adversary. Resentments are excessive. Time cannot allay them, nor death itself. They are left as an inheritance to future generations, and are removed only by satisfying them. Death for death is the general demand. Sometimes, however, the offended persons become appeased by presents, and especially by a captive taken in war, who is adopted into their family, and enjoys their friendship, and is supposed to supply the place of the murdered individual. Equally implacable were the ancient Germans

The resemblance holds in many other particulars The only material difference lies in the circumstance that many of the German tribes were more civilized than the Americans.

SPIRITUAL CONDITION OF THE HINDOOS.

THE knowledge of "the only true God," is connected with eternal life; but the Hindoos have *no knowledge of the one God* The greater part of their ancient teachers have declared that he is "the unknown Brumhu;" that he is not an object of worship, that he has no attributes, and has nothing to do with material things. They therefore worship the *gods*, who are to them the only objects of dread or hope, and to whom alone all worship, all praise, all petitions, and all offerings are presented. The histories of these gods exhibit them as in the highest degree capricious, weak, unjust, cruel, and licentious. That this is their real character is known to the most illiterate of the people; and therefore, in times of distress, they do not hesitate to reproach them in the most bitter expressions which disappointment can dictate; nor is it uncommon, in moments of anguish, for them to destroy the images of these gods which cannot save. This contempt of the gods is shown even in the most common occurrences of life: when a man's clothes are wet by an unexpected and undesired shower, he sometimes exclaims, "These rascally gods are sending more rain." To the Hindoos, therefore, the gods are not "a very present help in trouble." They cannot "cast all their care" upon them, nor call upon them in the time of trouble, with any hope of relief. But the Christian can refer his minutest wants to Providence, persuaded that his heavenly Father knoweth that he needeth all these things. Respecting this most important branch of divine knowledge, in what lamentable darkness are the Hindoos!

The Hindoos are not only without God, but without a Mediator. The lower orders, it is true, approach the gods through the brahmuns. Ignorant persons speak as though the gods were the medium of access to the one God; yet it is certain that the gods are never spoken of as intercessors, nor ever regarded as such, in any of the forms of prayer or praise found in the shastrus.

The worship of the Hindoo always terminates on the deity whom he addresses. If ever he looks further, his hopes are fixed on his meritorious actions: so that he expects by them to "obtain God," that is, absorption. But if he sin, he has no "advocate with the Father;" no one able to save to the uttermost, by ever living to make intercession.

Further, *a Hindoo has no hope in Divine mercy as it respects pardon:* that sin will be forgiven, or the punishment remitted, makes no part of Hindoo faith. The shastrus declare, that the sins both of gods and men never leave the offenders till expiated by personal sufferings through millions of births. If a person sin in the human shape, he is doomed to pass through eight millions of births, before he can again appear as high in the scale of existence as man. Supposing him to sin as often as he appears in the human form, when are those transmigrations to end? A bramhun once declared, that as long as men are possessed of wants, they must sin. From hence it appears, that the Hindoos, to a man, have no hope of happiness after death; for perfect ascetics are no where to be found, and a pardoning God, or a throne of grace, they know not.

The Hindoos have no idea of *seeking Divine assistance* to enable them to become virtuous according to their own ideas. They are quite of opinion with Dr. Priestley, that a man's virtue arises only from himself. The most painful duties are enjoined upon their yogees; but the praise of abstraction is wholly given to the ascetic himself, none to God. Hindoos sometimes speak of the divine favour resting upon a man, but they mean nothing more by this than a recognition of the doctrine of fate. But take from the Christian system the promise of assistance in duty, and it loses all its glory, and man becomes a certain prey to his spiritual enemies. Christ has said, "Without me ye can do nothing;" but he also says, "How much more [cheerfully than the tenderest earthly parent will give good gifts to his children] shall your heavenly Father give the Holy Spirit to them that ask him;" so that to a person enabled to trust in Christ and do the will of God, salvation becomes a matter of entire certainty. The Hindoo has never heard of such assistance.

The *government of the world is, according to the ideas of the Hindoos, in the hands of the gods*, and of as many gods as there are things over which they can preside; and these gods are so capricious and ignorant, that they are represented in many instances as counteracting and ruining each other. What must then become of the interests of mortals?—Hence a Hindoo has no confidence either in the wisdom or the benevolence of his god. In his misfortunes he not unfrequently reproaches his guardian deity, or resorts to some other power. He says, "The gods will do as they please;" but he is never able to say, God is too wise to be mistaken, and too good to be unkind. What a desolate creature is man, when we behold him stript of the tender care and wise direction of a "heavenly Father!" A Hindoo says, "O God, what art thou about? What have I done, that thou thus afflictest me?" But a Christian says, "It is the Lord, let him do as seemeth him good."

A Hindoo has no idea *that the present state is probationary*, and that if religion be truly cultivated, heaven may follow. He considers himself as placed under an inevitable fate, which he did not originate, and over which he has no control; that this fate will carry him forward as a floating atom, and bear him wherever it pleases. All the comfort therefore that arises to a Christian from the assurance, "Seek and ye shall find," and from a vast variety of "exceeding great and precious promises" scattered through the sacred volume, he never tastes. He quietly gives himself up to the current, and permits it to carry him wherever it will.

Finally, *his views of a future state neither awaken his fear, nor stimulate him to a course of virtuous action*, " seeking glory, honour, and immortality." He fears transmigration more than a state of misery;* and, as has been already observed, he has no hopes of heaven. If he had any, he has no idea that purity of mind is to qualify for its enjoyment, for sensual pleasures form the chief bliss promised in the Hindoo heavens. But the Christian hope leads the believer to purify himself even as Christ is pure; so that his hope, while it is as an anchor to the soul, is the best security for a life of holiness. But, when we add to all this, that unless the blessings of the Gospel are imparted to the Hindoos, either as sincere and holy seekers of God, or as actual believers in our Lord Jesus Christ, they must perish eternally, how heart-rending does their condition appear!

Thus the Hindoo system supplies no stimulus to a holy life—no examples of holy prophets, apostles, and martyrs—no means of religious instruction and improvement—no consolation and support in affliction—no hope and succour in death—no prospects of a glorious resurrection, nor of a blessed immortality. In short, it leaves its disciples " without hope, and without God in the world." Are we not then bound, by every motive which can operate upon us, as men made of one blood, and as Christians, to seek the diffusion of " the glorious gospel of the blessed God?" God grant that we may be faithful to these obligations, treating with deserved contempt and abhorrence the idle and unfeeling insinuation, that their conversion is hopeless, and that the word of God, as it respects these millions, *shall* return to him void. Let the means to accomplish their conversion be adequate to the case, and then we may hope, at no very distant period, that India shall be seen " stretching out her hands unto God," and saying, " What have we any more to do with idols?"

FRIEND OF INDIA

---

* Mukshya, or the liberation of spirit from every thing which is not spirit, is the highest felicity held out by the Hindoo writings. They believe that there is only one spirit, portions of which are individuated by portions of matter, thus forming sentient beings; this universal spirit is God. Hence Mukshya is the entire destruction of personal identity. The insulated portion of spirit, when liberated from all extraneous things, mixes with the divine essence, as the water contained in a vessel, when the vessel is broken, mixes with the general mass of water. The highest happiness therefore held out by their shastrus is, the less of personal identity by absorption in God, involving as a consequence the total destruction of the individual. A Hindoo cannot therefore expect future happiness, as that cannot be enjoyed by any one when his individuality is destroyed.

ON MINISTERIAL SUPPORT.

FROM the sacred writings it is evident that Jesus Christ appointed a gospel ministry, as the means of exhibiting the light of divine truth, and bringing to himself a chosen people out of every age and nation of the world, until time shall be no more. Under circumstances ever fluctuating and unpropitious, such a ministry has continued to exist; and is at this day employing, with astonishing success, its plans and exertions for the welfare of man, and the enlargement of the Redeemer's kingdom.

That such a ministry was instituted to show unto men the way of salvation, is generally acknowledged by professed Christians; but upon *the subject of giving a temporal support for ministerial services*, equivocation and dispute have taken rise. Though some persons consent to it as an act of charity, and others correctly regard it as a claim of right and justice; yet there are multitudes insensible to every consideration, who stubbornly deny that either justice or charity, requires any thing for such purposes. This is an evil widely extended, and fraught with ruinous consequences. To this it must be principally ascribed, that in many places the interests of true religion are languishing; houses of worship are seldom opened and thinly attended; churches are groping in darkness; ministers becoming earthly-minded; the word of God feebly or foolishly expounded, and a sordid system of covetousness, instead of being held up to contempt and scorn, is furnished with the sanction of what is called Christian example.

From the nature of the case, it is very liable to escape public animadversion. Ministers often choose to suffer in silence the most embarrassing privations, rather than provoke the censures and illiberal imputations of avaricious men. But whatever respect may be generally due to acute sensibilities, perhaps we should not err in calling this a false and squeamish delicacy. The late celebrated Dr. Coke, after returning from his visit to our country, in his report to the *English Conference*, observed; "that one evil pervaded the Methodist churches in America, which was deeply to be deplored:—that numbers of faithful and able ministers, annually located themselves to procure, by manual labour, a subsistence for themselves and families." The doctor then added, the " the fault was principally chargeable upon the preachers themselves, on account of their backwardness to urge upon the people, the duty of giving an ample support to the ministry." This remark claims serious consideration. Those especially whose circumstances exonerate them from the suspicion of in terested views, should never fail, upon suitable occasions, to bear their decided testimony against this abuse.

By claiming a temporal support for the ministry, we do not require a provision for that parade, and pride, and expense of living which is affected by the men of this world; but we contend that the faithful minister of the gospel has a *sacred right* to such a temporal remuneration for his labours, as may render his situation comfortable, and allow him a moderate surplus. If any standard be required, we would say, *Whatever it might be supposed that the talents, learning, industry, or secular occupation of the minister, if otherwise employed, might secure, of income for himself and family; ought to be given by the people for whose sake he toils in the gospel, and foregoes all secular advantages.*

Before we exhibit proofs of this position, it is necessary to premise, that the ministerial office requires all the time and attention of the preacher. This must be evident from the examples of our Lord and his apostles, and also from the strict charge of Paul to Timothy: " Till I come give attendance to reading, to exhortation, to doctrine. Neglect not the gift that is in thee—meditate upon these things; *Give thyself wholly to them,* that thy profiting may appear to all." 1 Tim. iv. 13—15.

The attentive reader of the word of God will not fail to observe, that under every dispensation previous to the advent of Christ, divine worship was maintained at considerable expense. After the departure of the Hebrews from Egypt especially, the expenses were such as cannot be computed by us. This was probably intended to impress their minds with a sense of the superior value of spiritual things. The church having now passed into a higher stage of spiritual refinement, these burdensome rites are done away, and *all we with open face behold the glory of the Lord* in the gospel. Yet we are not entirely exempt from expense in maintaining public worship. But since the gospel evidently retrenches nearly all those expenses which Jewish worshippers had to encounter; and, on the other hand, confers spiritual advantages upon us which are far superior to theirs; why should we feel reluctant to contribute for the support of the gospel ministry? Very reasonable and pointed is the interrogation of the apostle: " If we have sown unto you spiritual things, is it a great thing that we shall reap your carnal things?" But we shall have occasion to revert to this topic again, when we take up the arguments of the apostle on the subject.

In attempting a direct proof of the point, our first attention is due to the testimony of our great Redeemer. When he sent out his disciples to preach the kingdom of God in Judea, he warned them against the abominable sacrilege of working miracles and preaching the gospel for the purpose of amassing property or filthy lucre—"*freely ye have received, freely give;*" but immediately adds, " Provide neither gold nor silver nor brass, in your purses, nor scrip for your journey, neither two coats, neither shoes, nor yet staves. "*for the workman is worthy of his meat:*" της τροφης αυτω, *his maintenance,* including other necessaries besides *food.* No doubt this admonition was given partly on account of the short tour they were to make, and partly with a view to teach them dependence upon the Master who employed them; —if he judged them worthy of their maintenance, his omniscient providence would secure it; but it teaches also, with equal, if not greater evidence, that it is the indispensable duty of Christians to maintain those who preach the gospel among them. He who labours among men in word and doctrine, is as worthy of his maintenance, as is the man who reaps down their fields; and if it be kept back by them, is it not *fraud,* which the Lord of Sabbaoth will punish? James v. 4.

The apostle Paul, in the ninth chapter of his first letter to the Corinthians, has established this point by a series of very cogent arguments. He had probably discovered in the Corinthians a captious and parsimonious disposition, and therefore determined to act with the utmost caution among them:—certain it is that he was *in want,* while with them. 2 Cor. xi. 9. To prevent any suspicions of interested views, he laboured with his hands, to preach the gospel to them without charge. He ever afterwards exulted in the disinterested course of conduct which he had pursued, because the subsequent character of that church gave ample evidence of its correctness; and when he was totally beyond the reach of suspicion, he boldly declared his right to a maintenance from them. Now, that the apostle should decline to avail himself of his *right,* where circumstances might render it prejudicial to the interest of souls, reflects a glory upon his character, while it gives tenfold force to his arguments in favour of the principle we are vindicating. He is very careful to guard against a misconstruction of his conduct, both in this and a similar passage, in 2 Thess. iii. 9. *Not because we have not* POWER,—*or right.*

But we solicit the attention of our readers, more particularly, to the whole of the passage above cited. Paul asserts his apostolic character and authority, which must have been peculiarly manifest to the Corinthians, from the success of his labours; ver. 1, 2. He declares his right to a maintenance among them, not only for himself, but for a wife also, had he thought proper to take one, as did the other apostles; ver. 4, 5. And asks, whether himself and Barnabas only had no *right to forbear working;* which most obviously implies that the rest of the apostles *did not labour for their subsistence*, but *derived it from those to whom they ministered in holy things.* He then proceeds to adduce a number of arguments to establish the principle. He argues,

1. From the common sense of mankind: verse 7. " Who goeth a warfare at any time at his own charges? Who planteth a vineyard, and eateth not of the fruit thereof? Or who feedeth a flock, and eateth not of the milk of the flock?" The soldier, at the risk of his life defending his country, is supported at the public expense; the vine dresser and the shepherd, derive their subsistence from the fruit of the vine, and the milk of the flock. These things were customary and right; and hence the apostle infers the right of the minister to his maintenance. He is a soldier of the cross, a labourer in the Lord's vineyard, and a feeder of his flock. It is plainly a matter of strict justice, that he should have a remuneration in temporal things. Again, in the 11th verse he asks, " If we have sown unto you spiritual things, is it a great thing if we shall reap your carnal things?"—Evidently the force of the reasoning is this: if spiritual things be superior in value to temporal things—if the whole world be unequal to the value of one soul; Matt xvi 26. then can it be considered *a great thing*, that while we are labouring to effect the salvation of your souls, we should receive a remuneration in carnal things—*all of which* bear no comparison with the blessings we are instrumental in conferring upon you? Very reasonable then is the precept of the apostle, Gal vi 6. " Let him that is taught in the word, communicate to him that teacheth in all good things."

An additional consideration may be included under this head. Paul says, 1 Tim. v. 8 " If any provide not for his own, and specially for those of his own house, he hath denied the faith, and is worse than an infidel." This is the dictate of nature as well as inspiration. Heathen writers concur in the general sentiment. Tacitus says, " Liberos cuique ac propinquos natura carissimos esse voluit:" ' Nature dictates, that to every one, his own children and relatives should be most dear.' Cicero says, " Suis quisque debet tueri" ' Every man should take care of his own family.' For this purpose, our Creator has allotted us six days out of seven, for labour. With health, industry, prudence, and the divine blessing, any man may acquire a sufficiency for his own maintenance and that of his family. But the faithful minister of the gospel, though by no means exempt from this obligation, is compelled to forego every advantage which he might derive from labour. Can it be pretended, then, that he ought not to receive ample remuneration for his ministerial services? But the apostle argues,

2. From the law of Moses: ver. 8, 9, 10. "Say I these things as a man? or saith not the law the same also? For it is written in the law of Moses, (Deut. xxv. 4.) thou shalt not muzzle the ox that treadeth out the corn. Doth God take care for oxen? Or saith he it altogether for our sakes? For our sakes no doubt this is written: that he that plougheth should plough in hope; and that he that thrasheth in hope, should be partaker of his hope."—This precept of the Mosaic law, displays the amazing kindness of God, in providing for the sustenance of irrational animals, but the apostle declares that it is written for our sakes. The import of the passage is, that it cannot be supposed that God will provide for the maintenance of oxen, and forget or neglect to make provision for his ministering servants. Nay, this precept is designed to evince the contrary: that he that plougheth should plough in hope of enjoying the fruit of his labours; and that he that thrasheth in hope, should be partaker of his hope, of having a supply out of that which he is thrashing.—Again, in the 13th verse, he adverts to the provision made for the ancient ministers of religion: " Do ye not know that they which minister about holy things live of the things of the temple? and they which wait at the altar are partakers with the altar?" All the officers employed in conducting the temple worship, had a right to their maintenance out of the sacred revenues. They had their different spheres of sacred employment, and different secular advantages; the Levites were they which ministered about holy things, inferior officers, who, though they had no inheritance in Canaan, received about the fifth part of the incomes of the Hebrew nation, the privilege of 48 cities, and other immunities. The priests, belonging to the same tribe with the Levites, were the highest officers of the temple, and *waited* alone *at the altar* The Lord provided that they should *partake with the altar;*—they had the skins of all the burnt offerings; the skin and the flesh of all the sin and trespass offerings; the shewbread, after it was removed from the golden table; a considerable portion of all the peace-offerings; all of what was called the poll-money, with small reservations; the tenth part of the tythes from the Levites; and numerous perquisites beside. Now, this was the Divine appointment, and from this the apostle argues, that the ministers of the New Testament should be supported also. From the Old Testament we learn, that in times of declension in religion, these sacred claims were neglected; and it evinces that vital godliness is at a low ebb, among those who neglect the claims of the Lord's public servants at

this day. God did give a very solemn charge to the people, Deut. xii. 10. "Take heed to thyself that thou forsake not the Levite, as long as thou livest upon the earth." Hezekiah, agreeably to the Divine will, commanded the people "to give the portion of the priests and Levites, that they might be encouraged in the law of the Lord." 2 Chron. xxxi. 4. The sum of what we have to say upon this argument, is, that the ministry of the Old and New Testament are parallel; both instituted by the same high authority; both concerned in promoting the spiritual and eternal interests of men; and both, as it were, disinherited of the world. If provision was made for the temporal maintenance of the former, why not for that of the latter? But though we give them both a similar character, it must be remembered that the gospel ministry has the pre-eminence. Yet if the institutions of the Old Testament, which were so far inferior to the gospel, as to come under the denomination of *a worldly sanctuary and carnal ordinances*, if they made ample provision for the priest and Levite, and would not permit them to be encumbered with the cares of life; how can it be supposed that the ministry of a better testament shall be unprovided for, or left to contend with the world for their living, under every disadvantage? We will now turn our attention to the apostle's last argument.

3. From the law of Christ, verse 14. "Even so hath the Lord ordained, that they who preach the gospel should live of the gospel." What we inferred from the reasonings under the last head, is here declared to be the ordinance of the Lord; alluding to that language of our Redeemer already cited from Matt. x. 10. Luke x. 7. And is not this conclusive? Can a Christian ask any thing more? or neglect his duty henceforth? There is an absurd explanation given of this language by some, which the reader may possibly learn from the following paraphrase: "They that preach the gospel, shall derive their own spiritual life from the gospel." Who is so blind as not to perceive that this is an intended quibble? Who so ignorant of the scriptures, as not to see that it is a manifest departure from every just rule of scripture interpretation? The apostle is not speaking of spiritual life; but evidently drawing a parallel between the priest partaking with the altar, in the manner we have explained, and the minister living by the gospel. It is presumed, however, that there is a danger of giving too much importance to the errour, by an elaborate reply. Let the common sense of mankind decide. We will merely remark, that the apostle refers to our Lord's language, which is, *the labourer is worthy of his meat*—his maintenance; or as Luke has it, *worthy of his hire*.

Having discussed the arguments contained in the first epistle to the Corinthians, let us now turn to a passage in 2 Cor. xi. 7—9. Here the apostle places the subject in a very interesting point of light. "Have I," says he, "committed an offence in abasing myself that ye might be exalted, because I have preached to you the gospel of God freely? I robbed other churches, taking wages of them to do you service. And when I was present with you, and wanted, I was chargeable to no man: for that which was lacking to me, the brethren which came from Macedonia supplied."—Without pretending to illustrate what is sufficiently plain, let us simply remark,

1. Though the apostle voluntarily surrendered his right and authority for special purposes, yet the spirit of this language is *censure*. They were lacking in *duty* to him—he was *in want* among them: therefore, it was the duty of the Corinthians to have maintained the apostle; and their's is the fault, whatever induced him to decline receiving it of them. It is but too evident, however, that they were as silent about giving as he was about asking. A shrewd commentator observes, "if the preachers of the gospel were as parsimonious of the bread of life, as some congregations and christian societies are of the bread that perisheth; and if the preacher gave them a spiritual nourishment as base, as mean, and as scanty, as the temporal support which they afford him, their souls must, without doubt, have nearly a famine of the bread of life."

2. That brethren from Philippi, (see Phil. iv. 15, 16.) a city of Macedonia, did contribute to the necessities of the apostle while he was labouring for a distant church. If the apostle received assistance from a people not immediately under his care, and while preaching for another people; surely it cannot be pretended that the pastor of a church, should not be maintained by those who are almost exclusively the objects of his ministry.

3. That what the apostle received from the brethren of Macedonia he called WAGES. The original signifies "the *pay of money and provisions* daily given to a *Roman soldier.*" He calls it *robbery*, not because it was unjust, or that he practised any extortion in the case; but simply because it seemed to make the liberal and dutiful brethren of Macedonia, in a certain sense, tributary to the narrow-minded Corinthians.

What has been said will sufficiently obviate the principal objection that has been alleged against ministerial support: viz. that borrowed from *this example of Paul labouring for his own maintenance.* But some would ground it not so much upon his *example*, as upon the supposed *inspiration of those who are truly called to the ministry.*

They suppose it will be given the preacher in the hour of public duty what to say, and that it is, therefore, at least *unnecessary*, to devote any time to previous preparation. Indeed many profess to consider it worse than *unnecessary*—a circumstance involving very weighty suspicions against his religious character. Though wisdom requires, even in the smallest matters, *that we think before we speak*, yet in those things which involve the eternal interests of men, such a practice would be *criminal!* Thus Satan sports with the imbecility and the prejudices of mankind! But is it concluded that genuine ministers act always under Divine inspiration in their public duties? Inspiration, in the proper sense of the term, having accomplished its design in the establishment of Christianity, has long been dismissed from the church of Christ. Preachers of the gospel must expect no special *afflatus* of the Divine Spirit. They must seek knowledge from the divine word by prayer, meditation, and laborious research. These, and these alone, are the means which the Spirit of God will aid and bless, and precisely according to the diligence used, will the preacher's profiting appear. Divine assistance in the ministry may be expected, and will be given to our pious and persevering exertions. It is presumption, therefore, for that man to expect it, who either wastes his time in idleness, or devotes it to the pursuit of gain.

It has been objected, that *this doctrine tends to introduce unworthy persons into the ministry*. We acknowledge that the sacred office is not exempt from mercenary incumbents, who will devote the liberalities of the church to avarice or prodigality. But this is a difficulty which no device of man can obviate. Even where the greatest precautions are used, there will be found a Simon Magus. We deplore the fact; but do not perceive the *tendency* of this doctrine to promote it. Where exorbitant salaries are given, it may have such a tendency; but this is by no means what we propose. It is a LIVING, a MAINTENANCE for which we contend; and if unprincipled men seek it by deception and perjury, the guilt is theirs.

After all, it will be alleged by some, "*we are poor*, and hence we can give little or nothing for ministerial support." This, undoubtedly, is *possible;* but not always *strictly true*. It is frequently urged by churches as an apology for their neglect, when disinterested judges, possessing ample information, decide otherwise. We grant that it is *possible:* churches just constituted, few in number, the members generally destitute of property, and not in lucrative employments; or churches weakened by internal dissentions, or external disasters, may indeed be unable to support a minister. In such cases, the conscientious man would feel it his duty to serve them with a very modeerate subsistence, or even gratuitously. But we have reason to suspect that such pleas of poverty are *not always strictly true*. Minds even slightly tinctured with the principle of covetousness, are easily induced to fancy themselves *too poor* to give any thing for those advantages which they conceive to be more imaginary than real, and at best very distant. Where the spirit and power of religion lie dormant, and the chilling influence of the world has taken hold of the church; though their circumstances be generally affluent, they will declare themselves *too poor*. It would not be difficult to show the absurdity of such a plea in most instances. Let us suppose a church to consist of 150 members. Say 100 of them will each have an average income of *one dollar* per day. In one week they will have 600 dollars; which, in most situations, would maintain a minister with a family. This supposed case, which certainly embraces very moderate calculations, proves that the united labour of one hundred members during *one week*, will maintain a stated ministry for one year. None would be sensible of the loss. Nay, the remark would generally hold, that nine out of ten of those churches who complain of poverty, expend more time and money, in the forms and superfluities of fashionable life, than is needful for the maintenance of the ministry, even at *ten* or *twelve hundred dollars* per annum.

In some instances there is found to be a difficulty in raising money by a general and efficient plan. There will always be a diversity of characters and views in religious, as well as civil communities, which may create some embarrassment. But where there is in any one a manifest unwillingness to bear a part in the necessary expenses of public worship, it would be well for the church to consider seriously, whether such an one be not a subject of discipline: yet it must be observed, that forbearance and long suffering ought always to be exercised, as far as it shall be consistent with the honour of the church. The plans that are in operation are various. Some accomplish their views by voluntary subscriptions, perhaps aided by weekly, monthly, or quarterly collections; others by general contributions of all alike, in a manner similar to the modern *mite societies*, in connexion with pew-rents, &c. &c. But the most efficient and satisfactory plan, is that of *an equitable assessment upon every member*—a sum levied upon the property or income of every individual, by a fair valuation. In this service the congregations will usually with cheerfulness unite.

It is needless, however, to say much upon this part of the subject. The greatest and most formidable of all difficulties is that of an unwilling mind. Where this impediment does not exist, plans will be devised and promptly executed; the cause of Immanuel will flourish, and the best interests of men be substantially promoted. It cannot be pretended that we overrate the importance of a faithful and enlightened ministry. It always exerts a happy influence upon the manners and morals of society, as well as upon the future hopes of the believer. Both reason and observation attest the truth of the remark, that where the ministerial character is lightly esteemed, and a reasonable support neglected, religion seldom prospers. There are many churches in our country, who, for an age or two, have maintained little more than the shadow of existence; destitute of the stated ministration of God's word, and scarcely distinguishable from the mass of irreligious men, yet well able to support a stated ministry. The spirit of Laodicea is prevalent among them to an alarming degree. The Lord sends out labourers into the harvest; but they endeavour to starve them, either as a test of sincerity, or from the wretched apprehensions of want. Deplorable indeed, and almost hopeless, is the case of those churches where *worldly-mindedness*, or *covetousness*, or *unbelief*, predominate. Well might we address to them the language of the Redeemer: *Behold! your house is left unto you desolate:* nay, your hearts also must be desolate. Covetousness has rifled you of the elevated comforts of true religion; rendered you in a great degree chargeable with the contempt that is brought upon the gospel; and answerable for the blood of those that perish in your families and neighbourhoods for lack of spiritual knowledge; your own minds become sordid, and the language of your practice is, that "gain is godliness," and wealth "the one thing needful." You support not the gospel, because you deem it a matter of secondary importance, and distrust the providence of God. You will not believe that he has a right to remand your possessions; or that he will repay with interest what you expend for his glory. But remember that you are likely to defeat your own intentions. God has the entire disposal of your life and interests. If ye *dwell in ceiled houses*, and neglect *the house of the Lord*, ye take the most effectual means to exclude the blessing of God from *your basket and store*. It may be said of you, as the Lord said to Judah: "Ye have sown much and bring in little; ye eat, but ye have not enough; ye drink, but ye are not filled with drink, ye clothe you, but there is none warm; and he that earneth wages, earneth wages to put them into a bag with holes." Haggai i. 2—6.

O! ye that love the Lord, arouse from your stupor! The time for action will soon pass away. Ye repose upon the promises of God; go forth in mighty exertions to promote the interests of Zion upon an extended scale. *Seeking first the kingdom of God and his right-*

ousness, ye have the unfailing promise, that *all these* necessary *things for life shall be added unto you.* Then you have every reason to consecrate your all to God. The spirit of the gospel is a spirit of *benevolence.* Ye enjoy an exquisite happiness, in the prospect or the hope of diffusing the blessings of the gospel among men. Maintain your confidence and your zeal for God; hold every other concern in due subordination; and by widely-extended, and well-directed efforts to promote the salvation of others, endeavour to effect *an abundant entrance* into the kingdom of glory. And though we are unable to ascertain, at present, the proportion of influence which individual exertions may have in the advancement of the great cause, *we shall know hereafter*—it shall be told in the hearing of an assembled universe, at that day when a final estimate shall be made of all the characters and actions of man. Π. Σ.

GALILEO.

THE name of this eminent mathematician and astronomer will, probably, be held in veneration to the latest ages. Availing himself of a discovery relative to the power of certain glasses made by the children of one Jansen,* a Dutch optician, he formed the TELESCOPE. Directing this instrument to the heavens, he, *first of his species*, beheld the surface of the Moon diversified with profound vallies and lofty hills. Mercury and Venus he observed to vary in their phases like the Moon. He saw that Jupiter was attended with four satellites, which he denominated Medicean stars. Saturn appeared oblong, consisting of the orb and its *ansæ*, or extreme parts of its ring, while the sun exhibited large spots, from the motion of which the revolution of that immense body on its axis was inferred.

When this intelligence was sounded through Europe, by some astronomers these discoveries were applauded, while others treated his statements as visionary. These new appearances in the heavens,

---

* Bonnycastle, in his Introduction to Astronomy, states, that an incident effected "what philosophy might have sought for in vain: the children of one Zachariah Jansen, a spectacle-maker of Middleburgh in Holland, being at play in their father's shop, happened, by chance, to place a convex and concave glass in such a manner, that in looking through them at the weather-cock of the church, it appeared to be nearer, and much larger than usual. The surprise they expressed at this circumstance, exciting their father's curiosity, he examined the same object himself, and finding what the children said to be true, improved the hint, by fixing the glasses upon a board, that they might be always ready for observation."

added to the conviction he felt of the truth of the Copernican system, and he wrote in its defence. The ignorant and prejudiced clergy, not aware that the language of scripture is designed for popular use, cited him before the inquisition, first in the year 1615, when he was incarcerated for five months,—and afterwards in 1633, when, after a trial of two months, he was *forced to renounce his own views*, detained in prison at the pleasure of the cardinals, and enjoined, as a means of his salvation, to repeat, once a week, the seven penitential Psalms. He died a few years after, in the vicinity of Florence, having previously lost his eye-sight, from the perpetual use of the telescope, and exposure to midnight air.

The following is a copy of the ABJURATION he made.

"Soutenir qui le soleil immobile & sans mouvement local, occupe le centre du monde ; est une proposition absurde, fausse en philosophie, & hérétique, puisqu'elle est contraire au temoignage de l'écriture. Il est également absurde & faux en philosophie de dire que la terre n'est point immobile au centre du monde ; & cette proposition considerée théologiquement, est au moins erronnée dans la foi.— Moi Galilée, à la soixante-dixieme annee de mon âge, constitué personnellement en justice, etant à genoux, & ayant devant les yeux les saints evangiles, que je touche de mes propres mains, d'un cœur & d'une foi sinceres, j'abjure, je maudis & je deteste les absurdités, erreurs, heresies," &c.

To assert that the sun is immoveable, and without local motion, is stationed in the centre of the world, is an absurdity, false in philosophy, heretical, and contrary to the testimony of scripture. It is alike false and absurd to say that the earth is not immoveable in the centre of the world ; and this declaration, theologically considered, is at least erroneous in point of faith. Wherefore, I Galileo, in the seventieth year of my age, in public court, being on my knees and having before my eyes the holy evangelists, which I touch with my own hands, from my heart, and with sincere faith, *do* abjure, execrate, and detest these absurdities, errours, heresies, &c.

The above is certainly a curious document, viewed in a philosophic light, and may serve to exhibit a useful contrast between the power of the gospel and the power of science to sustain the mind in the fires of persecution. Christianity can breathe and rejoice in an atmosphere where philosophy faints and expires.

MISSIONARY INTELLIGENCE.—FOREIGN.

MISSION TO BURMAH.

Extract of a letter from Mr. Hough to the Cor Sec. dated Serampore, March 4, 1819.

REV. AND DEAR SIR,

ON inquiry I have ascertained it to be a fact, that the king of Burmah has demanded of this government both Chittagong and Dacca, and that the demand is not to be complied with. What the event will be, is yet uncertain, but should it be a trial of strength, it must turn in favour of the christian government and christian missionaries.

You will receive by this conveyance a printed plan for a college in Serampore, together with a memorial relative to translations. "Attempt great things, expect great things," is a maxim manifest in all the missionary pursuits in Serampore. Should the plan for a college succeed, it will, with the other plans of education now in operation in this country, be of incalculable advantage, if not to the present, yet certainly to the succeeding generation

I received a letter a few days since, from brother Meigs of Jaffna, informing me that brother Warren had finished his labours upon the earth, and that brother Richards was in very low state of health. I collected from the letter, that although the mission was afflicted, yet the Lord is pleased to give it prosperity.

Extract of a letter from the Rev. Dr. Carey to a friend in London, dated Serampore, October 4, 1818.

MY children are now all about me. We have employed Felix to assist in the operations of the printing-office, particularly reading and correcting proofs. William is at Cutwa, Jabez going to Rajpoothana, and Jonathan in Calcutta, practising law.

Brother Marshman's eldest daughter was lately married to a Mr. W. the first of the Company's civil servants who has been baptized.

Brother Ward's health is so bad, and his whole frame so relaxed, that the medical men all agree in the necessity of a voyage to England, and he will therefore, in all probability, embark in two months' time. This is much to be regretted, but cannot be prevented.

Through mercy, I am well. My work is rather heavier than ever, but I rejoice in it. My wife has been unable to walk for several months. I went with her on the river last week, to try whether that would be beneficial to her; but we were very near meeting with a serious accident. Our vessel, a pinnace, ran foul of a sloop lying at anchor, which carried away three or four of the stanchions of the windows; had we been a foot or two from the place we were in, we should have just run on the bow of the sloop, which would have infallibly sunk us, as the stream ran with amazing rapidity. God, however, mercifully preserved us. Our danger was the greater, as another sloop lay at anchor about half a mile from us, in a direct line; we, however, got a tow line fastened to the one on which we ran, which they gradually let out till we were alongside the one I feared, so that we were preserved from every harm.

Extract of a letter from Dr. Marshman to the Cor. Sec. dated

MY DEAR BROTHER, Serampore, March 4, 1819.

I have been longing for these many months to get time and opportunity to communicate ideas with you once more. Our cause is one with yours in the Burman country, and we hope ere long in other countries too, and ours in Hindoosthan are precisely the same —the same gospel to spread—the same errours to root out—the same means to be used—the same joy in success—the same adorable Redeemer to glorify. We do not wish to arrogate to ourselves any superior knowledge; all we have been enabled to obtain of knowledge and experience, in these twenty or twenty five years, we find quite little enough to enable us to do the work committed to us; but we are convinced that the gospel will never be effectually spread throughout any country merely by FOREIGN missionaries. It is theirs to carry the gospel thither, to sow wholly a right seed, and to nourish native converts, till they grow up to the stature of men in Christ Jesus: but these native converts must be the men who shall take the gospel and spread it through every city, and town, and village, till it shall fill the whole land. This is the course we have pursued from the beginning, and it is through these means that the Lord has granted us such abundant success. Such was indeed the case, both at the first promulgation of the gospel, and at the time of the reformation. A few foreign evangelists carried the gospel into the various countries, kindled the sacred flame in the minds of their native converts,—and these propagated the gospel where, perhaps, their revered teachers received the crown of martyrdom.

We now, through rich mercy, are placed in new circumstances. About 18 years ago our beloved Krishnoo led the way, and formed our only Hindoo convert. Now, in addition to the numerous European churches in the army, seven or eight at least, and other European brethren, we have a NATIVE Christian population, which includes above a thousand persons, men, women, and children, and which is rapidly increasing every year. These are indigenous in this country, and will remain, whatever may become of us. The great question is—shall their rising youth be cultivated to the utmost—be trained up in the knowledge of the sacred writings—of the doctrines and duties of the gospel—of the history, geography, and science of the ancient and modern world—of the Sungskrit language, the Latin of India—of the futility and falsehood they will have continually to withstand,—or shall they be left naked and defenceless—ignorant of the gospel they must disseminate—of the errours they have to combat every moment—of their own language,—and on this account alone be trampled under foot by their more learned adversaries? But how shall this be done but by a college over which a Carey shall preside, and to which he shall give the tone while yet in the flesh? The certainty of this course being likely, with the Divine blessing, to spread the gospel, will appear to most, but the *economy* of the course may not strike every one, though it will occur to a reflecting mind. Does it cost a thousand dollars annually to support a foreign missionary in India; a sum which the most rigid economy will, in many instances, feel insufficient, *sixty dollars* annually will support a native christian brother and his family with equal comfort. Then their outfit, their weakness of constitution, require many things which christian love and even humanity enjoins. It is quite unnecessary to add another word on the importance of improving native gifts to the utmost, while we hail every one whom the Lord renders willing to put his life in his hand and venture to the burning climes of India to carry the gospel thither.

We have purchased a piece of ground contiguous to the mission premises, on which to erect the college edifice. We are about to erect buildings without delay, for the accommodation of a hundred native christian students. We have already thirty christian native youths collected on the mission premises, and placed under a course of elementary instruction. We well know that you have in view another theological seminary with you, which we most cordially approve, and believe the Lord will bless. But he will not bless it the less for your lending your aid to encourage this, of such pressing and immediate necessity. The silver and the gold are the Lord's, and the hearts of all his people are in his hands,— AND SUCH IS THE NOBLENESS OF SOUL OF MANY OF HIS PEOPLE IN AMERICA, THAT IF HE STIR THEM UP, THE DONATION OF POSSIBLY TEN OF HIS PEOPLE THERE, MAY ESTABLISH THIS NATIVE CHRISTIAN COLLEGE, AND MAKE IT A BLESSING TO INDIA TO THE LATEST AGES.

Extract of a letter from Mr. Ward to the Cor. Sec. dated

MY DEAR BROTHER,   At Sea, April 13, 1819.

I WROTE to you a short time before I left Serampore, mentioning that I expected to go to England for my health, and on business, and that if I could be sure of pretty large subscriptions for a Hindoo college, in America, I would pay you a visit. I hope to be in England in three weeks, or a month, if spared; and I write now that I may send this off on the day we arrive at Liverpool, if possible; and with it a copy of the plan of the college. I much wish to visit America, and if you give me encouragement to hope that I shall be a successful beggar for our college, I will come over on purpose, should I be detained in England, or I will return to Serampore by America.

I was very ill during the last year in India, and thought at one time that I was about to appear to give up my account; but I was spared, and on getting a little better, this journey was projected. I grew better before I left Bengal, but as I had other concerns, relating to the future settlement of things at Serampore, and as it was hoped I might be able to obtain a pretty good sum to begin the college, I did not give up my journey, and by the help of God I am thus far advanced.

I was very sorry to hear of the illness of the two brethren lately sent out to strengthen the Burman mission, which lies under the greatest obstructions of any perhaps in India, owing to the capricious and despotic nature of the government; but the greater will be the honour of conquering these difficulties, and, once conquered, the field is immense. The people themselves are a fine race of men.

Should I come to see you, I shall bring testimonials from my brethren at Serampore, and from the society in England. Should this college be established, there will then be a gradation of means for the evangelizing of India, well suited to the work. The native schools will take the rising generation, and prepare them for reading the scriptures, and inquiring further into the nature of the kingdom of Christ as they grow up, of which they will have acquired some idea. The distribution of the scripture and tracts will be adding to the general illumination, and the preaching of missionaries, blessed to the souls of the heathen, will tend to the planting of churches. The college will train up a large body of youth, in such learning as will qualify some for respectable situations in life; thus raising such as have hitherto been the most ignorant and vicious of the population, because most neglected, and enabling them to recommend Christianity by their general knowledge and influence; and it will prepare converted youth for the ministry, for whom a college is more wanted than for young men in Europe and America, as the Hindoo has every thing to learn. The college lectures and instructions being also open to the heathen, if they will support themselves, much scientific and general knowledge will be diffused amongst them. There are already a number of young persons, the children of converted natives, ready to enter this college; and a house and a large piece of ground adjoining the mission premises, was bought just before I left Serampore. Some subscriptions had been collected in India, but much more was wanted before the buildings for the students could be raised.

I think that from this account you will be able to form some idea of what we have in view, and of the importance of the object; and should American baptists and others put a hand to this good work, they will have reason to think they have been laying up treasure in heaven, matter to increase their everlasting joy, seeing hereby the kingdom of the Redeemer may be so effectually advanced. I dare say that our brethren in America can rely upon us, for the application of their contributions, so that not a cent shall be wasted.

On the 24th of next month it will be twenty years since I left England. During this time I have lost my mother and eldest brother. I have yet a sister and three brothers living, I hope. To see them, to see my brethren in the Society, and many dear friends, and to retrace the scenes of my childhood and youth, forms a pleasing prospect; but I shall think my journey unprofitable, if it shall not subserve the interests of that kingdom which embraces the highest glory of God and the eternal happiness of myriads of the human race.

I shall be happy to receive accounts of fresh revivals amongst you. In the day of Pentecost, and in American revivals, we see what the Saviour can do in the earth, and in how short a time He can do it, when one sermon calls thousands. It is this day of power that is wanted, a day of power which He can call for whenever it shall please him. To display their energy, men need many days of preparation, and many instruments; but "He speaks, and his Almighty breath fulfils his great decrees." But as He chose to be six days in the work of creation, when he might have accomplished it at once, so he shows that the work of the new creation in the hearts of his elect, should be a work of time. We may think his promise fails, but we are utterly incompetent to form any opinion on his unrevealed will. This we may know, that one day with him is as a thousand years, and a thousand of our years as one day.

I have preached most Sabbaths since I embarked on board the ship, the Princess Charlotte of Liverpool, the captain is very obliging, but he is not a professor, nor are any of the officers. The carpenter seems to be a truly good man, he is member of an independent church at Whitehaven. The men sit and hear with attention; but I fear there is in none of them the revelation of God's power. Oh! what heavy work to preach, and yet see no fruit! But it is the Lord's work to save, ours to preach as he may enable us. I find it highly difficult to rely on him singly and wholly in the delivery of the word. I am ready to confide in the arguments I use, the persuasions I offer, the illustrations I attempt, and the force of the subject, rather than on the power of the Lord: this is an awful defect. I am ready to be angry with the hearers for not yielding themselves to the force of my arguments, when my grief should be that they do not yield themselves to God.

From Mr. Ward to the Rev. Joseph Maylin of Philadelphia, dated

MY DEAR BROTHER, At Sea, April 14, 1819.

I WAS favoured with yours, of June 9, 1818, some little time before I left Serampore, on a journey to England for my health, and on various other business connected with the mission in India, and especially to obtain subscriptions for raising a native college for christian and other youth at Serampore, of whom a number are ready to enter, and for whom such an institution is absolutely necessary.

I have a strong desire to visit America, that I may receive her contributions to this college, the ground for which was bought just before I left. It joins the other premises. Here, I hope, when we are laid in the dust, many will be training up for usefulness, to teach the sweet words of salvation to their fellow-countrymen sitting in the dark regions of sin, and kept prisoners by Satan, so that at his command they worship the destroyer.—Here native missionaries, taught the various languages of India, may go forth, bringing the Gentiles to be obedient to the faith. And may I not hope for your exertions, you who assisted us so affectionately in our first struggles at Calcutta —In this good work you may find an opportunity of helping that cause, which I know still lies near your heart. Inquire amongst your friends, and stir them up, and I may indulge the hope that Philadelphia, and New York, and Boston, and other cities of the United States, will patronize the cause. I will cheerfully come, either on purpose from England, or on my return to Serampore. I shall be in England (God willing) till May next year. Any letter you may favour me with, directed to the care of Dr. Ryland, Bristol, or W. Hope, Esq. Hope-street, Liverpool, I shall duly receive; and shall be glad to hear whether there be any encouragement to come over about the college, or if you can give me any good news respecting the cause of Christ in America, I shall rejoice.

You know in what state nominal Christianity has appeared in India hitherto; how ignorant, how vicious the native Portuguese are, and how the Christian cause has suffered in the eyes of the heathen, on this account. To prevent this being the case with the numerous native Christian youth, now rising up among the baptized Hindoos; to qualify some for respectable situations in life, to enable them to bring up their families well, and give them an education, and thus empower them to support the Christian cause by their influence and property, but more especially to train up really pious youth, and even persons more advanced, and fit them to teach others, by giving them a good knowledge of divinity, and enabling them to read the word fluently, (which few of them can now do,) is this college wanted. As the heathen reject the Christians, and cast them out of their land, it is necessary to meet the case as well as we can hence a number are supported by their labour at Serampore, and we have begun to take lands and form them into christian villages in other places, and if this college be erected, others may be well employed as clerks and attornies in the courts, and other respectable situations. When the body of Christians in India shall possess a good portion of christian knowledge, shall have christian teachers among them capable of teaching and defending the christian doctrine, and they shall be capable of supporting themselves by their own labour, and of contributing to the support of the cause, we may consider the gospel as having taken firm root in India, and that, under the blessing of God, the leaven thus hid will leaven the whole lump.

I know not that there has been any great alteration in the state of affairs lately; schools for native children have been begun by different denominations; nearly 8000 children are taught in the schools supported by the fund collected at Serampore from all parts of India, the Benevolent Institution is well filled up with children, and well supported; additions to the different churches are made from time to time, but the increase is not great any where. The additions at Calcutta had been fewer, but several under the instructions of Sibuk Ram were likely to be baptized soon after my departure. The translations are going forward under Dr. Carey successfully; and, upon the whole, though extensive success in the conversion of the heathen is not yet granted, there is much ground for gratitude and encouragement.—The chapel, however, is not full, a few are gone to Mr. Townley, the Independent missionary, and a few have given up all profession of religion. The health of brethren Carey and Marshman, when I left them, was very good. May they be long, long spared, even to a good old age.

Extract from Mr. Ward's account of his late journey from Serampore to Chittagong.

FEBRUARY 17, near *Kalee Ghat.*—This morning before breakfast went up to the temple of the great goddess, and found several bramhuns in the covered area before the temple, reciting different Sungskritu books, one the Chundee, and another the Shree-Bhaguvutu. As the doors of the temple were not yet opened, I began a conversation with an old man who professed to be here as a devotee of the goddess. I pressed him to examine the ground of his expectations from the goddess, reminding him that he would not purchase the slightest article of food or clothing without a thorough inspection; and that if all his hopes of future salvation should end in disappointment, that disappointment would be most grievous. He declared that he had no fears, that there existed the most convincing proofs of the power of the goddess. I told him that I had just seen, close to the temple, a poor woman lamenting the loss of her mother in the loudest cries, so as to fill the whole street with her complaints, and that therefore it was plain, that, notwithstanding the thousands of offerings presented to this goddess for health and prosperity, she did not save even those who lived close to her temple. A bystander said, that all these things were regulated by fate. "If then," I replied, "a person cannot die before his time, nor live beyond it, all these devotions are fruitless." The old man remarked, that at any rate the blessing of Kalee would be efficacious in a future state. I shook my head, and then changed the discourse, turning to a young man, who seemed eager to enter the lists; but when I saw he could not lay hold of the argument, I put an end to the conversation, by telling him that he afforded but a discouraging proof of the power of the goddess, who was famed for imparting wisdom to the simple. The bramhun, who continued reading the Chundee, smiled at his brother thus silenced, and in the midst of this, we were entreated to attend and pay our respects to the goddess, as the doors were now opened. After a little delay, that I might discover no eagerness in going to look at this mighty enchantress, we went up to the front of the temple, before the doors of which were placed a large heap of flowers to adorn the image. This black stone appears to be about three feet long, and one foot wide, the upper part, or the head, so painted as to represent the human countenance, with large oyster eyes, and a golden tongue hanging out even to the chin, to represent the feeling of surprise: no hands, or arms, or legs. We were pressed to ascend the steps, and take a nearer view of the goddess, or present our offering, but, recollecting what would be required, we turned about just as the bramhun was requesting us to pull off our shoes. Still, under the hope that we would make a present, the bramhun began to hint that the taking off the shoes would be dispensed with; but he gave up further entreaty when I assured him, that I would sooner submit to have both my hands chopped off, yea, rather part with life itself, than perform an act so treasonable against the true God.

We next went behind the temple, further to examine the building, which was undergoing a repair, when I asked a Hindoo in the group which accompanied us, how long the temple had been erected. Instead of giving a direct answer, he said, the temple had been already ten years undergoing the present repairs. I expressed my surprise, reminding him that if the goddess really possessed the extraordinary powers ascribed to her, the temple might surely have been repaired in one night; and at any rate it was a great proof of their want of devotion. The company smiled, and nodded an unwilling assent. We now went to an open area beyond the covered one, and in front of the image, where the animals are slain, and where two posts excavated at the top are erected, the one longer than the other, to receive the necks of the animals. I here asked the surrounding group how they could pretend that they did not take away life, while the ground around these parts was daily soaked with blood. The old plea was set up, that Kalee was the representative of time [from kalu, time] who devoured all his children, and that the shrastru commanded them to sacrifice animals, as well as to abstain from taking away animal life; and that both commands were therefore to be obeyed.

The old man whom I had addressed at first, now took up the discourse again, and pleaded for the truth of the Hindoo system, on account of its being honoured with so many martyrs, in the persons of the widows perishing on the funeral pile. I urged that these were positive murders, and murders of the most horrible nature, since the person who lighted the pile, and thus perpetrated the murder, was the offspring of the widow's own bowels. To this it was replied, that these widows were under the influence of God, for that they could endure coals of fire in their hands, without shrinking, before they departed to the pile; and further, it had been seen, that when widows had been hindered from thus sacrificing themselves, they had died at home in a day or two. I declared my disbelief of these things, and added that it was impossible to change the nature either of sin or of holiness, as of black and white, and that these would be found to be atrocious murders another day. I told them that I felt the greatest heaviness of mind on their account, at seeing them so much under the power of delusion: it appeared that, notwithstanding they professed to shrink from the destruction of animal life, they thought it meritorious to slay whole hecatombs of animals, yea, and their own mothers too, and gloried in these things as acts of merit. I again urged the old man to examine the grounds of his religious confidence, on which he seemed so much to value himself. I told him faith was nothing, unless it was built upon a right foundation; that he might have the greatest confidence in the virtue of his wife, but his confidence would not save him from disgrace if she proved unfaithful.—One of the company was rather sullen under these attacks on their religious hopes, and said, I might go my own way, but that they would not be persuaded from persevering in theirs. I told him I would leave one word with him before I took leave, which was, that if he died trusting in the idols, he would find himself miserably deceived, and even ruined for ever and that my words would be remembered by him in a future state. He professed to treat this admonition with contempt.

In leaving the temple yard, I was shown another small temple, containing the images of Krishnu and Radha. This led me to enter on the evil of images in worship, and to point out to one of the company, that the image of Kalee could not fail to impress on the mind of the beholder the idea that God was a ferocious being, and these of Krishnu and Radha that he was an impure being. A young man, who entered into the controversy with much zeal, pleaded that the Pouranic story relative to Krishnu, and his favourite mistress, the wife of Ayunu-Ghoshu, was capable of a religious interpretation. I asked him if he could be persuaded to put a religious construction on the affair, if some one were to seduce his own wife. All, however, produced little beside a smile from these deluded creatures, who treat the subjects of life, death, and eternity, with perfect levity. It is true, they wonder that I should have thought so much about their shastrus. and they asked from whence I had come. But before these people can begin to doubt, they must begin to think, and that is not done without an effort, to which they are wholly averse, and the consequences of which are too serious for them to encounter.—" *Can these dry bones live? Ah! Lord God, thou knowest.*" Still He who is the Resurrection and the Life hath said, " The hour cometh, and now is, when the dead shall hear the voice of the Son of God; and they that hear shall live." In passing the gateway, I saw another paltry temple containing an image or two covered with garlands, and two or three decently dressed bramhuns sitting before them. The priest asked me for an offering, upon which I asked if he received cowries and pice, and upon his smiling and nodding assent, I asked the spectators, whether, since this man's temple was surrounded with shops, he might not be considered as a real shopkeeper? They laughed, and said I had hit the mark. We now returned to our boats.

During our journey this morning, I passed through scenes which filled me with a horrour which time can never erase. It would seem that Providence, as a mark of its displeasure, had turned all those places into Golgothas, where the Hindoos are most deluded and God most dishonoured. In the whole way from Kalee-Ghat, for two or three days, we did not sail a hundred yards without seeing a dead body, or the remains of one. In one place I saw more, I think, than one hundred bedsteads on which the sick and dying had been carried to this cemetery, and three or four funeral piles were then preparing. A number of bodies in different places were half eaten by vultures, which birds were to be seen hovering on one or other side of the canal in almost every spot for miles. Other bodies were floating down the stream; others were seen sunk by weights in the water; and the sick in various places were waiting amidst the funeral piles till their turn should come. Never, never can the horrid impression be removed,—and the stench for two or three miles was almost intolerable. The mortality has probably been increased by the prevalence of the cholera morbus; but I could not help attaching much of it to the temple, which is constantly visited by crowds of emaciated pilgrims.

During our stay at Kulee-Gunj, a bramhun, sick of the above disease, was brought to the canal, and placed in the water up to the middle, while his friends called on the gods, and urged the dying man to follow their example. I stood near while this was going forward, and watched their motions with much interest. Several young men, of very respectable appearance, were engaged in these last offices. A female or two were present, who seemed somewhat affected, but I did not see either in them, or in the young men, or even in the son of the old man, who also was present, any real sorrow. The woman apparently most sorrowful, really smiled while she sat over the dead body half immersed in the canal. All the young men, four or five, appeared eager to enter upon the funeral ceremonies. They sent to the village for wood, for a new garment, for red lead, and for a morsel of gold. When it was observed, that there was no gold in the house, a person was directed to break a knob from the nose-ring of some female member of the family. Four rupees were given to meet the present expenses. One of the young men complained that he had not had time to perform his daily ablutions, and, that as he had touched the body, and could not be purified till the whole was over, it was then too late. Another of the young men said, "Pshaw, there are twelve months in the year, never mind one omission." The whole exhibited the appearance of hurry and bustle in passing through the ceremonies, without the least honourable feeling in any of the parties: a decent man among the spectators observed to me, that in this way we were all passing away. Respecting the man just expired, one or two said, it was a happy death, for he died quite sensible; he had the benefit of the Ganges, and repeated the names of the gods with his last breath. Another observed, that the day and the lunar signs were inauspicious, but that it was of no consequence, as the old man had enjoyed the benefit of dying in the Ganges. Veneration for whatever is connected with Greece and Rome, has made some persons think favourably of this mode of interment; but the universal want of feeling on these occasions, is a strong presumption that the process of burning a body, like that of cutting off limbs, or slaying cattle, deadens the sensibility of the parties, and extinguishes those feelings which a more decent mode of interment might excite. The persons assisting on these occasions are the male children or other near relations: the eldest son sets fire to the pile; after which all engage in supplying fuel, keeping up the vigour of the flame, or adjusting the parts of the body as they lie on the pile, and ensuring the speedy destruction of every part. It might be thought that these persons, so nearly related to the deceased—these children, dandled on the father's knees, or fed from the mother's breasts, would, in thus silently watching, for nearly two hours, the destruction of a frame once so dear to them, exhibit the strongest emotions of grief, but the very contrary is the case; and in no family ceremony, that of marriage excepted, is there more the appearance of thorough apathy than in this, no signs of grief whatever, the time in general is spent in conversations on the most common topics, and the only concern is to complete the business as rapidly as possible, and in a manner which shall be strictly conformable to the customs of the country. Could the lowest order of Europeans ever be brought to break the limbs of a father or a mother before interment; and so soon after death, to throw the body into the river, perhaps to be devoured by dogs,—or to throw the unburnt bones into the river?—What a contrast does a Christian funeral present to this! The closing of the coffin—the departure of the corpse, and the last farewell at the grave!——Ah! Christian parents, you can best describe what is felt at these moments, and how calculated all these awful ceremonies are to awaken the tenderest sensibilities of the heart. The Romans preserved the ashes of their parents in urns, but a Hindoo washes them all into the river adjoining the funeral pile, and would consider his house polluted by the presence even of his father's ashes!

Extract of a letter from Mr Lawson to the Cor. Sec. dated

MY DEAR BROTHER, Calcutta, March 6, 1819

Your last communication came to hand, I believe, through the politeness of Mr Rivardi. He has been extremely ill here, but is now restored to good health. Yesterday I had the pleasure of dining with him and Mr. B—— and several American gentlemen. At the last meeting of the Committee of the Calcutta Auxiliary Baptist Missionary Society, Mr B—— was chosen a member of the Committee. A vote of thanks to the American gentlemen in Calcutta, for their liberality, was also passed. These friends will have the pleasure of soon seeing two meeting-houses in existence for the poor heathens, built entirely through their benevolence, as also a school, to be called their own. A native has nobly come forward and offered to be at the expense of the latter for the American gentlemen, with whom he is connected in some way of business; but the expenses of the school will be defrayed by themselves. I hope this is an example which will be followed by many. How much good may be done in this way!

We struggle on in our missionary labour. To our view prospects are a little brightening. A good deal of work is done now amongst the natives. We have three bungalow meeting-houses for the Bengalees, besides those in prospect for the Americans. They are well attended, and already there have been several inquirers. Last Sabbath day I baptized two natives, one of whom is a very good preacher, and two Portuguese women. O may they be enabled to hold out to the end! We preach constantly to the soldiers in Fort William. There are many pious people in some of the regiments here, and their numbers are increasing. Brother Chamberlain has been very ill, but is now much better, and as much engaged in the cause the Lord Jesus as ever. He is building a meeting-house for English preaching at Mongbyr. He is a most useful man. May his life be long spared to us.

Since I last wrote to you I have not received any account from Rangoon. Dr. Johns and family are again in this country. They are not connected with the mission, but as friends. They reside at Serampore. Mr. Pearce, (son of the late Samuel Pearce,) lives with us in Calcutta. Mrs. L. and Mrs P. conduct a young ladies' seminary, which prospers, and brother Pearce has two or three printing presses in full employ. Brethren Carey, Yates, Adam, and Penny, live in another house in Calcutta, and are very active among the natives. Indeed nothing was done of any particular importance on a large scale, till these brethren began to go about, first in the lanes, alleys, &c. and afterwards to preach in the Mat meeting-houses. This place was almost an untouched field, though a place presenting every possible facility in the work of a missionary, to say nothing of its immense population. We hope soon to send you the first report of our Auxiliary Baptist Missionary Society. This will give you a better idea of what is going forward amongst the baptists in this city. Our pedobaptist brethren are very laborious, and we are on the best terms with them. I pray that a spirit of love may prevail more than ever

ROMAN CATHOLICS AT BETTIYAH.

About sixty miles to the north of Patna, in the neighbourhood of Bettiyah, there are several villages of Roman Catholic christians which have now been established for more than three quarters of a century. Christianity was first introduced into that part of Hindoost'han by P. Joseph Maria, about the year 1740, under the reign of raja Dhroova-sha. A few days after the arrival of this missionary, the ranee or queen, who had been long indisposed, was completely restored to health through his medical skill. The performance of this cure induced the raja to entreat the missionary to abandon his original design of proceeding to Nepal, that he might settle at Bettiyah. P. Joseph told him that his intention, in leaving his native land, was to propagate Christianity, and that in whatever situation he might be placed, he should always pursue the object of his mission. The raja, without any hesitation, immediately gave him the residence of his dewan, who had recently fallen into disgrace. The intelligence of his medical skill, and of the raja's attachment to him, caused numbers to flock around him, either to hear his new doctrine, or to obtain bodily relief. Among others, Prem-sha, an opulent goldsmith, generally called Lak-puti, (the lord of lacs of rupees,) who was well versed in the Hindoo writings, visited him to display his own learning and to defend the doctrines of Hindooism For seven years he maintained a controversy with P. Joseph, at the end of which time he publicly renounced idolatry, and was received into the communion of the church of Rome. His wife invariably refused to follow her husband's example The descendants of Prem-sha are very numerous; they now form a considerable portion of the population in the village of Bettiyah His son was alive in 1816, and was then sixty years of age he was highly respected by the present raja, who is rather unfavourable to the Christians.

P Joseph Maria lived in Bettiyah twenty-five years, during this period six other Hindoos renounced idolatry. On his death, the raja, his wife, his daughter, and chief servants, repaired to the missionary's house, and lamented his decease with every expression of grief; and the poor of Bettiyah, and the surrounding villages, seemed to feel his loss as that of a common father

For fourteen years after the commencement of the establishment, the distinctions of cast were retained among the Christians at length Prem-sha, the first convert, convened a meeting of his brethren, and exhorted them to divest themselves of this badge of idolatry, and live together as brethren. To this proposal they acceded; and from that period the Christians have lived in great harmony, without any reference to their previous mark.

Since the death of father Joseph, eighteen priests have officiated among the Christians in these parts. At Bettiyah fifty families have embraced Christianity since the arrival of the first missionary, and their descendants, who are very numerous, constitute the population at that place. Children are admitted to the communion table at the age of twelve, and fourteen is regarded as a fit age for the marriage of females. The establishment is possessed of 200 bigahs of land, which the native Christians cultivate, appropriating a tenth of their produce to the support of the priest. Their occupations are various some possess carts, which they lend to their heathen neighbours, others nourish turkeys, fowls, geese, ducks, or hogs, as a means of support. Others apply to the occupations of goldsmiths, carpenters, or retail dealers; they are altogether so useful, that the credit of the grand market is supported chiefly through their industry. Their dress, with the exception of a metal crucifix, differs in no respect from that of their heathen neighbours.

In the year 1816, a school was established in Bettiyah for the christian children, where they were taught to read, write, and commit to memory selections from the gospels, translated by the catholic clergy into the language of the province. One for girls was likewise opened, but the want of funds obliged the priest to abandon it. The boys' school was placed under a christian teacher, and the number of children in it amounted to twenty.

At Chooriya, there is likewise a christian school, where the children are taught the prayers and catechism in the Nepal language by a Nepal christian, born at Katmandoo. At the same place there is likewise an Italian and Nepal grammar in manuscript, composed by the catholic missionaries.

About the year 1769, P. Alberto, and three other missionaries, were expelled from Nepal by raja Prit'hee-Narayun, and, with sixteen families who had embraced Christianity from among the Nepalese, came and settled at Chooriya. The occasion of their expulsion was the attachment of the raja's two sons to the priest, whom they frequently visited, and their intention to embrace Christianity. One of these young men afterwards gave fifteen or twenty thousand rupees to the Bettiyah mission. P. Alberto lived thirty years at Chooriya, but his congregation received little or no addition from Hindoosthan; he baptized none but the offspring of those who had escaped with him from Nepal. In Nepal there are said to be now three churches one at Katmandoo, one at Bhat-ga, and the third at Patun; but no priests.

In Bootan there are said to be churches and native Christians, but no priests. They were expelled from thence many years back; on which they commenced the Nepal mission.

The churches which the catholic clergy formerly planted in India, subsist to this day, though we believe with very few additions. The zeal which originated the missions, has apparently vanished, and within the last twenty years no attempt appears to have been made to establish new missions in places where they do not exist. The present congregations are indebted for their continuance, in a great measure, to the donations of land which the priests formerly obtained. These are under the immediate direction and patronage of the clergy, the native Christians are their tenants, and are hereby relieved from those vexations which Hindoo landlords might have inflicted on them.

From this account we may conclude that Christianity, when once planted in Hindoosthan, can never be wholly extinguished. The Christians will always remain a distinct race; and their being freed from those horrid customs which involve such a waste of human life among their idolatrous neighbours, together with the privilege which widows amongst them enjoy of marrying a second time, cannot fail to increase their numbers far beyond what would be the case with an equal number of their heathen neighbours, among whom widows even of the tenderest age are for ever excluded from any participation in the duties of life. Were few or no additions therefore made to the present number of Christians, they must still be constantly on the increase but in proportion as men read, and examine, and weigh things, truth is certain of gaining new friends. Hindooism indeed contains within itself the seeds of extinction. With respect to receiving new converts into its bosom, it differs from every other creed in the world it prohibits all extension and all proselytism, and thus the same laws by which its integrity is preserved, serve constantly to diminish its numbers.

MEETING AT ALBION CHAPEL, MOORFIELDS.

The concluding service in aid of the Baptist Missions, was held on Thursday evening the 24th, at six o'clock, at Albion Chapel, Moorfields, which had been kindly lent by the Rev. Mr. Fletcher and his friends for the occasion. Prayer was offered by Mr. West of Dublin, and Mr. Coles of Bourton; after which a report, comprising the substance of the intelligence received from the various missionary stations during the last year, was read by Mr. Dyer of Reading. Mr. Ward followed, in a brief but energetic address, in which he particularly aimed to impress upon the minds of his audience, the supreme importance of imploring, with greater fervour and distinctness, the outpouring of the Holy Spirit. These divine influences, he remarked, had been granted to cheer the hearts of the bereaved disciples of Christ, after his departure from them—had been continued in the church from that day to the present—and were *indispensably* necessary to the success of Christian missions. On this topic Mr. W. dwelt with that earnestness which the subject so imperiously demands; and enumerated various most formidable obstacles, which nothing but the power of that divine Agent can remove. Among these he specified the *difficulty of acquiring a foreign tongue;* the *levity of character* so prevalent among the Hindoos, the *dreadful state of superstition to which they are reduced,* the *errors which have been propagated* among them, the *alienation of mind from all intercourse with Europeans;* and the *cast,* which imposes upon every convert the agonizing necessity of renouncing father, and mother, and wife, and children, for the sake of the gospel. We cannot but hope that the impressive appeals made by this experienced missionary, especially to his brethren in the ministry, will be productive of much good. The meeting was closed in prayer by the Rev. Mr. Campbell of Irvine, in Scotland, now supplying the chapel in the absence of Mr. Fletcher. We believe that this, as well as the meetings which preceded it, was found by many to be a season of refreshing from the presence of the Lord.

DOMESTIC MISSIONARY INTELLIGENCE.

STATION AT ST. LOUIS.

Extract of a letter from Mr. Welch to the Cor. Sec. dated

MY DEAR BROTHER,   St. Louis, August 2, 1819.

THE mission, at least within my circle, presents nothing worthy of particular notice, only that we have at length commenced worship in the vestry room of our meeting-house; but when or where we shall obtain means to finish it, I have not the most distant idea. Did the churches in the States only but know the good that would result, would they not send over to Macedonia " a few cedars for the Lord's house!" Although we have no increase or revivals, yet it is my decided opinion that opposition is not so general as it has been.

The appropriations which have been made, together with other advantages in favour of the station occupied by brother Peck, will enable him to live, after a little, without much expense to the Board, while my situation will be materially different, so long as I remain in this place. These facts, I hope, will not be overlooked by our patrons; for I am more jealous of injury to the mission on account of expense than any other; and such is the importance of this station, that to abandon it now would be to yield all for which the enemy contends. I am determined, by the grace of GOD, to persevere.

STATION AT ST. CHARLES.

Extract of a letter from Mr. Peck to the Cor. Sec. dated

REV. AND DEAR SIR,   St. Charles, July 20, 1819.

WE are still trying to promote the cause in which we profess to be engaged, in the use of such means as Divine providence puts into our hands, but, alas! our progress is extremely slow! I feel more and more the absolute necessity of the Holy Spirit to give success. No human efforts can produce much in this country, even to promote external religion, without the aim of Omnipotence. Still, I trust, the doctrine of the Cross will prevail. The Moravians first began to instruct the untutored tribes of men, by holding forth, and proving from the light of nature, the existence of God—his divine perfections—the inspiration of the holy scriptures—the odious nature of vice, and the loveliness and blessed consequences of a life of holiness and devotion to God. Finding but little success attending their labours, they agreed to alter their mode of preaching, and dwell more on the sufferings of Christ—the virtue of his atoning sacrifice, as the way of salvation to lost sinners. The Holy Spirit delights to own and bless the doctrine of the Cross. I have often reflected with pleasure on this idea, and have endeavoured, as much as possible, to make this mode of preaching my own. If it has not been attended with the same effects as followed the Moravians, it has been a source of consolation to myself.

Brother Welch still resides in St. Louis, and keeps up our school there. Our institution in St. Charles appears, on the whole, in a prosperous way. We have about 50 students, on an average, and more come in almost every week. Brother

Craig, who teaches with me, is a very useful, active man, and is a great acquisition as a labourer in this part of the vineyard. I don't know but he is equally devoted, and as useful in the cause, as if he was a missionary in due form. We endeavour to render a partial supply to about seven different settlements besides St Charles. Once a month I visit St. Louis, when brother Welch goes to Herculaneum, 30 miles down the Mississippi.

One person (a black woman) was baptized in St. Charles on the 11th instant. Brother Craig has baptized one or two at Femme Osage, 25 miles west of this. Four persons have been recently baptized in the church at *Boeuf*, (Buffalo,) 40 miles up and on the south side of the Missouri At that place is some little seriousness more than usual.

My health and that of my family continues good, though I have been excessively afflicted with biles. This is partly owing to the use of the Missouri river water, the tendency of which is to throw off morbid affections by eruptions on the skin. By this you will infer the healthiness of the Missouri. The season thus far has been very pleasant. Though pretty warm, I do not think the heat so oppressive as last season. I believe the thermometer has not exceeded 98°. The month of May was very rainy; June extremely dry The present month we have alternately rain and fair weather. Thunder is much heavier and lightning much more vivid, than where I have been accustomed to live. It frequently strikes among the timber. though seldom or never are lives destroyed I have counted nine and ten trees on different sides, when I have been in the woods, on which lightning had taken effect.

INDIANS OF ILLINOIS

Extract of a letter from elder M'Coy to the Cor. Sec dated

REV. AND VERY DEAR BROTHER,   Mission House, Wabash, July 29, 1819.

In my last (May 13th) I intimated that I was about to make another tour in the Indian country This rout was shorter than I had intended, owing to some late changes in the Indian agency, and other circumstances, between the government and the Indians. On the 28th of May, in company with a Wea, I left home, visited two Wea and several Delaware villages, and one of the Miamies. In many places they were in such a deplorable state of intoxication, that little could be done They treated me with great respect, but, having lately disposed of much of their land, they seemed to be so unsettled in their minds, the Delawares in particular, that they declared they could do nothing for their children until they had arrived at their new country, and then they would send for me. Among the Weas and Miamies I think we could do well, were we further from their settlements. Such is the situation of affairs between some of the frontier settlers and the Indians, that the latter object to leaving their children so near the former as we are at present situated. In addition to the blessing of God, I am persuaded that all that is wanting to ensure a good degree of success, is, to be placed further in their country, to be *re-enforced with missionaries*, and amply furnished with means.

To enable you to form a faint idea of the obstructions with which we meet, I mention the following circumstance. When I had agreed with an Indian to accompany me, his relatives appeared to be so envious, that, fearing he would be placed in a better condition than they, they endeavoured to dissuade him from going with me. He agreed to leave with us, until his return, a boy about six years old, but it was some time before I could persuade his relations to consent to the measure, which was an essential point. The Indian soon became so attached to me, that I felt pretty certain of retaining his boy as a scholar, but falling in company with some of his friends at a town, he became determined in his mind to take away the boy on his return. When we came home he found his boy doing so well that he consented to leave him. He attended school with pleasure, but a few days since his mother took him away, promising to bring him back shortly. Thus you will perceive, that in the case of an individual, we have to combat the prejudices of whole families. We must get right in among them, where we can carry every thing forward regularly at the same time. They are very often at our house; and a few days past, when I was from home, they had a drunken frolic at some camps which they have about ten poles from our door. The sober ones take good care that they who are drunk shall not insult us. I had a striking instance of this on my late tour. On my way homeward I was one day so unwell when passing through a Wea town, that I concluded not to stop, but the principal chief, hearing that I had gone along, rode after us, and requested me to return and have a *talk* I did so, and being directed by him to the proper place, I lay down to rest while he assembled his chiefs; but scarcely had I done so, until some drunken Indians became so troublesome to myself and others, that I expected to see them and the sober ones, who could not silence their loquacity, proceed from loud talk to severe blows, and Indian blows are not like those of a common boxer, but are performed with large knives. The chief at length told me we had better make *short* speeches, as there were some bad men among them, and that I had better not tarry long. I had, you may be sure, no objection to this proposal; and when we set out, they directed us out of the town by a way which would not lead in view of a certain house in which they were drinking.

Although I cannot for a moment lose sight of the condition of the Indians, yet the revival of religion mentioned in my last, takes much of my time and attention. The blessed work is spreading, 84 persons have been baptized. A wonderful change in affairs indeed has lately taken place. Maria church, which has, for years, been but slowly progressing, has latterly broke forth on the right hand and on the left, and enlarged the place of her tent, and stretched forth the curtains of her habitation. Prairie Creek church, in a little more than a year, has increased her numbers from 28, to 100, and in many neighbourhoods and families, where, till lately, the name of Jesus was scarcely mentioned, except profanely, some are begging for mercy, and others are singing his praise. Almost every meeting is a truly interesting one: but I must say a little about one which was particularly so. It was in a neighbourhood where the vices of the people had become proverbial. Although I felt a desire that the people should be benefited, yet, being worn out with exercise and want of sleep, I was much indisposed, and felt more like praying than preaching: the latter I think was more imperfectly performed than usual, yet such a deeply affected auditory I had never seen before. They were so desirous to observe order, that at first several left the room until they had recovered a little from their deep affection, but scarcely would they be returned, until their eyes, which were hardly wiped half dry, would pour forth a double flood. At length the weeping became general, though not loud or distracted. You will pardon me, if it was a crime, for mingling my tears with theirs; yes, indeed, I can hardly avoid crying while I write. As there was no display of talent, or artificial manoeuvre by the preacher, which could have such an effect, I had no doubt of the presence of God's Spirit. Three persons who gave perfect satisfaction respecting a work of grace on their hearts, have lately been baptized, who dated their awakenings to meetings of the Brucevile Mission Society. Should that institution do nothing more, this alone will be sufficient cause of eternal gratitude to God.

But at these happy meetings, in which, at times, I almost forget that I am still an inhabitant of earth, I often think of my red brothers, and say in my soul, O, God, when shall I see them trembling under a sense of sin, or wetting their faces with tears of penitential sorrow! When shall I hear them singing the songs of Zion! Or must I die without the sight! Even if this should be the case, nevertheless, let me live among them, let me die among them, and let me hope to hear them sing in heaven.

I think, sir, that at a time like the present you will allow me to indulge my feelings a little; so much, at least, as to say, that I believe there are only two things that keep me from being as happy a man as any in the world the one is, the want of opportunity to be more useful, and the other is my wicked heart. The former, I hope, will begin to vanish the next time I hear from you but, alas! who shall deliver me from the body of this death? Ah! brother, when you hear that the hand which has written this, has been consigned to the grave, then be glad for me, for the true cause of all my griefs will have been removed.

From Rev. Mr. Ranaldson to the Corresponding Secretary, dated

REV. AND VERY DEAR BROTHER, St. Francisville, June 29, 1819.

It has been long since I wrote to you. Indeed, the *incessant severity* of my labours, together with the feebleness of my constitution, has deprived me, in a great measure, of the happiness of writing often to my numerous and dear correspondents. I hope soon to enjoy, by an accession of labourers in this part of my Master's vineyard, more time for conversing with my distant friends. I have nothing of a very interesting nature to claim your attention at this time; yet it may afford you some satisfaction to hear from us, and to know what we are doing.

In September last I performed a tour to the Alabama territory, of 600 or 700 miles, accompanied by brother Estes. On leaving home, I contemplated as one object of the journey, a visit to the "Creek African Church" in the wilderness; but finding we should not have time to do this, and be at the Mississippi Association, we were compelled to return without making them a visit. An astonishing change has taken place in the Alabama wilderness since I passed through it on my way to New Orleans. The *solitary places* are literally made glad—places where the nightly howlings of ravenous beasts, and the more horrible yell of savage tribes affrighted the traveller, are converted into the peaceful abodes of civilized life,—into the fruitful fields of the husbandman. Some churches are constituted, and the joyful sound is heard in the land,—*the wilderness is glad, the desert blossoms,*—the fields are white unto harvest, and Zion's labourers are invited to enter!—I did not attempt, in this newly settled country, to make any collections for the mission; but on Pearl River, in the older settlements, a very laudable zeal was manifested towards the cause of missions.

Since my return, my labours have been confined chiefly to my own congregations. There have been small additions to the church, but no special revival of religion yet! We long for the salvation of God. Two Sabbaths past I had the pleasure to baptize 6 persons; two of whom were natives of Africa, whose clear and bright experience evinced to all that they were taught of God. These humble sons of Africa have been brought hither to hear the gospel,—who can tell but they may return hence to publish it to their brethren, that know not the liberty of the gospel!

The two schools, male and female, which have been established at Society Hill, have claimed a large portion of my time. Here are about 60 students, who receive daily instruction in the principles of morality and religion. They are generally diligent in their application to classical studies, amiable and correct in their moral deportments, solemn and attentive in divine worship. Some of these, I may say, were ignorant of the *existence of a God,* and had never been taught by minister, parent, or preceptor, the scheme of salvation! And yet I have never seen a collection of youth more easily disciplined, or more ready to listen to the words of truth and soberness. Some of the most flattering prospects are seen here, and this institution will, I hope, be continued, not only as a seminary of learning, but also as a *nursery of piety,* for generations to come. God has received praise from the mouth of one of these little ones, about 10 years of age, who gave testimony of her love to him in a manner truly astonishing to her family. She sleeps in Jesus. At a late public examination of the students, the committee of learned gentlemen appointed as inspectors, announced their entire approbation of the progress of the pupils, and of the utility of the institution.—Rev. Elisha Andrews is daily expected from Brown university to join me in these labours, which I hope will not be in vain in the Lord.

I have reiterated the *Macedonian cry* in the ears of my Atlantic brethren. They have heard the cry with tenderness and compassion. Some have come over to our help. We feel particularly grateful to the Board for sending brother Samuel Eastman to this destitute region. He has commenced his labours in Natchez, where he was baptized, and where he is likely to do much good. Brother M'Call is much beloved, and is settled in the vicinity of Port Gibson, a place recommended to him before he left Philadelphia. Brother John Smith, with whom you were once acquainted, is also a beloved fellow-labourer. He was regularly restored to the fellowship of his church in Ohio, and has been received into our church. He now serves the newly constituted church at Pinckneyville, and a destitute congregation in this parish.

Allow me, my dear brother, to continue my plea for Louisiana—but especially for *New Orleans.* True, there are many places in the state more needy and destitute than this city is at present, but they are of minor consideration in many respects. Many parts of this large and populous parish may be still regarded as good missionary ground. I did not know for some time after I came to the country, that there was a minister of any denomination settled in the parish; but have since learned that the Jepzibah church is situated below the Mississippi

...line, which has been blessed with some delightful seasons, and a considerable increase under the ministry of their worthy pastor, Rev Ezra Courtney. Beyond this church there are two others in the eastern parishes, and on the west side of the Mississippi river there are about five more, which were formed into an association last November. In this large and growing state, there may be 10 small churches of our order, and not ministers enough, I apprehend, to supply these. But your attention is called to New Orleans as a place of the first magnitude. Brother Davis has been continued 15 months by the Mississippi Society, as missionary to the poor of that city. His usefulness has been great in the hospitals and prison, as well as in the houses of the poor. The pious and benevolent are desirous for him to remain in this important sphere of usefulness, but it is uncertain whether he can be supported long by the society. Yet it is desirable, not only that he should continue to offer the consolations of the gospel to the *poor*, the *sick*, and *afflicted*, and teach the unlettered to read the bible, but that another should join him in his labours. A small church has been constituted in the city, which requires nourishing. Will it not be practicable for the Board to send out a suitable missionary for this place the ensuing winter? One recommended and patronized by you, would, I think, meet with encouragement at this time, and would probably receive some support from the country adjacent to New Orleans

---

Extract of a letter from Mr Eastman to the Cor Sec. dated

DEAR SIR, Natchez, July 25, 1819.

Since my last, which was dated 23d of March, I have spent my time principally in the city of Natchez, making short and occasional excursions into the country. The Rev Mr. Smith, a presbyterian brother, who had assiduously laboured in this city, left it about three months since, without the expectation of returning to renew his sanctuary efforts. His absence rendered this place more destitute of preaching than any other portion of country of equal population known to me in this state. Providence seemed to point it out to me as the most appropriate and promising missionary ground on which I could spend my labours. I have therefore endeavoured, in the name of the Lord, industriously to occupy it.

We have obtained a suitable place for worship, and have had recourse to the establishment of a school. I have rented, in partnership with a Mr. Smith, a large room, and opened an institution for the instruction of youths of both sexes, and at the same time repaired and put it in order for the accommodation of those who were desirous of hearing the everlasting gospel of Christ. It is a spacious and pleasant hall, 60 feet long, and 30 wide, has a neat pulpit, and is well furnished with seats. We opened it for meeting about the first of April, and have continued to assemble in it every Lord's day, unless providentially prevented. We have also held prayer and exhortation meetings on each Wednesday evening, which I trust have been profitable to us.

The number of hearers was at first quite small, but has gradually increased beyond our expectations. Our house is crowded with attentive, serious, and sometimes weeping congregations. Many seem to have been seriously awakened, and some are earnestly inquiring what they must do to inherit eternal life. It has pleased the Lord to encourage us with the prospect of a revival in this city.

How our expectations will terminate we know not. We desire to submit the whole to Him who worketh all things according to his own pleasure, whose ways are not as our ways, and whose thoughts are not as our thoughts; but we desire, we hope, and pray that many of the citizens of Natchez may experience like precious faith with us, and be introduced into the glorious liberty of the sons of God.

The house where we hold our meetings has become too small to accommodate our congregation, and the presbyterian brethren have generously offered us the use of their house, which is at this time unoccupied. We shall gratefully accept the indulgence. The people of Natchez consider it their duty to give temporal aid to those who minister spiritual things to them. They are about to do something for your unworthy missionary by way of subscription. Should this equal the expectation of my friends, I shall probably relinquish the labours and the profits of the school, and also be relieved from the necessity of dependency on the generosity of the Board for my support.

The number of pious believers in this part of the country is small. They are divided into various denominations. May the Lord increase the number and the graces of his people, that others seeing their good works may also glorify our Father who is in heaven.

Let our efforts be exerted in his name, however feeble they may be, the strong holds of Satan will tumble to the ground. Let our prayers, perfumed with the incense of a Saviour's intercession, be offered to God in faith, and let us wait with patient and pious expectation for the fulfilment of his promises.

RECENT INTELLIGENCE FROM BURMAH

The following interesting communication from Burmah was not received in time to be inserted in its proper place. We think it contains matter of too much importance to lay over for our next number, and therefore break into the ordinary arrangement, that we may present it to our readers.

From Mr. Colman to the Corresponding Secretary, dated

RESPECTED AND DEAR SIR,   Rangoon, February 20th, 1819.

WITH much pleasure I inform you of our arrival in Burmah. Five months we were on board the Independence, four in Bengal, and one upon our passage from Calcutta to this port. Various circumstances conspired to make the shores of this heathen land appear agreeable to us. We had long been in an unsettled state, and exposed either to the dangers of the ocean, or to the influence of a sickly clime. It was delightful to find ourselves at the end of our tedious journey, and safe from all the perils through which we had passed. But another consideration served much to animate us —we had reached the field in which we were destined to labour. Here we hoped to spend the remainder of our days, to scatter the good seed of the kingdom, and to see some plants of righteousness springing up, and yielding fruit to the glory of God. When we arrived at the landing place, we found our beloved brethren waiting to receive us. Our feelings, for a short time, destroyed the power of utterance. We could do no more than take each other by the hand. In about an hour the females came on shore, when the whole mission family met, and by mutual expressions of joy and love, attracted universal attention. From the shore we were conducted to the king's Godown, where we were strictly searched. We then proceeded to the mission house. Our feelings were indescribable when we stepped beneath its roof, and found ourselves encircled by that dear company which we had desired, so long, to enjoy. That was a season of rejoicing. How swiftly and pleasantly the hours passed away! How cheering and varied was the conversation! How fervent were the prayers and thanksgivings to Almighty God!

For more than a week we were assiduously employed in getting our things through the custom house. Our articles were strictly examined. The most trifling of them did not escape minute investigation. Having undergone this tedious operation, we were compelled, by the custom of the country, to make several presents to persons in authority. It is admitted that the viceroy has the first claim. Feeling the importance of securing his favour by every lawful means, we thought the opportunity good to pay him a visit, and, in presenting our gift, to request his protection. We found him seated in an open house, situated in the midst of a spacious garden. Before him were a number of his officers, and a few persons presenting petitions. Behind him, at a short distance, were a group of artisans of different occupations, whom he constantly employs. His Excellency received us in a very gracious manner, appeared much pleased with our present, and gave us the assurance that we should remain free from molestation beneath his authority. Surely there is reason for gratitude, that we are permitted to stay in this heathen land! Little dependence, however, can be placed upon the government. Things here are continually changing. The lives and property of the people, are at the arbitrary disposal of a single individual. The whole country, and all which it contains, are supposed to be his property. Hence he gratifies his inclination, without the least restraint. While, therefore, we acknowledge with gratitude, the protection of earthly rulers, we feel the necessity of putting all our confidence in the Lord Jehovah. He can either dispose them to favour us, or defend us from their injustice and cruelty. There is, certainly, no reason to fear, while we have such a powerful Friend. It is true that, in consequence of several reports that reached us, we once entertained some serious apprehensions respecting our personal safety in Burmah; but as we approached its shores, these apprehensions vanished; and, since that time, we have felt as secure amidst these habitations of cruelty, as though we were in a christian land, and enjoyed the protection of an equitable government.

Sickness and the want of a teacher have greatly impeded my progress in the language. I had studied but five days, when I was suddenly taken with an expectoration of blood from my lungs. The discharge was but small, but it greatly reduced my strength. My weakness was so great that I was compelled to relinquish my studies, and almost entirely to abstain from conversation. This was a severe trial. It caused great searchings of heart. It led me seriously to examine the motives which induced me to come to this heathen land. For two months I was extremely weak. But He who took away my health, has, to a considerable degree, restored it again. Once more I have returned to my studies. By the assistance of a teacher I have read the catechism, tract, and a few of the first chapters of Matthew. I have copied brother Judson's grammar, and half of his dictionary. The latter I hope to finish in two or three months. With real pleasure I look forward to the time when I shall obtain a knowledge of this difficult language. Brother Judson has performed a mighty task. He has now the great satisfaction of preaching to the poor heathen the words of eternal life. Hitherto he has principally confined his exertions to those who visit him, but soon his labours will be more public. We have recently purchased a small piece of land, adjoining the mission premises, on which a place of worship is now erecting. Here brother Judson intends to spend the principal part of his time. Among other considerations, I will mention two which induced us to adopt this plan. We concluded that this method of communicating divine truth, would be least calculated to offend the "powers which be." And as the necessity of preaching the gospel is acknowledged, it is best also, if possible, to pursue that course which will not excite the suspicions of a cruel and despotic government. The secluded situation of the house which we now occupy, had considerable influence upon our minds. It is situated upon no public road, and is almost entirely concealed from the view of passengers by lofty trees. This we conceive to be an important reason why so few inquire concerning the gospel. The house which is now building, stands upon one of the roads which lead to the great Pagoda. The passing here is immense, especially on worship days. We trust our American friends will pray, that from the house which we devote to the service of God, streams of salvation may flow to all the surrounding country.

DOMESTIC INTELLIGENCE, REVIVALS, &c.

From Rev. Daniel M'Call, dated Port Gibson, August 19, 1819.

WITH much pleasure I resume my pen, although I have no interesting intelligence to communicate. Since my last I assisted in the organization of a baptist church ten miles east of Port Gibson. I visit and administer to them the Lord's supper once a month. I have also a stated meeting near the Mississippi; but, as heretofore, devote more than half the Lord's days to Port Gibson. The people seem desirous of my labours, and are circulating, as I have been told, a subscription in my behalf.

My school is flourishing. The last four months I have usually had 26 or 28 pupils. There is now a recess of ten days, after which Mrs M'Call intends taking the female part of the school, and expects a number more, who have been waiting for her to commence teaching.

I unite with brother Peck in the desire to have a missionary employed in the Arkansas territory. If the project suggested by brother Ranaldson of employing a missionary in New Orleans, in addition to brother Davis, should not succeed, I hope, at least, that a person will be found who can devote his whole time to missionary labours in these regions of spiritual darkness. Having thought it my duty to consecrate A FIFTH OF MY INCOME to the cause of Christ, I would be willing to board the family of a missionary four months, towards aiding in his employment in the Arkansas territory.

Extract of a letter from Mr. William Polke, dated Bruceville, August 10, 1819.

THE Baptist Church on Maria Creek was constituted on the 20th of May, 1809, and consisted of 13 members, seven males and six females, who resided on the frontiers, from ten to twenty miles north and northwest of Vincennes, and was one of five churches that formed the "Wabash Association," which was organized on the 8th of July following. A few months after the constitution of the church, the Rev. Isaac M'Coy, then a licentiate, became a member, and preached to us regularly. October 14th, 1810, our brother M'Coy was ordained; on which occasion the Rev George Waller of Kentucky preached. The next morning we had the pleasure, for the first time, of hearing a female declare the goodness of God in revealing Jesus precious to her soul, and of witnessing the administration of the ordinance of baptism. From this time there were small additions made to the church, but no general revival. By the spring of 1812 eleven had been added by baptism, and the church, though small, was in a prosperous condition. From this period to the conclusion of the late war, our church shared largely in the common calamity. but, blessed be the name of the Lord, for his goodness and mercy endureth for ever, after bringing us through these trying scenes, He has granted us the smiles of his countenance.

In the summer of 1816, there was a partial revival in a small settlement on the lower side of the Wabash, where a few of our members resided, which so increased their numbers that they were dismissed and constituted as a church in the month of February 1817, which is called the "*Little Village Church*," from the circumstance of its being located in a deserted Indian village. In the spring of 1818, several of our members removed to a new settlement forming up the Wabash, and being joined by others from different parts, were dismissed by us and formed into a separate church, known by the name of the "*Prairie Creek Church*" The Lord has since enlarged her borders by the outpouring of his grace Since the third of February last, there have been added to her by baptism, 48 members, and the blessed work is still increasing. Aaron Frakes, a young brother in the ministry, is settled among them, and preaches with zeal and to good acceptance.

A short time previous to the removal of our brother M'Coy to the mission-house, there was more than common attention to his preaching. At our last October meeting he requested of the church that a special meeting might be appointed at his house on Monday evening the 26th of the same month, for the express purpose of praying for the success of the mission, and that our brother might be directed in the right way and preserved from evil When the evening arrived, all were surprised at the large and attentive congregation that assembled. The services were solemn and interesting in a high degree Many were deeply affected, and the most decent attention given by all. From this time meetings of prayer were better attended than formerly, and many appeared serious. In February we were visited by our brother Frakes, who preached with much engagedness In March he repeated his visit. Appearances still increasing, at our monthly meeting in April last our brother M'Coy, for the first time since his removal, visited us, and on that day two persons, the first fruits of this precious revival, were by him baptized in presence of a large and deeply affected congregation. Since that time 36 have been baptized, and appearances are still promising. The work appears to be spreading, but is yet mostly confined to the two churches above-mentioned. Our brother M'Coy, has for some time past visited us once a month, as also has brother Frakes; but still they cannot supply the pressing requests for preaching, as the destitute bounds are so extensive. There are some few preachers of other denominations—but nothing like a sufficient supply

This has been the greatest revival that ever has been experienced in this part of the country; it has been effected without noise or confusion, and with a solemnity becoming the religion of Jesus. I could relate some interesting anecdotes, but fear I have already trespassed on your time. I cannot, however, deny myself the pleasure of stating to you, that several persons, in relating their experience, mentioned that the first serious impressions they had was on becoming members of the Bruceville Missionary Society, from the reflection that, as they had become instrumental in sending the gospel to the destitute, there was a necessity of attending to the same themselves. May we not with rapture exclaim, the Lord hath done great things for us, whereof we are glad, in causing the wilderness and solitary place to rejoice and blossom as the rose! Where lately only the howling of beasts of prey were heard, and the savage yell resounded, the songs of Zion now are chanted, and a holy zeal fills the breasts of many to impart the blessings of the gospel and civilized life to our red neighbours of the forest.

From Rev Dr Billings, dated Edenton, (N. C.) August 16, 1819.

EDENTON has about two thousand inhabitants,—say one thousand whites. Of these but about five hundred go to a place of worship, and are about equally divided between the Episcopalians, Methodists, and ourselves. However, our congregation increases, and we are living in the utmost harmony with the other denominations; and, if I am not mistaken, we shall soon have a revival among us. I was yesterday about twenty-two miles from home, at a church called Wiccacon, where a revival has broken out. Such a scene I never before beheld. There were four ministers present. Brother Spivey and myself preached to about two thousand people in the open air, but the cries of the people at last totally overwhelmed us. Some despairing,—some crying for mercy,—others rejoicing,—some saying they had found Him,—others exclaiming, Glory, glory, glory! &c. Young men, by dozens, holding each other, weeping, groaning, and rejoicing! The old members, men and women, embracing each other, weeping and rejoicing! Some of us kept the stage, others went among the distressed. In a word, we preached, prayed, sung, and exhorted, till we were all entirely exhausted. We assembled at 10 o'clock, and departed about 2, leaving not less than five hundred persons, under various exercises of mind,—the male and female members staying to exhort and pray with them.

Brother Meredith is succeeding at Newbern beyond expectation. I received two letters last week from him A revival has broke out there. He has baptized eight or ten, and there is a general inquiry.

From Rev. Charles G. Sommers, dated Troy (N. Y.) August 23, 1819

THE Lord continues to be very gracious to us.—During this spring and summer we have had an addition of 55, and others stand prepared to follow the Lord in his appointed ways.—We continue to dwell together in love O! that our love to God may superabound!

Extract from the journal of Mr. West, dated January 24, 1819.

RODE 10 miles to Mantua, and found there a great time of awakening, which had commenced in a grammar school. This school had been very immoral. A female scholar, who was first struck with conviction, wrote a letter to the tutor, stating her great concern for her soul. He conversed with her, and her relation threw the school into tears, and all are still deeply concerned for their souls. This took place eight days before my arrival, during which time none had been able to attend to grammatical studies. Such a sight I never saw before. Thirty students, and many others, old and young, at once deeply affected! I stayed here three days, held four meetings, and preached five sermons; three of which were delivered in the seminary. I conversed much with them; and leaving them in a good way, I returned home.

MISCELLANEOUS.

THE supreme God is a Being eternal, infinite, and absolutely perfect; but a being, however perfect, without dominion, cannot be said to be LORD GOD. we say, my God, your God, the God of Israel, the God of gods,—but we do not say my Infinite, or my Perfect. On account of his dominion he is wont to be called LORD GOD or Universal Ruler. *Sir I Newton.*

IT is a circumstance worthy of observation, that, excepting the rotation of the earth upon its axis, there is no one body in nature, with which we are acquainted, whose motion is perfectly uniform and regular. *Bonnycastle.*

IN the year 1712, being the latter end of the reign of queen Anne, when the protestant interest in England was threatened with ruin, a paper was dispersed abroad in Great Britain and Ireland from London, entitled "A serious call from the city to the country, to join with them in setting apart some time; namely, from seven to eight every Tuesday morning, for solemn seeking of God, each one in his closet, now, in this so critical a juncture' The call was complied with. The death of the queen succeeded; and the affairs of the nation changed just at the time when the enemies of religion and liberty had their designs ripe for execution.

ON the ascent of Charles the 5th to his throne, he gave orders that he should be addressed by the title of " his majesty," before this period kings were never accosted in higher terms than "your honour," or " your grace" Surrounding sovereigns, jealous of the ambition of the young prince, decreed that they would bear the same title. It has since been worn by all the kings and queens of Europe.

INTERESTING LITTLE OCCURRENCES.

A PIOUS lady of Georgia, in April last, carried a Bible to present to a poor woman in her neighbourhood. The woman was absent, but the husband received it with thankfulness. The next day she hastened to the house of the lady, and told her that "six weeks before she dreamed she was very sick; and that she (the lady) had brought her medicine, which soon removed the complaint; and she now trusted that her dream would soon find its interpretation." She was greatly affected, and though unable to read much, spells the words in the Bible with prayerful attention.

A boy who had been present at a missionary meeting in the north of England, was so deeply impressed by what he had witnessed, that, on the next day he was overheard addressing himself thus to a little thrush, which he had taught to perch on his finger:—"You are a sweet little fellow, and I love you dearly; but, much as I love you, if any body would give me three-pence for you, you should go, and I would give it towards sending the gospel to the heathen."—A minister, who overheard this, was too highly gratified to suffer the poor lad to part with his darling bird, or to deprive him of the pleasure of contributing to the missionary cause; he therefore gave him double the sum he had set upon his bird.

A BENEVOLENT gentleman in the vicinity of London, was induced to visit a poor woman who was sick. When he entered the room, he perceived a little girl kneeling at the bed side, who immediately withdrew. He then inquired who that child was. The sick woman replied, Oh! sir, it is a *little angel*, who frequently comes to read the Scriptures to me, to my great comfort, and has just now given me six-pence. On further inquiry, he found she was one of the girls belonging to a neighbouring Sunday school. On the following Sabbath, our friend paid a visit to the school, and expressed a wish to speak to the child. She approached with trepidation;—when he asked her if she knew the poor woman just referred to, and had been to read the Bible to her? She replied that she had. He then asked, what had induced her to do so. She answered, 'Because, Sir, I find it said in the Bible, that pure religion, and undefiled before God and the Father, is this,—to visit the fatherless and widows in their affliction,' &c. 'Well,' said he, 'did you give her any money?' 'Yes, Sir.' 'And where did you get it?' 'Sir, it was the reward given me in this school.'

The gentleman who related this fact, said, (alluding to the expression of the sick woman,) 'I clasped the *little angel* in my arms, and prayed that the latter part of the text she quoted might also be accomplished in her,—that God would "keep her unspotted from the world."—*Evangel. Magazine.*

It is delightful to observe the tokens of the divine approbation which so frequently, in late days, attend the benevolent and pious efforts of Sabbath school teachers. And happy will that youth be, who regards such a public notice of the Lord's goodness to any unknown young fellow-sinner, as a call on him, from his great God and Saviour.

In a distant village lived a careless family, who seldom darkened the door of any church, and never, it is believed, did they raise the voice of prayer but when they were calling on the Almighty to damn those who had offended them. Under such dreadful instruction and example, and *parents* too! Samuel and James —— lived. As might naturally be expected, when they had attained, the one to his 12th, the other to his 14th year, both were regarded with sorrowful concern, by many, as swift travellers to ruin.

But it pleased that Being who endowed a dear little band with a "charity which was not rash, or vaunted not itself—but suffered long and was kind"—to establish a Sabbath school. It was conducted in an interesting and able manner. Many were induced by the rewards which were given to read and memorize the sacred scriptures. Samuel and James were at last to be seen repeatedly among the interesting group—and after some months, by the Divine blessing on the efforts of those who acted like dutiful parents, both of the little brothers deserted the ranks of young blustering swearers, and lounging ignorant Sabbath-breakers. It was evident to the estimable gentlemen, their teachers, " that these boys were not content with mere negative goodness"—that they were not content with mere labouring to cease from evil—but were learning to do well. In a little barn they daily met for retired social prayer. Here they probably often held sweet communion with the Father of their spirits. But they did not long enjoy the concealment of this little Bethel. By an imprudent action of a stranger, which evinced his hardihood in guilt, as well as the determinate but retired devotion of the youth, who were rudely disturbed while engaged in social duty, they were induced to search out a more private place in which to hold communion with Him whom they regarded as their Maker, their Redeemer, and their Judge. This place was no other than a dark disagreeable cellar—so that they could not conveniently address the Hearer of prayer in that posture which is so becoming and expressive in poor, sinful, dependent creatures. Ah! Samuel and James had not the deep shades of the grove, or the distant chamber, or the lonely closet, into which they might have retired, as many of their unknown young brothers, (and namesakes too,) now have. Shortly after this retired place was selected, a bundle of straw was conveyed into it, privately, by the elder brother. And here those dear young followers of the Redeemer were accustomed to meet, and jointly to pray to that God who saw them in the dark. Only a few weeks had elapsed before another removal was deemed proper; but it was a happy removal; and both parents and children will think of it with peculiar joy and delight through all eternity. Accidentally the father discovered the straw in the cellar. He asked his son Samuel, " what it was put there for?" The boy, with a firmness of resolution and coolness of temper which might have thrown a lustre even round aged piety, replied, " Father! James and I used to go into the barn to pray, but some one threw stones at the door; and when we came into the cellar it was so muddy that I brought the straw down—and it was I that spread it there, that we might *kneel on it*" The reply was enough for a prayerless father. With a downcast eye, and with a sinking heart, he went into a room; but when his hand was on the lock of the door he exclaimed, " Oh, God! is it possible my children are entering into heaven, and I am staying back!" What his vows and engagements were after he closed the door, are only known to Him who looketh on the heart. In a very little time a striking and complete reformation became apparent in both father and mother. All took their stand decidedly for God and for holiness—all gave full satisfaction to the officers of a respectable church, and were admitted into full communion. The voice of prayer and praise is no longer a stranger to their dwelling. Now peace dwells within its walls, and prosperity is perched upon its roof, and the happy inhabitants are not without the cheering hope of being translated to " a house not made with hands, eternal in the heavens."

ORDINATIONS.

ON the 29th of July last the Rev. JOHN FINLAY was ordained to the pastoral care of the Baptist church in Albany. The Rev Archibald Maclay of New-York preached a very impressive and appropriate sermon, from Colossians i 28. "*Whom we preach, warning every man, and teaching every man in all wisdom, that we may present every man perfect in Christ.*" The Rev. Francis Wayland, of Saratoga Springs, offered up the consecrating prayer, and was assisted by all the ministers present in the imposition of hands. Immediately after the prayer, the Rev Charles G. Sommers of Troy delivered an address to the candidate, and a special charge to the members composing the church. The Rev. Joshua Bradley, late pastor, presented the right hand of fellowship, and the Rev Stephen Olmstead of Schodack, made the concluding prayer. The assembly was large, and peculiarly solemn. The services were performed in a manner highly interesting, and it was believed by many that the approving presence of the Lord was enjoyed.

Mr. Finlay is a graduate of the University of Glasgow, where, as an alumnus he resided during a term of seven years. In prosecuting his collegiate career, it appears, not merely from a diploma, by which is conferred on him the degree of A. M., but, from testimonials the most satisfactory, and signed by the different professors, that his deportment was unexceptionable.

He arrived in America on the 17th of September, 1817, and was elected rector of the Richmond Academy in Augusta, on the 1st of January, 1818. On the 22d of the same month he was chosen a chaplain of the Georgia militia, and on the 29th of June he was called to the care of the Presbyterian church in Augusta, Georgia, over which he presided until he formed the resolution to locate himself in a more northerly section of the United States. On his way to New York it pleased God to enlarge his views of the kingdom of Christ, and on his arrival he was baptized by the Rev. Archibald Maclay.

ON the 15th of August, 1819, at a yearly meeting in the *High Point Chapel*, Monmouth county, New Jersey, Mr. JOHN HAGAN, a licentiate from the *church of Lower Dublin* (Pa.) was set apart to the work of the ministry as an itinerant. The order of services as follows. The introductory prayer by the Rev. John Cooper of New Jersey; sermon by Joshua P Slack of Pennsylvania from, Eph. iii. 8. *Unto me who am less than the least,* &c. The examination of the candidate by Mr. Cooper; prayer during the imposition of hands by the Rev. S. Bijotat of New York. The Rev. Mr. Cooper then delivered a solemn charge, and the Rev. Mr. Bijotat gave the right hand of fellowship.

After an intermission of thirty minutes, the Rev. Mr Hagan delivered a very impressive discourse from Ezek xxxvii. 1—10. which was immediately followed by the ordinance of the Lord's supper. The services were such as to impress the minds of a large assembly with the dignity of divine things; while the believing followers of Jesus found it a season of refreshment from the presence of the Lord.

ON the 23d of September, 1819, at the Baptist meeting house in Montgomery, JOHN S. JENKINS was ordained to the work of an evangelist. Rev Mr. Roberts of the Great Valley commenced the services, and preached the sermon from Matthew xxviii. 18—20 "*And Jesus came and spake unto them, saying, All power is given unto me in heaven and in earth Go ye, therefore, and teach all nations, baptizing them in the name of the Father, and of the Son, and of the Holy Ghost; teaching them to observe all things whatsoever I have commanded you; and, lo, I am with you alway, even unto the end of the world.*" Rev. Dr. Hough proposed the usual questions; Rev Mr. Griffin offered the ordination prayer, and the imposition of hands was performed by the ministering brethren present. Rev. Mr. Matthias delivered the charge, and Rev. Dr. Hough concluded the solemnities. The services were pleasing and impressive.

On Monday, August 23, 1819, at the meeting house of the Rock Springs Baptist church in Little Briton township, county of Lancaster, state of Pennsylvania, THOMAS POTEET was solemnly ordained pastor of the said church. Rev. Thomas Barton preached from 1 Cor. ix. 16. "*Wo is me if I preach not the gospel*" The usual questions were asked by Mr. Ferrell; Mr. Strawbridge offered the ordination prayer, and the rite of imposing hands was performed by the ministering brethren present; after which Mr Strawbridge presented him the bible. The Rev. Thomas Barton gave the right hand of fellowship; the Rev. Mr Ferrell gave the charge, and concluded with prayer and an appropriate hymn.

On Lord's day, August 29, 1819, at the meeting-house, Lower Dublin, Mr. JOSEPH WRIGHT, member of the Baptist church there was solemnly ordained to the work of the ministry, with a view to his taking charge of the Baptist church in Pleasant Valley, New York. The services were opened by singing and prayer by Rev. Mr. Slack, after which Dr. Staughton delivered a discourse from Isaiah lii. 7 "*How beautiful upon the mountains are the feet of him that bringeth good tidings, that publisheth peace, that bringeth good tidings of good, that publisheth salvation, that saith unto Zion, thy* GOD *reigneth,*" and afterwards proposed to the church and candidate the customary questions. The ordination prayer was offered by Rev. Mr. Slack, and the right hand of fellowship given by the Rev. Dr. Hough, of Montgomery; the bible was presented to Mr Wright, and an affectionate and impressive charge delivered by the Rev. Mr. Montanye from Col. iv. 17. "*And say unto Archippus, take heed to the ministry which thou hast received in the Lord, that thou fulfil it.*" The assembly was very large, and the services solemn and delightful. After the charge, the following hymn was sung, composed by one of the members of the church for the occasion·

O THOU who seers and prophets sent,
　And didst their mission seal,
By whom ordained th' apostles went,
　The Gospel to reveal.

To us thy guiding Spirit lend,
　While we with one accord,
Another labourer would send
　Into thy harvest, Lord

Saviour divine, assist his youth,
　To him thy grace impart;

While he divides the word of truth,
  With wisdom fill his heart.

As thou Isaiah's lips didst touch
  With coals of hallowed fire,
So may thy power in him be such
  As may his soul inspire.

Aid him with knowledge to unfold
  Thy pure and holy laws;
Make him like Paul or Peter bold
  To combat in thy cause

Then while he publishes around
  The sacred truths he feels.
Lord may his ministry be crown'd
  With multiplied seals.

OBITUARY.

REV. JEREMIAH MOORE.

For the following communication we are indebted to Rev. FRANCIS MOORE, the son of the deceased, who, in Jefferson county, Virginia, is pursuing a course of useful labours similar to those from which his venerable father has rested. The memory of the just is blessed, and deserves to be cherished. The toils, the sufferings, the successes that attended the deceased, have found their equal in few. Our only regret is, that the subsequent detail has been published no sooner.

JEREMIAH MOORE was born in Prince William county, Virginia, June 7th, 1746. His parents were respectable without opulence, as far as wealth may be supposed to establish distinctions among men. From a very early period in life serious impressions filled his mind relative to eternity, which he supposed were the cause of his not running into many of the excesses of the times. This excepted, nothing of an extraordinary character marked his progress through life until he reached his 17th year, when a considerable revolution took place in the neighbourhood where he was brought up, under the preaching of the Rev. David Thomas, who was the first baptist he ever heard of. Until now he never heard a doubt suggested with regard to the truth of the established religion. Curiosity induced him to go and hear this newlight, as Mr. Thomas was then called. He returned home greatly astonished at the gentleman's manner of preaching, the doctrines insisted on, together with his apt quotations from the scriptures in support of the whole. This brought him to confess it was something entirely new, and looked so much like the New Testament, with which he had some acquaintance, that it afforded him much matter for serious meditation: and although it was several years before he was made to understand the principles of the gospel, he never could obliterate from his mind the effect of this sermon. As his acquaintances were generally Episcopalians, he resolved, as much as possible, to hide his views from them, and this he found no difficulty in effecting, as his convictions went little further than to persuade him that Mr. Thomas and his baptist friends were good people, and did not deserve the abuse generally bestowed on them. The first of November, 1765, being a few months more than 19 years old, he was married to Lydia Renno, the daughter of Mr Francis Renno, whose ancestors were under the necessity of flying from France, their native land, on account of their religion, and taking refuge in the then British dominions. Settled in the world, he was tempted to fly to that false refuge, the conclusion of many, namely, that it was no matter what religion a man adopt, provided he be only sincere and moral. His having fallen into this snare himself he has said was the reason why, in his public preaching, he so earnestly warned others to escape it — Having come to this conclusion, he became more attentive to the established church, and carefully avoiding the baptists, would never go to hear them preach, nor see any of them if he could help it. By this time, 1771, they had much increased, and had advanced near his residence. Several of his acquaintances had joined them; while every mention of them brought up recollections that goaded him to the heart. On easter Monday of this year he went from home on business, and on his return his servant informed him that their mistress had gone with his mother to baptist meeting. As it was now some time in the afternoon, he made no doubt but they would soon return. But the evening came on without bringing any intelligence. As several of his father's family were at the place of worship, he was sure if any thing out of the ordinary course had taken place they would have informed him At about 11 o'clock at night he heard the company ride up, and Mrs. Moore call for a servant. He went out, and on inquiring if any thing had happened, was informed they had waited to hear a man preach by candle light In conversation with Mrs. Moore relative to the preaching, he soon discovered her mind was much affected. She observed, " Until now I never knew any thing about my situation as a poor miserable sinner, against the best of Beings." The conversation was like a dagger to his heart, a heavy gloom oppressed his mind, and fearful apprehensions filled him with horror, to a degree he had never felt before. A few days after he went to meeting The service was introduced by singing Watts' 30th Hymn, 2d book.

> " Come we that love the Lord,
> And let our joys be known,
> Join in a song with sweet accord,
> And thus surround the throne."

But the following words, " Let them refuse to sing, that never knew our God," came with power. He felt he knew not God. Deep distress filled his soul. For a considerable time he was left to mourn that he could not mourn. He was tempted to believe he had committed the unpardonable sin; that with him it was too late; God would not have mercy on him; and though he strove to pray, he was often led to conclude the mercies he sought were not for such as he. At length through the goodness of God he was enabled to feel the remission of his sins through the blood of the Lamb, to the unspeakable joy of his heart. No wonder then that the blood and righteousness of Jesus Christ should be the theme that he dwelt on and delighted in for more than 40 years! How could he who knew his own salvation was all of grace, preach a conditional Gospel to others! Soon after this he became a member of the baptist church at Chopawamsic, in Stafford county, Virginia. His baptism made no small stir among his friends, the most of whom were Episcopalians, and some of them enemies to the baptists—

Some pretended to pity his folly, while others treated him with contempt; and all agreed to give him up for lost as to any future usefulness to himself or family. By becoming a baptist he gave up a small office in the establishment worth 2400 pounds of tobacco yearly, and with it the friendship of many influential characters. When elder D. Thomas baptized him, he observed to a friend, I think I have this day baptized a preacher, and so the event proved. Soon after this event a lady, (it is believed to have been the mother of judge French, of Kentucky,) proposed the opening a meeting in the neighbourhood for singing God's praise, reading his word, and prayer, to which he consented, not imagining the work was in any way to devolve on him. Here, however, it may be said commenced that ministerial work in which he was engaged near 45 years, through difficulties and trials, with a zeal and abilities that have fallen to the lot of but few. Three times he was apprehended by the officers of the crown, and conducted to the town of Alexandria, to be lodged in the public gaol, and once committed by one of his majesty's justices of the peace to gaol, for preaching the gospel of Jesus Christ. This mittimus is yet in the hands of his family, and will, it is hoped, be preserved as an evidence of his faithfulness in his Master's cause. He was blessed with an uncommon degree of health, and with seeing many churches planted as the fruit of his labours. One in the town of Alexandria, now under the care of S. H. Cone, he mentions with peculiar pleasure, on account of its being located in the place where he was thrice called to answer at the bar of his country for preaching the gospel of a precious Christ, and where he received the sentence of the judge *to be in gaol during life*. From all these afflictions he was wonderfully and in an unexpected way in providence delivered, not without a hope of meeting in a happy eternity many of these his enemies and their posterity. No doubt is entertained but that the church of Alexandria, at this time, is in part composed of the families that have descended from his most bitter persecutors! The ways of God, O how unsearchable! About two years before his death, his friends saw, with unspeakable regret, that his accustomed health was fast declining. He nevertheless continued to travel and preach through a district of country from 50 to 60 miles diameter. His last attempt to speak for his Divine Master was in the village of Centerville. In the early part of the winter of 1814, it is thought by those who are qualified to judge, that his journeying to preach the gospel from place to place would, if directed to that end, have carried him twice round the globe. His preaching was principally confined to Maryland and Virginia, yet he visited North and South Carolina, Tennessee, Kentucky, Pennsylvania, Delaware, the Jersies and New-York. A few days before his death he observed to his son,*
"I have finished my course: the doctrines that I have tried to preach are the stay and comfort of my heart. I know in whom I have trusted. There is one thing, and only one, that gives me the least uneasiness, and that is, that I have not travelled more, preached more, and written more, and in all things, been more industrious in the best of causes." His last moments appeared to be employed, as was his life, in a desire to spread abroad the savour of His name whose blood and righteousness were all his hope. On the 24th of February, 1815, he left this for a better world on high, leaving a widow, five sons, and four daughters, to lament a loss to them irreparable.

* Elder F. Moore.

INDEX

TO

THE LATTER DAY LUMINARY,

Vol. I.—1818, 1819

ABYSSINIAN Church, condition of the, 203
Accounts of the Agent of the Board, 140—143, 392—395
―― of the Eastern Committee, 144
―― of Messrs Peck & Welch, *ibid.*
―― Treasurer's, 138, 390
Acrostic, 264
Address to the American Society for colonizing free people of colour, *reviewed*, 291
―― of the Rev. Dr. Wharton, to the New-Jersey Bible Society, 257
―― of the Merchant Seaman's Auxiliary Bible Society of London, 201
ADDRESSES OF THE BOARD, 113, 125, 239, 369
Affghanistan, where situated, 79
Affghans, secrets of the, 79; professors of Mahometanism, 80, hence their studiousness to conceal their origin, *ib.*; supposed to be the remnant of the ten tribes, 53; reasons for the supposition, 77; first suggested by Sir Wm. Jones, 79, opinion of Dr. Carey, 53, of Prideaux, 78, of several Jewish writers, 80; writers on the subject may be divided into three classes, 77, the argument concentrated, 78, new light on the subject expected, 81.
Africa, letters from, 297, 300
―― mission to, 400
Africans, colonization of, 263, 293, 400, 404
AGENT OF THE BOARD, letters from, 118, 375, additional items connected with the agency, 396
Albion Chapel, meeting at, 501
Alexander, emperor of Russia, conversion of, 18, conversion of his sister,
19, his Ukase to the synod of Moscow, *ibid.*
Alexander Galitzin, prince, conversion of, 17
American Bible Society, 2d report of the, 194, number of auxiliaries to, 416, sums received the last year, *ib.*
―― *Colonization Society* See *Africans*
―― *Indians*. See *Indians*.
Anecdotes, 61, 109, 460, 513, 514
Angus W. H. letter from, 353
Animals, all after their kind, 364
Annual meetings of the Board, 130, 388
Apocalypse, the prophet of the christian church, *ibid.*
Apostles, the, their number was small, 267, were missionaries, 269; called to office by the Redeemer, 265, carefully trained for their services, 267; inspired of God, 270, persons of real piety, solid sense, and active zeal, 266; were all, except Judas, real converts, 267; qualifications necessary to form their character, 268; surreptitiously assumed, 265; diversity of rank observable among them, 268; state of the world when they commenced their labours, 269, preached the gospel on the very soil which had been stained by their Master's blood, 270, enter the largest cities, and dispute with the learned, *ibid.*; their miraculous success in spreading the gospel under every opprobrium, 271; their disregard of sufferings and death, 270, seal their testimony with their blood, 329, contrasted with the followers of Mahomet, 270
Apostolic Mission tours, 328
Arimathea, Joseph of, the first missionary to England, 15

Aristobulus, introduces the gospel into England, 16
Arrival of the missionaries, 257
Art of Printing, remark of the vicar of Croydon on its introduction into England, 107
Association, Long Run, Kentucky, 459
———— Bethel, *ibid.*
Associations, tables of, 136, 383
Asylum for the Deaf and Dumb, 456
Aviragus, the British king, patronizes the early missionaries, 15

BAPTISM, duty and advantages of improving, sermon on, *reviewed*, 344
———— of Messrs. Judson and Rice, 23
Baptists, Dutch, some account of the, 254, 353
BAPTIST BOARD OF FOREIGN MISSIONS, addresses of the, 113, 125, 259, 369, annual meetings, 130, 382, general circular of the, 38, minutes of the, 130, 133, 379, 382
Baptist Education Societies, 102, 125, 135, 233, 381, 385, 397
———— Female Missionary Societies in Troy and Lexington, New-York, 101
Barrow, Rev. David, letter from, 206
Batchelder, Rev. Wm obituary of, 110
Bethel Association, 459
Bettiyah, Roman Catholics at, 499
Beza, conversion of, 19
Bible bought by a drunkard, 109
Bible Society, American, extracts from the 2d annual report of, 194, number of auxiliaries, amount of receipts in one year, and issues of books in three years, 416
———— ———— Boston Marine, 435
———— ———— Bremen, *ibid*
———— ———— British and Foreign, extracts from its reports, 54, 57, 97, 197, 198, 454
———— ———— Calcutta Auxiliary, 97
———— ———— Philadelphia, 194
———— ———— Russian, 416
———— ———— Tobolsk, in Siberia, 59
Billings Rev Dr letter from, 512
Blackwood's Magazine, extracts from, 85
Bombay, Jewish school at, 433
Bonnycastle's account of the origin of the telescope, 487, *note*; observation on the earth's rotation, 513
Boyle, the philosopher, 107
Booth, Mrs Elizabeth, obituary of, 110
Bradford, Rev John, martyr, instructions to be observed concerning prayer by, 338
Bright Cloud of righteousness, a drop of mercy from the, *reviewed*, 345

Brook, Rev Mr obituary of, 461
Brown, Rev O B letter from, 400
Bruceville Mission Society, formation of the, 43; Female Society, *ib.*
Bryce, Mrs Sophia, obituary of, 462
Bucknall, Mrs obituary of, 212
Burckhardt, Rev Mr letter from, 431
Burkitt on Philippians i. 29. 210
Burman and English tract, 145
———— *Mission*, origin of the, 23; for accounts of, see *Judson, Hough, Colman*, and *Wheelock*
Burning of two women, 254
Bushnel, Anna, letter from, 101
Buttolph, Rev. J. letter from, 408

CALCUTTA Auxiliary Bible Society, 97
Calmuc prince, letter from a, 98
Carey, Rev Dr. See *Letters*
Cartilages in the vertebræ of the back, 262
Catholics in Germany, zeal of, 57
Catskill Female Mite Society, 100
Centenary of the reformation, commemoration of the third at Frankfort, 97
Ceylon, inquiry excited among the natives of, 98
Chadbourn, Rev. John, ordination of, 460
Charleston school in India, 456
Character of the apostles, 265
Chamberlain, Rev J. letter from, 350
Chalmer's Discourses, notice of, 85, extracts from, 426
CHASE, professor, letter from, 384, answered, 386
———— *Rev Johnson*, letter from, 359
Chater, Rev. Mr letter from, 249
Cherokee woman, letter from a, 453
Cherokees, mission to the, 44, 45, 46, 154, 185, 410, 452
Chickasaws, desirous of a school among them, 42
Cholera morbus, ravages of in India, 247
Christians, selfishness among, 315
CHRIST JESUS, the first of missionaries, and the encourager, example, and supporter of succeeding ones, 68, state of the world when he took upon him the form of man, *ibid*, how far as a missionary he travelled, 71, 72; his mission not restricted to the Jews, 69; reveals to man the glories of the Father, 68, a contrast between him and the missionaries of his Cross, absurd, if not blasphemous, 70, yet from his example missionaries may deduce instructive lessons, *ibid*
Chronologers like clocks, 316
Churches and Meeting-houses, 69
Circular, general, 38

College at Serampore, 491, 493
COLMAN, REV. MR missionary to Rangoon, letter from, 508
Colonization of free people of colour, 265, 291—297, 400—404
Colonization Societies, 457
Comet lines on the, 464
Commandment, a new, 316
Comparison between the North American Indians and the ancient Germans, 472
Comstock, Rev Oliver, ordination of, 460
Convention of the Baptist denomination in the United States, origin of the, 39
Conversion of Alexander, emperor of Russia, his sister, and prince Alexander Galitzin, 16—19
——— of Beza, 19
——— and restoration of the Jews, 430
——— of sailors, 354—357
——— of the World, *reviewed*, 278—291. 340—345
Cooper. Rev David, letter from, 38
Cornelius, Rev. Samuel, ordination of, 106
Crane, Rev Mr letter from, 401
Creation, absurd conjectures of philosophers respecting the, 421, rational, succinct, and sublime description contained in the bible, *ibid*; work of each day, 422—426
Crusades, origin and intention of the, 432, undertaken with a bad spirit, *ibid*, defeat and infamy of the, 433; the object will be effected by better means, *ibid*
Curwen, Mrs Mary, obituary of, 62

DEAF AND DUMB, Asylum for the, 456
Death of my mother, on the, 63
——— of a child, on the, 319
De Bruyn, Rev Mr. account of his murder, 301, 444
Delhi, interesting accounts from, 248
De pastorali cura, 107
Deus vult, motto of the crusaders, 433
Devil, worshipped by American Indians, 362
Discourse on the duty and advantages of improving our baptism, *reviewed*, 344
Divine revelation, importance of its being committed to writing, 428
Drake, elder, letter from, 454
Drop of Mercy from the bright cloud of righteousness, *reviewed*, 345
Drunkard, bible bought by a, 109
Dutch Baptists, some account of, 254, 353
Dying infant to a weeping mother, 216

EARTHEN VESSELS, 104
Eastern Committee, accounts of the, for outfit, &c of missionaries to Burmah, 144
Eastman, Rev. Samuel, ordination of, 263, instructions to, *243; letters from, 413, 507
End of Affliction, 319
English mission to India, view of the, 441
Epistle to the Hebrews, remark on the style of the, 460
Epitaph on Thomas Tallis, 317
Errour no where stable, 316
——— efforts of philosophers for removing it, feeble and unavailing, 270
Ethiopic Manuscript, 203
Expenditures connected with the business of the Agent, 142, 395

FATHER'S best wishes for the welfare of his son, exemplified in the prayer of Jacob, 231
Female sex, 317
Ferris, Rev E letter from, 313
Ficklin, Rev Mr report of on the subject of the Indian school, 448
Finlay, Rev John, ordination of, 516
Fisher, Rev Mr letter from, 247
Fisk, Rev Pliny, missionary to Jerusalem, 431
Flood, Dr generous conduct of, 181
Fuller, Rev Dr. Andrew, biography of, 161; his opinion of Robinson's History of Baptism, 87, of the millennium, 364
Furman, Mrs obituary of, 365

GALILEO, his calculations of the spots in the sun, 107, invents the telescope, 487; forced by the inquisition to abjure his opinion of the Copernican system, 488
Ganges, exposure of the sick on the banks of the, 496—498
General Circular, 38
——— state of religion, 155, 414
——— survey of Baptist missionary stations in India, 441
George, Rev Mr letters from, 308, 309
Glasgow, Mission Society, 53
Godden, Thomas, set apart as a missionary for Jamaica, 255
GOSPEL, introduction of into England and Wales, 15, 83, the remedy for the disorders of our fallen world, 280; how it is to be published, 281; must be preached to every creature, *ibid*.
Graves, Rev Absalom, letter from, 206
Green, Rev T. P letter from, 459

Greene, *Rev Samuel* ordination of, 461
Grotius, his proofs of the truth of the Christian religion, 232

Hagan, Rev. John, ordination of, 516
Hall, *Rev. Gordon,* letter from, 450
Handy, *Rev Joy,* letter from, 312
Heart power of the, 262
Henderson, *Rev Mr.* letters from, 409, 410
Henry, *Matthew,* on the creation, 364
—— anecdote of, 109
Herschel, *Dr.* opinion of, 107
Hill, *Keturah,* letter from, 100
Hindoos, spiritual condition of the, 473; believe in the transmigration of the soul, 474; have no knowledge of God, 473; no hope in Divine mercy, 474; are of Dr Priestley's opinion respecting virtue, 475; have no idea that the present state is probationary, *ibid;* entertain the doctrines of fatalism, *ibid;* their views of a future state neither excite fear nor inspire virtue, *ibid;* liberation of spirit from every thing not spirit, the highest felicity held out in their writings, *note,* 476; duty of Christians to attempt their conversion, 476
Hinton, *Rev James,* letter from, 51
History of Baptism, Robinson's, edited by D Benedict, A M. reviewed, 86
Hodgen, *Rev Mr.* letter from, 348
Holcomb, *Rev Hosea,* letter from, 313
Holiness, internal principle of, defined, 272; false opinions of some respecting it, 273
Holy Spirit, influences of the, variously experienced, 14; necessary to missionary success, 332, 502
Hough, Rev George H missionary to Burmah See *Letters.*
Howell's History of the Bible, quotation from 83
Hymns, 64, 111, 112, 367, 517

Iceland, state of religion in, 260
Importance of having Divine revelation committed to writing, 428
India, native preachers in, the supporting of them from private funds originated with Mrs Dr. Carey, 53
Indians, *American,* accounts from missionaries among them, 33, 47, 88, 91, 148, 154, 175, 185, 242, 243, 301, 309, 404, 413, 448, 454, 502, 505
Indians, *American,* difficulties to be overcome in teaching them, 195; are attentive to the word, 183; importance of setting them examples of industry, 305; compared with the ancient Germans, 472; worship the *evil spirit,* 362; worship the planet Venus, and sacrifice human victims, 244; worship idols of their own formation, 309
Indian School in Kentucky, 409, 448
—— woman, letter from an, 453
Influences of the Holy Spirit, variously experienced, 14; necessary to missionary success, 332. 502
Instruction for pious young men called to the Christian ministry, 125, 135, 283, 381, 385
Instructions to missionaries, 31, *243
—— to be observed concerning prayer, 338
Internal principle of holiness, definition of, 272; false opinions respecting it, 273
Introduction to the Latter Day Luminary, iii.
—— of the gospel into England and Wales, 15, 83; various opinions on the subject, 15, 16, 83, 84
Ireland, propagation of the gospel in, 52
Items connected with the general agency, &c. &c. 396
Ivimey, *Rev. J.* letter from, 253

Jailor's household baptized, 106
Jenkins, *John S* ordination of, 516
Jerusalem, present state of the Jews at, 431
—— mission to, *ibid*
Jesus, Dr Newton on the name, 363; probable reason of his going to Jerusalem with his parents, 364. See Christ.
Jewish children in London, schools for, 456
—— History, occupies a large portion of Divine revelation, 430; exhibits man's depravity and God's perfections, *ibid*
—— school at Bombay, 433
Jews, the, were an honoured people, 430; faithful guardians of the sacred scriptures, 429; obligations of christians to, 430; vigorous exertions making for their conversion, *ibid;* favourable appearances, 430, 431
Johnson, *Col Richard M* his zeal in favour of the Indians, 39
Jones, *Elizabeth L.* obituary of, 317
Joseph of Arimathea, supposed to introduce the gospel into England, 15
Journal, extracts from Mr Welch's, 178
—— from Mr. Posey's, 185
—— from Mr Ward's, 494
—— from Mr. West's, 512

JUDSON, REV. ADONIRAM, missionary to Burmah, baptized in Calcutta, 23, his tract in Burman and English, 145, letters from See *Letters*.
—— Mrs letter from, 27
Junior brethren at Calcutta, letter from the, 440

KALEE-GHAT, affecting scenes at, 496
Kalee ghuny, exposure of a sick bramhun at, 497
Kentucky, revivals in, 205, 206, 312
—— Indian school in, 376. 382. 409. 448
Kingdom of the stone and kingdom of the mountain, explained, 336
2 *Kings*, v 18. criticism on, 20
Kitching, Rev Christopher, missionary to Jamaica, setting apart of, 255
Krishnu, worshippers of, 496

LATTER DAY GLORY, 63
—— —— *Luminary*, reasons for publishing the, v, vi. 41 121
Lent, reason for eating fish in, 864
Letters from the Agent of the Board, 118 375
—— from W H. Angues, 353
—— from elder David Barrow, 206
—— from Rev. Dr. Billings, 512
—— from Rev O B Brown, 100
—— from Rev. Mr. Burckhardt, 431
—— from Anna Bushnel, 101
—— from Rev John Buttolph, 408
—— from a Calmuc prince, 98
—— from Rev. Dr Carey, 48. 93. 439. 489
—— from Messrs Carey, Marshman and Ward to the missionaries at Rangoon, 26
—— Rev. J. Chamberlain, 95. 350
—— Rev Ira Chase, 384, reply, 386
—— Rev. Johnson Chase, 359
—— Rev. Mr. Chater, 249
—— from a Cherokee woman, 453
—— from Rev S. COLMAN, missionary to Rangoon, 508
—— from elder David Cooper, 38
—— from Mr. W. Crane, 401
—— from elder Drake, 454
—— from Rev. Mr. EASTMAN, missionary, 413. 507
—— from Rev. E. Ferris, 313
—— from Rev. Mr. Fisher, 247
—— from Rev. Henry George, 308, 309
—— from Rev. Absalom Graves, 206
—— from a gentleman in London, 197
—— from T. P. Green, 459
—— from Rev. Joy Handy, 312
—— from Rev. Gordon Hall, 433
—— from Rev. Mr. Henderson, 409, 410

Letter from Keturah Hill, 100
—— from Rev Dr. Hinton, 51
—— from Rev Mr Hodgen, 348
—— from Rev Hosea Holcomb, 313
—— from Rev G H HOUGH, missionary to Rangoon, 28 173 300 489
—— from Rev Mr Ivimey, 253
—— from Rev ADONIRAM JUDSON, missionary to Rangoon, 23 25 45 173 242 397. 399
—— from Mrs N JUDSON, 27
—— from the Junior brethren at Calcutta, 440
—— from Rev J Lawson, 94 247. 498
—— from Mr Le Jeune, 458
—— from Rev Dr Marshman, 490
—— from Rev Daniel M'Call, 510
—— from Rev. ISAAC M'COY, missionary, 43, 44, 90, 182, 412, 450, 503
—— from T L M'Kenney, Esq. 41, 42
—— from Rev E Montague, 314
—— from Rev. Mr Morrison, 51
—— from Rev Mr. Pearce, *244
—— from Rev John Peck, 205
—— from Rev JOHN M PECK, missionary, 34, 90, 175, 242, 243, 301, 303 304, 502
—— from Messrs Peck and Welch, 89, 149, 150, 404, 405
—— from Rev. S Pillsbury, 314
—— from Mr Wm Polke, 314 415 510
—— from Rev. HUMPHREY POSEY, missionary, 44, 45, 46 154. 185 410 452
—— from Rev J A RANALDSON, missionary, 36, 37 91 153 160. 505
—— from E Reynolds, 99
—— from Rev LUTHER RICE, Agent of the Board, 118 375
—— Rev I Roberts, 254
—— from Mrs Rowe 43, 49 95 311
—— from Rev Silas Shelburne, 206
—— from Rev. Joseph Sheppard, 312
—— from Sierra Leone, 297, 298, 299
—— from Rev Mr Siers, 251
—— from Rev Mr. Sommers, 512
—— from Benjamin Stout, Esq 205
—— from Edward Tanner, Esq. 362
—— from Anstis Titus, 101
—— from Rev A. Waller, 313
—— from Rev George Walker, 459
—— from Rev Wm Ward, 50, 51. 310, 311 349 491 493
—— from Rev J E WELCH, missionary, 33 89. 177 306 502
—— from Rev E. W WHEELOCK, missionary to Burmah, 31 456
—— from Mrs. WHEELOCK, 437
—— from Rev John Young, 312
Liberty, religious, triumphs of, in France, 353

Lights in which the future glory of the church is exhibited, 465
Long Run Association, 459
Lord's Prayer in Burman, 174
Louisiana, mission to, 36. 38 91. 153. *243. 413

MAGAZINES, when first published, iv; their utility, v. vii
Mahomet, his doctrines propagated by the terrours of the sword, 271
Man, apostacy of, iii.; his limited capacity, 426; motives for humility, 427
Manuscript, valuable Ethiopic, 203
Marine Bible Society of Boston, 455;
Massachusetts Baptist Education Society, address of the, 102
M'Call, Rev D. ordination of, 263; letter from, 510
M'Coy, Rev. Isaac, missionary. See *Letters* from
M'Kenney, T L Esq. letters from, 41, 42.
Meetings of the Board, annual, 133 382
Melancholy, lines on, by Mrs. Hough, 159
Merchant Seamen's Auxiliary Bible Society, London, 201
Microscope, wonders of the, 108
Millennium, Mr. Fuller on the, 364; hymn on the, 368
Ministerial support, reasonableness of, 477, moderate support only required, 478. 484, objections answered, 484, design of the ministry, 477, the duty of those they minister to proved from our Saviour's commands, and from the apostle Paul's arguments 478.—483; other reasons, 486, plan for raising funds for the purpose, 485
Minutes of the Board from the meeting of the Convention in May 1817 to May 1818, 130—133, from May 1818, to May 1819, 379—382
Mission to Burmah, 22. 30 133 145, 173 242 300 397. 436 489 508
—— to St Louis. See *Letters* from J. M PECK and J. E WELCH.
—— to St. Charles, 502
—— to New-Orleans and vicinity, 36, 37. 91. 134. 153 180. 413. 505 508
—— to the Cherokee Indians. See *Letters* from Mr Posey
—— to the Indians of Illinois. See *Letters* from Mr M'Coy
—— to the Wyandot Indians, 308, 309 454
—— to Africa, 40
—— to Jerusalem, 431

Mission, British, to India, general survey of the, 441, &c
Missionaries, instructions to 31, *243; sailing of more, 30, appointment of to labour in Africa, 400, number and stations of, 283, duty and ability of christians to augment their number, 280 291, means for their support, 285. See CHRIST.
Missionary, observations on the term, 65. its meaning among the Romans, *ibid*; incorrectly defined, *ibid*; its real import, 66, the office contrasted with that of a prophet, an apostle, and an ordinary minister, *ibid*; how far Christ travelled in that capacity, 71, 72. travels of St. Paul, 417, of the other apostles, 328 331
Monies expended by the Agent, 142. 396; by Mr. Peck, 143, by Mr Welch, *ibid*; by the Eastern committee, 144
—— received by the Agent, 140. 392; by Mr Peck, 143, by Mr. Welch, *ib*.
Montague, Rev E letter from, 314
Moore, Rev Jeremiah, obituary of, 518
Morrison, Rev Robert, letter from, 51
Moscow, Ukase to the synod of, by the emperor Alexander, 19
Mugs, some account of the, 443, 444
Mukshya, or liberation of spirit, the highest felicity held out in the Hindoo writings, *note*, 476
Murder of Mr De Bruyn, 444
Murphy, John C. ordination of, 106

NAAMAN, healed of leprosy, discovers a heart converted to God, 20, his language, 2 Kings v 18 seems to imply a contradiction, *ibid*; its meaning correctly stated, 21, the original conveys a very lively idea of his feelings, *ibid*.
Naomi, her pious conduct, 12
Natchez, awful visitation of, 37
Native preachers in India, the idea of supporting them from private funds originated with Mrs Dr. Carey, 53
New Commandment, 316
New Market street Baptist church, 61
New Orleans, reformation in, 37
Newton, Dr on the name JESUS, 363,
—— on the use of fish in Lent, 364
—— *Sir Isaac*, on the names of GOD, 513

OBITUARY of Rev. Wm Batchelder, 110
—— of Mrs E Booth, *ibid*
—— of Rev Mr Brook, 461
—— of Mrs. Sophia Bryce, 462

Obituary of Mrs Bucknall, 212
—— of Mrs Curwen, 62
—— of Mrs Furman, 365
—— of Mrs E L. Jones, 517
—— of Rev. Jeremiah Moore, 518
—— of Mrs. Rhoda G Paul, 366
—— of Mrs Eleanor Richards, 211
—— of Captain Paul Titcomb, 365
Observations on the term Missionary, 65
—— of an old writer, 210
Ordination of John Chadbourn, 460
—— of Hon. O C. Comstock, *ibid*
—— of Samuel Cornelius, 106
—— of Samuel Eastman, 263
—— of Samuel R Greene, 461
—— of John Hagan, 516
—— of John S Jenkins, 516
—— of Daniel M'Call, 263
—— of John C. Murphy, 106
—— of Thomas Poteet, 517
—— of Silas Shelburn, 60
—— of Joshua P Slack, *ibid*
—— of Joseph Wright, 517
—— and setting apart of Messrs Wheelock and Colman, 31
Ordination hymn, 517
Owen, Dr on Ephesians i. 20—23, observation of, 231

PARSONS, REV. LEVI, missionary to Jerusalem, 431
Parting stanzas, 264
PAUL, the apostle, his conversion, 417, is visited by Ananias, 418, preaches the gospel from Jerusalem round about 'Illyricum, 417; supposed to have visited England, 16, his advice to Timothy 107 to Titus, *ibid.*
Paul, Mrs Rhoda G obituary of, 366
Pawnees, some account of he, 244
Peck, Rev. J letter from, 205
PECK, REV JOHN M. missionary See *Letters* from.
Persia, Christians in, tolerated, 352
Parka, the apostle, supposed to be the first to introduce the gospel into England, 16, travels and death of, 329
Philosophy, efforts of, for meliorating the condition of man, feeble and unavailing, 270
Plan of the Institution for pious young men called to the gospel ministry, 237
Poetry, 63, 64. 111, 112 159, 160 215, 216 264. 319, 320 367, 368 464
Polk, Esq Robert biography of, 332
Polke, Wm, letters from, 314 413. 510
Pomponia supposed to introduce the gospel into England, 15
Poor family in Germany, anecdote of, 107

Population of the globe, 282
POSEY, REV. HUMPHREY, missionary—See *Letters* from.
Posey, Esq Thos governor of Indiana, friendly to Indian reform, 43, 44
Poteet, Thomas, ord nation of, 517
Power of the heart, 262
Prayer, the Christian's duty and privilege, 83. reasonableness of, 81, its tendency, 82, answers of, an inducement to, 83; instructions to be observed concerning, 338 340
Propagation of the gospel in Ireland, 52
Psalms, 111. 160 464

RADHA, worshippers of, 496
Raikes, Robert, the founder of Sabbath schools, 188
Ranaldson, Rev J A See *Letters.*
RANGOON See *Burman Mission*
Reason for eating fish in Lent, 364
Reason of difference among christians, 315
Religion not a hinderance to the student, 275; reasons for the reverse stated and refuted, 275. 278
Report of the Calcutta Auxiliary Bible Society, 97
—— of Rev. Mr. Ficklin, 448
—— of the Washington Missionary Society, 99
—— of committees appointed to audit the Treasurer's accounts, 139, 391, the Agent's accounts, 142, 395
Restoration and conversion of the Jews, 166, inferred from Deut. xxx. 1 6, Isaiah xi 12 and xxvii. 12, Ezek xxxvi. 24 and xxxvii. 21. 167; circumstances that render the event probable, 167, 168, Dr. Gill's opinion, 169. See *Jews*
Revelation, Divine, importance of having it committed to writing, 428
Revelations, ii. 9. Trappe on, 109
REVIEW of Chalmer's Discourses, 85.
—— conversion of the World, 278 340
—— Address of the American Society for colonizing free people of colour, 291
—— Discourse on the duty and advantage of improving our baptism, 344
—— drop of Mercy from the Bright Cloud of Righteousness, 345
Review of the mission to St. Louis, 405
—— British mission to India, 441
Revivals in Illinois, 451. 504 511., in Kentucky, 205, 205. 312, in New-Hampshire, 314, in New-Jersey, 313.

in New-York, 357 362 512, in North Carolina, 512, in South-Carolina, 313, in Ohio, 513, in Virginia, 206. 313 345

Reynolds, E letter from, 99

RICE See *Agent of the Board*

Richards, Mrs Eleanor, obituary of, 211

Riches, instability of, 230. 317, often unjustly obtained 229, not a source of happiness, *ibid*

Right hand of fellowship to Messrs Wheelock and Colman, by Mr Sharp, 170

Roberts, Rev T letter from, 254

Roman Catholics at Bettiyah, 495

Rowe, Mrs. letters from, 48, 49, 95. 311

Ruth, observations on the history and character of, 9, her departure from Moab considered emblematic, 12

SAILING of missionaries for Burmah, 30

Sailors, conversion and account of, 354, deprived of religious instruction, 356, 201, duty of christians toward them, 202

Schools, in St Louis, 176, Indian, in Kentucky, 376 448, Jewish, in Bombay, 433, in London, 456

Scripture Criticism, 2 Kings v. 18 20 John xx 17 337. See *Naaman*

Selfishness among Christians, 315

Serampore, works in the press at, 349, letters from, see *Carey, Ward* and *Marshman*

Setting apart of missionaries, 255

Shelburn, Silas, ordination of, 60

Sheppard, Rev Joseph, letter from, 312

Siam an extensive mission field, 173

Siamese, religion of the, 207

Sierra Leone, letters from, 297

Slack, Joshua P. ordination of, 60

Snuff and Segars, use of relinquished, and the saving appropriated to pious uses, 435

State of religion in France, 458, general state of, 155 414

Sunday schools, origin of, 188

Sunday School Teacher, 215

Survey of Baptist mission stations, 441

Sutcliffe, Rev. John, biography of, 217

TABLES OF ASSOCIATIONS, 136. 388

Tanner, Edward, letter from, 362

Tartars. See *Affghans.*

Telescope, origin of the, 487

Theatre at Albany turned into a meeting house 314

Theological Institution, 130. 135. 125 385

Theophilus, a boodhist priest, conversion and death of, 251

Titcomb, captain Paul, obituary of, 365

Titus, Anstis, letter from, 101

Tobolsk Bible Society, 59

Tract in Burman and English, 145

Translation of the scriptures into Burman, 130

Trappe on Revelation ii 9.
—— on the text, "I and my Father are One," 210

Treasurer's accounts, 138, 390

Triumph of religion in France, 353

Truth of the christian religion, 232
—— the word of, 61

UKASE of the emperor Alexander, 19

United Society for the spread of the gospel, 307

VALUABLE Ethiopic manuscript, 203

View of the history, literature, and religion of the Hindoos, 208

WALDENSES, the missionaries of the dark ages, some account of the, 225

Waller, Rev Absalom, letter from, 313

Waller, elder George, letter from, 459

Ward's view of the history, &c of the Hindoos, 208, some account of his journey from Serampore to Chittagong, 494 See *Letters*

Washington Mission Society, 99

Wealth, reflections on 229

WELCH, Rev. JAMES E missionary See *Letters* from

WHELOCK, REV E. W. missionary, letters from, 31, 436
—— Mrs letter from, 437

Wistar, Dr Caspar, anecdote of 210

Wonders of the microscope, 108

Worthy of imitation, 434

Wright, Joseph, ordination of, 517

Writing, advantages of, 428

Wyandot Indians, 308 310 454

YOUNG, *Rev John,* letter from, 312

ZEAL of Catholics in Germany, 57

CPSIA information can be obtained
at www.ICGtesting.com
Printed in the USA
BVHW011150180222
629445BV00009B/176